YOUNG CONSUMER BEHAVIOUR

Although one perspective depicts young consumers as vulnerable and passive in the marketplace system, our knowledge of this consumer group will be inadequate if limited to this contention. Their roles and relevance in family consumption activities are becoming increasingly profound. Available evidence shows that they cannot be ignored in the marketplace dynamics as they consume goods and services in their households and are involved in various other active roles in their household consumption including making decisions where applicable. Hence, the landscape of young consumer behaviour is changing.

Young Consumer Behaviour: A Research Companion focuses on exploring the behaviour of young consumers as individuals and societal members. The chapters address different aspects of consumption activities of children as individuals like motivation, involvement, perception, learning, attitude, the self and personality. Similarly, chapters on consumer behaviour in social settings contextualised to young consumers including culture, subculture, family and groups are incorporated into the book. This book fills a gap in the literature by addressing the dynamics of consumption patterns of this consumer group in relation to various marketing stimuli and different stakeholders. It combines eclectic perspectives on the topic and specifically, bridges the gap between historical perspectives and contemporary issues.

Building on the extant literature in the field of marketing and consumer behaviour, this book is a compendium of research materials and constitutes an essential reference source on young consumer behaviour issues with both academic and managerial implications.

Ayantunji Gbadamosi (BSc (Hons), MSc, PhD, FHEA, FCIM) lectures at Royal Docks School of Business and Law of the University of East London, UK. He was formerly the Leader for Research and Knowledge Exchange in the school. He is listed in *Who's Who in the World*.

YOUNG CONSUMER BEHAVIOUR

A Research Companion

Edited by Ayantunji Gbadamosi

Routledge
Taylor & Francis Group

LONDON AND NEW YORK

First published 2018
by Routledge
2 Park Square, Milton Park, Abingdon, Oxon OX14 4RN

and by Routledge
711 Third Avenue, New York, NY 10017

Routledge is an imprint of the Taylor & Francis Group, an informa business

© 2018 selection and editorial matter, Ayantunji Gbadamosi; individual chapters, the contributors

The right of Ayantunji Gbadamosi to be identified as the author of the editorial material, and of the authors for their individual chapters, has been asserted in accordance with sections 77 and 78 of the Copyright, Designs and Patents Act 1988.

All rights reserved. No part of this book may be reprinted or reproduced or utilised in any form or by any electronic, mechanical, or other means, now known or hereafter invented, including photocopying and recording, or in any information storage or retrieval system, without permission in writing from the publishers.

Trademark notice: Product or corporate names may be trademarks or registered trademarks, and are used only for identification and explanation without intent to infringe.

British Library Cataloguing-in-Publication Data
A catalogue record for this book is available from the British Library

Library of Congress Cataloging-in-Publication Data
A catalog record for this book has been requested

ISBN: 978-0-415-79008-6 (hbk)
ISBN: 978-0-415-79009-3 (pbk)
ISBN: 978-1-315-21359-0 (ebk)

Typeset in Bembo Std
by Swales & Willis Ltd, Exeter, Devon, UK

CONTENTS

List of contributors   *viii*
Preface   *xvii*
Acknowledgements   *xx*

PART I
Introduction and theoretical background   1

1 The changing landscape of young consumer behaviour   3
 Ayantunji Gbadamosi

PART II
Young consumers as individuals   23

2 Children's consumer perception   25
 Nashaat H. Hussein

3 Learning and consumer socialisation in children   37
 Adya Sharma

4 Young consumers' motivation and involvement: uses and gratifications perspective   59
 Emmanuel Adugu

5 Exploring personality, identity and self-concept among young consumers   79
 Abdullah Promise Opute

6 Attitudes and persuasion in young consumer behaviour 98
Ayodele C. Oniku, Achi E. Awele and Olawale Adetunji

PART III
Young consumers and marketing strategies   **117**

7 Brand, branding and brand culture among young consumers   119
Andrew Hughes

8 Pricing, income and brand symbolism: exploring young consumers' understanding of value   138
Diliara Mingazova and Ayantunji Gbadamosi

9 The young ones, shopping and marketing channels: what actually shapes their mind?   155
Zubin Sethna, Rebecca Fakoussa and David Bamber

10 Marketing communications and the young consumer: evidence from a developing country   170
Nicolas Hamelin, Ayantunji Gbadamosi and Lucas M. Peters

11 Digital marketing and the young consumer   188
Vishwas Maheshwari, Karl Sinnott and Bethan Morris

12 Services and relationship marketing: perspectives on young consumers   208
Yiwen Hong, Anh N. H. Tran and Hsiao-Pei (Sophie) Yang

13 Segmenting the children's market   230
Mahama Braimah, Cynthia A. Bulley and Janet A. Anore

14 Amplifying the voices of young consumers in food advertising research   246
Anna Maria Sherrington, Steve Oakes and Philippa Hunter-Jones

PART IV
Young consumers in social and cultural contexts   **269**

15 Reference groups and opinion leadership in children's consumption decisions   271
Ayodele C. Oniku and Achi E. Awele

16 Youth subcultural theory: making space for a new perspective   288
    Ofer Dekel, Elizabeth Dempsey and Emily Moorlock

17 Young consumer misbehaviour: a perspective from
    developing countries   307
    Richard Shambare, Nyasha Muswera and Jane Shambare

18 Faith, religion and young consumer behaviour   334
    Eddy Kurobuza Tukamushaba and Dan Musinguzi

19 Children's consumer behaviour in developing countries
    in the twenty-first century   347
    Ndivhuho Tshikovhi and Richard Shambare

PART V
Social marketing and consumerism: perspectives on young consumers   **367**

20 Social marketing and the protection of the young consumer   369
    Chahid Fourali

21 Consumerism and consumer protection: a focus on young
    consumers   391
    Ayantunji Gbadamosi, Kathy-Ann Fletcher, Christiana Emmanuel-Stephen and Idowu Comfort Olutola

Index   *414*

CONTRIBUTORS

Olawale Adetunji works as a Lecturer in the Department of Marketing of Moshood Abiola Polytechnic, Abeoukuta, Nigeria. He is presently a doctoral student at Babcock University, Nigeria.

Emmanuel Adugu, PhD, is a Research Methodologist and Lecturer in Applied Statistics, Statistical Computing, Research Design and Analysis and Social Development at the Department of Government, Sociology and Social Work, University of West Indies, Cave Hill Campus. His current area of research focuses on public opinion data in decision-making and citizens using the marketplace to influence public policy with the goal of promoting sustainable development and global welfare.

Janet A. Anore holds an MPhil in History and an MBA in Marketing, from the University of Ghana. Janet is an experienced educationist and has worked in various positions in the education sector in Ghana, including a position at the tertiary level. Janet also has rich experience in the not-for-profit sector. Janet is interested in international relations and politics, marketing and entrepreneurship.

Achi E. Awele works as a marketing consultant and teaches marketing and business-related courses on a part-time basis with several institutions in Nigeria. He is presently preparing to commence his doctoral degree in the last quarter of 2017.

David Bamber is Director of PhD Studies at Bolton Business School at the University of Bolton, UK, and is Visiting Professor of Management Education at the Organisational Learning Centre, UK. He is a Foundation Member and Historic Affiliate of the Chartered College of Teaching, UK. He was Research Fellow in Organisational Learning at the University of Salford, UK; Visiting Research Fellow at Christ University, Bangalore, India; Senior Lecturer in Marketing at

Liverpool Hope University, UK; and has been an External Examiner in Business and Marketing at several UK universities including Leeds Becket University, Southampton Solent University, the University of East London and Canterbury Christ Church University.

Mahama Braimah is a Senior Lecturer at the University of Ghana Business School. He has published several research papers and has rich experience in industry, having served in various top-level management positions in different industries and firms. He has also developed and facilitated several executive development programmes, inside and outside of Ghana. Dr Braimah is interested in service marketing, business strategy, SMEs, tourism and hospitality.

Cynthia A. Bulley is a Senior Lecturer in Marketing and Organisational Research with the Central University, Ghana. She has had a varied career in industry and academia. She has facilitated workshops and training programmes for organisations in Ghana. Her considerable research, teaching and consulting activities focus on the application of marketing practices and organisation capacity building. She is interested in organisational management, experiential marketing and international business.

Ofer Dekel is a Senior Lecturer at Sheffield Hallam University. His work tells the story of the individual consumer. Traditional marketing treats consumers as the outcome of structures, patterns and regularities. Ofer makes the claim that this traditional approach leads to marketing failure. Instead, marketers need to focus on individual differences, learn how consumers move from one discourse to another and how they assemble these discourses to negotiate their lives and circumstances in an ever-changing social reality. Ofer promotes mass customisation, visual research, participatory research, non-representational marketing concept, crowdfunding and network analysis.

Elizabeth Dempsey is a Senior Lecturer in Marketing at Sheffield Hallam University, UK. Before entering academia Elizabeth worked in a range of commercial marketing roles focusing on communications and brand development. Her PhD research is centred on brands, teenagers and presentation of self and her research interests are customer psychology and branding.

Christiana Emmanuel-Stephen is a consumer research professional with an academic background in public relations, advertising, branding and marketing. Currently a PhD researcher at the University of East London, her research focuses on luxury fashion consumption and identity creation of Black African women in London.

Rebecca Fakoussa is a Senior Lecturer at the University of Northampton in the UK, where she enthusiastically teaches and publishes. She is an international family business consultant and mediator working with small to multi-national businesses on issues ranging from succession to strategy. Rebecca has particular expertise in start-up, nextGen, marketing, consumer behaviour, international business, cross-cultural management, decision-making and women on boards. She has started and run several of her own companies and gained her PhD in Family Business Governance from Kingston University, UK.

Kathy-Ann Fletcher is a PhD researcher at the University of East London. She is investigating the influence of social media brand communities on consumer identity. Her research interests lie in branding, consumer behaviour and digital media.

Chahid Fourali has a background in psychology, education and marketing and has published in all three areas. He led the consultation with the UK Government to set up the Marketing and Sales Standards Setting Body, which he then led for eight years, as well as the development of three sets of world-class national occupational standards (in marketing, sales and social marketing) that were supported by many internationally recognised marketing and business gurus. These standards are now the basis for all nationally recognised qualifications in the UK in the three professional areas. Dr Fourali is Senior Lecturer in Management at the London Metropolitan Business School and is Examiner/Subject Expert for Cambridge University and the University of Hertfordshire. He has achieved fellowship or professional membership status from several international organisations including FRSA, FCIM and BABCP. His recent book *Social Marketing: A Powerful Tool for Changing the World for Good* received very encouraging reviews including being selected for one of the Levitt Group 5 Great Minds events organised by the Chartered Institute of Marketing.

Ayantunji Gbadamosi, BSc (Hons), MSc, PhD, FHEA, FCIM, lectures at Royal Docks School of Business and Law at the University of East London, UK. He was formerly the Leader for Research and Knowledge Exchange in the school. He received his PhD from the University of Salford, UK, and has taught marketing courses at various institutions including the University of Lagos, Nigeria; the University of Salford, UK; Manchester Metropolitan University, UK; Liverpool Hope University, UK; and various professional bodies. He is a Fellow of the Chartered Institute of Marketing (FCIM) and a Fellow of the Higher Education Academy (FHEA). Dr 'Tunji Gbadamosi has several research outputs in the form of journal articles, chapters in edited books, co-edited books, monograph, conference papers and case studies. His papers have been published in a variety of refereed journals including *Journal of Brand Management*, *Thunderbird International Business Review*, *International Journal of Market Research*, *International Journal of Retail and Distribution Management*, *Marketing Intelligence and Planning*, *Social Marketing Quarterly*, *Young Consumers*, *Journal of Fashion Marketing and Management*, *Society and Business Review*, *International Journal of Consumer Studies*, *International Journal of Small Business and Enterprise Development*, *Entrepreneurship and Regional Development* and *International Journal of Entrepreneurship and Innovation*. He is the author of *Low-Income Consumer Behaviour* (2010) and the editor of *The Handbook of Research on Consumerism and Buying Behaviour in Developing Nations* (2016). His co-edited books are: *Principles of Marketing: A Value-Based*

Approach (2013) and *Entrepreneurship Marketing: Principles and Practice of SME Marketing* (Routledge, 2011). Dr Gbadamosi is a member of the editorial board of several academic journals. He has supervised several undergraduate and postgraduate students including PhD students to successful completion and served as an examiner for several doctorate degree examinations. He is the current Programme Chair of the International Academy of African Business Development (IAABD). His research interests are in the areas of consumer behaviour, SME marketing, marketing to children and marketing communications. He is listed in *Who's Who in the World*.

Nicolas Hamelin is an Associate Professor of Marketing at S P Jain School of Global Management and Adjunct Professor at Franklin University Switzerland. He is also an In-Country Analyst for Euromonitor International, a London-based global marketing research agency. Dr Hamelin holds a PhD in Physics from Sussex University, UK; an MSc in Environmental Management from Ulster University; and a PhD in Business at the Royal Docks Business School, University of East London. He has worked as a Research Fellow at the City University of Hong Kong, the Foundation for Fundamental Research on Matter and the Energy Centre of the Netherlands. In international business, he has worked at ST-Ericsson within the Nokia BU, as a Business Development and Strategic Marketing Manager. Since 2007, he has been Assistant Professor of Marketing at the American University Al Akhawayn University in Ifrane. Dr Hamelin has a diploma in TV Journalism from INA (Institut National de l audiovisuel in Paris). His main research interests are in the fields of consumer behaviour, neuromarketing, social marketing and environmental management.

Yiwen Hong is a PhD student at Coventry University, based in the Department of Marketing. Yiwen graduated from the University of Stirling with an MSc in Marketing. Her research interests include entrepreneurial marketing and online marketing. Yiwen's PhD is examining the impact of entrepreneur's characteristics upon the adoption and exploitation of the Internet by Chinese e-commerce firms. She is exploring these ideas through in-depth interviews with the entrepreneurs and staff members of the e-commerce firms, as well as observation of the firm's webpages.

Andrew Hughes is a Lecturer in Marketing at the Research School of Management at the Australian National University, where he teaches various marketing units at both the undergraduate and postgraduate levels. He currently serves as the convenor of the Master of Marketing Management programme and is immediate past convenor of the MBA programme. His research has examined the role of stakeholders in political marketing, personal brands, the role of negative advertising and how consumers respond emotionally to different types of information. His thesis, 'The Relationship Between Advertisement Content and Pacing on Emotional Responses and Memory for Televised Political Advertisements' was nominated for ANU's prestigious thesis prize, the J. G. Crawford Award. He is currently researching the role of information in different media types and environments on emotional responses and brand resonance and the use of video sharing to change attitudes towards stakeholders in sustainability. Connect with him at @marketingandrew.

Philippa Hunter-Jones, PhD, is a Reader in Marketing within the University of Liverpool Management School, UK. Her research interests examine the experiences of vulnerable consumers within the context of service, service design and service systems. She is currently working on multiple projects in this area linked to transformative service research, particularly within the context of health and well-being. Alongside this she has completed research linked to children, social tourism, the role of the third sector in tourism and the holiday-taking experiences of cancer patients. Her work has been published in a range of outlets, which include *Tourism Management*, *Annals of Tourism Research*, *Journal of Marketing Management* and *Journal of Business Research*.

Nashaat H. Hussein is Assistant Professor of Childhood Sociology in the Alsun and Mass Communication Department of Misr International University in Cairo. He has published extensively in *Cairo Papers in Social Sciences*, *Journal of the History of Childhood and Youth* and the *International Journal of Sociology and Social Policy*. He is author of *The Social Stigma of Divorce in the Cultural Sociology of Divorce: An Encyclopedia* (2013), *Sport and Schools in the Sociology of Education: An A–Z Guide* (2013) and is currently writing a book entitled *Sociology of Childhood: An Alternative for Understanding Children and Adolescents in Egypt*.

Vishwas Maheshwari is Head of Business Management and Marketing at Staffordshire University. Previously, he has worked as Director of Postgraduate programmes at the University of Chester, UK. He is Co-Founding Chair for Place Marketing and Branding Special Interest Research Group at the Academy of Marketing, UK. He also contributes as editorial board member for *International Journal of Organisation Analysis* and *Journal of Global Responsibility*. He has published research in the areas of branding, digital marketing communication and management. He is an experienced academic having taught and managed a range of courses and programmes in the marketing discipline.

Diliara Mingazova is a Lecturer in Marketing at the Royal Docks School of Business and Law, University of East London. Her research areas are consumer culture theory (CCT), consumer–brand relationships, marketing to children, strategic brand management, sociocultural brand management and branding. She is currently at the final stage of her PhD, which has a focus on children as consumers and their relationship with brands.

Emily Moorlock is a Lecturer at Sheffield Hallam University. Prior to this role she worked in various marketing positions, most recently as a consumer insight analyst. In this role she undertook extensive market research into young consumers, an area she is particularly passionate about. Her primary research interests focus on consumer behaviour and branding.

Bethan Morris is a Visiting Lecturer at Warrington School of Management, University of Chester. Beth's specialisms include digital marketing communications, digital PR and social media management. Beth is a member of the teaching team for undergraduate programmes including marketing and public relations, business management, hospitality management and events management.

Dan Musinguzi is an Assistant Professor at Stenden University Qatar. He holds a PhD in Tourism Management from the Hong Kong Polytechnic University and a Master's degree in Heritage and Cultural Management from the University of the Witwatersrand, South Africa. His research interests are tourism impacts, residents' attitudes and perceptions to tourism, pro-poor tourism, sustainable tourism, cultural heritage preservation, tourism planning and development, leveraging sports events, service quality in tourism and knowledge development. Dan has published research papers in academic journals and is an active reviewer of research papers for journals (including *Tourism Management, International Journal of Contemporary Hospitality Management, Tourism Management Perspectives*) and conferences.

Nyasha Muswera is a PhD candidate in the Business Management Department at the University of Venda, South Africa. She is studying towards a dissertation on culture and rural entrepreneurship. Her research interests revolve around the areas of marketing, consumer behaviour, customer relationship management and entrepreneurship.

Steve Oakes, PhD, is a Senior Lecturer in Marketing at the University of Liverpool Management School whose inter-disciplinary research focuses upon consumer responses to music in advertising and service environment contexts. An additional strand of his research examines key issues for arts (especially music) marketing. He has published in various journals including *Psychology and Marketing, Journal of Advertising Research, Marketing Theory, Journal of Marketing Management, Applied Cognitive Psychology, Critical Perspectives on Accounting, Accounting and Business Research, Journal of Marketing Communications, The Service Industries Journal, Accounting Forum* and *Journal of Services Marketing*, among others.

Idowu Comfort Olutola is a PhD candidate with particular interest in entrepreneurship, ethnic minority entrepreneurship and sustainable food production in Africa. Prior to enrolling at the University of East London, she worked as a scientific officer at the Federal Institute of Industrial Research in Nigeria facilitating training and market research for SMEs. She holds an MA in International Business and Entrepreneurship from De Montfort University and a BSc in Agriculture. She does peer mentoring and charity work in Africa.

Ayodele C. Oniku teaches marketing and related business courses at both undergraduate and postgraduate levels at the University of Lagos, Nigeria. His experience spans nearly two decades in both academic and business consulting. He is a consultant and market analyst to some Europe-based companies on West-African markets.

Abdullah Promise Opute, PhD, is a researcher and freelance academic and management consultant. Dr Abdullah Promise Opute has mentored, tutored and supported six PhD students (with analysis – SPSS, SEM and qualitative analysis including Grounded Theory analysis) to successful completion of their PhDs. He also supports corporate bodies with technical advice in several areas of management and also undertakes strategic change-driven researches for organisations.

Currently, Dr Abdullah Promise Opute works as an examiner in the areas of global marketing, corporate strategy and organisational behaviour at UK and African universities. He has worked in Nigeria, Germany and the UK. He received his PhD from the University of East Anglia, Norwich, UK and has teaching and examining experience in the areas of accounting (financial and management), business management, corporate strategy, marketing and organisational behaviour. Dr Abdullah Promise Opute has several research outputs in the form of peer-reviewed journal articles, chapters in edited books and conference papers. Being multi-disciplinary, his research straddles the fields of organisational behaviour, marketing and strategic management accounting (SMA). His research interest includes inter-functional integration, relationship conflict management, cross-cultural management, consumer behaviour, ethnic minority businesses (EMBs), strategic human resource management (SHRM) and strategic management accounting (SMA). He received the 'Best Paper' award at the Academy of Marketing Conference, 2007.

Lucas M. Peters is the author of the country guidebook *Moon Morocco* (2017), as well as a number of other essays and stories that have appeared in diverse publications such as *Creative Nonfiction*, *Ploughshare* and *Veg News*. He has been a consultant for the Travel Channel and holds an MFA from Goddard College, an MA from Central Washington University and a BA from the University of Washington. He lived in Morocco from 2009 to 2015 and currently lives with his family in Paris, where he teaches at the Sorbonne.

Zubin Sethna is a Principal Lecturer (Associate Professor) in Entrepreneurial Marketing at Regent's University London. Dr Sethna is Editor-in-Chief of the prestigious *Journal of Research in Marketing and Entrepreneurship* and regularly reviews for a variety of other marketing and entrepreneurship journals. He is a qualified marketing practitioner as well as an entrepreneur. He has successfully launched five businesses (one of which won a UK National Award) and in his capacity as Managing Consultant at Baresman Consulting (www.baresman.com), he has integrated marketing strategy/communications with management consultancy and training for numerous organisations both in the UK and internationally and across a variety of industry sectors (health care, professional services, music, travel, manufacturing, retail, IT, education and 'cottage' industries). This passion for entrepreneurship and marketing is very evident in his book (with Dr Roz Jones and Dr Paul Harrigan) *Entrepreneurial Marketing: Global Perspectives* (2013). His latest publication, *Consumer Behaviour* (2016), is fast becoming the UK and Europe's most popular textbook on the subject. Dr Sethna has conducted research in the UK, Europe, India and China and has raised external funding of nearly £500k for various academic projects. He is Co-Chair of the Academy of Marketing's Special Interest Group on Entrepreneurial and Small Business Marketing and has been invited to conduct keynote lectures at HE institutions in the UK, EU, China and India. In 2017, he was unanimously elected to become a member of the advisory board of the acclaimed Global Research Symposium on Marketing and Entrepreneurship.

Jane Shambare holds a BA (Hons) in Criminology from the University of South Africa. She currently works at Muelmed Mediclinic. Her research interests are in the areas of youth delinquency and criminological profiling.

Richard Shambare is a Senior Lecturer in the Business Management Department at the University of Venda, South Africa, where he teaches entrepreneurship and business management. Dr Shambare has published in peer-reviewed journals and presented papers at several international conferences. He specialises in research in the disciplines of technology adoption, marketing and consumer (mis)behaviour.

Adya Sharma is the Director at Symbiosis Centre for Management Studies of Symbiosis International University, India. She is a PhD holder and a double postgraduate. She has been part of the academic team instrumental in restructuring the marketing syllabus for university level at Symbiosis International University. She started her career with one of the leading trading houses of India under the Government of India. She brings with her more than two decades of rich practical experience from both the corporate and academic world. She has conducted training sessions for various companies including Goldman Sachs Women Entrepreneurship Program, Tata Motors, Amdocs, McDonalds, Wipro and Godrej. Dr Sharma has also been the second supervisor for Master's theses of students conducted under Berlin School of Economics and Law, Germany. Dr Sharma has several research outputs in the form of journal articles, chapters in edited books, conference papers and case studies. She is currently working on a book titled *Marketing Techniques for Financial Inclusion and Development*.

Anna Maria Sherrington, PhD, is a Senior Lecturer in Marketing at the University of Central Lancashire, UK, where she specialises in marketing communications, marketing management and social marketing. Her main research interest is advertising to young consumers with an emphasis on topics related to the conflict between healthy eating and fast-food advertising. She has worked in a range of marketing communication positions in the UK, Sweden and Germany, covering industries including marketing consultancy, manufacturing industry and the not-for-profit sector. Her research mission is to understand how marketing can be used to address the rapidly growing problem of childhood obesity.

Karl Sinnott has extensive experience in the development and delivery of undergraduate, postgraduate and professional programme (CIM) modules covering all aspects of marketing including digital marketing. He currently works as a Programme Leader for the Marketing and PR and Marketing and Advertising Management Programmes at the University of Chester, UK, having worked previously at both GSM and BPP Universities. His academic experience is underpinned by sound commercial background and extensive industry experience across different sectors including financial services, telecoms, travel and leisure, sports and retail.

Anh N. H. Tran is a PhD student at Norwich Business School of the University of East Anglia. She holds an MA in Marketing Management from Coventry

University, UK, and a BA in Business Administration from Southern Cross University, Australia, before joining a PhD. She works as a full-time Marketing Lecturer at Banking Academy (Vietnam). She also has experience working as a Research Assistant at Coventry University. Her research interests are in service marketing, electronic word of mouth and consumer behaviour.

Ndivhuho Tshikovhi is a PhD student in Social and Political Sciences at the Université Libre de Bruxelles, Belgium.

Eddy Kurobuza Tukamushaba is an Associate Professor at Stenden University Qatar in the department of International Hospitality Management. He holds a PhD in Hotel and Tourism Management from the Hong Kong Polytechnic University, Hong Kong and a Master's in Business Administration (Marketing) from Makerere University, Uganda. Eddy has published several journal articles and book chapters and conference papers. Some of his research work has been published in *International Journal of Sustainable Society*, *Journal of Hospitality Marketing and Management*, *European Journal of Hospitality and Tourism Research*, *International Journal of Market Research*, *Journal of International Entrepreneurship*, *Journal of China Tourism Research*, *Journal of Teaching in Travel and Tourism* and *Journal of Managerial Psychology*. He has received 'Best Paper' awards at different international conferences.

Hsiao-Pei (Sophie) Yang held several marketing posts in industry prior to joining academia. She has a PhD in Marketing and an MA in International Marketing. Her research interests are in the marketing of higher education and the consumption of services. Since acquiring her doctorate, Sophie has published in a number of journals such as *Journal of General Management*. In addition, she has written book chapters and case studies in mainly services marketing areas.

PREFACE

It is crystal clear that the relevance of young consumers in family consumption activities is increasing by the day. A point of convergence among researchers and practitioners is that issues associated with this consumer group and their interactive roles in the marketplace are very intriguing. On the one hand, they are noted as vulnerable consumers and on the other they appear as active participants in consumption issues and could not be described as naïve to marketplace dynamics. Hence, they are actively involved in family buying roles as initiators, influencers, buyers, deciders, users and even gatekeepers in varying circumstances. In this context, they influence family and societal consumption pattern differently at one age or another and even in some cases, before birth. Meanwhile, the profundity of scholarship attention on them as a consumer group is evident and still gaining momentum. Nevertheless, the rapid changes in the marketing environment across various areas such as the technological and sociocultural dimensions set a limit on the extent to which we can rely on the existing knowledge in this research field for various business related decisions. Simply put, the landscape of marketing is changing rapidly and there is a compelling need not only to keep up with this pace, but also to make a meticulous link between the past and the present. Accordingly, there are lacunae in the extant literature on the dynamics of consumption patterns of this consumer group in relation to various marketing stimuli and different stakeholders. Hence, this edited book, which combines eclectic perspectives on the topic, is introduced to address these gaps. It specifically bridges the gap between historical perspectives and contemporary issues on this topic.

Scope of the book

Essentially, this book focuses on exploring the behaviour of young consumers as individuals and societal members. The terms child consumers and young consumers are used interchangeably in various ways in this book as it covers issues relating to various categories of young consumers. Hence, the book comprises 21 chapters, which address different aspects of consumption activities of children as individuals like motivation and involvement, perception, learning, attitude, the self and personality. Similarly, chapters on consumer behaviour in social settings contextualised to young consumers ranging from culture, subculture, income and social class, family and groups are incorporated into the book. Apart from postmodernism, consumerism, ethics and marketing research on children's consumer behaviour, services and relationship marketing, branding and brand culture, the book also covers more contemporary issues with regards to young consumer behaviour such as social media and consumer misbehaviour. Hence, the scope is considerable.

Target audience

This comprehensive publication is intended as a compendium of research materials that will constitute an essential reference source, building on the extant literature in the field of marketing and consumer behaviour. Essentially, the primary target markets of the book are postgraduate students, researchers, managers and policy makers for insight into consumption practices of young consumers and the relevance of these to business and societal developments.

The secondary target market of the book consists of students studying marketing at the undergraduate level who will need to deepen their knowledge on children's interactive activities and roles vis-à-vis the marketing stimuli. By and large, it is hoped that this text will illuminate the field and serve as a key source of research materials for these target markets.

Objectives of the book

Young Consumer Behaviour explores these broad objectives:

1. Enable readers to develop a coherent understanding of the basic underpinnings of children's consumer behaviour as they relate to individual and group-oriented consumption decisions.
2. Robustly unpack the historical discourses on young consumer behaviour.
3. Provide readers with insight into how consumer behaviour concepts may be applicable to children's contemporary real-life situations.

In more specific terms, the text aims to:

1. Highlight the individual aspects of child consumers from perception to motivation, personality, learning, the self and attitude.
2. Discuss young consumer behaviour in the context of cultural and social settings to cover social class, culture, subculture, values and how these factors interrelate to influence family and societal consumption issues.

3. Explore and explain customer relationship management, consumer misbehaviour and their implications for the formation of a sound marketing strategy in relation to children's roles in the marketplace.
4. Examine children's roles in consumer decision-making processes through the use of relevant models, multi-culturalism, diffusion of innovations and contemporary issues in consumer behaviour including social networks and the evolving virtual relationships.
5. Discuss the ethical issues in children's roles in the marketplace and marketing research activities.
6. Explore children's reactions to the marketing mix elements both in the physical product and service offerings contexts.

Dr Ayantunji Gbadamosi
University of East London, UK
May 2017

ACKNOWLEDGEMENTS

Certainly, many people worked to make this book a reality. As the editor of the book, I am greatly indebted to colleagues who have demonstrated great enthusiasm and strong commitment to the work in their various chapter contributions. Without this, the book would not have been possible. Evidently, their expertise and time devoted to the project are invaluable. Indeed, they are great scholars to work with. The huge support of the Routledge team, Kristina Abbotts, Kelly Cracknell, Mathew Ranscombe and Emma Redley concerning this project is noteworthy. To them I say a big thank you.

I owe many thanks to my family, my wife, Remilekun Gbadamosi and children (Miracle, Favour and Joy) for the encouragement and support concerning the work. Their understanding is well appreciated. Above all, the inspiration to work on this book comes from God, for which I am eternally grateful. To many others who I have not specifically mentioned, especially our students who are often interested in discussing marketing issues with us and thereby stimulating a beneficial research climate, I think of you and thank you nevertheless.

PART I
Introduction and theoretical background

1
THE CHANGING LANDSCAPE OF YOUNG CONSUMER BEHAVIOUR

Ayantunji Gbadamosi

Introduction

In its holistic form, consumer behaviour is a fascinating phenomenon. It is even more intriguing when considered from the viewpoint of the associated heterogeneity among consumer groups. One of the underpinning principles in marketing is the theory of market segmentation, which underscores the fact that we are considerably constrained in our knowledge of consumer behaviour without recourse to the typically obvious and subterranean factors that differentiate one consumer group from the other. Using demography as an example indicates that it is intelligible to distinguish between old and young consumers. Accordingly, the extant literature is replete with definitions of young consumers mainly due to varying circumstances that characterise such studies and write-ups. As indicated by McCarthy (2010), childhood could be conceptualised at several age levels. Meanwhile, most societies recognise that a child reaches adulthood at age 18, implying that this age could possibly be used as a boundary of definition of young consumers. However, in several other contexts, consumers slightly over this age boundary are also considered as young consumers. Hence, the discussion in this chapter straddles all categories of young consumers. So, adapting Solomon's (2015) definition of consumer behaviour, young consumer behaviour can be conceptualised as the study of the processes involved when these young people individually, or in groups select, purchase, use or dispose of products, services, ideas or experiences to satisfy needs and desires. This is somewhat similar to another perspective offered by Schiffman *et al.* (2010). If adapted to the context and focus of this chapter, young consumer behaviour can also be defined as the behaviour exhibited by young people while searching for, purchasing, using, evaluating and disposing of products and services that they expect will satisfy their needs (Schiffman *et al.*, 2010). Clearly, both of these definitions emphasise the process this consumer segment undertakes in their quest to satisfy their needs. So, this chapter examines the changing landscape of young consumer behaviour by drawing together the historical viewpoints and contemporary perspectives on this issue and in doing so sheds light on what this consumer group consumes, how it consumes and why it does so.

According to Griskevicius and Kenrick (2013), at the proximate level, we as consumers seek a number of goals including self-esteem, meaning, novelty, identity and reliability, so humans' need to solve the inherent evolutionary challenges has a significant influence in the modern product choices and the various economic decisions made. In his paper on evolutionary consumption, Saad (2013) emphasises the pride of consumer scholars as the discipline's quest for an interdisciplinary ethos but he still states that a reflective scrutiny of the status quo shows substantial room for improvement. In a related publication several years ago, Trentmann (2004) observes that there were too few historical building blocks for a general debate on the changing physiology of modern consumer society in its various narrative forms. A meticulous literature search reveals that this trend still persists especially in relation to young consumers. In the view of Kopnina (2013), the subject of consumption is linked to a child's feeling of responsibility, identity and perceived status among many other issues indicating that it is socially conditioned. Hence, it will be helpful to take social economic differences into account when teaching consumption issues (Kopnina, 2013). In a somewhat related view, the dynamic nature of the media landscape has been highlighted, showing that new online platforms through which people could interact with one another has changed dramatically (Hollenbeck and Kaikati, 2012). Accordingly, increasing evidence now shows that young consumers are more open to innovative technologies and could actually be described as agents of change (see, for example, Steenkamp *et al.*, 1999; Spero and Stone 2004; Gurtner and Soyez, 2016). In specific terms, available evidence also shows that the average child is exposed to approximately three hours of TV a day and this time is exclusive of the time spent on playing video games or watching videotapes (Mares, 1998; Nielsen Media Research, 1998; American Academy of Pediatrics, 2001). So, putting this in context, by the time the average consumer reaches the age of 70, the individual would have spent approximately seven years to one decade watching television (Strasbuger, 1993). Interestingly, apart from TV, a plethora of other things are associated with children's consumption and some of these have experienced significant changes over these years, hence this is the terrain explored in this chapter.

Historical perspectives on young consumer behaviour

As shown by Griskevicius and Kenrick (2013, p. 373):

> An evolutionary perspective asserts that all living organisms evolved to behave in ways that gave those organisms an evolutionary advantage . . . [implying that] modern humans are endowed with psychological mechanisms that incline them to process information and make decisions in ways that have enabled our ancestors to survive, thrive, and replicate.

Accordingly, they proceed through distinct stages of a somatic (birth to puberty), a mating (puberty to parenthood) and parenting stage, which also includes grandparenting for humans (Griskevicius and Kenrick, 2013). So, historically, young consumers have always been a part of existence all along. Although our consumption patterns change by age over time (Gbadamosi, 2016), we were all once children at a stage in life. It is therefore not surprising that much modern behaviour is influenced by deep-seated evolutionary motives, such as avoiding disease, making friends, evading physical harm, attaining status, acquiring a mate, keeping a mate and caring for the family (Griskevicius and Kenrick, 2013). More often than not, having an understanding of the past is key to gaining insight into the present. As indicated by Laslett and Brenner (1989), while historians tend to be more interested in context, sociologists tend to focus more on abstraction and generalisation but the tension between the two is useful to historical sociologists. It has been argued that people are 'backpackers' through time as they carry the remains of experiences from one place to another, including those relating to them and others, so it is logical to assemble historical narratives by exploring documents (Schmidt and Garcia, 2010). Although in the research context related to young consumers, this segment of the chapter is reminiscent of this viewpoint as it traces lines of developments in the research inquiry about this consumer segment showing key contributions in this research domain.

At the basic level, we can trace the discussion of human consumption to the work of Charles Darwin who, according to Downes (2013), was the first to appeal to evolution for the purpose of having an understanding of aspects of human behaviour. Similarly, it is very common to trace the history of the systematic study of children to the early observational work of Charles Darwin (Smith and Greene, 2014). Unlike the developmental psychology that has placed the discourse of children in its mainstream focus since it was recognised as a discipline at about the end of the nineteenth century to the beginning of the twentieth century (Kessen, 1990; Smith and Greene, 2014), other social science disciplines like anthropology and sociology rather position the discourse of issues relating to children at the margin and simply embed it into the family or household issues (Smith and Greene, 2014). This view is somewhat related to the claim that while children have been noted as consumers right from the eighteenth century since the development of a specific culture of children's toys and games, but their potential as a consumer group in society was only fully realised during the nineteenth century (James and James, 2012). Cross (2010) presents the historical issues around the children's market using the framework of the 'cute' and 'cool' concepts. One could tease from this viewpoint that the former explains specific ways that children interact with adults indicating their vulnerability, vitality and dependency on adults, whereas the latter is a rejection of the former by the child, suggesting expression of freedom from adults' possessive needs (Cross, 2010, pp. 83–86). In this article, with reference to a body of literature, it was noted that developing products for children was an afterthought of producing those meant for adults, while miniature coasters and ferris wheels developed for children only began in the 1920s (Mangels, 1952; Cross, 1997; Register, 2001). So, it is reasonable to concur with the claim of Bullock and Gable (2006) that while several advocates acted to speak on behalf of adults as far back as 400 BC, the focus of similar actions on children did not really take place until the latter part of the nineteenth century in the US. An example corroborating this position could be seen in the claim that articles published about African American children were at a very low rate between 1936 and 1965, the trend changed upward slightly between 1966 and 1970, experienced a further sharp increase between 1971 and 1975, but thereafter reduced (Mclloyd, 2006). Nonetheless, it is important to note the interest in a specific type of young consumer group that developed shortly after this. These are the 'Generation Y' consumers. According to Cekada (2012, cited in Moore *et al.*, 2010), this group of consumers are children born between 1980 and 2000. The existing literature shows that they were brought up in an era characterised with notable changes, which are economic, cultural and technological in nature (Schewe and Noble, 2000; Moore *et al.*, 2010). From a different perspective but also emphasising the delayed full recognition of children as a consumer segment, Gunter and Furnham (1998) citing Davis (1990) note that the emergence of 'teenager' as a distinct group and the 'youth market' was not given much particular marketing importance until the mid-1950s. But in specific terms, the emergence of the baby boomer generation after the Second Word War actually ushered in the keen interest in young consumers as a significant consumer group (McNeal, 1992; Gunter and Furnham, 1998).

One of the marketing literature areas that has been used to uncover the discourses of historical issues about children's consumption behaviour is their socialisation and a good number of papers have been written on this, such as the seminal papers of Ward (1974) and John (1999). Some of these papers have revealed other publications. For example, one is able to tease from John's (1999) that early scholarship effort in this research area could be traced to the 1950s, citing papers like Guest (1955) on brand loyalty and that of Reisman and Roseborough (1955) written on conspicuous consumption; and acknowledging further efforts in other research domains including consumption patterns authored by Cateora (1963), children's understanding vis-à-vis the retail function (McNeal, 1964) and the parents' influence in purchase decisions (Wells and LoSciuto, 1966; Berey and Pollay, 1968). John (1999) also pinpoints the 1970s as a period of a more blossomed part of scholarship in this important research area. This is a very helpful hint on the build-up of literature around children's role in the marketplace.

Past studies have also looked into issues around financial resources and these also have some far reaching implications for our understanding of the dynamics of children's consumption and the marketplace. In a paper on parental attitude to pocket money allowance for children, Furnham (2001) highlights some scholarship efforts on this issue over past decades in various countries, including studies conducted in the UK (Newson and Newson, 1976; Furnham and Thomas, 1984); the US (Marshall and Magruder, 1960; Mortimer *et al.*, 1994) and France (Lassarre, 1996) among very many others. By and large, while scholarship attention on issues around young consumers was markedly sparse before the nineteenth century, this has not only changed now but also follows the related recent trends in the society.

Contemporary issues in young consumer behaviour

Virtually everything around us endorses the common saying that 'change is a permanent phenomenon'. Change is experienced in virtually every ramification of human life, be it the way we see the world around us, the way we react to the stimuli, the nature of these stimuli, and many more. The scale of changes in the marketing world and the way consumers respond to them have changed dramatically in the past couple of years and the trend continues. Hence, it will be theoretically and managerially relevant to explore some of these changes in relation to young consumers in the contemporary period. As noted by Trentmann (2004), while there may be some discrepancies in the perspectives of theorists of modernity and those of post-modernity, there is agreement between them that consumption is central to modern capitalism and contemporary culture. So exploring it is clearly a worthwhile endeavour. With reference to Vygotsky's cultural-historical theory, Edwards (2013), in a study that revolves around a digital play in the early years and the use of technology in early childhood curriculum, posits that patterns of development are unlikely to remain static over time as children acquire cultural knowledge and tools that they will use in their adulthood stage. Specifically, in the digital world it has been shown that children now interact online. In the consumption context, Hollenbeck and Kaikati (2012) indicate that the media landscape has changed recently as people now interact in a myriad of ways. One notable example here is the blossomed use of social media across the world. By definition, social media could be described as online application, platform and media that aid collaboration, interaction and sharing of content (Richter and Koch, 2007, in Kim and Ko, 2012). Generally, social media in its various forms, such as socio blogs, pictures, microblogging and weblogs, has revolutionised our way of life in various ways. They offer marketers opportunities to reach consumers in their social communities (Kelly *et al.*, 2010; Godey *et al.*, 2016). As an example, Hollenbeck and Kaikati (2012) show how consumers use brands on their Facebook pages to depict themselves. Interestingly, young consumers are at the centre stage when it comes to the use of these tools. In a study that revolves around social media marketing activities, brand equity and luxury fashion brands, Kim and Ko (2012) show five social media marketing activities as:

- Entertainment
- Trendiness
- Interaction
- Customisation
- Word of mouth.

By and large, these authors (Kim and Ko, 2012) found that Social Media Marketing (SMM) activities were effective in luxury brands' future profit and provide more novel value to customers than the traditional marketing media. It is therefore not surprising when it is claimed that the power to shape brand image has been transferred from marketers to consumers in the form of online contents and connections (Tsai and Men, 2013; Godey et al., 2016). Clearly, this is the world where young consumers thrive. They typically end the day clutching one gadget or another and start the next day in similar manner. So, it will not be outlandish to claim that their consumption pattern is considerably guided by these devices. Nevertheless, developments in the world of technology could be seen in the light of the usual aphorism of two sides of a coin, as some of the impacts are not so positive in relation to societal welfare. As far back as 2010, it was noted that between 10 per cent and 20 per cent of real-life violence could be linked to media violence (Comstock and Strasburger, 1993). DuRant et al. (1997, in American Academy of Paediatrics, 2001, p. 423) report four key findings of the National Television Violence study as (a) approximately two-thirds of all programming contains violence, (b) children's shows contain the most violence, (c) portrayal of violence is often glamorised and (d) perpetrators often go unpunished. Nonetheless, the overall impact of the recent developments in the dynamics of young consumer behaviour is considerable.

One of the key fundamental developments in the study of young consumers revolves around the new sociology of children, which the literature indicates climaxed around the 1990s, in which childhood became increasingly conceptualised as a legitimate and problematic research phenomenon in sociology and related areas (James and Prout, 1997) in that children are now viewed as actors in sociocultural interactions in society rather than mere absorbers in the system (Freeman Mathison, 2009; James and Prout, 1997). For example, it has been reported that there are growing concerns about excessive misuse of alcohol by young consumers in recent times, such that in Europe some young people start drinking alcohol at the age of 12 (Moore et al., 2010). It makes sense to see things around this in a holistic perspective. In the submission of John (1999), issues like an increase in the number of single-parent families, technological advancement and other cultural changes in the society limit the extent to which we can totally rely on existing findings about socialisation.

Although a good number of studies have emphasised the huge impact of culture on consumption including the consumption pattern of young consumers, there are noteworthy developments in this line of reasoning that call for caution in how one interprets these postulations. One notable example is the child–parent relationship in developing countries. The common argument is that children in these countries have very limited access to global marketplace information, operate under autocratic parental guidance and hence have very little or no control over their consumption issues. Nevertheless, the spread of the technological development across the world (albeit in a limited way to developing countries) seems to have subtly introduced children in these contexts to marketplace information. So, children in

Ghana, Nigeria, Tanzania and other developing countries are also aware of marketplace myths such as Spiderman and Batman stories, which are commonly associated with Western culture (Gbadamosi, 2015a). In fact, Gbadamosi (2012) found that, the very 'thick' cultural divide between developed and developing countries in terms of children's roles in family decisions is waning by the day as children in developing countries, especially those in metropolitan centres, also participate as initiators, influencers, buyers, users and deciders in some cases. Gbadamosi's (2012) findings show that these children have opportunities to take decisions relating to routine products and even have a say in some crucial decisions that relate to them. So, things are changing in the dynamics of children's consumption.

Young consumer decision-making process

It is now very well established that consumers pass through several stages in their consumption process. Although this could vary depending on circumstances of the purchase involved, the stages are typically as depicted in Figure 1.1, which comprises the need for recognition, search for information, evaluation of alternatives, purchase and post-purchase evaluation. This is discussed in this section in relation to exploring the changing landscape of consumption among young consumers.

Need recognition

The needs of young consumers these days are considerably different from what they used to be several years ago. The needs trail developments in every sphere of life. Basically, needs refer to states of felt deprivation (Kotler and Armstrong, 2018), so the scope of this discussion is considerably wide (see Figure 1.2).

At the very basic level, young consumers' need for food is well established in the literature (Marshall and O'Donohoe, 2010). Very many examples of food items relating to young consumers in society in recent times abound, ranging from cereals to confectioneries. These in turn prompt marketers to feature children in most of the related ads. One of the concerns around this phenomenon is the low intake of some nutritious foods. Minaker and Hammond (2016) report that in the 2010 Global Burden of Disease study, worldwide low fruit consumption is ranked number 5 alongside other causes of disability-adjusted life years. Meanwhile, in a study about low frequency of fruit and vegetable consumption among Canadian youth, Minaker and Hammond (2016) found that only 10 per cent of Canadian

FIGURE 1.1 Consumer decision-making process

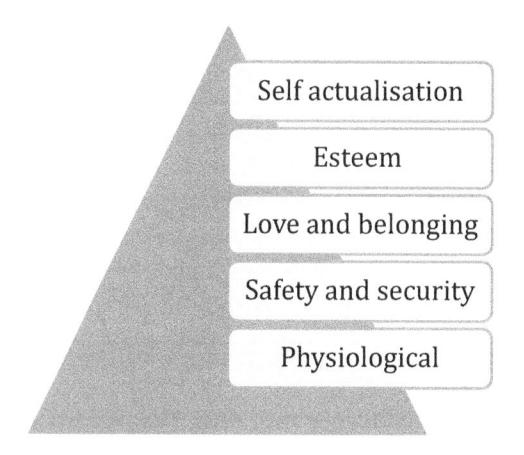

Self actualisation
Esteem
Love and belonging
Safety and security
Physiological

FIGURE 1.2 Hierarchy of needs

students in Grades 6–12 met the food guide fruit and vegetable (FV) consumption recommendation in the year 2012–2013. Unfortunately, this is not an isolated case. Ironically, such food items are very useful to guard against most of the diseases including cardiovascular diseases and cancers. While some of their needs are very basic, others transcend this level. Perhaps it will be useful to make reference to the very commonly cited Abraham Maslow hierarchy of needs in the explication of this phenomenon. Given the prior view of children as 'inactive' members of the family, it is tempting to concur that their needs will basically be at the physiological level, safety/security levels, or at best the love and belonging stage. But an increasing number of studies show that children also battle to meet higher-level needs. Increasing numbers of young adults now accumulate unmanageable amounts of debt, abuse credit cards and battle an insatiable appetite for life demands (Robert and Jones, 2001; Duh, 2016). With reference to Webley *et al.* (1991), Otto *et al.* (2006) indicate that at least two types of understanding influence the saving behaviour of children, which are (a) the need to understand 'temptation', and (b) the need to understand saving strategies as an effective way of handling the problem of temptation. In her seminal paper on consumer socialisation of children, John (1999) notes that our culture encourages children to embrace materialism. In other words, they look to material products as a source of achieving personal happiness, success and self-fulfilment. In fact, at higher levels of need, some children now see alcohol, tobacco and in some cases some illegal drugs as needed items to belong, and to be respected among their peers. More often than not, an increasing amount of academic evidence points to the fact that young consumers are vulnerable to messages they receive through TV and other media (Gbadamosi *et al.*, 2012). Hence, these could trigger need recognition. Some young consumers' social needs also revolve around avoiding ridicule among friends and peers. Wooten (2006) specifically examines the effect of ridicule in the consummation of adolescents and found that ridicule affects how these young consumers perceive belongingness.

He then suggests that the psychological and social pressures felt by children in relation to wearing expensive brands, and the associated financial pressure on parents, could be reduced by maintaining a policy of mandatory school uniforms. According to Wooten (2013), if wearing uniform is made optional, it could become a symbol of stigma for those that choose to wear it. All of these point to a change in the pattern of needs of the young consumer in recent times.

Search for information

More fundamentally, consumers explore a number of options when searching for information concerning products and services to buy to fulfil their needs. These could be categorised in a number of ways but it is very common to conceptualise them as internal and external. The internal source of information is obtained by searching memory to recall experience or encounter with offerings and what they could offer. Sources outside of this, such as from friends, neighbours and advertisement are categorised as external. Gbadamosi (2012) notes that children often resort to 'reference to others' as a tactic to convince their parents that the products or services being demanded are of good fit. This is an example of external source. Evidence shows that young consumers now have a superfluity of sources of information on their day-to-day consumption. The literature specifically shows that they are more open to innovative technologies and tend to be more aware of the current and upcoming environmental issues (Bentley et al., 2004; Spero and Stone, 2004; Franzen and Meyer, 2010; Gurtner and Soyez, 2016). Furthermore, evidence shows that young consumers search more for product information online than adults (Source et al., 2005; Chaffey and Ellis-Chadwick, 2016). Similarly, there is a claim that younger, better-educated consumers who love shopping/fact-finding process tend to engage in more information searches, while women tend to search more than men (Punj and Staelin, 1983; Huang et al., 2009; Solomon et al., 2016). Platforms like Google, Yahoo and many related others now serve as great sources of marketplace information about products and services for these young consumers. One may be tempted to think that the digital expedition is only amenable to older children like teenagers and others in older categories, but children of lower age now interact with technology frequently as well and could use this to influence their parents who control resources and/or will make decisions concerning the purchase.

Evaluation of alternatives

Given the numerous sources of information available to the young consumer and the limited resources at their disposal, there is a need to evaluate the alternatives towards making the 'right' choice. A number of criteria could be used to evaluate available options depending on the product and circumstances associated with the purchase. Some of the common factors are price, quality, availability, suitability and a host of other factors. All of these could be categorised as personal, social-cultural, and commercial as shown in Figure 1.3. Considering price as an example, in some cases, children depend on the evaluation of the parents as they control the family budget in most cases, especially for special products (Gbadamosi, 2012). Besides, it has been shown that children inhabit some unique niches or microenvironments within their family's ecology that can influence their socialisation as consumers (Kerrane and Hogg, 2013). Accordingly, their evaluation of which market offerings to buy and how to buy them could follow the family tradition which is a position attested to by the study of Fournier (1998) entitled 'Consumers and their brands' in which family tradition was found as a possible influence on people's future consumption choices. Nonetheless, evidence still shows that young consumers' spending power is high (Moses, 2000, in Gurtner and Soyez, 2016), which suggests that they also could be in a position to evaluate the offerings to buy and might not be as price sensitive as their parents who will most likely be more conscious in spending due to maturity in the experience of the marketplace system. In fact, Davies and Lea (1995) indicate that students are relatively low income and have tolerant attitude to debt. Gurtner and Soyez (2016) also found that while young consumers are interested in ecological products, they also crave for enjoyment in these products, hence hedonic value will be a key criterion for them when evaluating their options of ecological factors. From another perspective, the young consumers' identities could be another crucial criterion as they hold multiple identities and will want to favour market offerings that help them realise these identity goals.

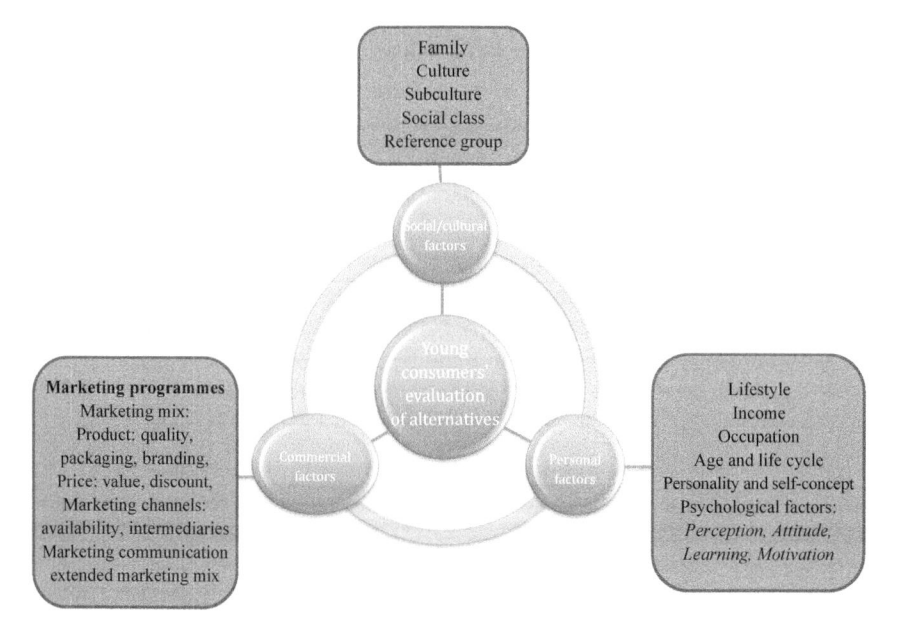

FIGURE 1.3 Young consumers' evaluation of market offerings

Source: Adapted from Gbadamosi (2016).

This is what Gbadamosi (2015b) found about young ethnic consumers in the UK whose consumption goals are about meeting their social needs and revolve around brand personification.

The purchase act

At the stage of purchase, consumers are expected to make the choice based on the evaluation in the previous stage. It is very common to state that some categories of young consumers depend on their parents for purchases especially in relation to some key items. So, the gatekeeping role of parents is very key in this regard. For instance, studies have shown mothers as primary socialisation agents in children's consumption system (Roberts et al., 1980). This aligns closely to the claim of McLeod (1974) that a child's participation in the family purchase decision begins as soon as s/he can hold a coin. Similarly, it is noted that as they accompany their parents on shopping trips they load their parents' shopping trolleys with many products of which some may be unwanted items, while some children pester their parents concerning specific market offerings they would like to buy. These young consumers are known as 'trolley loaders' and 'pesters' respectively (*Snacks Magazine*, 1993, in Gelperowick and Beharrell, 1994). Nonetheless, research shows that students also have their own money, which they obtain from various sources. It has been shown that young consumers obtain disposable income from two main sources, namely those they receive from parents or guardians and others received from paid employment (Miller and Yung, 1990; Darlin et al., 2006; Chen et al., 2013). From another perspective, their income sources have been explained as regular and special income. While the former category of income comes from parents, guardians or grandparents, the latter, which is the special income, is obtained on special occasions during birthdays, anniversaries, Christmas Day, New Year's Day and through reward for good behaviour (Liebeck, 1998; Gbadamosi, 2012). In their study, Haynes et al. (1993) found that older children were more involved in the selection of their clothing than the younger children, while Backett-Milburn et al. (2010) found teenagers' food practices as grounded in past contexts, present family life as well as future aspirations. Overall, it has been shown that young consumers between the age of 11 and 16 are more active economically as some of them have part-time jobs and others have a bank account that is in the name of their parents (Furnham, 1999). So, young consumers are becoming more powerful in the purchase act of many market offerings.

Post-purchase evaluation

Conventionally, the consumer decision-making process is not deemed to have ended effectively until the consumer has been able to compare his or her actual experience of the product or service with his or her expectation. This is the post-purchase evaluation stage. In doing the post-purchase evaluation, these young consumers could experience a match between the performance of the product and their experience, their expectation could be exceeded by the performance of the product or the product's performance could fall short of their expectation. The literature indicates that the first could be described as a neutral feeling, the second could cause what is known as disconfirmation of experience that results in satisfaction and the third results in negative confirmation of expectation and dissatisfaction (Cadotte *et al.*, 1987; Schiffman *et al.*, 2012). Many factors could be at play here, just as those highlighted concerning the evaluation of alternative stages (Figure 1.3). For example, the evaluation of the fit of the purchase could be around cultural values. This is related to the claim of Treviño *et al.* (2015) that there is a need for preschool children, families, food service staff and teachers to have culturally relevant nutrition education towards improving health knowledge and eating behaviour that meets dietary recommendations.

Meanwhile the post-purchase evaluation results in a number of actions, such as engaging in repeat purchase of the brand, complaining about the experience, or engaging in word of mouth (WOM) communication, which could be positive or negative, depending on the experience. The impact of WOM in sales of consumer goods is considerable. It has been shown, based on a McKinsey & Company study, that 67 per cent of consumer goods sales revolve around personal information sources (Taylor, 2003; Okazaki, 2009). But of specific interest in this discussion of WOM is the increasing use of e-word of mouth communication (eWOM), which is very common among young consumers and involves spreading information about the experience of the use of products and services through chat and blogs, website bulletin boards, email lists and a host of other online communication modes. As a practitioner in that area, Needham (2008) stresses the notion of value co-creation. He notes that the strategy is now no longer about 'marketing at young people', but 'marketing with them'. He notes that 13–14 percent of these young consumers create and upload their own content, while 8 per cent write their blogs regularly, 17 per cent of 16–25 year olds are friends with one brand or another on their social network profile pages. Interestingly, we can still have distinction between laptop- and desk computer-based word of mouth on the one hand, and mobile devices word-of-mouth (mWOM) on the other, which have been described as very easy to manage and especially common among young people (Sato and Kato, 2005; Okazaki, 2009). This word of mouth communication associated with mobile devices (mWOM) has been described as relatively popular among young consumers, and it is characterised with a high level of intrinsic enjoyment in that it gives consumers a gratifying experience in a ubiquitous way (Okazaki, 2009).

The young consumer and the family: examining the dynamics

As shown in the previous sections of this chapter, a lot of things have changed concerning research around young consumers, and the factors that influence their consumption behaviour. Nonetheless, given the specific nature of family, the trend of developments around this key factor vis-à-vis young consumer behaviour is also examined in this section. The great relevance of families in the consumption pattern of young consumers is well acknowledged. In fact, some authors have argued that family is the most important decision-making and consumption unit (Assael, 1998; Shoham and Dalakas, 2005). Stated differently, Sidin *et al.* (2008) argue that while there are many factors that interplay to influence children's consumer decision-making, family is one of the most influential of these. Young consumers of all categories belong to one family or another. As argued by Laslett and Brenner (1989), be it from the perspective of family strategies, or a socio-reproduction standpoint, the implications of families for the society as a whole is wide-ranging. No wonder, it is posited, that the impact of various psychosocial outcomes that emerge from childhood family experiences, such as money attitudes, should be incorporated into the life-course model of consumption orientations (Benmoyal-Bouzaglo and Moschis, 2010; Moore *et al.*, 2010). Early research on family and young consumers approaches the study of family dynamics in terms of the communication pattern between parent and children. McLeod and Chaffee (1972) looked at family communication patterns and then came up with a typology showing four types of family communication structures, which are:

- Laissez-faire families
- Protective families
- Pluralistic families
- Consensual families.

In this typology, they describe the laissez-faire families as those where there is little parent–child communication, while protective families emphasise obedience and social harmony in the way they communicate. Meanwhile, according to McLeod and Chaffee (1972), in pluralistic families, children are not only encouraged to explore new ideas, but are also allowed to express them without fear of retaliation, but in consensual families while the children are encouraged to be interested in the world of ideas, this should be done without affecting the existing internal harmony and hierarchy of opinion in the family (McLeod and Chaffee, 1972; Moschis, 1985). As expected, these different communication styles in the family influence the young consumer behaviour in the marketplace dynamics. Accordingly, Moschis (1985) argues that parents' influence on the development of the consumption behaviour of their children could be direct or indirect. In the direct form, they could engage in purposive training, and the indirect approach could be by moderating the interaction of these children with other sources of consumer influence. Meanwhile, in positioning children's socialisation within the family, Cram and Ng (1999) show that children's experience of ownership starts with objects such as toys given to them at the early stage of life, while adults and older siblings in the family help them during infancy (6–9 months) to know what belongs to them and what is off limits, to avoid environmental hazards (Furby, 1980; Cram and Ng, 1999).

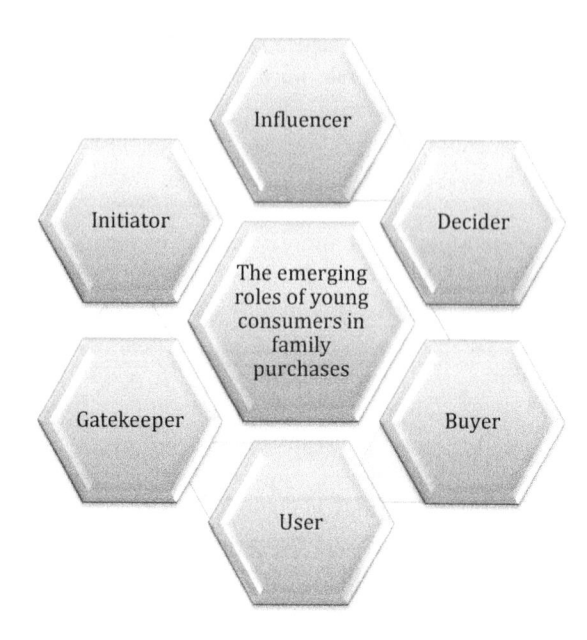

FIGURE 1.4 The emerging roles of young consumers in family purchases

In terms of what has changed over the years, Cram and Ng (1999) note that materials that used to be household items gradually became things that young consumers were able to buy on their own, citing the example of TV sets with reference to the publication of McNeal (1992). While this was the case in 1999 when this work was published, it is clear that this has now changed dramatically with children taking decisions on their own mobile phones, the types of hair style they have and which brands of clothes they wear in order to fit societal trends. As shown in Figure 1.4, it is now increasingly difficult to argue about the limiting role of youths in family consumption as increasing evidence now shows that their roles in family purchases could be any of these – initiator, influencer, decider, buyer and gatekeeper. Statistically, at the global level, it was highlighted that children spend $300 billion of their own pocket money and influence another $1.88 trillion of purchases made by their family (Lindstrom and Seybold, 2003, in Kerrane and Hogg, 2013). Solomon (2015, p. 456) shows that students spend over £11 billion a year on purchases of snacks and beverages, another $4 billion on personal care products and around $3 billion on the purchase of CDs. Kerrane and Hogg (2013) found children to be early adopters of technically complex products within the family. Overall, young consumers constitute a significant force within the family settings.

Concluding remarks

Young consumers constitute an important market segment in the society. This explains the profundity of the scholarship attention directed at it as an area of interest in recent times. It has also attracted the attention of practitioners. Historically, young consumers were not considered as significant a market segment as spouses in the family, especially in the early research endeavours. Existing literature indicates that considerable research attention on young consumers as a research area became significantly noticeable from around the nineteenth century and gradually developed in many ramifications. But a lot has changed since then and these changes cannot be ignored. If we use the common macro-environmental framework to decipher the discourse, a number of interesting developments around young consumer behaviour are noteworthy. Politically, marketers are no longer having an easy ride in terms of dealing with young consumers. Accountability is improving in various areas of marketing practices, from product suitability to marketing communications (Gbadamosi, 2010). Governments' attention on children's consumption is improving across the world by calling for more socially responsible marketing. Examples, on this include sugar consumption, access to tobacco and alcohol, exposure to inappropriate marketing communication messages and many others. Economically, increasing evidence now shows that young consumers have access to more money and exert more control on such resources than they did several decades ago. The huge changes in the socio-cultural environment concerning children are remarkable. The realisation of children as 'active' consumers especially from the new sociology perspective is a notable development. Their participation in the family buying roles has now been significantly extended beyond the mere simple requests for goods and services. Young consumers now have a say in the holiday destination for the family, the brands of clothes to wear for festive seasons, their food consumption and a host of other consumption issues.

Young consumers are active from the stage of need recognition right to the state of post-purchase evaluation. It is even more interesting that these changes are sidestepping the cultural divide between societies. This is because, as globalisation has made the world a global village, children in cultural settings characterised with considerable autocratic parental upbringing are catching up with their counterparts in other parts of the world in relation to products and services they consume and their participation in such decisions. The changing landscape in the technology arena is huge in terms of scale and significance. These developments permeate every stage of the decision-making process of these young consumers. The advent of the Internet, the experience of mobile technologies, the excitement that characterises the functioning of social media tools, all add to the evidence that the tide is turning concerning young consumer behaviour. The implications of this phenomenon is not limited to the relevant academic discourse, it also suggests to practitioners that the young consumer market has evolved and that managing the strategic response to it would require a dynamic mindset that can capture the salient factors that characterise this market, including value co-creation with them in all areas that underpin the marketing system.

References

American Academy of Paediatrics (2001). Children, adolescents, and television: Committee on public education. *Paediatrics, 107*(2), 423–426.

Assael, H. (1998). *Consumer behavior*. Boston, MA: South-Western College Publishing.

Backett-Milburn, K. C., Wills, W. J., Roberts, M. and Lawton, J. (2010). Food, eating and taste: Parents' perspectives on the making of the middle-class teenager. *Social Science and Medicine, 71*, 1316–1323.

Benmoyal-Bouzaglo, S. and Moschis, G. P. (2010). Effects of family structure and socialization on materialism: A life course study in France. *Journal of Marketing Theory and Practice, 18*(1), 55–71.

Bentley, M., Fien, J. and Neil, C. (2004). *Sustainable consumption: Young Australians as agents of change*. Canberra, Australia: National Youth Affairs Research Scheme.

Berey, Lewis A. and Pollay, R. W. (1968). The influencing role of the child in family decision making. *Journal of Marketing Research, 5*, 70–72.

Bullock, L. M. and Gable, R. A. (2006). Programs for children and adolescents with emotional and behavioral disorders in the United States: A historical overview. *Current Perspectives, and Future Directions, Preventing School Failure, 50*(20), 7–13.

Cadotte, E. R., Woodruff, R. B. and Jenkins, R. L. (1987). Expectations and norms in models of consumer satisfaction. *Journal of Marketing Research, 24*(3), 305–314.

Cateora, Phillip R. (1963). *An analysis of the teenage market*. Austin: University of Texas Bureau of Business Research.

Chaffey, D. and Ellis-Chadwick, F. (2016). *Internet marketing: Strategy, implementation and practice* (6th edn). Essex: Pearson Education.

Chen, C., Lin, I., Huang, S. L., Tsai, T. and Chen, Y. (2013). Disposable income with tobacco smoking among young adolescents: A multilevel analysis. *Journal of Adolescent Health, 52*, 724–730.

Comstock, G. and Strasburger, V. C. (1993). Media violence: Q and A. *Adolescent Medicine, 4*(3), 495–510.

Cram, F. and Ng, S. H. (1999). Consumer socialisation. *Applied Psychology, 48*(3), 297–312.

Cross, G. (1997). *Kids' stuff: Toys and the changing world of American childhood*. Cambridge, MA: Harvard University Press.

Cross, G. (2010). Children and the market: An American historical perspective. In D. Marshall (ed.), *Understanding children as consumers* (pp. 81–95). Los Angeles, CA: Sage.

Darling, H., Reeder, A. I., McGee, R. and Williams, S. (2006). Brief report: Disposable income, and spending on fast food, alcohol, cigarettes, and gambling by New Zealand secondary school students. *Journal of Adolescence, 29*, 837–843.

Davies, E. and Lea, S. E. (1995). Student attitudes to student debt. *Journal of Economic Psychology, 16*(4), 663–679.

Davis, J. (1990). *Youth and the condition of Britain: Images of adolescent conflict (Vol. 1)*. London: Athlone Press.

Downes, S. M. (2013). Research dialogue evolutionary psychology is not the only productive evolutionary approach to understanding consumer behaviour. *Journal of Consumer Psychology, 23*(3), 400–403.

Duh, H. I. (2016). Childhood family experiences and young Generation Y money attitudes and materialism. *Personality and Individual Differences, 95*, 134–139.

DuRant, R. H., Rich, M., Emans, S. J., Rome, E. S., Allred, E. and Woods, E. R. (1997). Violence and weapon carrying in music videos: A content analysis. *Archives of Paediatrics and Adolescent Medicine, 151*(5), 443–448.

Edwards, S. (2013). Digital play in the early years: A contextual response to the problem of integrating technologies and play-based pedagogies in the early childhood curriculum. *European Early Childhood Education Research Journal*, 21(2), 199–212.

Fournier, S. (1998). Consumers and their brands: Developing relationship theory in consumer research. *Journal of Consumer Research*, 24(4), 343–373.

Franzen, A. and Meyer, R. (2010). Environmental attitudes in cross-national perspective: A multilevel analysis of the ISSP 1993 and 2000. *European Sociological Review*, 26, 219–234.

Freeman, M. and Mathison, S. (2009). *Researching children's experiences*. New York and London: The Guilford Press.

Furby, L. (1980). The origins and early development of possessive behaviour. *Political Psychology*, 2, 30–42.

Furnham, A. (1999). The saving and spending habits of young people. *Journal of Economic Psychology*, 20(6), 677–697.

Furnham, A. (2001). Parental attitudes to pocket money/allowances for children. *Journal of Economic Psychology*, 22(3), 397–422.

Furnham, A. and Thomas, P. (1984). Adults' perceptions of the economic socialization of children. *Journal of Adolescence*, 7(3), 217–231.

Gbadamosi, A. (2010). Regulating child-related advertising in Nigeria. *Young Consumers*, 11(3), 204–214.

Gbadamosi, A. (2012). Exploring children, family, and consumption behaviour: Empirical evidence from Nigeria. *Thunderbird International Business Review*, 54(4), 591–605.

Gbadamosi, A. (2015a). Family consumption systems in Africa: A focus on children. In S. Nwankwo and K. Ibeh (eds), *Routledge companion to business in Africa* (pp. 146–159). Oxford: Routledge.

Gbadamosi, A. (2015b). Brand personification and symbolic consumption among ethnic teenage consumers: An empirical study. *Journal of Brand Management*, 22(9), 737–759.

Gbadamosi, A. (2016). Consumer behaviour in developing nations: A conceptual overview. In A. Gbadamosi (ed.), *Handbook of research on consumerism and buying behaviour in developing nations* (pp. 1–29). Hershey, PA: IGI Global.

Gbadamosi, A., Hinson, R., Eddy, T. K. and Ingunjiri, I. (2012). Children's attitudinal reactions to TV advertisements: The African experience. *International Journal of Market Research*, 54(4), 543–566.

Gelperowic, R. and Beharrell, B. (1994). Healthy food products for children: Packaging and mothers' purchase decisions. *British Food Journal*, 96(11), 4–8.

Godey, B., Manthiou, A., Pederzoli, D., Rokka, J., Aiello, G., Donvito, R. and Singh, R. (2016). Social media marketing efforts of luxury brands: Influence on brand equity and consumer behavior. *Journal of Business Research*, 69(12), 5833–5841.

Griskevicius, V. and Kenrick, D. T. (2013). Fundamental motives: How evolutionary needs influence consumer behavior. *Journal of Consumer Psychology*, 23(3), 372–386.

Guest, Lester P. (1955). Brand loyalty: Twelve years later. *Journal of Applied Psychology*, 39, 405–408.

Gunter, B. and Furnham, A. (1998). *Children as consumers: A psychological analysis of the young people's market*. London: Routledge.

Gurtner, S. and Soyez, K. (2016). How to catch the generation Y: Identifying consumers of ecological innovations among youngsters. *Technological Forecasting and Social Change*, 106, 101–107.

Haynes, J. L., Burts, D. C., Dukes, A. and Cloud, R. (1993). Consumer socialization of preschoolers and kindergartners as related to clothing consumption. *Psychology & Marketing*, 10(2), 151–166.

Hollenbeck, C. R. and Kaikati, A. M. (2012). Consumers' use of brands to reflect their actual and ideal selves on Facebook. *International Journal of Research in Marketing*, 29, 395–405.

Huang, P., Lurie, N. H. and Mitra, S. (2009). Searching for experience on the web: An empirical examination of consumer behavior for search and experience goods. *Journal of Marketing*, 73(2), 55–69.

James, A. and James, A. (2012). *Key concepts in childhood studies*. London: Sage.

James, A. and Prout, A. (1997). *Constructing and reconstructing childhood: Contemporary issues in the sociological study of childhood*. London: Routledge.

John, D. R. (1999). Consumer socialization of children: A retrospective look at twenty-five years of research. *Journal of Consumer Research*, 26, 183–213.

Kelly, L., Kerr, G. and Drennan, J. (2010). Avoidance of advertising in social networking sites: The teenage perspective. *Journal of Interactive Advertising*, 10(2), 16–27.

Kerrane, B. and Hogg, M. K. (2013). Shared or non-shared? Children's different consumer socialisation experiences within the family environment. *European Journal of Marketing*, 47(3/4), 506–524.

Kessen, W. (1990). *The rise and fall of development*. Worcester, MA: Clark Atlanta University Press.

Kim, A. J. and Ko, E. (2012). Do social media marketing activities enhance customer equity? An empirical study of luxury fashion brand. *Journal of Business Research*, 65, 1480–1486.

Kopnina, H. (2013). An exploratory case study of Dutch children's attitudes toward consumption: Implications for environmental education. *The Journal of Environmental Education*, 44(2), 128–144.

Kotler, P. and Armstrong, G. (2018). *Principles of marketing* (17th edn). Harlow: Pearson Education.

Laslett, B. and Brenner, J. (1989). Gender and social reproduction: Historical perspectives. *Annual Review of Sociology*, 15, 381–404.

Lassarre, D. (1996). Consumer education in French families and schools. *Economic Socialization*, 13, 130–148.

Liebeck, L. (1998). Children under 13. *Discount Store News*, 37(20), 55–58.

Lindstrom, M. and Seybold, P. (2003). *Brandchild*. London: Kogan Page.

McCarthy, M. (2010). Keynote from RIME 2009: Researching children's musical culture – historical and contemporary perspectives. *Music Education Research*, 12(1), 112.

McLeod, J. M. (1974). Commentaries on Ward, 'consumer socialization'. *Journal of Consumer Research*, 1(2), 15–17.

McLeod, J. M. and Chaffee, S. H. (1972). The construction of social reality. In T. Tiedeschi (ed.), *The social influence process* (pp. 50–99). Chicago, IL: Aldine-Atherton.

McLloyd, V. C. (2006). The role of African American Scholars in research on African American children: Historical perspectives and personal reflections. *Developmental Psychology: Monographs of the Society for Research in Child Development*, 71(1), 121–144.

McNeal, J. U. (1964). *Children as consumers*. Austin: Bureau of Business Research, University of Texas at Austin.

McNeal, J. U. (1992). *Kids as customers: A handbook of marketing to children*. New York: Lexington Books.

Mangels, W. F. (1952). *The outdoor amusement industry: From earliest times to the present*. New York: Vantage Press.

Mares, M. L. (1998). Children's use of VCRs. *The Annals of the American Academy of Political and Social Science*, 557(1), 120–131.

Marshall, D. and O'Donohoe, D. (2010). Children and food. In D. Marshall (ed.), *Understanding children as consumers* (pp. 167–183). Los Angeles, CA: Sage.

Marshall, H. R. and Magruder, L. (1960). Relations between parent money education practices and children's knowledge and use of money. *Child Development*, *31*(2), 253–284.

Miller, J. and Yung, S. (1990). The role of allowances in adolescent socialization. *Youth Socialisation*, *22*, 137–159.

Minaker, L. and Hammond, D. (2016). Low frequency of fruit and vegetable consumption among Canadian youth: Findings from the 2012/2013 youth smoking survey. *Journal of School Health*, *86*(2), 135–142.

Moore, G. F., Rothwell, H. and Segrott, J. (2010). An exploratory study of the relationship between parental attitudes and behaviour and young people's consumption of alcohol. *Substance Abuse Treatment, Prevention, and Policy*, *5*(6), 1–14.

Mortimer, J. T., Dennehy, K., Lee, C. and Finch, M. D. (1994). Economic socialization in the American family: The prevalence, distribution, and consequences of allowance arrangements. *Family Relations*, *43*(1), 23–29.

Moschis, G. P. (1985). The role of family communication in consumer socialization of children and adolescents. *Journal of Consumer Research*, *11*(4), 898–913.

Moses, E. (2000). *The $100 billion allowance: Accessing the global teen market*. New York: Wiley.

Needham, A. (2008). Word of mouth, youth and their brands. *Young Consumers*, *9*(1), 60–62.

Newson, J. and Newson, E. (1976). *Seven years old in the home environment*. London: Allen & Unwin.

Nielsen Media Research (1998). *Nielsen report on television*. New York: Nielsen Media Research.

Okazaki, S. (2009). Social influence model and electronic word of mouth: PC versus mobile internet. *International Journal of Advertising*, *28*(3), 439–472.

Otto, A. M. C., Schots, P. A. M., Westerman, J. A. J. and Webley, P. (2006). Children's use of saving strategies: An experimental approach. *Journal of Economic Psychology*, *27*, 57–72.

Punj, G. N. and Staelin, R. (1983). A model of consumer information search behavior for new automobiles. *Journal of Consumer Research*, *9*(4), 366–380.

Register, W. (2001). *The kid of Coney Island: Fred Thompson and the rise of American amusements*. Oxford: Oxford University Press.

Reisman, D. and Roseborough, H. (1955). Careers and consumer behavior. In L. Clark (ed.), *Consumer behavior. Volume 2: The life cycle and consumer behaviour* (pp. 1–18). New York: New York University Press.

Richter, A. and Koch, M. (2007). *Social software: Status quo und Zukunft*. Technischer Bericht, Nr. 2007-01. Fakultät für Informatik. München: Universität der Bundeswehr München.

Roberts, J. A. and Jones, E. (2001). Money attitudes, credit card use, and compulsive buying among American college students. *Journal of Consumer Affairs*, *35*(2), 213–240.

Roberts, M., Wortzel, L. and Berkeley, R. (1980). Mothers' attitudes and perceptions of children's influence and their effect on family consumption. *Advances in Consumer Research*, *8*(1), 730–735.

Saad, G. (2013). Research dialogue: Evolutionary consumption. *Journal of Consumer Psychology*, *23*(3), 351–371.

Sato, N. and Kato, Y. (2005). Youth marketing in Japan. *Young Consumers*, *6*(4), 56–60.

Schewe, C. D. and Noble, S. M. (2000). Market segmentation by cohorts: The value and validity of cohorts in America and abroad. *Journal of Marketing Management*, *16*(1–3), 129–142.

Schiffman, L. G., Kanuk, L. L. and Hansen, H. (2012). *Consumer behaviour: A European outlook* (2nd edn). Harlow: Pearson.

Schiffman, L. G., Leslie Lazar Kanuk, L. L. and Wisenblit, J. (2010). *Consumer behavior: Global edition* (10th edn). Boston, MA: Pearson.

Schmidt, M. A. and Garcia, T. M. F. B. (2010). History from children's perspectives: Learning to read and write historical accounts using family sources. *Education*, *38*(3), 289–299.

Shoham, A. and Dalakas, V. (2005). He said, she said . . . they said: Parents' and children's assessment of children's influence on family consumption decisions. *Journal of Consumer Marketing*, *22*(3), 152–160.

Sidin, S. M., Abdul Rahman, M. K., Abdul Rashid, Z., Othman, N. and Abu Bakar, A. Z. (2008). Effects of social variables on urban children's consumption attitude and behavior intentions. *Journal of Consumer Marketing*, *25*(1), 7–15.

Smith, C. and Greene, S. (2014). *Key thinkers in childhood studies*. Bristol: Policy Press.

Solomon, M. R. (2015). *Consumer behaviour: Buying, having, and being* (11th edn). Harlow: Pearson Education.

Solomon, M. R., Bamossy, G. J., Askegaard, S. and Hogg, M. K. (2016). *Consumer behaviour: A European perspective* (6th edn). Harlow: Pearson Education.

Source, P., Perotti, V. and Widrick, S. (2005). Attitude and age differences in online buying. *International Journal of Retail and Distribution Management*, *33*(2), 122–132.

Spero, I. and Stone, M. (2004). Agents of change: How young consumers are changing the world of marketing. *Qualitative Market Research: An International Journal*, 7, 153–159. http://dx.doi.org/10.1108/ 13522750410530057.

Steenkamp, J. B. E. M., Hofstede, T. F. and Wedel, M. (1999). A cross-national investigation into the individual and national cultural antecedents of consumer innovativeness. *Journal of Marketing*, *63*, 55–69. http://dx.doi.org/10.2307/1251945.

Strasburger, V. C. (1993). Children, adolescents, and the media: Five crucial issues. *Adolescent Medicine*, *4*(3), 479–494.

Taylor, J. (2003). Word of mouth is where it's at. *Brandweek*, 2 June, p. 26.

Trentmann, F. (2004). Beyond consumerism: New historical perspectives on consumption. *Journal of Contemporary History Copyright*, *39*(3), 373–340.

Treviño, R. P., Vasquez, L., Shaw-Ridley, M., Mosley, D., Jechow, K. and Piña, C. (2015). Outcome of a food observational study among low-income preschool children participating in a family-style meal setting. *Health Education and Behavior*, *42*(2), 240–248.

Tsai, W. H. S. and Men, L. R. (2013). Motivations and antecedents of consumer engagement with brand pages on social networking sites. *Journal of Interactive Advertising*, *13*(2), 76–87.

Ward, S. (1974). Consumer socialization. *Journal of Consumer Research*, *1*(2), 1–14.

Webley, P., Levine, M. and Lewis, A. (1991). A study in economic psychology: Children's saving in a play economy. *Human Relations*, *44*, 127–146.

Wells, W. D. and LoSciuto, L. A. (1966). Direct observation of purchasing behavior. *Journal of Marketing Research*, *3*(August), 227–233.

Wooten, D. B. (2006). From labeling possessions to possessing labels: Ridicule and socialization among adolescents. *Journal of Consumer Research*, *33*, 188–198.

PART II
Young consumers as individuals

2
CHILDREN'S CONSUMER PERCEPTION

Nashaat H. Hussein

Introduction

Children play an increasingly significant role as consumers. They have become 'an important consumer group' (Ramzy et al., 2012, p. 30). In a growing consumer society, children are socialised at an early age to become responsible consumers, which usually starts as young as 5 years of age when 'children increasingly make independent purchases' (Valkenburg and Janssen, 1999, p. 3). Currently, children have become active participants in family purchase decisions (Martin and Bush, 2000), in brand selection, and also in the orientation of overall familial consumption.

The scale of marketing to children has substantially increased. Although marketing various products that only target children is relatively new, it is considered a key element of the general development of a modern consumer society. Therefore, children increasingly encounter commercial messages in a wider range of contexts and forms. With the development of new marketing technologies, the nature of marketing to children has also changed significantly. Advertising is now only one aspect of a much broader range of strategies that are being used to reach the children's market. Commercial forces play an important role in many areas of children's lives, including play, education and recreation. Recognising children as a separate age group, particularly separate from the adult world, took place in the late nineteenth century. It was accompanied by a growing acknowledgement of the significance of children as a specific market in its own, and by the emergence of advertising to children that began to grow quite rapidly in the early twentieth century. This was accompanied by what some have seen as a symbolic 'valorization of childhood' (Fass, 2007), which is a view of childhood as a special time that deserves special attention and recognition, and accordingly special expenditures. Recognising children from that perspective, especially as a potential segment of consumer society, has resulted in driving attention to children's perception of consumption and to the nature and dynamics that influence their consumer lifestyles. Additionally, in the last few years, children's income has doubled and their spending has almost tripled. They have become inclined to compare prices, prefer certain brand names and are highly influenced by the power of product advertisements, which have an impact on their decision-making behaviour and selection process of consumer goods (Dotson and Hyatt, 2000). Therefore, children are able to show signs of early consumer purchasing behaviour and decision-making processes that relate to being consumers at an early age.

The growing children's market potential has motivated marketers to reach this emerging segment of consumers. Significant means of influencing these young consumers included, among other means, packaging (with specific graphics and colours used as extrinsic product attributes). As explained by McNeal and Ji (1999, p. 349), children respond better to colour and graphics due to their limited reasoning abilities and inability to read. It could therefore be argued that if child consumers preferred colour and graphics applied to the packaging of products, specifically aimed at the children's market, their behaviour as consumers could be predicted to some extent. This would confirm that the product is bought by the child consumer at whom the product was targeted. Product characteristics represent another means for targeting children. Ted Mininni (2005), for example, found that the relationship between product characteristics and consumption intensity in children is moderated by their perception of the character (i.e. supporting character, like a celebrity) or endorser of the product. Children's perception of consumption does not only affect other children's behaviour, but can also affect the perception of adults towards certain products. It is argued that children can be used as 'props or associates to influence the perception of adults associated with them' (Collett, 2005, p. 331).

Children's consumer behaviour can be defined as the process and activities children engage in when searching for, selecting, purchasing, using, evaluating and disposing of products and services so as to satisfy their needs and desires. This process is highly influenced by a child's perception. Knowledge of how young consumers obtain and utilise information from external sources is important to marketers in formulating communication strategies. Marketers are particularly interested in how consumers sense external information, how they attend to various sources of information, how this information is interpreted and given meaning and how the information is retained. These four processes are all part of perception, the process by which an individual receives, attends to, interprets and stores information to create a meaningful picture of the world. Perception, as an individual process, depends on internal factors such as a child's beliefs, experiences, needs, moods and expectations. The perceptual process is also influenced by the characteristics of a stimulus (such as its size, colour and intensity) and the context in which it is seen or heard. Selectivity occurs throughout the four stages of the consumer's perceptual process. Therefore, perception can be viewed as a filtering process in which internal and external factors influence what is received and how it is processed and interpreted. The sheer number and complexity of the marketing stimuli a person is exposed to in any given day requires that this filtering occur. Therefore, selective perception may occur within all four stages of the perceptual process. Understanding that there is a direct link between perception and consumption, specifically among children, this chapter highlights the process of children's consumer perception and examines the link between children's consumer perception and their consumer lifestyles.

The nature of children's perception

Most cultures consider a child to be any boy or girl under 18 years of age. This indicates that the definition entails the existence of different age groups within that broad age range, including adolescents. It also means, from a social psychological perspective, that different cognitive abilities and skills may be characteristic of each age group of children. Based on age variations and developmental stages, 'children realize that differences exist in the world and realize this to a greater or lesser extent, depending upon their mental development and chronological age' (Young, 1985, p. 47), as well as their abilities to interpret and distinguish the different forms of stimuli they are exposed to on a day-to-day basis.

Perception can be defined as the process by which an individual receives, attends to, interprets and stores information to create a meaningful picture of the world. It can also be considered as 'a process which involves the recognition and interpretation of stimuli, which register on our senses' (Rookes and Wilson, 2000, p. 1). Accordingly, perception as a process depends on internal factors such as a person's beliefs, experiences, needs, moods and expectations, as well as the characteristics of a stimulus (such as its texture, size, colour and intensity), and the context in which it is seen or heard. These are all factors that affect attitudes of individuals towards certain stimuli and appreciation or disdain of others. Perception is based on the link between the outer and inner worlds of an individual. The mechanism by which perception works depends on the idea that stimuli of the outer environment create signals (visual, auditory, etc.) that can be sensed. The perceiver who receives those signals converts them into psychologically meaningful representations that define his/her inner experience of the world. Hence, 'once a meaningful percept is achieved, it serves as input to higher-order cognition, including inferences about the target's goals and intentions. This interpretation of target input then, guides the perceiver's response' (Bodenhausen and Hugenberg, 2009, p. 2).

Infants and young children learn about mechanical causality from the perceptual information they receive (Leslie, 1994). Perception organises itself fairly rapidly around a core framework representing the arrangement of cohesive, solid, three-dimensional objects, which are rooted in a series of mechanical relations such as pushing, blocking and support. Action is crucial to the development of these explanatory frameworks: as the child becomes able to manipulate different causes and observe the effects, further learning occurs. Causal principles such as temporal order, intervention in situations and real world knowledge about likely causes and effects (for example, that a switch is probably a cause of something) are all important for understanding the causal structure of physical events, and can already be observed in 2 and 3 year olds (Bullock *et al.*, 1982; Shultz *et al.*, 1982). Furthermore, 4 year olds can use co-variation data to induce causal structure (Gopnik *et al.*, 2001). Causal reasoning is well developed early in childhood. However, the ability to deal effectively with multiple causal variables – scientific reasoning – develops more slowly.

One of the central problems of cognition, and consequently perception, is the problem of selecting which stimuli will receive attention and which will be denied or overlooked. For example, when customers are searching the market for their favourite food or other specific items, their attention must select significant or goal-related stimuli while simultaneously ignoring or even subduing the processing of distracting other types of food or items or other stimuli in general. These two separate needs, attention and inattention, are sub-served by different cognitive mechanisms, leading to an outcome called selective attention (Bodenhausen and Hugenberg, 2009), which is the process of paying attention to only certain stimuli and not others.

In adopting Piaget's (1952, p. 245) approach to children's perception of stimuli brought on by aspects such as colour and graphics, it is possible to study the way in which children in the preoperational stage (2–7 years old) of cognitive development perceive the colour and graphics in packaging design. Therefore, perception is a vehicle through which the meaning that a consumer attaches to a specific stimulus, such as colour or graphics, could be determined (Solomon, 2004, p. 325). In particular, preferences form one dimension of the perceptual process that can be used to understand the meaning a consumer attaches to the above-mentioned stimulus. These preferences are formed through the selection process a consumer applies during the process of perception, which in the case of colour and graphics may be considered as external attributes of the product, which the consumer perceives (Du Plessis and Rouseau, 2003, p. 218). In connection with colour and graphics of children's consumer behaviour, Piaget's (1952, p. 245) work on cognitive development aims at understanding the dynamics of a child's perception of colour and graphics. Perception of children takes place in the form of stages of cognitive development, or what Piaget called the perceptual process. During those stages, children are characterised by focusing only on a single stimulus, for example, the stimuli found in the colour and graphics of packaging, and develop later as children move from stage to another. These stimuli are captured through the perception of the child. Such a stimulus might be the only meaningful interpretation the child consumer is able to make at an early age, as other skills have not yet been developed through which communication occurs.

Understanding that children represent a special social group, a question raised is how marketers reach this emerging segment of consumers. In this regard, packaging (with specific reference to the graphics and colours used as extrinsic product attributes) can be highlighted as a significant means of influencing these young consumers. Accordingly, if child consumers preferred colour and graphics applied to the packaging of products, specifically aimed at the children's market, their behaviour as consumers could be predicted to some extent (Gorn *et al.*, 1997, p. 1387), which would ensure that the product is bought by the child consumer at whom the product was targeted. In general, colour is considered a primary communicator of the intended message of packaging and is used to maximise attention.

Graphics, cartoon and animal characters in packaging design are yet another factor that affect children's consumer perception. Many researchers argue that the use of cartoon and animal characters act as an attractive medium to catch the attention of child consumers. This attraction may also be found in the association that the child consumer has with different graphical characters. The influence that such graphical categories of characters have on the child consumer may also be considered an important instigating factor in child consumers' purchasing and decision-making. Many researchers also believe that children are usually eager to try new brands and commodities to consume, which makes them increasingly dismiss products that fail to cater to their immediate needs due to the plethora of choices at their disposal. They seem to be always in the 'what's next' mode quickly demanding the next, upgraded things once the initial desires have been fulfilled (Lindstrom, 2004). Behavioural attitudes like brand switching, impulsive decisions and constant aspirations for self-extensions of personality through materialistic symbols prompt many marketers to constantly approach or target children's indecisive mindedness. Exposure to various products at an early age leads to increasing consumerism in this generation.

Concerning food preferences among children, for example, 'positive role modeling correlates with an increased interest in food and less food fussiness among children' (Gregory *et al.*, 2010). Poor role models influence children's perceptions of foods and mealtimes (Matheson *et al.*, 2002). For example, negative comments about the taste or texture of a particular food will make a child less willing to try it. On the other hand, a child is more likely to try a particular type of food if he or she observes an adult enjoying it. Families are typically children's first significant models of eating behaviour (Golan and Weizman, 2001). However, peer pressure and peer cultures play a decisive role in children's food preferences when children reach their adolescent years. A good example was presented by Laura Bellows and Jennifer Anderson (2006) in their article entitled, 'The Food Friends: Encouraging Preschoolers to Try New Foods', when they found that most children choose their favourite product based on taste perceptions, which can be influenced by food packaging, such as their choice of salty snacks most frequently. They also reported that visual elements influence children's selection of favourite packaging (i.e. characters, colours) and healthiest product (i.e. images). When children generated their own drawings of a new product, the most frequently included packaging elements in the drawings were product name, price, product image and characters, suggesting those aspects of the food packaging were most significant to them.

Children's perception and consumer lifestyle

Research findings indicate that 'consumption is now an intrinsic part of children's everyday lives and identity formation' (Hill, 2016, p. 15). It is noteworthy to realise that children have increasingly become active in the process of consumption. Studies of the process of consumption among children reveal that 'children consumers show certain characteristics that make them active in the consumer purchasing environment. For one, they are said to have become more aware of brands than their parents' (Dotson and Hyatt, 2000, p. 223). Children have become able to compare prices, select brand names and become highly affected by the impact of product advertisements. These characteristics have made them, to a certain extent, able to make decisions and behave accordingly and have a tremendous effect on their selection of consumer goods (Ozgen, 2003). Martensen and Gronholdt (2008, p. 17) found that

> children tend to suggest buying the product category, brand and model much more often and be much more influential with regard to products typically aimed at children (e.g. juice, soft drinks, cereals) than product categories aimed at the family in general (vitamin pills, shampoo and toothpaste).

Therefore, children have become active participants in the consumer market.

Perhaps the most significant issue in a child consumer's purchasing behaviour is the growing influence children have on their parents' shopping behaviour (Wilson and Wood, 2004). Much research carried out on children's influence in family decision-making emphasises that children have at least some influence on decisions for a wide array of products and some even report that children have an increasing role in family purchase decisions (Caruana and Vassallo, 2003; Chavda and Dunn, 2005; Tufte, 2003). The influence that children have on parental purchase decisions appears to increase with age (Laczniak and Palan, 2004). As children grow older, their influence on their parents' choices of consumer goods increases since, from the perspectives of both children and their parents, they have become more rationally oriented to the global culture of consumption.

James McNeal (1992) considers the child consumer market as a growing global phenomenon. From his perspective, it is a holistic approach whereby the child is considered to be characteristic of three different markets. These markets are the primary market, where child consumers are able to spend their own money; an influential market, where the child consumer influences his/her parents' buying decisions and behaviour; and a future market, where the child will become a consumer of all products and services as they grow older. On the other hand, children have become one of the fastest growing market segments of end user (Wilson and Wood, 2004). Not only do marketers see children as part of the current market, but also as the most important part of the future market.

Although early research findings concerning the consumer socialisation of children emphasise that parents are responsible for the consumer socialisation of their children, current research findings seem to highlight the fact that it may only apply to children at a very young age (during early childhood). As children grow older, other elements seem to interfere with the consumer socialisation of children, including peer pressure, advertisements and attitude development, and also through the development of children's perception and cognitive abilities. The dilemma over the role of parents in the consumer socialisation of children stems from the fact that parents are responsible for giving pocket money to children. However, researchers rarely discuss the way children engage in the process of determining the socially and culturally appropriate amount of pocket money they should receive from their parents and the factors that affect children's preferences. Therefore, it would be misleading to ignore the active role of children in the development of their consumer lifestyles.

Consumer socialisation is defined as the process by which children and young people acquire skills, knowledge and attitudes relevant to their functioning in the marketplace. While the concept of 'consumer socialisation' is still debated in the literature, many would accept Ward's definition of consumer socialisation as 'the process by which young people acquire skills, knowledge, and attitudes relevant to their functioning in the market place' (Ward, 1980, p. 380). Many researchers believe that the consumer socialisation of children takes place on the basis of 'ages and stages' (Ward et al., 1977). Therefore, children's development as consumers is related to the development of more general cognitive skills and capacities, such as the ability to process information, to understand others' perspectives, and to take account of multiple factors that might be in play in consumption decision-making. Influenced by parents and peers, as well as media and marketing institutions, children's consumer behaviour is seen to become gradually more autonomous, consistent and rational. As children get older, they also draw on a greater range of information sources in making purchasing decisions (Haynes et al., 1993).

Understanding that children's consumer socialisation is influence by the socio-economic status of the family and its parental style, or as Ali et al. (2012, p. 1) stated: 'differences in parental style reflect differences in shopping behavior for children', children's conception of consumption is not a homogenous whole. Children of parents with higher educational levels are able to perceive persuasive intent in commercials. Adolescents from families of higher socio-economic status were found to socialise faster and were better in a consumption role. Also, female adolescents were perceived to communicate overtly with their parents (Russell and Tyler, 2002), while male adolescents had more probability of receiving a negative reinforcement. Social orientation for the mother is found to be higher for daughters than sons. Also intergenerational influence was found to be mainly from mothers to daughters (Mandrik et al., 2005). With regard to gender-based differences toward consumption, research revealed that girls prefer discussing shopping with their parents, while boys have distinctly more 'own' money at their disposal (weekly pocket money, earned income, presents, etc.) than girls, especially among most cultures in the developing world (Russell and Tyler, 2002).

Girls' and boys' consumption styles begin to differ from each other already before school age. The most important socialising agents for gendered consumption at a young age are still parents, but differentiated marketing and product segmentation have an increasingly important role. Boys also have more materialistic attitudes, and economic matters are more important for them. The consumption styles of young boys are characterised by a great emphasis on technology and leisure time equipment. Young boys' attitudes towards consumption also include indifference to environmental and ethical consumption. Young girls are regarded as an important consumer group today, but in marketers' minds, there is also an image of a future mother who makes most of the purchase decisions in the family (Russell and Tyler, 2002). However, according to several studies, women and girls are more economical, green and ethical in their consumption than men and boys. Women also control their consumption better than men do, and women sacrifice their own needs for their loved ones. Girls are being socialised as caring consumers (Wilska, 2003).

Children's food preferences, for example, 'are influenced by the people around them' (Bellows and Anderson, 2006). The eating behaviours children practise early in life affect their health and nutrition and contribute to significant factors in childhood such as being overweight and obesity and may continue to shape food attitudes and eating patterns through adulthood (Campbell and Crawford, 2001; Westenhoefer, 2002). Eating environments – mealtimes and snacks – that make food fun, offer a variety of new foods and encourage children to taste and choose the foods they want, let children develop food attitudes and dietary practices that ultimately support good health (Campbell and Crawford, 2001). Poor role models influence children's perceptions of foods and mealtimes (Matheson et al., 2002). For example, negative comments about the taste or texture of a food will make a child less willing to try it.

Based on viewing children as a growing potential market, children today are open to a growing number and range of commercial messages, which extend far beyond traditional media advertising, and involve activities such as online marketing, sponsorship and peer-to-peer marketing. Commercial forces also increasingly impact on children's experiences in areas such as broadcasting, education and play. The commercial world offers children significant opportunities in terms of entertainment, learning, creativity and cultural experience, despite the fact that many parents and researchers see those opportunities and exposure to the global marketing elements as harmful on children's well-being, especially on their mental and physical health (John, 1999). These roles are reflected in the whole range of marketing and promotional appeals that target children. They are apparent not only in the advertisements for toys or breakfast cereals on children's television, but also in the many ads for fancy cars or financial services that feature children; and indeed in the intensive marketing of educational goods and services to parents. Children are also of course exposed to a great deal of advertising and promotion that does not directly target them at all, yet may well influence their perceptions of particular brands. This process is often particularly apparent in debates about the impact of media and popular culture (Schor, 2014). Concerns about the harmful effects of popular culture on children and young people have a very long history, dating back well before electronic technology. These concerns reflect much more general anxieties about the future direction of society; but, as several studies have shown, they can also be inflamed and manipulated by those with much broader political, moral or religious motivations.

Conclusion

Although the kinds of products marketed to children have remained much the same, the buying power of children and adolescents has increased exponentially over time. By understanding the way children and adolescents' consumer perception works, marketers learn the most significant ways for targeting children. Children's perception of consumption progresses as children are becoming more involved in the global culture of consumption. Children's ability to consume has started to play a significant role in the definition of childhood throughout the world, and 'children are more and more defined and evaluated by their spending capacity. Living in a culture of consumption is to be exposed to enormous pressures to conform to the beliefs and values of that culture' (Hill, 2016, p. 16). Understanding that children have become a valued source for marketers due to their participation in the global market, 'children are exposed to numerous advertising stimuli and because they are relying on these stimuli to perform consumer actions, more insights are needed on our youngest consumers. These insights could help young consumers to make more solid consumer decisions' (Vermeir and Van de Sompel, 2014, p. 339).

Undoubtedly, marketers typically see children as playing three roles: they are consumers in their own right. They spend the pocket money they receive from their parents on their own behalf (under the influence of peers and parents). They also influence the purchasing decisions of their families. Finally, they can be perceived as a long-term market potential. These roles are reflected in the whole range of marketing and promotional appeals that target children. They are clear not only in the advertisements on children's TV channels, but also in the many ads that feature children's reality, and indeed in the intensive marketing of educational goods and services to parents. Children are also exposed to a great deal of advertising and promotion that does not directly target them at all, yet may well influence their perceptions of particular brands.

When examining the process of perception, one can find that three steps are notable in the perceptual process: selection, organisation and interpretation (Pride *et al.*, 2015). Concerning the perception of consumption, perception can be thought of as a consumer's awareness and analysis of reality. It mainly represents one's subjective reality. During the perceptual process, consumers are exposed to stimuli, devote attention to stimuli and attempt to comprehend the stimuli. Comprehension occurs when the consumer attempts to derive meaning from information that is received. The mechanism by which consumers develop perceptions takes place through the perceptual process: sensing some stimuli by seeing, hearing, smelling, tasting or touching; organising the input from these human senses; and reacting as a result of this organisation. This perceptual process allows consumers to interpret stimuli and develop an attitude to either proceed buying an item or ignore it. Recognising those elements of the perceptual process makes it easy for marketers to target children since they typically target their senses in a number of ways.

Since parents are perceived as the primary socialisation agents for children, they play a role in modifying the influence of other socialisation agents such as mass media upon their children (Charbonneau and Garland, 2005). Although children's consumer behaviour largely takes place in the context of the family and children also remain economically dependent upon their parents for a longer period, children have a growing degree of autonomy and independence in their consumer behaviour and they may exercise a major influence on family purchasing decisions. Many older children in particular also earn income on their own behalf. To this extent, children – and especially older children – can be seen as economic actors in their own right. The greater significance of children as economic actors, both within and beyond the family, raises significant questions about learning. Several studies suggest that parents feel a responsibility to educate their children about responsible consumption, and fear that they may be 'reckless' spenders; although young people disagree, believing that they know more about money and finance than previous generations, precisely because of their exposure to the commercial world (Ranjbarian et al., 2013). With regard to the pocket money they receive, parents strongly aim to prepare their children for adulthood or at least for some form of self-sufficiency. This desire takes the form of providing skills to the youngsters so that they may cope without the assistance of parents. Being a consumer is one of these skills. It seems clear that children are turned into consumers at a very early age through the desire and inspiration of their parents, who also provide the youngsters with the necessary financial support in the form of pocket money. Although this might be a reason for giving children pocket money, especially when they go to school, many parents do this as a form of creating the status of the child among his or her peers.

References

Ali, A., Batra, D., Ravichandran, N., Mustafa, Z. and Rehman, S. (2012). Consumer socialization of children: A conceptual framework. *International Journal of Scientific and Research Publications*, 2(1), 1–5.

Bellows, Laura and Anderson, Jennifer (2006). The food friends: Encouraging preschoolers to try new foods. *Young Children*, 61(3), 37–39.

Bodenhausen, Galen and Hugenberg, Kurt (2009). Attention, perception, and social cognition. In Fritz Strack and Jens Förster (eds), *Social cognition: The basis of human interaction* (pp. 1–22). New York: Psychology Press.

Bullock, M., Gelman, R. and Baillargeon, R. (1982). The development of causal reasoning. In W. J. Friedman (ed.), *The developmental psychology of time* (pp. 209–254). New York: Academic Press.

Campbell, Karen and Crawford, David (2001). Family food environments as determinants of preschool-aged children's eating behaviors: Implications for obesity prevention policy. A review. *Australian Journal of Nutrition and Dietetics*, 58(1), 19–25.

Caruana, Albert and Vassallo, Rosella (2003). Children's perception of their influence over purchases: The role of parental communication patterns. *Journal of Consumer Marketing*, 20(1), 55–66.

Charbonneau, Jan and Garland, Ron (2005). Talent, looks or brains? New Zealand advertising practitioners' views on celebrity and athlete endorsers. *Marketing Bulletin*, 16(3), 1–10.

Chavda, Haley and Dunn, Chris (2005). Adolescents' influence on family decision-making. *Young Consumers*, 6(3), 68–78.

Collett, Jessica (2005). What kind of mother am I? Impression management and the social construction of motherhood. *Symbolic Interaction*, 28(3), 327–347.

Dotson, Michael and Hyatt, Eva (2000). A comparison of parents' and children's knowledge of brands and advertising slogans in the United States: Implications for consumer socialization. *Journal of Marketing Communications*, 6(4), 219–230.

Du Plessis, F. P. J. and Rousseau, D. (2003). *Buyer behaviour: A multi-cultural approach* (3rd edn). Cape Town: Oxford University Press.

Fass, Paula (2007). *Children of a new world: Society, culture and globalization*. New York: New York University Press.

Golan, Moria and Weizman, Abraham (2001). Familial approach to the treatment of childhood obesity. *Journal of Nutrition Education*, 33(2), 102–107.

Gopnik, A., Sobel, D. M., Schulz, L. E. and Glymour, C. (2001). Causal learning mechanisms in very young children: Two-, three-, and four-year-olds infer causal relations from patterns of variation and covariation. *Developmental Psychology*, 37(5), 620–629.

Gorn, Gerald, Chattopadhyay, Amitava, Yi, Tracey and Dahl, Darren (1997). Effects of colour as an executional cue in advertising: They're in the shade. *Management Science*, 43(10), 1387–1400.

Gregory, Jane, Paxton, Susan and Brozovic, Anna (2010). Maternal feeding practices, child eating behavior and body mass index in preschool-aged children: A prospective analysis. *The International Journal of Behavioral Nutrition and Physical Activity*, 7, 55–65.

Haynes, Janice, Burts, Diane, Dukes, Alice and Cloud, Rinn (1993). Consumer socialisation of preschoolers and kindergartners as related to clothing consumption. *Psychology and Marketing*, 10(2), 151–166.

Hill, Jennifer (2016). *How consumer culture controls our kids: Cashing in on conformity*. Santa Barbara, CA: ABC-CLIO.

John, Deborah (1999). Consumer socialization of children: A retrospective look at twenty-five years of research. *Journal of Consumer Research*, 26(3), 183–213.

Laczniak, Russell and Palan, Kay (2004). Under the influence: Targeted advertising pinpoints how kids sway parents' buying decisions. *Marketing Research*, 16(1), 34–39.

Leslie, A. M. (1994). Pretending and believing: Issues in the theory of ToMM. *Cognition*, 50(1), 211–238.

Lindstrom, Martin (2004). *Brand child: Remarkable insights into the minds of today's global kids and their relationships with brands*. London: Kogan Page.

McNeal, James (1992a). *Kids as customers: A handbook of marketing to children*. Lanham, KY: Lexington Books.

McNeal, James and Ji, Mindy (1999). Chinese children as consumers: An analysis of their new product information sources. *Journal of Consumer Marketing*, 16(4), 345–365.

Mandrik, Carter, Fern, Edward and Yeqing, Bao (2005). Intergenerational influence: Roles of conformity to peers and communication effectiveness. *Psychology and Marketing*, 22(10), 813–832.

Martensen, Anne and Gronholdt, Lars (2008). Children's influence on family decision-making. *Innovative Marketing*, 4(4), 14–22.

Martin, Craig and Bush, Alan (2000). Do role models influence teenagers' purchase intentions and behavior? *Journal of Consumer Marketing*, 17(5), 441–454.

Matheson, Donna, Spranger, Kristina and Saxe, Amy (2002). Preschool children's perceptions of food and their food experiences. *Journal of Nutrition Education and Behavior*, *34*(2), 85–92.

Mininni, Ted (2005). Kids want it cool and true. *Journal of Brand Identity and Consumer Promotion*, *64*(August), 64–73.

Ozgen, Ozlen (2003). An analysis of child consumers in Turkey. *International Journal of Consumer Studies*, *27*(November), 366–380.

Piaget, Jean (1952). *The origins of intelligence in children*. New York: International Universities press.

Pride, W., Ferrell, O. C., Lukas, B., Schembri, S. and Niininen, O. (2015). *Marketing principles* (2nd edn). Melbourne: Cengage Learning Australia.

Ramzy, Omar, Ogden, Denise, Ogden, James and Zakaria, Mohamed Yehia (2012). Perception of children's influence on purchase decisions: Empirical investigation for the US and Egyptian families. *World Journal of Management*, *4*(1), 30–50.

Ranjbarian, Bahram, Shekarchizade, Zahra and Fathi, Saeed (2013). Social class influence on child's perception of TV advertisement messages by the elementary students. *International Journal of Academic Research in Business and Social Sciences*, *3*(6), 93–106.

Rookes, Paul and Wilson, Jane (2000). *Perception theory, development and organisation*. London: Routledge.

Russell, Rachel and Tyler, Melissa (2002). Thank heaven for little girls: 'Girl heaven' and the commercial context of feminine childhoods. *Sociology*, *36*(3), 619–637.

Schor, Juliet (2014). *Born to buy: The commercialized child and the new consumer culture*. New York: Simon & Schuster.

Shultz, Thomas (1982). Rules of causal attribution. *Monographs of the Society for Research in Child Development*, *47*(1), 1–51.

Solomon, Joshua (2004). The effect of spatial cues on visual sensitivity. *Vision Research*, *44*(12), 1209–1216.

Tufte, Birgitte (2003). Children, media and consumption. *Advertising and Marketing to Children*, *5*(1), 69–76.

Valkenburg, Patti and Janssen, Sabine. (1999). What do children value in entertainment programs: A cross-cultural investigation. *International Communication Association*, *49*(2), 3–21.

Vermeir, Iris and Van de Sompel, Dieneke (2014). How advertising beauty influences children's self-perception and behavior. In Avinash Kapoor and Chinmaya Kulshrestha (eds), *Dynamics of competitive advantage and consumer perception in social marketing* (pp. 327–347). Hershey, PA: IGI Global.

Ward, S. (1980). Consumer socialization. In Harold H. Kassarjian and Thomas S. Robertson (eds), *Perspectives in consumer behavior* (pp. 380–396). Glenville, IL: Scott Foresman.

Ward, S., Wackman, D. B. and Wartella, E. (1977). *How children learn to buy: The development of consumer information processing skills*. Beverly Hills, CA: Sage.

Westenhoefer, Joachim (2002). Establishing dietary habits during childhood for long-term weight control. *Annals of Nutrition & Metabolism*, *46*, 18–23.

Wilska, Terhi-Anna (2003). Mobile phone use as part of young people's consumption styles. *Journal of Consumer Policy*, *26*(3), 441–463.

Wilson, George and Wood, Katie (2004). The influence of children on parental purchases during supermarket shopping. *International Journal of Consumer Studies*, *28*(4), 329–336.

Young, Bernard (1985). Children's perception about art. *Art Education*, *38*(6), 47–49.

3
LEARNING AND CONSUMER SOCIALISATION IN CHILDREN

Adya Sharma

> Where did you come from, baby dear?
> Out of the everywhere into the here.
> Where did you get those eyes so blue?
> Out of the sky as I came through.
>
> *('Baby' by George MacDonald, 1895)*

Introduction

French Historian-Philippe Aries in his book, *Centuries of Childhood: A Social History of Family Life*, has concluded that childhood is a recent idea. Before the seventeenth century, children were represented as mini adults. The concept of childhood started emerging from the seventeenth century onwards and children's books did not exist before the seventeenth century (Tunnell and Jacobs, 2013). John Locke, the English philosopher, proposed the concept of childhood in *Some Thoughts Concerning Education* in 1693. It was only towards the end of the nineteenth century that systematic study of larger groups of children began. The modern attitude to children is characteristic of the late nineteenth century. The role of the family, sanctity of the child, compulsory education and the child's personality are all concepts that were introduced in the late nineteenth century. The study of Indian childhood needs to be looked at with a different lens, as the Indian political and social scenario had no similarity with that of the Western world. Indian childhood gained prominence in Hindi literature from the 1930s.

Times have definitely changed. Children who were seen as young adults at one time are now being addressed as three markets in one – the current market who spends on their desire, future market and the market that has a strong influence (McNeal, 1987). With the advent of technology, the boundaries have been blurred between regions and cultures. In this techno-romantic era, this is the age of liberalisation of the child from adult control and supervision (Kumar, 2016).

With this background, this chapter aims at tracing the changing role of children as consumers in society. The objective of the chapter is as follows:

a) To trace the history and journey of consumer socialisation.
b) To understand the major factors affecting consumer socialisation.
c) To introduce and discuss the counter view of reverse socialisation.
d) To view the two theories of consumer socialisation and reverse socialisation as complementary to each other and propose a theoretical model combining the two theories.
e) To highlight the ethical issues in marketing to children.
f) To identify areas of future research related to learning and consumer socialisation in children.

Definition of children

It is interesting to note the definition of children in different contexts. Most English dictionaries define the child as a human infant, an unborn human offspring, boy or girl in the period before puberty. The dictionary definitions are based on biological factors and even borderline on emotional factors. Another component that has been used to define the child is age. As per the UN Convention on the Rights of the Child (Article 1), the child is anyone under 18 years of age, unless under the law applicable to the child, majority is attained earlier. The convention takes no position on the life of an unborn child. Many countries have ratified this convention. Thus as per the Juvenile Justice (Care and Protection of Children) Act 2000, India; any person below the age of 18 is considered as a child. Similarly the Federal Civil Code in Mexico provides that the age of majority is 18. Article 4 of the Child Welfare Law in Japan defines the child as anyone below 18 years of age. Under Israel law, a child is defined as any human being below the age of 18. Under Australian law also the age of majority is 18. Though many countries have ratified this convention it may be noted that there are still a number of different laws that specify age limit in different circumstances in different countries.

Learning and some theories of learning

Learning is defined as the process of acquisition of knowledge or skills through study, experience or teaching. Over the years researchers and academicians have proposed a number of theories to describe the process of learning. Broadly speaking, these theories can be grouped as follows:

- Behaviourism
- Cognitivism
- Constructivism.

Behaviourism

Behaviourism theories perceive that learning is the equivalent of a change in behaviour and is determined by factors in the environment. It does not recognise unobservable mental processes (Kretchmar, 2016a). Two key individuals who contributed to this field were Ivan Pavlov and B. F. Skinner who proposed classical conditioning theory and operant conditioning theory respectively. Pavlov's classical conditioning theory is hugely recognised with the experiment he did with a dog, where the dog began salivating not just in response to food but also to other environmental cues. The classical conditioning model works on the principle that unconditioned stimulus (UCS) leads to unconditioned response (UCR). With repeated pairing of neutral stimulus (NS) with unconditioned stimulus (UCS), the neutral stimulus becomes a conditioned stimulus that evokes conditioned response (CR) (Kretchmar, 2016b). The same is illustrated in Figure 3.1.

Operant theory by Skinner states that individuals will continue behaviour that is positively reinforced and eliminate behaviour that is punished (Lovata, 1987). Behaviourism theories have been criticised by the cognitive school of thought for not preparing the learner for problem solving or creative thinking.

Cognitive theories

The cognitive school of thought believes that what happens inside the mind is an important part of learning. Schunk (2004) proposed the two-store memory model. He highlighted short-term memory and long-term memory. Long-term memory is our brain's system for storing, managing and retrieving information. On the other hand short-term memory is closely related to 'working' memory. Short-term memory is about 'now' or 'at the moment'. Items stored in short-term memory are either dismissed or transferred to long-term memory.

Cognitive theories too have had their fair share of criticism, where it was pointed out that importance of interaction and environment is too focused on the individual learner and his/her mental processes.

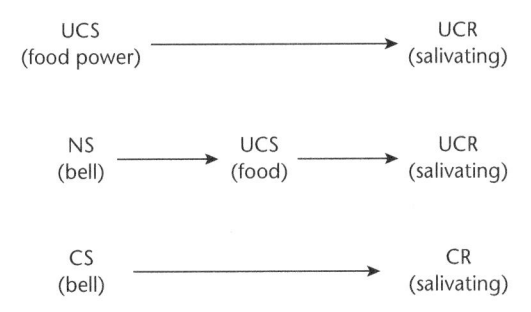

```
UCS                  ─────────────▶    UCR
(food power)                            (salivating)


NS           ────▶    UCS      ────▶    UCR
(bell)                (food)             (salivating)


CS                   ─────────────▶    CR
(bell)                                  (salivating)
```

FIGURE 3.1 Classical conditioning theory

Source: www.psychestudy.com/sites/default/files/styles/articles/public/pavlovs-classical-conditioning-diagram_0.jpg?itok=-cwsW4eV.

Constructivism

Constructivism posits that learning is an active, constructive process. People construct their representations of objective reality by linking it to prior knowledge and thus mental representations are subjective. Two main contributors to this school of thought are Jean Piaget and Lev Vygotsky. Piaget introduced the concept of accommodation, adaptation and assimilation. These are discussed later in the chapter. Vygotsky's major contribution has been the zone of proximal development (ZPD), which is the distance between the learner's ability to perform a task under guidance and his/her own problem-solving ability. Learning occurs in this zone (Yoders, 2014).

The three different schools of thoughts have together contributed in understanding and implementing the process of learning. The discussion on learning provides a multi-dimensional framework for analysing the different perspectives on consumer socialisation in the next section.

Consumer socialisation

It is believed that childhood experiences play an important role in shaping a child's behaviour as he becomes an adult. With changes in the political, social and economic scenario, the role of children also started changing in society and family. Marketers saw the opportunity and potential for products designed and made especially for children. Many reasons have been cited by researchers for the growing importance of children as consumers. Some of them include:

a) There is a new trend of accepting and encouraging children as co-decision makers in family (Sharma and Dasgupta, 2009).
b) There is a rising influence and affluence of children due to socio-economic changes in the 1970s and 1980s that resulted in indulgent parental behaviour (Valkenburg and Cantor, 2001).

Hence it is important to understand how children become consumers. As a first step it is imperative to understand what socialisation is. Brim (1966) described socialisation as a process by which individuals acquire the knowledge, skills and dispositions that enable them to participate as more or less effective members of groups and the society. Ward (1974) worked on this definition to define consumer socialisation as the process by which young people acquire skills, knowledge and attitudes relevant to their functioning as consumers in the marketplace. Moschis and Churchill (1978) proposed a consumer socialisation framework. It comprised of antecedent variable, process and outcome.

According to the framework, the antecedent variables affect the consumer learning properties both directly and indirectly. More specifically, socio-cultural variables and age were defined as antecedent variables. Further, the socio-structural variables identified were parents, the mass media and peers. The socialisation process incorporates both the socialisation agent and type of learning actually operating. The acquiring of cognitive and behavioural properties are often referred to as consumer skills.

This model is considered to be the most widely applied model in consumer socialisation research (Hunter-Jones, 2014). In the next section we will understand how the socialisation agents, which are widely believed to be family, peers, mass media and age, affect the socialisation process.

How age affects consumer socialisation

Jian Piaget developed a theory of cognitive development that explains how children learn differently at different stages in development (Piaget, 1964). He identified four stages in development to childhood. In the first stage, which lasts from birth to 2 years of age, he learns about himself and his environment through motor and reflex actions. This is also called the sensori motor stage. The next stage until the age of 7 is called the pre-operational stage, where he learns how to deploy his new linguistic capabilities. He begins to use symbols to represent objects. The concrete operational phase lasts until early adolescence and in this stage the child begins to think abstractly and make rational decisions based on observable concrete phenomenon.

Piaget's theory of cognitive development is a comprehensive theory about the nature and development of human intelligence and explains how individuals perceive and adapt to new information through processes of assimilation and accommodation. The last stage is the formal operational stage, where the child demonstrates abstract thinking including logic, reasoning, comparison and classification.

The theory had its share of criticism. Vygotsky, a contemporary of Piaget, argued that a child's learning always occurs in a social context in cooperation with someone more skilful (Vygotsky, 1978). Furthermore, he suggests that this interaction provides language opportunity and that language is the foundation of thought (McLeod, 2014). In a more practical language, it is understood that children learn to be consumers. It is a process and hence involves active learning and participation. Marketers also need to understand the notion of readiness. There are stages for concepts to be taught.

Another framework to understand consumer socialisation stages was proposed in 1999 by Deborah Roedder John. Three stages were described to understand the consumer socialisation of children with age as the central theme (see Table 3.1). The perceptual stage, from 3–7 years, is highlighted by the unidimensional approach of the child, looking at things only from his own perspective. Decision-making is based on single attributes and salient features. The age from 7–11 years is the analytical stage. The child starts to look at things from a dual perspective and this decision is based on two or more attributes and relevant features. The last stage is the reflective stage and lasts from 11–16 years. In this stage the child views things from a dual perspective in a social context. He is able to take decisions on multiple attributes and relevant features.

Calvert (2008) wrote that while an older child may view the product from various dimensions and think in a logical manner, a younger child will struggle to see things from the perspective of others. Thus a young child easily buys the fantasy of fairies and ghosts while an older child can reason abstractly and analyse logically.

Integrating all these perspectives, it becomes clear that age definitely plays a role in the socialisation of children. What is missing is the effect of the environment. Will two children of the same age but brought up in two different environments be socialised in the same manner? The consumer socialisation theory and model also encompass the role of environment or social factors on consumer socialisation. In the next section, we will discuss the role of major social factors.

Family as a consumer socialisation agent

Family represents the most potent influencing agent in a child's socialisation (Carlson and Harrison, 2010; Sharma, 2011). Ward *et al.* (1977) defined three

TABLE 3.1 Stages in children's development as consumers

Characteristics	Perceptual stage 3–7 years	Analytical stage 7–11 years	Reflective stage 11–16 years
Knowledge structures			
Orientation	Concrete	Abstract	Abstract
Focus	Perceptual features	Functional/underlying features	Functional/underlying features
Complexity	Unidimensional Simple	Two or more dimensions Contingent (if–then)	Multi-dimensional Contingent (if–then)
Perspective	Egocentric (own perspective)	Dual perspectives (own + others)	Dual perspectives in social context
Decision-making and influence strategies			
Orientation	Expedient	Thoughtful	Strategic
Focus	Perceptual features	Functional/underlying features	Functional/underlying features
	Salient features	Relevant features	Relevant features
Complexity	Single attribute Limited repertoire of strategies	Two or more attributes Expanded repertoire of strategies	Multiple attributes Complete repertoire of strategies
Adaptive	Emerging	Moderate	Fully developed
Perspective	Egocentric	Dual perspectives	Dual perspectives in social context

Source: John (1999).

alternative roles of the family in the development of consumer information processing skills:

a) directly impacts the development of general cognitive abilities and indirectly impacts the development of consumer skills;
b) motivates children to apply general cognitive abilities in areas of consumer behaviour;
c) teaches consumer skills that are not highly integrated with cognitive abilities.

Researchers have studied the contribution of family as a socialisation agent from different perspectives, with the most popular being family communication and child demographics in the family. In recent years, interest has also been centred on the working status of the mother (Lee, 1994; Isin and Alkibay, 2011).

Child demographics in the family and consumer socialisation

Research has found that the female child is more influential than the male child in the family, both as an individual and as a group (Lee, 1994; Tomko, 2012) and three females within a family have been found to be more influential than three males acting together (Lee and Collins, 2000). The gender of the child has not been found to be a determining factor on the decisions of the family to purchase products for the children in the age group of 5–6 years. Gender difference has been highlighted for socially desirable consumer behaviour where female adolescents scored more than male adolescents. However, male adolescents appeared to know more about consumer matters (Moschis and Churchill, 1978; Isin and Alkibay, 2011). Adolescents were influenced by family members' participation in gaming and males were more likely to have a favourable perception towards gaming and the gaming industry (Shields, 2009). Research indicates that home is where children first learn about money (Danes and Haberman, 2007; Lusardi *et al.*, 2010) and school as a source of monetary information was only true to the extent of 10 per cent (Mandell and Xiao, 2008). Male children on average have their first financial discussion at home at an earlier age than female children (Agnew and Agnew, 2015). Further more, studies show that male and female children differ in their socialisation behaviour, which may be due to the desire to remain consistent with gender role expectations. In a study by Jadva *et al.* (2010), girls were found to look significantly more at dolls than boys did and similarly, boys were found to look significantly more at cars than girls did. Gender divide is observed in terms of preference of products and companies may consider designing different advertising appeals and communication towards girls and boys.

The effect of family communication on consumer socialisation

Family communication has been measured on two dimensions: Concept-oriented and socio-oriented (Bakir *et al.*, 2006). Socio-oriented parents emphasise harmonious relationships and encourage children to avoid any conflict. Children exposed to this type of communication usually defer to parental authority. They are not encouraged to ask questions or share their views, especially when theirs are in contradiction to existing views. Parents with concept-oriented communication emphasise individual ideas, beliefs and feelings. They encourage children to express ideas and to challenge others' views. Moschis and Moore (1985) indicated that socio-oriented families were found to encourage the children to evaluate their consumer behaviour on the basis of its perceived effect on others. Children's exposure to online advertising has been explained by the type of communication within their family (Wonsun Shin, 2010) and a positive correlation has been found between socio-oriented communication and restrictive mediation. At the same time, restrictive mediation has been found to be the second largest contributor to child materialism (Adib and El-Bassiouny, 2012). Ayadi and Bree (2010) defined family communication as synonymous with values and consumption skills sharing, in contrast other research suggests that concept-oriented family communication has no effect on youth's development of materialistic values, regardless of cultural background (Moschis et al., 2011). McLeod and Chaffee (1972) developed a typology that characterises the family communication pattern.

Laissez-faire families are low on both socio-orientation as well as concept orientation. Protective families encourage socially acceptable behaviour and discourage questions. Plurastic families encourage airing one's views with less regard to socially acceptable norms. Consensual families encourage reasoning and yet seek societal approval. Studies on the effect of family communication on consumer socialisation have shown that children from plurastic families seem to be the most competent consumers and those from laissez-faire families appear to be the least competent (Moschis et al., 1986). The difference between different family patterns was reiterated in another study by Carlson et al. (1990), which highlighted that plurastic families encourage consumer learning without emphasising monitoring and control of consumption behaviour and that protective and laissez-faire families de-emphasise concept messages.

The role of father and mother in consumer socialisation of the child

The mother's role has been acknowledged by researchers in consumer socialisation and is seen as playing a prominent role in helping the child become a consumer (Flouri, 1999; Kim, Lee and Tomiuk, 2009; Minahan and Huddleston, 2010). Comparatively father's role appeared to be less than mothers (Kim, Lee and Tomiuk, 2009). Also, mothers are preferred in consumption investigations specifically related to children because of their great familiarity with the market and their relation to children (Aldous, 1974). Mothers act as mediators of the influence of various socialisation agents and hence have an impact on consumption choices of children (Alsop, 1988; Abrams, 1984). Also, adolescents' perspective of parent–child communication about consumption has typically been studied by investigating mothers' views (Carlson et al., 1992). In India, the mother's role in the family is greater and more significant in that the family revolves around the child and the child around the mother. The Indian mother has been described as the socialiser of the new generation (Chakrapani and Vijay Kumar, 1994). In the Indian context, also, findings have suggested the gendered nature of communication between parents and children. While content is limited, there is more communication between mother and child. Mothers reported a closer relationship with their children and also children reported that communication with their mother is more relaxed than with their father (Jejeebhoy and Santhya, 2011). Mothers' employment status has also been defined as a factor influencing consumer socialisation of children. Children of mothers with part-time or no employment shopped for their clothing less as compared to children of mothers with full-time employment (Haynes et al., 1993). This provided more exposure to children of mothers with full-time employment. Further, mothers from higher-income families perceived that their children expressed more interest in apparel shopping (Haynes et al., 1993). It was also indicated that mothers' level of materialism and communication style could predict a child's level of materialism. Influence from one generation to another was also passed from mothers to daughters (Flouri, 1999; Mandrik et al., 2005) and girls have been found to trust their mothers to help them gain shopping experience. The strength of maternal influence appears to be so pronounced that it continues throughout the daughter's life including after the mother's death (Minahan and Huddleston, 2010). The father's role appeared to be much less than the mother's in the family communication pattern. However, in a study conducted on single-mother households, girls and black children were more positively affected by relations with their fathers and father figures than were boys and white children. Divorced fathers were more influential in children's achievement than were married fathers (Coley, 1998). Mothers' concept-oriented communication was positively linked to children's use of utilitarian, social and conspicuous decision-making styles, while mothers' socio-oriented communication was positively linked to children's use of undesirable decision-making styles and negatively to children's influence in family purchase decisions (Kim, Lee and Tomiuk, 2009).

Research shows that family is a major socialisation agent for children (Moschis et al., 2011; Wonsun Shin, 2010). However, what needs to be debated is the relevance of the family definition as defined in many research studies. Hughes and Southall (2012) describe the family at its core as two different sex partners who may or may not have children who are the biological product of their relationship and who have taken a formal affirmation of their relationship, usually marriage. Galvin et al. (2004) describe family as networks of people who share their lives over long periods of time, bound by ties of marriage, blood or commitment-legal or otherwise, who consider themselves as a family and who share a significant history and anticipated future of functioning in a family relationship. In a changing social and economic scenario the above definitions have limited applicability. While the West has witnessed rising single-parent families/step-families, India has witnessed the move from joint families to nuclear families. Family as a socialisation agent therefore, needs new research with a changed definition of the family.

The role of media as a socialisation agent

Media is another socialisation agent that over the years has garnered much interest. Media entails values, attitudes and interpretations of reality because it is embedded within specific social, cultural, economic and political contexts (Baltruschat, 2004). Children learn to use media to become aware of new products (Ward, 1974). TV commercials and in-store experiences have been found to be the primary sources of new snack foods for Chinese children (Fan and Li, 2009). Interestingly, further studies suggest that paediatricians almost universally believe that children's media use negatively affects children in many different areas, such as aggressive behaviour, eating habits, physical activity levels, risk for obesity, high-risk behaviour and school performance (Gentile et al., 2004). Research suggests that children do not comprehend the symbolic nature of television until they reach the preschool years. At the same time, television programmes designed with a specific goal to teach academic or social skills can be effective with potentially long-lasting effects (Kirkorian et al., 2008). Children aged 11–15 years were found to be influenced by media representations of a stigmatised neighbourhood, but also they were not passive reproducers of these messages and some of them were able to offer counter messages (Van der Burgt, 2008). In a study conducted among children aged from 6 months to 5 years, results indicated that parents perceived subjective norms regarding various categories of media were significantly related to actual child consumption, and positive attitudes towards media were significantly related to higher ratios of child consumption (Cingel and Kremar, 2013). Results of a study showed that those children who had more knowledge about advertisers' tactics were more likely to identify brands and commercial content in the advert game and less likely to be influenced (Waiguny et al., 2014). Parents may believe that they are filtering the information reaching their children but studies have proved that not only are children being exposed to adult-oriented information but appear adept at processing that information (Dotson and Hyatt, 2000). The role of the media as a socialisation agent can no longer be restricted only to television or radio. The Internet has taken the world by storm and changed the dynamics. Studies related to various Internet platforms as socialisation agents is limited, but many researchers believe that new media are contributing to a social shift from a media-rich living-room home where family members shared their views by sitting together and talking over dinner or watching their favourite show together, to a media-rich bedroom where every member follows his/her own individual interests. The Internet may therefore be contributing to the individualised family 'living together separately' (Livingstone, 2006). Another school of thought believes that new media may be producing a global 'children's culture' that transcends national differences, but this may not be necessarily disadvantageous for children themselves (Buckingham, 2007), and that media ratings may help minors decide whether or not they want to watch a certain movie or programme or play a certain game (Gosselt et al., 2012).

Reverse socialisation

The world dynamics are changing very fast. Transformed by a digital revolution, advances in medicine and human knowledge, the world has witnessed many changes in the last two decades. Coupled with changing social, cultural and economic dimensions, the role of children has also changed. Researchers started questioning the uni-directional process of socialisation (Ekstrom *et al.*, 1987). Children were no longer observers but participants in family decision-making. A new area of research started gaining ground. Children were not just learning the skills but also teaching new skills to the family. Research on reverse socialisation started gaining strength and importance (Belch *et al.*, 1985; Lee and Beatty, 2002; Wilson and Wood, 2004). It was proposed that the traditional model of socialisation needs to be revaluated (Dotson and Hyatt, 2000). We will now try to understand the influence of children with different parameters.

The relationship between types of product and children's influence in family consumption

Studies have shown that children have more influence on products related to their use (Tinson and Nancarrow, 2005; Beyrouti and Houssami, 2013). Children's influence was more pronounced on products that were routinely consumed, were inexpensive and with low risk (Isin and Alkibay, 2011; Gbadamosi, 2012). There was also a positive relation found between the influence of the child and his/her knowledge of the product (Thomson *et al.*, 2007). In recent years, attempts have been made to understand the influence of the child with respect to product category rather than a single product. Thus children were found to have maximum influence on purchase decisions of products used by the child (e.g. ice cream, bicycles, shoes, chocolate, children's spare time activities) and minimum influence on everyday products used by the family (e.g. dairy products, fruits and vegetables, bread) (Sharma and Sonwaney, 2015a, 2015b). Thus children's influence is a function of their interest and knowledge.

The relationship between family communication and the child's influence in family consumption

We have seen that family communication is an important parameter in understanding the socialisation of the child. We will now see how it also plays a decisive role in understanding the influence of the child. Researchers have proved that concept-oriented communication is a positive predictor of the influence of the child. Concept-oriented communication encourages the child to develop his/her views and this thereby increases the influence of the child. Similarly, socio-oriented communication that discourages discussion and arguments is a negative predictor of the influence of the child (Rose *et al.*, 1998; Caruana and Vassallo, 2003; Kim,

Lee and Tomiuk, 2009). Concept-oriented parents seek the input of children, which in turn helps the children to play an active role in decision-making (Youn, 2008; Wonsun, 2010). Findings suggest that children's perceived influence has generally been found to be highest for pluralistic and consensual parents (Caruana and Vasallo, 2003; Bakir *et al.*, 2006). Studies have also indicated that adolescents in concept-oriented families had greater influence in decision-making (Wang *et al.*, 2007; Sharma and Sonwaney, 2015a, 2015b). Interestingly, the parent–child relationship has been viewed as a game by parents and children with both having a clear understanding of their role (Nash, 2009). The level of 'expertness' or the level of knowledge that a family attributes to the child affects the influence of the child. In other words, if a child is perceived to have knowledge for a particular product, he becomes a strong influencing agent (Watne and Winchester, 2011).

Child demographics and the influence of the child in family consumption

Research has also tried to understand the effect of various child demographic factors on the influence of children. Males were found to have stronger influence during the search and decision stage, while females had more influence during the initiation phase (Beneke *et al.*, 2011). Overall, the initiation stage witnessed the maximum influence of the child, followed by the final decision stage, with least influence on information found to be during the search stage (Wang *et al.*, 2004; Chaudhary and Gupta, 2012). Almost unanimously all studies have reported an increase in the influence of children as they get older (Ahuja and Stinson, 1993; Akinyele, 2010; Tomko, 2012). The size of the family has also been found to affect the influence of the child. Children in small families had more influence, perhaps because they spent more time together, whether co-shopping or because there was more scope for conversation (Suwandinata, 2011; Geuens *et al.*, 2003; Watne *et al.*, 2011). Studies suggest that children are intelligent and that they can often employ various strategies when they feel they deserve to have their way. In contrast, however, children have been shown to use a positive influence strategy when they feel that parents have a right to make consumer decisions for them. Children were also found to use a direct strategy of placing demands on parents, or a cooperative strategy by helping parents (Williams and Burns, 2000; Marshall *et al.*, 2007; Pedersen *et al.*, 2012).

The relationship between parents and children has witnessed changes over the years. A study by Foxman *et al.* in 1989 proposed that a difference exists between the views of children and parents in terms of children's influence. Studies done some 20 years later, however, propose that parents appreciate the views of children and their influence (Gram, 2006; Thomson *et al.*, 2007). Culture also plays its role in defining the influence of children. Parents in the US were defined as more concept-oriented and more socio-oriented than Egyptian parents (Ogden *et al.*, 2012). The influence of Chinese-Canadian children was found to be greater than the influence of Caucasian-Canadian children for convenience products related to children (Kim, Yang and Lee, 2009). The influence of the child in family decision-making has also witnessed changes and age, size of the family, culture and the stage of decision-making have been some of the factors studied by researchers. The changing role of children in family decision-making has brought into focus a more interactive and bidirectional process of family decision-making.

The changing role of children: a new perspective

The role of children has witnessed dramatic changes in the past few decades. The changing social, economic scenario has contributed to changing family dynamics. Smaller families, more disposable income and both parents working have led to families where children have so much power that some families are becoming child led (Cowell, 2001). Socialisation has been defined as the process by which people acquire skills, knowledge and attitudes relevant to their functioning as consumers in the marketplace (Ward, 1974). For a long time the only area of interest was how children acquired skills to become consumers. Recent studies have shown that children are not just learning, but are also now teaching the skills to their family. Parents are once again learning, acquiring skills and knowledge, only this time from children. Parents too are getting re-socialised. Interestingly there is also a similarity of factors affecting the socialisation of children and re-socialisation of parents.

The role of family communication in the socialisation of children is well researched. Simultaneously, research has proved that family communication also defines the influence of children and shown the importance of family communication style in determining children's participation in the shopping process (Haselhoff *et al.*, 2014). Demographics such as age and gender have also been shown to affect the socialisation of children. Interestingly children's demographics also play a role in defining the influence of children. Similarly, the size and type type of family and the roles of father/mother are again common factors affecting both socialisation of children and the influence of children. There exists a common thread linking the socialisation of children by family and re-socialisation of the family by children and yet these have been treated as two different areas of research. The two are related to each other because in one case the children are acquiring skills to become consumers and in the other parents are re-acquiring and updating their skills to become consumers. The result is re-socialisation of parents. The following model attempts to integrate consumer socialisation and reverse socialisation and in this way the model is unique of its kind and has responded to a call for research on reverse socialisation (Easterling *et al.*, 1995). A review of the two leading theories, consumer socialisation theory and reverse socialisation theory, helps us understand the link between the two. Consumer socialisation theory focuses on the learning process of children to become consumers. It focuses on different factors such as age, family, media, etc. However, consumer socialisation has been criticised for viewing socialisation as a one-sided process and does not acknowledge the role of children as influencers (Peterson and Rollins, 1987). Separate areas of research focus on children's influence. This theoretical overview provides a premise to integrate consumer socialisation theory and reverse socialisation theory in order to understand how children and parents acquire skills to become consumers (Sharma and Sonwaney, 2014).

Figure 3.2 integrates the consumer socialisation theory and reciprocal theory to present a comprehensive diagram that highlights the changing dynamics of family decision-making. Children learn from parents but parents also learn/re-learn from children. Learning and socialisation is therefore a lifelong process for both children and parents.

Ethical issues in marketing to children

Marketing to children is considered ethically problematic. The central premise of ethical business practice is informed consumer decision-making. Researchers believe that children are not immune to persuasive marketing and are affected consciously or unconsciously (Moore, 2004). A number of ethical concerns are identified by parents and children about children's exposure to food marketing in particular pester power, family conflict and use of powerful techniques through Internet (Mehta *et al.*, 2014). Advergames are used by marketers to shape children's minds. Through them marketers do not just get the attention of children but also know how long the user is engaged with the brand and can track exact behaviour. Thus it not only informs children, but also monitors them

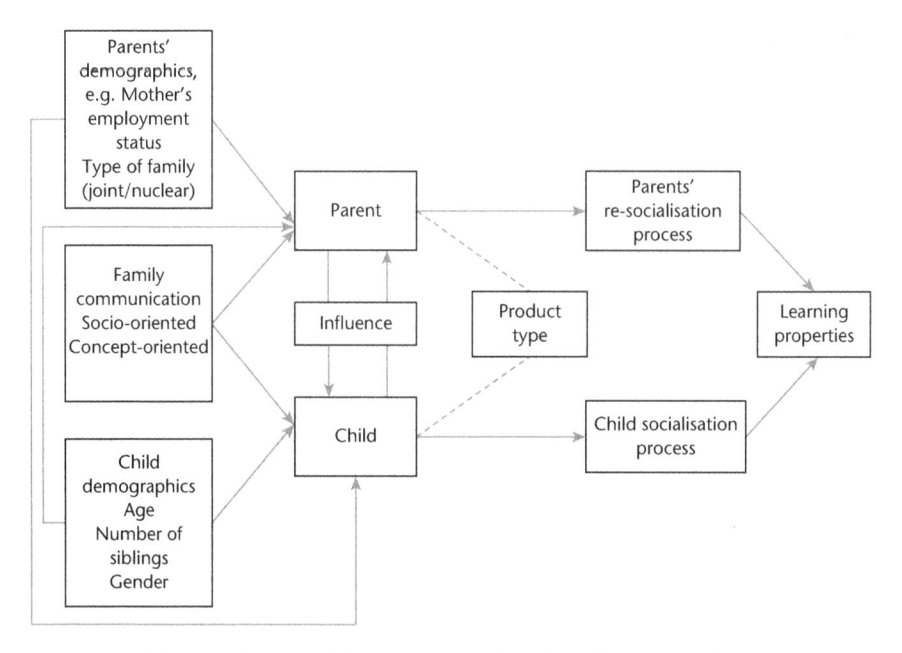

FIGURE 3.2 Socialisation of children and re-socialisation of parents; relation to family variables

Source: Sharma and Sonwaney (2014).

(Calvert, 2008). It is interesting to note that there were no objections related to the ethical marketing practices of the situation in which both parents are willing to focus their financial efforts primarily on their children with the desire to ensure a higher than average standard of living. As an ethical marketing practice, there was a consensus in requirement of the submission of the actual quality of the product (Aldea and Brandabur, 2015). There are compelling reasons on both sides, i.e. for advertising to children and against advertising to children. Some have argued that advertising to children remains an economic necessity in need of adjustment and regulation (Preston, 2004). Rapidly changing technology is giving birth to new products and services, which are marketed with new strategies and it is needless to say that new ethical issues will also keep emerging. Researchers have pondered if the power of the Internet itself to spotlight issues will be a significant force in providing a kind of self-regulation that supports an ethical e-commerce environment (Stead and Gilbert, 2001). It has also been highlighted that definition of best interest standards is usually related to children as a protective measure. At the same time, studies have shown that children are influencing family decisions and hence there has been a demand for defining standards with consideration of children as agents. Thus, a new framework is proposed where best interest standards should be reconciled with recognition of children as agents (Carnevale et al., 2015). In order to reach out to children through digital content, some salient points to reinforce the 'child-first' ethos include: acknowledging parents, a child-friendly, easy to read and easy to find privacy policy for children. Transparency, accountability and child-friendly design are advocated as ethical ways to reach out to children. In order to nurture a culture of ethics, it is required that researchers continue to examine their assumptions, values, attitudes and beliefs about children and childhood. It is important to engage more critically with key ethical considerations linked to informed consent, harm and benefits, privacy and confidentiality (Graham et al., 2016). A child-centric view of research ethics opens up a whole new perspective and refocuses current thinking onto children as agents, their power and impact. Researchers have proposed a participatory ethical approach that promotes the inclusion and empowerment of young people in research and policy (Houghton, 2015). Ultimately, the most vital ingredient in the recipe for better ethical behaviour by marketers remains the force of will to always keep ethics at the heart of a company's purpose (Laczniak, 2008).

The road ahead

Concepts of childhood and socialisation of the child are part of culture and have transformed through time. The research on child socialisation is more or less traced to the last century. The central assumption was on the unidirectional nature of the concept, which emphasised that children learn the skills to be consumers from various socialisation agents such as family, media and peers. The role of family and media as socialisation agents has received much attention and the changing social and economic environment has also impacted on the role of children in the family. The unidirectional process came under scrutiny and the role of (only) parents as teachers was re-conceptualised. Children too were found to be influencing the purchase decisions of the family and thus while socialisation portrays the child as a learner and the parent as a teacher, re-socialisation portrays the parent as a learner and the child as a teacher (Sharma, 2016). A new area of research – reverse socialisation – started gaining ground. Marketers, researchers, policy makers were interested in understanding the factors that affect the influence of children. The power equations in the family have witnessed changes and it is important to understand the new role of children. The proposed model in this chapter is based on theoretical premise and is an attempt to integrate two theories that have a common base – the theory of child socialisation and the theory of reverse socialisation. The testing of this model can greatly enhance our understanding of the process and the outcomes associated with it.

Marketers also need to acknowledge and understand the changing dynamics of family decision-making. Yes, children have substantial influence, but this influence needs to be understood in the context of different product categories. Thus, for products where children have more influence, communication needs to be designed with the child in focus. The influence also needs to be understood with respect to age, gender and other family demographics. For public policy makers the importance of understanding the changes cannot be overemphasised. Children play an important role in purchase decisions. Providing correct information to the child would play a crucial role in his/her customer orientation. Products for which policy makers are seeking to deter or change children's views can be done by developing appeals that provide information to the child.

Society has witnessed new family structures, media has been redefined by the Internet, the global boundaries have become virtual and the intermixing of cultures is more pronounced. Perhaps it is time to redefine family and media and understand the effect of this redefined family and new media on consumer socialisation. The old definition of family, the old media comprising mainly of television has limited applicability. In this dynamic environment the socialisation of children and re-socialisation of parents provides rich possibilities for future research.

References

Abrams, Bill (1984). T.V. ads shows struggle to replace bygone images of today's mothers. *The Wall Street Journal*, *204*(5), 27.

Adib, Hagar and El-Bassiouny, Noha (2012). Materialism in young consumers. *Journal of Islamic Marketing*, *3*(3), 255–282.

Agnew, S. and Cameron-Agnew, T. (2015). The influence of consumer socialisation in the home on gender differences in financial literacy. *International Journal of Consumer Studies*, *39*(6), 630–638. doi:10.1111/ijcs.12179.

Ahuja, R. D. and Stinson, K. M. (1993). Female-headed single parent families: An exploratory study of children's influence in family decision making. *Advances in Consumer Research*, *20*(1), 469–474.

Akinyele, S. T. (2010). The influence of children on family purchasing decisions in Ota, Nigeria. *Journal of Contemporary Management Research*, 4(2), 1–11.

Aldea, R. L. and Brandabur, R. E. (2015). The perception of ethics related to the marketing targeted to children in Romania. *International Journal of Academic Research in Economics and Management Sciences*, 4(1), 125–140.

Aldous, J. and McLeod, J. M. (1974). Commentaries on Ward, 'consumer socialization'. *Journal of Consumer Research*, 1(2), 15–17.

Alsop, Ronald. (1988). Mom leaves her mark in loyalty to products. *The Wall Street Journal*, 19 January, 33.

Aries, Phillipe (1965). *Centuries of childhood: A social history of family life*. New York: Vintage.

Ayadi, K. and Bree, J. (2010). An ethnography of the transfer of food learning within the family. *Young Consumers*, 11(1), 67–76. doi: 10.1108/17473611011026028.

Bakir, A., Rose, G. M. and Shoham, A. (2006). Family communication patterns: Mothers' and fathers' communication style and children's perceived influence in family decision making. *Journal of International Consumer Marketing*, 19(2), 75–95. doi: 10.1 300/J046v19n02.05.

Baltruschat, D. (2004). The ABCs of media education: A hands-on-approach. *Feliciter*, 50(5), 190–192.

Belch, G. E., Belch, M. A. and Ceresino, G. (1985). Parental mid-teenage child influences in family decision-making. *Journal of Business Research*, 13(2), 163–176.

Beneke, Justin, Silverstone, Grant, Woods, Alastair and Schneider, Greg (2011). The influence of the youth on their parents' purchasing decisions of high-technology products. *African Journal of Business Management*, 5(10), 3807–3812. doi: 10.5897/AJBM10.359.

Beyrouti, N. and Houssami, R. (2013). The kids market: Kids' influence and family buying decision making. The case of Lebanon. *Business Journal for Entrepreneurs*, 3, 138–173.

Brim, Orville G. (1966). Socialization throughout the life cycle. In O. Brim and S. Wheeler (eds), *Socialization after childhood* (pp. 1–49). New York: John Wiley.

Buckingham, D. (2007). Childhood in the age of global media. *Children's Geographies*, 5(1), 43–54.

Calvert, S. L. (2008). Children as consumers: Advertising and marketing. *The Future of Children*, 18(1), 205–234.

Carlson, L., Grossbart, S. and Stuenkel, J. (1992). The role of parental socialization types on differential family communication patterns regarding consumption. *Journal of Consumer Psychology*, 1(1), 31.

Carlson, L., Grossbart, S. and Walsh, A. (1990). Mothers' communication orientation and consumer-socialization tendencies. *Journal of Advertising*, 19(3), 27–38.

Carlson, L. and Harrison, R. (2010). Family public policy in the United States. *Journal of Macromarketing*, 30(4), 320–330. doi 10.1177/0276146710378169.

Carnevale, F. A., Campbell, A., Collin-Vézina, D. and Macdonald, M. E. (2015). Interdisciplinary studies of childhood ethics: Developing a new field of inquiry. *Children and Society*, 29(6), 511–523. doi:10.1111/chso.12063.

Caruana, A. and Vassallo, R. (2003). Children's perception of their influence over purchases: The role of parental communication patterns. *Journal of Consumer Marketing*, 20(1), 55–66.

Chakrapani, C. and Vijay Kumar, S. (1994). *Changing status and role of women in Indian society*. New Delhi: M. D. Publications.

Chaudhary, M. and Gupta, A. (2012). Children's influence in family buying process in India. *Young Consumers*, 13(2), 161–175. doi:10.1108/17473611211233512.

Cingel, D. P. and Kremar, M. (2013). Predicting media use in very young children: The role of demographics and parent attitudes. *Communication Studies*, 64(4), 374–394. doi: 10.1080/10510974.2013.770408.

Coley, Rebekah Levine (1998). Children's socialization experiences and functioning in single mother households: The importance of fathers and other men. *Child Development*, 69(1), 219–230.

Cowell, P. (2001). Marketing to children: A guide for students and practitioners – part 2. *Marketing Review*, 2(1), 71–87.

Danes, S. M. and Haberman, H. R. (2007). Teen financial knowledge, self-efficacy, and behavior: A gendered view. *Journal of Financial Counseling and Planning*, 18(2), 48–60.

Dotson, M. J. and Hyatt, E. M. (2000). A comparison of parents' and children's knowledge of brands and advertising slogans in the United States: Implications for consumer socialization. *Journal of Marketing Communications*, 6(4), 219–230. doi:10.1080/135272600750036346.

Easterling, D., Miller, S. and Weinberger, N. (1995). Environmental consumerism: A process of children's socialization and families' resocialization. *Psychology and Marketing*, 12(6), 531–550.

Ekstrom, K. H., Tansuhaj, P. S. and Foxman, E. R. (1987). Children's influence in family decisions and consumer socialization: A reciprocal view. *Advances in Consumer Research*, 14(1), 283–287.

Fan, Ying and Li, Yixuan. (2009). Children's buying behavior in China: A study of their information sources. *Marketing Intelligence and Planning*, 28(2), 170–187. doi: 10.1108/02634501011029673.

Flouri, E. (1999). An integrated model of consumer materialism: Can economic socialization and maternal values predict materialistic attitudes in adolescents? *Journal of Socio-Economics*, 28(6), 707–724.

Foxman, E. R., Tansuhaj, P. S. and Ekstrom, K. M. (1989). Family members' perceptions of adolescents' influence in family decision-making. *Journal of Consumer Research*, 15(4), 482–491.

Galvin, K. M., Brommel, B., Galvin, K. and Bylund, C. (eds) (2004). *Family communication: Cohesion and change*. New York: Allyn & Bacon.

Gbadamosi, A. (2012). Exploring children, family, and consumption behavior: Empirical evidence from Nigeria. *Thunderbird International Business Review*, 54(4), 591–605. doi:10.1002/tie.21486.

Gentile, D. A., Oberg, C., Sherwood, N. E., Story, M., Walsh, D. A. and Hogan, M. (2004). Well-child visits in the video age: Pediatricians and the American Academy of Pediatrics' Guidelines for Children's Media Use. *Pediatrics*, 114(5), 1235–1241. doi:10.1542/peds.2003-1121-L.

Geuens, M., De Pelsmacker, P. and Mast, G. (2003). How family structure affects parent–child communication about consumption. *International Journal of Advertising and Marketing to Children*, 4(2), 57.

Gosselt, J. F., De Jong, M. T. and Van Hoof, J. J. (2012). Effects of media ratings on children and adolescents: A litmus test of the forbidden fruit effect. *Journal of Communication*, 62(6), 1084–1101. doi:10.1111/j.1460-2466.2012.01597.x.

Graham, A., Powell, M. A. and Truscott, J. (2016). Exploring the nexus between participatory methods and ethics in early childhood research. *Australasian Journal of Early Childhood*, 41(1), 82–89.

Gram, M. (2006). 'If we're not going to Italy, I'm not coming': Children as co-decision-makers in the family? The case of family holidays. *Advances in Consumer Research – European Conference Proceedings*, 7112–7118.

Haselhoff, V., Faupel, U. and Holzmüller, H. H. (2014). Strategies of children and parents during shopping for groceries. *Young Consumers: Insight and Ideas for Responsible Marketers*, *15*(1), 3–13.

Haynes, J. L., Burts, D. C., Dukes, A. and Cloud, R. (1993). Consumer socialization of preschoolers and kindergartners as related to clothing consumption. *Psychology and Marketing*, *10*(2), 151–166.

Houghton, C. (2015). Young people's perspectives on participatory ethics: Agency, power and impact in domestic abuse research and policy-making. *Child Abuse Review*, *24*(4), 235–248. doi:10.1002/car.2407.

Hughes, H. and Southall, C. (2012). Gay and lesbian families and tourism. In H. Schanzel, I. Yeoman and E. Backer (eds), *Family tourism: Multi-disciplinary perspectives* (pp. 125–139). Bristol: Channel View Publications.

Hunter-Jones, P. (2014). Changing family structures and childhood socialisation: A study of leisure consumption. *Journal of Marketing Management*, *30*(15–16), 1533–1553. doi:10.1080/0267257X.2014.930503.

Isin, F. and Alkibay, S. (2011). Influence of children on purchasing decisions of well-to-do families. *Young Consumers*, *12*(1), 39–52. doi:10.1108/17473611111114777.

Jadva, V., Hines, M. and Golombok, S. (2010). Infants' preferences for toys, colors, and shapes: Sex differences and similarities. *Archives of Sexual Behavior*, December 2010, *39*(6), 1261–1273.

Jejeebhoy, S. J. and Santhya, K. G. (2011). Parent–child communication on sexual and reproductive health matters: Perspectives of mothers and fathers of youth in India. www.popcouncil.org/uploads/pdfs/2011PGY_ParentChildCommunication.pdf. (accessed 17 December 2014).

John, D. (1999). Consumer socialization of children: A retrospective look at twenty-five years of research. *Journal of Consumer Research*, *26*(3), 183–213.

Kim, C., Lee, H. and Tomiuk, M. A. (2009). Adolescents' perceptions of family communication patterns and some aspects of their consumer socialization. *Psychology and Marketing*, *26*(10), 888–907.

Kim, C., Yang, Z. and Lee, H. (2009). Cultural differences in consumer socialization: A comparison of Chinese-Canadian and Caucasian-Canadian children. *Journal of Business Research*, *62*(10), 955–962. doi:10.1016/j.jbusres.2008.08.005.

Kirkorian, H. L., Wartella, E. A. and Anderson, D. R. (2008). Media and young children's learning. *Future of Children*, *18*(1), 39–61.

Kretchmar, J. (2016a). Behaviorism. *Behaviorism: Research Starters Education*, 1–5. doi:10.3331/ors_edu_419.

Kretchmar, J. (2016b). Social learning theory. *Social Learning Theory – Research Starters Education*, 1–5. doi:10.3331/ors_edu_404.

Kumar, Krishna (2016). Studying childhood in India. *Economic and Political Weekly*, *51*(23). www.epw.in/journal/2016/23/commentary/studying-childhood-india.html#sthash.kh44NiD8.dpuf (accessed 16 December 2016).

Laczniak, Gene R. (2008). Ethics of marketing. In Robert W. Kolb (ed.), *Encyclopedia of business ethics and society* (pp. 1336–1343). Thousand Oaks: Sage.

Lee, C. K. (1994). Influence of children in family purchase decisions. PhD thesis, University of Auckland. https://researchspace.auckland.ac.nz/handle/2292/1137/ (accessed 10 May 2011).

Lee, C. K. and Collins, B. A. (2000). Family decision-making and coalition patterns. *European Journal of Marketing*, *34*(9/10), 1181–1198.

Lee, K. C. C. and Beatty, S. E. (2002). Family structure and influence in family decision making. *Journal of Consumer Marketing*, *19*(1), 24–41.

Livingstone, S. (2006). Drawing conclusions from new media research: Reflections and puzzles regarding children's experience of the internet. *Information Society*, *22*(4), 219–230. doi:10.1080/01972240600791358.

Locke, John (1909–1914). *Some thoughts concerning education: Vol. XXXVII Part 1.* New York: Collier & Son.

Lovata, L. M. (1987). Behavioral theories relating to the design of information systems. *MIS Quarterly*, *11*(2), 147–149.

Lusardi Annamaria, Mitchell, Olivia S. and Curto, Vilsa (2010). Financial literacy among the young: Evidence and implications for consumer policy. www.dartmouth.edu/~alusardi/Papers/Financial_literacy_young.pdf (accessed 10 December 2016).

McDonald, George (1871). *At the back of the north wind.* www.samizdat.qc.ca/arts/lit/PDFs/BackoftheNorthWind_GM.pdf (accessed 13 November 2016).

McLeod, S. A. (2014). Lev Vygotsky. www.simplypsychology.org/vygotsky.html (accessed 13 November 2016).

McLeod, J. M. and Chaffee, S. H. (1972). The role of family communication in consumer socialization of children and adolescents. *Journal of Consumer Research*, *11*(4), 898–913.

Mandell, Lewis (2008). Financial literacy in high school. In Annamaria Lusardi (ed.), *Overcoming the saving slump: How to increase the effectiveness of financial education and saving programs* (pp. 257–259). Chicago: University of Chicago Press.

Mandrik, C. A., Fern, E. F. and Yeqing, B. (2005). Intergenerational influence: Roles of conformity to peers and communication effectiveness. *Psychology and Marketing*, *22*(10), 813–832.

McNeal, J. U. (1987). *Children as consumers: Insights and implications.* New York: Lexington Books.

Marshall, D., O'Donohoe, S. and Kline, S. (2007). Families, food, and pester power: Beyond the blame game? *Journal of Consumer Behaviour*, *6*(4), 164–181. doi:10.1002/cb.217.

Mehta, K. P., Coveney, J., Ward, P. and Handsley, E. (2014). Parents' and children's perceptions of the ethics of marketing energy-dense nutrient-poor foods on the internet: Implications for policy to restrict children's exposure. *Public Health Ethics*, *7*(1), 21–34.

Minahan, S. and Huddleston, P. (2010). Shopping with mum–mother and daughter socialization. *Young Consumers*, *11*(3), 170–177.

Moore, E. S. (2004). Children and the changing world of advertising. *Journal of Business Ethics*, *52*(2), 161–167.

Moschis, George P. and Moore, Roy L. (1985). Racial and socioeconomic influences on the development of consumer behavior. In Elizabeth C. Hirschman and Moris B. Holbrook (eds), *NA – Advances in Consumer Research* (Vol. 12, pp. 525–531). Provo: Association for Consumer Research.

Moschis, G. P. and Churchill, Jr., G. A. (1978). Consumer socialization: A theoretical and empirical analysis. *Journal of Marketing Research*, *15*(4), 599–609.

Moschis, G. P., Prahato, A. E. and Mitchell, L. G. (1986). Family communication influences on the development of consumer behavior: Some additional findings. *Advances in Consumer Research*, *13*(1), 365–369. 46.

Moschis, G. P., Sim, Ong Fon, Anil, Mathur, Yamashita, Takako and Bouzaglo, S. B. (2011). Family and television influences on materialism: A cross-cultural life course approach. *Journal of Asia Business studies*, *5*(2), 124–144.

Moschis, G. P. and Churchill, Gilbert, A., Jr. (1978). Consumer socialisation: A theoretical and empirical analysis. *Journal of Marketing Research*, *15*, 599–609.

Nash, C. (2009). *Parent–child purchase relationship.* PhD thesis, Dublin Institute of Technology. http://arrow.dit.ie/cgi/viewcontent.cgi?article=1025&context=busmas) (accessed 12 April 2014).

Ogden, Denise T., Ogden, James R. and Ramzy, Omar (2012). Perceptions of children's influence on purchase decisions: A comparison between US and Egypt. www.wbiconpro.com/516-Denise.pdf (accessed 22 June 2014).

Pedersen, Susanne, Grønhøj, Alice and Bech-Larsen, Tino. (2012). Family members' roles in healthy-eating socialization based on a healthy-eating intervention. *Young Consumers: Insight and Ideas for Responsible Marketers*, *13*(3), 208–223. doi:10.1108/17473611211261610.

Peterson, Gary W. and Rollins, Boyd, C. (1987). Parent–child socialization. In Marvin B. Sussman, Susan K. Steinmetz and Gary W. Peterson (eds), *Handbook of marriage and the family* (pp. 471–507). New York: Plenum.

Piaget, J. (1964). Part I: Cognitive development in children: Piaget development and learning. *Journal of Research Science Teaching*, *2*, 176–186. doi:10.1002/tea.3660020306.

Preston, C. (2004). Children's advertising: The ethics of economic socialisation. *International Journal of Consumer Studies*, *28*(4), 364–370. doi:10.1111/j.1470-6431.2004.00401.x.

Rose, G. M., Bush, V. D. and Kahle, L. (1998). The influence of family communication patterns on parental reactions toward advertising: A cross-national examination. *Journal of Advertising*, *27*(4), 71–85.

Schunk, D. H. (2004). *Learning theories: An educational perspective* (6th edn). Harlow: Pearson Education.

Sharma, A. (2011). Role of family in consumer socialization of children: Literature review. *Researchers World Journal of Arts, Science and Commerce*, *2*(3), 161–167.

Sharma, A. (2016). Exploring the changing role of children as consumers in India: Are are they learning from us or are they teaching us? In *Handbook of research on consumerism and buying behavior in developing nations*. New York: IGI Global.

Sharma, R. W. and Dasgupta, P. (2009). Marketing to children: A planning framework. *Young Consumers*, *10*(3), 180–187. doi:10.1108/17473610910985991.

Sharma, A. and Sonwaney, V. (2014). Theoretical modeling of influence of children on family purchase decision making. *Procedia Social and Behavioral Sciences*, *133*, 38–46.

Sharma, A. and Sonwaney, V. (2015a). Exploring the role of family communication and brand awareness in understanding the influence of child on purchase decisions: Scale development and validation. *International Journal of Business Excellence*, *8*(6), 748–766.

Sharma, A. and Sonwaney, V. (2015b). Family communication patterns and children's influence on purchase decisions. *Indian Journal of Marketing*, *45*(10), 7–22.

Shields, P. O. (2009). Coming of age: The college market and the gaming entertainment industry. *Journal of Hospitality Marketing and Management*, *18*(1), 68–88. doi:10.1080/19368620801989220.

Stead, B. A. and Gilbert, J. (2001). Ethical issues in electronic commerce. *Journal of Business Ethics*, *34*(2), 75–85.

Suwandinata, H. (2011). *Children's influence on family decision-making process in food buying and consumption*. PhD thesis. http://geb.uni-giessen.de/geb/volltexte/2012/8589/pdf/SuwandinataHanny_2012_01_19.pdf. (accessed 13 December 2013).

Thomson, E. S., Laing, A. W. and McKee, L. (2007). Family purchase decision-making: Exploring child influence behaviour. *Journal of Consumer Behaviour*, *6*(4), 182–202. doi:10.1002/cb.220.

Tinson, J. and Nancarrow, C. (2005). The influence of children on purchases. *International Journal of Market Research*, *47*(1), 5–27.

Tomko, Paul R. (2012). Understanding the factors affecting the influence of children on their parents total purchases. PhD thesis, Capella University. http://media.proquest.com/media/pq/classic/doc/2662550201/fmt/ai/rep/NPDF?_s=xTqZvWcg%2FEYgxQjxIzJZcW9m7Y4%3D (accessed 31 March 2013).

Tunnell, M. O. and Jacobs, J. S. (2013). The origins and history of American children's literature. *Reading Teacher*, *67*(2), 80–86. doi:10.1002/TRTR.1201.

Valkenburg, Patti M. and Cantor, Joanne (2001). The development of a child into a consumer. *Journal of Applied Developmental Psychology*, 22(1), 61–72. http://dx.doi.org/10.1016/S0193-3973(00)00066-6.

Van der Burgt, D. (2008). How children place themselves and others in local space. *Geografiska Annaler Series B: Human Geography*, 90(3), 257–269. doi:10.1111/j.1468-0467.2008.291.x.

Vygotsky, L. (1978). Interaction between learning and development. In G. Auvain and M. Cole (eds), *Readings on the development of children* (pp. 34–40). New York: Scientific American Books.

Waiguny, M. J., Nelson, M. R. and Terlutter, R. (2014). The relationship of persuasion knowledge, identification of commercial intent and persuasion outcomes in advergames: The role of media context and presence. *Journal of Consumer Policy*, 37(2), 257–277. doi:http://dx.doi.org/10.1007/s10603-013-9227-z.

Wang, Hsieh and Yeh, Tsai. (2004). Who is the decision maker: The parent or the child in group package tour? *Tourism Management*, 25(2), 183–194.

Wang, S., Holloway, B. B., Beatty, S. E. and Hill, W. W. (2007). Adolescent influence in family purchase decisions: An update and cross-national extension. *Journal of Business Research*, 60(11), 1117–1124.

Ward, S. (1974). Consumer socialisation: Initial study results. *Advances in Consumer Research*, 1(1), 120–125.

Ward, S., Wackman, D. and Wartella, E. (1977). The development of consumer information-processing skills: Integrating cognitive development and family interaction theoris. *Advances in Consumer Research*, 4(1), 166–171.

Watne, T., Lobo, A. and Linda, B. (2011). Children as agents of secondary socialization for their parents. *Young Consumers: Insight and Ideas for Responsible Marketers*, 12(4), 285–294. doi:10.1108/17473611111185841.

Watne, T. and Winchester, T. (2011). Family holiday decision-making: The knowledge and influence of adolescent children and parents. Australia and New Zealand Marketing Academy Conference. www.academia.edu/1324896/Family_holiday_decision_making_the_knowledge_and_influence_of_adolescent_children_and_parents (accessed 23 May 2013).

Williams, L. A. and Burns, A. C. (2000). Exploring the dimensionality of children's direct influence attempts. *Advances in Consumer Research*, 27(1), 64–71.

Wilson, G. and Wood, K. (2004). The influence of children on parental purchases during supermarket shopping. *International Journal of Consumer Studies*, 28(4), 329–336.

Wonsun, S. (2010). Consumer socialization online: Antecedents and consequences of children's skepticism toward online advertising. *American Academy of Advertising Conference Proceedings*, 115.

Yoders, S. Y. (2014). Constructivism theory and use from a 21st-century perspective. *Journal of Applied Learning Technology*, 4(3), 12–20.

Youn, Seonmi (2008). Parental influence and teens' attitude toward online privacy protection. *The Journal of Consumer Affairs*, 42(3), 362–388.

4
YOUNG CONSUMERS' MOTIVATION AND INVOLVEMENT

Uses and gratifications perspective

Emmanuel Adugu

Introduction

Consumption is viewed by some scholars as a process whereby consumers are the end users of products (Dixon, 1999; Firat, 2001). Generally, consumption includes activities of buying goods, social relations connected to the provision, allocation and use of goods and services and can also be viewed as part of the social space in which people participate in creating and reproducing meanings about the occurrences of everyday life (Luckmann, 1989). In developed nations, consumption is increasingly being viewed as one way that individuals and groups express themselves and their values (Katz-Gerro, 2004), but little is written about such issues in developing and emerging nations (Stolle and Micheletti, 2013). Commodities within this perspective not only have a use value for the consumer, but also have an abstract value that consists of the cultural, symbolic and emotional meanings around the good (Lupton, 1997). Consumers are believed to actually enhance a commodity's economic value when they attach or add value to a product that is not intended by the producer (Dixon and Banwell, 2004). Unfortunately, much of the literature on consumption normally focuses on food, energy, clothing, etc. and much less on social media and Internet use (consumption), especially uses and gratifications associated with them in emerging and developing countries.

Social media includes a multitude of sources of online information normally created, circulated and used by consumers to educate one another about products, services and brands available in the marketplace (Murugesan, 2007). Social media has become an important area of interest for academicians, marketing professionals, researchers, internal development practitioners, etc. For example, businesses can make contact with consumers through a variety of social media channels. In spite of that, there is a gap in the literature on young consumers' motivation and involvement in social media. This chapter examines young consumers' use (consumption) of social networking sites (Facebook, Twitter) and the Internet in

31 emerging and developing countries around the world. The chapter will specifically explore the types of needs/gratifications that motivate young consumers to use social networking sites and the Internet. In view of this, there is the need to first discuss motivation (specifically, Maslow's hierarchy of needs), followed by consumer involvement construct. The relationship between uses and gratifications theory, social networking sites and Internet use are then discussed. Research questions, data, variable measurement, analysis and discussion are then presented and finally, conclusions are drawn.

Maslow's hierarchy of needs

There are many conceptual definitions of motivation. Buford *et al.* (1995) define it as a predisposition to behave in a purposive manner to achieve specific, unmet needs. For Higgins (1994), it is an internal drive to satisfy an unsatisfied need; and in the view of Kreitner (1995), it is the psychological process that gives behaviour purpose and direction. Thus motivation can be linked to internal and external factors that may stimulate an individual to take agency in order to satisfy a specific need or achieve an objective.

Scholars have proposed many theories of motivation over the years. Some of these are: Maslow's hierarchy of needs, equity theory, three-dimensional theory of attribution and Hertzberg's two-factor theory. In this chapter, Maslow's hierarchy of needs is considered to be particularly appropriate because it has been widely used to explain individuals' social media usage (Kuan-Yu and His-Peng, 2011).

Maslow's hierarchy of needs model conceptualises human needs in terms of a hierarchical structure. The model is usually portrayed in the form of a pyramid, where basic needs are at the bottom and self-actualisation needs are at the top. As a result, the dominant motivational need at each level is an antecedent to the next higher level. Maslow used the concepts of physiological, safety, belongingness/love, esteem and self-actualisation to portray the hierarchical structure of human motivations as shown in Figure 4.1 below. According to Maslow, the most basic level needs must be met before the individual could be motivated to direct focus on the next higher level of need or secondary needs. In that respect, at the basic level, physiological needs such as air, water and food are required for survival. Next on the hierarchy are safety needs such as job security, financial security, health and well-being, stability, predictability, physical and psychological safety. Following that are needs for belongingness in relation to family, friends and community. The fourth need on the hierarchy is esteem – to be accepted and valued by others. Esteem needs are operationalised in terms of a motive for a stable and high evaluation of humans themselves, for self-respect, self-esteem, and for the esteem of others (Maslow, 1954, p. 90). At the apex of the hierarchy is the need for self-actualisation. This need deals with the motivation for personal development, in order to realise full potential and fulfilment. In essence, self-actualisation needs are connected to the desire to become more and more what one is, to become everything that one is capable of becoming (Maslow, 1954, p. 94).

Self-
actualisation

Esteem

Love/belonging

Safety

Physiological

FIGURE 4.1 Maslow's hierarchy of needs model

Maslow's model is applicable to media use such as Internet and Social Network Sites (SNSs). In that context, individuals may seek to satisfy their physiological and safety needs through reliance on media that is supportive of interpersonal dialogues (Kang and Jung, 2014). As Huizinga (1970) noted, it is also possible for individuals to build social connections, belongingness and love for others physically and emotionally through mediated channels. Huizinga continued that satisfaction of individuals' needs for belongingness, safety in addition to their physiological needs, develops self-esteem and self-actualisation. Similarly, exposure to the media may stimulate self-esteem where its content (for example, news and entertainment) is supportive of the audience (Chia and Yip, 2009; Knobloch-Westerwick and Hastall, 2010). For example, as Smock *et al.* (2011) noted, youth involvement on social media in activities (such as socialising, entertainment, gathering facts and knowledge, etc.) are motivated by the desire for self-exploration and the need to experiment with their identities. Consequently, satisfying consumers' esteem needs may influence their involvement.

Consumer involvement construct

There are various conceptualisations of consumer involvement. Consumer involvement is defined as a person's perceived relevance of an object based on inherent needs, values and interests (Zaichkowsky, 1985, p. 342). It may be influenced by the personal characteristics of the consumer (Lastovicka and Gardner, 1978); physical characteristics of the product (Wright, 1974); and the situational factors related to the purchase decision (Clark and Belk, 1978). Consumer involvement can be viewed as goal-directed capacity (Park and Mittal, 1985), where a perceived need (motivation or stimulus) is necessary for involvement. With reference to products or technology, consumer involvement refers to feelings of interest and enthusiasm toward the product (Goldsmith and Emmert, 1991); or in relation to technology, it is conceptualised as a trait to influence a consumer's technology perceptions (Ranaweera et al., 2005). Involvement is viewed by scholars as an individual difference variable that influences consumers' decision-making and communication behaviours (Michaelidou and Dibb, 2008, p. 3); and may also moderate different aspects of consumer behaviour (Dholakia, 2001).

A number of studies revealed that consumer involvement may lead to higher levels of use intention (Kamarulzaman, 2007) and continuance intention (Wang et al., 2006). It is in that context (Michaelidou and Dibb, 2008, p. 2) aptly noted that involvement can be used to segment consumers into low, moderate and high involvement groups, which can subsequently be targeted with different promotional strategies.

Measuring level of involvement is challenging due to its multi-dimensional nature. In that context, no single construct can individually and satisfactorily describe, explain or predict involvement (Rothschild, 1979, p. 78). Zaichkowsky (1985, p. 342) noted the following areas that affect a person's level of involvement:

1. *Personal* – inherent interests, values or needs that motivate one toward the object.
2. *Physical* – characteristics of the object that cause differentiation and increase interest.
3. *Situational* – something that temporarily increases relevance or interest toward the object.

Other scholars also support the notion that involvement is a multi-dimensional construct. In that vein, Kapferer and Laurent (1985) suggested that involvement should be measured along five facet (dimensions). Table 4.1 lists the five dimensions. These are: interest, pleasure, sign, risk importance and risk probability. According to Kapferer and Laurent, in a minimal involvement type of profile, consumers score lowest on all five dimensions (facets), whereas in a total involvement type of profile, consumers score highest on all dimensions.

TABLE 4.1 Consumer involvement profile scale: the five facets/antecedents of involvement

Facets of involvement (CIP)	*Description of facets*
Interest	The personal interest a person has in a product category, its personal meaning or importance
Pleasure	The hedonic value of the product, its ability to provide pleasure and enjoyment
Sign	The sign value of the product, the degree to which it expresses the person's self
Risk importance	The perceived importance of the potential negative consequences associated with a poor choice of the product
Risk probability	The perceived probability of making such a poor choice

Source: Kapferer and Laurent (1985, 1993).

Implicit themes that run through the above conceptualisations of involvement are perceived personal importance, interest, product, service or good, characteristics, motivation, risk assessment and consumption. In essence, involvement is the perception that the 'product or object' has the capacity to satisfy important values and needs of the consumer in a specific situation with minimal undesirable consequences. Involvement may ultimately lead to consumers' gratification for engaging with the product or object in focus. Available research reveals that there is a link between consumer involvement with a technology and attitude toward using it. In that context, ease of use, usefulness, and enjoyment of a technology are linked to its involvement (Wan-I et al., 2011).

Uses and gratification theory, social networking sites and Internet use

One of the most influential theories of media research is uses and gratifications theory (Roy, 2009). The basic premise of uses and gratifications theory is that individuals seek media that satisfy their needs ultimately leading to gratification (Lariscy et al., 2011). Needs are the combined product of psychological dispositions, sociological factors and environmental conditions (Katz, Haas and Gurevitch, 1973, p. 178). Individuals' needs motivate their media choices for the gratification of their needs. In that regard, Swanson (1979, p. 4) aptly noted that the uses and gratifications approach shifts the emphasis of communication research from answering the question 'what do the media do to people?' to 'what do active audience media members do with the media?' Uses and gratifications theory is one of the first research approaches to consider the active role of the audience in media choice, suggesting that individuals actively search for, identify with and use media to satisfy specific gratification needs (Ku et al., 2013). It provides an analytical framework for examining consumer media usage (Jere and Davis, 2011), where gratifications received are useful as core predictors of media use and recurring media use (Palmgreen and Rayburn, 1979; Kaye and Johnson, 2002; Reiss and Wiltz, 2004).

Stafford et al. (2004) identified three types of gratifications sought by consumers, namely, content gratifications, process gratifications and social gratifications. Content gratifications relate to consumers' use of a particular media due to the content it provides. Process gratifications deal with consumers' use of a medium due to the enjoyment associated with the use of that medium. Social gratifications relate to the use of a particular medium to satisfy consumers' need for social interaction.

Some scholars believe that the uses and gratifications research approach is appropriate for Internet study (Ruggiero, 2000; Weiser, 2001; Johnson and Kaye, 2003). Consumers' Internet usage may be associated with various gratifications (motives). Song et al. (2004) found seven gratifications associated with Internet use. These are: virtual community, information seeking, aesthetic experience, monetary compensation, diversion, personal status and relationship maintenance. Similarly, Eighmey and McCord (1998), Papacharissi and Rubin (2000) noted that motives for information seeking and entertainment are strongly related to Internet use.

Economic motivations, privacy and transactional security have also been uncovered as gratifications linked to the Internet (Korgaonkar and Wolin, 1999). Another study revealed that most gratifications related to Internet use are: global exchange (keeping in touch with others); seeking career opportunities; provision of wide exposure; and self-development (Roy, 2009). Some of Roy's findings concur with Choi et al. (2004), who compared Internet use in the US, Netherlands and South Korea. Findings showed that self-improvement and information seeking were major gratifications/motives across all the three countries.

Social network sites like Facebook, Twitter, etc. are Internet-based services where individuals design their public profile and engage in interactions with family, friends and professional contacts. As a result, social network sites enable users to connect to or join a social network, develop and continually keep relationships with others (Ellison et al., 2007). A pertinent question is: what are the motivations for users to join a social network and what kinds of gratifications are derived from using a particular medium? In other words, what are the needs or motives of users of social networks? Are they goal-oriented users seeking to satisfy personal needs?

Katz, Gurevitch and Haas (1973, p. 167) specified five needs (motivations) for media consumption. These are: cognitive needs, which deal with strengthening information, knowledge and understanding; affective needs, in terms of strengthening aesthetic, pleasurable and emotional experience; integrative needs, related to strengthening credibility, stability and status; social integrative needs, which are related to strengthening contact with family, friends and the world; and escape or tension release needs, which relate to escape or release from tension originating from society and oneself.

Even though there are exceptions, research suggests that most social network sites primarily support pre-existing social relations, where relationships may be weak ties, with some offline element (Boyd and Ellison, 2007). Similarly, research also shows that gratifications (motives) for using social network sites may be for information sharing about self and academic purposes, socialising to keep in touch with friends, feel connected, post social functions, etc. (Stassen, 2010; Santos et al., 2009).

Currently, social networking sites are popular, especially among the youth (Fewkes and McCabe, 2012; Junco, 2012). Research shows that most college students of traditional college age are using social network sites for significant periods of time for gratifications such as making new friends, and keeping in touch with friends (Raacke and Bonds-Raake, 2008). Other young people use it to cultivate and maintain relationships with friends, in addition to entertainment and passing time (Sheldon, 2008).

Several recent studies seek to unearth consumers' motivation for social media use such as: Facebook (Krause et al., 2014); Instagram (Sheldon and Bryant, 2016); Twitter use (Chen, 2011); and digital photo sharing on Facebook (Malik et al., 2016). In connection with motivations (uses and gratifications) for social media use, results from a recent study identify ten uses and gratifications for using social media (such as Facebook, Twitter, LinkedIn, YouTube, etc.). These uses and gratifications are social interaction, information seeking, passing time, entertainment, relaxation, communicatory utility, expression of opinions, convenience utility, information sharing, surveillance and watching of others (Whiting and Williams, 2013, p. 368).

Research questions

Throughout the world, young media consumers are labelled based on their habits and values. For example, they are labelled as digital natives (Prensky, 2001) for their modes of information consumption in the digital world, and Generation C (Bruns, 2007), due to their dominant willingness to create content. Some specific gratifications underpinning social network and Internet habits of young consumers are: active engagement in content production, integrating Internet into their leisure and entertainment activities, going first to the Internet for all their information needs, willingness to share personal information compared with earlier generations (Rissanen and Luoma-Aho, 2016). This chapter is focused on young consumer motivation and involvement in relation to their engagement with social network sites and the Internet from a uses and gratifications perspective using nationally representative data sets from 31 emerging and developing nations.

Three major questions that the chapter seeks to answer are:

1. What gratifications are associated with youth in emerging and developing nations through using social network sites and the Internet?
2. Do youth in emerging and developing nations combine social network-related gratifications with Internet-linked gratifications?
3. To what extent do youth in emerging and developing nations engage in more than one form of social network-related gratification in combination with Internet gratification and vice versa?

Data and measurement of variables

As noted earlier, this chapter fills the gap in the literature focusing on young consumers' motivation and involvement in social network sites and the Internet based on data from 31 emerging and developed countries throughout the world. Data for this chapter comes from the Pew Research Center, US. The Pew Research Center is a nonpartisan 'fact tank' that is based in Washington DC. It provides information on social issues, public opinion and demographic trends shaping the US and the world.

The author assessed data gathered from the following countries: Senegal, Tanzania, Kenya, Nigeria, Ghana, South Africa, Uganda, Chile, Brazil, Peru, Colombia, Nicaragua, Venezuela, Mexico, El Salvador, Argentina, China, Philippines, Malaysia, Vietnam, Indonesia, Thailand, Bangladesh, India, Lebanon, Tunisia, Jordan, Egypt, Ukraine, Russia and Poland.

Youth or being young is a socio-cultural concept. In that regard, its conceptualisation varies. For example, the United Nations defines youth as those between 15 and 24 years of age, whereas NU Habitat (Youth Fund) defines it as those between ages 15–32 (United Nations, 2017); African Youth Charter defines youth as 15–35 (African Union, 2006). According to the United Nations Educational, Scientific and Cultural Organisation (UNESCO), youth is a fluid category rather than a fixed age group (see unesco.org). In that connection, different definitions of youth can be adopted depending on the context. This research adopts the African Youth Charter's definition of youth for the following reason: it allows a broad age range to cater for the prolonged period of dependency characteristic of most emerging and developing nations. This is consistent with the generally high levels of unemployment and cost of setting up independent households in such nations. In essence, due to financial, economic and socio-cultural reasons, the period of transition from dependence to independence is wide – necessitating the use of a broad age group (15–35) in order to capture diverse members of youth living in emerging and developing nations.

The data for this chapter is nationally representative and was gathered from 36,619 face-to-face interviews in 31 countries, conducted from March to June 2014. For statistical consistency across all regions covered by the data, the definition given by the African Youth Charter where youth means 'every person between ages 15 and 35 years' is used in this research. In that context, consistent with the focus of this chapter, the analysis of the data is restricted to respondents from ages 18–35. Consequently, the sample size of the data used in relation to the youth dropped from 36,619 to 21,159. Thus the effective sample size is 21,159. Consistent with recommendations by the Pew Research Center for the use of its research data, the final dataset was weighted to ensure that each country (stratum) is proportionally represented. This data will provide the much needed insight into young consumers' use of social media and the Internet in relation to the above questions. This has implications for effective marketing, international development, etc. Below is a detail of the construction of variables used in the analysis, coupled with the descriptive statistics associated with these variables.

Socio-demographics

Socio-demographic variables collected include age, gender, level of education and employment status. Data collected on income could not be used due to the currency metric used, which posed comparability challenges across nations. Age is measured in years. The median age, mean and mode are 26, 26.25 and 30 respectively. Gender is coded as a dichotomous variable (female coded 1 and male coded 0). In the sample of about 49.4 per cent (10,449) were male (coded 1 and recoded 0), and 50.6 per cent (10,710) female (coded 2 and recoded 1).

Respondents' level of education is measured in terms of the total number of years of schooling or education they have completed. The average number of years of schooling completed by the youth respondents (ages 18 to 35) is 13.3 whereas the mean and median are both 12.

The employment status of respondents were: in paid work (coded 1); unemployed and looking for a job (coded 2 and recoded 0); in education (not paid for by employer), in school, student even if on vacation (coded 3 and recoded into 0); apprentice or trainee (coded 4 and recoded into 0); permanently sick or disabled (coded 5 and recoded into 0); retired (coded 6 and recoded 0); doing housework, looking after the home, children or other persons (not paid), (coded 7 and recoded into 0); don't know (coded 8 and recoded into 0); and refused (coded 9 and recoded into 0). Following this classification, 10,550 (49.9 per cent) of respondents are employed and the rest unemployed.

Uses and gratifications of Internet use (consumption)

Based on a synthesis of the substantive literature reviewed, the following gratifications associated with Internet consumption are employed: buy a product online; get news and information about politics; make or receive payments; get information about health and medicine for you or your family; look for or apply for a job; stay in touch with family and friends; get information about government or public services; take an online class or take an online course that leads to a certificate. Respondents (Internet and smartphone users) were asked whether they have used the Internet to engage in any of the above behaviours (gratifications). The response categories were dichotomous, with Yes = 1 and No = 2. These responses were recoded into Yes = 1 and No = 0. Consistent with Pew (2015), for analytical purposes, the responses were classified as follows: socialising (stay in touch with family and friends); getting information (get political news, get health information, get government or services information); career and commerce (look/apply for a job, make or receive payments, buy products, take an online class). The descriptive statistics associated with gratifications in terms of socialising, getting information, carrier and commerce in the 31 countries surveyed are shown in Table 4.2 below.

Internet users (for youth – ages 18 to 35) in the emerging and developing countries surveyed overwhelmingly (about 90 per cent) used the Internet for the gratification to stay in touch with friends and family. With respect to those online, 100 per cent of Senegalese, 93 per cent of Chileans and 92 per cent of Ukrainians socialise with friends and family via the Internet. Following staying in touch with friends and family, 89 per cent and 56 per cent of the youth use the Internet for the gratifications of getting information on government services and political news respectively. Gratifications in terms of career and commerce are at the bottom tier. In that context, 41 per cent of youth surveyed used the Internet to take an online class and look/apply for a job respectively. Few youth Internet users used it for the gratification of online banking (buying products and making/receiving payments).

Uses and gratifications of social networking

Similar to the uses of gratifications of Internet use and based on a synthesis of the substantive literature reviewed, the following gratifications associated with social network sites are employed: share views about music and movies, share views about sports, share views about products, share views about politics and share

TABLE 4.2 Internet use to socialise, get information, career and commerce

	Socialising	Getting information				Career and commerce			
	Stay in touch with family and friends	Get political news	Get health info	Get government or services info	Look/apply for a job	Make or receive payments	Buy products	Take an online class
	%	%	%	%	%	%	%	%
Africa								
Senegal	100.0	49.2	37.7	100.0	38.7	24.1	11.0	49.2
Tanzania	87.8	55.6	30.9	87.8	34.3	37.5	12.9	53.2
Kenya	81.3	63.9	41.4	81.3	60.5	39.9	16.7	47.7
Nigeria	80.8	54.8	42.6	80.8	29.5	18.3	12.1	51.3
Ghana	78.9	52.3	33.9	78.9	28.0	25.8	6.2	31.9
South Africa	74.6	29.7	27.5	74.6	48.2	19.9	13.1	29.5
Uganda	74.1	51.3	41.5	74.1	29.6	25.9	5.2	36.6
Latin America								
Chile	97.1	51.3	62.6	97.1	48.9	44.2	38.6	52.1
Brazil	92.7	57.8	59.0	92.7	46.7	24.4	30.2	48.3
Peru	93.2	54.5	61.5	93.2	43.4	13.4	11.1	37.9
Colombia	91.7	48.6	55.3	91.7	48.7	20.6	19.6	33.5
Nicaragua	90.3	49.4	61.0	90.3	29.6	8.6	6.0	33.3
Venezuela	88.3	41.3	63.6	88.3	28.5	27.7	23.5	36.9
Mexico	90.1	31.4	53.1	90.1	36.5	16.9	13.2	33.9
El Salvador	91.3	51.6	47.1	91.3	36.0	11.0	7.3	32.5
Argentina	86.1	43.0	42.8	86.1	43.8	22.4	25.6	40.2
Asia								
China	91.3	65.7	49.4	91.3	39.0	51.7	62.1	46.5
Philippines	90.6	45.8	54.6	90.6	44.2	8.3	7.5	43.9
Malaysia	89.9	38.9	38.3	89.9	47.2	25.9	23.4	42.5

Vietnam	91.6	79.8	72.7	91.6	24.4	16.4	29.3	46.5
Indonesia	89.8	46.3	46.0	89.8	45.7	6.8	10.8	41.0
Thailand	91.9	57.1	60.3	91.9	37.6	16.3	26.8	40.5
Bangladesh	72.2	57.1	24.8	72.2	61.0	8.4	20.6	28.2
India	73.1	40.7	32.7	73.1	62.2	25.2	21.9	47.0
Middle East								
Lebanon	91.9	72.8	2.6	91.9	20.1	2.4	1.4	1.2
Tunisia	93.4	71.1	69.2	93.4	52.3	22.0	18.9	58.4
Jordan	91.4	47.0	38.4	91.4	32.6	31.2	29.6	25.7
Egypt	80.0	69.6	41.8	80.0	23.0	11.0	2.7	23.6
Eastern Europe								
Ukraine	97.2	80.1	61.4	97.2	40.9	33.6	48.4	51.0
Russia	88.0	68.1	61.9	88.0	45.2	43.9	47.5	52.8
Poland	90.5	62.2	60.8	90.5	52.8	71.1	73.3	48.1
All countries	89.0	56.0	49.0	89.0	40.0	27.0	27.0	41.0

views about religion. In that regard, respondents were asked whether they have ever used social networking sites like Facebook or Twitter to share their views about music and movies, sports, products, politics and religion. The response categories were dichotomous, with Yes = 1 and No = 2. These responses were recoded into

TABLE 4.3 Sharing views on social networking sites

	Music and movies	*Sports*	*Products they use*	*Politics*	*Religion*
Africa	%	%	%	%	%
Kenya	81.3	73.6	35.0	60.9	56.6
Uganda	76.5	67.4	36.1	34.2	45.6
Ghana	70.0	72.7	31.0	39.4	53.5
Senegal	70.6	70.6	24.3	37.6	45.3
South Africa	74.6	42.0	37.8	26.4	30.2
Nigeria	65.5	60.8	34.6	48.2	59.3
Tanzania	57.9	63.4	28.4	33.3	36.3
Latin America					
Mexico	86.7	63.8	41.6	19.6	14.2
Brazil	82.3	63.5	59.2	32.5	33.9
Venezuela	83.0	60.8	54.2	29.4	26.2
Chile	87.3	61.1	64.4	30.4	16.6
Peru	80.6	56.2	37.2	25.4	25.0
Colombia	77.4	56.4	34.6	31.7	28.7
Argentina	73.8	54.7	38.6	25.6	18.5
Nicaragua	71.2	59.4	27.5	16.2	30.6
El Salvador	62.5	55.7	26.1	35.7	44.2
Asia					
Vietnam	89.0	70.6	69.9	16.8	13.7
Thailand	89.4	67.2	41.7	35.4	32.2
China	86.8	64.1	67.5	43.5	9.8
Indonesia	84.1	59.3	36.8	17.3	21.1
India	81.9	72.5	44.9	43.2	38.3
Malaysia	80.8	53.5	44.7	30.5	46.6
Philippines	76.6	53.6	21.0	17.2	28.0
Middle East					
Jordan	76.1	54.1	15.4	63.1	64.7
Egypt	79.2	62.5	5.3	64.0	55.7
Tunisia	73.0	67.6	77.6	40.7	40.4
Lebanon	64.9	31.1	21.1	75.8	11.6
Eastern Europe					
Russia	69.5	46.6	46.4	23.5	6.5
Ukraine	65.0	39.8	42.5	35.8	8.5
Poland	60.6	44.9	47.0	16.7	9.4
All countries	77.0	58.0	42.0	36.0	29.0

*Bangladesh not included due to insufficient sample size.

Yes = 1 and No = 0. The descriptive statistics associated with gratifications in terms of socialising, getting information, carrier and commerce in the 32 countries surveyed are shown in Table 4.3. Overall, most youth (77 per cent) in emerging and developing nations who use social networks predominantly share their views about music. This is followed by 58 per cent of social networkers. Sharing views on religion was the least used.

Analyses and discussion

The analyses are presented in terms of the relationship between Maslow's physiological, safety, belongingness, esteem and self-actualisation needs and gratifications such as socialising, getting information, career and commerce and sharing views. Following that, count occurrences of Internet and social networking gratifications are discussed and finally the influence of Internet on economy, education, personal relationships, politics and religion.

Linking concepts of motivation, involvement and uses and gratifications

Based on the gratifications for using Internet and social networking sites, Table 4.4 was constructed to show the link between Maslow's model and gratifications in terms of socialising, getting information, career and commerce, and sharing views.

Socialising

Staying in touch with friends and family is linked to love/belonging because it is essential in forming and maintaining relationships and may help mitigate loneliness. It may also be an esteem need because it shows how a person is valued by a network of friends and family.

Getting information

Health information, political news, and government information services may protect individuals from danger.

Career and commerce

Looking/applying for a job may be considered physiological because it may potentially lead to earning income to provide food, shelter, clothing and others for the individual. It is about safety since it may lead to economic and financial security. It is related to self-actualisation since an individual's job may be a conduit to realise his/her perceived potentials. Making or receiving payments and buying products can meet physiological needs as well as fulfil safety needs. For online classes, they may foster self-actualisation needs.

Sharing views

Music and movies, sports, products, politics and religion are connected to love and belonging because they connote a sense of affiliation and connectedness to a common philosophy. These may also foster esteem needs since sharing views on pertinent issues may lead to gaining recognition and respect from friends, family, community and the wider society.

Cross tabulations between Internet and social networking sites

Table 4.5 is a cross tabulation of count occurrences of Internet use and social networking site gratifications. It shows that 11,638 (55 per cent) of respondents (youth) did not engage in any of the social network and Internet-based gratifications. A total of 1,958 youth in emerging and developing nations engaged in Internet-related gratifications but not in gratifications associated with social network sites. Similarly, 146 (less than 1 per cent) respondents engaged in social network gratification only. A good number of the youth are engaged in one or more types of Internet-related gratification compared with the corresponding social network site gratifications.

TABLE 4.4 Maslow's model: Internet socialising, getting information, career and commerce and sharing views on social network sites

	Physiological	Safety	Love/belonging	Esteem	Self-actualisation
Socialising					
Stay in touch with family and friends			✓	✓	
Getting information					
Get political news		✓	✓	✓	
Get health info		✓		✓	
Get government or services info	✓	✓			
Career and commerce					
Look/apply for a job	✓	✓	✓	✓	✓
Make or receive payments	✓	✓		✓	
Buy products	✓	✓	✓	✓	✓
Take an online class		✓	✓	✓	✓
Sharing views					
Music and movies			✓	✓	
Sports			✓	✓	
Products they use		✓	✓	✓	
Politics		✓	✓	✓	
Religion		✓	✓	✓	

TABLE 4.5 Cross tabulations of count occurrences of Internet- and social network-related gratification

		Social network						
		.00	1.00	2.00	3.00	4.00	5.00	Total
Internet	.00	11638	45	43	29	16	13	11784
	1.00	130	26	23	20	10	5	214
	2.00	492	337	334	176	47	27	1413
	3.00	433	310	480	377	133	38	1771
	4.00	312	238	427	404	161	73	1615
	5.00	284	180	351	496	255	118	1684
	6.00	165	124	256	388	261	152	1346
	7.00	80	64	126	216	167	110	763
	8.00	62	28	58	129	168	127	572
Total		13596	1352	2098	2235	1218	663	21162

For example, 337 individuals were engaged in two forms of Internet-related gratification and one form of gratification associated with social network sites. Similarly, 427 individuals were engaged in four types of Internet gratification and two forms of social network gratification. On the other hand, 47 individuals engaged in four forms of social network-related gratifications and two forms of Internet gratification. The general pattern is that less people engage in many forms of social network-related gratifications compared with Internet gratifications.

Internet influence and effectiveness

Youth surveyed in emerging and developing countries hold the view that increasing use (consumption) of the Internet has good influence on certain aspects of their lives. The aspects surveyed are: morality, politics, education, economy and personal relationships. As shown in Figure 4.2, most youth surveyed believe that increasing use of the Internet has a good influence on education (72 per cent). This is followed by influence on personal relationships. These levels of Internet influence have implications for youth education and economic policies.

Based on a specific question that asked respondents about their views on the effectiveness of trying to influence what the government does through posting personal comments on political or social issues online, 26 per cent and 10 per cent are of the view that it is somewhat effective, and very effective respectively. Table 4.6 shows the relationship between type of influence and the effectiveness of trying to influence what the government does through posting personal comments on political or social issues online. The relationship is positive and statistically significant across all types of influence investigated. Finally, background characteristics such as employment status (being employed), gender (male), and number of years of education are all positively and significantly associated with youth Internet use (consumption).

Figure 4.2

Bar chart showing Good Influence (%) by Type of Influence:
- Morality: 38%
- Politics: 46%
- Education: 72%
- Economy: 60%
- Personal Relationships: 62%

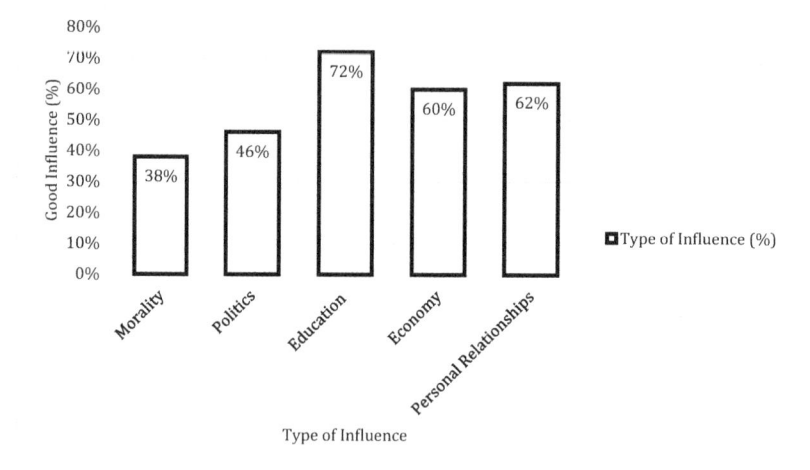

FIGURE 4.2 Influence of Internet use in various aspects of life

TABLE 4.6 Relationship between type of influence and posting personal comments online

Variable	Morality	Politics	Education	Economy	Personal relationship
Posting personal comments	✓	✓	✓		✓

✓ Means positive and statistically signification correlation.

Conclusion

Analyses reveal diversity of uses of social network sites by the youth in emerging and developing nations. Findings show that the gratifications associated with social network sites and the Internet are: stay in touch with family and friends, getting information such as political news and health information and information sharing. The youth surveyed have to a large extent integrated social networking and the Internet into their economic life, entertainment and much less into the political and religious spheres of life. Consistent with Maslow's hierarchy of needs model, social network sites and the Internet provide gratifications that fulfil physiological needs such as entertainment, job searching, etc. They may also fulfil safety needs by providing platforms for youth to validate views on safety of products, financial security, etc. Consistent with Park and Lee (2012), social network sites and the Internet also maintain human relationships and develop feelings of belongingness. In terms of taking online classes as a form of gratification, they may enhance job performance as noted by Hawkes *et al.* (2013) since it facilitates self-actualisation needs.

As noted by Zaichkowsky (1985, p. 342), consumer involvement may be influenced by personal, physical and situational factors. It may also be argued that youth's level of involvement with these media are influenced by such factors. The gratifications above may be the dominant influencing factors for some youth to engage in the use of social network sites and the Internet. For some, the need (gratification) of being in a particular network may be a major influence factor associated with their social media usage. For others, a combination of those factors determine their levels of involvement.

It is in that regard that both forms of gratifications (related to social network sites and the Internet) are combined by the youth. This provides evidence that a good number of the youth are engaged in both forms of gratification. It follows that the youth who engage in Internet-related gratification are likely to be the same people who engage in social network gratification. They complement each other and are not mutually exclusive modes of gratifications associated with the youth.

This chapter has revealed that youth in emerging and developing nations actively share, search and consume information on social media platforms. Many domains of their lives are profoundly affected by social media. These have managerial/marketing implications, given the needs that drive their social media use. Media campaigns of new products can be targeted at social media users to engage and influence them for desirable outcomes. Uses and gratifications that attract and firmly hold youth to specific social media can be used as focal points of such campaigns. In that vein, marketers can adopt popular social media among the youth to shape their identity, brand involvement, brand loyalty and purchase behaviour.

Finally, it is important to note that due to the fact that data for this chapter is based on nationally representative data from 31 emerging and developing nations around the world, the findings are generalisable and applicable to other nations in similar settings and contexts.

References

African Union. (2006). *African youth charter*. *African Union*. www.africa-union.org (accessed 15 January 2017).
Boyd, D. and Ellison, N. (2007). Social network sites: Definition, history, and scholarship. *Journal of Computer-Mediated Communication, 13*, 210–230.
Bruns, A. (2007). Proceedings from Produsage, Generation C, and their effects on the democratic process. *MiT 5 (Media in Transition) Conference*. Boston, MA: MIT.
Buford, J. A., Jr., Bedeian, A. G. and Lindner, J. R. (1995). *Management in extension* (3rd edn). Columbus: Ohio State University Extension.
Chen, G. M. (2011). Tweet this: A uses and gratifications perspective on how active Twitter use gratifies a need to connect with others. *Computers in Human Behavior, 27*(2), 755–762.
Chia, S. C. and Yip, L. P. (2009). Media, celebrities, and fans: An examination of adolescents' media usage and involvement with entertainment celebrities. *Journalism and Mass Communication Quarterly, 86*(1), 23–44.
Choi, J., Dekkers, A. and Park, S. (2004). *Motives of Internet use: Cross-cultural perspectives in the US, the Netherlands and South Korea*. Eindhoven, the Netherlands: Fontys Publicaties.
Clarke, K. and Belk, R. W. (1978). The effects of product involvement and task definition on anticipated consumer effort. In H. K. Hunt (ed.), *Advances in consumer research* (Vol. 5, pp. 313–318). Ann Arbor, MI: Association for Consumer Research.
Dholakia, U. M. (2001). A motivational process model of product involvement and consumer risk perception. *European Journal of Marketing, 35*(11–12), 1340–1367.

Dixon, J. (1999). A cultural economy model for studying food systems. *Agriculture and Human Values*, *16*, 151–160.

Dixon, J. and Banwell, C. (2004). Re-embedding trust: Unravelling the construction of modern diets. *Critical Public Health*, *14*, 117–131.

Eighmey, J. and McCord, L. (1998). Adding value in the information age: Uses and gratifications of sites on the worldwide web. *Journal of Business Research*, *41*(3), 187–194.

Ellison, N., Steinfield, C. and Lampe, C. (2007). The benefits of Facebook 'friends': Social capital and college students' use of online social network sites. *Journal of Computer-Mediated Communication*, *12*, 1143–1168.

Fewkes, A. M. and McCabe, M. (2012). Facebook: Learning tool or distraction? *Journal of Digital Learning in Teacher Education*, *28*(3), 92–98.

Firat, A. F. (2001). Consumer research for the benefit of consumers. *Journal of Research for Consumers*, *1*. www.jrconsumers.com/academic_articles/issue_1/Firat.pdf (accessed 5 December 2016).

Goldsmith, R. and Emmert, J. (1991). Measuring product category involvement: A multitrait–multimethod study. *Journal of Business Research*, *23*, 363–371.

Hawkes, C. P., Walsh, B. H., Ryan, C. A. and Dempsey, E. M. (2013). Smartphone technology enhances newborn intubation knowledge and performance amongst pediatric trainers. *Resuscitation*, *84*(2), 223–226.

Higgins, J. M. (1994). *The management challenge* (2nd edn). New York: Macmillan.

Huizinga, G. (1970). *Maslow's need hierarchy in the work situation*. Groningen, Germany: Wolters-Noordhoff.

Jere, M. G. and Davis, S. V. (2011). An application of uses and gratifications theory to compare consumer motivations for magazine and Internet usage among South African women's magazine readers. *Southern African Business Review*, *15*(1), 1–27.

Johnson, T. J. and Kaye, B. K. (2003). Around the worldwide web in 80 ways. *Social Science Computer Review*, *21*(3), 304–325.

Junco, R. (2012). The relationship between frequency of Facebook use, participation in Facebook activities, and student engagement. *Computers & Education*, *58*(1), 162–171.

Kamarulzaman, Y. (2007). Adoption of travel e-shopping in the UK. *International Journal of Retail and Distribution Management*, *35*(9), 703–719.

Kang, S. and Jung, J. (2014). Mobile communication for human needs: A comparison of smartphone use between the US and Korea. *Computers in Human Behavior*, *35*, 376–387. doi:10.1016/j.chb.2014.03.024.

Kapferer, J.-N. and Laurent, G. (1985). Consumer involvement profiles: New empirical results. In E. Hirschman and M. Holbrook (eds), *Advances in consumer research* (Vol. 12, pp. 290–295). Provo, UT: Association for Consumer Research.

Kapferer, J.-N. and Laurent, G. (1993). Further evidence on the consumer involvement profile: Five antecedents of involvement. *Psychology and Marketing*, *10*(4), 347–355.

Katz, E., Gurevitch, M. and Haas, H. (1973). On the use of the mass media for important things. *American Sociological Review*, *38*(2), 164–181. http://repository.upenn.edu/asc_papers/267 (accessed 1 October 2016).

Katz, E., Haas, H. and Gurevitch, M. (1973). On the use of the mass media for important things. *American Sociological Review*, *38*, 164–181.

Katz-Gerro, T. (2004). Cultural consumption research: Review of methodology, theory, and consequence. *International Review of Sociology*, *14*, 11–29.

Kaye, B. K. and Johnson, T. J. (2002). Online and in the know: Uses and gratifications of the web for political information. *Journal of Broadcasting and Electronic Media*, *46*(1), 54–71.

Knobloch-Westerwick, S. and Hastall, M. R. (2010). Please your self: Social identity effects on selective exposure to news about in- and out-groups. *Journal of Communication*, 60(3), 515–535. http://dx.doi.org/10.1111/j.1460-2466.2010.01495.x.

Korgaonkar, P. and Wolin, L. (1999). A multivariate analysis of web usage. *Journal of Advertising Research*, 39(2), 53–68.

Krause, A. E., North, A. C. and Heritage, B. (2014). The uses and gratifications of using Facebook music listening applications. *Computers in Human Behavior*, 39, 71–77.

Kreitner, R. (1995). *Management* (6th edn). Boston, MA: Houghton Mifflin.

Kuan-Yu, L. and Hsi-Peng, L. (2011). Why people use social networking sites: An empirical study integrating network externalities and motivation theory. *Computers in Human Behavior*, 27, 1152–1161.

Ku, Y.-C., Chu, T.-H. and Tseng, C.-H. (2013). Gratifications for using CMC technologies: A comparison among SNS, IM, and e-mail. *Computers in Human Behavior*, 29, 226–234.

Lariscy, R. W., Tinkham, S. F. and Sweetser, K. D. (2011). Kids these days: Examining differences in political uses and gratifications, Internet political participation, political information efficacy, and cynicism on the basis of age. *American Behavioral Scientist*, 55(6), 749–764.

Lastovicka, J. L. and Gardner, D. M. (1978). Components of involvement. In J. C. Maloney and B. Silverman (eds), *Attitude research plays for high stakes* (pp. 53–73). Chicago, IL: American Marketing Association.

Luckmann, T. (1989). On meaning in everyday life and in sociology. *Current Sociology*, 37, 17–30.

Lupton, D. (1997). Consumerism, reflexivity, and the medical encounter. *Social Science and Medicine*, 45, 373–381.

Malik, A., Dhir, A. and Nieminen, M. (2016). Uses and gratifications of digital photo sharing on Facebook. *Telematics and Informatics*, 33(1), 129–138.

Maslow, A. H. (1954). *Motivation and personality*. New York: Harper.

Michealidou, N. and Dibb, S. (2008). Consumer involvement: A new perspective. *Marketing Review*, 8(1), 83–99.

Murugesan, S. (2007). Understanding Web 2.0. *IT Professional*, 9(4), 34–41.

Palmgreen, P. and Rayburn, J. D. (1979). Uses and gratifications and exposure to public television: A discrepancy approach. *Communication Research*, 6, 155–180.

Papacharissi, Z. and Rubin, M. A. (2000). Predictors of Internet use. *Journal of Broadcasting and Electronic Media*, 44(2), 175–196.

Park, N. and Lee, H. (2012). Social implications of smartphone use: Korean college students' smartphone use and psychological well-being. *Cyberpsychology, Behavior, and Social Networking*, 15(9), 491–497. http://dx.doi.org/10.1089/cyber.2011.0580.

Park, W. C. and Mittal, B. (1985). A theory of involvement in consumer behavior: Problems and issues. In J. N. Sheth (ed.), *Research in Consumer Behavior* (Vol. 1, pp. 201–231). Greenwich, CT: JAI Press.

Pew Research Center. (2015). Internet seen as positive influence on education but negative influence on morality in emerging and developing nations. www.pewglobal.org/2015/03/19/internet-seen-as-positive-influence-on-education-but-negative-influence-on-morality-in-emerging-and-developing-nations/ (accessed 28 August 2017).

Prensky, M. (2001). Digital natives, digital immigrants part I. *On the Horizon*, 9(5), 1–6.

Raacke, J. and Bonds-Raacke, J. (2008). MySpace and Facebook: Applying the uses and gratifications theory to exploring friend-networking sites. *CyberPsychology and Behavior*, 11(2), 169–174.

Ranaweera, C., McDougall, G. and Bansal, H. (2005). A model of online customer behavior during the initial transaction: Moderating effects of customer characteristics. *Marketing Theory*, 5(1), 51–74.

Reiss, S. and Wiltz, J. (2004). Why people watch reality TV. *Media Psychology*, 6(4), 363–378.

Rissanen, H. and Luoma-Aho, V. (2016). (Un)willing to engage? First look at the engagement types of millennials. *Corporate Communications: An International Journal*, 21(4), 500–515.

Rothschild, M. L. (1979). Advertising strategies for high and low involvement situations. In J. C. Maloney and B. Silverman (eds), *Attitude research plays for high stakes* (pp. 74–93). Chicago, IL: American Marketing Association.

Roy, S. (2009). Internet uses and gratifications: A survey in the Indian context. *Computers in Human Behavior*, 29, 878–886.

Ruggiero, T. E. (2000). Uses and gratifications theory in the 21st century. *Mass Communication and Society*, 3(1), 3–37.

Santos, I., Hammond, M., Durli, Z. and Chou, S.-Y. (2009). Is there a role for social networking sites in education? In A. Tatnall and A. Jones (eds), *Education and technology for a better world* (pp. 321–330). Berlin Heidelberg: Springer.

Sheldon, P. (2008). The relationship between unwillingness-to-communicate and students' Facebook use. *Journal of Media Psychology*, 20(2), 67–75.

Sheldon, P. and Bryant, K. (2016). Instagram: Motives for its use and relationship to narcissism and contextual age. *Computers in Human Behavior*, 58, 89–97.

Smock, A. D., Ellison, N. B., Lampe, C. and Wohn, D. Y. (2011). Facebook as a toolkit: A uses and gratification approach to unbundling feature use. *Computers in Human Behavior*, 27, 2322–2329. doi:10.1016/j.chb.2011.07.011.

Song, I., Larose, R., Eastin, S. M. and Lin, A. C. (2004). Internet gratifications and Internet addiction: On the uses and abuses of new media. *Cyber Psychology and Behavior*, 7(4), 384–394.

Stafford, T. F., Stafford, M. R. and Schkade, L. L. (2004). Determining uses and gratifications for the Internet. *Decision Sciences*, 35(2), 259–288.

Stassen, W. (2010). Your news in 140 characters: Exploring the role of social media in journalism. *Global Media Journal*, 4(1), 1–16.

Stolle, D. and Micheletti, M. (2013). *Political consumerism: Global responsibility in action*. Cambridge: Cambridge University Press.

Swanson, D. L. (1979). The continuing evolution of the uses and gratifications approach. *Communication Research*, 6(1), 3–7.

United Nations. (2017). Frequently asked questions. *Youth: Social policy and development division*. http://social.un.org (accessed 2 January 2017).

Wang, H. C., Pallister, J. G. and Foxall, G. (2006). Innovativeness and involvement as determinants of website loyalty: Determinants of consumer loyalty in B2C e-commerce. *Technovation*, 26(12), 1366–1373.

Wan-I, L., Chiu, Y., Chia-Chu, L. and Che-Yuan, C. (2011). Assessing the effects of consumer involvement and service quality in a self-service setting. *Human Factors and Ergonomics in Manufacturing and Service Industries*, 21(5), 504–515.

Weiser, E. B. (2001). The functions of Internet use and their social and psychological consequence. *CyberPsychology and Behavior*, 4(6), 723–743.

Whiting, A. and Williams, D. (2013). Why people use social media: A uses and gratifications approach. *Qualitative Market Research: An International Journal*, 16(4), 362–369. doi: 10.1108/qmr-06-2013-0041.

Wright, P. (1974). Analyzing media effects on advertising response. *Public Opinion Quarterly*, 38, 192–205.

Zaichkowsky, J. L. (1985). Measuring the involvement construct. *Journal of Consumer Research*, 12, 341–352.

5
EXPLORING PERSONALITY, IDENTITY AND SELF-CONCEPT AMONG YOUNG CONSUMERS

Abdullah Promise Opute

Introduction

The motivation research in the 1940s and 1950s has been a critical precursor to the field of consumer behaviour. Emphasising that importance, Converse and Huegy (1952) note that while marketing texts of the 1920s through to the 1950s covered several subject areas, it had almost nothing to say about consumer behaviour. These motivation researches, which focused on enhancing the understanding of why the consumer did what he/she did, laid many of the foundations for the theoretical domain of consumer behaviour to date (Fullerton, 2013).

Motivation research 'represents the introduction into consumer or market research of new concepts drawn from the whole range of the social sciences' (Gardner, 1959, p. 36). In 1950, a committee convened by the American Marketing Association concluded that

> motivational research is so important to the development of the applied science of marketing that a constant effort should be made to see that the truest insights of the other social sciences be made available to marketing in a form in which they can be made to bear on marketing problems.
> *(Woodward, 1950, p. 32)*

Advocating for greater use of the behavioural foundation, Newman (1957, p. 386) argued that the case

> rests on the recognition that buying and consumption are human acts serving human purposes about which marketing has known too little . . . They can be better understood if . . . behavioural theories, concepts, and methods enter the picture.

Essentially, motivation research has attempted to uncover underlying motivations in consumer behaviour. As captured by Smith (1954, p. 5), it attempted to 'focus attention on the whole battery of inner conditions that play a dynamic part in a person's buying or not buying, responding favourably or unfavourably to some communication' (Smith, 1954, p. 5).

In the recent past, the importance of this marketing perspective has been increasingly emphasised. The need for further efforts towards enhancing knowledge in this area has been underlined repeatedly (e.g. Kleine et al., 1993; Escalas and Bettman, 2005; Gbadamosi, 2016). In a recent publication, *Handbook of Research on Consumerism and Buying Behaviour in Developing Nations* (2016, p. 1), the guest editor Ayantunji Gbadamosi commented thus: 'Irrespective of the differences between us, one of the binding cords that explain our homogeneity is that we all are consumers. However, there are idiosyncratic issues that might still differentiate consumption in one society from another.'

Gbadamosi (2016) comments further that consumers are all different in many ways: demographically, emotionally, culturally or in various other contexts and can act differently to the same stimulus. Concurring to this view of idiosyncratic issues, as well as cultural, emotional and other behavioural codes that condition the response to a stimulus, this chapter contextualises an identity perspective of consumer behaviour. According to that perspective, an organising construct for understanding everyday activities is the self – a sense of who and what we are (e.g. Kleine et al., 2004; White et al., 2012) or personalities (e.g. Holbrook, 1992).

The young consumers' domain is a core context for knowledge development (e.g. La Ferle and Chan, 2008; Cody, 2014; Syrjälä et al., 2015; Mau et al., 2016). Very little is known about young consumers and how they enact selfhood, socialising behaviour, identity transformation and purchase preference formation. Inspired by this gap in the literature, this chapter draws on the theoretical advocacy of Cody (2014) who has noted a pattern of theoretical inclinations that has seemed foundational in many studies of young consumers and their interaction with consumption. Reinforcing the problematic in that approach, Cook (2009) argued that such studies have been compromised by a fixation on the effects approaches, and by so doing sacrifice richer and interpretive explorations of the social relationships that emerge between young consumers and various realms of consumer culture and practices, taking into consideration the boundaries and hierarchies that characterise their social world. Concurrent with this desire to enhance the understanding of young consumers' preference formation, the conceptualisation in this chapter is tailored to contribute to the understanding of how identity (driven by family role and affiliation to social groups) and identity transformation (through networking and socialising influence) and preference formation impact. This chapter aims to contribute to the understanding of the psychological attributes of consumer behaviour among young consumers. In other words, this chapter contributes to marketing and psychology literature and in doing so presents a framework that combines symbolic interactionism and identity theories (e.g. Stryker, 1968, 1987).

The central thesis underpinning this chapter is that preference formation among consumers generally is contingent on the conceptualisation of self. Next, 'young consumers' is conceptualised and core characteristics are pinpointed and relevant literature on self-concept and association to consumer preference formation is reviewed. Given the psychological approach in this chapter, literature on culture is also discussed, underlining its significance as a core factor that shapes the psychological mindset and self-concept of an individual. The chapter explains identity, collective identity and collective identity transition among young consumers. In the final section, the conclusions are presented, underlining the importance for marketers to adopt a pro-active approach towards responding effectively to the needs of the consumers and directions for further knowledge development are flagged.

Young consumers: conceptualisation and characteristics

The importance of young consumers to marketers has often been underlined in the literature (e.g. La Ferle and Chan, 2008; Goldberg et al., 2003; Cody, 2014; Mau et al., 2016). Before explaining 'young consumers' as the premise of this chapter and typical characteristics of this consumer domain, it is important to clearly define who a consumer is. Lee (2009) defines a consumer as 'an individual with a distinctive personality'.

Prior literature on young consumers shows that contributors have diversely defined young consumers. For example, Chan and Prendergast (2007) conceptualise adolescents as people within the age category of 11–20 years old (inclusive). Exploring the celebrity-mediated social world among Chinese university students, Chan and Zhang (2007) defined young consumers as including students within the age of 18–24 years. In a further study, Chan (2006b) categorised Chinese children aged between 13 and 19 years (inclusive), while Davis and Lang conceptualised consumers who are 25 years old or under, as young consumers. A central foundation in the focus of this chapter is the important role that mobile multi-media devices play in enabling young consumers to achieve a bundle of benefits: functional, experiential and symbolic brands. Aligning that foundation to the conceptual thread in the aforementioned literature, young consumers are conceptualised in this chapter to include consumers aged 25 or under (Chan, 2006a; Chan and Zhang, 2007; La Ferle and Chan, 2008; Davis and Lang, 2013).

Until the twentieth century, research that examined the role of young people as consumers was rare (Mau et al., 2012). In recent times however, the increasing significance of mobile media and changed social and cultural perspectives, have led to an overdue change – young consumers have increasingly become the focus of research and of companies (Wimalasiri, 2004). Developments in that regard even point to the fact that adolescents are becoming very active in the marketplace, and even at an increasingly younger age (Brusdal, 2007). As reported in further literature, the self-image of young consumers has also changed as materialism has become increasingly important for children (Chaplin and John, 2010; Otto, 2013; Goldberg et al., 2003).

One core factor that has contributed massively to this development is the growing exposure of children to media, such as television, smartphones and social networking sites (Dotson and Hyatt, 2005; Watne et al., 2011). Furthermore, as these scholars argue, with more competencies in technology and media, children even assume important roles as agents of secondary socialisation for their parents (Dotson and Hyatt, 2005; Watne et al., 2011).

With the increasing wave of information technology, cyber technology (mobile phones, i-pads, tablets, etc.) and attached multi-fun (e.g. games, photo and texting applications) and learning devices, customers are exposed to a vast range of features and applications for meeting experiential as well as functional benefits. For example, most people use a smartphone 'for internet browsing, email, navigation, social media, listening to music, reading news, games, finance, health and fitness, taking notes, calendar, weather forecast, and a lot of other things' (Nagarkoti, 2009, p. 5). Young consumers are not only one major patronising group for such devices, but also having these devices has become a symbol of social group identity.

McNeal (2007) notes that children are not only actively beginning to make their own purchase decisions between the ages of 6–8 years, but also have access to a significant budget at their disposal, which they can use independently. Insights about Germany show that the income based on pocket money for children aged 7–12 years is US$569.40 per month per child (Klein, 1997). Consequently, children are able to realise their individual desires through independent purchase decisions (Fan and Li, 2010). The importance of young customers as a core market segment is gaining increasing recognition as they are being targeted by a multitude of marketing messages from manufacturers and dealers.

Empirical investigations of the Chinese context lend support to the above arguments. Chinese children and adolescents are increasingly accessing mass media for information and entertainment (Bu, 2001; Chan and Zhang, 2007). Other contributors add that young Chinese consumers are exposed more to commercial than interpersonal sources, for new product information (e.g. McNeal and Ji, 1999; Chan, 2005). The young consumers' market will continue to increase in its importance to marketers as their discretionary income and power to influence parent purchases increase over time. Consequently, marketers are recognising this importance and are utilising the growing media space that digital interactive technologies offer to reach out to children.

The self-concept: definition, typologies and consumer preference formation association

The importance of understanding the personality-related concepts of a person's self-image or self-concept and consumption behaviour influence has been reinforced by several scholars (Aaker, 1999; Govers and Schoormans, 2005; Sirgy et al., 1997; Ashmore et al., 2004; Lee, 2009). According to Lee (2009, p. 25), 'personality' refers to 'the unique psychological characteristics eliciting consistent and lasting responses to one's own environment'.

Several schools of personality theory exist in the literature. According to the Freudian perspective, which was influenced by earlier thinking that there is activity within the mind at a conscious and unconscious level, personality develops from the interaction among the three fundamental structures of the human mind: the id ('I want to do that now'), the ego ('Maybe we can compromise'), and the superego ('It's not right to do that') (Freud, 1937). Freud (1937) notes that there are conflicts among the three structures, and how we behave and approach the world hinges on our ability to strike a balance among these desires. Furthermore, he notes that the ability to strike this balance is instrumental to our ability to resolve two over-arching behavioural tendencies and conflicting issues: our biological aggressive and pleasure-seeking drives vs. our socialised internal control over those drives.

Freud's personality theory was criticised, among others, for its narrow focus and for the fact that some elements of the theory cannot be empirically validated. In contrast to the Freudian perspective, the trait theory of personality identifies and measures the degree to which certain personality traits – recurring patterns of thought and behaviour, such as shyness or openness to new things – exist from individual to individual. One of the pioneers of formal personality psychology, Allport and Odbert (1936) examined the dictionary and identified 4,000 words that describe the human personality. While the toolbox of Allport's trait theory contained 4,000 words, he grouped them into three main categories, but underlined that only a few traits really define who we are. These defining and central traits, as he called them, dominate a person's behaviour, and can include, for example, describing a person as being shy, intelligent or honest.

Despite the continued influence in personality theory, Allport's 4,000 traits were considered impractical for applications. Consequently, other scholars have attempted to address that limitation. The first attempt to prune down the trait theory to a manageable size was by Raymond Cattell in the 1940s. Examining the list, Cattell (1945) combined similar traits and eliminated those that seemed very rare, and obtained a list of 171 characteristics. Subsequently, he performed a factor analysis of the 171 characteristics to determine the traits that were closely related in a sample. Sixteen main factors (personality traits) were captured. According to him, every individual has these main traits (characteristics such as warmth, dominance and apprehension) and our personalities are contingent on the measure of each in every individual.

Raymond Cattell was applauded for significantly cutting down on Allport's list of traits, but also criticised for his broad 16PF theory. Responding to this criticism, Hans Eysenck, in collaboration with his wife Sybil Eysenck, improved on the work of Raymond Cattell and proposed three main characteristics – extroversion vs. introversion, neuroticism vs. stability, and psychoticism vs. socialisation (Eysenck, 1953; Eysenck and Eysenck, 1993). Personality theorists consider the Eysenck traits theory to be more legitimate, as it is one of the first to make the approach more quantifiable, and by so doing, responded to the critical criticism of psychological theories of not being empirically verifiable. That notwithstanding, the Eysenck theory was, like other personality theories preceding it, criticised for being too narrow. With time, similar, recurring theories and character traits have been suggested, and many have settled upon five key personality traits, leading to a further theory called the Big Five. The Big Five theory, also called OCEAN (acronym for the traits) includes the traits of openness, conscientiousness, extraversion, agreeableness and neuroticism. The theory suggests that all of the other minor traits would fall within these five.

Thus, several theories have been suggested and utilised towards enhancing the understanding of what drives individual behaviour. Another foundation that has been utilised in the personality discourse is the self-concept. According to Baumeister (1999), self-concept implies 'the individual's belief about himself or herself, including the person's attributes and who and what the self is' (p. 247). There are three different components of the self or self-concept (Rogers, 1959):

1. The view you have of yourself (self-image).
2. How much value you place on yourself.
3. What you wish you were really like (ideal self).

Self-image relates to what a person sees in himself/herself, and is affected by several factors such as parental influences, friends, the media, etc. (Rogers, 1959; Kuhn, 1960), while self-esteem describes the extent to which an individual will like or approve of himself/herself or how much that individual values himself/herself. It always involves a degree of evaluation that may have a positive or negative view (see also Baumeister, 1999 and Figure 5.1). On the other hand, the ideal self relates to what one would like to be. When there is a mismatch between one's self-image and his/her ideal self, it affects how much that individual values himself/herself. Actual happenings in life and a person's experience are rarely consistent with a person's ideal self, thus incongruence – difference between a person's ideal self and actual experience – is to be expected (Rogers, 1959; Baumeister, 1999). The reverse – congruence, is the case when one's ideal self and actual experience are consistent or very similar (Rogers, 1959; Baumeister, 1999. As Rogers (1959) notes, for a person

SELF-ESTEEM

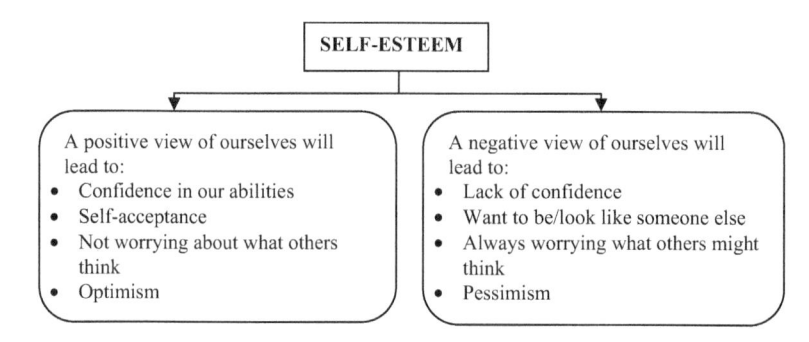

A positive view of ourselves will lead to:
- Confidence in our abilities
- Self-acceptance
- Not worrying about what others think
- Optimism

A negative view of ourselves will lead to:
- Lack of confidence
- Want to be/look like someone else
- Always worrying what others might think
- Pessimism

FIGURE 5.1 The levels of self-esteem

Source: Author. Materials collated from Kuhn (1960), Rogers (1959) and Baumeister (1999).

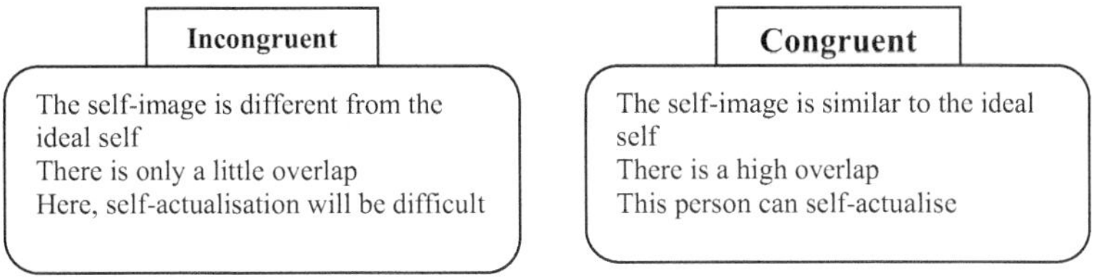

Incongruent	Congruent
The self-image is different from the ideal self There is only a little overlap Here, self-actualisation will be difficult	The self-image is similar to the ideal self There is a high overlap This person can self-actualise

FIGURE 5.2 Distinguishing congruence and incongruence levels

Source: Author. Materials collated from Rogers (1959) and Baumeister (1999).

to achieve self-actualisation, he/she must be in a state of congruence. Figure 5.2 highlights what distinguishes congruence from incongruence.

Four major factors influence the extent to which an individual may achieve congruence (Argyle, 2008):

1. The ways in which others (particularly significant others) react to us.
2. How we think we compare to others.
3. Our social roles.
4. The extent to which we identify with other people.

Another foundation that has featured in the discourse of self or self-concept is the extended self. Belk (1988) presented the concept of the extended self and posited that 'knowingly or unknowingly, intentionally or unintentionally, we regard our possessions as part of us' (p. 139). According to that concept, the individual self encompasses an inner core of self as well as aggregate selves that range from family to neighbourhood to nation. As further elaborated by Belk (1988), these self constructions are enhanced by various possessions that are viewed by their owners as having different degrees of centrality to one or more of their individual or aggregate senses of self (see also Belk, 2013). The extended self is composed of a person's mind, body, physical possessions, family, friends and affiliation groups (Belk, 1988).

Digital technologies are increasingly becoming a central factor in modern-day society. With these digital technologies, e.g. web pages, online games, search engines, virtual worlds, social media, Internet, email, smartphones, MP3, etc., the possibilities for self extension are becoming extensive (Belk, 2013). These digital technologies are fundamentally changing consumer behaviour and have implications for the formulation of the extended self. Belk (2013) identifies five digital technology-induced changes with regards to the formulation of the extended self – dematerialisation, re-embodiment, sharing, co-construction of the self and distributed memory.

Grounded in the psychological foundation, the self-concept is premised on the view that people's possessions contribute to and reflect their identities. Therefore, personality can be useful in analysing an individual consumer's responses to certain product or brand options. From a marketing point of view therefore, understanding the personality notion of customers and how that drives their preference formation is a *sine qua non* towards ensuring competitive advantage in a global and dynamic marketplace where cyberspace technologies have increased the marketing options available to customers.

Understanding the psychological traits that shape the personality construct in the mind of an individual has been the focus of social identity theory (Tajfel and Turner, 1986) and its extension, self-categorisation theory (Turner, 1985). An individual's construct of self – identity – comprises two levels: personal identity and social identity. The former is related to a person's individual notion of self, while the latter relates to the various identities associated with groups to which a person belongs. Thus, an individual has a repertoire of identities that reflect individual-level identity and other social identities. Based on these theories, the extent to which each of these identities drive behaviour is dependent on the context. As a consequence, an individual's response to a stimulus would depend on the extent to which the given situation corresponds with either that individual's personal identity or one of many possible social identities (e.g. Tajfel and Turner, 1986; Brewer, 1991). Expanded, the factors that influence what a consumer decides to buy include the following:

1. *Social* – core social factors include reference groups (and social groups), family, role and status.
2. *Cultural* – culture is the most critical factor in the preference formation of decision-making and includes buyer culture, subculture and social class. It includes norms, values, perceptions, etc. (see Figure 5.1).
3. *Personal* – typical personal factors that influence an individual's buying behaviour include age, lifestyle, economic situation, personality and self-concept.
4. *Psychological* – four core psychological factors affect a consumer's buying behaviour, namely perception, motivation, learning and beliefs. A consumer can be affiliated to a variety of reference groups where he/she finds a feeling of association and attachment, sources information and standard of behaviour.

Marketing perspectives on consumer behaviour propose that consumers are seemingly emotional and engage in identity-congruent behaviours. Driven by that identity congruency, products that are linked with an aspect of social identity are evaluated more favourably, especially when it involves a social identity that is chronically viewed as important (e.g. Kleine *et al.*, 1993). This is the central underlying theoretical foundation for this chapter. The young consumers are typically social identity driven. In the modern-day world where digital technologies have become 'a must get' for young consumers, due to their functional, experiential and symbolic benefits, young consumers are increasingly staying connected to like minds, both locally and globally. The implication of this development is increased social identity congruent behaviour in their preference formation patterns.

Embedded in the social identity driven consumer behaviour conceptualisation in this chapter is the psychological understanding that culture shapes the psychological mindset of individuals. Therefore, before delving into the association between social identity (or collective identity) (e.g. Ashmore *et al.*, 2004) and consumer preference formation, it is important to pinpoint critical artefacts that feed into the psychological mindset of individuals and eventually their identity construction, as this is also instrumental to an enhanced understanding of that association.

According to psychology literature, the decision-making tendencies of individuals are driven by their psychological frame of mind, which is further a consequence of their culture – a shared pattern of categorisations, attitudes, beliefs, definitions, norms, values and other elements of subjective culture (Triandis *et al.*, 2001, p. 74). Newman and Nollen (1996, p. 754) add to this view and conceptualise culture as the 'values, beliefs, assumptions learned in early childhood that distinguish one group of people from another'. Figure 5.3 pinpoints some features that constitute and form the core of a given culture.

Based on the sequence of theoretical development, this chapter conceptualises two levels of artefacts that constitute culture – conventional and post-conventional. This chapter offers a psychological perspective on the behavioural characteristics that drive consumer preference formation among young consumers. Therefore the conceptualisation of culture in this chapter draws from cross-cultural psychology literature (Shteynberg *et al.*, 2009), which posits that efforts to demystify cultural influence should consider using a wider range of psychological constructs to develop broader theoretical accounts of cultural influence. Responding to that call, this chapter proposes a conceptualisation that builds on insights from diverse streams of literature: organisational culture literature (e.g. Schein, 1991); relationship marketing literature (e.g. Kotler *et al.*, 2006; Opute, 2014); sports marketing literature (e.g. Opute, 2015); and management literature (e.g. Hofstede, 1980; Kanter and Corn, 1994; Opute, 2012). The conventional culture artefacts include attitudes, definitions, norms, beliefs and values as captured in mainstream literature. Depending on the complexities of the specific societies (countries), these culture features may reflect homogeneity across the ethnic and regional enclaves within the society. On the other hand, the post-conventional artefacts that include national-level features – religion, war history of a country and colonialism experience

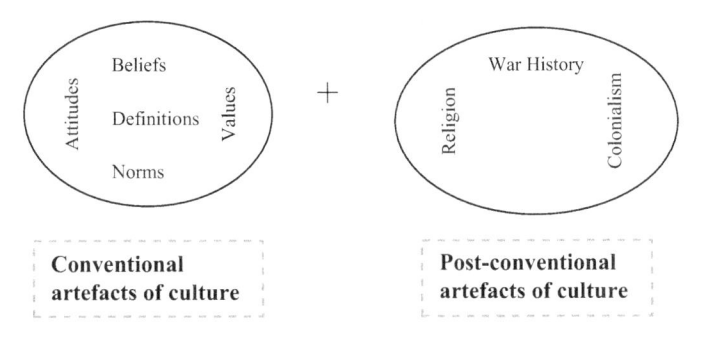

FIGURE 5.3 The artefacts of culture

Source: Author.

(e.g. Hagos, 2015; Opute *et al.*, 2016), that shape the psychological mindset and cultural frame of a group or society. In other words, such national-based culture would exert a homogenous influence across the ethnic and subcultures within the society (or country), except for the religion artefact. In societies (countries) where multiple religious orientation is the norm, heterogeneous forms of religion-induced culture would exist as the ethnic and sub-groups may be guided by different religious principles. Post-conventional artefacts exert significant influence on relational behaviour and the identity structure of people (e.g. Hagos, 2015; Opute *et al.*, 2016). Elaborating on this, Opute *et al.* (2016) add that post-conventional artefacts, and especially war history can create an indelible mark that will significantly shape the mindset of an individual. In extreme circumstances, this could lead to individuals developing a tendency to reject other people. Each culture contains subcultures that are demarcated on such bases as nationality, religion, racial groups or groups of people sharing the same geographical location.

Psychological theory captures social network as a significant factor of consumer preference formations, whether high-involvement (e.g. Batra *et al.*, 2008; Bian and Moutinho, 2009) or low-involvement (e.g. Chang and Zhao, 2003) products. This significance is, however, driven by the cultural artefacts that shape the psychological mindset of consumers. Hence, entrepreneurial activity among some ethnic minority businesses is characterised by cultural enclave social networking (e.g. Hagos, 2015; Opute *et al.*, 2016).

Identity, collective identity and collective identity transition among young consumers

Consumers often use possessions not only to actively create their self-concept, but also to reinforce and express self-identity. Thus, individuals can differentiate themselves and assert individuality based on their possessions (e.g. Kleine *et al.*, 1993). Within this psychological foundation of consumer behaviour, it is also a fact that possessions can be used to make a statement about one's social reference – reflecting social ties to one's family, community, and/or cultural groups, as well as brand communities (Muniz and Thomas, 2001; Escalas and Bettman, 2005). Thus, consumers use their behaviour patterns to make a statement about their identity. According to Ting-Toomey (2015), an individual's composite identity has group membership, relational role and individual self-reflective implications. Typical sources for acquiring individual composite identity include social-cultural conditioning processes, individual lived experiences and the repeated intergroup and interpersonal interaction experiences (Ting-Toomey, 2015).

Evidence on store preference formation identifies word of mouth as instrumental in shaping the store preferences of various social groups including relatives, friends and entire generations (e.g. Chen and Xie, 2008). Given the propensity to engage intensively and frequently with their peers, friends, school mates and social networks via multi-media devices, young consumers are highly likely to exhibit collective identity that reflects a self-concept that is positive and prototypical of their immediate social groups described above. In addition, they would attach a high degree of importance of their particular group membership to their overall self-concept. Consequently, young consumers in such social groups merge their sense of self with the group. Hence:

1. People do not necessarily buy products just for what they do, but mainly for what the product means.
2. Thus, people buy brands they believe to have meanings that create and define their self-concept.

(Levy, 1959)

Escalas and Bettman (2005) elaborate that consumers enact their self-identity based on the congruency between brand-user associations and self-image associations. Thus, driven by the image factor, consumers would chronically view such products as important, regardless of the attached cost, because they value the need to boost their ego and self-esteem, and by doing so the desired psychological utility – affiliating or sharing belongingness and similar identity with their idols and heroes. In other words, their ego is boosted as a signal effect of using a brand is triggered. Their opinion of self is boosted because of their view of what the brand says about them as consumer and to others.

Propelled by the word-of-mouth factor and multi-media induced engagement propensity, the young consumers social group would be characterised by a strong collective identity transition. Globally, the use of interpersonal as well as computer-mediated interaction is increasing and it has become a norm for young people to have access to such modern multi-media devices. Indeed, the Internet plays a prominent role among young people. For example, in Japan, the majority of young people aged 15–24 spent between one and three hours per day on the Internet (Chan and Fang, 2007). This implies that family- and parent-based cultural norms and values would over time diminish in their level of importance in shaping the social group, self-concept and consumption preferences of young consumers, as their preference becomes strongly defined by the norms, values and interests of their immediate social groups (peers, friends, school mates and social networks). The comment below shows the extent to which young people's consumption is influenced by their social group affiliation. Here, a young woman describes how her social context strongly defines her consumption preference.

> When I'm hanging out with students, I drink way more alcohol than when I'm with my other friends. That's because I try to fit in by drinking as much as they do, although I'd rather be outside kicking a soccer ball around.
> *(Excerpt taken from Syrjälä et al., 2015, p. 301)*

Thus, their 'personal self categorisation' (Ashmore *et al.*, 2004) becomes essentially based on differentiations between oneself as a unique individual and other in-group members and less on differentiations between groups of people (e.g. race or nationality) (Turner and Oakes, 1986). Thus, in the interactionist notion, the self-categorisation theory of social influence argues that the influence is predominantly a factor of the shared social categorical nature of the psychological group formation (Abrams and Hogg, 2004; Ashmore et al., 2004).

Globalisation, 'the increasing interconnection of economic, social and technological processes across regions and countries' (Reed II et al., 2012, p. 311), has strong implications for psychological processes (Arnett, 2002) and consumer responses to market offerings (Alden et al., 1999). One of the central engines of globalisation, technological progress – in the form of improvement in computing and communication technology, is radically changing people's lives through new ways of communicating and by leading to a reassessment of established behaviours. Such improvements in information technology and other technology forms enable more people to interact and join an integrated world economy. Indeed, the world has become a global village (McLuhan, 1964), and computer-mediated communication channels (social networks, email and Internet-based communication platforms) have ushered in new and effective ways for people to relate to one another across the globe, developments that have important ramifications for identity processes (McKenna and Bargh, 2000). It is important to note that a new psychological group pertinently emerges, and swiftly, among young consumers, especially young consumers who interact frequently (e.g. school pupils, students, young members of sports clubs) and who easily buy into multi-media devices that are fitted with a good range of fun and interacting features. Since young consumers are highly connected through multi-media devices, a high level of consumer socialisation would be expected. Given that culture is not a stagnant system (Zhao, 1997), it would also be expected that a process of constant interacting with other cultural systems would lead to norms, attitudes, motivations and behaviours being transmitted among young consumers. Over time, since 'attitudes, motivations and values are learned through modeling, reinforcement and social exchange' (Chan, 2006a, p. 127), the original culture and resultant personal identity, gained, for example, though parental influence will erode, while the consumer-socialisation-driven collective identity becomes a core driver of behaviour and preference formation for young consumers. When consumers reach this transformation point, a strong emotional attachment to their social group (young consumers' community) is the rational response. In this state, their view of self is highly collective-identity congruent. Especially for this group of consumers, who are not only engaging in symbolic buying but as reflected in recent marketing literature are increasingly gaining a higher purchasing power, marketers must devise a marketing strategy to effectively respond to their needs.

Conclusion, marketing/managerial implications and research agenda

The core aim of this chapter is to enhance the understanding of consumer preference formation among young consumers in modern-day society where the marketing landscape has globalised. Income, technology and lifestyles of consumers are changing, and purchasing function is gaining increasing importance.

Within the aforementioned aim, this chapter seeks to contribute to literature on the psychological perspective of marketing by pinpointing critical psychological artefacts that shape the mindset of an individual, self-concept (an individual's mental representation of self, which comprises two levels – personal identity and social/collective identity), identity transformation capacity and influence on young consumers' preference formation. In that regard, this chapter also identifies core directions for research towards further knowledge development in this area. For marketers, this chapter draws attention to young consumers' behavioural trend in a globalised marketing landscape where young consumers are exploiting multi-media devices to stay connected, network and exercise their purchasing power, nationally and globally. Marketers aiming to take advantage of this strategic young consumers' market segment need to devise a pro-active approach that utilises this knowledge of the psychological features and the emergent self-concept and transformation dynamism and influence on buying behaviour, in order to respond effectively to these consumers.

The young consumers' market segment is a major market for international marketers, given its size, homogeneity, increasing purchasing power and acceptance of cyberspace technologies-based marketing approaches. According to recent studies, young consumers have an increasingly higher disposable income due to more generous allowances and income from part-time jobs (e.g. Sharma, 2002; Nugent, 2006). Multi-media mobile applications usage has increasingly become more pertinent in today's modern society.

Without doubt, the young consumers form a core part of the passionate patronisers of these multi-media applications, a trend that has benefited from the aforementioned increasing spending power of young consumers.

A central notion in the social identity theory indicates that people become emotionally attached to the groups to which they belong and also derive self-esteem from that group membership. Increased usage of multi-media mobile applications among young consumers will undoubtedly intensify in the future, as these offer them great fun and allow them to stay interactive and engage with their peers, friends and role models across the globe. Notably, young consumers are more hedonic consumers – they prefer a more experiential view of consumption (Mäenpää et al., 2006). Unlike the less hedonic consumer, more hedonically orientated consumers attach higher value to almost every proposed service dimension.

Thus, understandably there are several motivations why young consumers patronise multi-media devices, one of which is the experiential function. These devices offer them options to overcome stress in the family and immediate environment on the one hand, while also allowing them to stay abreast of trends and developments in their social communities. In particular, this attachment to their friends, peers and other social community domains is a paramount driver of young consumers' preference formation. This is noted in socialising theory, which underlines that while parental influence exerts influence on young consumers' consumption behaviour, peer-induced influence is much more significant (e.g. McGinnis *et al.*, 2006), a logical consequence of the fun factor and stress escape benefits as in the case of multi-media media applications. This notion of lesser parental influence is supported by food consumption literature (Kelly *et al.*, 2006) which suggests that due to the push effect of food advertisement, young consumers would mount pressure on their parents to allow them to purchase their desired food options, even though they may be unhealthy. For these young consumers, social norms, situations and peer groups govern their consumption and could lead to them engaging in the extremes of harmful consumption, for example, drinking alcohol (Smith, 2013), smoking (Ferguson and Phau, 2013) or compulsive shopping (Saraneva and Sääksjärvi, 2008).

The young consumers are active and pass through socio-cultural processes and individual lived experiences with their friends, peers, schoolmates, etc. They engage in regular and repeated inter-group, inter-cultural and interpersonal interaction experiences in their age-category domains. These tendencies enable them to generate the much needed knowledge to guide them in making strong collective identity transition, which makes them exhibit active consumer preference formations driven mainly by their identification with their friends, peers, schoolmates and other social communities that share the same feelings, values and categorisations. In other words, their consumer preference formation is highly social-identity congruent. In their mindset, the personal identity component, which to a large extent would be shaped by parental influence, plays a less significant role in their preference formation decision-making. These outcomes are rational, especially in circumstances where an individual chronically views an aspect of social identity as important. Under such a level of emotional attachment to a social group, individuals engage in identity-congruent behaviours and evaluate products more favourably (Kleine *et al.*, 1993).

The young consumer market segment is one of critical importance to marketers, not only for their ever-increasing purchasing power, as emphasised earlier in this chapter, but also for the fact that the future lies ahead of them. Furthermore in this latter regard, given the analytical evidence that young consumers have a high propensity for collective identity transition, they are a strategic segment for marketers. Finally, the young consumers segment is the more critical for marketers given the unique characteristic that in most of their product preferences, they are able to achieve the three basic categories of benefits: (1) functional, (2) experiential and (3) symbolic brand benefits. One typical example of such products is mobile phones. Mobile phones offer value in terms of their shared symbolic meaning (Holt, 1995), offer economic value that provides particular benefits to the consumer (Holt, 1995), and offer experiential value as a consumption practice (Taylor and Harper, 2001). Marketers must therefore pay due attention to this significant market segment and map out a suitable strategy for adequately responding to their needs.

No doubt, this chapter contributes in several ways to enhancing the understanding of young consumers' behaviour from a personality and identity perspective. More research is needed to enhance the understanding of the ways that socially generated reasons and behaviours influence young people's consumption and life in general. A core argument in this chapter is that their attachment to their friends at school, peers and other social community domains exert significant influence on their preference formation. While the conceptualisation for this chapter draws from cultural notions, religion – a core artefact of culture (e.g. Aldraehim *et al.*, 2012) and identity (Ting-Toomey, 2015) – has not been considered. Given this limitation, future knowledge development efforts should aim to examine how religion may shape young consumers' behaviour. Furthermore, given that some societies are conservatively oriented, and parents' role in their children's behaviour might take more authoritative and stringent forms in some societies, there is need for more understanding of young consumers' behaviour in such settings. For example, to what extent does consumer socialising take place in such settings and what factors moderate the level of socialising, if at all existent? Furthermore, future efforts should also strive to improve general understanding about the product-type contingencies surrounding collective identity-congruent behaviour among young consumers. Finally, one concern about consumer socialising is that it drives materialism behaviour among young consumers (e.g. John, 1999; Goldberg *et al.*, 2003), and in the long run, materialism is negatively associated with happiness and subjective well-being (Kasser, 2002). Further research is also pertinent in this area to illuminate the association between consumer socialising and materialism on the one hand, and between materialism and happiness and subjective well-being on the other (Chan and Zhang, 2007).

References

Aaker, J. L. (1999). The malleable self: The role of self expression in persuasion. *Journal of Marketing Research*, 36(1), 45–57.

Abrams, D. and Hogg, Michael A. (2004). Metatheory: Lessons from social identity research. *Personality and Social Psychology Review*, 8, 98–106.

Alden, D. L., Steenkamp, J. and Batra, R. (1999). Brand positioning through advertising in Asia, North America, and Europe: The role of global consumer culture. *Journal of Marketing*, 63(1), 75–87.

Aldraehim, M. S., Edwards, S. L., Watson, J. A. and Chan, T. (2012). Cultural impact on e-service use in Saudi Arabia: The role of nepotism. *International Journal for Infonomics*, 5(3/4), 655–662.

Allport, G. and Odbert, H. (1936). Trait-names: A psycho-lexical study. *Psychological Monographs*, 211.

Argyle, M. (2008). *Social encounters: Contributions to social interaction*. Piscataway, NJ: Aldine Transaction.

Arnett J. J. (2002). The psychology of globalization. *American Psychologist*, 57, 774–783.

Ashmore, R. D., Deaux, K. and McLaughlin-Volpe, T. (2004). An organizing framework for collective identity: Articulation and significance of multidimensionality. *Psychological Bulletin*, 130(1), 80–114. doi:10.1037/0033-2909.130.1.80. PMID 14717651.

Batra, R., Ahuvia, A. and Bagozzi, R. (2008). Brand love: Its nature and consequences. Working paper, Michigan Dearborn University, Ann Arbor.

Baumeister, R. F. (ed.) (1999). *The self in social psychology*. Philadelphia: Taylor & Francis.

Belk, R. W. (1988). Possessions and the extended self. *Journal of Consumer Research*, 5 (September), 139–168.
Belk, R. W. (2013). Extended self in a digital world. *Journal of Consumer Research*, 40(3), 477–500.
Bian, X. and Moutinho, L. (2009). An investigation of determinants of counterfeit purchase consideration. *Journal of Business Research*, 62(3), 368–378.
Brewer, M. B. (1991). The social self: On being the same and different at the same time. *Personality and Social Psychology Bulletin*, 17(5), 475–482.
Brusdal, R. (2007). If it is good for the child's development then I say yes almost every time: How parents relate to their children's consumption. *International Journal of Consumer Studies*, 31(1), 391–396.
Bu, W. (2001). *The influence of mass media on children*. Beijing: Xinhua Publishing.
Cattell, R. B. (1945). The description of personality: Principles and findings in a factor analysis. *American Journal of Psychology*, 58, 69–90.
Chaplin, L. N. and John, D. R. (2010). Interpersonal influences on adolescent materialism: A new look at the role of parents and peers. *Journal of Consumer Psychology*, 20(2), 176–184.
Chan, K. (2005). Materialism among children in urban China. In H. Cheng and K. Chan (eds), *The proceedings of the 2005 Asia Pacific Conference of the American Academy of Advertising* (pp. 22–33). Ohio: American Academy of Advertising.
Chan, K. (2006a). Consumer socialisation of Chinese children in Schools: Analysis of consumption values in textbooks. *Journal of Consumer Marketing*, 23(3), 125–132.
Chan, K. (2006b). Young consumers and perception of brands in Hong Kong: A qualitative study. *Journal of Product and Brand Management*, 15(7), 416–426.
Chan, K. and Fang, W. (2007). Use of the internet and traditional media among young people. *Young Consumers*, 8(4), 244–256.
Chan, K. and Prendergast, G. (2007). Materialism and social comparison among adolescents. *Social Behaviour and Personality: An International Journal*, 35(2), 213–228.
Chan, K. and Zhang, C. (2007). Living in a celebrity-mediated social world: The Chinese experience. *Young Consumers*, 8(2), 139–152.
Chen, Y. and Xie, J. (2008). Online consumer review: Word-of-mouth as a new element of marketing communication mix. *Management Science*, 54(3), 477–491.
Cody, K. (2014). Hearing muted voices: The crystallisation approach to critical and reflexive child-centric consumer research. *Young Consumers*, 16(3), 281–300.
Converse, P. D. and Huegy, H. (1952). *The elements of marketing*. Englewood Cliffs, NJ: Prentice Hall.
Cook, D. T. (2009). Knowing the child consumer: Historical and conceptual insights on qualitative children's consumer research. *Young Consumers: Insight and Ideas for Responsible Marketers*, 10(1), 269–282.
Davis, R. and Lang, B. (2013). Does game self-congruity increase usage and purchase? *Young Consumers*, 14(1), 52–66.
Dotson, M. J. and Hyatt, E. M. (2005). Major influence factors in children's consumer socialization. *Journal of Consumer Marketing*, 22(1), 35–42.
Escalas, J. E. and Bettman, J. (2005). Self-construal, reference groups, and brand meaning. *Journal of Consumer Research*, 32(3), 378–389.
Eysenck, H. J. (1953). *Uses and abuses of psychology*. Baltimore, MD: Penguin.
Eysenck, H. J. and Eysenck, S. B. G. (1993). *The Eysenck personality questionnaire revised*. London: Hodder & Stoughton.
Fan, Y. and Li, Y. (2010). Children's buying behaviour in China: A study of their information sources. *Journal of Marketing Intelligence and Planning*, 28(2), 170–187.

Ferguson, G. and Phau, I. Y. (2013). Adolescent and young adult response to fear appeals in anti-smoking messages. *Young Consumers*, *14*(2), 155–166.

Freud, A. (1937). *The ego and the mechanisms of defence*. London: Hogarth Press and Institute of Psycho-Analysis.

Fullerton, A. A. (2013). The birth of consumer behaviour: Motivation research in the 1940s and 1950s. *Journal of Historical Research in Marketing*, *5*(2), 212–222.

Gardner, B. B. (1959). The ABC of motivation research. *Business Topics*, 7, 35–41.

Gbadamosi, A. (2016). Consumer behaviour in developing nations. In *The handbook of research on consumerism and buying behaviour in developing nations* (pp. 1–29). Hersey, PA: IGI Global book series Advances in Marketing, Customer Relationship Management, and EServices (AMCRMES).

Goldberg, M. E., Gorn, G. J., Peracchio, L. A. and Bamossy, G. (2003). Understanding materialism among youth. *Journal of Consumer Psychology*, *13*(3), 278–288.

Govers, P. C. M. and Schoormans, J. P. L. (2005). Product personality and its influence on consumer preference. *Journal of Consumer Marketing*, *22*(4), 189–197.

Hagos, S. B. (2015). An interpretive phenomenological analysis of Eritrean refugee entrepreneurs in the UK. PhD thesis, University of Teesside, UK.

Hofstede, G. H. (1980). *Culture's consequences: International differences in work-related values*. Beverly Hills, CA: Sage.

Holbrook, M. B. (1992). Patterns, personalities, and complex relationships in the effects of self on mundane everyday consumption: These are 495 of my most and least favourite things. In John F. Sherry, Jr. and Brian Sternthal (eds), *Advances in consumer research* (Vol. 19, pp. 417–423). Provo, UT: Association for Consumer Research.

Holt, D. B. (1995). How consumers consume: A typology of consumption practices. *Journal of Consumer Research*, *22*, 1–16.

John, D. R. (1999). Consumer socialising of children: A retrospective look at twenty-five years of research. *Journal of Consumer Research*, *26*, 183–213.

Kanter, R. M. and Corn, R. I. (1994). Do cultural differences make a business difference? Contextual factors affecting cross-cultural relationship success. *Journal of Management Development*, *13*(2), 5–23.

Kasser, T. (2002). *The high price of materialism*. Cambridge, MA: MIT Press.

Kelly, J., Turner, J. J. and McKenna, K. (2006). What parents think: Children and healthy eating. *British Food Journal*, *108*(5), 413–432.

Klein, L. (1997). More than play dough. *Brandweek*, *38*, 24 November.

Kleine, R. E., Kleine, S. S. and Kernan, J. B. (1993). Mundane consumption and the self: A social-identity perspective. *Journal of Consumer Psychology*, *2*(3), 209–235.

Kleine, S. S., Kleine, III, R. E. and Laverie, D. A. (2004). Exploring how role identity development stage moderates person–possession relations. *Research in Consumer Behaviour*, *10*.

Kotler, P., Rackham, N. and Krishnaswamy, S. (2006). Ending the war between sales and marketing. *Harvard Business Review*, July–August, 68–78.

Kuhn, M. H. (1960). Self-attitudes by age, sex and professional training. *Sociological Quarterly*, *1*, 39–56.

La Ferle, C. and Chan, K. (2008). Determinants for materialism among adolescents in Singapore. *Young Consumers*, *9*(3), 201–214.

Lee, J. W. (2009). Relationship between consumer personality and brand personality as self-concept: From the case of Korean Automobile brands. *Academy of Marketing Studies Journal*, *13*(1), 25–44.

Levy, S. J. (1959). Symbols for sale. *Harvard Business Review*, *34*(4), 117–124.

Mäenpää, K., Kanto, A., Kuusela, H. and Paul, P. (2006). More hedonic versus less hedonic consumption behaviour in advanced internet bank services. *Journal of Financial Services Marketing*, *11*(1), 4–16.

McGinnis, J. M., Gootman, J. and Kraak, V. I. (2006). *Food marketing to children and youth: Threat or opportunity*. Washington DC: The National Academies Press.

McKenna, K. Y. and Bargh J. A. (2000). Plan 9 from cyberspace: The implications of the Internet for personality and social psychology. Personal. *Social Psychology Bulletin*, *4*, 57–75.

McLuhan, M. (1964). *Understanding media: The extension of man*. New York: McGraw-Hill.

McNeal, J. U. (2007). *On becoming a consumer: The development of consumer behaviour patterns in childhood*. London: Butterworth-Heinemann.

McNeal, J. U. and Ji, M. F. (1999). Chinese children as consumers: An analysis of their new product information sources. *Journal of Consumer Marketing*, *16*(4), 345–364.

Mau, G., Schuhen, M., Steinmann, S. and Schramm-Klein, H. (2016). How children make purchase decisions: Behaviour of the cued processors. *Young Consumers*, *17*(2), 111–126.

Mau, G., Steffen, C., Schramm-Klein, H. and Steinmann, S. (2012). The impact of health warnings on children's consumption decisions. In M. Eisend, T. Langner and S. Okazaki (eds), *Advances in advertising research* (Vol. III, pp. 93–103). Wiesbaden, Germany: Gabler.

Muniz, A. M., Jr. and Thomas, C. O. (2001). Brand community. *Journal of Consumer Research*, *27*, 412–432.

Nagarkoti, B. (2009). Factors influencing consumer behaviour of smartphone users. BBA thesis International Business. Arcada.

Newman, J. W. (1957). *Motivation research and marketing management*. Boston, MA: Harvard University Press.

Newman, K. L. and Nollen, S. D. (1996). Culture and congruence: The fit between management practices and national culture. *Journal of International Business Studies*, *27*, 753–779.

Nugent, R. (2006). *Youth in a global world*. Washington DC: Population Reference Bureau.

Opute, A. P. (2012). Maximizing effectiveness in team sports: The personal audit tool. *Team Performance Management*, *18*(1/2), 78–101.

Opute, A. P. (2014). Cross-functional bridge in dyadic relationship: Conflict management and performance implications. *Team Performance Management*, *20*(3/4), 121–147.

Opute, A. P. (2015). Optimizing team and organizational performance in sports setting: A diversity management perspective. In E. S. Linton (ed.), *Advances in sports research* (pp. 39–60). New York: Nova Science.

Opute, A. P. and Madichie, N. (2016). An interrogation of accounting-marketing interface in UK financial services organisations: Mixing cats with dogs? *Australasian Marketing Journal*, *24*(3), 214–225.

Otto, A. (2013). Saving in adulthood and adolescence: Insights from developmental psychology. *Economics of Education Review*, *33*, 8–18.

Reed II, A., Forehand, M. R., Puntoni, S. and Warlop, L. (2012). Identity-based consumer behaviour. *International Journal of Research in Marketing*, *29*, 310–321.

Rogers, C. R. (1959). A theory of therapy, personality and interpersonal relationships, as developed in the client-centered framework. In S. Koch (ed.), *Psychology: A study of science* (pp. 184–256). New York: McGraw Hill.

Saraneva, A. and Sääksjärvi, M. (2008). Young compulsive buyers and the emotional rollercoaster in shopping. *Young Consumers*, *9*(2), 75–89.

Schein, E. H. (1991). What is culture? In P. J. Frost, L. F. Moore, M. R. Louis, C. C. Lundberg and J. Martin (eds), *Reframing organizational culture* (pp. 243–254). Newbury Park: Sage.

Sharma, A. (2002). The use of generation Y Euromonitor archive. www.euromonitor.com/The_lure_of_generation_Y (accessed 19 April 2007).
Shteynberg, G., Gelfand, M. J. and Kim, K. (2009). Peering into the magnum mysterium of culture: The explanatory power of descriptive norms. *Journal of Cross-Cultural Psychology*, 40(1), 46–69.
Sirgy, M. J., Grewal, D., Mangleburg, T. F., Park, J. O., Chon, K. S., Claiborne, C. B., Johar, J. S. and Berkman, H. (1997). Assessing the predictive validity of two methods of measuring self-image congruence. *Journal of the Academy of Marketing Science*, 25(3), 229–241.
Smith, A. (2013). Smartphone ownership 2013. Pew Research Center Report. www.pewinternet.org/2013/06/05/smartphone-ownership-2013/ (accessed 28 August 2017).
Smith, G. H. (1954). *Motivation research in advertising and marketing*. New York: McGraw-Hill.
Stryker, S. (1968). Identity salience and role performance. *Journal of Marriage and the Family*, 4, 558–564.
Stryker, S. (1987). The interplay of affect and identity: Exploring the relationships of social structure, social interaction, self, and emotion. Paper presented at the annual meetings of the American Sociological Association, Chicago.
Syrjälä, H., Leipämaa-Leskinen, H. and Laaksonen, P. (2015). Social needs in Finnish young adults' mundane consumption. *Young Consumers*, 16(3), 301–315.
Tajfel, H. and Turner, J. C. (1986). The social identity theory of intergroup behaviour. In S. Worchel and W. G. Austin (eds), *Psychology of intergroup relations* (pp. 7–24). Chicago, IL: Nelson-Hall.
Taylor, A. and Harper, R. (2001). The gift of the gab: A design-oriented sociology of young people's use of mobiles. *Computer Supported Co-Operative Work*, 12(3), 267–296.
Ting-Toomey, S. (2015). Identity negotiation theory. In J. Bennett (ed.), *Sage encyclopaedia of intercultural competence* (Vol. 1, pp. 418–422). Los Angeles, CA: Sage.
Triandis, H. C., Carnevale, P., Gelfand, M., Robert, C., Wasti, A. Probst, T., Kashima, E., Dragonas, T., Chan, D., Chen X. P., Kim U., Kim, K., de Dreu, C., van de Vliert, E., Iwao, S., Ohbuchi, K.-I. and Schmitz, P. (2001). Culture, personality and deception. *International Journal of Cross-Cultural Management*, 1, 73–90.
Turner, J. and Oakes, P. (1986). The significance of the social identity concept for social psychology with reference to individualism, interactionism and social influence. *British Journal of Social Psychology*, 25(3), 237–252.
Turner, J. C. (1985). Social categorization and the self-concept: A social cognitive theory of group behaviour. *Advances in Group Processes*, 2, 77–122.
Watne, T., Lobo, A. and Brennan, L. (2011). Children as agents of secondary socialisation for their parents. *Young Consumers*, 12(4), 285–294.
White, K., Argo, J. J. and Sengupta, J. (2012). Dissociative versus associative responses to social identity threat: The role of consumer self-construal. *Journal of Consumer Research*, 39(4), 704–719.
Wimalasiri, J. S. (2004). A cross-national study on children's purchasing behaviour and parental response. *Journal of Consumer Marketing*, 4(21), 274–284.
Woodward, J. L. (1950). Depth interviewing. *The Journal of Marketing*, 14, 721–724.
Zhao, S. (1997). *In search of a right place? Chinese nationalism in the post-cold war world*. Hong Kong: Chinese University of Hong Kong.

6
ATTITUDES AND PERSUASION IN YOUNG CONSUMER BEHAVIOUR

Ayodele C. Oniku, Achi E. Awele and Olawale Adetunji

Introduction

The issues of marketing communication and accomplishment of persuasion towards products among young consumers has long been a popular debate in academic circles and it has been discussed across cultures, nationalities, family orientations, family social class and other demographic features such as age and sex. In order to advance study on this topical issue, this study looks at it distinctively from an academic community. The fact remains that the roles and impacts of marketing communication tools like advertising for adults are quite different to those for young consumers. Young consumers in this case cover children and teenagers; the development of cognitive and affective senses has to do with age and experiences, thus the different behavioural tendencies exhibited by the group in buying decisions when compared to adults. It becomes imperative for more studies to be developed on the topical issue, especially when previous studies have shown that effectiveness of advertising and other marketing communication programmes of organisation are a function of culture that varies across nationalities and invariably affects and determines the perception and attitudinal behaviour of consumers towards product acceptability and consumption in every market.

Attitude formation is the expected result of every marketing communication to show its effectiveness, and it becomes more favourable when a positive attitude formation is achieved. This relies solidly on message, graphic effects, the medium used, adaptation to people's culture and celebrity used, where it is necessary. Thus, the persuasion objective of marketing communication is a function of medium features and integration of environmental factors that are best suited to the market.

Nigeria has witnessed rapid increase in advertisements that focus on children and younger generations and the popularity cannot be disconnected from the environment created by the government and policy makers as long as such advertisements do not infringe on the rights of children and create undesirable consumption patterns among them. For instance, in the late 1970s, Nestle PLC's Milo wrestled the beverages market with dominant brands like Cadbury's Bournvita, Twining & Company Ltd., UK's Ovaltine and Pronto with advertisements that focused on children between the ages of 6–15 years – basically children in primary and secondary schools – with persuasive information on energy building and athletic lifestyle. The Nestle PLC's Milo is now a leader in the industry and the company has not deviated from advertisements and other marketing communications that focus on youths.

Presently, the noodles industry, in spite of the fact that the food is non-African, has gained grounds and become a popular menu choice among children courtesy of the advertising strategy that focuses on children in order to penetrate the market. The two leading companies in the industry, Indomie and Honeywell, develop their respective advertisements with different music slogans that have become popular among children, hence a child's choice of noodles is a function of the music he/she likes or prefers.

The experiences in other countries that measurement largely relies on application of the CSI dimension (consumer style inventory) reveals what shape consumers' persuasion in different markets among youths. In the Chinese market, the work of Fan and Xiao (1998) unfolded how the modified CSI scale shapes youths' purchase decisions. Also, another study compares the South Korean and USA youths' purchase decisions based on the CSI dimensional scale and the findings reveal how CSI shapes youths' purchase decisions differently across nations and cultures (Hafstrom et al., 1992). The scale dimensions are: brand conscious, perfectionist, recreational-shopping conscious, confused by overchoice, impulsive, time-energy, habitual, brand loyal and price-value conscious.

Attitude and persuasion

The earlier work of Fishbein (1963) and Fishbein and Ajzen (1972, 1975) form the bases upon which contemporary debates and discourses on attitudes depend (Jorgensen and Sonstegard, 1984; Herr, 1995; Peter and Olson, 1999). According to Fishbein,

> an individual's intention to perform any behaviour is a direct function of his/her attitude towards performing the behaviour, his/her beliefs about what significant others think he/she should do and the motivation to comply with the beliefs of those significant other.
>
> *(Jorgensen and Sonstegard, 1984)*

Thus, attitude is all about an individual's overall evaluation of a concept; this concept may be a brand, advertising or price of a product and other product and market variables. In marketing, consumers' attitudes focus on their evaluation of the marketing activity of organisations, which might involve promotion or marketing communication action, product/brand, price or distribution strategies or tools. Evaluation can be created by both the affective and cognitive systems. According to Peter and Olson (1999, p. 121) the 'affective system automatically produces affective responses – including emotions, feelings, moods, and evaluations or attitudes – as immediate, direct responses to certain stimuli'. The development leads to favourable or unfavourable affective responses that happen without consumers' consciousness or cognitive processing, and ultimately the evaluations become associated with a product or brand, service or organisation, which thereby helps to form the consumers' attitude towards the product.

Therefore, when advertising or any marketing communication tool is integrated into the framework of attitude operations, it becomes imperative to understand and acknowledge that the affective and cognitive systems rely on the contents of the message, graphic illustration or medium used to generate persuasion, which depend on the consumers' responses to the stimuli. In other words, the experience of individual consumers with the communication process goes a long way to determine the persuasive effect of the marketing communication tool; and emphatically it is a function of message contents, medium used, appropriate target or understanding of the target market. Therefore, a favourable attitude is formed towards a brand when affective and cognitive systems are moved towards the persuasion point. However, consumers are dissuaded from a brand when the affective and cognitive systems are negatively affected due to inappropriate message contents, the wrong target market and poor or wrong medium.

The self and attitude formation

The roles of self as a formidable factor in role identity cannot be downplayed in understanding attitude formation of consumers towards brand preference and selection. The roles of self largely affect and influence advertising reception and the processing of the message by consumers. The implication goes wider than purchasing a product to the extent that consumers want his/her personality identity and behaviour identity to be understood by the product, which might in turn influence purchase decision. In a practical sense, the fusion of self and advertising message is what forms organisation strategies to influence purchase decisions in the appropriate target market.

Self-concept focuses on different concepts of people and how they relate to others, and the personality and lifestyle consumers want to be associated with (Chang, 2008; Peter and Olson, 1999). Chang (2008) reveals that self-concepts built by consumers manifest in the form of self-categorisation and development of salient cues that form the basis of comparison with others to create self-categorisation.

Self-congruence on the other hand, stresses the match-up between consumers' self-image and brand-user image and this brings about self-image congruence (Berkman et al., 1996). In other words, consumers easily form positive attitude towards a product when product features and promotional objectives emphasise the similarities that match consumers' expected or planned self-image for themselves.

The self-image is what differentiates consumers from one another, and forms the basis for self-categorisation. Thus, it is strategic for organisations to impute product features that match up with the target market self-image and to support such features with market communication that emphasise the message of consumers' self-image to achieve self-congruence. Consumers' self-images of being bold, adventurous, sexy, cool, etc. are imputed in products' features and consumers who seek such personalities establish self-congruence when they purchase and consume such products. The work of Mitchell (1986) and Chang (2008) shows the strategic linkage between consumers' self and attitude formation.

Self-referencing occurs when advertising and other marketing communication project a product's features in a way that makes cognitive processing influence the consumer to relate their self with the product. This invariably leads to positive attitude formation because the communication message emphasises attributes that makes consumers relate with the product, which equally leads to a self-congruent attitude towards the product. The importance of self-referencing is that marketing communication promotes a product to a target market or a segment by emphasising what makes the market identify with a product. Berger and Mitchell (1989) and Chang (2008) emphasise self-referencing as a way for organisations to achieve attitude change and behaviour relationship towards products.

Young consumers and attitudes to TV ads

Studies have shown that attitudes to TV ads and other marketing communication tools are strategic in understanding attitude formation, which invariably affects buying decisions and purchase patterns among consumers irrespective of culture, age and family orientation (Riecken and Samli, 1981; Mitchell, 1986; Berger and Mitchell, 1989; Langrial et al., 2014). The earlier work of Rossiter (1977) shows support to the connection and positive relationship between TV adverts and children's attitude formation towards a brand. Thus, a scale was developed to measure the attitude. The essence is that organisations may know what could trigger children's affective and cognitive reactions in TV advertisements, which would aid the formation of positive attitudes towards a brand. The test–retest correlations and test–retest validity show the basis on which the measuring scale is built – truth, annoy, good only, like, persuade, believe and best buy. The simplicity and brevity of the scale makes it more adaptable and reliable for children's evaluation and study. Equally, studies have shown that teenagers are trendsetters and have more and better information than parents in certain purchase decisions and consumption patterns; likewise adolescent girls are more informed than their mothers when it comes to purchase decisions on fashion (Zollo, 1995; Gavish et al., 2010).

Berger and Mitchell (1989) further note that attitude accessibility, attitude confidence and attitude–behaviour relationship determinations are paramount in achieving attitude formation towards a brand. In other words, the level of attitude confidence and attitude accessibility consumers enjoy are crucial in determining attitude towards a brand. Importantly, advertising repetition is fundamental to achieving attitude confidence and accessibility (Berger and Mitchell, 1989). The issue of repeated advertisement or advertising frequency is corroborated by the work of Mitchell (1986).

Mitchell (1986) emphasises the dual roles of verbal and visual components of advertisements in which the author shows that visual and verbal components of advertisements directly affect consumers' attitude towards the advertisement and product attribute benefits, which ultimately determine brand attitudes. Consequently, the rating of verbal and visual components of advertisements in terms of positive or negative determines attitude towards the advertisement and product attribute benefits that finally determine brand attitudes. Peter and Olson (1999), Kisielius and Sternthal (1984) and Berkman et al. (1996) emphasise the strategic roles of exposure to verbal and visual components of advertisement to stimulate and generate attitude formation and persuasive effects. Succinctly, the cognitive effects on consumer reactions are established. However, Edell and Staelin (1983) found that where visual components of advertisements differ or run contrary to the verbal component of the same advertisement, it may cause distraction on the part of consumers.

Another dimension to children's TV advertisements is the cultural-based content of their modality and application to influence brand attitude and achieve positive attitude formation towards a brand or product. Kashif et al.'s (2011) work focuses on Pakistani fathers' roles in children's attitude towards TV adverts; Chan and McNeal's (2003) work looks at Chinese children; Langrial et al.'s (2014) work focuses on a comparison of Canadian and Pakistani children's attitudes; and McGinnis et al. (2006) carry out a cross-cultural study of nine countries: Austria, Belgium, Denmark, Iceland, the Netherlands, Norway, Portugal, Spain and Sweden. The bottom line is that TV advertising needs to be culture-based for it to be effective in attitude formation and to generate persuasive effects. In other words, adaptation rather that standardisation is more strategic and effective in TV advertising policy. The work of Langrial et al. (2014) employs Hofstede's (1993a, 1993b, 2001) dimensions of culture to make comparisons between children from the two countries. Practically, the dimensions of individual, power distance, uncertainty avoidance, masculinity and long-term orientation form the basis of explaining the differences and similarities between Canadian and Pakistani children's perception of TV advertising. The findings reflect the differences in cultural dimensions that exist between the two countries based on Hofstede's (Hofstede and Bond, 1998).

Chan and McNeal's (2003) study focuses on family type or orientation to determine the effect of parent–child communication about consumption and advertising to determine purchase decision. The study shows that two types of family orientation exist – socio-orientation and concept orientation, and the types of orientation determine the communication line between parents and children (Neulinger and Zsoter, 2014). The determined relationship ultimately affects parents' or children's domination in TV advert viewing and purchase decision. The study of Chan and McNeal (2003) shows the children's permissible right in TV viewing that affects their buying decisions and behaviours. The study also shows the outcome of consumption and purchase decisions when there is co-viewing between parents and children, and the type of purchase decisions that may exist when there is presence of perceived parental influence and control of the TV viewing of children.

On the issues of orientation, the works of Chang and McNeal (2003) and Neulinger and Zsoter (2014) corroborate each other in that type of family orientation determines a family communication structure, which invariably determines children's role in purchase decisions and hence their consumption patterns, and that the source of information influences consumers' attitude formation or persuasive effects. For instance, according to Neulinger and Zsoter (2014), families with pluralistic and consensual communication are more concept-oriented whereby children are 'encouraged to develop their own views, skills and competencies in the market place' (p. 397). Chan and McNeal's (2003) study stresses that pluralistic and consensual parents are largely educated and hold professional or administrative positions. *Laissez-faire* families are found to be less careful and less involved in their children's TV viewing and shopping, thus the children lack the skills and competencies to be involved in planned and careful shopping, but instead tend toward more recreational and hedonistic shopping (Chang and McNeal, 2003; Neulinger and Zster, 2014).

The work of Moore and Lutz (2000) argues that children's experience with product consumption and buying behaviour based on advertising is a function of product trial and advertisement exposure. Also, the study further suggests that cognitive and affective reactions of children towards advertisements vary between older and younger children. In other words, the older and younger children exhibit different receptions and reactions in purchase decision when advertisements are the only source of information about products; and may have different reactions and receptions when product trial precedes advertising exposure. There is also a difference in reaction and behaviour among children who adopt product trial only and those that are exposed to advertisement only.

Persuasion in advertising and attitude formation

The work of Chang (2008) shows the importance of models in advertising and how younger consumers seek self-concept in modelling activity to determine brand preference, brand affinity and positive attitude formation. In other words, every young consumer is motivated to form preference for a brand advertised by a model when there is a congruency between the model's age and the participants – young consumers. The study clearly shows that self-concept in consumers drives them to look for self-congruency in advertising, thus where modelling or advertising information self-categorisation is found by consumers there is plausibility for brand preference, brand attitude and brand affinity (Chang 2000; DeSarbo *et al.*, 2002).

Phillips and McQuarrie (2010) use the term 'narrative transportation' to stress the experience of consumers when stories and other narratives found in magazines and other print media lure or persuade them to form favourable intent and attitudes towards a brand. The veritable roles of print ads, aesthetic factors and aesthetics in advert imagery and the grotesque are found to be a platform for consumer transportation into advertising engagement towards attitude formation. The study shows that 'grotesque imagery was associated with the consumers' outcomes of transportation and immersion' (p. 389). Immersion is described as a way to achieve 'intense experience with the brands, eliciting positive brand outcomes' (p. 389). By and large, the roles of ad imagery are strategic in advertising especially among women to experience narrative transportation (Gerrig, 1993; Green and Brcok, 2000; Till and Baack, 2005).

Hypotheses

Based on the literature and existing constructs on persuasion (Moore and Lutz, 2000; Chang, 2008; Phillips and McQuarrie, 2010) adopted for the study, we hypothesise that:

- H1: Brand information from reliable sources like close associates and family members will not heighten purchase preference among young consumers.
- H2: Shared information about brand features and attributes that meet the latest popular trends will not influence purchase decisions among young consumers.
- H3: Information that fits into and identifies with self-concept and self-congruency is not mandatory for purchase decisions among young consumers.

Methodology

The scale for the study was developed based on the previous works of Feick and Price (1987) and Beatly and Talpade (1994). Thus, consumer purchase decision and persuasion scales were combined to measure youths' attitude and persuasion.

The questionnaires were administered on 400 people comprising 200 young adolescents and 200 parents/guardians. The returned and processed questionnaires are 363 respondents made up of 176 young adolescents and 187 parents/guardians. The inclusion of parents in the study is to create robustness in data collection because of their roles in children's purchase decisions and consumption patterns, and previous studies have adopted the method either wholly or complementarily (Chang, 2008; Kashif et al., 2011; Neulinger and Zsoter, 2014). Under the demographic background of parents in the questionnaire, the designated role of parents are sought in order to understand their manners and patterns of influence on the youths' consumption patterns and buying decisions.

The samples for the young adolescents were persons from senior secondary school (SSS), which is the last three years of secondary education in Nigeria, and first-year freshman students in university. Thus, the focus was on teenagers who previous studies have shown to have the capability to handle and understand questionnaire administration with less involvement from the interviewee (Zollo, 1995; Gavish et al., 2010). The study was carried out on the Akoka Campus of the University of Lagos, where the International Secondary School (ISS) was selected for the senior secondary school students and the freshers on the Akoka-Yaba University campus were selected for the study. Accidental sampling technique was employed for the freshers, and this happened during their registration exercise as fresh intakes.

The researchers first visited the schools and explained to the pupils the need for the research and how to go about filling in the questionnaires. A new date was set for the exercise, which coincided with the end of the year students–parents gathering, which usually takes place towards the end of a session or term. This provided a good platform to meet the parents in one location. Hence, the questionnaire was administered to the parents/guardians on that day. However, because of the length of the questionnaire items and the busy schedule of teachers, we were told to come back for collection of the questionnaires meant for students the following day. Before the researchers left the school, the researchers re-explained to the respondents individually the purpose and importance of the study and pleaded with them for their honest response to the items on the questionnaire.

Results

Reliability: internal consistency test

The constructs for the study; persuasion and consumer purchase decision were subjected to an internal consistency test after a pilot study was conducted by the researchers. Cronbach Alpha coefficients were computed for the items. A leading figure in reliability testing notes that a Cronbach Alpha coefficient of .70 or higher is considered 'acceptable' in most social science research based on a standard alpha value of .7 (Pallant, 2007).

TABLE 6.1 Reliability test statement

Constructs	No. of items	Alpha coefficients (α)
Information from close people	2	.744
Shared information about brands	2	.737
Information fit congruency	2	.780
Consumer purchase decision	2	.860

Respondents' profile

TABLE 6.2 Demographic background of the 176 children

Variable		Frequency
Gender	Male	95
	Female	81
Age (years)	13–15	109
	16–19	67
Education	SSS 1–3	137
	First-year undergraduate	39
	Total	176

TABLE 6.3 Demographic background of parents/guardians

Variable		Frequency
Gender	Male	95
	Female	92
Age (years)	25–35	63
	36–45	52
	46–55	52
	56 +	20
Status/Role	Parent	62
	Guardian	45
	Grandparent	30
	Teacher	23
	Religious leader	13
	Professional counsellor	10
	Sports trainer	4
Occupation	Government worker	62
	Self-employed	74
	Private firm worker	51
Frequency of meeting the child	Regularly	73
	Daily	47
	Occasionally	48
	On request	19
Marital status	Single-parent	77
	Married	102
	Divorced	8
Educational status	Below/above WASC	59
	'O' level	67
	BSc/HND	50
	MSc/MBA	11
	PhD	
	Total	187

From Table 6.3, the frequency of each variable reveals the weight in each case. For instance, under status/role, the categories of status are in biological parents, guardian, grandparents, teachers, religious leader, counsellor and sports trainers, and the frequency shows that biological parents score 33.1 per cent followed by guardians at 24.1 per cent. Also, the frequency of meeting the child, which was measured on the variables of regularly, daily, occasionally and on-request, the results showed that regularly factors scored 39 per cent; occasionally 25.7 per cent, daily 25.1 per cent and on-request 10.2 per cent.

Mean and standard deviation

TABLE 6.4 Standard deviation statistical analysis

Constructs	N	Mean	Standard deviation
Information from close people	363	3.9876	.8468
Shared information about brands	363	3.9118	.7352
Information fit congruency	363	4.1295	.8233
Consumer purchase decision	363	4.1115	.5883

Hypothesis testing

- H1: Brand information from reliable sources like close associates and family members will not heighten purchase preference among young consumers.

TABLE 6.5 Brand information sources and students' preferences

		Consumer purchase decision	Brand information from reliable sources
Consumer purchase decision	Pearson correlation	1	.591**
	Sig. (2-tailed)		.000
	N	363	363
Brand information from reliable sources	Pearson correlation	.591**	1
	Sig. (2-tailed)	.000	
	N	363	363

** Correlation is significant at the 0.05 level (2-tailed).

In Table 6.5, the correlation result of Hypothesis 1 (H1), shows that brand information from reliable sources like close associates and family members has a correlation coefficient (r) of 0.591 with consumer purchase decision, meaning that they are positively associated. This invariably means that an increase in brand information from reliable sources like close associates and family members will lead to an increase in consumer purchase decision and vice versa. Also, since the p-value is <0.05, hence the hypothesis is significant at 5 per cent. Therefore, the hypothesis that brand information from reliable sources like close associates and family members will not heighten purchase preference is not supported.

- H2: Shared information about brand features and attributes that meet the latest popular trends will not influence purchase decisions among young consumers.

TABLE 6.6 Shared information about brand features and popular trends and students' purchase decision

		Consumer purchase decision	Shared information about brand features
Consumer purchase decision	Pearson correlation	1	.429**
	Sig. (2-tailed)		.000
	N	363	363
Shared information about brand features	Pearson correlation	.429**	1
	Sig. (2-tailed)	.000	
	N	363	363

** Correlation is significant at the 0.05 level (2-tailed).

From Table 6.6 above, the correlation result of Hypothesis 2 (H2) shows that shared information about brand features has a correlation coefficient (r) of 0.429 with consumer purchase decision, meaning that they are positively associated. The implication of this is that an increase in shared information about brand features and attributes will influence consumer purchase decision and vice versa. Also, since the p-value is <0.05, hence the hypothesis is significant at 5 per cent. Therefore, the hypothesis that shared information about brand features and attributes that meet the latest popular trends will not influence purchase decisions is not supported.

- H3: Information that fits into and identifies with self-concept and self-congruency is not mandatory for purchase decisions among young consumers.

In Table 6.7, the correlation result of Hypothesis 3 (H3) shows that information that fits into and identifies with self-concept and self-congruency has a correlation coefficient (r) of 0.380 with consumer purchase decision, meaning that they are positively associated. The implication of this is that when there is an increase in information that fits into and identifies with self-concept and self-congruency of teenagers, their purchase decision will also increase and vice versa. Also, since the p-value is <0.05, hence the hypothesis is significant at 5 per cent. Therefore,

TABLE 6.7 Information on self-concept and self-congruency and students' purchase decision

		Consumer purchase decision	Information that fits
Consumer purchase decision	Pearson correlation	1	.380**
	Sig. (2-tailed)		.000
	N	363	363
Information that fits	Pearson correlation	.380**	1
	Sig. (2-tailed)	.000	
	N	363	363

** Correlation is significant at the 0.05 level (2-tailed).

TABLE 6.8 Construct inter-correlations and correlations matrix

Constructs	1	2	3	4
1. Consumer purchase decision	1			
2. Information from close people	.591**	1		
3. Shared information about brands	.429**	.587**	1	
4. Information fit congruency	.380**	.441**	.604**	1

**Correlation is significant at the 0.05 level (2-tailed).

the hypothesis that information that fits into and identifies with self-concept and self-congruency is not mandatory for purchase decisions is not supported.

Guilford and Frutcher (1973) noted that item-correlations and inter-correlations should fall between 0.10–0.60 (for inter-correlations) and 0.30–0.80 for item-correlations respectively. The test results for this study falls between 0.42–0.60, designating a good test fitness.

From Table 6.8, it is revealed that there is a positive association between consumers' purchase decisions, information from close people, shared information about brands and information fit congruency.

Discussions, conclusions and implications

The study succinctly looks at three factors that attitude depends on and that influence buying decisions and consumption patterns or market behaviours of young consumers. The factor of sources of information is strategic in attitude of information as revealed in the study. Practically, consumers are differently biased to reliable sources of information, so what is reliable to one set of consumers may not play the same role for another set of consumers. The findings show that young consumers depend on certain sources of information that they deemed reliable to trigger attitude formation. In other words, once a source of information is found to be reliable, young consumers continually look toward that source to generate right and dependable information on buying decisions, consumption patterns and market behaviours. In this instance, reliable information about products and markets are found to be dependable when they come from family members and close associates. The findings further reveal that reliable information from relatives and close associates is very strong with biological parents. Young consumers largely and reliably depend on counsels, instructions, directives and orders from the biological parents to form attitudes that enhance market behaviours, consumption patterns and purchase decisions. The findings corroborate the research of Kashif et al. (2011) and Jay (2012), who concluded that the opinions of both fathers and mothers are strategic in children's buying decisions.

Strategically, the study further examines the roles of information provided or made available to consumers as a way of forming attitudes towards certain products or brands. In other words, the availability of information on products' function, performance, features and other attributes are crucially important to young consumers to form attitude. Thus, the findings show that provisions and sharing of such information among young consumers is strategic to their attitude development and formation. The study of Mitchell (1986) stresses the connection between advertising's visual and verbal components and product attributes to achieve attitude formation that ultimately leads to achievement of brand attitude among consumers. In the same vein, Moore and Lutz (2000) corroborate the importance of stressing and sharing product attribute information to aid attitude formation through emphasis of product trial and advertisement exposure among children, though comparison is made in the study between older and younger children. Phillips and McQuarrie (2010) elaborate further on the roles narratives and story via aesthetics and imagery play in advertising to emphasise product attributes in order to generate positive attitude formation among consumers.

The work of Chang (2000, 2008) gives credence to the finding that creating self-concept, self-referencing and congruency of ages with models led to positive attitude formation among consumers. The work of Chang (2000) specifically emphasises that age congruency of models with participants or consumers would enhance attitude formation and generate persuasive effects on young consumers. By and large, recognition and implanting of concepts of self-referencing, self-concept and age congruency that allow consumers to see themselves in all or many definitions in product information or product attributes can speedily enhance persuasive effects and positive attitude formation that generate brand attitude for products.

Thus, it is clear that the roles of advertising messages and other marketing communication tools are very strategic in achieving positive attitude formation towards products. The study has thrown more light on what should form organisation strategies when creating marketing communication messages, which, according to the study, should strategically be premised on sourcing information from links that the youth consumers find more reliable. Importantly, organisations should recognise the relevance and efficacy of self in product design and attributes, and its integration into market communication messages in order to achieve positive attitudes towards product formation.

Conclusively, the study has added to knowledge especially among young consumers who are transiting from secondary to university education. Indeed, the study was carried out in a university environment in order to understand the peculiarities of that particular stage in social life. Importantly, the findings have also thrown more light on the relationship between attitude formation and marketing communication tools in order to achieve generating positive attitude towards a brand. Largely, the work has unfolded the facts that decision makers in marketing need to know about factors that are strategic to persuasion and positive attitude formation in order to create effective demand among young consumers.

References

Beatly, S. E. and Talpade, S. (1994). Adolescent influence in family decision making: A replication with extension. *Journal of Consumer Research*, *21*(2), 332–341.

Berger, I. A. and Mitchell, A. A. (1989). The effect of advertising on attitude accessibility, attitude confidence and attitude–behaviour relationship. *Journal of Consumer Research*, 16(12), 269–279.

Berkman, H. W., Lindquist, J. D. and Sirgy, M. J. (1996). *Consumer behaviour*. Chicago, IL: NTC.

Chan, K. and McNeal, J. U. (2003). Parent–child communications about consumption and advertising in China. *Journal of Consumer Research*, 20(4), 317–334.

Chang, C. (2000). The effects of personality differences on product evaluation. In S. Broniarczyk and K. Nakamoto (eds), *Advances in consumer research* (Vol. 28, pp. 26–33). Valdosa: Association for Consumer Research.

Chang, C. (2008). Chronological age versus cognitive age for younger consumers. *Journal of Advertising*, 37(3), 19–32.

DeSarbo, W. S., Juyoung, K. S., Chan, C. and Melinda, S. (2002). A gravity-based multidimensional scaling model for deriving spatial structures underlying consumer performance/choice judgements. *Journal of Consumer Research*, 29(1), 91–101.

Edell, J. and Staelin, R. (1983). The information processing of pictures in advertisements. *Journal of Consumer Research*, 10(1), 45–60.

Fan, J. X. and Xiao, J. J. (1998). Consumer decision-making styles of young-adult Chinese. *The Journal of Consumer Affairs*, 32(2), 275–294.

Feick, L. F. and Price, L. L. (1987). The market maven: A difference user of marketplace information. *Journal of Marketing*, 51, 83–97.

Fishbein, M. (1963). An investigation of the relationship between beliefs about an object and the attitude toward an object. *Human Relations*, 16, 233–240.

Fishbein, M. and Ajzen, I. (1972). Attitudes and opinions. *Annual Review of Psychology*, 23, 487–544.

Fishbein, M. and Ajzen, I. (1975). *Belief, attitudes, intention and behavior*. Reading: Addison-Wesley.

Gavish, Y., Shoham, A. and Ruvio, A. (2010). A qualitative study of mother–adolescent daughter–vicarious role model consumption interactions. *Journal of Consumers Marketing*, 27(1), 43–56.

Gerrig, R. J. (1993). *Experiencing narrative worlds*. New Haven, CT: Yale University Press.

Green, M. C. and Brock, T. C. (2000). The role of persuasion in transportation in the persuasiveness of public narratives. *Journal of Personality and Social Psychology*, 79(5), 701–721.

Guildford, J. P. and Fruchter, B. (1973). *Fundamental statistics in psychology and education* (5th edn). New York: McGraw-Hill.

Hafstrom, J. L., Chae, J. S. and Chung, Y. S. (1992). Consumer decision-making style: Comparison between United States and Korean young consumers. *The Journal of Consumers Affairs*, 26(1), 146–158.

Herr, P. M. (1995). Whither fact, artifact, and attitude: Reflections on the theory of reasoned action. *Journal of Consumer Psychology*, 4(4), 371–380.

Hofstede, G. (1993a). Cultural constraints in management theories. *Academy of Management Executives*, 7, 81–94.

Hofstede, G. (1993b). The cultural relativity of organisational practices and theories. *Journal of International Business Studies*, 14, 75–89.

Hofstede, G. (2001). *Culture consequences: Company values, behaviour, institution and organisations across nations*. Thousand Oaks, CA: Sage.

Hofstede, G. and Bond, M. (1988). The Confucius connection: From cultural roots to economic growth. *Organisational Dynamics*, 16(4), 5–21.

Jay, Y. (2012). Mothers' perceptions of the negative impacts on TV food ads on children's food choices. *Appetite*, 59(2), 372–376.

Jorgensen, S. R. and Sonstegard, J. S. (1984). Predicting adolescent sexual and contraceptive behaviour: An application and test of the Fishbein model. *Journal of Marriage and Family*, 46(1), 43–55.

Kashif, M., Ayyaz, M. and Basharat, S. (2011). TV food advertising aimed at children: Qualitative study of Pakistani fathers' views. *Asia-Pacific Journal of Marketing and Logistics*, 26(1), 647–658.

Kisielius, J. and Sternthal, B. (1984). Detecting and explaining vividness effects in attitudinal judgements. *Journal of Marketing Research*, 21(February), 54–64.

Langrial, S., Kashif, M. and Ehsan, U. (2014). Exploring attitudes of Pakistani and Canadian children towards television advertisements: A cross-cultural comparative analysis. *Asia-Pacific Journal of Management Research and Innovation*, 10(3), 191–201.

McGinnis, J. M., Gootman, J. A. and Kraak, V. I. (2006). *Committee on food marketing and the diet of children and youth institute of medicine food marketing to children and youth: Threat or opportunity?* Washington DC: National Academies Press.

Mitchell, A. A. (1986). The effect of verbal and visual components of advertisements on brand attitudes and attitude towards the advertisement. *Journal of Consumer Research*, 13(6), 12–24.

Moore, E. S. and Lutz, R. J. (2000). Children, advertising, and product experiences: A multi-method inquiry. *Journal of Consumer Research*, 27(6), 31–48.

Neulinger, A. and Zsoter, B. (2014). Mother–child interactions in youth purchase decisions. *Society and Economy*, 36(3), 387–406.

Pallant, J. (2007). *SPSS survival manual* (3rd edn). London: McGraw Hill Open University Press.

Peter, J. P. and Olson, J. C. (1999). *Consumer behaviour and marketing strategy* (5th edn). New York: McGraw Hill.

Phillips, B. J. and McQuarrie, E. F. (2010). Narrative and persuasion in fashion advertising. *Journal of Consumer Research*, 37(10), 368–392.

Riecken, G. and Samli, A. C. (1981). Measuring children's attitudes towards television commercials extension and replication. *Journal of Consumer Research*, 8(1), 57–61.

Rossiter, J. R. (1977). Reliability of a short test measuring children's attitudes towards commercials. *Journal of Consumer Research*, 3(4), 179–184.

Till, B. D. and Baack, D. W. (2005). Recall and persuasion: Does creative advertising matter? *Journal of Advertising*, 34(3), 47–57.

Zollo, P. (1995). Talking on teens. *American Demographics*, 17(11), 22–28.

Appendices: SPSS output

Teenagers

Sex

		Frequency	%	Valid %	Cumulative %
Valid	Male	95	54.0	54.0	54.0
	Female	81	46.0	46.0	100.0
	Total	176	100.0	100.0	

Age

	Frequency	%	Valid %	Cumulative %
Valid 10–12 years	36	20.5	20.5	20.5
13–15 years	73	41.5	41.5	61.9
16–19 years	67	38.1	38.1	100.0
Total	176	100.0	100.0	

Education

	Frequency	%	Valid %	Cumulative %
Valid JSS 1–3	56	31.8	31.8	31.8
SSS 1–3	81	46.0	46.0	77.8
First-year undergraduate	39	22.2	22.2	100.0
Total	176	100.0	100.0	

Adults (parents/guardians)

Sex

	Frequency	%	Valid %	Cumulative %
Valid Male	95	50.8	50.8	50.8
Female	92	49.2	49.2	100.0
Total	187	100.0	100.0	

Age

	Frequency	%	Valid %	Cumulative %
Valid 25–35 years	63	33.7	33.7	33.7
36–45 years	52	27.8	27.8	61.5
46–55 years	52	27.8	27.8	89.3
56 years and above	20	10.7	10.7	100.0
Total	187	100.0	100.0	

How frequently do you meet the child?

		Frequency	%	Valid %	Cumulative %
Valid	Regularly	73	39.0	39.0	39.0
	Daily	47	25.1	25.1	64.2
	Occasionally	48	25.7	25.7	89.8
	On request	19	10.2	10.2	100.0
	Total	187	100.0	100.0	

Marital status

		Frequency	%	Valid %	Cumulative %
Valid	Single parent	77	41.2	41.2	41.2
	Married	102	54.5	54.5	95.7
	Divorced	8	4.3	4.3	100.0
	Total	187	100.0	100.0	

Educational qualifications

		Frequency	%	Valid %	Cumulative %
Valid	Below/above WASCE 'O' Level	59	31.6	31.6	31.6
	BSc/HND	67	35.8	35.8	67.4
	MSc/MBA	50	26.7	26.7	94.1
	PhD	11	5.9	5.9	100.0
	Total	187	100.0	100.0	

Occupation

		Frequency	%	Valid %	Cumulative %
Valid	Government worker	62	33.2	33.2	33.2
	Self-employed	74	39.6	39.6	72.7
	Private firm worker	51	27.3	27.3	100.0
	Total	187	100.0	100.0	

Status/role

		Frequency	%	Valid %	Cumulative %
Valid	Parent	62	33.2	33.2	33.2
	Guardian	45	24.1	24.1	57.2
	Grandparent	30	16.0	16.0	73.3
	Teacher	23	12.3	12.3	85.6
	Religious leader	13	7.0	7.0	92.5
	Professional counsellor	10	5.3	5.3	97.9
	Sport trainer	4	2.1	2.1	100.0
	Total	187	100.0	100.0	

Test results

Statistics

		Consumer decision	Brand information from reliable sources	Shared information about brand features and attributes	Information that fits into and identifies
N	Valid	363	363	363	363
	Missing	0	0	0	0
Mean		4.1115702	3.98760	3.91185	4.12948
Std. deviation		.77286760	.970126	.984941	.844080

Correlations

		Consumer decision	Brand information from reliable sources	Shared information about brand features and attributes	Information that fits into and identifies
Consumer decision	Pearson correlation	1	.591**	.429**	.380**
	Sig. (2-tailed)		.000	.000	.000
	N	363	363	363	363

(continued)

(continued)

		Consumer decision	Brand information from reliable sources	Shared information about brand features and attributes	Information that fits into and identifies
Brand information from reliable sources	Pearson correlation	.591**	1	.587**	.441**
	Sig. (2-tailed)	.000		.000	.000
	N	363	363	363	363
Shared information about brand features and attributes	Pearson correlation	.429**	.587**	1	.604**
	Sig. (2-tailed)	.000	.000		.000
	N	363	363	363	363
Information that fits into and identifies	Pearson correlation	.380**	.441**	.604**	1
	Sig. (2-tailed)	.000	.000	.000	
	N	363	363	363	363

** Correlation is significant at the 0.01 level (2-tailed).

PART III
Young consumers and marketing strategies

7
BRAND, BRANDING AND BRAND CULTURE AMONG YOUNG CONSUMERS

Andrew Hughes

Chapter outline

Anyone who looks at a young child at play in a room full of toys will realise how intrinsic the relationship is between children and brands. While movies like *Toy Story* or the *Lego Movie* may have made that relationship explicit for all to see, as soon as a child is born they are building relationships and sharing experiences with brands.

Some of these relationships endure for far longer than our childhood – many of you reading this may still own a toy given to you at a time in life when your only concerns were eating, sleeping and cuddles. These enduring relationships form a bridge with our memories from past and present and shape our future behaviour as adults. In a marketing context, this is truly what is meant by customer lifetime value.

This chapter will discuss some of the more important theories of children and branding. It will start with a very brief background on branding and then define who young consumers are in both an age and a developmental context. This is important as they are not necessarily directly correlated with each other.

Next there will be a discussion on brands, branding and young consumers. Why should brands even target children and young people, and what value or relationship can they build to them? The importance of the 3Es of branding to children – emotions, enjoyment, and experience – will then be discussed, with two new conceptual models being introduced in this area – the Brand Emotional Response Model for Young People (BERMY) and for children the Brand Adoption Curve (BAC).

The chapter will then examine how some influence and try to influence children, and also the power of children on others in making consumer decisions. The role of emerging technology, such as virtual reality (VR), is also discussed here as this is a new way brands are using to influence the minds of the young.

Some future thoughts on children and branding will then be discussed, such as the role of ethics in this area, before the chapter will conclude with some final points for researchers, practitioners and parents.

A very brief background on branding

To understand how and why an organisation may co-create value with children and their brands, it is important to briefly address some of the background theory in the area. A brand can be defined as being a name, term, sign, symbol or design, or a combination of these, intended to identify the goods or services of one seller or group of sellers and to differentiate them from those of competitors (American Marketing Association, 2017). A brand easily identifies a product or service and is a seller's promise to deliver consistently a specific set of features, benefits and services to buyers (Kotler, 2000) and has four important characteristics: attributes, benefits, values and personality (Kapferer, 1992; Keller, 1993). A brand's meaning to a consumer is based around each of these four values, and it is up to the marketer to decide on what emphasis to place on each so that a brand can be established (Kapferer, 1992).

The choice of a brand name, and the use of other brand elements such as a logo or URL, has been recognised as important in establishing brand equity for a new product (Aaker, 1991, 1996; Keller, 1993, 1998; Keller et al., 1998). The right brand name can also enhance brand awareness, help create a favourable brand image for a newly created product and enhance recall of the product (Keller et al., 1998). Prior studies in memory have also found that the choice of a brand name is important in associating images with a product in a consumer's mind (Anderson, 1983; Wyer and Srull, 1989; Keller, 1993), and that once a strong association is established with the brand, the rate of decay of this association in the mind is slow (Loftus and Loftus, 1980). The more information that can be associated with a brand name due to its attributes, benefits and attitudes, the higher the level of consumer association (Russo and Johnson, 1980; Johnson, 1984; Alba and Hutchinson, 1987; Chattopadhyay and Alba, 1988).

Brand research conducted by Keller (1993) and Aaker (1982, 1991) state that branding strategies and principles can be applied to all products and services without exception. The essence of any brand positioning strategy is that the brand has a sustainable competitive advantage or 'unique selling proposition' that gives consumers a compelling reason for buying that particular brand (Ries and Trout, 1979; Aaker, 1982; Wind, 1982; Keller, 1993). These differences can be communicated explicitly by making direct comparisons with competitors or may be highlighted without stating a competitive point of reference (Keller, 1993), which makes the application of this strategy ideal when it comes to branding with children. A brand can also be positioned as being exemplar in its category, and can use its specific attributes and benefits, such as name, with consumers to position itself as the leading choice of consumers (Rosch and Mervis, 1975; Ward and Loken, 1986; Nedungadi and Hutchinson, 1990; Keller et al., 1998).

From a relationship marketing perspective, brands form an integral part of a relationship between consumer and brand (Grönroos, 1994). This may even be more so between a child and a brand because a child's cognitive developmental stage may make them more likely to see a toy as a brand, and less as a product with different utilities of use.

Defining young consumers and the young consumer life cycle

Defining who young consumers are is important in many contexts. It is not just as simple as using demographic brackets as it needs to also provide a deeper picture of a child in a learning and developmental context. This helps contextualise how young consumers move through the young consumer life cycle from birth to blowing out the candles on their eighteenth or twenty-first birthday cake. This aids in the understanding of the variation in how young consumers respond to different marketing methods.

Then there is the societal aspect of how children are treated in different nations around the world in terms of their ability and age where they assume independence of their consumption process. In some nations, for example, working ages are closely linked to obtaining control of bank accounts and other financial decisions excluding more formal contracts such as those for cars or smartphones.

For researchers and practitioners interested in this field a wider context is important when it comes to assessing just how developed a young consumer is mentally as age is not everything, or as they say you should not judge a book by its cover. Table 7.1 for that reason is not a specific rule but more a general one when it comes to age and the early types of relationships children form with brands. However, these ages are critical times for brands and their youngest consumers as the experiential aspect of the relationship is not just at its most simplistic but also its most formative as memory nodes and associations are connected to the experiential triumvirate of brand, experience and memory.

It is also important to consider how different areas of childhood developmental theory, as elaborated in Table 7.1, may influence how a child or young person is affected by marketing and branding methods. As Table 7.1 shows, there are several areas of childhood developmental theory that may be helpful in understanding how children may respond to marketing techniques as they move through the various stages of childhood and adolescence.

The principles of each of these theories may be able to assist marketers and researchers not only to design, implement and monitor marketing programmes but also how they may be able to best go about positioning a brand. This is of course helpful for brands as they can start to develop brand salience, awareness, imagery and performance associations at an age where there may be few other competitors for a child's heart and mind.

But these theories also serve as a reminder that each child may be at a different stage of life and learning and to allow for a high degree of flexibility and latitude in their branding so that they can maintain a strong relationship through these early years of consumer life which in turn helps maintain a positive association once they become adults.

The three stages of branding and marketing development in a child: kids, tweens and early adulthood

Two of the most seminal researchers on marketing, children and developmental stages, John (1999) and Valkenburg and Cantor (2001), have models that relate to how children move through a consumer developmental process. While they differ on the number of steps, John (1999) only has three steps, Valkenburg and Cantor (2001) have four and they stop respectively at 12 and 16 years of age and both take an integrative approach to their construction. Although both models include developmental steps from some of the major theorists listed in Table 7.1, they do share in common an emphasis, from a developmental perspective, on the work of Piaget.

TABLE 7.1 Major theorists of childhood development

Theoretical approach	Principles of the theory	Theorist
Maturation	Growth and development occur in orderly stages and sequence. The individual genetic timetable affects rate of maturation	Arnold Gesell (1880–1961)
Psychodynamic	Behaviour is controlled by unconscious urges. Three components of the mind are id, ego and super ego	Sigmund Freud (1856–1939)
Psychosocial	Personality develops in eight stages throughout a lifetime. Development is influenced through interactions with family, friends and culture	Jean Piaget (1896–1980) Lev Vygotsky (1896–1934)
Cognitive	Qualitative changes in the way children think. The child is considered an active learner going through stages	Erik Erikson (1902–1994)
Behaviourist	Learning is gradual and continuous. Development is a sequence of specific conditional behaviours. Main emphasis is on the environment, not heredity. Observable behaviours are considered most important	John Watson (1878–1958) B. F. Skinner (1904–1990) Albert Bandura (1925)
Ecological	Balance between nature and nurture. Child is placed in the middle of concentric factors that all influence the child. Emphasis is placed both on environment and heredity	Uri Bronfenbrenner (1917–2005)
Information processing theory	We all have an innate learning ability. Children are born with specialised information processing abilities that enable them to figure out structure of development	Noam Chomsky (1928–)

Source: NSW Centre for Learning Innovation (2006).

With these models capped at age 16, this chapter has taken a broader perspective on the classification of branding to children to the age of 21, or what some parents call the empty nest stage of life when their children finally leave home and become truly independent. This is because in some parts of the world childhood can legally extend in some product categories, such as alcohol or even finance, until the age of 21. Then there is the developmental perspective from some theorists in Table 7.1, which states that age is merely a loose guide on how psychologically or mentally developed a person may be as not every 18-year-old is the same for a myriad of reasons. Even marketers implicitly recognise this as media and marketing habits do change markedly in each of these stages.

Tables 7.2, 7.3 and 7.4 therefore provide a guide to each stage of childhood development in a marketing and branding context and are based on the works of both marketing and childhood development theorists.

Baby, toddlers and childhood

This stage discusses some typical marketing or consumer behaviour that may be displayed by children aged from 0–11. This is a wide range of ages in terms of learning and developmental steps, but it is important to differentiate each age bracket here in terms of how they may not just act and behave as early consumers, but also how they experience, interact and engage with brands and then the impact of this on their later behaviour as consumers.

TABLE 7.2 Some marketing or consumer behaviour of children aged 0–11

Age/other descriptor	Marketing or consumer behaviour that may be displayed
0–2/baby and toddler	Interest in toys with bright and colourful designs, lights and sounds. Toys with textures, and easy learning based around elemental fine and gross motor skills. Sharing is difficult and need satisfaction based on immediacy. Basic building block and simple reward games popular. Still attached to teething or baby toys
3–4/early childhood	Develops an independent sense of humour based on conditioning and exposure to media such as a smart device, or TV shows like *Sesame Street*, starts to enjoy the company of others through possible attendance at a childcare centre, creative toys and activities (painting, drawing, sandpit) starts to become more popular, enjoys role-playing activities such as using cars or other brand characters such as Lego or Barbie. Brand resonance is usually restricted to products in a few distinct categories
5–7/mid-childhood	Starts schooling, skilled at colouring-in, puzzles, certain games, may enjoy organised sports and recreation activities such as football, dance, running, very adept at using a mobile or smart device, has a more independent sense of fashion style and is starting to identify and relate to brands across several categories. Early signs of emotional responses being based on cognitive processing

(continued)

124 Andrew Hughes

TABLE 7.2 *(continued)*

Age/other descriptor	Marketing or consumer behaviour that may be displayed
8–11/late childhood	May start to independently purchase more and more in different categories, especially if earning pocket money, has a developed social network based across school, social and recreation activities and family, may have their own account to use a mobile device on, usually their own, very engaged in organised activities such as sport and recreation, has a strong sense of relationship with 2–3 brands in several categories, and understands the difference between needs and wants, but still lacks a wide knowledge of all brands in categories. Emotional responses start to move from primary to primary and cognitive

Source: Adapted from John (1999) and Valkenburg and Cantor (2001).

Tweens

Tweens is one of the more interesting stages of children and marketing. Tweens are generally considered to be children too old to be considered children but too young to be seen as early adults and there are a wide range of definitions and debate based on age on what a tween is (Martensen, 2007). They cover some of the teen years but like all stages development is contextual to the individual. Importantly for marketers, economically this segment spend on their own, just in the US, $30 billion annually but influence $150 billion of their parents', spending (Chaet, 2012). This makes this segment alone worthy of significant interest from brands.

TABLE 7.3 Some marketing or consumer behaviour of children aged 12–15

Age/other descriptor	Marketing or consumer behaviour that may be displayed
12–15/ tweens	Emotional development and responses start to be based on deeper, more cognitive thoughts and actions, to be active on social media and will by the end of this period have accounts with several websites or apps, extensive social network based on school, family and friends, become very conscious of fashion style and brands and aware of several brands in each category where they have a higher social risk in consumption, 2–3 where the risk is lower, can recognise and express brand loyalty. Celebrity endorsement may be important in some categories Emotional responses more cognitive than primary, may have a job to supplant pocket money and have a medium degree of disposable income and financial independence. Primary source of influence starts to move away from parents and family to those outside the home and may experiment with illicit or adult substances or behaviours

Early adulthood

While many marketing and children researchers only have models until the end of the tween years or late teens, this chapter extends that to the age of 21, as many young consumers really don't have fully developed consumer minds until early adulthood. In a way, for some, their marketing and consumer childhood only ends when they have purchased that first car, got that first loan or finally signed a tenancy agreement.

This stage is more noticeable in the current day and age for the influence of digital in all aspects of their lives. From devices, to media, to experiences and how they purchase and consume, digital is the key influencer on their behaviour. As evidence of this the average weekly spend on mobile phones for someone aged between 16–24 in first-world nations is $US26 (Microsoft, 2013).

It is also the stage of childhood where brand experiences from earlier stages now become noticeable in consumer behaviour and relationships.

TABLE 7.4 Some marketing or consumer behaviour of children aged 16–21

Age/other descriptor	Marketing or consumer behaviour that may be displayed
16–18/ early adult	Emotional development and responses primarily cognitive in most normal situations and environments. Active on social media and has also probably embraced dark social apps like Snapchat and WeChat. May even be active content producers on social media such as Facebook, Instagram or other sites
	Toys are now primarily consigned to the attic or have been disposed of, may still be active in same sports and recreational activities that they first started in mid-childhood, independent consumers in several categories now probably due to increased financial and social independence from the family unit, may have 1–2 jobs to provide income and possibly is starting to consider higher involvement longer-term purchases such as cars, mobile devices or even holidays. Reaching end of physical development for some
18–21/ adult or college student	Although an adult, many consumers may retain some sort of relationship or affection for toys, games or brands from their tweens or childhood. This may be displayed through possession of these items even if they have moved out of home or started tertiary studies
	Most are now making their first adult high-involvement, high-risk purchases, such as cars, study, holidays, renting, mobile devices and possibly even loans and credit cards. Extensive knowledge, identity and relationships with several brands in several categories, even those that may be special or unique purchases
	While physical development has usually ended, many are still gaining maturity and true independence in a social, financial, psychological and personal sense. Some at this age may even be settling down or becoming parents themselves

Brands, branding and young consumers

Why brand to children?

Value

The economic and financial value of branding to children is staggering – in Italy alone the market is worth $US5 billion a year, with half of this on toys, and is currently growing at 9 per cent per annum (ANSA, 2017). Across the other side of the world in New Zealand the demand for that nation's milk products from parents in Asian markets drawn to its brand attributes of cleanliness, pristine environments and organic production values, has led to budget surpluses that are paving the way for the future of that nation (Field, 2017). It is no wonder then that so many brands are seeking ways to enter or develop these markets!

Then there is the lifetime customer value perspective. As Sasser *et al.*'s (1997) seminal paper notes, the value of having a customer for their lifetime is not just being able to create a sustainable business model but also the value that is gained through exposure to the brands and positive word-of-mouth recommendations from within the consumer's key reference groups. For a $5 pizza this may translate into literally tens of thousands of dollars over a consumer's lifetime. So if a child has a positive lifetime memory of family holidays that happened in a certain brand of car, and then that creates a flow-on effect to their own lifetime purchasing of the same brand of car, that could equal hundreds of thousands of dollars.

Even if the definition of lifetime is narrowed down to that of a product category or age bracket in childhood, the value could still be high in all metrics. An example here might be nappies or diapers, or even a movie franchise like *Harry Potter*, which is now worth $US25 billion due to the brand value in merchandising and movies, despite the fact that there have been no new books for several years now (Meyer, 2016).

With money such as this, and the marketing benefits of a strong relationship with brands over a customer's lifetime, it is no wonder so many brands are active in this space.

Relationship

Keller's customer-based brand equity model (1993) and Aaker's brand equity model (1991, 1996) are two good reasons why brands target children, even if not explicitly. That is, the relationship a brand can develop with a child can form the start of a consumer journey that may last literally from cradle to grave. It could be as simple as happy memories of a family holiday – from the car that took them there, and the toys they had with them, to what music was being played, where they stayed, their experiences at that place and even the food consumed or enjoyed – all brands that they developed a stronger attachment and connection with yet while probably having purchased very few of them.

Ownership of brands and relationships with brands is therefore something similar to what Vargo and Lusch (2004) discussed, that is something neither owned nor being necessarily tangible. While they called this service-dominant logic (SDL) perhaps in this area a more appropriate term would be kid-dominant logic (KDL) as for many children it is the intangible relationship, consumption, experience and emotions that are what they seek to own more than just their favourite toy.

For many children though the early years are formative in how they position, attach salient attributes and develop meaning for brands. The importance of these variables in the long term is reflected in Keller's and Aaker's models – that is, when they become adults these aspects of a brand transfer into very valuable components of brand equity.

For some children, this process can span generations from when perhaps their grandparents first developed their own relationship with a brand. Gresham and Shimp (1985) might describe this more as a case of classical conditioning, but exposure and experience to the brand is important for children (Phelps and Hoy, 1996). Lego is one such example of this, but also FMCG brands such as Nestle, Kellogg's or even Cadbury who likely owe much of their revenue to brand loyal customers that first sampled the product as a child and whose own parents probably were exactly the same when they were children.

Relationship between brands and consumers has always been important though, and not because of the value that may be co-created in one (Grönroos, 1994). In some cultures the relationship has significance across many variables (Palmer, 1997) such as meaning, identity, performance, personality, attributes, personality, judgement and quality (Grönroos, 1990). If a brand is able to establish positive and strong levels of these attributes during a child's formative years in a natural and authentic way then this is likely to translate into high levels of brand loyalty and brand equity when the child becomes an adult and starts their own family.

The 3Es of branding to children: emotions, enjoyment and experiences

Inextricably linked into relationship are the 3Es of branding to children – emotions, enjoyment and experiences. While these three could be broadly based under cognition and feeling, for many children the presence of each of these in any brand is critical to how they form a relationship and resonance with that brand.

The smarter and more nimble brands recognised this a long time ago and actively work to use these elements combined, creating brands that can connect and engage with consumers across many different segments and many different cultures (Gbadamosi, 2012).

Although not all of the variables that represent the 3Es can be listed here, two good examples that relate more specifically to children, and that are being used by brands, are brand characters and brand community.

Brand characters and heroes

Creating brand heroes is one way of building positive emotions, enjoyment and experiences with a brand. And if you create enough of them they can then even be turned into a billion dollar theme park like Disneyland or the Universal Studios Tour, or a multi-movie franchise such as *Toy Story*.

For those brands that target primarily a young market, such as Pixar, creating brand heroes is a non-stop process based on extensive market research. Recent brand valuations of some popular brand heroes, such as Postman Pat, the Wiggles, Peppa Pig, Thomas and Friends, and Disney and Pixar characters reveals the economic value alone in creating brand heroes (Costa, 2010).

Then there is the appeal of using brand characters, especially cartoon or animated ones. Their image will never be tarnished by scandal or gossip, they endure across generations and cultures, and they can easily be transferred on platforms of traditional or new media such as apps. The most successful children's brand campaign created in Australia in the last decade, *Dumb Ways to Die*, involves brand characters advocating safety around trains, has seen their videos viewed over 100 million times on YouTube, with 4.8 million shares, had a number one song on iTunes, and the app was downloaded 106 million times and was number one on its second edition release in 83 countries (McCann, 2016).

In an ethical context concerns have been raised over the use of animated characters in children's branding and marketing, especially in some categories such as food (Kraak and Story, 2015). Considering the widespread use of animated characters in this part of marketing these concerns do have validity, and policy formulators and governments should be considering ways to ensure that concerns don't transform into problems without restricting the development of brands either.

Brand community

Being part of a brand community is becoming more and more important to young consumers and in maintaining their relationship to a brand through to their journey to adulthood. As Muniz and O'Guinn's (2001) seminal article notes, the influence that brand communities have on consumers and consumer behaviour is becoming a key factor on their final purchase intentions. While Facebook, the biggest brand community in the world, is a great example of the power and importance of a brand on young consumers, other digital and non-digital elements have become important outlets for young brand consumers to interact with others from their brand community.

Sporting clubs like football giants Manchester United, Chelsea, and even the Olympics themselves have realised this in years past. Yet they are still far, far behind the massive online open brand communities (MOOBCs) established decades ago by the major entertainment brands such as Sony (PlayStation), Microsoft (XBox), and the size and sophistication of social media brands such as Pinterest and Instagram that are appealing to younger and younger audiences.

Both Sony and Microsoft's online gaming communities number in the tens of millions and many children enjoy playing every day against other children from all parts of the world via the popular PlayStation and XBox gaming platforms, highlighting how creating and investing in brand communities isn't just a fad but now a successful brand strategy (Fournier and Lee, 2009).

BERMY

The brand emotional response model for youth (BERMY) is a conceptual model aimed at recognising how young people and children engage, co-create and relate with brands and is unique due to the developmental concepts and their age in the young consumer life cycle as explained earlier. It is primarily designed for children from the mid-childhood stage and older.

While the model has its foundations in Keller's customer-based brand equity (CBBE) model, in no way is this intended to replace or supersede that. Instead it is more about being able to provide a conceptual framework on how brands and young people relate to one another in the early stages of life. It is therefore more general than specific, but also attempts to encapsulate the emotional responses a child or young person may show towards a brand that will end up in a relationship being formed.

It does have some unique steps and ladders that relate to each of the steps in the process, which applies to children due to their current level of learning and developmental growth. It also recognises that children are very rarely until later in their lives able to act as consumers in full control of the entire decision-making process as instead they are usually fulfilling other roles such as influencers or end-consumers (Calvert, 2008).

The first step, for example, considers how important the initial emotional response (IER) between a child and a brand can be. This could be as simple as a child being at the shops with their parents, and just by chance, walking down a toy aisle in a supermarket where they may be exposed to a new brand, even though

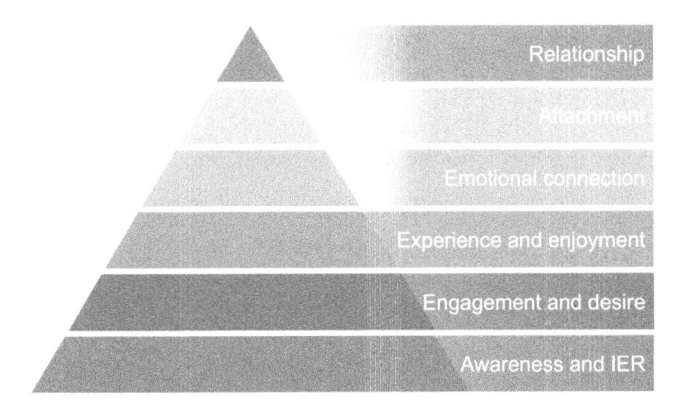

FIGURE 7.1 Brand emotional response model (BERMY): youth

they may not have been aware of it or have the intention of purchasing the brand. However, they may be likely to pick up that toy, despite the frowning looks or protestations from their parents, and thereby have that very first initial emotional response to the brand and attain awareness of it all at the same time.

The second step, engagement and desire, is concerned with explaining the level and intensity of desire and engagement by a young consumer after their first initial experience response and awareness of a brand. This is linked to salience in Keller's model, that is once the brand identity has been established after the first step, then a child is likely to move to a need to engage further with the brand through experiences such as media and toys. This further experience then creates a desire within the child for that to transition to the next stage of their relationship with the brand.

This stage can be identified by researchers and practitioners by measuring the levels of emotions such as desire, interest and passion. The higher the levels, the more likely that a child will progress to the next level in the relationship with the brand, a finding most parents already know. Some children may have a plateauing out of their desire for a brand at this stage as they may have further experiences of the brand that may see their interest and engagement levelling off.

Experience and enjoyment is about recognising that for many children having positive and significant levels of these means that they are starting to build a strong relationship with the brand. Typically at this stage a child will have purchased or be in regular contact with the brand and moved past desire to a more sustainable and stable emotional state with the brand. The need or want to have that toy or experience has been replaced by now by being able to really enjoy and experience everything that the brand has to offer. This builds on the associations and benefits of the brand with the child, strengthening the relationship and creating positive and powerful memories.

This level quickly transforms into an emotional connection with the brand, which could be based around many different needs and wants that are being satisfied through the enjoyment and experience of the brand. This is not as needy as that demonstrated in desire, but can, however, become an attachment to the brand, something commonly seen in how attached tweens become to social media. Although this attachment may wane as they get older, it never really disappears but rather morphs into a more mature attachment to the brand whose meaning and perception may alter as adult life is entered into.

And this is recognised in the relationship between brand and consumer. Although it is important to note here that what is unique is those earlier stages and emotional responses and experiences with the brand are now attached to powerful, positive, childhood memories that may mean that even if the consumer ceases using the brand, their association and relationship with it may last decades longer until they buy that same brand for their own children or grandchildren. A good example of this is Mickey Mouse and its longevity and strength as a brand across multiple cultures and markets.

For younger children, especially those at or below mid-childhood, this chapter proposes a further conceptual model that more closely matches developmental and learning abilities at that age. There is some similarity to BERMY, but the key point of the brand adoption curve (BAC) is that the emotional, experiential and engagement aspects are more relative for a child who is younger and looking for simplified but enriching experiences in their own context. This model is conceptual and based on the developmental authors in Table 7.1, but also on John (1999) and Valkenburg and Cantor (2001) and observational research, and is the subject of current research.

Having a model like this will go some way to helping researchers, practitioners, society and families understand just how their child may be engaging and relating to brands in their life.

Influencing the young consumer: family, tribes, belonging and fads

Media and information processing: keep it simple marketers!

Nursery rhymes demonstrate very simply how to convey information to children and young consumers – keep the information simple, fun, engaging and allow for information to be stored in long-term memory through some simple repetitive methods such as the use of music or characters. Recent work on the effect of television advertising by Gbadamosi *et al.* (2012) supports these findings, and follows on from the seminal work conducted by Rossiter and Robertson (1974).

Earlier work in attention capture, such as by Posner (1980) and Droit-Volet (2008), found that the less information on a screen and the slower that information is shown then the more likely that information can be retained. This is true for children as it is for adults – the simpler the message, the easier it can be retained, remembered and then recalled at the appropriate time by the child (Robertson and Rossiter, 1974). TV shows such as *Sesame Street*, *Postman Pat* and *Bob the Builder* are designed to allow a child to process, store and then recall that information when the time is right, but also in a fun and enjoyable way. This allows these shows to

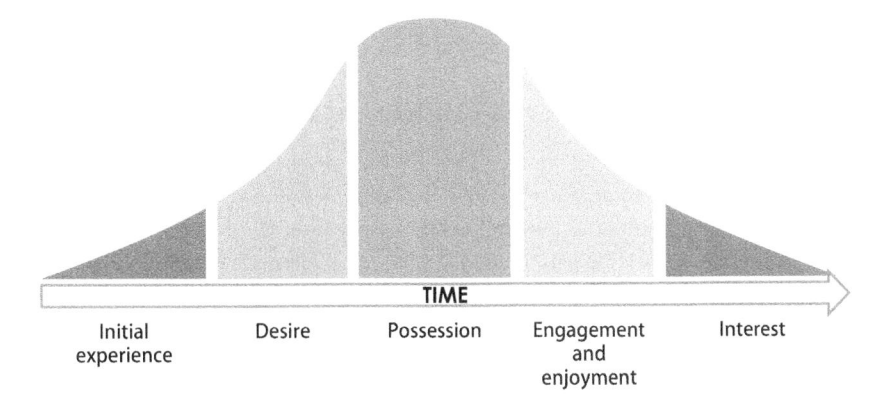

FIGURE 7.2 Children's brand adoption conceptual model

create brand personalities that closely match that of the child. As Aaker (1997) found, all brands have personalities that allow consumers to engage with them, or not as the case may be. But brand personalities also tell stories and help position a brand, evoking feelings and associations between themselves and consumers that create a resonance.

Even in experiential spaces, such as theme parks, it is important to keep the co-created experiences simple. Schmitt's (2010) five areas of experiences that a marketer can create can be applied to children as for adults but with the exception of keeping the experience simplistic and with the child's developmental and age in mind.

Brand experiences: happy memories and long-lasting relationships

Many theme parks stand in testament to the power of memories on long-term, strong and loyal relationships in us all – Disneyland and Legoland are both classic examples here. As Vargo and Lusch (2004) note in their seminal paper on the co-creation of value and service-dominant logic, ownership is moving from the physical to the intangible. This means that a consumer will possess a memory or a consumption experience for their lifetime, and for children this is no different.

Positive memories have been shown for a long time to have significant influence on attitudes to the brand and as antecedents on predictive consumption behaviour towards brands (Keller, 1987). This is evidenced through how many adults have strong connections with brands that they may not have had any experiences with since they were children, yet despite this gap of time, which may stretch into decades, they will usually end up buying the same toys that they had as youngsters.

Recreational brands such as zoos can build relationships with families, one of their key markets, because of their ability to create and maintain positive experiences. This can even extend to place branding, with resort destinations such as the Caribbean, Spain or even the French and Swiss Alps all being able to provide experiences that are hard to replicate but also that allow children to have fond memories of long after they were last there.

Keeping it in the family: the role of parents and grandparents

The importance of family in the brand behaviour of children cannot be underestimated by any marketer. Sheth (1974) recognised this and wrote a consumer behaviour decision model that highlighted the importance of families on individual and joint purchases made by people living together in a house, something that is no different in all cultures around the world (Gbadamosi, 2012).

As noted (Sheth, 1974) a person in the house can fulfil different roles for the same purchase. They can be either an influencer, consumer, purchaser and decision maker and sometimes even a combination of all of these roles. This means in a practical sense that a child could also be all of these things, so their knowledge of branding starts to grow from being restricted to just a few categories that they have direct engagement with, to ones associated with them fulfilling one of these roles in the house.

It is not just the stereotypical influences either of parents or grandparents that may be important here – it could be the integrated aspects of what they share with their children through shared experiences, culture, subculture and extended family that also have an influence on brand behaviour.

As parents or primary caregivers are undisputedly the biggest influencers on the brand behaviour of children, so can children be the biggest influencers on the brand behaviour of parents. Many a parent, for example, lists the quality of a camera as being a key heuristic when purchasing a smartphone simply because it means that they can capture the best possible images of their children. And of course there are many parents out there who can attest to the power of the child on their decision to visit certain fast-food outlets!

Even though parental influence starts to wane in the tweens, this does not necessarily dilute the impact of them on a child's behaviour with all of the various attributes of branding from salience, identity, performance, imagery, judgements, personality and resonance. As Braun-LaTour *et al.* (2007) point out, a child's memories of these brands and experiences are important in how adults perceive a brand's meaning later in life.

FOMO, YOLO and digital: rewarding the adventurers and pioneers

There is no doubt that as the young consumer hits the middle to later stages of the tween years all of a sudden FOMO (Fear of Missing Out), YOLO (You Only Live Once) and digital become key drivers of their brand relationships. A great many social influencers owe their success and wealth to these young consumers wanting to identify more with their future adult selves than their past child ones.

At the same time, many young consumers seek to become the brand adventurers and pioneers among their peers and their behaviour will move from being passive in some categories to very active – it is not uncommon for the friends count list on Facebook of many young people to be in the thousands by the time they hit 16 or 17, despite Facebook being only legal from the age of 13.

There is also a greater identification of brands that may be linked to rebellion – many a young teenager in Europe, for example, has a Spanish party resort (Ibiza or Majorca anyone?) as being high on their list of things to do without parents or someone wiser and more sane. It is also at this stage that any good social marketer will tell you that alcohol and illicit brands now move from being cognitive thoughts and aspirations into behavioural actions due to some young consumers' embrace of the dark side as they move from being dependent to independent of not only their family home but also that of their childhood.

This is not to say that brands that had a relationship with a child are then just cut adrift, more that they are buried in long-term memory (remember *Inside Out?*) until they are recalled at a different stage of life.

Consumers at this age are now chasing more adult and mature experiences and relationships with brands where they are able to connect their personality with that of the brand. Emerging technologies, such as virtual reality (VR) and augmented reality (AR), will probably be, within five years from you reading this page, common experiences with children in some parts of the world. They represent a new frontier on how brands will interact with children, being able to offer near complete sensory experiences that surpass any that have come before it. With over $US120 billion in revenue forecast in AR and VR by 2020 (Digiday, 2017) it is no wonder that brands are starting to invest more heavily in experiences in this area that are directly targeted at children and young people. Ethical questions though are being raised about limits needing to be placed on this technology, especially on how it may affect the cognitive and developmental learning of children (Foremski, 2017) so marketers do need to be careful.

Future thoughts

Branding to children should not be seen as exploitative by major brands. Indeed, for many of us reading this right now there are brands that we have had decades-long relationships with that we have now passed onto our own children.

Ethical behaviour of brands is becoming an important influence on consumer behaviour in this area, especially from a parental or care-giver perspective. Any brand that wants to operate successfully in this area should always be transparent about any potential harms or ill effects to children, even if they haven't been raised yet. Doing so is not just ethical, but smart business as these brands are likely to be perceived as having values that consumers seek out in relationships that they see as having decades-long time frames. With ethical concerns high, making research advances can be difficult in this area. Many researchers have turned to newer research methods such as social media or observational research and experimental to advance knowledge and further understand behaviour.

That aside, however, branding to children shows no signs of abating and as such there are many new areas of theory being explored such as the relationship between obesity, television advertising and children. Cross-culture research is also increasing as most studies to date have been limited to Western markets but with growing consumption in places such as India, China and emerging markets such as Africa, there is a growing need to understand how children in these markets relate, attach, engage and are influenced by brands.

Researchers have many areas in which they can explore and gain further understanding of how children and brands relate to one another and any further research findings will be gratefully received by practitioners and society alike.

Conclusion

This chapter was by no means an exhaustive examination of all of the theories and brand examples that relate to children and brands. The focus of this chapter was four-fold. First, to provide a definition and foundations of some of the factors and definitions, such as age and developmental cycle and to provide a broader frame to practitioners and researchers in which to consider how brands and children relate to one another.

Second, to define, describe and discuss the relationship between the three primary stages of childhood development and brands and branding methods. Third, to briefly discuss some of the reasons behind the importance of branding to children, such as being able to create and build relationships with children in a more natural and authentic way that allows for brand resonance and positive attitudes to the brand to last across generations. Finally, understanding how to communicate to young consumers through communication and information, and the importance of experiences on relationships between child and brand. The role of family and the ever-increasing influence of social media on children was also briefly discussed.

While the chapter may have only briefly examined the influence of brands on children there is no doubt that this area is far, far wider and more in-depth than any single chapter can convey due to the dynamic and fluid nature of what childhood is and how markedly it can differ due to many internal and external variables.

Regardless of age, development or variables brands will always be seeking their fame and fortune in this area of branding because of the importance of developing endearing relationships with the youngest of consumers that will possibly last for decades thereafter. Many brands from many categories can attribute their sustainability and competitive advantage to the relationship they developed with children but there are a great many more who regret that they did not develop such a relationship.

For those brands thinking of whether or not to co-create brands and brand relationships with children, as long as they can do this with transparency and a firm set of ethical values, there is no reason why they should not, as the opportunities are much like a child's imagination: endless.

References

Aaker, D. (1982). Positioning your product. *Business Horizons*, *25*(May/June), 56–62.
Aaker, D. (1991). *Managing brand equity*. New York: The Free Press.
Aaker, D. (1996). *Building strong brands*. New York: The Free Press.
Aaker, J. L. (1997). Dimensions of brand personality. *Journal of Marketing Research*, *34*, 347–356.
Alba, J. and Hutchinson, W. (1987). Dimensions of consumer expertise. *Journal of Consumer Research*, *13*(March), 411–453.
American Marketing Association. (2017). *Common language marketing dictionary*. http://marketing-dictionary.org/ama (accessed 23 August 2017).
Anderson, J. (1983). *The architecture of cognition*. Cambridge, MA: Harvard University Press.
ANSA. (2017). Spending on Italian children worth 3 bn. www.ansa.it/english/news/general_news/2017/03/09/spending-on-italian-children-worth-3-bn_cca92582-b2c5-4d78-a32d-94e63e7d1283.html (accessed 10 March 2017).
Braun-LaTour, K. A., LaTour, M. S. and Zinkhan, G. M. (2007). Using childhood memories to gain insight into brand meaning. *Journal of Marketing*, *71*(2), 45–60.

Calvert, S. L. (2008). Children as consumers: Advertising and marketing. *The Future of Children*, *18*(1), 205–234.
Chaet, H. (2012). The tween machine. *Adweek*. www.adweek.com/brand-marketing/tween-machine-141357/ (accessed 1 March 2017).
Chattopadhyay, A. and Alba, J. (1988). The situational importance of recall and inference in consumer decision making. *Journal of Consumer Research*, *15*(June), 1–12.
Costa, M. (2010). Brand characters can bring home the bacon. www.marketingweek.com/2010/11/09/brand-characters-can-bring-home-the-bacon/ (accessed 1 March 2017).
Digiday. (2017). How to drive marketing success with AR & VR technology. http://digiday.com/sponsored/deloittesbl-005-843-how-to-drive-marketing-success-with-ar-vr-technology/ (accessed 24 February 2017).
Droit-Volet, S. (2003). Alerting attention and time perception in children. *Journal of Experimental Child Psychology*, *85*(4), 372–384.
Droit-Volet, S., Clément, A. and Fayol, M. (2008). Time, number and length: Similarities and differences in discrimination in adults and children. *The Quarterly Journal of Experimental Psychology*, *61*(12), 1827–1846.
Field, M. (2017). Growing up with New Zealand's 'white gold'. http://asia.nikkei.com/magazine/20170302/Tea-Leaves/Growing-up-with-New-Zealand-s-white-gold (accessed 10 March 2017).
Foremski, T. (2017). Technologies of persuasion: Virtual reality and the dream marketing machine. *ZD Net*. www.zdnet.com/article/technologies-of-persuasion-vr-is-a-dream-marketing-machine/ (accessed 9 March 2017).
Fournier, S. and Lee, L. (2009). Getting brand communities right. *Harvard Business Review*, *87*(4), 105–111.
Gbadamosi, A. (2012). Exploring children, family, and consumption behavior: Empirical evidence from Nigeria. *Thunderbird International Business Review*, *54*(4), 591–605.
Gbadamosi, A., Hinson, R. E., Tukamushaba, E. K. and Ingunjiri, I. (2012). Children's attitudinal reactions to TV advertisements. *International Journal of Market Research*, *54*(4), 543–566.
Gresham, L. G. and Shimp, T. A. (1985). Attitude toward the advertisement and brand attitudes: A classical conditioning perspective. *Journal of Advertising*, *14*(1), 10–49.
Grönroos, C. (1994). From marketing mix to relationship marketing: Towards a paradigm shift in marketing. *Management Decision*, *32*(2), 4–20.
Grönroos, C. (1999). Internationalization strategies for services. *Journal of Services Marketing*, *13*(4/5), 290–297.
John, D. (1999). Consumer socialization of children: A retrospective look at twenty-five years of research. *Journal of Consumer Research*, *26*(3), 183–213.
Johnson, M. D. (1984). Consumer choice strategies for comparing noncomparable alternatives. *Journal of Consumer Research*, *11*(December), 741–753.
Kapferer, J. (1992). *Strategic brand management: New approaches to creating and evaluating brand equity*. London: Kogan Page.
Keller, K. L. (1987). Memory factors in advertising: The effect of advertising retrieval cues on brand evaluations. *Journal of Consumer Research*, *14*(3), 316–333.
Keller, K. L. (1993). Conceptualizing, measuring and managing customer-based brand equity. *Journal of Marketing*, *57*(1), 1–23.
Keller, K., Heckler, S. and Houston, M. (1998). The effects of brand name suggestiveness on advertising recall. *Journal of Marketing*, *62*, 48–57.
Kotler, P. (2000). *Marketing management* (10th edn). Upper Saddle River, NJ: Prentice Hall.
Kraak, V. I. and Story, M. (2015). Influence of food companies' brand mascots and entertainment companies' cartoon media characters on children's diet and health: A systematic review and research needs. *Obesity Reviews*, *16*(2), 107–126.

Loftus, E. and Loftus, G. (1980). On the permanence of stored information in the human brain. *American Psychologist*, *35*(May), 409–420.
McCann (2016). Dumb ways to die. http://mccann.com.au/project/dumb-ways-to-die/ (accessed 1 March 2017).
Martensen, A. (2007). Tweens' satisfaction and brand loyalty in the mobile phone market. *Young Consumers*, *8*(2), 108–116.
Meyer, K. (2016). Harry Potter's $25 billion magic spell. http://time.com/money/4279432/billion-dollar-spell-harry-potter/ (accessed 11 March 2017).
Microsoft. (2013). Young adults revealed: The lives and motivations of 21st-century youth. www.iabaustralia.com.au/uploads/uploads/2013-10/1382482800_c2c193f455812b00f573e82911cbf963.pdf (accessed 8 March 2017).
Muniz, A. M. and O'guinn, T. C. (2001). Brand community. *Journal of Consumer Research*, *27*(4), 412–432.
Nedungadi, P. and Hutchinson, W. (1990). Recall and consumer consideration sets: Influencing choice without altering brand evaluations. *Journal of Consumer Research*, *17*(December), 263–726.
NSW Centre for Learning Innovation. (2006). A basic introduction to child development theories. http://lrrpublic.cli.det.nsw.edu.au/lrrSecure/Sites/LRRView/7401/documents/theories_outline.pdf (accessed 1 February 2017).
Palmer, A. (1997). Defining relationship marketing: An international perspective. *Management Decision*, *35*(4), 319–321.
Phelps, J. E. and Hoy, M. G. (1996). The Aad–Ab-PI relationship in children: The impact of brand familiarity and measurement timing. *Psychology & Marketing*, *13*(1), 77–105.
Posner, M. I. (1980). Orienting of attention. *Quarterly Journal of Experimental Psychology*, *32*(1), 3–25.
Ries, M. and Trout, J. (1979). *Positioning: The battle for your mind*. New York: McGraw Hill.
Robertson, T. S. and Rossiter, J. R. (1974). Children and commercial persuasion: An attribution theory analysis. *Journal of Consumer research*, *1*(1), 13–20.
Rosch, E. and Mervis, C. (1975). Family resemblences: Studies in the internal structure of categories. *Cognitive Psychology*, *7*(October), 573–605.
Rossiter, J. R. and Robertson, T. S. (1974). Children's TV commercials: Testing the defenses. *Journal of Communication*, *24*(4), 137–144.
Russo, E. and Johnson, E. (1980). What do consumers know about familiar products? In Richard J. Lutz (ed.), *Advances in consumer research* (Vol. 7, pp. 417–423). Provo, UT: Association for Consumer Research.
Sasser, W. E., Schlesinger, L. A. and Heskett, J. L. (1997). *Service profit chain*. New York: Simon & Schuster.
Schmitt, B. H. (2010). *Customer experience management: A revolutionary approach to connecting with your customers*. New York: John Wiley & Sons.
Sheth, J. N. (1974). A theory of family buying decisions. *Models of Buyer Behavior*, 17–33.
Valkenburg, P. M. and Cantor, J. (2001). The development of a child into a consumer. *Journal of Applied Developmental Psychology*, *22*(1), 61–72.
Vargo, S. L. and Lusch, R. F. (2004). Evolving to a new dominant logic for marketing. *Journal of Marketing*, *68*(1), 1–17.
Ward, J. and Loken, B. (1986). The quintessential snack food: Measurement of product prototypes. In Richard J. Lutz (ed.), *Advances in consumer research* (Vol. 13, pp. 126–131). Provo, UT: Association for Consumer Research.
Wind, Y. (1982). *Product policy: Concepts, methods and strategy*. Reading, MA: Addison-Wesley.
Wyer, R. and Srull, T. (1989). Person memory and judgement. *Psychological Review*, *96*, 58–83.

8
PRICING, INCOME AND BRAND SYMBOLISM

Exploring young consumers' understanding of value

Diliara Mingazova and Ayantunji Gbadamosi

Introduction

The discourse of price as a key element of marketing mix is now well established in the marketing literature. This is commonly associated with the fact that it is the only element that yields revenue out of all of the marketing mix factors, while others represent costs (Armstrong *et al.*, 2017). Indeed, price is crucial to a firm's marketing strategy and overall profitability. Fundamentally, the discussion of price covers a myriad of issues including costs, pricing objectives, competition, perceived value, customers' reaction to price as a marketing stimulus and many others. The main focus of pricing strategy has been stated as maximising the profit of the sellers by capturing the heterogeneous product valuation of the customers and accounting for competition and cannibalisation (Kim *et al.*, 2009). It is important to state that the significance of price is not limited to the business organisations offering their goods and services to fill the needs in the marketplace but also relates to consumers using these goods and other stakeholders such as government and non-government agencies. For instance, Khan *et al.* (2012) show that public health pricing instruments like taxation could be used to reduce the consumption of energy-dense food and possibly the predominance of obesity among young consumers in the US. While this finding is US related, it is logical to contend that the postulation will have a wider relevance in the society beyond the context of this study. By and large, economic activities linking pricing strategies of marketers, consumers' income, and how consumers react to the issues is a focal subject in the marketplace dynamics. Similarly, this is a potent topic when considered in the context of young consumer behaviour. As a relevant example, family income has been a major influence in various areas of children's development and well-being. In a study by Gibb *et al.* (2012) on childhood family income and life outcome in adulthood, it was found that low family income during the childhood stage of life could be linked to a range of economic and educational disadvantages in adulthood. This is not surprising as income creates opportunities for purchases, some of which are goods, services and experiences that are beneficial for children's upbringing. For instance, children consume several food items, wear clothes, shoes, attend amusement parks, benefit from the services of hairstylists and a host of many others. Gbadamosi (2012) categorises these products into routine products and special products. According to Gbadamosi (2012), the routine products, as indicated by their name, are consumed frequently and tend to be relatively cheaper when compared to the special products that are only consumed once in a while. Clearly, some of these market offerings could be gender specific, age related or known in various other possible categorisations. Meanwhile, in this day and age, children in households are becoming increasingly involved in some of the consumption-related roles and some of these include pricing issues. So, given that the impact of pricing and consumers' interpretation of price and value of market offerings can be different across different consumer groups, this chapter focuses on young consumers' understanding of value and how these are linked to income and the symbolic aspect of brands. Meanwhile, research on children as consumers is growing (e.g. Ji, 2002, 2008; Cook, 2008, 2010; Marshall, 2010 and others) because both academics and practitioners now recognise that the young consumer segment is attractive for businesses and is relatively un-researched. For example, in such disciplines as consumer culture and consumer behaviour, little is known about children as consumers. The young consumer segment can be seen as distinctive and valuable and if a greater understanding could be gained of how young consumers perceive and understand consumerism and elements of the marketing mix, it will be enriching from both the academic and practitioner's perspectives (Berey and Pollay, 1968; Leigh and Gabel, 1992; McNeal, 1999).

Marketing mix: price and young consumers

It is widely accepted that careful management, organisation and planning of the marketing mix are important undertakings for practitioners because they contribute to the creation of competitive advantages. Interestingly, some scholars and practitioners argue that the price element of the marketing mix is the *most* important because it generates revenue and has a direct and immediate effect on consumer behaviour (Robicheaux, 1976; Kellerman *et al.*, 1995; Gbadamosi *et al.*, 2013). Also, price-related activities can and do affect other significant business performance aspects, for instance Yoo *et al.* (2000) argue that price selection and frequency of use of the price promotions can affect brand equity. Brand equity is an important financial asset for organisations and one that can create competitive advantages (Aaker, 1991; Lassar *et al.*, 1995; Yoo *et al.*, 2000, p. 195). Furthermore, despite the significance of the price factor in relation to other aspects, such as consumer purchasing decisions and customer knowledge, it is surprising that very little is known about children as consumers and the price factor (Damay *et al.*, 2011, 2014).

Young consumers or children as consumers are a very attractive and distinct segment for a wide range of businesses in a variety of industries because children have their own spending power and they do influence family purchasing decisions. Moreover, they are not only *current* consumers but also *future* consumers once they move from childhood to adulthood (Berey and Pollay, 1968; McNeal, 1999). Therefore, it is important to gain an understanding of how children understand the concept of the marketing mix of which price is one of the most significant elements from a broader marketing perspective. Scholars and business practitioners, for example, can better understand their product choices and shopping behaviour if such understanding can be gained. For example, it is well accepted among marketers that price is an information cue for consumers, which influences their decision-making process (Helgeson and Beatty, 1987).

There are many definitions of 'price' in a wide variety of academic literature and for the purpose of this chapter, the definition formulated by Zeithmal (1988, p. 10) from the consumer's perspective is considered the most suitable, which is that 'price is what is given up or sacrificed to obtain a product'. Furthermore, Zeithmal (1988) acknowledges the relationships between price, quality and consumers' buying decisions and states that there is a firm link between a high price and consumers' high-quality expectations. However, the high-price/high-quality expectation leads to a greater economic sacrifice and it is the collision of these two factors that leads to the complex buying decisions. Despite these sophisticated relationships between price and consumers' buying behaviour, there are some interesting ideas that can be teased out from it in relation to *children as consumers* and the way they make *buying decisions*.

Children's price decision-making

Decision-making about price as one of the marketing mix elements can vary with the type of customer involved. Pagla and Brennan (2014, p. 698) argue that 'older children perceive brands to be better value-for-money than do younger children'. Relevantly, Bowen (2000, p. 20) argues that '72% of children say you must pay more to get good quality. Consequently, price has an effect on children just as it does on adults, maybe even more.' Furthermore, Williams *et al.* (2016, p. 5881) argue that children perceive price in terms of affordability. They further clarify that,

> by 9–10 years of age, children had started to incorporate price magnitude and comparative prices into their decisions in addition to affordability, and by 11–12 the majority considered these first-order concepts. However, in the 13–14-year-old age group, children were less likely to mention affordability.
> *(Williams* et al.*, 2016, p. 5881)*

In a related study, Turner and Brandt (1978) identify that children (4–8 years old) can compare and compute unit price in order to make efficient purchase decisions. Similarly, Lindstrom and Seybold (2003) argue that children as young as

6 years old understand the value of money and by 8 years old they are able to make a purchase decision on the basis of the value that they can gain from the product. Furthermore, a slightly different perspective on price and young consumers in relation to purchase decision-making is provided by Moschis and Moore (1979), who investigated how young consumers (7–12 years old) use price and brand names as the most important criteria for their purchase decision-making. They posit that 'apparently, perceived product attributes at this stage outweigh social influences, although the relative importance of these factors seems to depend on the type of product being evaluated' (Moschis and Moore, 1979, p. 110). Interestingly, Damay *et al.* (2014) clarify that price is not the only factor that can influence children's buying decisions and that they tend to prefer well-known brands regardless of their higher prices. Therefore, it is important to recognise such elements of price as value, more specifically the concept of perceived value for young consumers as they can have profound implications on how they make consumption decisions.

Major pricing strategies and perceived value among young consumers

Traditionally, scholars start explaining the concept of price from the point of view of its multi-faceted nature, as it contains various elements from accounting, psychology and economics, which combine to contribute to our understanding of the subject (e.g. Gbadamosi *et al.*, 2013; Baines *et al.*, 2017). Consequently, it takes an understanding of various issues including supply and demand, costing, price perception and many others in order to set the price that is economically effective for organisations and psychologically appealing and satisfying for consumers. Fundamentally, the marketing literature often recognises four main pricing strategies/orientations, which are depicted in Figure 8.1.

A great deal of research attention has been paid to how *consumers perceive the value* of market offerings, which can be linked to the way they react/respond to price changes. These have been very helpful in providing insight into the topic. Meanwhile, in the context of young consumers, Webley (2005, p. 54) posits an interesting idea in relation to children as economic agents. He states that,

> while children may observe the functioning of the adult economy by going shopping with their parents, watching TV reports about unemployment, by reading, and by talking to teachers and others, they also participate in it and create their own autonomous economic world.

The issue of how young consumers interact with price and understand value in the marketplace can be examined in relation to their stages in life. For example, Burris (1983) shows that development of economics knowledge among children is stage-orientated and consistent with the Piagetian view on children and development of their social knowledge, which, they argue, occurs in a linear way. In this study, he shows that, at an early age (4–5 years old), children perceive value/price

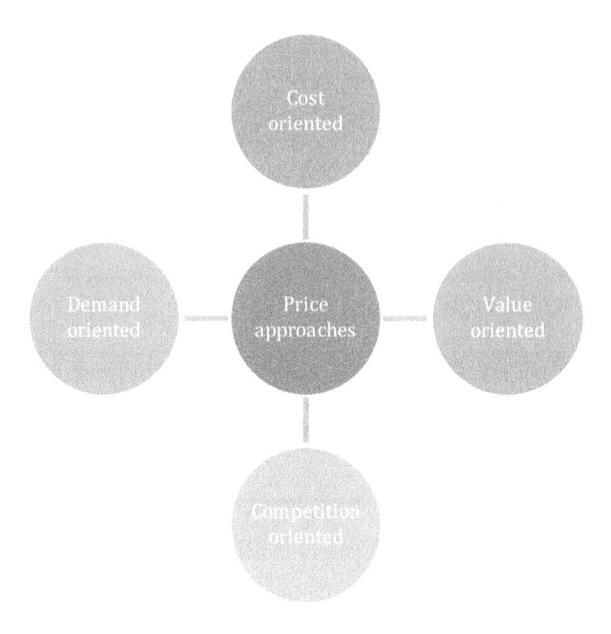

FIGURE 8.1 Price orientations

Source: Adapted from Baines et al. (2017).

on the basis of the object's material/physical characteristics (e.g. diamonds cost less than a wristwatch because diamonds are smaller). At the next stage (7–8 years old) children perceive price and value on the basis of object's usefulness and functions (e.g. a car is expensive because it takes people from one place to another, a wristwatch is more expensive than a book because a wristwatch shows the time). Then, children in the next category (11–12 years old) understand price/value on the basis of inputs/costs that occur during the production process (e.g. shoes cost more than candy because shoes need more time to be made). So, it is not surprising that in another related view, Webley (2005, citing Berti and Bombi, 1988) simply states than children's perception and understanding of price is primarily based on the characteristics of the goods and does not necessarily connect to the categories of supply and demand, which are well used in economics theories of which some are depicted in Figure 8.1. So, this idea of the importance of product characteristics to children could logically be linked to the concept of product value and then extended to the well-developed ideas about brand symbolism. This resonates with the common saying of beauty being defined best in the eyes of the beholder.

Product/brand perceived value and young consumers

The notion of customer perceived value is multi-dimensional and has been explained in a myriad of ways (El-Adly and Eid, 2017). One of these perspectives is offered by Woodruff (1997, p. 142) in a definition that explains customer value as 'a customer's perceived preference for and evaluation of those products attributes, attributes' performances, and consequences arising from use that facilitate (or block) achieving the customer's goals and purposes in use situation'.

If we examine this critically, it could be stated that it is not a radical departure from the claim of Zeithaml (1988, p. 14) who shows that perceived value can be viewed as a 'consumer's overall assessment of the utility of a product (or service) based on perceptions of what is received and what is given'. In a somewhat similar theoretical position, Sweeney and Soutar (2001) suggest that the notion of perceived value could be conceptualised as the value for money concept, which is based on the relationship between quality and price. But how does this happen within the discourse of young consumer behaviour? What we know is that despite the growing stream of research that addresses consumer perceived values among adults, very little is known about how children perceive value from their own perspective (Williams et al., 2016). In a study that centres on how value is perceived by children, Williams et al. (2016) note that children's perceptions of value are formed through such categories as benefits (what they received) and sacrifices (what they have to give up). They identify a number of benefits associated with market offerings to include the following types: emotional, social, functional value and curiosity. Furthermore, in this study, price and risk (monetary risk and product performance risk) perceptions have been identified as sacrifices for children. These findings are based on the ideas in the consumer socialisation process and the linear development of consumer knowledge originally developed by John (1999). Overall, it could be stated that as children grow older, their value perception changes in a linear way.

Meanwhile, the existing viewpoints regarding customer value have been criticised on the grounds that they fail to include the aspects of experiential and hedonic, symbolic and expressive values but rather are based on functional and instrumental values (Smith and Colgate, 2007; El-Adly and Eid, 2017). However to have a deeper level of understanding of this phenomenon, this point cannot be ignored. It is not surprising that Holbrook (2006) proposes that fantasies, feelings and fun, which are three key aspects of the consumption experience, all significantly contribute to customer-perceived value. Understandably, these are the terrains where young consumers thrive. Accordingly, their perceptions of value are most likely to be driven by these elements. This is demonstrated in the claim of Woolley (1997) who acknowledges that children enjoy fantasy and have a propensity towards it, which supports the claim of Rose et al. (2012, p. 84) that 'they [children] like fantasy and generally react positively to fantasy-based advertisements'. This provides a reasonable justification for the findings of Nairn et al. (2008, p. 633) who argue that for children, 'the major benefit a brand can provide is entertainment and fun'.

Brand, branding and perceived value

The importance of brand in the marketing parlance cannot be overemphasised. The classic definition of a brand provided by Keller (1998, p. 5), which could be linked to the concept of perceived value sees it as 'a set of mental associations, held by the consumer, which add to the perceived value of a product or service'. Clearly, the value-oriented approach to pricing requires organisations to gain great understanding of their market segments and gain deep understanding of the true value that consumers gain from the products or services they acquire. It is therefore understandable that branding and the associated elements such as brand symbolism, brand awareness, brand image, identity, personality and others contribute to the formation of perceived value. Hence, if young consumers constitute the targeted segment, marketers have to gain a deep understanding of how children engage, perceive and use brands.

There is a well-developed stream of literature that addresses young consumers' brand awareness mainly by using developmental principles of psychology. The brand awareness concept could be linked to the price element and children's price sensitivity (Williams *et al.*, 2016). Consequently, it is important for practitioners to be aware of existing research and the associated findings on the brand awareness concept in relation to children. We will now explore some of these findings. Achenreiner and John (2003) argue that children recognise brand names at the age of 3–4 years old. However, as children grow older, their level of brand recognition and recall increases. By the time they reach the age of 7–8 years old they are able to name and recognise several brands under many product categories (Rubin, 1974; Rossiter, 1976; Ward *et al.*, 1977; McNeal, 1992). It is also recognised that children do request products by brand names, as it is a source of product information (Otnes *et al.*, 1994). These findings highlight the relevance and importance of brands to the world of children. Furthermore, Achenreiner and John (2003) identify that children who have reached the age of 12 are using brand names as cues to make consumer judgements. In this research, they further argue that, as they develop, children are able to use brands at the conceptual level and not just the perceptual level. Brand awareness, which refers to the child's brand preferences, starts to appear around the age of 3, and increases over time. Essentially, brand awareness might vary between different brands and can be influenced by the child's level of cognitive development and the economic group to which he/she belongs (Guest, 1964). Interestingly, research has been carried out with children to seek to establish at what age they recognise logos. Valkenburg and Buijzen (2005, p. 464) were able to report that 'by the age of 2, children are able to recognise 8 out of 12 brand logos and by the age of 8, they are able to recognise 100% of the logos'. It is evident that children have great levels of brand awareness from a very early age, which may have an effect on their price/value sensitivity.

Meanwhile, despite much successful research using the Piaget mode of developmental psychology in the marketing field in order to study young consumers, it still faces criticism from researchers who recognise the importance of consumer culture theory (CCT) as an approach to improve our understanding of how the child relates to brands and this has consequences for their understanding of price and value. For example, Nairn *et al.* (2008) explain three reasons why the socialisation approach of studying the child's relationships with the brand needs to be expanded through the application of CCT. The first reason is that CCT would enable not only age factors, but also factors such as gender, ethnicity, social class, family income and others. The second reason relates to the emotional aspects of consumption, peer-group influence and the changes in social interpretations of symbols. The final reason is that it would enable researchers to consider the social and cultural influences on the process of interaction between the child and symbolic brands. Consequently, insightful knowledge about young consumers can be gained and their own perception of value can be understood, which can then be used to identify the effective price.

In order to gain a better understanding of young consumers' perceived value, it is expected that different aspects of branding will be studied and there are two main theoretical approaches used by marketers to study this phenomenon. These are: (1) the principle of the child cognitive development model and (2) CCT. The first stream of researchers study children by using the principle of child cognitive development where the fundamental principles of socialisation are used. John's (1999) research is a fundamental paper in this area. In the study in question, John (1999) used the Piaget (1968) model in order to explain the consumer socialisation of children and she explains how the child develops as a consumer as his/her knowledge, skills and values develop over the different age ranges. As has been shown earlier in this chapter, this approach has been successfully used to add to our knowledge of such aspects as children's price understanding, buying decisions and others. Therefore, the way young consumers understand and perceive value is useful for marketers in order to make predictions in relation to supply and demand and fix an appropriate price for young consumers.

Young consumers and price sensitivity

Wakefield and Inman (2003, p. 201) suggest that 'price sensitivity refers to the extent to which individuals perceive and respond to changes or differences in prices for products or services'. Also, existing research proposes that in different product categories consumers react differently to the price changes (Gardner, 1971). For example, in the situation where the high level of product risk occurs (pharmaceutical products for example) consumers are less price sensitive. Tellis (1988, p. 340) explains 'the reason is probably consumers' concern with the safety, effectiveness and timing rather than with the price of pharmaceutical products'. Furthermore, promotional frequencies have also been recognised as factors that can influence consumers' price sensitivity for both functional and hedonic goods (Wakefield and Inman, 2003). Additionally, the income of consumers has been a factor influencing our understanding of price sensitivity. For example, Jones et al. (1994) identify a relationship between low-income consumers and a variety of product categories. Therefore, scholars are keen to understand better consumers' price sensitivity in order to set economically effective prices. Gbadamosi (2009) also demonstrates this in the context of low-involvement products in which low-income women consumers simply show loyalty to the price of these products rather than to any particular brands as they switch between stores' own brands and manufacturer brands when they are on special offers. This clearly shows the incidence of price sensitivity.

In relation to young consumers, McNeal (2000) argues that by the age of 7, children are 'active shoppers', influencers of their parents' decision-making and consumers who use their pocket money and understand price variations of different products in different stores. Moreover, children have been perceived as not being price-sensitive agents, however, this view has changed in recent years. Children's price sensitivity is affected by their experiences, brand and product knowledge, motivations and wealth. Not surprisingly children's price sensitivity decreases in situations with higher-priced products with which they have little experience and/or knowledge. Gbadamosi (2012) raises a relevant point in the context of developing countries, he proposes that marketers whose target audience is children should apply the consumer-oriented approach in order to develop their marketing strategies directed at this group of consumers. Furthermore, he clarifies that, in relation to price:

> [I]t is important that marketers consider the fact that while children are mostly not as price sensitive as adults and could own their resources; in most cases it is their parents who might be price sensitive as they are the ones in control of the resources. So, pricing strategies for relevant products could be formulated to have a reflection of this complexity.
>
> *(Gbadamosi, 2012, p. 601)*

Therefore, it is clear that young consumers could be price sensitive, however the parents' influence is significant especially in terms of higher-value goods. Children as consumers acquire knowledge about prices from their parents through the well-known socialisation processes, however, children *themselves* are considered to be powerful consumers and it is important to gain an understanding of how price changes might influence their buying decisions. In their research, Boland *et al.* (2011) argue that children's purchasing decisions, like those of adults, are also influenced by sales promotions, which can be linked to their price perception and sensitivity towards it. It is therefore intelligible to concur with McNeal (2000) that marketers have to be honest, straightforward, enthusiastic and use language that is understandable to children when they price to them.

Income and brand symbolism

Children have been recognised as active and powerful consumers since 1960 and recent statistical data reveals their great spending power. For instance, the Office of National Statistics records that in 2000 the value of the children's market in the UK was £117 billion and furthermore that around 70 per cent of children under 16 years old in the UK receive pocket money (UK ONS Social Trends, 2009). Additionally, the Childwise Monitor Report (2009, cited in Marshall, 2010) found that 84 per cent of children in the age category of 5–16 have a regular income. It has to be kept in mind that children not only have their own disposable income, which tends to be sourced through pocket money/allowances and gifts of money, which they spend for their own needs, but they also influence their parents' purchasing decisions (McNeal and Yeh, 1997; John, 1999). Kuhn and Eischen (1997) argue that children participate in both impulse and planned purchasing decisions. Children have their own spending power and scholars recognised that children's income (especially their pocket money) supports the children's economic socialisation, which is mainly facilitated by their parents. Interesting insights have been identified in relation to the low-income families and symbolic meaning of brands and their values for these families. Middleton *et al.* (1994) suggested that between 1983 and 1993, Britain had a clear socio-economic division for children. Consumption processes could be linked to the increased level of income inequality (Harvey, 2001). It was identified that parents from families with a low level of income tend to believe that their children should not stand out from their peers, and therefore they buy almost everything that they request (everyday basic necessities) and deprioritise expenses on social activities, holiday and other major purchases (Kempson, 1994; Middleton *et al.*, 1994). A study by Elliott and Leonard (2004) identifies the symbolic role of brands for low-income families' purchase decisions. The authors argue that in low-income families children have less control over their parents' purchase decisions and parents very often do not have sufficient knowledge about less expensive products and therefore they buy the most popular brands. Similar ideas are supported by Hamilton (2009), who proposes that in low-income families, consumption decisions are based on careful budgeting because money is central to their lives. Consequently, children are very often excluded from grocery shopping in order to keep budgeting in balance and take children's attention away from unaffordable products. Also, parents in low-income families reduce parent–child disagreement and gain emotional benefits when they satisfy some of the children's shopping requests because this helps them to insure that children are not affected by their financial situation (Hamilton, 2009). Elliott and Leonard (2004, p. 349) recognise the symbolic value of brands in low-income families (in relation to Nike trainers) and argue that 'a poor family may be more likely to buy their child branded trainers because they are aware of the absence of money in their life and are using the symbolic meaning of branded goods to fill that gap'.

Leigh and Gabel (1992) show that for young consumers, feelings of group affiliation is very important, therefore symbolic consumption is highly relevant for them. Also, Bowen (2000) clearly states that children are not junior adults, but rather that peer-group support is more important for them than for adults and that they tend to choose products/brands that hold a specific symbolic meaning, which helps them to overcome peer pressure. Consequently, the concepts of consumer behaviour, product/brand symbolism and segmentation should be carefully connected to the classic marketing mix tool, meaning to the pricing element of the marketing mix. By doing so, as proposed above, practitioners are better able to create a more competitive position and strategy.

Brand symbolism, price and young consumers

As has been briefly pinpointed earlier in this chapter, there are two main theoretical approaches that might be used to study young consumers towards gaining a better understanding of their knowledge of marketplace issues including pricing. Cook (2008, 2010) argues that children have, to date, largely been 'invisible' in the different aspects of consumerism. Moreover, he stresses that children should be included in the consumer culture research area to further our overall understanding as they are consumers and members of society who are active, valuable and who tend to develop their own identity. Martens *et al.* (2004, p. 158) contend that studies of the types of children's goods, toy culture and other 'marketing, media and cultural studies have primarily been interested in the nature of markets for children's goods' as opposed to the children themselves. Essentially, they posit that researchers' interest in the symbolic meanings that children create around goods is neglected. Moreover, the importance of studying children themselves, rather than considering them as a homogeneous social group, and also the lack of the empirical research is emphasised (e.g. Martens *et al.*, 2004; Cody, 2012). Consequently, Martens *et al.* (2004, p. 161) argue that 'relatively little is known about how children engage in practices of consumption, or what the significance of this is to their everyday lives and broader issues of social organisation'.

Symbolic meanings of brands and social and cultural aspects of branding can contribute to our understanding of price in relation to young consumers because these issues uncover the symbolic aspects of young consumers' purchasing behaviour, which, as Holbrook (2006) argues, are missing in our understanding of perceived value. Consumption symbolism and the symbolic meanings of brands play a significant role for children's integration into a consumer world (Achenreiner and John, 2003). Putting it in more specific perspective, Achenreiner and John (2003) argue that children who are aged 7–8 years old are able to recognise consumption symbols because they are able to think symbolically. John (1999) makes a valuable contribution by reviewing the findings of 25 years of research on consumer socialisation. The phenomenon of children's development as consumers is assessed by John (1999) through the following categories: development of consumer knowledge, skills and values, which are developed through the different age periods. Additionally, she draws attention to the relation between 'age-related improvements in cognitive abilities' and 'consumer knowledge' (John, 1999, p. 184). It becomes clear from this study that the ability to think more abstractly within symbolic thoughts refers to the 'analytical stage' (ages 7–11). The next stage is called the 'reflective stage' (ages 11–16) where the child starts to recognise social meanings and begins to form his/her own identity. Meanwhile, in the 11–16 age group, the child pays more attention 'to the social aspects of being a consumer, making choices, and consuming brands' (John, 1999, p. 184). Significantly, at the analytical stage, the child does understand the value of material possessions and this refers to their skills of social comparison. This can also be linked to the concept of value perception and price. In another interesting study, Menzel *et al.* (2006) studied children aged 8–13 in order to explain the symbolic meanings that they allocate to souvenirs. Their research shows that children at ages 10–12 do understand the symbolic meanings of their possessions. Furthermore, scholars pay attention to the cultural and social aspects of consumption and children's different social contexts. For example, Elliott and Leonard (2004) emphasise the significant influence of peer pressure over children's consumer behaviour. Moreover, the authors argue that the need of the child to fit in with his/her peers is one the prime motivations for desiring a particular brand with particular symbolic meanings. Additionally, Elliott and Leonard (2004, p. 357) stress 'how children want to own the branded trainers that their peers do in order to enable them to have equal status in the eyes of their friends'. Recently, Rodhain and Aurier (2016) claim that children's relationships with brands constitute a highly social phenomenon. In their research the focus is on the school context and peers. In general, they conclude that the child–brand relationship concept is very dynamic and highly social in its nature.

Easterbrook *et al.* (2014) also show that children aged 8–15 years do have an understanding of consumer culture, 'symbolic meanings', and 'culture ideals' how they can be used in order to gain social status, or used in order to 'fit in' and be accepted by peers. These authors argue that media plays the role of facilitator of such processes. Significantly, Ross and Harradine (2004, p. 21) indicate the following themes in their research of children and branding: 'cool', 'older' and such that they 'would not be left out'. Nairn *et al.* (2008) also explore the 'cool' concept and children's interpretations of it in relation to brand symbolism. They note that 'cool' is 'a highly negotiated concept which does not adhere to an object or person in a straightforward manner' (Nairn *et al.*, 2008, p. 633). More recently, Granot *et al.* (2014) highlight 'cute' as another significant phenomenon and language of popular consumer culture. In this perspective, Granot *et al.* (2014) emphasise that this concept is organised around different theoretical categories of CCT: consumers' personal and collective identities, lived worlds of consumers, their experiences and sociological categories. By and large, marketers can create and deliver value to young consumers in myriad ways both implicitly and explicitly (e.g. a cool brand that they would desire because it would help them fit in). Therefore, marketing practitioners would be more able to establish an economically effective and psychologically appealing and satisfying price for young consumers if addressed from a holistic perspective.

Conclusion

The hallmark of contemporary marketing is about creating and delivering value to the target market. Achieving this is inextricably linked to the effective management of all of the marketing mix elements, among which is price. Meanwhile, apart from their increasing spending power as a consumer group, children influence a plethora of consumption decisions of their families including which type of products to buy, where to buy them, and in some cases the decision of which of the available alternatives offers the best value for what is being paid. Hence, the notion of children's understanding of value is crucial for successful marketing, especially in cases where these young consumers are closely involved. This brings to the fore the importance of understanding the numerous factors that underpin pricing of market offerings such as costs, demands, price sensitivity, income and many others. Clearly, highlighting each of these factors or a combination of them in young consumers' marketplace transactions is a worthy research endeavour. For instance, young consumers' incomes, which they earn from a variety of sources such as gifts from parents, grandparents, and part-time jobs, could be very significant to the notion of perceived value in their consumption context. Similarly, the disposable income available to their families could be of crucial relevance to how each child's consumption system is structured. Meanwhile, in this consumption system is the notion of brand symbolism, which emphasises the behind the surface meanings of brands to these young consumers. In this discussion context, the meanings of brands go beyond the functional attributes of the products but also extend to other realms such as using brands to construct and communicate identity, for self-esteem and to feel they belong in socio-cultural settings.

Theoretically, this chapter updates the extant literature in relation to young consumer behaviour concerning price as an element of the marketing mix as synthesised with income as a key factor that is significant in the family consumption system. It also links these to a number of issues within the brand discourse such as brand awareness and brand symbolism. The managerial implications of the issues discussed are huge and numerous. As shown in this chapter, practitioners targeting young consumers need to understand that they are becoming increasingly relevant as consumers in their own right and in some instances define value differently from what we have in conventional understanding. This tends to vary with different age groups. From the viewpoint that they contribute to their family consumption decisions, it is logical to incorporate this understanding into marketing strategies orchestrated to target families in various transactions. Similarly, integrating the role of brand symbolism associated with these young consumers into firms' strategic direction will be greatly valuable.

References

Aaker, D. (1991). *Managing brand equity: Capitalizing on the value of a brand name*. New York: Free Press.

Achenreiner, G. B. and John, D. R. (2003). The meaning of brand names to children: A developmental investigation. *Journal of Consumer Psychology*, 13(3), 205–219.

Armstrong, G., Kotler, P. and Opresnik, M. O. (2017). *Marketing: An introduction* (13th edn). Harlow: Pearson Education.

Baines, P., Fill, C., Rosengren, S. and Antonetti, P. (2017). *Fundamentals of marketing*. Oxford: Oxford University Press.

Berey, L. A. and Pollay, R. W. (1968). The influencing role of the child in family decision making. *Journal of Marketing Research*, 5(1), 70–72.

Berti, A. E. and Bombi, A. S. (1988). *The child's construction of economics*. Cambridge: Cambridge University Press.

Boland, W. A., Connell, P. M. and Erickson, L. M. (2012). Children's response to sales promotions and their impact on purchase behavior. *Journal of Consumer Psychology*, 22(2), 272–279.

Bowen, M. (2000). Kids culture. *International Journal of Advertising and Marketing to Children*, 2(1), 19–23.

Burris, V. (1983). Stages in the development of economic concepts. *Human Relations*, 36(9), 791–812.

Childwise. (2009). Monitor report 2008/2009. www.childwise.co.uk (accessed 10 January 2016).

Cody, K. (2012). 'No longer, but not yet': Tweens and the mediating of threshold selves through liminal consumption. *Journal of Consumer Culture*, 12(1), 41–65.

Cook, D. T. (2008). The missing child in consumption theory. *Journal of Consumer Culture*, 8(2), 219–243.

Cook, D. T. (2010). Commercial enculturation: Moving beyond consumer socialization. In *Childhood and consumer culture* (pp. 63–79). Basingstoke: Palgrave Macmillan.

Damay, C., Guichard, N. and Clauzel, A. (2011). When children confront prices: An approach based on price presentation. *Journal of Product & Brand Management*, 20(7), 514–525.

Damay, C., Guichard, N. and Clauzel, A. (2014). Children's price knowledge. *Young Consumers*, 15(2), 167–177.

Easterbrook, M. J., Wright, M. L., Dittmar, H. and Banerjee, R. (2014). Consumer culture ideals, extrinsic motivations, and well-being in children. *European Journal of Social Psychology*, 44(4), 349–359.

El-Adly, M. I. and Eid, R. (2017). Dimensions of the perceived value of malls: Muslim shoppers' perspective. *International Journal of Retail and Distribution Management*, 45(1), 40–56.

Elliott, R. and Leonard, C. (2004). Peer pressure and poverty: Exploring fashion brands and consumption symbolism among children of the 'British poor'. *Journal of Consumer Behaviour*, 3(4), 347–359.

Gardner, D. M. (1971). Is there a generalized price-quality relationship? *Journal of Marketing Research*, 8(2), 241–243.

Gbadamosi, A. (2009). Cognitive dissonance: The implicit explication in low-income consumers' shopping behaviour for 'low-involvement' grocery products. *International Journal of Retail and Distribution Management*, 37(12), 1077–1095.

Gbadamosi, A. (2012). Exploring children, family, and consumption behavior: Empirical evidence from Nigeria. *Thunderbird International Business Review*, 54(4), 591–605.

Gbadamosi, A., Bathgate, I. and Nwankwo, S. (eds) (2013). *Principles of marketing: A value-based approach*. Basingstoke: Palgrave Macmillan.

Gibb, S. J., Fergusson, D. M. and Horwood, L. J. (2012). Childhood family income and life outcomes in adulthood: Findings from a 30-year longitudinal study in New Zealand. *Social Science & Medicine*, 74(12), 1979–1986.

Granot, E., Alejandro, T. B. and Russell, L. T. M. (2014). A socio-marketing analysis of the concept of cute and its consumer culture implications. *Journal of Consumer Culture*, 14(1), 66–87.

Guest, L. (1964). Brand loyalty revisited: A twenty-year report. *Journal of Applied Psychology*, 48(2), 93.

Hamilton, K. (2009). Consumer decision-making in low-income families: The case of conflict avoidance. *Journal of Consumer Behaviour*, 8(5), 252–267.

Harvey, D. (2001). *Spaces of capital: Towards a critical geography*. London: Routledge.

Helgeson, J. G. and Beatty, S. E. (1987). Price expectation and price recall error: An empirical study. *Journal of Consumer Research*, *14*(3), 379–386.

Holbrook, M. B. (2006). Consumption experience, customer value, and subjective personal introspection: An illustrative photographic essay. *Journal of Business Research*, *59*(6), 714–725.

Ji, M. F. (2002). Children's relationships with brands: 'True love' or 'one-night' stand? *Psychology & Marketing*, *19*(4), 369–387.

Ji, M. F. (2008). Child–brand relations: A conceptual framework. *Journal of Marketing Management*, *24*(5–6), 603–619.

John, D. R. (1999). Consumer socialization of children: A retrospective look at twenty-five years of research. *Journal of Consumer Research*, *26*(3), 183–213.

Jones, E., Chern, W. S. and Mustiful, B. K. (1994). Are lower-income shoppers as price sensitive as higher income ones? A look at breakfast cereals. *Journal of Food Distribution Research*, *25*(1), 82–92.

Keller, K. L. (1998). *Strategic brand management: Building, measuring, and managing brand equity*. Upper Saddle River, NJ: Prentice Hall.

Kellerman, B. J., Gordon, P. J. and Hekmat, F. (1995). Product and pricing courses are underrepresented in undergraduate marketing curricula. *Journal of Product & Brand Management*, *4*(1), 18–25.

Kempson, E. (1994). *Outside the banking system*. London: HMSO.

Khan, T., Powell, L. M. and Wada, R. (2012). Fast food consumption and food prices: Evidence from panel data on 5th and 8th grade children. *Journal of Obesity*, 1–8. www.hindawi.com/journals/jobe/2012/857697/ (accessed 17 January 2016).

Kim, J. Y., Natter, M. and Spann, M. (2009). Pay what you want: A new participative pricing mechanism. *Journal of Marketing*, *73*(1), 44–58.

Kuhn, M. and Eischen, W. (1997). Leveraging the aptitude and ability of eight-year-old adults: And other wonders of technology. In *European Society for Opinion and Marketing Research conference proceedings* (pp. 160–170). www.warc.com/SubscriberContent/Article/leveraging_the_aptitude_and_ability_of_eight_yearold_adults,_and_other_wonders_of_technology/9276 (accessed 17 January 2016).

Lassar, W., Mittal, B. and Sharma, A. (1995). Measuring customer-based brand equity. *Journal of Consumer Marketing*, *12*(4), 11–19.

Leigh, J. H. and Gabel, T. G. (1992). Symbolic interactionism: Its effects on consumer behaviour and implications for marketing strategy. *Journal of Services Marketing*, *6*(3), 5–16.

Lindstrom, M. and Seybold, P. B. (2003). *Brandchild: Remarkable insights into the minds of today's global kids and their relationship with brands*. London: Kogan Page.

McNeal, J. U. (1992). *Kids as customers: A handbook of marketing to children*. Lanham, MD: Lexington Books.

McNeal, J. U. (2000). *The kids market: Myths and realities*. Ithaca, NY: Paramount Market.

McNeal, J. U. and Yeh, C. H. (1997). Development of consumer behavior patterns among Chinese children. *Journal of Consumer Marketing*, *14*(1), 45–59.

McNeal, R. B. (1999). Parental involvement as social capital: Differential effectiveness on science achievement, truancy, and dropping out. *Social Forces*, *78*(1), 117–144.

Marshall, D. (ed.) (2010). *Understanding children as consumers*. London: Sage.

Martens, L., Southerton, D. and Scott, S. (2004). Bringing children (and parents) into the sociology of consumption: Towards a theoretical and empirical agenda. *Journal of Consumer Culture*, *4*(2), 155–182.

Menzel Baker, S., Schultz Kleine, S. and Bowen, H. E. (2006). On the symbolic meanings of souvenirs for children. In R. W. Belk (ed.), *Research in consumer behavior* (pp. 209–248). Bingley: Emerald.

Middleton, S., Ashworth, K. and Walker, R. (1994). *Family fortunes.* London: Child Poverty Action Group.

Moschis, G. P. and Moore, R. L. (1979). Decision making among the young: A socialization perspective. *Journal of Consumer Research, 6*(2), 101–112.

Nairn, A., Griffin, C. and Gaya Wicks, P. (2008). Children's use of brand symbolism: A consumer culture theory approach. *European Journal of Marketing, 42*(5/6), 627–640.

Otnes, C., Kim, Y. C. and Kim, K. (1994). All I want for Christmas: An analysis of children's brand requests to Santa Claus. *Journal of Popular Culture, 27*(4), 183.

Pagla, M. and Brennan, R. (2014). The development of brand attitudes among young consumers. *Marketing Intelligence and Planning, 32*(6), 687–705.

Piaget, J. (1968). Quantification, conservation, and nativism. *Science, 162,* 976–979.

Robicheaux, R. A. (1976). How important is pricing in competitive strategy? Circa 1975. In H. W. Nash and P. R. Donald (eds), *Proceedings: Southern Marketing Association 1975 Conference* (pp. 55–57). Atlanta: Southern Marketing Association.

Rodhain, A. and Aurier, P. (2016). The child–brand relationship: Social interactions matter. *Journal of Product & Brand Management, 25*(1), 84–97.

Rose, G. M., Merchant, A. and Bakir, A. (2012). Fantasy in food advertising targeted at children. *Journal of Advertising, 41*(3), 75–90.

Ross, J. and Harradine, R. (2004). I'm not wearing that! Branding and young children. *Journal of Fashion Marketing and Management: An International Journal, 8*(1), 11–26.

Rossiter, J. R. (1976). Visual and verbal memory in children's product information utilization. *ACR North American, 3,* 523–527.

Rubin, R. S. (1974). The effects of cognitive development on children's responses to television advertising. *Journal of Business Research, 2,* 409–419.

Smith, J. B. and Colgate, M. (2007). Customer value creation: A practical framework. *Journal of Marketing Theory and Practice, 15*(1), 7–23.

Sweeney, J. C. and Soutar, G. N. (2001). Consumer perceived value: The development of a multiple item scale. *Journal of Retailing, 77*(2), 203–220.

Tellis, G. J. (1988). The price elasticity of selective demand: A meta-analysis of econometric models of sales. *Journal of Marketing Research, 25,* 331–341.

Turner, J. and Brandt, J. (1978). Development and validation of a simulated market to test children for selected consumer skills. *Journal of Consumer Affairs, 12*(2), 266–276.

UK ONS. (2009). *Social trends, 39.* file:///Users/philipclark/Downloads/social_trends_39_tcm77-137023.pdf (accessed 10 January 2016).

Valkenburg, P. M. and Buijzen, M. (2005). Identifying determinants of young children's brand awareness: Television, parents, and peers. *Journal of Applied Developmental Psychology, 26*(4), 456–468.

Wakefield, K. L. and Inman, J. J. (2003). Situational price sensitivity: The role of consumption occasion, social context and income. *Journal of Retailing, 79*(4), 199–212.

Ward, S., Wackman, D. B. and Wartella, E. (1977). *How children learn to buy: The development of consumer information-processing skills.* London: Sage.

Webley, P. (2005). Children's understanding of economics. In M. Barrett and E. Buchanan-Barrow (eds), *Children's understanding of society* (pp. 43–67). London: Psychology Press.

Williams, J., Ashill, N. and Thirkell, P. (2016). How is value perceived by children? *Journal of Business Research, 69*(12), 5875–5885.

Woodruff, R. B. (1997). Customer value: The next source for competitive advantage. *Journal of the Academy of Marketing Science*, *25*(2), 139–153.

Woolley, J. D. (1997). Thinking about fantasy: Are children fundamentally different thinkers and believers from adults? *Child Development*, *68*(6), 991–1011.

Yoo, B., Donthu, N. and Lee, S. (2000). An examination of selected marketing mix elements and brand equity. *Journal of the Academy of Marketing Science*, *28*(2), 195–211.

Zeithaml, V. A. (1988). Consumer perceptions of price, quality, and value: A means-end model and synthesis of evidence. *The Journal of Marketing*, *52*, 2–22.

9

THE YOUNG ONES, SHOPPING AND MARKETING CHANNELS

What actually shapes their mind?

Zubin Sethna, Rebecca Fakoussa and David Bamber

Introduction

An introduction to 'the young ones'

Let's transport ourselves back to 350 BCE for just a second and assume we were reading the *Nichomachean Ethics* in which Aristotle wrote the famous words 'for the things we have to learn before we can do them, we learn by doing them'. Thus, learning is the 'behaviourial changes that result from experience' (Sethna and Blythe, 2016). This surely has to be at the crux of studying young consumer behaviour?

While to many young consumers in the twenty-first century Sir Cliff Richard maybe akin to a *singing dinosaur*, there is no doubt that at the height of his career he and The Shadows were big business. In fact, upon closer inspection we now find that their lyrics may indeed have contained a profound message. The young ones we know are not *afraid* of anything. Many of the fears that young people develop are as a result of conditioned fear responses to fear-relevant stimuli (Öhman and Mineka, 2001; Olsson *et al.*, 2005). There is no doubt that our young ones will like some things better than others; and will sometimes have a preference for learning about some associations more than others.

'They live, love while the flame is strong.' Indeed. Young consumers are members of a highly consumption-orientated society. Whether that's consumption of products, services, knowledge, communications or entertainment – they love to live life to the full, and *consume* using a variety of channels. According to Chang (2015), the majority (precisely 57.1 per cent) of the 'web generation' (also known as Generation Z) use mobile Internet devices while watching television. This of course bodes well for advertisers and those trying to encourage the 'learning' – Duff *et al.* (2014) revealed a positive relationship between media multi-tasking and advertising utility. It gets even better knowing that these young consumers who have become habitual media

multi-taskers can continue to think about a particular medium even after they've shifted to looking at another medium (Oviedo et al., 2015).

'Tomorrow, Why wait till tomorrow, tomorrow sometimes never comes.' You'd think that tomorrow really is never going to come when you see the statistics on latency; the amount of time that a young consumer is, for example, willing to wait for the search results to appear in an Amazon search is maybe as little as 6 seconds (Dixon, 2014). Other commentators had previously pitched the figure somewhere between 8 to 15 seconds for a web page to load on any given device (Nah, 2002; Galletta et al., 2004) but of course our technological capability has since increased many fold.

'There's a song to be sung.' Underlying this technological capability there is still a dichotomy between those children from 'Eastern and Western' societies. Research by Larson and Verma (1999) examined children in East Asian post-industrial societies who spend their 'free' time doing schoolwork (a use associated with lower intrinsic motivation but high achievement and economic productivity) as compared to children in North America who spend more time on leisure (associated with greater self-direction but of an uncertain relation to development).

So, in sum, the young ones of today really are learning and adapting to different channels at an incredible pace. From birth they start to behave in a particular way. And a large part of that behaviour is centred on and around consumption. For the purposes of clarity, we are informed by Bennett's (1995) definition of consumer behaviour: 'The dynamic interaction of affect and cognition, behaviour and environmental events by which human beings conduct the exchange aspects of their lives'.

Who and what are we talking about?

In this chapter we start to investigate the marketing channels that young consumers use. The conventional definition of marketing channels is how goods and services reach the marketplace (Stokes and Wilson, 2017). The understanding of this element of what used to be known as the marketing mix (place) acknowledges that for any firm, there is a fundamental choice of channels: from producer to wholesaler, through retailer and distribution direct to end-users or through various intermediaries. It is from this basic choice that other options then emerge, often in the planning stages (Sethna, 2013). Stokes and Wilson (2017) further note that these could take a variety of forms. Currently, commonly known channels include direct sales, specialist outlets, online sales, mail order and agents/distributors, to name but a few. These are all amenable to serving young consumers depending on the circumstance. What is important for organisations to remember is 'where else can we sell our products, and what changes do we need to make in order to reach our target market?' (Neck et al., 2018). However, words such as dynamic and changing are prevalent when we're talking about young consumers. Their needs, wants and the channels they use to consume are changing on a daily basis and the way in which they express them continues to change too. Thus we can only begin to highlight some of the channels that are *currently* being used and hope that by the time this chapter is published, the channels haven't changed drastically. However, what remains constant is the general model of consumer behaviour (Sethna and Blythe, 2016), which highlights the basic attitudes that young minds will form over time (that of thought, emotion and intended behaviour) – and not always in that order either!

So let's first go back to the very beginning of a child's life. Babies are able to use their fine motor skills long before they are able to speak. Goldin-Meadow and Feldman (1975, 1977) alluded to this notion by suggesting that this may explain how some deaf children have spontaneously developed 'gestural communication'. Other commentators have reported that this is simply the result of hearing infants who have been systematically exposed to American Sign Language (ASL) (Prinz and Prinz, 1979; Holmes and Holmes, 1980; Bonvillan et al., 1983). What we do know is that as far back as 1963, Werner and Kaplan wrote a narrative that described symbolic gestures as a natural transition between action and words. Examples can include the 10-month-old baby who suddenly stops crying when her father 'signs' to her that milk is on its way. The baby understands that her needs are about to be met and thus there is no need to cry any longer! Acredolo and Goodwyn (1990) provide an example of a 15-month-old infant who rubs her fingers together having seen something on the floor – her mother confirms to her that she has seen a spider! So sign language communications are crucial in the early ability to partake in two-way communication channels, and thus to start to play a part in the decision-making processes allied to consumption.

According to the last UK Census in 2011 there are just over 10.5 million children aged 0–15 in England and Wales (National Archives, 2011), while there are 2.2 billion children worldwide (UNICEF, 2014). Children have their own purchasing power and a huge influence on their direct and indirect carers (parents, grandparents and other families). In the US, children's direct spending of their own money has steadily increased for the past three decades. Preadolescent children (ages 4–12 years) spent $17.1 billion in 1994 and over $40 billion in 2002. And if you take a sub-section of this market – 'tweens' (those aged 9–13 who are considered 'too old for toys and too young for boys [and girls]' it is estimated that this market is responsible for $200 billion in annual sales. These figures do not even tap into the huge influence children have on their parents' purchases. Raised in dual income and single-parent households, children are 'deeply involved in family purchases, be they groceries or a new car' (Neuborne, 1999, p. 86). Research suggests that at an age as early as 6 months old, babies are forming mental images of corporate logos and mascots (McNeal and Yeh, 1993). Further, at 3 years of age, one out of five American children are already making direct requests for specific name brand products (Center for a New American Dream, 2002). It is of course no surprise that the older children get, the more they become brand aware. They distinguish and begin to prefer brands over non-branded items (Ward *et al.*, 1977; Borzekowski and Robinson, 2001). Wherever children go, from supermarkets to fast-food restaurants to toy stores to clothing stores, they will find licensed characters they know from their hours of daily television viewing (Wechsler, 1997a). Their task is to convince their parents that the product is worth spending their money on. Allied with the product's marketing campaign, this more often than not works in the child's favour. Take, for example, Kotex's successful marketing to both parents and children. 'U by Kotex Tween' appealed to both tweens and parents, and the resultant sales secured a 15.9 per cent share of the tampon market and 19.4 per cent of the sanitary napkin and liners segment. In another example, Hummerkids.com have offered games and colouring pages to entice and educate children about the joys of owning a huge sports-utility vehicle (SUV). In 2007, Honda also launched an advertising campaign on Disney's ABC Kids channel. But of course it's worth noting that there are many campaigns that have been a catastrophic disaster. For instance, take the Abercrombie Kids' Ashley Push-Up Triangle. This bikini top lined with push-up padding was marketed to girls as young as 8 years old. Parents were understandably very angry about the marketing and sales of such a product, and wanted to 'keep their kids kids' – even though tweens may occasionally want to seem grown-up. Abercrombie & Fitch found themselves in a situation where they changed their story by claiming that the product was intended for girls aged 12 and up. Very soon the bikini was removed from shelves, and Yahoo Finance's 24/7 Wall Street placed the Ashley Push-Up Triangle in its number one slot for biggest product failure of the year.

The changing environment in terms of channels available is also an important factor. Children have websites, TV and social media channels (cable, terrestrial and online) that are entirely dedicated to them. Thus the exposure to marketing content is far higher (and growing at a phenomenal rate) than for previous generations. And so it stands to reason that as their media access grows, so does their power to influence those around them. In the UK, a charity called Childwise (2017) suggests 'children now don't remember a time before the Internet'. Based on nearly 2,000 respondents aged 5–16 years old, the charity reported that these children spend an average of six and a half hours a day in front of a screen (television, computer or mobile device). Furthermore, they have become the chief technology officer in the household and often have a significant and important say in the purchase of computers and audio-visual equipment. Childwise (2017) further highlights the changing habits of children:

> The main difference from the 1990s is that then TV and magazines were the main ways for connecting kids to the media and now they have different devices from tablets, mobiles, games consoles and they have a much higher screen time.

Their research shows YouTube is the most popular on-demand service and paid-for on-demand services, such as Netflix, have also risen rapidly in recent years with predictions to continue. Companies have discovered that it is often more effective to recruit a child as an in-home marketer than to try to convince a parent to buy their products. That may explain why Nickelodeon (a cable and satellite television network) is Viacom's most profitable division – advertisers are lining up to pay a premium for access to their most valuable targets. Furthermore, every child represents a new chance to build cradle-to-grave brand loyalty. In contrast, terrestrial channels, for example, BBC1 has seen its audience of 7–16 year olds drop from over 80 per cent in 1995 to just over 40 per cent in 2014 (Childwise, 2017). The use of the Internet has given children freedom and independence to identify and discover their own interests and pursue these in their time at their pace. They may make decisions based on content from them and for them.

As alluded to already, some marketers have created different sub-teen groups. Because of the continuous changing tastes of, and the channels being utilised by these 'sub-teens' towards consumer electronics and fashion goodies, we now see that in this highly interactive and personalised environment, marketing for this age group has now been further segmented into four distinct under-13 age groups: newborns–1 year olds, 3–5 year olds, 5–8 year olds and 8–12 year olds.

Historically, there are two main theories that have informed both stages and child categories commonly used in child psychology and early childhood education. These are cognitive development theory (Piaget) and psycho-social development theory (Erikson). While both suggest various development stages and build on the idea that personality development takes place across a person's lifespan, the stages that are used somewhat differ. Cognitive development theory (Piaget) focuses on the various stages of a child where transition from one stage to the other follows a sequence; that cognitive development was a progressive reorganisation of mental processes resulting from biological maturation and environmental experience. He developed the stages with key ideas as his building blocks and created four stages through observation of children. Child-centred classrooms and 'open education' are direct applications of Piaget's views (Gorman, 2008). He believed all children passed through the stages sequentially throughout their lifetime.

A number of criticisms have been levelled at Piaget's stage theory: Carlson and Buskist (1997) note weaknesses with Piaget's terminology: his concepts are ill-defined operationally so that both the reputed changes in child behaviour and the child's mind cannot be exactly and precisely measured and therefore the theory cannot be confirmed or refuted and cause–effect relationships between Piaget's various concepts cannot be determined. Hence, it is no surprise that further criticisms ensue from Weiten (1992) that the stages may be incorrect and erroneous: and there are confusing results from Flavell *et al.* (1981) and Bower (1982). Additionally, Piaget is not alone in being criticised for basing his theory on a cohort of children who are steeped in Western schooling, in this case from Geneva. Indeed, Kenway *et al.* (2017) propose that the model of the Western public schools, in particular the notion of the English public school, has been exported throughout the former British Empire thus promoting the elitism of that mercantile system and that very educational system that would provide individuals who could perform the various administrative duties required to rule and maintain economic trade. So, through the drive for economic power, education has become a prime global commodity that is consumed not only by children but by adults also, with most governments' education spending between 5 and 8 per cent of gross domestic product on education (Tanzi and Schuknecht, 2000) and the majority of that spending being for the education of children. Additionally, Vygotsky (1926) provides alternative theories to those of Piaget. For Vygotsky (1962 and 1934/1987), thought and language are initially separate systems from the beginning of life, merging at around 3 years of age, producing verbal thought, called 'inner speech' and 'private speech', which is the connecting point between social and inner speech. Thus, cognitive development arises from an internalisation of language. Vygotsky (1978) places great emphasis on culture and social factors affecting cognitive development. Cognitive development grows from social interactions through guided learning that takes place within the 'Zone of Proximal Development' (ZPD). Children and their playmates co-construct knowledge in their own environment, which in turn influences how they think and what they think about marketing channels and adults, who are within the child's ZPD, transmit their own culture's tools of intellectual adaptation, which children then internalise (Vygotsky, 1926).

Within the ZPD of the individual, both child and adult, are things that are known and outside the ZPD are things that are not known. Close to the innermost self of the child are the parents, carers or significant adults of the child and similarly the child is in the innermost part of the ZPD of the parent. Soon after birth, little is known of the external environment by the child. Gradually the child experiences more. Most experiences will be new for the child and where those experiences are pleasurable they will be delightful (Plutchick, 1980) and as they are new experiences that the child is interested in they will be a delightful surprise for the individual, in this case the child (Kumar et al., 2001).

The notion of ZPD is useful for the marketer. The cake, the candles and the balloons at the birthday party will all be a surprise (outside the child's ZPD) and a delight for the child but the grandparents will have experienced these many times before (well inside the adult's ZPD). Nevertheless, the occasion of the child's birthday will be a delight for the adults mainly because the experience will contribute to the adults' own delightful memories. Thus, such occasions are a delight for both the adult and child. The occasion, behaviours and products within the adult's ZPD are placed by the adults inside the child's ZPD. The knowledge of the significant adults is already in the child's ZPD and that knowledge is easily extended to include the behaviours such as blowing out of the candles, making a wish, eating cake and playing with balloons. On such occasions the child learns mainly about happy emotions but also sad emotions, perhaps when the balloons are popped, or sometimes when the presents received are not 'as expected'! The not previously known products: the cake, the candles, the balloon and the birthday presents are now placed within the child's ZPD. Words are important too in Vygotsky's theories and words are important in marketing to children. Clearly the child has a more limited vocabulary than the adult and the words known to the child will generally have fewer syllables than the majority of adult words. Promotional campaigns, such as those adopted by Kellogg's (2017) have remained lucrative for over 80 years. The 'snap, crackle and pop' campaign promoting the Rice Krispies breakfast cereal has been successful because short, mono-syllable words such as 'snap' and 'pop' are close to mono-syllable words, like 'mum' and 'dad', which are already known by the child. 'Crackle' has a short syllable extension and is placed between the two words 'snap' and 'pop', which are close to the ZPD of the child. Hence, 'crackle' is carried into the ZPD by the two surrounding words. One can hear the young child sounding out 'snap' and 'pop' and attempting but initially mispronouncing 'clackle'. This is the beginning of brand recognition by the child: first knowledge of the words, then knowledge of the product and then knowledge of the brand: 'snap, crackle, pop', 'Rice Krispies' then 'Kellogg's'. The words are within the ZPD, and they place the product in the mind of the child and then the product carries the brand into the child's ZPD.

Consider a supermarket shopping experience. A young child will be taken in a car on the child seat to the supermarket and placed in the supermarket trolley with a fixed child seat in it. Even though the child is a passive observer of the supermarket shopping experience, it is the adult's shopping and purchasing behaviours that are placed in the ZPD of the child. As the child grows and continues to encounter the supermarket shopping experience, then the child may point out or vocalise products to the adult, which are by now already placed in the child's ZPD. Following this, there comes a point when the child walks and is allowed to walk holding the trolley with the adult. Trolley-pushing behaviour is learnt then when the child is allowed to walk more freely, which provides freedom for further product recognition and selection. At such a point conversation about pricing may occur (although knowledge and understanding about pricing may still be scant): when the adult states that there is a cheaper but equally acceptable product available or conversely the adult may explain that the more expensive product may be preferable because it has better features.

Just as the idea of the ZPD helps us understand how consumer knowledge may develop in the child, so too can the ZPD help demonstrate how consumer behaviour develops in the child: this is represented in Bamber's model of placement and consumer behaviour development (Bamber, 2017), see Figure 9.1 below.

The notion of *children's consumer socialisation* is defined in research as 'processes by which young people acquire skills, knowledge, and attitudes relevant to their functioning as consumers in the marketplace' (Ward, 1974). In addition to three major socialisation agents that influence children's consumer behaviour (parents, peers and mass media) there are also three stages of this process, which have been identified by John (1999). First is the perceptual stage, where children begin to distinguish ads from programmes, associate brand names with product categories, and understand the basic script of consumption. During the second, analytical stage, children capture the persuasive intent of ads, begin to process functional cues regarding products and develop purchase influence and negotiation strategies. During the last 'reflective' stage, children understand the tactics and appeals of ads, become sceptical about them, understand complex shopping scripts and become capable of influencing purchases. Given the drastic changes in channels available, media-usage patterns (Bardhi *et al.*, 2010) and households, companies know that

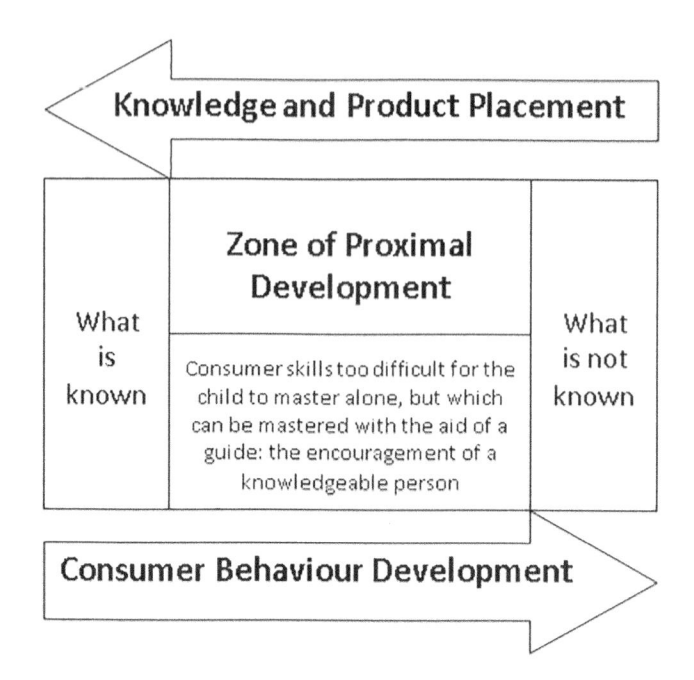

```
                 Knowledge and Product Placement

              ┌─────────────────────────────────────────┐
              │         Zone of Proximal                │
              │         Development                     │
     What     │                                         │   What
      is      │  Consumer skills too difficult for the  │  is not
    known     │   child to master alone, but which      │   known
              │   can be mastered with the aid of a     │
              │   guide: the encouragement of a         │
              │     knowledgeable person                │
              └─────────────────────────────────────────┘

                 Consumer Behaviour Development
```

FIGURE 9.1 Bamber's model of placement and consumer behaviour development

Source: Bamber (2017).

the child's brand knowledge is ignited first with food products and toys and food and quite often by the time they have reached the age of 8, they are able to recall a vast variety of products in categories within which they have been targeted. One of the first 'channels' that children unconsciously use for marketing information are their parents, and specifically their mothers. Wisenblit et al. (2013) investigated the influence of parental styles on children's consumption. Their study examined parental styles based on levels of nurturing and authoritarianism to determine mothers' awareness of children's media exposure, likelihood of setting media and consumption limits and communications with children about commercial messages. The results suggested that nurturing mothers are more aware of advertising aimed at children and talk more to children regarding advertising and consumption than authoritarian mothers. Mothers who are nurturing and not authoritarian are more likely to yield to requests and favour more regulation than other parents. There are many implications that result from such studies. A marketer may view a nurturing mother as a barrier to reaching children with persuasive messages. These mothers will not only limit the access to such messages, but furthermore train children to be sceptical of such advertising messages. Wisenblit et al. (2013) note that 'marketers who deal honestly with customers will be more successful in appealing to nurturing mothers and their market-savvy children'. There are also some wider, macro-level social implications. For instance, by recognising the distinctions in parental style, policy makers can develop and promote more defined policy regulating food-marketing practices. Thus, nurturing mothers are more supportive of regulation than are authoritarian mothers, and efforts to promote such regulation should target nurturing mothers. The factors that influence mothers to intervene and limit children's media and consumption behaviour also affect attitudes toward regulation of food-related advertising. With the uprising of media multi-tasking (the practice of participating in multiple exposures to two or more commercial media forms at a single point in time, including traditional, online, social and entertainment media), behaviours and experiences among young consumers, lobby groups around the world have campaigned against the undermining of families by 'rampant consumerism' by repeatedly asking a themed question 'How can one family in isolation combat this $15 billion industry that's working night and day to undermine parental authority?'

Thus, building on the five circles of sensory experiences (and the insight from Erikson, 1968) our interpretation of communication leads to consumption. Every human has five senses – smell, sound, sight, taste and touch. Hultén et al. (2009, p. 17) suggest that 'the sensory experience is the result of the reactions of the senses to different elements or triggers in marketing'. They further identify that in the traditional psychological context, elements or triggers are often called 'stimuli'. As a child develops and grows, different senses develop and change. In the taste area, foods one might like become too bitter or sweet while visually one might have a pink, blue or black phase. Sensory input and human senses are of vital importance for existence and development and without them it would be impossible to develop, learn, think or build on one's understanding. Humans using their mouth, nose, eyes, ears and skin send information to their brain, which creates emotions and feelings and finally a reaction. Babies initially have phases where they put everything in their mouths to explore, while much later in childhood they develop an awareness of smell and reactions.

Marketing channels: place, distribution and social media marketing

It is of course common knowledge that 'place' in marketing terms not only refers to the location where exchanges take place but is also quite often an integral part of the product itself. The place, whether it be the plethora of online or offline shopping options, has led to a rise in two industry terms: multi-channel and omni-channel. Multi-channel refers to a retailer who sells in multiple online channels (e.g. a web store, marketplaces and via social media). Omni-channel refers to retailers with both a physical and digital presence. However, many commentators have battled with defining exactly what omni-channel is. Google defines it as: 'ensuring retailer marketing strategies are geared toward enabling customers to convert on any channel'. While Hubspot defines it as: 'the ability to deliver a seamless and consistent experience across channels, while factoring in the different devices that consumers are using to interact with your business'.

Take for instance, the famous Hamley's toy store in central London, where the physical store is as important as the products contained within it, which is as important as the website showcasing new products and providing information on existing products. So for companies to ask the question 'how will we distribute and deliver our products and services to our customers?' they need to do this by having their young consumers in the forefront of their minds at all times – because young consumers will generally shop wherever is the most convenient. We've already established that Generation Z, around the world, is savvy when it comes to mobile technology. But are companies successfully executing on all of their omni-channel initiatives? Anecdotal evidence suggests not. Even with the momentum toward integrating commerce across channels, the one big piece of the puzzle that is missing is the answer to the question 'what does our young customer want and when do they want it?!' Omni-channel really should be about providing a holistic omni-channel customer experience by transcending any one channel or platform and simply providing young consumers with what they want, when they want it. Many organisations recognise that nobody today shops exclusively through a single medium. Young consumers buy from a variety of channels that are forever fluid; meaning that they are continually changing. Nearly half of all online product searches (48 per cent) begin on marketplaces like Amazon, for instance. In comparison, 31 per cent of Americans first turn to larger retailers, 12 per cent to category-specific retailers and 7 per cent to webstores. So if an organisation is selling their product using a webstore without using Amazon as part of a multi-channel strategy, they're missing out on a huge number of searches and therefore potential conversions. Product discoverability is crucial for online retailers, and even more so for big brands. What is interesting though is how this is panning out in different parts of the world. You may be surprised to read that more than one-third of Kenya's entire economy is traded using the M-Pesa platform; a mobile phone-based money transfer, financing and micro-financing service, launched in 2007 by Vodafone. Apart from the obvious interaction online via a computer, even if the young consumer is shopping *offline* by physically visiting shopping malls or the high street locales, you can be sure that there is an integrated element of checking competitor prices/available colours/locations, etc. online through a mobile device, which is always on hand, and thus does not limit where and when people shop online. And even if a lot of the visitors to a particular website are not immediately ready to purchase, pre-transactional conversion opportunities let the company trade something site visitors find valuable. So content becomes king. Ensuring that young customers find the content and style, etc. of a website valuable is key. User Experience (UX) and User Interface (UI) trends are coming from the likes of Apple, Uber, Tinder, Buzzfeed and Instacart.

> *User Experience (UX)* – the internal experience that a person has as they interact with every aspect of a company's products and services.
>
> *User Interface (UI)* – the series of screens, pages and visual elements (like buttons and icons) that you use to interact with a device.

Customer experience – in the form of 'entrepreneurial marketing' (Sethna *et al.*, 2013) – is the new battle ground and the gap between design, user preferences and marketing delivery channels is where companies invite disruption and competition (Miles *et al.*, 2015). We now live in a world where there is a fusion of online and offline. This means that it is no longer valid to refer to outdated models of distribution/marketing channels in the network such as 'producer, wholesaler and retailer'. We are fast moving towards a world where 'online' means entirely mobile, which means that the most important item of information an organisation needs to know is exactly where is the person right now and where is the transaction taking place? Note, it's not about what webpage they are visiting, but where the consumer is physically, because this gives us a clue as to how they are feeling. What are they surrounded by? 'Location-based marketing' enables a company to build a picture of the 'journey' a customer has made (i.e. where were they 10 minutes ago, etc.), and then using big data and predictive analysis, you can predict where they will be in 10 minutes time, and thus estimate how many of the company's products can be exposed to them and eventually sell to them! The fusion between online and offline has already caused chaos as well as opportunity for retailers in many parts of the world. Their traditional roles have been altered to the point where they no longer know whether they are online, offline or mobile retailers! Individual and organisational consumption is affected the world over (Sethna, 2006). Take, for example, the retail scene in Brazil over the past five years. Some 50 per cent of young consumers will research online but buy in store, 40 per cent will research in store but buy online, 89 per cent want digital information in store. Customers do their online shopping from a variety of locations and wherever is most convenient. Nearly half (43 per cent) of Americans who have shopped online have made a purchase while lying in bed. Another 20 per cent admit to purchasing from the bathroom or while in a car. So exactly what kind of state of mind are these consumers in? Then of course there is an added complication of exactly when and where does one collect or have the product delivered? Do you buy online and have it delivered to the store, or do you buy in store and have it delivered at home or to a 'click and collect' facility somewhere? Given that we as a society are so mobile-driven, the 'traditional' process of e-commerce, i.e. ordering at home for delivery to home, seems so outdated now. Gone are the days of having to wait at home for the courier to arrive. M-commerce and m-technology now enable distribution using 'mobile, wherever someone is' or 'collected, mobile, wherever someone is'. Apps using geo-location will enable a courier to track you down, wherever you are, to deliver your ordered product. The marriage between telecommunications companies and banks, which has resulted in cashless transactions enabled by digital technology – mobile payments – will further make the whole process seamless (recent examples include Apple Pay, PayPal, Google Wallet, etc). For Generation Z – who are self-confident, quick, competent, global, tech savvy and demanding, who have very high expectations when it comes to transparency and flexibility – these are the kinds of things that create an amazing experience and that 'customer magic', which they constantly crave.

Having consumed that magic, young customers will be all too ready to share their experiences online with others. The surfacing of Internet-based social media [also referred to as consumer-generated media] has made it possible for one-to-many communications (Mangold and Faulds, 2009) (sometimes with hundreds or even thousands of other people) about products, services and the companies that provide them. This has resulted in a significant impact on consumer-to-consumer communications. While social media services like Facebook, Twitter, Instagram, Pinterest and Snapchat require account holders to be at least 13 years old, most children have access online before this age. On Safer Internet Day, a survey found that three-quarters of children aged between 10 and 12 have social media accounts despite being below the age limit. The most popular site for the under 13 year olds was Facebook, which 49 percent said they used.

But a survey by the BBC's news programme for children, Newsround, found that more than three-quarters of younger children at primary-leaving age were using at least one social media network (*Telegraph*, 2016). There is, of course, legislation that has been introduced initially by the US Government, which passed the Children's Online Privacy Protection Act (COPPA) of 1998 to safeguard and protect the interests and privacy of those children aged under the age of 13, by placing rules on online marketing techniques. Marketing channels therefore encompass the content, timing and frequency of the social media-based conversations occurring between consumers; and quite often these are outside an organisation's direct control. Traditionally of course, organisations would have a high degree of control, especially when devising their own integrated marketing communications programmes. It would therefore be beneficial for organisations to harness the conversations that these young consumers are having online and hopefully learn how to shape those young consumers' discussions by providing them with appropriate tools such as networking platforms, blogs, social media and promotional tools to engage eager customers.

Summary

From the very early 'animistic' thinking that very young children develop (for instance, buying into fantasies that lead them to believe that Santa really will fly in being pulled by reindeer), to adolescents being able to reason abstractly and understand the motives of advertisers, children 'live and grow up in a highly sophisticated marketing environment that influences their preferences and behaviours' (Calvert, 2008) and will engage in the shopping process using a multitude of marketing channels, but mainly centred around 'on-demand'. Organisations will have to use their adapted marketing channels in order to remain relevant as well as to be responsive to the young consumer's craving for marketing that gives them what they want – when they want it. This continuous evolution of consumer expectations as technology advances is what is fuelling on-demand marketing. As we've seen through this chapter, social media encourages consumers to share, compare and rate experiences; and mobile devices continue to add a 'wherever' dimension to the digital environment. The coming of age really is NOW, with young consumers wanting to interact anywhere at any time.

References

Acredolo, L. P. and Goodwyn, S. W. (1990). Sign language among hearing infants: The spontaneous development of symbolic gestures. In V. Volterra and C. Erting (eds), *From gesture to language in hearing and deaf children* (pp. 68–78). New York: Springer.

Bamber, D. (2017). Bamber's model of placement and consumer development. Personal email communication with T. Gbadamosi, 24 April.

Bardhi, F., Rohm, A. J. and Sultan, F. (2010). Tuning in and tuning out: Media multitasking among young consumers. *Journal of Consumer Behaviour*, 9, 316–332.

Bennett, P. D. (1995). *Dictionary of marketing terms*. Chicago, IL: American Marketing Association.

Bonvillian, J. D., Orlansky, M. D., Novack, L. L. and Folven, R. J. (1983). Early sign language acquisition and cognitive development. In D. Rogers and J. Sloboda (eds), *The acquisition of symbolic skills* (pp. 207–214). New York: Plenum Press.

Borzekowski, D. L. G. and Robinson, T. N. (2001). The 30-second effect: An experiment revealing the impact of television commercials on food preferences of preschoolers. *Journal of the American Dietetic Association*, 101(1), 42–46.

Bower, T. G. R. (1982). *Development in infancy* (2nd edn). San Francisco: W. H. Freeman.

Calvert, S. L. (2008). Children as consumers: Advertising and marketing. *Future Child Spring*, 18(1), 205–234.

Carlson, N. R. and Buskist, W. (1997). *Psychology: The science of behaviour* (5th edn). Boston, MA: Allyn & Bacon.

Center for a New American Dream. (2002). Just the facts about advertising and marketing to children. http://epsl.asu.edu/ceru/Articles/CERU-0502-115-OWI.pdf (accessed 28 August 2017).

Chang, Y. (2015). Media multitasking across generations: Simultaneous mobile internet and television usage behaviors and motives. *Mass Communication Research*, 124(8), 3–116.

Childwise. (2017). *The monitor report 2017: Children's media use and purchasing*. www.childwise.co.uk/reports.html#monitorreportBasedonwww.bbc.co.uk/news/technology-32067158.

Dixon, P. (2014). Take hold of the future: Six faces of global change. USI Lecture. www.youtube.com/watch?v=GwMpWUxNtGM (accessed 1 February 2017).

Duff, B. R. L., Yoon, G., Wang, Z. and Anghelcev, G. (2014). Doing it all: An exploratory study of predictors of media multitasking. *Journal of Interactive Advertising*, 14, 11–23.

Erikson, E. H. (1968). The human life cycle. In D. L. Sillis (ed.), *International encyclopedia of the social science* (Vol. 9, pp. 286–292). New York: Crowell-Collier.

Flavell, J. H., Speer, J. R., Green, F. L. and August, D. L. (1981). The development of comprehension monitoring and knowledge about communication. *Monographs of the Society for Research in Child Development*, 46(192).

Galletta, D. F., Henry, R., McCoy, S. and Polak, P. (2004). Web site delays: How tolerant are users? *Journal of the Association for Information Systems*, 5(1), 1–28.

Goldin-Meadow, S. and Feldman, H. (1975). The creation of a communication system: A study of deaf children of hearing parents. *Sign Language Studies*, 8, 225–233.

Goldin-Meadow, S. and Feldman, H. (1977). The development of language-like communication without a language model. *Science*, 197(4301), 401–403.

Gorman, R. F. (2008). *Great lives from history: The 20th century*. New York: Salem Press.

Holmes, K. M. and Holmes, D. W. (1980). Signed and spoken language development in a hearing child of hearing parents. *Sign Language Studies*, *28*, 239–254.

Hultén, B., Broweus, N. and Van Dijk, M. (2009). What is sensory marketing? In *Sensory marketing* (pp. 1–23). London: Palgrave Macmillan.

John D. R. (1999). Consumer socialization of children: A retrospective look at twenty-five years of research. *Journal of Consumer Research*, *26*(3), 31.

Kellogg's. (2017). Rice crispies speak to you. www.kelloggsfamilyrewards.com/content/dam/kelloggsfamilyrewards/en_US/promotions/games/ricekrispies/frosted/puzzle.pdf (accessed 25 April 2017).

Kenway, J., Fahey, J., Epstein, D., Koh, A., McCarthy, C. and Rizvi, F. (2017). *Class choreographies: Elite schools and globalization*. London: Palgrave Macmillan.

Kumar, A., Olshavsky, R. W. and King, M. F. (2001). Exploring the antecedents of customer delight. *Journal of Consumer Satisfaction, Dissatisfaction and Complaining Behavior*, *14*, 14–27.

Larson, R. W. and Verma, S. (1999). How children and adolescents spend time across the world: Work, play and developmental opportunities. *Psychological Bulletin*, *125*(6), 701–736.

McNeal, J. U. and Yeh, C. H. (1993). Born to shop. *American Demographics*, *15*(6), 34–39.

Mangold, W. G. and Faulds, D. J. (2009). Social media: The new hybrid element of the promotion mix. *Business Horizons*, *52*(4), 357–365.

Miles, M., Gilmore, A., Harrigan, P., Lewis, G. and Sethna, Z. (2015). Exploring entrepreneurial marketing. *Journal of Strategic Marketing*, *23*(2), 94–111.

Nah, F. F. H. (2002). *A study of web users' waiting time, in intelligent support systems technology: Knowledge management*. Edited by V. Sugumaran. Hershey, PA: IGI Global.

National Archives. (2011). http://webarchive.nationalarchives.gov.uk/20160105160709/www.ons.gov.uk/ons/rel/wellbeing/measuring-national-well-being/measuring-children-s-well-being/art-measuring-children s well being.html (accessed February 2017).

Neck, H. M., Neck, C. P. and Murray, E. L. (2018). *Entrepreneurship: The practice and mindset*. Thousand Oaks, CA: Sage.

Neuborne, E. (1999). Generation Y. *Business Week*, 15 February, 81–88.

Öhman, A. and Mineka, S. (2001). Fears, phobias and preparedness: Toward an evolved module of fear and fear learning. *Psychological Review*, *108*, 483–522. doi:10.1037/0033-295x.108.3.483.

Olsson, A., Ebert, J. P., Banaji, M. R. and Phelps, E. A. (2005). The role of social groups in the persistence of learned fear. *Science*, *309*, 785–787. doi:10.1126/science.1113551.

Oviedo, V., Tornquist, M., Cameron, T. and Chiappe, D. (2015). Effects of media multitasking with Facebook on the enjoyment and encoding of TV episodes. *Computers in Human Behavior*, *5*, 407–417.

Plutchik, R. (1980). *Emotion: A psychoevolutionary synthesis*. New York: Harper & Row.

Prinz, P. M. and Prinz, E. A. (1979). Simultaneous acquisition of ASL and spoken English (in a hearing child of a deaf mother and hearing father): Phase I – early lexical development. *Sign Language Studies*, *25*(4), 283–296.

Sethna, Z. (2006). An investigation into how individual and organisational consumption is affected when dealing with SME organisations from emerging economies. *Asia Pacific Journal of Marketing and Logistics*, *18*(4), 266–282.

Sethna, Z. (2013). Marketing planning for value delivery. In A. Gbadamosi, S. Nwankwo and I. Bathgate (eds), *Principles of marketing: A value-based approach* (Chapter 11). London: Palgrave Macmillan.

Sethna, Z., Jones, R. and Harrigan, P. (2013). *Entrepreneurial marketing: Global perspectives*. Bingley: Emerald.

Sethna, Z. and Blythe, J. (2016). *Consumer behaviour* (3rd edn). London: Sage.
Stokes, D. and Wilson, N. (2017). *Small business management and entrepreneurship* (7th edn). Hampshire: Cengage Learning.
Tanzi, V. and Schuknecht, L. (2000). *Public spending in the 20th century: A global perspective.* Cambridge: Cambridge University Press.
Telegraph. (2016). Children ignore age limits by opening social media accounts. www.telegraph.co.uk/news/health/children/12147629/Children-ignore-age-limits-by-opening-social-media-accounts.html (accessed February 2017).
UNICEF. (2014). www.unicef.org/sowc2014/numbers/documents/english/SOWC2014_In%20Numbers_28%20Jan.pdf (accessed February 2017).
Vygotsky, L. S. (1926). *Educational psychology*. Translated by R. Silverman. Florida: St Lucie Press.
Vygotsky, L. S. (1962). *Thought and language*. Cambridge, MA: MIT Press.
Vygotsky, L. S. (1978). *Mind in society: The development of higher psychological processes.* Cambridge, MA: Harvard University Press.
Vygotsky, L. S. (1934/1987). Thinking and speech. In R. W. Rieber and A. S. Carton (eds), *The collected works of L. S. Vygotsky, Volume 1: Problems of general psychology* (pp. 39–285). New York: Plenum Press.
Ward, S. (1974). Consumer socialization. *Journal of Consumer Research*, *1*(2), 1–14.
Ward, S., Wackman, D. B. and Wartella, E. (1977). *How children learn to buy*. Thousand Oaks, CA: Sage.
Wechsler, D. (1997). *WAIS-III administration and scoring manual*. San Antonio, TX: The Psychological Corporation.
Werner, H. and Kaplan, B. (1963). *Symbol formation: An organismic-developmental approach to language and the expression of thought*. New York: John Wiley & Sons.
Weiten, W. (1992). *Psychology: Themes and variations* (7th edn). London: Brooks Cole.
Wisenblit, J. Z., Priluck, R. and Pirog, S. F. (2013). The influence of parental styles on children's consumption. *Journal of Consumer Marketing*, *30*(4), 320–327.

10
MARKETING COMMUNICATIONS AND THE YOUNG CONSUMER

Evidence from a developing country

Nicolas Hamelin, Ayantunji Gbadamosi and Lucas M. Peters

Introduction

Marketing communications constitute a strategic part of the marketing programmes of businesses. For example, it is a crucial element in the jigsaw of activities involved in the planning process while developing new products or services. So, well-developed market offerings need marketing communications so that the target market could be made aware of the value they offer. Interestingly, evidence around us in this day and age shows a plethora of products, services and the associated brands that are targeted at children because not only do they consume in their own right but they also do so in other circumstances with other family members. So, it is not surprising that many marketing communication tools are targeted at these young consumers. From conventional understanding, a number of marketing communications tools are mixed interactively to communicate value to consumers. These are noted as advertising, sales promotion, personal selling, publicity and public relations and direct marketing (see Figure 10.1). As shown in the huge scale of evidence in the marketing world, all of these tools are used in various measures to reach out to these young consumers.

One erroneous view that is sometimes associated with marketing communications is the use of the term synonymously with advertising. According to De Pelsmacker *et al*. (2010), this misconception is due to the fact that advertising is the most visible of these tools. Hence, it is very common to hear the expression, 'advertising to children' when in actual fact the intention relates to how businesses use marketing communications to reach these young consumers. Figure 10.1 shows the basic categorisation of marketing communication tools often used to reach their target audience, which indicates that the scope is relatively broader. In fact, a more detailed presentation given by De Pelsmacker *et al*. (2010) presents the tools as:

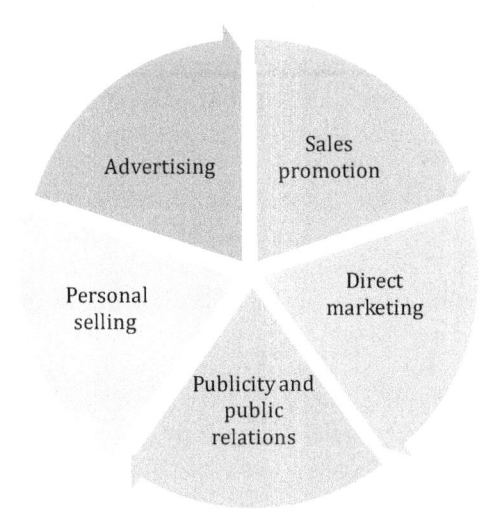

FIGURE 10.1 Basic marketing communication tools

- Advertising
- Sales promotion
- Public relations
- Sponsorship
- Personal selling
- Direct marketing
- Point-of-purchase
- Exhibition and trade fairs
- Electronic communications.

Hence, marketers have a range of opportunities for communicating with the consumers. As businesses use these tools directly or indirectly to make favourable mention of their offerings to their target consumers, which could include young consumers, the relevance of the term, integrated marketing communications (IMC) cannot be ignored. As explained by Fill and Turnbull (2016, p. 337), 'IMC requires that organisations coordinate their various strategies, resources and messages in order that they enable meaningful engagement with audiences . . . to develop a clear positioning and encourage stakeholder relationships that are of mutual value'. Adopting this stance ensures synergy, creativity and integration such that planning, execution and monitoring of all communication activities are geared towards the same goals and relate to each other (Ouwersloot and Duncan, 2008). Clearly the children's market and the associated marketing communications constitute an interesting phenomenon for so many reasons including their consumption pattern (Gbadamosi, 2012; Gbadamosi et al., 2012). Available evidence shows that they are dynamic following the trend of the development in the digital world. Findings show that alcohol groups and nightclubs explore Facebook as a tool for reaching young adults and through this tool, they co-produce and generate alcohol-related content with this consumer group (Moraes et al., 2014). Meanwhile, Grant and O'Donohoe (2007) cite the work of Haste (2005) to show that in a survey of 1,058 young British consumers aged 11–21, 95 per cent of them had access to a mobile phone while the proportion of the respondents who 'could not bear to be without' it, was 77 per cent. This is one of the obvious reasons marketers are keeping up with the communication 'game' by exploring these and various means of reaching these young consumers. Grant and O'Donohoe (2007) found that mobile phones have a universal appeal to a young audience and that they specifically love the social and entertainment-related content part of it. Their findings led them to suggest that marketers should offer this consumer segment content that aids in maintaining and developing personal relationships that matter to the young consumer (Grant and O'Donohoe, 2007). This also corroborates the findings of Gao et al. (2010), but from the context of Chinese youth consumers. Therefore, it is clear that the dynamics of young consumers and marketing communication is a global interesting phenomenon.

The detailed discussion of each of the elements shown in Figure 10.1 and how they are mixed by various organisations are beyond the scope of this chapter but the chapter contextualises the discussion in relation to young consumer behaviour. This is considered useful as identifying, analysing and ultimately understanding the target market and its buying behaviour is identified as the first step in formulating a good marketing communication strategy (Smith and Zook, 2011). More specifically, the chapter focuses on advertising and uses a developing country as the theoretical platform.

Background of the study

Children under 14 years of age spend nearly 40 billion dollars every year (McNeal, 2006) and influence an additional 500 billion dollars of their parents' purchases (Campbell et al., 2000). Children spend money, or influence their parents to spend money, on clothing, food and toys, segments of the market that are all well-trod territories for advertisers. To capitalise on this segment, these advertisers craft their media in such a way that most of their commercials and print advertisements target children, not their parents (Abideen and Salaria, 2010). The statistics expressed in this chapter, and many others, affirm that the advertising market catering to the underage demographic is lucrative (Gulla and Purohit, 2013). In today's capitalist market, not only do children make their own purchases directly, usually with money obtained through allowances or presents, but they are also pushing their parents to buy things they want or perceive as needing (Gulla and Purohit, 2013) – and these types of purchases are growing continually over time (Euromonitor International, 2012). Essentially, marketing specialists are now attempting to respond to the particular interests and demands of children, not to better the children or out of any altruism, but solely in order to financially profit from this large and growing market (Akhtar et al., 2010).

Clearly, children constitute one of the most important population segments for marketers and researchers to concentrate on (Calvert, 2008; Akhtar et al., 2010). This is illustrated in the statistics. While in 1983, corporations allocated around $100 million of their total annual marketing budget to children, today this number has reached nearly $17 billion. This represents an extraordinary increase of 1700 per cent in funds that are earmarked expressly for advertising campaigns that target children (McNeal, 2006). Not only are children immediately lucrative (Gulla and Purohit, 2013), successful advertising also helps to build long-term consumer relationships (Harrison, 2008), which means that marketers can build brand loyalty. Marketers realise that targeting children at an early age with an effective advertisement may make them loyal to their brands for the rest of their life (Asadollahi and Tanha, 2011). Marketers target children at an early age solely in order to maintain their fidelity (Calvert, 2008), using techniques such as the ominously-titled 'cradle to grave' technique, wherein babies are targeted by advertisers with the express purpose of creating a brand loyalty that will last a lifetime, quite literally, from their cradle to their grave (Horovitz, 2006).

Due to the fast-paced developments in media and its ubiquity, children are increasingly affected by advertisements in ways that haven't been seen in previous generations (Harrison, 2008). Because millennials are exposed to more advertising than their predecessors, the media space dedicated to them has grown exponentially over the last decade (Calvert, 2008) and in ways previously unseen. Projected movies, television, video games and Internet content have all allowed the insertion of commercial products that target children throughout the programme. Today, the average child has 147 conversations about brands throughout the week, nearly twice the amount their parents do (Corcoran, 2007). Marketers today attempt to develop advertisements that are persuasive enough to tug at the emotions of the children (Calvert, 2008). They use every means at their disposal to attract the attention of children, particularly their favourite cartoon characters (Linn, 2008). To that end, there are now more than 40,000 princesses marketed by Disney (Linn, 2008). Repetition, remunerated competitions and free gifts are other means that marketers use to reach larger underage audiences that drive product sales. These methods are found to stay longer in the memories of the child and directly affect their purchasing selections and attitude as well as the attitudes of their parents. Importantly for the emotional relevance of the children, these types of advertising tactics make children feel that they are up to date, or 'cool' (Akhtar et al., 2010).

The underage market in Morocco

The total number of children under the age of 18 in Morocco is roughly estimated at 11 million, which represents more than 35 per cent of the country's total population (Euromonitor International, 2012), and 3 million of these children are under the age of 5 as of the year 2013, while 27.8 per cent of the total population was under the age of 14, approximately 4.5 million males and 4.3 million females (CIA World Fact Book, 2013). Primary school enrolment registered in the year 2009 of the school-aged population was 87 per cent for girls and 92 per cent for boys (Euromonitor International, 2012), meaning that this is a market that is getting educated.

It is no surprise, then, that the market for children in Morocco has a tremendous potential for marketers. In Morocco, most brands show profits increasing where forecasts insured that the market would evolve for the coming years (Euromonitor International, 2012); in particular, products targeting children have shown increasing profits year after year. Children and baby product sales for the year 2013 reached a growth rate of 8 per cent (Euromonitor International, 2012). This growth is mostly due to the development of advertisers and marketers directly targeting children through their campaigns (Euromonitor International, 2012). Thus, the children of Morocco have become another underage target group for companies that find them a financially lucrative segment of the population to cater to, given their collective purchase power.

Because the underage market in Morocco is such a large percentage of the population, it has attracted the attention, not only of local brands, but of many international brands as well – such as L'Oréal and Beiersdorf (Euromonitor International, 2012). The leader in baby and child products in the Moroccan market continues to be the international giant Johnson & Johnson, with a 32 per cent value share in the year 2013, though Maphar Laboratories is a not too distant second with a value share of 22 per cent (Euromonitor International, 2012).

Overall, most brands have shown an increase of profits while economic forecasts have insured that the market will continue to evolve in the coming years. In fact, 2013 saw a total growth rate of 8 per cent with MAD 254 million (approximately 25.4 million Euros) registered for baby and child products (Euromonitor International, 2012).

Additional research has found that Moroccan parents, due to an increase in hygiene awareness, will likely spend more in the coming years on baby and child products (Euromonitor International, 2012). Forecasts claim that by 2018, the growth rate in this sector will increase to MAD 332 million, or roughly 33.2 million Euros (Euromonitor International, 2012).

Besides health and hygiene, the video game industry is another field that has tremendous potential for the underage market and many multi-nationals are trying to position themselves within the country to gain better shares. Gaming culture is very strong in the country and because of this, sales in units of games and consoles reached 23,000 units between 2007 and 2012, according to one study by Media 24 (Wamda.com, 2017).

Because of the increase in marketing to the underage market, and the fact that, going forward, this will likely do little more than increase – both in terms of money spent and the sheer amount of advertising that children will be subjected too – it is now important to measure the attitude of children towards advertising in the emerging economy of Morocco.

Literature review

What children understand of their attitudes towards advertising is one of the subjects that has attracted the attention of many researchers from around the world. At a very young age, children possess the capability to form an attitude towards a commercial (Abideen and Salaria, 2010), assess its advertising message(s) and respond to it accordingly (John, 1999). It has been found that a child's attitude, at all ages, is affected by advertising (Livingstone and Helpser, 2004) and Harrison (2008) points out that advertising affects children's implicit attitudes in their consumption while still other research has demonstrated that children are affected differently by advertisements depending on various reasons and conditions, such as age, social status and their surroundings (Goldberg and Gorn, 1978; Stephens et al., 1982).

Problematically, children are usually unable to differentiate between what is real and what is fictional (Gulla and Purohit, 2013). It is determined that a child's attitude towards commercials may differ depending on the way he or she perceives the commercials (Gulla and Purohit, 2013). However, specifically with animated advertisements, the credibility of the message is questioned or not fully believed, particularly with boys who do not trust what they see on these types of commercials (Ali et al., 2012). Given that advertisements, in general, exaggerate, children do not believe everything they see. However, the power of the moving images and sound in television commercials push children to hold a positive attitude towards advertising (Gulla and Purohit, 2013).

Being able to differentiate between commercials and common television programmes, and also having the ability to realise the intent to sell, is important in that it helps children to detect advertising; furthermore, children are then able to find the impact that advertising has had on their own attitude (Goldberg and Gorn, 1978; Stephens et al., 1982). Children generally improve their ability to distinguish between commercials and ordinary programmes as they grow, both intellectually and cognitively (John, 1999; Khan and Syed, 2014). As they develop their knowledge they realise the impact of advertising on their attitude due to their intellectual development and cognitive evolution (John, 1999).

The research on the impact of advertising on children has proven that advertising has both positive and negative effects on their attitude, though generally, the children themselves remain positively disposed toward advertising (Buckingham et al., 2007). Making use of four dominant factors determining children's attitudes – entertainment, credibility, informativeness and likeability – we can find that a child's attitude towards advertising is generally positive (Gulla and Purohit, 2013). Another research concerning the attitude of children towards commercials found that their attitude towards them is, for the most part, positive

(Ali et al., 2012). Mostly, children display this positive attitude towards advertising in four different elements of socialisation: parental communication, mass media, gender and race (Bush et al., 1999). Additionally, there are a few researchers who point out that advertisements do not have any negative impact on a child's memory or attitude (Akhtar et al., 2010) and suggest that advertisements normally target parents in order to guide their buying behaviour and not children, who normally insist on purchasing their goods once they are together with their parents (Akhtar et al., 2010). An additional study investigating the impact of television advertisement on children aged between 10 and 15 showed that the impact of commercial influence varies from one child to another (Khan and Syed, 2014). However, Calvert (2008) argues that the developing income of children, allocated specifically from their parents and relatives, enables their ability to directly impact the purchasing behaviour of their parents and this impact continues to grow, which serves to give children more power in purchasing the things they want.

Bush et al. (1999) explored the consumer socialisation impact on a child's attitude towards advertisements. They made a comparison of African-Americans and Caucasian children. They discussed the factors shaping children's African-American and Caucasian attitudes toward advertising. As a result, they found that parental communication, mass media, gender and race are significantly related to children's attitudes toward advertising. The researchers also discovered that African-Americans spend more time watching television and hold positive attitudes after watching a commercial.

Another study that explored the negative effects of commercials on a child's attitude found that television advertising enhanced the level of materialism among children, created more parent–child conflicts and caused unhappiness for children (Buijzen and Valkenburg, 2003). The writers think that children are unable to protect themselves from the power of these advertisements. The analysis was based on a vote-counting method and found that there is a correlation between children's viewing of television commercials and the effects mentioned previously on children's attitude (Buijzen and Valkenburg, 2003).

Though children might view advertising in a generally positive light, according to Harrison (2008), their exposure to advertising can be harmful on their attitudes (Harrison, 2008). Cantor (1998) also states that television advertising can be harmful for children, but also potentially beneficial – for instance, through television advertising, children can be encouraged to learn and investigate what they should do to avoid or report domestic violence, sexual predators, cyberbullying, as well as other unwanted sorts of contact or behaviour (Buckingham et al., 2007). After all, online social networks, video game websites and file sharing can all be sources of dangerous content or contact for children, though they aren't the only places to have cause for concern. After all, the average child still watches nearly 12,000 violent acts on television annually (Abideen and Salaria, 2010). This continuous exposure to violence has consistently been proven to be harmful to children and detrimental in how they grow emotionally, making them more prone to imitate the acts of violence they have witnessed (Buckingham *et al.*, 2007).

Beyond the copious amounts of violence witnessed in the media, advertising itself has also been found to be harmful to children (Jarlbro, 2001). Though some advertising might be positive, other types of advertising can be dangerous in that they promote materialism and implicitly endorse the philosophy that material possessions are the source of joy, beauty and success (Wulfemeyer and Mueller, 1992). Thus, children can suffer from many unwanted effects that may stem from their exposure to these types of commercials. Abideen and Salaria (2010) argue that significant impacts on children's attitude – such as unnecessary purchasing, materialism and the increased intake of food of little to no nutritional quality (that is, what we commonly term 'junk food') – may be easily associated with television advertising.

Unsurprisingly, children are more responsive than adults when exposed to advertising (Harris *et al.*, 2009). It has been determined that easy to understand, new commercials attract children effortlessly (Rice and Woodsmall, 1988). When a child watches a commercial repeatedly, it is more likely that this product will be found in that child's home (Goldberg, 1990). Repeated commercials push children to hold a positive attitude towards it for a longer period (Robertson *et al.*, 1979). Most children are aware of the advertisement's goal but the power of commercials push them to buy advertised products anyway or encourage their parents to do so on their behalf (Asadollahi and Tanha, 2011). The fact that imagined creatures and role models are exposed as powerful, smart and attractive pushes children to somehow adopt these fictional lifestyles (Abideen and Salaria, 2010). The good news is that children are less susceptible to these sorts of tactics when accompanied by their parents, though of course they remain more responsive and vulnerable when they watch TV alone (Pine and Nash, 2002). Thus, the persuasive intent of advertisements, and their accompanying negative effect on a child's attitude, can be mitigated. Parents who ignore the goal of these commercials run the risk of making the negative impact stay (Calvert, 2008). However, parents who accompany their child while watching programmes and then explain to them what they are viewing can protect the child from unwanted influence (Mulkan, 2007).

Another problem is that what a child sees in a television commercial generally decides their food choices and guides their attitude (Livingstone and Helpser, 2004). Because the majority of the commercials aired are for junk food, these advertisements have a direct effect on current and increasing levels of childhood obesity (Livingstone and Helpser, 2004; Asadollahi and Tanha, 2011). Hence, advertising directed to children has the effect of promoting both consumerism and contributing to childhood obesity (Asadollahi and Tanha, 2011). There are several studies that come to similar conclusions.

Abideen and Salaria (2010) examined the impacts of television advertising on children, especially with regards to eating disorders in children. They found that there are mainly three significant impacts on a child's attitude caused by television advertising: unnecessary purchasing, materialism and a low to poor nutritional diet (Abideen and Salaria, 2010).

Harris et al. (2009) state that children's exposure to advertising can actually help the prevailing obesity epidemic. Their study uses a test of both children and adults where they exposed both groups to junk-food advertising and gave them snacks while watching the commercials. They determined that children consumed 45 per cent more than adults when exposed to food advertising. In fact, children cannot control themselves when exposed to advertisements and, as a result, direct advertising contributes to increased food intake for children (Harris et al., 2009), though the argument took for granted the direct link between advertising and food consumption.

One of the interesting studies in the literature focused on the advertising effect on children's attitude in the UK (Livingstone and Helsper, 2004). This study primarily discusses the advertising of the food industry and how that affects a child's food choices. They stated that a child's attitude at all ages is affected by advertisements, and specifically that television commercials have a direct effect on childhood obesity. Children base their eating choices on what they watch on television (Livingstone and Helsper, 2004). The interaction of children with television commercials causes them to decide their food choices and guide their attitude. Livingstone and Helsper (2004) argue that daily exposure to advertising harms a child's health indirectly. Hence, their research suggests that media literacy education could help reduce the effects of advertising on a child's overall health and attitude (Livingstone and Helsper, 2004).

Conceptual framework

Media influence

The effect of the media has different aspects of impact on a child's attitude depending on various factors, such as social standing and role of the family (Asadollahi and Tanha, 2011). The media may help raise a child's self-recognition or it may sharply harm it when negatively perceived (Harris et al., 2009). Advertisements can cause violence, racism and bad stereotypes that may harm a child's attitude (Abideen and Salaria, 2010).

Socio-demographic factors

Socio-demographics are important due to the impact they hold on shaping a child's attitude towards advertising (Abideen and Salaria, 2010). Briefly, factors within this study include the age of the respondent, gender and socio-economic status.

Age

Age is an important factor that ought to be taken into consideration. In reality, data gathered for this purpose embrace ages from 6–12. It must be admitted that the responses would vary because the perception of commercials would also vary from a child of 6 to another child of 12 (Akhtar *et al.*, 2010). Consequently, this criterion will help in identifying the perception of children to advertisements and help us understand a child's attitude towards commercials (Abideen and Salaria, 2010).

Gender

Morocco is a traditional country where gender has a crucial role in framing a child's attitude as boys and girls are raised very differently (Sadiqi, 2003). Many studies show that this difference in gender is common in all societies due to many reasons, such as culture, society or religion (Sadiqi, 2002). A girl's attitude towards advertising differs from that of a boy (Lagorio, 2009). For this reason, we expect that gender may have an important role in defining a Moroccan child's attitude towards advertising (Wood, 1994; Lagorio, 2009).

Economic status

Economic information gathered was primarily concerned with the income of the children's parents. This information shows the family's economic status. Within the questionnaire we tried to use the 'car number' question to get an idea about the family income. This is estimated to provide an idea about the economic status of the child. Children with economically stable living situations are supposed to hold a different attitude towards commercials from those children from families with income difficulties (Livingstone and Helpser, 2004).

Family size

Another piece of information within this context was the size of the family. The children had to specify the number of members in their families. This should show whether family size affects a child's attitude towards commercials or not (Lagorio, 2009). This information is estimated to give an idea about the child's interaction with his or her family and the ability of the family to influence a child's attitude towards advertising (Akhtar *et al.*, 2010).

Social influence

Social norms

Another factor taken under valuation is the child's social norms. In reality, this factor deals with the child's surroundings. This is a crucial element in our study because it groups many norms that may influence a child's attitude (Abideen and Salaria, 2010). Generally, social norms are related to the child's family and friends who normally form the child's environment. In the survey, we gave questions primarily about the parents and friends and their impact on the child's choices.

Religion

According to research performed by the Moroccan Center for Studies and Contemporary Research about religiosity in the kingdom, females are more religious than males in Morocco, with 59 per cent for women and only 36 per cent for males. The Center states that females exceeded males in practising religion and doing ritual prayers (Arbaoui, 2012). Religion has an important role in influencing a person's behaviour and attitude towards many aspects (Horwath and Lees, 2008). In Morocco, as in other Muslim countries, Islam shapes the way people interact with each other and the way they behave (Arbaoui, 2012). Religion has an important role in organising the whole society from many levels (Arbaoui, 2012). Islam is the official religion of the country and the king represents the Emir of believers (Moroccan Constitution). The Constitution specifies that Islam is the official religion of the state where the king is 'Commander of the Faithful and Defender of the Community and the Faith'. Generally speaking, Moroccan parents try to raise their children in a way that respects religious rules and aspects (Horwath and Lees, 2008).

According to Delener (1994), Religion is 'a gathering of values and beliefs that regulate behavior and function as a code of conduct', while 'Religiosity is the amount of applying religion'. Normally, religiosity can be divided into two main parts. Allport and Ross (1967) clarify these two types of religiosity as first, intrinsic religiosity, which amounts to whether or not religion is necessary for daily life and second, extrinsic religiosity, which deals with its external use (Allport and Ross, 1967). Intrinsic religiosity represents the vitality of religion in people's daily life, while extrinsic religiosity refers to the way people use religion for external purposes, such as social activities (Allport and Ross, 1967; Delener, 1994). People are influenced by religion, both intrinsically and extrinsically in making decisions with regards to their attitudes and buying behaviours (Delener, 1994). They pay much attention to the religious side of their beliefs to make decisions and whether to choose or purchase one product or another (Delener, 1994). Bridges and Moore (2002) state that there is a reliable relationship between religious education and social and emotional functioning for children. Actually, this effect could be stronger for younger children (Bridges and Moore, 2002). One research conducted in the US found that religion influences a child's attitude and self-perception (Corriveau *et al.*, 2015).

Religious children are found to have more trust in commercials than non-religious children and religious children believe more in miracles, while non-religious children have less trust (Corriveau *et al.*, 2015). This is important to keep in mind as, in our case, Islam is the religion that should impact a child's attitude towards advertising (Delener, 1994).

Attitude towards television advertising

A child's attitude is divided into four important sub-elements: *credibility*, *self-entertainment*, *self-concept* and *ideal-self* (McLeod and O'Keefe, 1972; Pecheux and

Derbaix, 2003). First, *credibility* measures the degree of belief that children have with regard to commercials. Second, *self-entertainment* helps us measure whether children find commercials entertaining or not. Third, *self-concept* helps measure the way children see themselves. Lastly, the *ideal-self* determines the child's status versus their idealised version of themselves after watching commercials. A research model based on the above literature review of media influence, socio-demographic factors, social influence, values and children's attitudes toward advertising is presented in Figure 10.2.

Survey development

The survey was written simply to make the task easy for children. It was translated to French using back translation to make it easier for children to respond. All measures were assessed using established scales. The attitude of children towards advertising was measured using a 5-point Likert-type scale (where 1 = strongly disagree and 5 = strongly agree) developed by Rossiter (1977) and Pecheux and Derbaix (2003), which was used to gather data on attitudes toward television commercials. The survey, which was conducted with children aged 5–12, was divided into three main sections. The first set of questions concerned the child's habits with regard to television and Internet viewing where the children were questioned

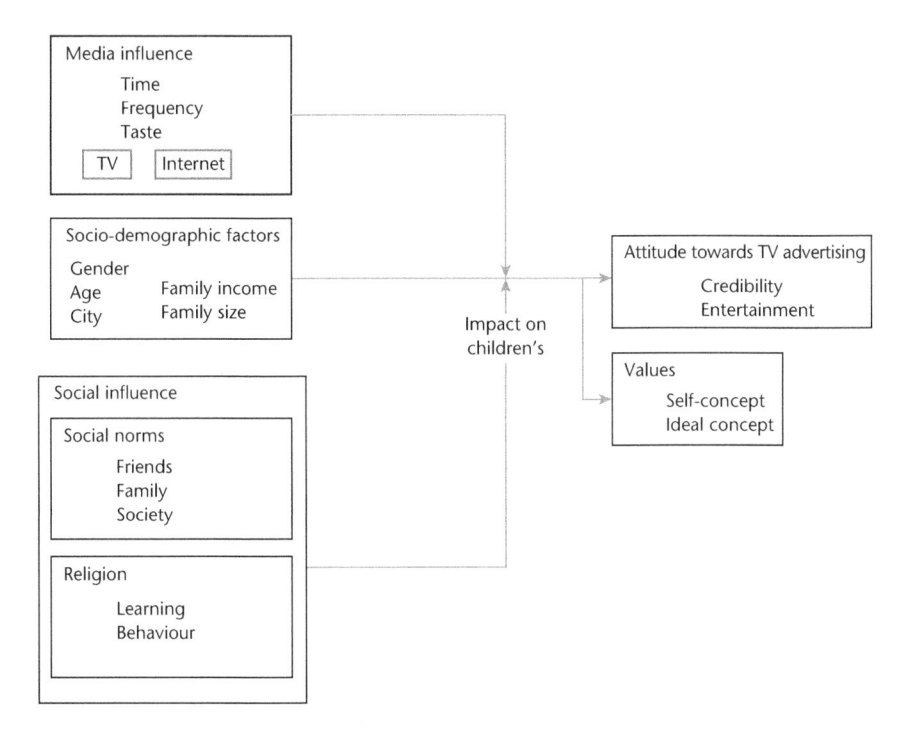

FIGURE 10.2 Children's attitudes towards advertising

about the hours spent using different types of media. The second concerned the child's point of view with regard to different statements related to advertisements and in this context children stated their degree of approval on what they saw advertised. The third was more general information such as age, gender, income and family size. The survey was distributed to children around Morocco using simple random sampling. It was distributed in Agadir, Taroudant, Inzgan, Marrakech, Casablanca and Azrou. The study was conducted in the following schools: Paul Signac, Kalb Almaarifa, Ashbal Alhouda, Mimosana, Elmawrid, Galois, Alwaha, Le Petit Champion, Moulay Ismail, Alkastalani, Lalla Soukayna and Dar Alhikma. With the help of the teachers and administrators of each school selected, the questionnaire was explained to the children directly in their classrooms in order to help them understand the purpose of the survey. Every question was explained to the children and they were given plenty of time to complete the survey. Some students admitted that their parents helped them fill in the survey questions.

Conclusion and implications

The overall results demonstrated that children hold a positive attitude towards advertising in Morocco. This is firmly supported by Gbadamosi *et al.* (2012) whose study in four countries indicates that children like television advertising especially in relation to its entertainment features. In this current study, the children's image of themselves is found changeable and can easily be influenced by the independent variables selected to identify their attitude towards advertising as a whole. Male children discovered that they believed more in the advertisements than females. This is endorsed by the findings of Wood (1994) who argues in her research that males have more trust in the advertisements they see than their female peers. Hendon *et al.* (1978) and Butter *et al.* (1981) also confirm this finding and argue that boys find commercials more credible than girls do. Boys believe more in miracles and they usually try to imitate popular fictional heroes, such as Spiderman and Batman.

Younger children are found to have more trust towards the commercials they view. Taking into consideration that the credibility measured is not taken the same way by children from all the ages selected for this purpose, we can state that younger children believe more in the advertisement they view than older ones. This means that the older the child, the less he or she trusts the advertisements he or she confronts. This finding was already proved in previous research carried out by Gulla and Purohit (2013) and Harris *et al.* (2009). These researchers found that the understanding a child has of the complexity of the world increases as they grow; meaning that the older the child is, the more realistic he or she becomes. They found that children aged between 12 and 14 have less trust in commercials than younger ones due to the growth of their cognitive defence development. This is due to their intellectual development and cognitive evolution (John, 1999). This is obvious since the older the child becomes, the more conscious he or she is and the more he or she realises that the goal of these commercials is simply to sell them things.

The results also found that children are less affected when watching programmes that their parents or tutors agree on. This was admitted by Pine and Nash (2002), who indicated that parental control decreases the degree of advertising's impact on a child. This means that children could be more affected by advertisements when watched alone and without parent approval. The presence of a parent helps reduce the effect of advertisements by commenting or controlling their child's perception of the programme. Calvert (2008) also states that children who are controlled by their parents while watching television are more realistic. Children tend to believe what they watch on commercials. Being accompanied by parents reduces the effect of advertising on their attitudes (Akhtar et al., 2010; Pine and Nash, 2002).

Religiosity among children also plays an important role in defining their choices. Religious children have more trust in commercials than non-religious ones (Corriveau et al., 2015). Religious children believe more firmly in miracles, which is why they also believe what they see in commercials (Corriveau et al., 2015), while non-religious children are typically more critical. Religiosity prevents children from drawing their ideal self in their own ways (Horwath and Lees, 2008). The rules and laws of religion block children, as well as adults, from constructing their ideal self or, in more melodramatic terms, stops them from achieving their dreams (Horwath and Lees, 2008). In fact, religiosity creates a gap between a child's real self and their ideal self since the child feels that they are somehow blocked by the rules and laws of their religion. In Islam, the question of 'Halal or Haram' is present in every aspect of a Muslim's daily life. Religious children always try to search for a religious explanation for their attitudes and decisions. It goes without saying that, in Morocco, Islam is present in every aspect of life and impacts a child's daily life, including their understanding of advertisements.

The more time spent watching television or surfing the Internet, the less trust a child has in the advertising. Usually, children have less trust in the commercials they face if they watch them repeatedly and for a longer time (Wellman, 1990). This finding is somewhat interesting concerning the time that children spend watching television or surfing the web. This could be explained by the frequency as the commercial becomes ordinary and does not strongly affect the intention of the child as it does if watched only a few times. Repeated commercial viewing, however, increases a child's attention towards the product, which is coupled with a loss of interest when the same advertisement is repeated (Wellman, 1990). Children are easily attracted by new waves and trends and new commercials are found to easily attract the attention of children (Rice and Woodsmall, 1988).

Children in families with higher incomes have a tendency to trust the commercials they see. Children with higher income also have more access to television, Internet and to different means of media advertising than children with lower income. Moreover, children coming from families with higher incomes have more belief in commercials as their parents contribute in allowing them to imitate their commercial heroes, to believe in miracles, and to play Spiderman or Batman (Goldberg, 1990).

Children growing in families with larger sizes have less trust in advertisements. This suggests that children from big families have less trust in the commercials they see. This is attributable to the impact that these children could have had from their older brothers and sisters. Calvert (2008) states that children in large families are always protected in the sense that their relatives explain to them what they see in these commercials. Children in large families are mostly accompanied while watching television. They are always watching programmes together and give their opinions. Older children always try to orient younger ones and explain to them the intent of these commercials, thus, younger children in the family are less affected by these commercials (Calvert, 2008).

Religion influences a girl's choice more than it does a boy's. This finding, as substantiated by research in the literature review, confirms that females are more religious than males. The answers received from the children confirm that a girl's religiosity is stronger than that of a boy's, even as a child. Religion has more impact on a female's purchasing choices and attitude where it does not really impact a male's at the same level (Arbaoui, 2012). This was also seen in the research performed by the Moroccan Center for Studies and Contemporary Research about religiosity in the kingdom that found females are more religious than males in Morocco. This can, in part, be explained by female scarf-wearing, lower rates of smoking and practise of rituals. The impact of mothers on their female children is stronger than that on their male children. Consequently, the impact of religion on a female's choices is stronger than that of her male peers. The older the child, the more impact extrinsic religiosity has on his or her attitude. This implication confirms that older children are more influenced by extrinsic religiosity. The impact of extrinsic religiosity on a child's development influences a child's attitude differently, depending on his or her age. The older a child becomes, the more he or she knows about extrinsic religiosity and its values. This is due to children's intellectual change and cognitive progress (John, 1999) and is attributable to different influences that come from parents, education and society (Horwath and Lees, 2008; Arbaoui, 2012). Thus, children raised in a religious country such as Morocco, are found to be more easily persuaded by advertising through both intrinsic and extrinsic religiosity, their belief in miracles and the social pressures, both in the family and in their social groups, to conform standards being advertised. Overall, if marketing communications are not clearly managed or effectively regulated, it could lead to a rise in childhood obesity and violence due in large part to marketers targeting children in their advertisements.

The contribution and implication of the discussion in this chapter are two-fold. It has extended knowledge on the dynamics between young consumers and marketing communications with specific reference to advertising. So, theoretically, it has updated the literature in this context. Meanwhile, there are huge implications for practitioners as well. It provides strategic direction to businesses on communicating with children as a consumer group, which could be a very useful input to a firm's segmentation, targeting and positioning strategy. While the study focuses on advertising, the relevance of the findings could be adapted to other tools as applicable and the application of the findings could have a far-reaching global impact beyond the research context.

References

Abideen, Zain Ul and Salaria, Rashid M. (2010). Effects of television advertising on children: With special reference to Pakistani urban children. *MRPA Paper-22321.* https://mpra.ub.uni-muenchen.de/22321/ (accessed 3 March 2016).

Ali Abid, Raza, Ali, Dileep, Kumar, Muhammad, Haroon and Bushra, Ghurfran (2012). Gender role portrayal in television advertisement: Evidence from Pakistan. *Information Management and Business Review, 4*(6), 340–351.

Allport, G. W. and Ross, J. M. (1967). Personal religious orientation and prejudice. *Journal of Personality and Social Psychology, 5*(4), 432.

Akhtar, Jam, F. A., Hijazi, S. T. and Khan, M. B. (2010). Impact of advertisement on children behavior: Evidence from Pakistan. *European Journal of Social Sciences, 12*(4), 1–8.

Arbaoui, Larbi (2012). Increase in religiosity in Morocco. Moroccan Center for Studies and Contemporary Research, Morocco World News. www.moroccoworldnews.com/2012/03/31700/increase-in-religiosity-in-morocco-moroccan-center-for-studies-and-contemporary-research/ (accessed 3 March 2016).

Asadollahi, A. and Tanha, N. (2011). The role of television advertising and its effects on children. *Interdisciplinary Journal of Research in Business, 1*(9), 1–6.

Bridges, L. J. and Moore, K. A. (2002). *Religion and spirituality in childhood and adolescence.* Washington DC: Child Trends.

Buckingham, D., Whiteman, N., Willett, R. and Burn, A. N. (2007). The impact of the media on children and young people with a particular focus on computer games and the internet. Paper prepared for the Byron Review on children and new technology.

Buijzen, M. and Valkenburg, P. M. (2003). The effects of television advertising on materialism, parent–child conflict and unhappiness: A review of research. *Journal of Applied Developmental Psychology, 24*(4), 437–456.

Bush, Alan J., Smitha, Rachel and Craig, Martine (1999). The influence of consumer socialization variables on attitude toward advertising: A comparison of African-Americans and Caucasians. *Journal of Advertising, 23*(3), 13–24. doi:10.1080/00913367.1999.10673586.

Butter, E. J., Popovich, P. M., Stackhouse, R. H. and Garner, R. K. (1981). Discrimination of television programs and commercials by preschool children. *Journal of Advertising Research, 21*(2), 53–56.

Campbell, K. and Davis-Packard, K. (2000). How ads get kids to say I want it. *Christian Science Monitor, 18,* 25.

Calvert, S. L. (2008). Children as consumers: Advertising and marketing. *The Future of Children, 18*(1), 205–234.

Cantor, J. (1998). 'Mommy, I'm scared': How TV and movies frighten children and what we can do to protect them. www.amazon.com/Mommy-Im-Scared-Frighten-Children/dp/0151004021 (accessed 3 March 2016).

CIA World Fact Book. (2013). www.cia.gov/library/publications/resources/the-world-factbook/ (accessed 3 March 2016).

Corcoran, M. (2007). These days, some teens covet expensive brand names in purses, accessories. *Los Angeles Times,* September 25.

Corriveau, Kathleen, Chen, Eva E. and Harris, Paul L. (2015). Judgments about fact and fiction by children from religious and nonreligious backgrounds. *Cognitive Science, A Multidisciplinary Journal, 39*(3), 353–382.

Delener, N. (1994). Religious contrasts in consumer decision behaviour patterns: Their dimensions and marketing implications. *European Journal of Marketing, 28*(5), 36–53.

De Pelsmacker, P., Geuens, M. and Van den Bergh, J. (2010). *Marketing communications: A European perspective* (4th edn). Harlow: Pearson Education.

Euromonitor International. (2012). Consumer lifestyles in Morocco. www.euromonitor.com/consumer-lifestyles-in-morocco/report (accessed 3 March 2016).

Fill, C. and Turnbull, S. (2016). *Marketing communications: Discovery, creation, and conversations* (7th edn). Harlow: Pearson Education.

Gbadamosi, A. (2012). Exploring children, family, and consumption behaviour: Empirical evidence from Nigeria. *Thunderbird International Business Review*, 54(4), 591–605.

Gbadamosi, A., Hinson, R., Eddy, T. K. and Ingunjiri, I. (2012). Children's attitudinal reactions to TV advertisements: The African experience. *International Journal of Market Research*, 54(4), 543–566.

Gao, T., Sultan, F. and Rohm, A. J. (2010). Factors influencing Chinese youth consumers' acceptance of mobile marketing. *Journal of Consumer Marketing*, 27(7), 574–583.

Grant, I. and O'Donohoe, S. (2007). Why young consumers are not open to mobile marketing communication. *International Journal of Advertising*, 26(2), 223–246.

Goldberg, M. E. (1990). A quasi-experiment assessing the effectiveness of TV advertising directed to children. *Journal of Marketing Research*, 27(4), 445–454.

Goldberg, M. E. and Gorn, G. J. (1978). Some unintended consequences of TV advertising to children. *Journal of Consumer Research*, 14(3), 22–29.

Gulla, A. and Purohit, H. (2013). Children's attitude towards television advertisements and influence on the buying behavior of parents. *International Journal of Marketing, Financial Services*, 2(6), 103–117.

Harris, J. L., Bargh, J. A. and Brownell, K. D. (2009). Priming effects of television food advertising on eating behavior. *Health Psychology*, 28(4), 404.

Harrison, P. (2008). Advertising and its effect on children's attitudes: '. . . At least, do no harm'. *Deakin Business Review*, 1(1), 14–21.

Haste, H. (2005). Joined-up texting: Mobile phones and young people. *Young Consumers*, 6(3), 56–67.

Hendon, D. W., McGann, A. F. and Hendon, B. L. (1978). Children's age, intelligence and sex as variables mediating reactions to TV commercials: Repetition and content complexity implications for advertisers. *Journal of Advertising*, 7(3), 4–12.

Horwath, Jan and Lees, Janet (2008). Assessing the influence of religious beliefs and practices on parenting capacity: The challenges for social work practitioners. *British Journal of Social Work*, 40(1), 82–99.

Horovitz, B. (2006). Six strategies marketers use to get kids to want stuff bad. USATODAY.com. (n.d.). http://usatoday30.usatoday.com/money/advertising/2006-11-21-toy-strategies-usat_x.htm (accessed 3 March 2016).

Jarlbro, G. (2001). *Children and television advertising: The players, the arguments and the research during the period 1994–2000*. Stockholm: Konsumentverket.

John, D. R. (1999). Consumer socialization of children: A retrospective look at twenty-five years of research. *Journal of Consumer Research*, 26, 183–213.

Khan, Shaista Kamal and Sheheryar, Syed (2014). Impact of TV advertisement on children's attitudes in Karachi. *Journal of Business and Management*, 16(3), 40–46.

Lagorio, C. (2009). Resources: Marketing to kids. CBS Evening News. www.cbsnews.com/news/resources-marketing-to-kids/ (accessed 3 March 2016).

Linn, S. (2008). *The case for make believe: Saving play in a commercialized world*. New York: The New Press.

Livingstone, S. and Helsper, E. (2004). *Advertising foods to children: Understanding promotion in the context of children's daily lives*. London: Office of Communications.

McLeod, J. M. and O'Keefe, G. J. (1972). The socialization perspective and communication behavior. In F. G. Kline and P. J. Tichenor (eds), *Current perspectives in mass communication research* (pp. 121–168). Beverly Hills, CA: Sage.

McNeal, James (2006). Young people and harmful media content in the digital age. *Nordicom*, June, p. 13.

Moraes, C., Michaelidou, N. and Meneses, R. W. (2014). The use of Facebook to promote drinking among young consumers. *Journal of Marketing Management*, 30(13–14), 1377–1401.

Mulkan, D. (2007). The effects of violence programs on Indonesian television: A literature study about the attempts to find solution for the effect of violence television programs on Indonesian children. Paper presented at the 10th Indonesia-Malayan Culture Symposium, Bangi, Selangor Malaysia, 29–31 May.

Ouwersloot, H. and Duncan, T. (2008). *Integrated marketing communications* (8th edn). Berkshire: McGraw-Hill Education.

Pecheux, C. and Derbaix, C. (2003). A new scale to assess children's attitude toward TV advertising. *Journal of Advertising Research*, 3(4), 390–399.

Pine, Karen and Nash, April (2002). Dear Santa: The effects of television advertising on young children. *International Journal*, 26(6), 529–539.

Rice, M. L. and Woodsmall, L. (1988). Lessons from television: Children's word learning when viewing. *Child Development*, 59, 420–429.

Robertson, T. S. and Rossiter, J. R. (1974). Children and commercial persuasion: An attribution theory analysis. *Journal of Consumer Research*, 1(1), 13–20.

Robertson, T. S., Rossiter, J. R. and Gleason, T. C. (1979). Children's receptivity to proprietary medicine advertising. *Journal of Consumer Research*, 6(3), 247–255.

Rossiter, J. R. (1977). Reliability of a short test measuring children's attitudes toward TV commercials. *Journal of Consumer Research*, 3, 179–184.

Sadiqi, F. (2003). *Women, gender, and language in Morocco (Vol. 1)*. Leiden: Brill.

Smith P. R. and Zook, Z. (2011). *Marketing communications: Integrating offline and online with social media* (5th edn). London: Kogan Page.

Stephens, N., Stutts, M. A. and Burdick, R. (1982). Preschoolers' ability to distinguish between television programming and commercials. *Journal of Advertising*, 11(2), 16–26.

Wamda.com. (2017). Wamda [online]. Available at: https://www.wamda.com/2014/02/is-morocco-ready-to-become-a-key-producer-of-video-games (accessed 18 September 2017).

Wellman, H. M. (1990). *The child's theory of mind*. Cambridge, MA: MIT Press.

Wood, J. T. (1994). *Gendered lives: Communication, gender, and culture*. Belmont, CA: Wadsworth Publishing.

Wulfemeyer, K. T. and Mueller, B. (1992). Channel One and commercials in classrooms: Advertising content aimed at students. *Journalism & Mass Communication Quarterly*, 69(3), 724–742.

11
DIGITAL MARKETING AND THE YOUNG CONSUMER

Vishwas Maheshwari, Karl Sinnott and Bethan Morris

Introduction

The digitalisation of media fuelled by remarkable technological advancement has changed the landscape of the business environment and the variety of functions within it since the initial development of the Internet. This includes key business operations of marketing and its relative activities such as advertising, direct and personal selling, relationship building, branding and brand development for enhancing communication to serve existing and increasing potential segments in a set market.

Moreover, significant development of digital media has led to the establishment of the term *digital marketing* where traditional models and frameworks of marketing could be applied in a more enhanced manner using a variety of digital platforms, drastically improving the promptness and effectiveness of marketing efforts. This includes use of innovative webpages, social media marketing through prominent platforms such as Facebook, Twitter, Instagram and Snapchat and digital channels such as YouTube and mobile marketing applications. The use of digital marketing mediums have been increasingly popular within all demographic segments, especially for the purpose of information searching, fact finding and establishing trustworthiness before committing to a particular product or a brand.

Digital marketing: terminology, transition and transformation

According to Chaffey and Ellis-Chadwick (2016, p. 10), 'Digital Marketing is a combined application of Internet and related digital media technologies in conjunction with traditional communications in order to achieve marketing objectives'.

The (digital) application has been further extended to marketing of products and services with the use of contemporary mobile technologies and other augmented digital channels. Digital marketing is actually becoming a key catalyst for companies' marketing reach and depth as far as engagement with customers, reference groups and stakeholders is concerned. With the continuous expansion of such engagement opportunities for companies, use of digital media applications for marketing and promotional activities also provides a platform for generating real-time analytics in relation to marketing campaigns. For example, companies are able to monitor, evaluate and analyse what specific marketing concepts and activities have worked for them and what does not effectively provide valuable insight into generating resource and cost efficiencies.

In addition, there is a transitional shift in marketing function overall, with more advanced and sophisticated digital marketing techniques and applications being put in place by companies for attracting, engaging, serving and maintaining relationships with customers. It has also seen active implementation of integrated multi-channel marketing activities combining both traditional and digital platforms. In effect, there has been a strategic- and operational-level transformation of traditional customer relationship management (CRM) into electronic CRM (E-CRM) and now social CRM (S-CRM).

A variety of digital approaches such as social media marketing, location-based marketing and mobile marketing predominantly planned with key demographic insights for accurate targeting are now commonly used in order to gauge customer expectations, identify their requirements, create awareness, initiate engagement and build relationships for establishing brand and products/services loyalty. However, an appropriate consideration is also given to incorporate traditional marketing channels such as TV adverts and print media, at the same time, to emphasise integrated communications.

Developing a digital marketing approach

Developing and implementing a distinct digital marketing plan is essential for the success of any campaign, especially with exceptional levels of competition due to better access to the market for all. Building from some of the key works (Chaffey and Ellis-Chadwick, 2016; Kingsnorth 2016; Econsultancy, 2017; IDM, 2017) into the strategic development of digital marketing, we discuss a staged approach to digital marketing that may provide useful understanding to key derivatives of this process, as shown in Figure 11.1.

The six derivatives including contemporary customer relationship dimensions should be tied together as outlined in Figure 11.1, as a systematic package to deliver a successful application of digital marketing strategy:

- *Market evaluation (online)* – researching and assessing potential market and relative activities, sector-wide or competitor specific, provides valuable insight to understand and establish influential factors of digital communication and more importantly the *digital age* of activities.

```
                    ┌─────────────────────────────┐
                    │  Evaluation of marketplace  │
              ┌────▶│         (online)            │
              │     └──────────────┬──────────────┘
              │                    ▼
              │     ┌─────────────────────────────┐
              │     │ Define target audience      │
              │     │ boundaries                  │
              │     └──────────────┬──────────────┘
              │                    ▼
              │     ┌─────────────────────────────┐
              │     │ Establish consumer          │
              │     │ expectations                │
              │     └──────────────┬──────────────┘
              │                    ▼
              │     ┌─────────────────────────────┐      ┌─────────┐
              │     │ Implement digital marketing │◀─────┤         │
              │     │ plan (integrated)           │      │         │
              │     └──────────────┬──────────────┘      │         │
              │                    ▼                     │ E-CRM   │
              │     ┌─────────────────────────────┐      │ S-CRM   │
              │     │ Campaign performance        │      │         │
              │     │ measurement                 │      │         │
              │     └──────────────┬──────────────┘      └─────────┘
              │                    ▼
              │     ┌─────────────────────────────┐
              └ ─ ─ ┤ Reset digital marketing     │─ ─ ─ ┘
                    │ approach                    │
                    └─────────────────────────────┘
```

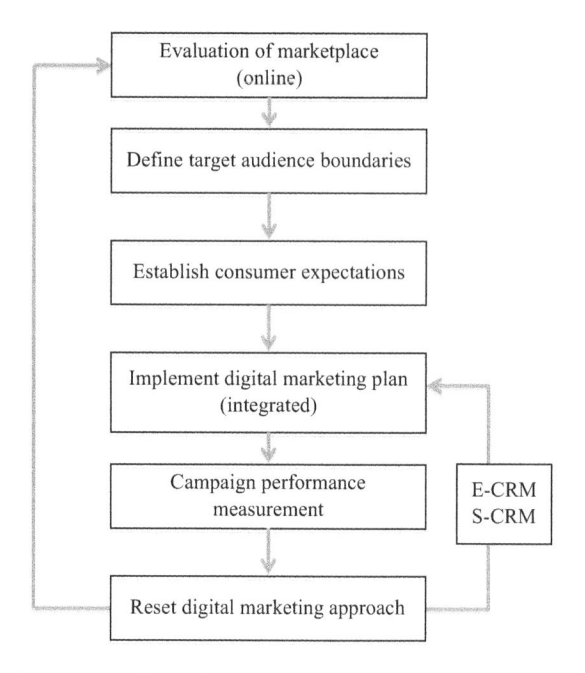

FIGURE 11.1 The process of developing digital marketing

- *Target audience* – segmentation has been essential for every marketing effort and digital marketing is no different. However, the main difference specific to digital marketing is setting up realistic boundaries by establishing online customer personas (*segment groups*) and their respective digital activities for sourcing product- or brand-specific information.
- *Consumer expectations* – having a clear understanding of consumer expectations could help in developing a digital experience personifying each consumer need and ensuring delivery of product or brand promise.
- *Integrated digital marketing plan* – it is essential to put together an integrated plan for enhanced marketing communication that is less invasive but more inviting and appealing for better conversion, i.e. use of various digital marketing channels such as social media marketing, search engine optimisation and display advertising.
- *Performance measurement* – measuring the effectiveness of digital marketing campaigns is an integral part of assessing the influence of various marketing activities in response to customer engagement and conviction. From a resource planning perspective, this is a very helpful activity since it suggests which digital technique(s) worked and which were less effective. Campaign measurement variables could further aid in exploring real-time market trends by use of appropriate analytics tools.
- *Resetting the digital marketing approach* – as a result of the above measurement and evaluation activity, a new or revised digital marketing plan, in line with marketing objectives, could be put in place addressing any specific market developments.

- *E-CRM and S-CRM* – digital customer relationship management by proactively engaging with consumers via web and social media applications also provides effective input to the performance measurement of digital marketing activities.

Digital marketing process or package is essential to support online market understanding and establish target audiences and their relative digital personas. In relation to this, we have made an attempt to shed light on aspects of digital marketing applications that are specifically linked to young consumers and their intent, capabilities and selectiveness for using these applications. We also provide further discussion into the role and importance of digital marketing in consumer behaviour, purchase-influence and consumption decision-making, specifically within young consumers.

Digital marketing communications and young consumers

The worldwide web has evolved from a space for information retrieval into a network that facilitates collaboration, connection and interaction. The Internet as we now know it, referred to as Web 2.0 was shaped during the late 1990s and early 2000s (Ryan, 2016). The advent of Internet-enabled phones and broadband has changed it from a luxury to a necessity. In fact, the demand for mobile data is rising at a rate that the current communications infrastructure itself is struggling to accommodate (National Infrastructure Commission, 2016). Today's children will be growing up knowing nothing other than the freedom that Web 2.0 has brought to enable them to choose the content they want to consume or create, when, where and how they please.

Households are becoming increasingly connected, 83 per cent of children aged 5–15 in the UK have access at home to a tablet and 99 per cent of all UK households with children have Internet access (Office for National Statistics, 2016). Smart TV ownership has risen since 2014 from one-eighth to just over a quarter of all UK homes. By the time they reach school age, children have consumed media on multiple devices, and have developed skills to access and navigate the basic functions of mobile phones and tablets. Unsurprisingly, as digital developments have paved the way for an array of new media and communication tools, consumers' media consumption has become more fragmented. This is no different for children, who are no longer passive consumers. We live in an always on, in-demand culture that the traditional marketing communications mix alone does not satisfy.

Internet use and the young consumer

Just as with traditional forms of marketing communication, we need to identify where, when and how to communicate with consumers. The Internet itself is not a communication tool; it is the medium through which digital communications are made. In order to select the most appropriate tools, it is necessary to understand how young consumers use the Internet. The home remains the main centre of children's Internet use, choosing PCs and laptops as more suitable for homework but preferring portable devices for entertainment and communication. Where pre-school and primary school-age children tend to play games and watch YouTube videos on tablets and smartphones, tweens (those aged between 9 and 12 years old) and teens use them primarily for messaging and social media. It has become more unusual for a teenager to not have a smartphone today. Teens spend on average over three hours a day using them, brands that are looking to engage with young consumers need to ensure that their communications can be accessed on mobiles, particularly through social media.

Although most social networking sites have a minimum age requirement of 13 years, nearly three-quarters of children aged 10–12 have signed up to at least one account (Coughlan, 2016). When connecting with family and friends, children's choice of platform will depend upon the audience. Facebook is used less by children for communication purposes. Facebook is a space also occupied by parents and older family members with whom they may not want to interact with in the way they would with their peers. Young consumers prefer to associate with peers on instant messaging and dark social platforms such as WhatsApp and Snapchat. Dark social, a term that is much less sinister than it sounds, refers to platforms that enable the sharing of web links that cannot be tracked by web analytics. These apps enable individual or closed group conversation and are preferred by young consumers to SMS messaging, as they are free to use. WhatsApp enables basic sharing of messages, photos and videos and is appealing as a simple and quick to use platform. For those that wish to enhance, embellish or simply have fun with messaging styles, Snapchat is the platform that young consumers turn to. In fact, Snapchat is used by over 80 per cent of the teenage population in the UK, and in the US almost a quarter of Snapchat's members are under 18 years old (Statista, 2017).

Snapchat: what's its appeal?

Snapchat is a messaging app that allows its users to send images and videos, which 'self-destruct' within a few seconds of the recipient opening them. Snapchat Stories are collections of snaps that last longer but still disappear after 24 hours. The ephemeral nature of Snapchat has come under scrutiny by Internet safety experts because of the potential for inappropriate material to be shared without trace. However, it also enables the young consumers to express themselves confidently with less anxiety about saying something that makes them appear foolish. Individual Snaps as they are known could be embellished with captions, electronic doodles and various filters and lenses enabling its users to tell their stories in a fun and novel way. It is this spontaneous, carefree style of communication that cements Snapchat's appeal with young people. At the close of its first day's trading on the New York Stock Market, *The Financial Times* (2017) reported that Snap Inc, the owner of Snapchat was valued at $28.3 billion.

Use of Snapchat to engage a young audience

Snapchat lenses are overlays that can be placed on an image, usually a selfie. Popular ones have included 'Puking Rainbows', an animated rainbow that comes out of a person's mouth, like vomit and 'Face Swap', where as it implies faces are swapped with other people, animals or objects in a photo. As it was possible to screenshot the results, Snapchat users delighted in sharing their face swap images on other social platforms. Many, including the one below, went viral.

Furthermore, 20th Century Fox used sponsored lenses to promote the Marvel film, *X-Men Apocalypse*. It worked with Snapchat to make all available lenses X-Men themed for a day. Snapchat users took pictures of themselves with the lens of their favourite X-Men character. Snapchat measured that the lenses received over 298 million views over the course of the day.

FIGURE 11.2 'Face Swap' image

Source: Imgur (www.imgur.com).

Generating engagement though, does not always require paid-for promotion. Brands that perform particularly well on Snapchat are those that convey an authentic, fun and entertaining personality and centre their stories on the people behind the brand. Among these is *Teen Vogue*, who take viewers behind the scenes at fashion shows, and whose editorial team give product reviews from within the publication's offices. *Teen Vogue* also provides its followers behind-the-scenes access to celebrities in the form of 'takeovers'. Takeovers are essentially account owners giving a third party access to temporarily broadcast from their account. In January 2017, popular girl band Fifth Harmony hosted a takeover of *Teen Vogue*'s Snapchat account. Takeovers using celebrities popular with a young audience provide incentives for *Teen Vogue*'s target market to follow them, and give celebrities exposure to an audience of potential fans.

Snapchat Stories: FEAT Socks

Another brand that uses Snapchat to showcase its fun and relatable brand personality is US apparel brand FEAT Socks who were ranked second in a list of the best brands on Snapchat by *Entrepreneur Magazine* in February 2017. Founded by Parker Burr, Taylor Offer and Elijah Grundel while in their final year in college, FEAT Socks started out by making and selling brightly coloured and patterned socks to fellow students on campus. According to its website, FEAT products are now stocked in just under 100 surf, skate and sports retailers. As it has grown, its focus has remained on catering for a young market.

FEAT centres its communications around the day-to-day lives of its founders, team and even the resident pet bulldog, Blake (who has his own sock design). Followers gain a very personal insight into the workings of the company and the dynamics of the team. One of their recent stories was based on a day in their headquarters, which looks more like a teenager's den than offices. They hold meetings at a ping-pong table, pack their products while eating chocolate gummy bears, shoot basketball hoops and order in pizza as a reward for working late in order to get orders out to their valued customers. This casual, cool but reliable ethos aligns well with the brand. Paradoxically, their peers influence teenagers but also strive to show their individuality. Regardless of whether they actually are or not, teens typically wish to view themselves as risk takers and thrill seekers (Global Web Index, 2015). FEAT incorporates this into its products and promotion. For example, it has launched a product range co-designed by Garett Hill, a well-known professional skateboarder. Snapchat's mission statement is very clear about facilitating self-expression, embracing the present and sharing experiences 'Our products empower people to express themselves, live in the moment, learn about the world and have fun together'. FEAT conveys a similar message in its strapline that also lends itself to the immediate and exciting nature of Snapchat, 'Live like this'. According to their website, 'Live like this is not a motto, but a way of life. Designed for doers, creators and anyone who embodies a positive lifestyle.'

Why Snapchat works so well for FEAT is the way that they combine stories with promotions. FEAT offers promotions exclusively on Snapchat, and directs its followers to take a screenshot of their coupon codes. As Snapchat notifies accounts when a user has taken a screenshot of their content, this provides a useful way to measure engagement and interest in their promotions. The user is not clicking directly on to a link to their online store. As the young consumer may not have access to their own funds online, making a coupon code available is a useful tactic if parents or guardians will be buying on their behalf. Unlike other social media platforms, Snapchat has limited search functionality. Until recently Snapchat has only allowed a user to add a contact by inputting their specific account handle into its search function or while in the app, scan in a Snapchat-generated QR code, known as a Snapcode. Teenage consumers will turn to social networks to research a brand, so it is important for brands to retain an active and customer-driven social presence. FEAT builds brand awareness by disseminating its content on other platforms; its own blog, high-quality close ups of socked feet usually also wearing brands of footwear popular with teens such as Vans, Converse and Nike often featured on Instagram. It engages with fans on Twitter and integrates imagery and featured products on Facebook. All platforms though point to Snapchat, offering exclusive promotions in order to encourage users to follow and engage with them.

WhatsApp

WhatsApp presents a greater challenge for brands. As discussed, WhatsApp provides a user-friendly, free experience and provides closed conversation to individuals or groups. WhatsApp was bought by Facebook in 2014, a once independent service with values at its core is now owned by the world's largest monetised social media platform (Statista, 2017). Inevitably, WhatsApp's privacy stance has eroded and in 2016 revealed that it would be sharing user data with Facebook for a more targeted Facebook experience. Users can opt-out of this service, however, when the digital environment has made individuals less patient, terms of service are often agreed without the user reading them. WhatsApp has an age restriction of 13 years old and data should not be collected for those under 16 according to its own website, however, as we know children under the age of 13 are readily signing up to social accounts, therefore age information may not be entirely accurate. The overarching structure of WhatsApp is of less concern in this section, it is more important that our understanding of how children use the platform informs marketing communication strategy. WhatsApp facilitates group conversations. Depending upon a child's network of peers, it is possible that they could be involved in multiple group conversations. A key concern among children is missing out on updates, gossip and conversation with friends. Conversely, children have also reported that the amount of WhatsApp notifications they receive when in group chats can be overwhelming. Even a few hours away from their device can mean they return to a large stream of unread comments. What this indicates is that children will screen their messages in order to find the most valuable information to them. Sending unsolicited messages through any means of digital communication is generally perceived as bad practice, whatever the age of the consumer. However, brands can effectively engage with consumers through WhatsApp if they have initiated contact with them, and several brands including Hellman's, and Boots have enjoyed relative success with adult consumers. For children this may differ, even if they reached out and instigated a conversation, once a response has satisfied their query, engagement via alternative social channels may be preferable. In addition to the risk of outbound messages through the app being perceived as intrusive, further in-app communications may well be lost within a stream of unread messages from peers.

Social media campaign measurement and analytics

Notably, the two platforms we have explored are among the most challenging to track in terms of campaign success, as neither has formal analytics built in. Social media analytics allow organisations to measure the performance of a campaign against the objectives they have set themselves. Social network sites such as Facebook and Twitter have in-built analytics where a wide variety of metrics can be measured and monitored; this includes the demographic profile of followers, how engaging content has been, and what time of day followers are using the social network. This is, however, not as limiting as it appears. Many software companies provide analytics programs, but this aside, valuable information is still available from within both Snapchat and WhatsApp. On both platforms it is possible to see how many times a message, snap or story has been opened. Also, for Snapchat it is possible to measure how many times a story has been followed to its completion. These could in essence help to identify which content is the most interesting and engaging. Second, analytics are used for much more than campaign measurement. Data is available for the 13–17-year-old segment of a Facebook or Twitter audience. If a brand has insight into this segment, it is possible to glean information about their interests and what content engages them the most, to inform the tactics used within both Snapchat and WhatsApp.

Digital marketing and young consumer behaviour

In this part of the chapter we will look at the influences of the young consumer on the digital or online decision-making process (the 'consumer decision journey') for a variety of relevant brand categories. Typically, young consumers will also be highly involved in the decision-making process for brands and products they consume as part of the wider family decision-making process, but this is outside the scope of this chapter. For our purposes the scope of the decision-making process for the young consumer will be determined by the brand categories in which the young consumer is the primary or only consumer from within the family unit, and the decision-making process itself is online rather than offline.

In the course of this part of chapter we will look to answer the following questions.

1. What is the typical online consumer decision-making process for these categories?
2. Given that the young consumer is not the actual purchaser, which stages of the process can the young consumer exert influence over?
3. What are the direct or indirect influencers at play on the young consumer at each stage of this process?

Let's start with the consumer decision-making process.

What is the typical online consumer decision-making process for those categories where the young consumer is the primary consumer of the brand category?

Given the fact that the young consumer is effectively part of the decision-making unit and NOT the purchaser, it is important to understand the overall online decision-making process from the purchaser's (parent, guardian, etc.) perspective before we look at how the young consumer influences the various stages of the overall process. Current thinking around the online consumer decision journey has developed from traditional customer decision-making (CDM) theories discussed in earlier chapters of this book.

So what is the typical consumer decision journey online?

The concept of the purchase funnel has been extensively used to outline the stages of the customer decision-making process and although it is now used in an online context, as a theoretical construct the purchase funnel pre-dates the move to online. Figure 11.3 outlines the basic concept. Most authors would seem to agree that the construct has become more popular in that it describes effectively the typical end-to-end customer journey across digital platforms and that the stages of the funnel reflect what we now call the (online) customer journey.

It is generally felt that the funnel shape is deemed useful to describe what is perceived to be the 'natural loss' of potential customers at each stage. Critiques of the purchase funnel approach seem to focus on the lack of complexity or linearity of the construct. As far back as 2007 Haven emphasised two important points in their research and review of thinking around the online consumer design-making process:

1. The actual purchase process online is much more complicated than the traditional funnel model describes.
2. There are some new factors to consider when using the funnel in a modern context (such as social media and online communities).

198 Vishwas Maheshwari et al.

1. Pre-awareness

2. Awareness

Purchase intent trigger

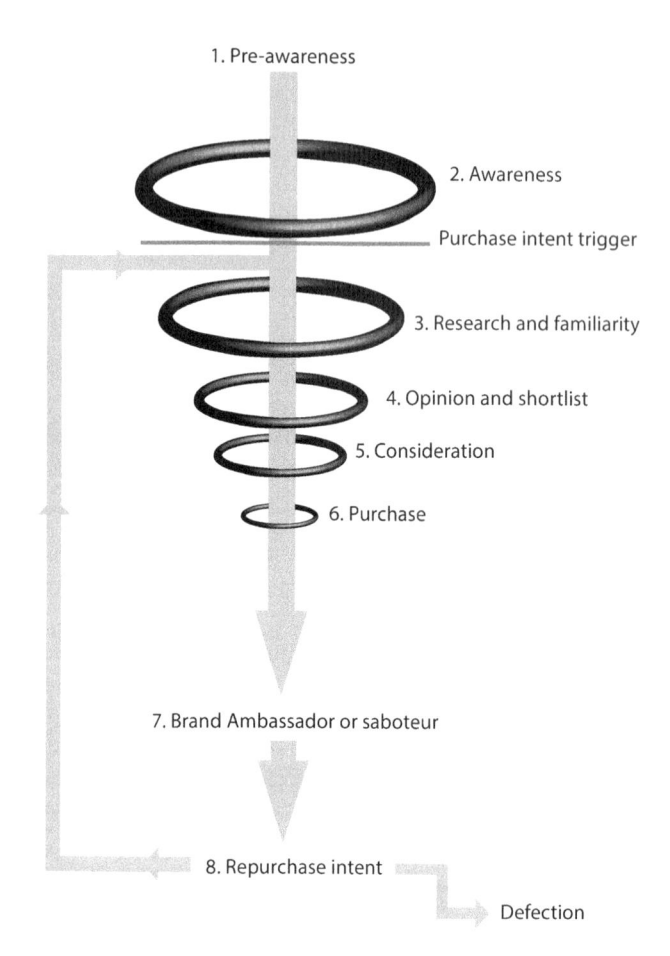

3. Research and familiarity

4. Opinion and shortlist

5. Consideration

6. Purchase

7. Brand Ambassador or saboteur

8. Repurchase intent

Defection

FIGURE 11.3 The consumer purchase funnel by Gibson (2015)

Source: marketing-made-simple.com.

The Forrester Report (Haven, 2007) first makes the point that the traditional purchase funnel may be too linear for meaningful application to the online environment and that a variety of complex factors are at work, with social media often at the centre. The lack of complexity led them to develop their own model as shown in Figure 11.3, which describes a much more complex consumer decision journey. As reflected in the model, the ultimate consumer decision may be influenced by a number of factors around the edge of the model. These range from the influence of recommendations from friends, peer reviews, competitive alternatives and even user-generated content. Haven's central point here seems to be that in the digital age, consumer purchase decisions are not that simple, and that people and in particular young consumers are influenced by a variety of different factors and influencers. Haven's (2007) critique of the purchase funnel as lacking in complexity also appears to be a foundational principle for the work of management consultants in the marketing field and more specifically consumer behaviour.

Court *et al.* (2009) have led the work in this domain and have taken the thinking in this area in quite a different direction. Court *et al.* (2009) suggest that the funnel analogy implies that consumers follow a systematic and staged process to narrow down the 'initial-consideration set' as they weigh options, make decisions, and then ultimately buy the product or service. Post-purchase evaluation is then regarded as a quasi trial period in which consumers determine their loyalty to brands and the likelihood of buying their products again (see re-purchase intention in Figure 11.3).

In their view the funnel concept fails to capture all the touch points and key buying factors resulting from the 'explosion of product choices and digital channels'. When these factors are coupled with the emergence of an increasingly discerning, well-informed young consumer then the need for a more complex, more sophisticated and less linear approach to understanding the consumer decision-making process would appear to be pertinent to help marketers navigate this environment.

While the linear purchase funnel approach (and model) is still, perhaps surprisingly, being deployed by many marketing professionals, Court *et al.* (2009) (and Haven, 2007) seem to regard the continued use of the purchase funnel approach as a very linear approach in what Haven (2007) and Court *et al.* (2009) would state is now a non-linear world.

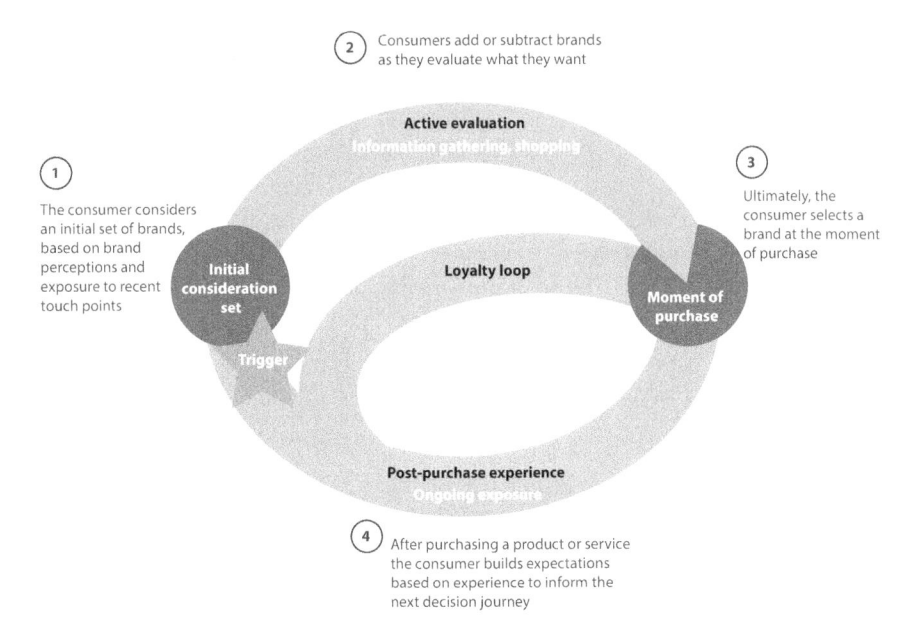

FIGURE 11.4 The McKinsey consumer decision purchase loop by Court *et al.* (2009)

Source: marketing-made-simple.com.

Court *et al.* (2009) recommend a loop model, as illustrated in Figure 11.2, instead of the usual straight-line approach reflected in the purchase funnel construct. The radically different approach is based on empirical research originally carried out in 2009, through interviews with 20,000 businesses in the US, Germany and Japan.

The model still reflects some of the core principles of consumer decision models (CDMs) so awareness, purchase and loyalty still underpin the McKinsey model. However, it is the 'looped' dimension to the model, which represents more of a radical shift from previous thinking, such as the purchase funnel.

The approach is termed the consumer decision journey and Court *et al.* (2009) strongly believe that the approach is applicable to any demographic market (including young consumers), any geographic market (even emerging markets), any decision-making unit and also has relevance across all digital media channels including what is now termed 'omni-channel'.

So how does the approach work?

Court *et al.* (2009) propose that the decision-making process is more of a circular journey, with four primary phases. They call these:

1. Initial consideration
2. Active evaluation, or the process of researching potential purchases
3. Closure, when consumers buy brands
4. Post-purchase, when consumers experience the brands.

This new way of thinking seems to have real resonance and the original work by Court *et al.* (2009) has now spawned lots of additional research and variants of these loop-based models. Google's ZMOT (Zero Moment of Truth) is a prime example of much vaunted work in this area and approaches that, it is felt, fit the more complex and sophisticated buying process of the modern consumer.

Bosomworth (2015) produced an infographic on Smart Insights, which they feel synthesises the latest thinking in this area. The stages of the model are described below in Figure 11.5 and the model will then be used to help explore the typical consumer decision journey for categories that involve young consumers as well as to understand the influences of the young consumer at the various stages in this process.

The stages of the model are defined as follows:

1. Trigger
2. Initial consideration set
3. Zero moment of truth
4. Purchase decision
5. Second moment of truth.

WHAT'S INFLUENCING PURCHASE?

A Google ZMOT x McKinsey&Company Mash-up

ZERO MOMENT OF TRUTH
Product or brand based research sees brands added and subtracted to the early consideration set. Based upon price, performance, online reviews, in-store browsing and social media.

INITIAL CONSIDERATION SET
Consumer's carry preference and preconceived ideas, often enabling a rapid forming of an early consideration set for research and exploration, in-store, at home online, or via mobile on the move.

FIRST MOMENT OF TRUTH
A final shortlist is set, based upon the evaluation phase products are viewed and reviewed either online (desktop and mobile) or at shelf in-store, possibly each at the same time.

McKinsey&Company LOYALTY LOOP
Some Triggers come with automatic brand selection based on previous experiences, advocacy born of emotions, trust, deep beliefs and a relationship.

TRIGGER
A consumer's journey is emotional, triggered by need or want, influenced by direct and indirect brand messages, friends, WOM. It is not, necessarily anything to do with brand owners, or their advertising.

SHARED OPINIONS
Positive & negative reviews become the next persons ZMOT or Trigger

PURCHASE DECISION
The moment of purchase and associated experience is central to how the consumer feels about the brand, as well as the retailer, before consumption takes place - are they excited or impartial?

SECOND MOMENT OF TRUTH
Unwrapping, unboxing and using - the consumer now has new information for future brand purchases, as well as the ease and means to share those experiences, creating a brand foot-print for future consumers to follow.

What kind of brand foot-print is your brand and the consumer making?

Purchase is no longer funnel orientated - people add and subtract both brands and products - to be effective marketing requires a thorough appreciation of buyer behaviour prior to, during and after transaction.

Complex consumer journeys demand brands to think beyond a transaction goal, instead infusing themselves into the consumer's community and across multiple touch-points.

Whether it's a new Honda Civic or a can of Diet Coke brands create a footprint, directly and indirectly by the experience they engender, building influence - good and bad - over time at one or more touch-points.

first10 & Smart Insights
www.first10.co.uk   www.smartinsights.com

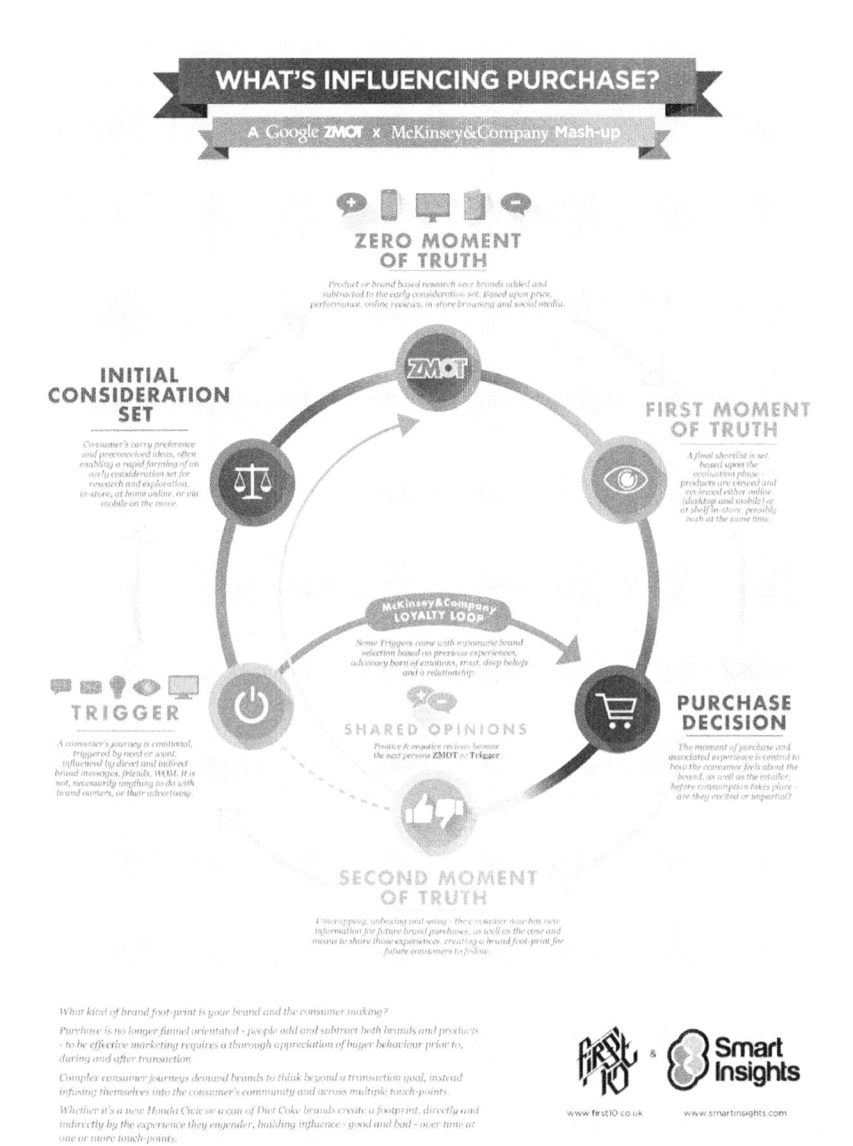

FIGURE 11.5 Customer decision journey by Bosomworth (2015)

Source: www.smartinsights.com.

Let's now use the model to help answer our final two questions:

- Given that the young consumer may not be the actual purchaser, at which stages of the process can the young consumer exert influence over the process?
- What are the direct or indirect influencers at play on the young consumer at each stage of this process?

Trigger

The first stage of the process looks at the initial triggers, which push the consumer to consider the product and look at the needs and wants of the consumer. Given the type of categories under consideration, the young consumer is likely to be highly involved in this stage and will often initiate the trigger.

So what are the influences at play? The central idea here is that the initial trigger often comes from indirect or direct brand messages, friends, as well as word of mouth. It is not necessarily anything to do with big brand messages and advertising.

This last point seems very relevant to the young consumer market. Imagine that our young consumer has decided they'd like a new video game. Given the very young consumer's lack of understanding about the principles of advertising as well as the constraints imposed by regulators, the importance of advertising at this stage is likely to be more limited.

It's much more likely that any initial triggers will come from (say) viewing a dedicated gaming YouTube channel for a certain genre of games. In other words, the relevance of peer pressure and word of mouth through social media platforms including YouTube channels cannot be underestimated. These aspects of digital marketing strategy are much more likely to be key influences on the young consumer at this stage in the process.

Initial consideration set

This stage of the model infers that the ultimate consumer carries preferences and preconceived ideas about the brand category now under consideration and that this will often enable the consumer to rapidly form an early consideration set.

Given that the young consumer is, in this context, the ultimate consumer of the product (as opposed to parents or guardians) they are much more likely to be highly involved in this stage of the customer decision journey. It's highly likely that the young consumer will immediately be able to name an initial consideration set of brands to purchase. For example, this might include the latest versions of Call of Duty, Battlefield, Grand Theft Auto, FIFA, Final Fantasy, etc.

Court *et al.*'s (2009) research with consumers (see Figure 11.5) suggested strongly that media fragmentation and the dazzling number of products now available in most categories has actually made it more difficult for all consumers, including the young, to reduce the number of brands they consider at the outset. According to Statistics Brain (2016), around 16,000 adverts are seen by young consumers in the US in an average year. Faced with such a plethora of choices and communications, our young consumers tend to fall back on the limited set of brands that have made it through the wilderness of messages. In this context, brand awareness does matter. Brands in the initial consideration set can be up to three times more likely to be purchased eventually than brands that aren't in it. Brand awareness is also very likely to be driven by peers and, therefore, online and offline word of mouth such as the social media platforms already mentioned. So, in our gaming example, if the young consumer is interested in 'Sports' games within the 'Soccer' category, the initial consideration set is likely to include those games used by peers or specifically referenced by peers on the various platforms or online communities they are using to engage with like-minded young consumers.

Zero moment of truth

At this stage of the journey product- or brand-based research conducted by the young consumer sees brands added and subtracted to the early consideration set. The objectives during this stage of the process are for the (young) consumer to attain what Google term the 'zero moment of truth'. Court *et al.* (2009) refer to this as the 'active evaluation' stage. Again, given the fact that the young consumer is the ultimate 'user', the degree of involvement in this important stage of the customer decision journey is likely to be high. In our gaming example, competitor brands outside the initial consideration set may 'interrupt' the decision-making process by entering into consideration and even force the exit of rivals. The number of brands added in later stages does differ by industry.

So what are the influences on the young consumer at this stage of the journey?

In today's decision journey, consumer-driven marketing is increasingly important as customers seize control of the process and actively 'pull' information helpful to them. Court *et al.*'s (2009) research found that two-thirds of the touch points during the active-evaluation phase involve consumer-driven marketing activities, such as Internet reviews and word-of-mouth recommendations from friends and family, as well as in-store interactions and recollections of past experiences.

So in our gaming example, typically, given the context and the demographic, online reviews on the websites of gaming and general online retailers such as Amazon will be a major influence on this crucial stage of the process. Peer-to-peer reviews on social media platforms and even in-store trialling are also likely to be influences.

First moment of truth

At this stage of the consumer decision journey a final shortlist is established based on the previous active evaluation phase. Given the direct involvement in the trialling and ultimate consumption of the product, this is also a stage in which the young consumer is likely to be highly involved and their input into any decision criteria is likely to be significant. It is worth stressing, however, that certain elements of the decision criteria are likely to be out of their sphere of control. Budget is the most likely criteria and also the element most likely to draw the purchaser into this stage of the process.

So, with the combined input of the young consumer and the purchaser (parent, guardian) the shortlist is then reviewed using the set of decision criteria either online, typically on a mobile or at shelf in store, possibly both at the same time.

Purchase decision

This stage is defined as the moment of purchase. Irrespective of the channel used to make the purchase and the age of the young consumer, the ultimate purchaser is very likely to drive the actual purchase transaction itself. So, in our gaming example, the purchaser completes the transaction online or accompanies the young consumer, if the transaction happens in store.

Second moment of truth

The 'second moment of truth' is a stage that reflects the associated experience right at the point of purchase, a critical stage in any customer decision process. The young consumer is at the focus of this 'second moment of truth' as it is he/she who undertakes the unwrapping, unboxing and actual usage of the product. Given the high propensity of young consumers to re-purchase updated versions of our video game (or similar games in this genre) this second moment of truth is regarded as pivotal in the whole consumer decision journey.

Post-purchase and the loyalty loop

When the young consumer starts to utilise the product, the marketer's work has just begun. The post-purchase experience mentioned in the second moment of truth (see above) will shape their opinions for every subsequent decision in the category, making the journey an ongoing cycle or loop. Hence the term, the 'loyalty loop'.

The strength (and significance) of the loyalty loop does depend on the type of loyalty shown by the young consumer. A proportion of our loyal young consumers will be active loyalists, who not only stick with the brand but the triggers to initiate re-purchase of the brand will be virtually automatic based on previous experiences, advocacy, emotional attachment, trust and a developing relationship. This type of active loyalist young consumer is also more likely to recommend the brand. So, in our gaming example, after having purchased the latest version of FIFA, for example, they will join online communities and share their experiences with others.

There may also be other types of loyalists who are deemed to be passive and, whether from lethargy or the confusion caused by the vast array of choices, they stay with a brand without being committed to it. Despite their claims of allegiance, passive loyalists of (say) FIFA are open to messages from competitors who give them a reason to switch.

Having explored the typical customer decision journey for the young consumer, it is important to recognise how this understanding might impact on digital marketing strategies focused on this segment.

However, two important questions seem pertinent in addressing this important issue:

1. How can digital marketers optimise their digital marketing strategies with this particular customer decision journey in mind?
2. What are the challenges here, given the different influences at play and the constraints imposed by different forms of regulation?

We will address these two questions together by looking at each of the opportunities.

Align digital marketing strategy with the consumer decision journey

Developing a deeper knowledge of how young consumers make decisions is the first step in the process. Understanding the key stages where the young consumer has high involvement as well as the most effective and responsible ways of influencing through appropriate digital marketing techniques at these key stages are also of paramount importance.

Tailor messaging

Given the complexities and the sensitivities of marketing to this segment, messages need to be tailored to the audience and rather than having one core message across all the stages, messages should be tailored to take account of the specific point in the journey (initial consideration vs. active evaluation for example) and the degree of influence exerted at that point by the young consumer. Consideration also needs to be given to tone of voice used in any communication given the sensitivities around exploiting this market and constraints imposed by the relevant regulation.

Invest in consumer-driven marketing

To look beyond funnel-inspired push marketing, brands must invest in vehicles that let marketers interact with young consumers as they learn about brands. The epicentre of consumer-driven marketing is the Internet, but social media and online communities are also vitally important for this segment and crucial during the active-evaluation phase as young consumers seek information, reviews and recommendations. Brands need to develop strong capabilities in these vital areas.

Integrating all customer-facing activities

Given the complexity of the new consumer decision journey and the multitude of channels available, the importance of integration across channels cannot be understated. Marketers have long been aware of profound changes in the way consumers research and buy products. The picture is much less clear for the young consumer. The shift in consumer decision-making and the complexities and sensitivities involved in the customer decision journey for the young consumer means that marketers need to configure their marketing resources so they regard loss of power over consumers not as a threat but as an opportunity. With this in mind brands will be better positioned to be in the right place at the right time, giving the young consumer relevant information and supporting them so they can exert influence over the process in an acceptable way and in a fashion that also favours the brand.

Conclusion and implications

The culture of instant messaging suggests that children interact with real-time communication well. An inbound approach, that is one that provides valuable content to bring consumers to the brand, is more appropriate in the case of young consumers. Social media is a boredom breaker for many children, so communications must not be too long, and offer them value. As young as some consumers are, they do show some understanding of the commercial nature of advertising and marketing and will see through any overtly sales-like messages. If young consumers want to engage with brands via social media, they have many avenues to do so, but most importantly, will do so on their own terms.

It is vital for brands to undertake serious strategic thinking while devising digital marketing plans for products and services for which the young adult is the ultimate consumer. The complexities of the decision-making process, the influence of the young adult in this process and the ethical parameters that need to be considered, all make this a challenging, but potentially very rewarding scenario for brands. Brands in a range of sectors such as finance and banking sectors, food and gaming sectors have a powerful incentive to rise to these challenges. Those brands that are successful in engaging with young consumers appropriately, at the right stage of the journey and with the appropriate emergent channels will put themselves in a very powerful position. They can utilise this to their advantage by further cementing the relationship with the young consumer as their purchasing power increases, with a very positive impact on lifetime customer value.

This chapter makes an updated case about the importance of digital marketing and the critical role it plays in terms of communicating with a varied target audience, especially young consumers. The conceptual model for development, implementation and monitoring of the digital marketing process presented in the chapter should assist marketers in effective planning and positioning of digital marketing communication strategies. Finally, we also resonate the fact that for brands to succeed and establish a loyal young consumer following, they have to be ready to adapt to the fast-changing and digitally enhanced marketing field but also be proactive in exploring possible opportunities that are innovative and creative.

References

Bosomworth, D. (2015). *The consumer decision journey*. Smart Insights. www.smartinsights.com/marketplace-analysis/consumer-buying-behaviour/what-influences-purchase/ (accessed 20 March 2017).

Chaffey, D. and Ellis-Chadwick, F. (2016). *Digital marketing: Strategy, implementation and practice* (5th edn). Harlow: Pearson.

Coughlan, S. (2016). *Safer internet day: Young ignore 'social media age limit'*. www.bbc.co.uk/news/education-35524429 (accessed 1 March 2017).

Court, D., Elzinga, D. and Vetvik, O. J. (2009). *The consumer decision journey*. www.mckinsey.com/business-functions/marketing-and-sales/our-insights/the-consumer-decision-journey (accessed 20 March 2017).

Econsultancy. (2017). *Content planning doesn't need hundreds of tools*. https://econsultancy.com/blog/68589-five-essential-ingredients-for-digital-marketing-success (accessed 4 March 2017).

Gibson, Jon (2015). *Consumer purchase funnel: Marketing made simple*. www.marketing-made-simple.com (accessed 20 March 2017).

Global Web Index. (2015). *Examining the attitudes and digital behaviours of teens*. Global Web Index. https://pro.globalwebindex.net/reports/17965 (accessed 3 March 2017).

Haven, B. (2007). Marketing's new key metric: Engagement. *Forrester Report*. www.forrester.com/report/Marketings+New+Key+Metric+Engagement/-/E-RES42124 (accessed 20 March 2017).

IDM. (2017). Institute of Direct and Digital Marketing blog. www.theidm.com/ (accessed 28 February 2017).

Kingsnorth, S. (2016). *Digital marketing strategy: An integrated approach to online marketing*. London: Kogan Page.

National Infrastructure Commission. (2016). *Connected future*. www.gov.uk/government/news/government-must-take-action-now-to-secure-our-connected-future-so-we-are-ready-for-5g-and-essential-services-are-genuinely-available-where-they-are-n (accessed 28 February 2017).

Office for National Statistics (2016). *Internet access: Households and individuals – 2016*. www.ons.gov.uk/peoplepopulationandcommunity/householdcharacteristics/homeinternetandsocialmediausage/bulletins/internetaccesshouseholdsandindividuals/2016#main-points (accessed 28 February 2017).

Ryan, D. (2016). *Understanding digital marketing: Marketing strategies for engaging the digital generation* (3rd edn). London: Kogan Page.

Snapchat. (n.d.) X-Men Apocalypse: *Sponsored lens campaign*. https://storage.googleapis.com/snapchat-web/success-stories/pdf/pdf_xmen_en.pdf (accessed 20 March 2017).

Statista. (2017). *Most famous social network sites worldwide as of January 2017, ranked by number of active users (in millions)*. www.statista.com/statistics/272014/global-social-networks-ranked-by-number-of-users/ (accessed 20 March 2017).

Statistics Brain Institute. (2017). *Television watching statistics*. www.statisticbrain.com/television-watching-statistics/ (accessed 23 March 2017).

WhatsApp. (2014). *Setting the record straight*. https://blog.whatsapp.com/529/Setting-the-record-straight (accessed 20 March 2017).

12
SERVICES AND RELATIONSHIP MARKETING

Perspectives on young consumers

Yiwen Hong, Anh N. H. Tran and Hsiao-Pei (Sophie) Yang

Child consumers, services and services marketing

Child consumers: a conceptual overview

Children can be defined as being aged between 0 and 12 years old (Valkenburg and Cantor, 2001) and are identified to be increasingly important and influential as consumers in marketing research, partly due to their higher levels of disposable income (Calvert, 2008; Šramová, 2014). This is primarily due to increasing amounts of pocket money being given to children. For example, Calvert (2008) states that around 87 per cent of young children's income is supplied by parents, compared to 37 per cent for teenagers. In 2002, it was found that children aged 4–12 years old spend around $30 billion USD per year (Calvert, 2008). They also influence family household purchasing decisions, including snacks, holiday and car-purchasing decisions. Indeed, estimates show that children (aged 2–14 years old) can hold influence over approximately $500 billion USD per year (Calvert, 2008).

There are deemed to be a number of 'special features', which distinguish child consumers from adult consumers. Here, children are learning to 'become' consumers, to be socialised in their purchasing decisions and consumer behaviour by external factors (Šramová, 2015). From a marketing perspective, it is proposed that children are able to

> (1) feel wants and preferences (as early as infancy and toddlerhood); (2) search to fulfill them (as early as the preschool period); (3) make a choice and a purchase (from the early elementary school period on); and (4) evaluate a product and its alternatives (as early as the later elementary school period).
> *(Valkenburg and Cantor, 2001, p. 69)*

McNeal (1992) distinguished child consumers, in terms of the markets they are seen to be influencing: primary, secondary and future. First, the primary market refers to the current consumption habits of the children and the purchases they are making. Second, the secondary market relates to the extent to which the child can influence family purchasing decisions. Third, the future market describes the potential future sales from children as they become older consumers with higher levels of disposable income (McNeal, 1992).

Regarding the primary market, the current consumption habits of children are affected by a number of different factors. These factors include advertising and marketing, familial influence and peer pressure. According to the literature, marketing and advertising does have an impact upon children's purchasing intentions, but is less important than familial or peer influence (Nicholls and Cullen, 2004; Ebster *et al.*, 2009; Šramová, 2014).

However, the nature of the children's purchases and the influences upon these is differentiated by age. Indeed, Valkenburg and Cantor (2001) identified four development stages of children according to consumer behaviour and preferences: 0–2 years old (infants and toddlers); 2–5 years old (pre-schoolers); 5–8 years old (early elementary school); 8–12 years old (later elementary school). Those children at the younger end of the age spectrum (0–2 years old and 2–5 years old) are more likely to be enticed by the physical aspects of a product, such as its colour or shape, whereas older children may be more influenced by the social meaning of their purchase (Lemish, 2007; Calvert, 2008; Šramová, 2015). The social meaning of purchases refers to the increasing sensitivity of older children to current trends and the norms of their peer group in order to gain their respect. Actually, children in the 8–12 age bracket were found to pay more attention to their peers' opinions than advertising when making purchase decisions, compared to children aged 2–5 (Valkenburg and Cantor, 2001; Nicholls and Cullen, 2004).

Concerning the secondary market, it is argued in the marketing literature that a significant proportion of family spending results from the influence of the child's desires, particularly in the supermarket (Calvert, 2008; Ebster *et al.*, 2009; Šramová, 2015). At the same time, the child's purchase decisions are not only controlled and monitored by family members, but also influenced to an extent by familial or cultural preferences. Therefore, child consumers are proposed to be not yet fully independent when making purchase decisions (Nicholls and Cullen, 2004).

Furthermore, in relation to the future market, as children become attached to a particular product or service at a young age, they are likely to continue using this product or service as they grow older. Thus, firms are increasingly focusing on advertising to children, particularly on modern forms of media, such as the Internet, in order to increase the likelihood of customer loyalty from a young age (Šramová, 2014). Thus, the future market can be seen to be captured if firms can become attractive to children.

In this way, child consumers are an important market segment for services marketing. It is therefore worthwhile for the company to pay more attention to attracting young customers as they can establish a strong customer–brand relationship from childhood. For example, customers who visited Disneyland theme park when they were young may be more likely to become attached to the Disney brand. They can influence their family to go with them on trips to the theme park. As well as this, when the customer is in adulthood, they are likely to take their own children to the theme park, having become attached to the Disney brand in their own childhood. This may influence their own purchasing habits, as well as that of their children.

Definition of services

In the marketing literature, services are defined as something distinguished from 'pure' goods. Services can be sold as a separate 'item', such as in the entertainment industry. At the same time, services can be sold alongside physical goods, to create added value and boost sales. Here, in increasing the value of the physical good, utilising a service allows firms to distinguish themselves from competition. This often appears in the form of insurance or an after-sales service when a customer is purchasing a high-end physical product, such as a car or house. Services are not sold exclusively in the service industry and can be utilised by any firm in increasing the business effectiveness of their goods, although they tend to be found in particular industries, e.g. banking, finance, insurance, etc. (Grönroos, 2011).

Four key defining characteristics of services have emerged in the marketing literature to highlight the distinction between goods marketing and service marketing: intangibility, inseparability, perishability and heterogeneity (Fisk *et al.*, 1993; Taherdoosta *et al.*, 2014). First, intangibility refers to the notion that services are based on experiences and are not physical items, like tangible goods (Taherdoosta *et al.*, 2014; Kushwaha and Agrawal, 2015). Here, actions are performed by the service provider, as unlike goods, services are not taken home by the consumer after the transaction has taken place. For example, this could be showing a movie at the cinema or serving food in a restaurant.

Second, perishability means that the services cannot be inventoried, nor returned or re-sold, in contrast to physical stocks of goods, which can be stored according to customer demand (Taherdoosta *et al.*, 2014; Kushwaha and Agrawal, 2015). Indeed, an under or over supply of services can present an issue for firms. Here, as the services during a period of low-demand cannot be stored for a period of high-demand, supply and demand of services needs to be carefully managed. For example, a bus tour needs to sell out its seats for that trip only as they cannot be inventoried for a later tour.

Thirdly, inseparability relates to the simultaneous occurrence of the production and consumption of services. Whereas goods are produced and consumed in separate locations, being first produced elsewhere and then consumed by the customer, the opposite is true for services (Taherdoosta *et al.*, 2014; Kushwaha and Agrawal, 2015). This highlights the fact that services are an experience, rather than a good being consumed.

Fourth, heterogeneity refers to the ways in which services vary between transactions, in contrast to the production line of physical goods. It is asserted that no two service experiences are the same and differ according to the service provider and the customer (Taherdoosta et al., 2014). Lovelock and Gummesson (2004) critiqued these four characteristics of services and propose a new paradigm, where 'non-ownership' becomes the defining aspect of services. According to this, services act as a way of renting or accessing some kind of benefit, e.g. having the right to gain access to expertise or to use facilities and networks.

Lovelock and Gummesson (2004) asserted that there is a lack of evidence to support the claims of these four characteristics. In their tests, Lovelock and Gummesson (2004) found that the four characteristics were only relevant for certain services, but not all of them. Therefore, it is argued that these characteristics cannot adequately explain the concept of services and that the characteristics have become increasingly less valid in relation to services, primarily due to changes in the service sector and technological advancements. For instance, the increasing use of automation and strict quality standardisation procedures has reduced the heterogeneity of service provision (Lovelock and Gummesson, 2004). As a result, several authors have extended the traditional '4Ps' marketing mix in order to modernise and improve the framework.

The development of technology has solved the problem of service perishability. For instance, university students may attend lectures through distance learning instead of coming to the class. The variability of services is also reduced based on innovative technology such as ATM or other banking services. Young customers do online shopping and might also pay for products through Internet banking. In other cases, service providers like language centres may assess the participant's prior knowledge to create homogenous groups of learners, resulting in better service provision.

Services marketing

Why services marketing?

Services marketing is an increasingly influential and important aspect of marketing, considering the expansion of the services economy in developed countries. Indeed, the service sector dominates around 70 per cent of developed economies today (Bureau of Economic Analysis, 2006). Services marketing is differentiated from traditional marketing, as services involve the marketing of experiences or activities, rather than of physical goods. It is for this reason that Rafiq and Ahmed (1995) proposed extending the marketing mix that has been employed as a framework for traditional marketing to be more applicable for services marketing. Therefore, McCarthy's (1960) 4Ps framework (*product, price, place* and *promotion*) has been extended to consist of a further 3Ps (*physical evidence, people* and *process*), making a 7Ps framework for services marketing. The importance of the 7Ps in services marketing has been highlighted throughout the marketing literature (Grönroos, 2004; Kushwaha and Agrawal, 2015).

The new marketing mix was used to identify aspects of services marketing that were not adequately addressed by the traditional marketing mix (Shamah, 2013; Kushwaha and Agrawal, 2015). Indeed, services marketing originally emerged as a critique of the traditional marketing paradigm (Skalen, 2009). Here, the extended services marketing mix accounts for the fundamental differences between goods and services (Fukey *et al.*, 2014). The additional 3Ps are proposed to account for the added complexities of services over goods and the importance of interaction with people, which is a necessary element of services. Thus, people, processes and physical evidence are deemed to be the 'interactive marketing dimensions' of the services marketing mix (Gummesson, 1999; Kushwaha and Agrawal, 2015). While much research in marketing has focused its efforts on single elements of the marketing mix, it is proposed by Kushwaha and Agrawal (2015) that it is not the individual 'Ps' that may be the most significant, but rather the interaction between them. In this way, the 7Ps framework is important to consider when taking into account services marketing in the context of child consumers. This will be discussed in further detail below.

Extended marketing mix: the 7Ps

First, the 'product mix' considers the 'service' products that are being offered to the customers. The firms aim to personalise such services to meet customers' specific needs, in contrast to a perceived standardisation of goods (Fine, 2008; Kushwaha and Agrawal, 2015). Thus, it is advocated in the marketing literature to develop the 'product mix' from the customer's perspective in meeting their particular expectations. Here, firms seek ways in which they can differentiate themselves from their competitors, with the quality of service products that they offer (Fine, 2008).

Second, the 'price mix' takes into account the firm's value of its service products. Here, a firm's service pricing needs to be fair and competitive in order to assure company loyalty and to entice new customers. If the prices are too high, it can result in customers switching to competitor firms, who offer a more reasonably priced service (Colgate and Hedge, 2001; Kushwaha and Agrawal, 2015). Price is deemed to have a significant impact upon customer satisfaction and loyalty, particularly in the services market where there are a number of competitive alternatives available for the customer to choose from (Bang and Philipp, 2013; Kushwaha and Agrawal, 2015). However, due to the higher costs of attracting new customers, firms using service marketing tend to focus on building customer loyalty (Fine, 2008).

Third, the 'place mix' refers to the distribution channels and outlets of services, which are identified to be significantly different to those used for goods (Grönroos, 1984). This relates to the inherent nature of services: the inseparability of production from consumption directs the way in which the service is distributed (Grönroos, 1984; Skalen, 2009; Kushwaha and Agrawal, 2015). For example, in the banking sector, banking services are produced and consumed at the bank itself. Furthermore, in restaurants, the service of providing food and drinks is produced and consumed at the same time. The 'place mix' also considers the physical location of the store or outlet where the service transaction is taking place. It is also worth noting that firms are increasingly moving to online stores to distribute their services (Purcarea et al., 2013; Kushwaha and Agrawal, 2015).

Fourth, 'promotion mix' relates to the ways in which firms promote their services. Here, firms need to consider the most appropriate and effective marketing communications channels and promotional tools to use. Certain firms in the service industry may not be able to make use of traditional promotional techniques such as TV advertising, due to financial constraints, and may instead focus on other more cost-efficient promotional tools, such as social media (Kushwaha and Agrawal, 2015; Šramová, 2015). The 'promotion mix' can include wider tools outside of advertising, such as sales promotion, PR and personal selling. For instance, firms may lower their prices during certain periods in order to increase sales and attract customers.

After having considered the traditional 4Ps framework, it is now necessary to take into account the supplementary 3Ps, which are part of services marketing. Fifth, the 'people mix' proposed by Judd (1987) considers the human actors who play a part in the delivery of services to customers. It was argued that the firm's frontline employees represent the organisation to customers and are of vital importance to the marketing of a service (Shanker, 2002; Kushwaha and Agrawal, 2015). Here, the performance of employees is seen to play an important role in determining the customers' perceptions of the service and its ultimate success (Grönroos, 1984; Skalen, 2009; Kushwaha and Agrawal, 2015). The customers are not only interested in the service itself, but how the service transaction takes place and the interaction between employees and customers. Here, customers are involved in co-producing the service product with the employees at the point of transaction (Grönroos and Voima, 2013). Furthermore, employees' training and professional education levels are vital for firms involved in service transactions. There is a need to ensure that the employees are more proactive and customer-oriented in service provision (Skalen, 2009).

Sixth, 'physical evidence' is the place in which the service transaction takes place and where customers and employees interact. Due to the intangibility of services, the service environment is often used as a proxy for service quality. The physical appearance and style of the environment plays a significant role in determining customers' perceptions of the firm (Shanker, 2002; Kushwaha and Agrawal, 2015). Thus, the environment acts as physical evidence of an intangible service (Fukey et al., 2014; Kushwaha and Agrawal, 2015).

Seventh, 'process mix' refers to the methods through which the service is delivered to customers, described as 'the architecture of services' (Kushwaha and Agrawal, 2015). The process facilitates the customer experience when engaging in a service transaction (Grönroos, 2011). In the marketing literature, it is argued that the processes need to be smooth, easy, convenient and fast, as well as customer friendly (Kushwaha and Agrawal, 2015). Similar factors are considered to be important when the process is moved online (Ibrahim et al., 2006).

Services marketing in the context of children

The marketing mix and young consumers

The marketing mix is vital in creating an efficient marketing system, by meeting the needs of a target market and co-operating with customers' preferences. The 7Ps subsequently serve as the basis of decision-making in the service industry (Aghaei et al., 2014; Kushwaha and Agrawal, 2015). Considering the importance of 7Ps in the services marketing framework, this section will explore the applicability of 7Ps in the context of child consumers. Each of the extended marketing mix elements will be evaluated according to how they align with children's consumption.

The 7Ps in the context of children

The 'product mix' considers the extent to which services are designed to meet the needs of customers, considering their preferences and different age groups (Fine, 2008; Kushwaha and Agrawal, 2015). Services can be sold in their own right to customers, or supplied as an extra when the customer is purchasing goods. In the context of children, particular services are offered to them to align with their needs and preferences. Services that could be appealing to children include entertainment or education. According to Calvert (2008), products should be marketed according to the age groups of children. Services should similarly align with this strategy. For example, older groups of children would be marketed different kinds of movies compared to younger children, while children who are interested in sports would be advertised swimming or football classes.

Furthermore, restaurants may give extra services that are specifically for children. This could include games, toys or an activity sheet. These are not necessarily paid services, but help to meet children's needs and preferences. It helps to add value to the goods being purchased, as well as to the brand itself. Added services create a connection between the brand and the children, which helps to build long-term brand loyalty, considering their importance in the 'future market' (McNeal, 1992; Šramová, 2014).

The price mix refers to the value of the service products and the price sensitivity of the customer (Colgate and Hedge, 2001; Kushwaha and Agrawal, 2015). It is proposed in the marketing literature that older children and teenagers are price sensitive (Šramová, 2015). With younger children, parents normally pay for any services they might wish to buy, but if they were to buy these themselves, price is argued to be an influential element. Older children and teenagers enjoy saving money from both pocket money and any part-time jobs that they may have. Price is therefore an important factor for them when making a purchasing decision

(Šramová, 2015). For instance, when purchasing a service such as entertainment, the time and seat chosen when watching a movie or performance can determine the price.

The place mix relates to the distribution channels of services and the location of service outlets. The location of the service outlet is considered to have an impact upon its success and the likelihood of consumers going there (Grönroos, 1984; Skalen, 2009; Kushwaha and Agrawal, 2015). In the context of children, it could be argued that the service location should be found in a convenient place where children are likely to go and not too far from where children normally visit. For instance, in a 2015 Mintel report, it was found that a significant proportion of customers chose their most frequently visited hair salon according to location (39 per cent), compared to price of services (46 per cent), loyalty (36 per cent) and good reviews (18 per cent). Therefore, the provision of services for children is highly dependent on convenience as well as price. Children are unlikely to make use of services if they are located too far away.

The 'promotion mix' takes into account the marketing channels that firms may use when promoting their products, such as television or the Internet (Kushwaha and Agrawal, 2015; Šramová, 2015). Child consumers are increasingly targeted by a number of different marketing techniques used by firms. Traditionally, this involved advertisements on television. Fan and Li (2010) found that television remained the most important source of information on new products for Chinese children. Advertisements are reliant on targeting children, due to their effectiveness in engaging child consumers to increase brand awareness and affect product-purchasing decisions. During the Christmas period in the Netherlands, it was found that children watched up to 25 advertisements during the commercial break (Valkenburg and Cantor, 2001). It is proposed that advertisements have a strong impact on the consumption habits of children (Valkenburg and Cantor, 2001; Calvert, 2008). Due to the strength of such influence, parents are no longer the primary influence on children's consumption values (Valkenburg and Cantor, 2001). However, it is worth noting that modern social studies have found that children may not be passive recipients of advertisements but rather 'active and motivated explorers of what they encounter in the media' (Valkenburg and Cantor, 2001, p.70).

Advertisements will often use what Calvert (2008) referred to as 'attention-getting production features' to engage children and attract their interest. This includes aspects such as bright, flashy imagery, sound effects, rapid movement and pacing and loud sounds. The message needs to be easily memorable and to the point (Calvert, 2008; Cairns et al., 2013). Celebrity endorsements are also commonly used in children's advertisements, linked to well-known brands and peer approval (Fan and Li, 2010). Alongside this, branded characters (i.e. media characters that promote a brand name) are often used in advertisements, which may appeal to children and become synonymous with the brand to its viewers. For instance, Ronald McDonald is a branded character used by McDonald's to promote the brand to children in a fun, entertaining way. This is used alongside premiums, whereby McDonald's gives away small toys in its Happy Meal to increase its appeal to children.

Indeed, brand knowledge and brand awareness are important drivers of advertising, where firms aim to ensure that children become loyal to their brand and, in turn, capture a segment of the future market. Brand loyalty is what firms strive for when they advertise to the youth (Šramová, 2015). Linked to this, it was found that children increasingly request particular brands when deciding to purchase products as they grow older (Fan and Li, 2010). Indeed, children's understanding of, and engagement with, advertisements evolves according to their developmental stage. For instance, pre-school aged children have difficulty in distinguishing between characters in advertisements and characters in TV shows and cannot identify the persuasive, manipulative nature of commercials, taking it at face value (Buijzen and Valkenburg, 2000; Valkenburg and Cantor, 2001; Cairns *et al.*, 2013). On the other hand, at a later stage in childhood, children become reflective and analytical, being able to understand and identify marketing practices and their intent, in a relatively sophisticated manner. It is for this reason that the marketing literature has identified the highest impact of advertising and marketing efforts being on children under 8 years old (Buijzen and Valkenburg, 2000; Valkenburg and Cantor, 2001). However, Calvert (2008, p. 215) did state that, 'Even so, all children can be influenced to purchase certain products if the products are made attractive enough to consumers'.

Despite television remaining the dominant marketing channel, firms have developed new venues for advertising to children in recent years: primarily through the Internet (Calvert, 2008). The Internet is being increasingly used by brands, who recognise its interactive and dynamic nature and can make use of flashy animations to market itself to children, who now spend the majority of their leisure time online (Cairns *et al.*, 2013). Children are now exposed to more discrete forms of marketing, where advertisements and marketing campaigns are often placed online, using a number of 'stealth marketing techniques' (Calvert, 2008). This is where, for example, the services may be advertised within the content of a video game or movie, i.e. product placement. For children, and particularly older children, advertisements not being overt or overly obvious are attractive and enticing (Cairns *et al.*, 2013). Viral marketing is also increasingly used by firms to advertise to children in order to enable or enhance brand loyalty (Calvert, 2008). The viral marketing technique is particularly directed towards teens, who are often pressured by peers into favouring particular brands (Cairns *et al.*, 2013).

The 'people mix' considers the need for a customer-oriented approach to services marketing, where the human element of service is vital. Here, human resources, and the interaction between customers and employees, are deemed to be key (Skalen, 2009). The way in which the service is produced is crucial in terms of the customers' perception of the brand. As a result, firms are encouraged to ensure that their service marketing is customer-oriented by training and educating their employees (Skalen, 2009).

'Personal selling' is considered to be a way in which firms can personalise their sales process and build relationships between the seller and the customer. Here, the customer can build a relationship in the long term with the brand. For children, this is found to be an important aspect in their purchase decision-making, where they are more likely to buy particular products and brands if they have already formed a strong bond with the salesperson (Šramová, 2015). Personal selling allows relationships to be formed between children and the brand, which can continue into adulthood, allowing brand loyalty to form. For instance, this could be personal selling at a hair salon or a restaurant. If the child can form a good relationship with the hair stylist, they are likely to continue going to the same hair salon into adulthood.

The process mix refers to taking into account *how* the service is carried out, rather than what the customer receives. In other words, the process mix focuses more on the 'functional quality', rather than the 'technical quality' (Grönroos, 1984; Skalen, 2009). The process mix strongly impacts service quality and customer service experience and is therefore inherently linked to the 'people mix'. Such measurements of service quality can include factors such as reliability, appearance, attitudes and behaviour of the employees (Skalen, 2011). Consequently, service marketers, as it is argued, should control or manage their 'human resources' to be more customer-oriented and proactive when they are dealing with children (Shostack, 1977). A proactive approach to services marketing comprises of anticipating children's needs and acting on their previous knowledge. Human resource management may involve middle-managers coaching their staff to be better communicators and their behaviour more customer-oriented, to 'model a service ethic' when dealing with children (Zeithaml *et al.*, 1990, p. 139). Here, employees may be trained to improve their knowledge about service quality and to understand how to provide a high level of service.

The physical evidence mix considers the environment in which the service transaction takes place. The quality or style of the environment is identified to have a significant impact upon how the customer perceives and experiences the brand (Shanker, 2002; Kushwaha and Agrawal, 2015). In the context of children, they would appreciate an attractive environment that is well decorated and brightly coloured (Zeithaml *et al.*, 2008). They are more likely to make a purchase in an environment that is inviting. Indeed, they tend to prefer environments that are visually appealing, including the use of cartoon figures (Kirkorian *et al.*, 2008). Furthermore, products need to be placed at an eye-catching level in the store to engage the interest of children. The physical evidence also applies to the online environment, where children will be attracted to websites that are user-friendly, easy to understand and have high levels of security.

The marketing mix and the 7Ps discussed here relate to ways in which firms target their marketing communication messages towards children. Here, they aim for the products to be attractive to children and for the children to form a relationship with their brand. There are concerns in the marketing literature about the ethics of companies targeting child consumers in their advertisements. These are partly social in nature, where, on the one hand, children may become increasingly 'drawn into the adult world' (Šramová, 2014, p. 1028) taking part in less traditional activities for children. On the other hand, children may spend an increasing amount of time in stores and online, instead of spending time with their friends or family outdoors, which could potentially affect the socialisation process and their cognitive development (Šramová, 2014, 2015).

As well as this, the marketing of high-calorie food to children has a negative impact upon their health and well-being, resulting in rising levels of children with obesity (Calvert, 2008; Šramová, 2015). The attractive, engaging nature of food advertisements is encouraging children to eat food with a higher fat, salt or sugar content than they normally would (Cairns et al., 2013). As a result of these concerns, there are guidelines on advertisements to children to protect them, considering younger children's inability to grasp the advertiser's intent and purpose. For example, the Federal Communications Commission (FCC) has limited the amount of time allocated to advertisements to be one hour of children's programmes in the US. The marketers need to abide by these guidelines when advertising to children.

Child consumers and relationship marketing

Theoretical overview of relationship marketing

In the past few decades, relationship marketing has taken a central position in business exchanges. Research in different fields of service marketing (Grönroos, 1994; Bolton et al., 2000) and business-to-business marketing (Bhardwaj, 2007) confirmed that long-term relationships bring benefits to both companies and customers.

Before exploring more about relationship marketing, it is worth looking at the definition of the term 'relationship' from a marketing perspective. Morgan and Hunt (1994) defined relationship as a marriage, of an enduring personal relationship between two people that repudiate all others. However, there are differences between social and personal relationships (Radley, 1996). Personal relationships focus on the psychological make-up of the engaged parties. In a personal relationship, the connection between people formed by emotional bonds and interactions is valued whereas in a social relationship people tend to behave in the same patterns over time. Social relationships are vital without being desired. The motives of social relationships are closely related to the needs of those involved in them. This raises a question of whether relationships should be considered as a 'marriage'. According to Tynan (1997), as marriage does not concern the number and nature of those involved in the relationship, it therefore cannot be considered in the same way as a relationship.

Shaker and Basem (2010) viewed relationships as the social process in which the interactions between people happen. People interact with each other according to different factors, such as their feelings, social pressure or based on rational factors. Therefore, it is hard to expect exclusivity from a social relationship. In the context of a company–consumer relationship, the customer might not consider the company as a marriage partner, whereas they might want to include other parties in that relationship. It enforces the findings of Szmigin and Bourne (1998) by stating that every relationship is enclosed in a network of other relationships. Morales (2005) emphasises that customers compared the outcomes within the relationship, which confirms the equity theory by highlighting that people compare the costs and rewards that the relationship brings them. When a person perceives injustice, he/she tends to adjust the equity in real terms (actual equity) or to adjust the perception of equity (psychological equity). Otherwise, the relationship would end. Therefore, the main concept of relationships is to fulfil customers' needs instead of focusing only on selling products to gain an equitable relationship (Arnett and Badrinarayanan, 2005).

Relationship marketing (RM)

Relationship marketing (RM) is an emerging marketing perspective that is well established in the marketing literature. Many researchers have identified that managing external relationships helps companies gain competitive advantages (Morgan and Hunt, 1994; Berry, 1995).

Although there is no agreement on a definition of RM, Grönroos's (1994) definition has been widely accepted among scholars. According to Grönroos (1994, p. 9),

> Relationship Marketing is to identify, establish, maintain and enhance and when necessary also to terminate relationships with customers and other stakeholders, at a profit, so that the objectives of all parties are met, and that this is done by a mutual exchange and fulfilment of promises.

This definition indicates that relationships are developed between 'customers and other stakeholders'. In the context of child consumers, companies can have different relationships with their children customers as well as other stakeholders such as key influencers of children.

According to Vyas and Raitani (2015), RM involves developing a lifetime relationship with customers rather than an individual dealing in order to increase short-term profit. Udegbe et al. (2010) argued that RM focuses on using different strategies to develop a long-term relationship with customers. Organisations therefore need to exceed customers' expectations to satisfy, maintain and develop a relationship with them.

RM emphasises a two-way commitment between stakeholders and firms. This mutual exchange creates a win–win situation where both stakeholders and the firm gain something. Developing loyalty between a firm and stakeholders can only continue if both parties benefit from the relationship exchange. However, RM has not been adopted in all situations with all customers (Palmer, 1996). According to Gummesson (1994), customers are not always in a relational mode. Thus, transaction marketing tends to be the most appropriate in some marketing situations. Grönroos (2011) also identified the differences between those customers who would like to have a transactional exchange with the company and those who wish to have either an active or passive relationship with the company. Therefore, RM should be applied depending on customers' preferences (Garbarino and Johnson, 1999).

Branding and RM

The similarity between RM and branding strategy is on building customer loyalty. Researchers suggest that the main idea of RM is to develop and maintain customers, whereas the principle of branding lies in customers' perspectives towards the company (Wood, 2000). According to Srivastava et al. (1998), both RM and branding activities focus on creating intangible customer assets that enhance customer loyalty. Rust et al. (2004) concurred with this and stated that there is a distinction between RM and branding. RM focuses on relationships and their extension to the firms, whereas branding is considered as a product-centred concept. Therefore, the difference between RM and branding is mainly based on the core level of relationships versus products. However, as customers develop attitudes and behaviour toward the company, the influences of brands and relationships are hard to separate. In addition, loyalty is also a primary goal of RM (Hennig-Thurau et al., 2002). A number of studies have explored the connection between loyalty and profitability and found that customer loyalty towards the brands positively impacts profitability through increasing revenues and decreasing costs (Berry, 1995; Hennig-Thurau et al., 2000).

Determinant of RM

The fundamental basis of RM emphasises the mutual exchange between the organisation and different stakeholders (Harker, 1999). RM thus is not about gaining new customers but about maintaining the relationship with the current customers. Companies should adopt RM from customers' perspective and understand why they enter into a relationship and react positively toward the firm (Palmer, 1996).

According to Gwinner et al. (1998), the main reason for firms to apply RM could be to gain social benefits. Social benefits focus on the relationship itself rather than on the result of transactions and were found to positively influence customers' commitment towards the relationship. Similarly, Berry (1995) suggested that there is a strong connection between social benefits and customer loyalty. When customers have a positive relationship with employees or other customers of the company, they tend to be more loyal to the brand. Other researchers such as Oliver (1999) confirmed that customers who are part of the social organisation are more motivated to maintain loyalty with the company.

Other reasons for firms to apply RM are to build trust and commitment. Commitment is defined as customer's long-term orientation towards the relationship with companies (Geyskens et al., 1996), whereas trust exists when customers believe in the reliability of the service provider (Morgan and Hunt, 1994). According to Hennig-Thurau et al. (2002), trust and commitment foster greater customer loyalty towards the company. Gounaris (2005) viewed trust and commitment as the two essential factors that lead customers to form a relationship with the company, while trust precedes the development of commitment. Both trust and commitment are crucial for building successful long-term customer relationships (Morgan and Hunt, 1994). For example, in order to gain back customers' trust, McDonald's added healthier product options to its menu to change customers' perceptions of the product. It highlights a significant change, by moving toward a healthy image of the brand that would enhance a customer–brand relationship.

A number of customers may be involved in a relationship as the consequence of their satisfaction (Ndubisi et al., 2008). Customer satisfaction is defined as the degree to which the customer perceives the difference between expectation and performance appraisal (Yi, 1990). Lo (2012) provided evidence for the significant impact of satisfaction on customer loyalty and argued that by forming a relationship, customers can gain different benefits such as profitability, cost reduction or comfort. In 2011, Coca-Cola ran the Share a Coke campaign that offers an affordable personalised product to attract teens. The beverage giant is also knowledgeable of how to target and satisfy young customers via social media and mobile phones. Through the campaign, Coca-Cola achieved a phenomenal result with an increase in sales of 7 per cent. More importantly, the Share a Coke campaign helped the brand through the tough times in persuading teens to consume its product, leading to better relationships with young customers.

Why RM?

According to Hanley and Leahy (2009), it is cheaper to maintain and develop an existing customer base than to acquire new customers. Thus, engaging in RM benefits the company through developing customer loyalty. Egan (2008) argued that the importance of RM varies by different sectors. In industries such as retailing, customers engage more with the sale personnel (the point of contact) instead of forming an extensive relationship with the company (Szmigin and Bourne, 1998). However, in other industries, particularly high-involvement purchases such as cars, real estate or luxury products, customers are looking for trust when dealing with the company. Thus, RM especially attracts those industries as it aids the long-term commitment between customers and the company (Egan, 2008). Moreover, in high-involvement purchases, it is easier to cross-sell new products/services within the product portfolio to existing customers; satisfied customers may generate positive word of mouth that is considered more effective than paid advertising (Egan, 2008). Companies thus can reduce the unproductive marketing practice to achieve greater customer responses.

RM also acts as an indicator for future sales and profits (Hougaard and Bjerre, 2002). RM provides companies with the opportunities to meet customers' needs in an effective way because after having a reliable relationship with the brand, other alternatives are less attractive to customers. However, there is no guarantee that customers are willing to form a relationship with the company (Berry, 1995). Therefore, companies need to motivate customers to build a relationship with them through offering more interpersonal interaction or value-added services that are not available from other sources (Dibb and Meadows, 2001), as it enhances customers' loyalty.

RM in the context of children

According to Brassington and Pettitt (2003), companies should aim to create loyalty with consumers as early as possible. It is important for marketers to understand the role of children, in order to develop a long-term relationship in the future. Holbrook and Schindler (1991) found that early childhood experiences have a great impact on customer purchasing behaviour. However, Hawkin and Coney (1974) argued that children carry their positive attitude towards the brands to their adulthood. Children relate to brands just as a person may form a relationship with somebody (Smit *et al.*, 2007).

A study by Ross and Harradine (2004) highlighted that children tend to express themselves through the brands they like. They will choose those brands that have higher congruity with their self-image in order to display their self-identity (Hur *et al.*, 2011). Moreover, Park and Lee (2005) emphasised that the function of brands not only describes the product/service but also expresses customers' personality. It impacts on both customers' satisfaction and brands' relationships with firms. Research conducted by Aaker *et al.* (2004) indicated that brand personality has an influence on the development of a customer–brand relationship, which ultimately leads to customer loyalty. If consumers see a brand as a signal of self-identity, they are more likely to purchase from that brand (Strizhokoya *et al.*, 2011). Children thus tend to have a positive attitude towards the brands that are most congruent with their personality. It motivates them to build a relationship with those brands (Haryanto *et al.*, 2016).

Smit *et al.* (2007) identified trust as a measurement of brand relationship. The finding reveals that trust is crucial in developing the relationship between company and customers. The feeling of confidence and trust fosters children to create a positive response towards a brand. Those responses can be classified in terms of positive word of mouth, loyalty, commitment and attitude. The establishment of commitment and positive attitude toward the brand leads to children re-purchasing buying behaviour. It then affects the establishment of relationships between children and brands (Haryanto *et al.*, 2016). Moreover, Moore and Lutz's (2000) study indicated that children would have a positive commitment and attitude with the brands that have a high level of awareness and salience. Brand salience is defined as the extent to which a brand is activated in a customer's mind (Miller and Berry, 1998). It refers to the top-of-mind awareness (Johnstone and Dodd, 2000) that results in purchases and brand usage (Raggio and Leone, 2007). Children will purchase more products/services from the brands with a higher level of salience, which evokes a higher degree of possibility to build a relationship with the brand.

Moreover, Ji and Wood (2007) indicate that past experience is an indication of customer purchasing habits. Their research showed that habits are unconsciously repeated in customers' daily lives. When children evaluate the company positively, they tend to have a strong commitment towards it and form a positive memory to always purchase products/services from the company (Rubin, 2006). The finding was also supported by the study of Kurniawan and Haryanto (2011), indicating how positive memories make children purchase products/services from certain brands. Past usage experience and customer satisfaction, therefore, influence the creation of customer loyalty and their relationship with the company.

Due to their lack of finances, children rely on parents to acquire desired goods (Neeley and Coffey, 2004). However, they also apply emotional strategies to influence their parents' purchases (Palan, 1997). Often, children act affectionately in verbal expression or behaviour to impact parental purchase decision-making. Specifically, children tend to be involved more in the purchasing process related to clothing and footwear products (Ross and Harradine, 2004). They do not generally pay for these yet as children, but they have the ability to pester parents to buy certain products. Thus, if companies satisfy children as users now, they are likely to become long-term customers.

Ross and Harradine (2004) highlighted that children frequently purchase electronic products, such as computers, games or gadgets, under peer pressure. They also search for information from peers concerning product features, quality, price or alternative products. However, if children have a positive relationship with a brand, they are likely to repurchase that brand consistently (Hur et al., 2011), as it saves them time and effort without searching for new products or services.

According to O'Dougherty et al. (2006), about half of the food purchase requests in supermarkets are initiated by children. Retailers are therefore advised to develop stronger relationships with children. Promotional and marketing strategies of retailers should be implemented to build an effective relationship with children, which leads to enhanced customer loyalty. Food retailers such as McDonald's offer toys and coupons as incentives, alongside food products, to attract children. Many companies have also used integrated marketing strategies to attract children (Calvert, 2008) such as using the same cartoon character in different media platforms like TV, movies or books. In the case of Burger King, the company used the television character SpongeBob to market the brand, which boosted sales significantly.

The research of Goksel et al. (2013) found that television, websites and online games are useful promotional tools to target children. Companies also recognise the power of promoting a brand to parents and children effectively in a school environment. However, it is argued that schools should be a place where children are protected from advertising techniques. Consequently, marketers need a different strategy to influence children at schools. For example, Kraft successfully attracted children through sponsored educational materials to be used in schools. They created 'healthy eating kits' to teach children the Canada Food Guide using Kraft products. In addition, CSR initiatives of companies, such as sponsoring school events, are found to enhance brand image (Gulla, 2013).

Marketing practices such as branded characters, product placement or celebrity endorsements are applied by firms to attract children's attention, meaning that products stay in children's memories and influence their parents' purchases (Ramzy et al., 2012). Branded characters that are associated with a company are often used to promote the brand name. Aiming at enhancing customers' interest toward the brand, many companies have used famous television cartoon characters to sell products such as cereals or vacations (Calvert, 2008).

Celebrity endorsement is another marketing strategy that companies use to build a relationship with children. Saraf (2013) investigated how celebrity endorsements enhance children's preference for products. The study found that children feel validated in their choice of products when a celebrity endorses it. Children are particularly influenced by an advertisement that has other children in it, as children could identify themselves closely with the 'child star'. For example, the sack race in the ad of Surf Excel or Boost attracted children, who then convince their parents to buy the product.

Moreover, companies also apply product placement to increase children's familiarity with products, which leads to favourable opinions of the brand (Calvert, 2008). Auty and Lewis (2004) found that children recognise products that appear over and over again on their favourite movies, which increases the likelihood of product purchases. Product placements are commonly seen in children's movies such as Coca-Cola in *Madagascar* or Burger King in *Scooby-Doo 2*. Apple is another example that gained the 2015 product placement award when appearing in *The Lego Movie*. Apart from movies, websites that target children could also carry product placements. For example, Pepsi put their logo on Bolt, a popular music webpage for children. Every time that children click into the music page, they are reminded of the brand name of Pepsi, thereby strengthening the brand image.

Conclusion

Marketing mix, both in its basic conceptualisation and the extended form (7Ps) are important in attracting children customers by meeting their needs and building relationship with them. Each 'P' serves different functions in services marketing, which increases brand awareness, boosts sales and creates loyalty with children. On the other hand, relationship marketing focuses on creating, maintaining and developing a long-term relationship with customers. This chapter suggested that when children experience a satisfactory service experience, they carry that positive attitude into their adulthood. They form a relationship with a brand as a person forms a relationship with another person.

In order to encourage children to join in a relationship with brands, companies need to be aware of children's needs and preferences and apply marketing strategies effectively. As children tend to express themselves through brands that they associate with, brands should aim to help express children's identity and seek ways to differentiate products from competitors by means of product/service personalisation.

The literature discussed in this chapter suggested that children are more price sensitive due to their lack of finance. Firms should take that into account in their price setting when targeting children. Moreover, personal selling plays an important part in building the relationship with children, which often allows the relationship between children and the brand to be formed and carried into adulthood.

The social environment, such as children's parents, also influences the relationship between children and brands. Parental influence on children should thus be considered by firms when targeting marketing strategies towards children in order to build a customer–brand relationship. Advertisements are influential to children's purchases. However, there are concerns about companies' ethics when using advertisements to target children, which might also reduce trust from parents on the brand. The marketing of high-calorie food to children, for example, has a negative impact on their health and well-being, resulting in rising child obesity levels (Calvert, 2008; Šramová, 2015).

Companies, therefore, need to listen to parents' concern over the influence of advertisements on their children and should be honest when using adverts to build trust and relationships with children. Moreover, companies should observe advertising guidelines that aim to protect children, considering younger children's inability to grasp the advertiser's intent and purpose.

In conclusion, a customer-oriented approach is recommended to firms when interacting with children. Tailored training sessions can also be provided to staff by firms to improve their knowledge concerning how to better communicate with children. Furthermore, the physical environment of a service provider significantly impacts on customer experience and in general, children prefer a well-decorated, brightly coloured environment. Firms, therefore, should pay attention to its physical evidence to impress children and facilitate a positive experience.

References

Aaker, J., Fournier, S. and Brasel, S. A. (2004). When good brands do bad. *Journal of Consumer Research*, *31*(1), 1–16.

Aghaei, M., Vahedi, E., Kahreh, M. S. and Pirooz, M. (2014). An examination of the relationship between services marketing mix and brand equity dimensions. *Procedia-Social and Behavioral Sciences*, *109*, 865–869.

Arnett, D. B. and Badrinarayanan, V. (2005). Enhancing customer needs-driven CRM strategies: Core selling teams, knowledge management competence, and relationship marketing competence. *Journal of Personal Selling & Sales Management*, *25*(4), 329–343.

Auty, S. and Lewis, C. (2004). Exploring children's choice: The reminder effect of product placement. *Psychology & Marketing*, *21*(9), 697–713.

Bang, N. and Philipp, P. K. (2013). Retail fairness: Exploring consumer perceptions of fairness towards retailers' marketing tactics. *Journal of Retailing and Consumer Services*, *20*, 311–324.

Berry, L. L. (1995). Relationship marketing of services: Growing interest, emerging perspectives. *Journal of the Academy of Marketing Science*, *23*(4), 236–245.

Bhardwaj, D. (2007). Relationship marketing in context to the IT industry. *Vision: The Journal of Business Perspective*, *11*(2), 57–66.

Bolton, R. N., Kannan, P. K. and Bramlett, M. D. (2000). Implications of loyalty program membership and service experiences for customer retention and value. *Journal of the Academy of Marketing Science*, *28*(1), 95–108.

Brassington, F. and Pettitt, S. (2003). Principles of marketing. *Journal of Small Business and Enterprise Development*, *10*(2), 137–138.

Buijzen, M. and Valkenburg, P. (2000). The impact of television on children's Christmas wishes. *Journal of Broadcasting and Electronic Media*, *44*, 456–469.

Bureau of Economic Analysis. (2006). *National economic accounts.* www.bea.gov/national/index.htm#gdp (accessed 11 January 2017).

Cairns, G., Angus, K., Hastings, G. and Caraher, M. (2013). Systematic reviews of the evidence on the nature, extent and effects of food marketing to children: A retrospective summary. *Appetite, 62,* 1209–1215.

Calvert, S. (2008). Children as consumers: Advertising and marketing. *The Future of Children, 18*(1), 205–234.

Colgate, M. and Hedge, R. (2001). An investigation into the switching process in retail banking services. *International Journal of Bank Marketing, 19*(5), 201–212.

Dibb, S. and Meadows, M. (2001). The application of a relationship marketing perspective in retail banking. *Service Industries Journal, 21*(1), 169–194.

Ebster, C., Wagner, U. and Neumueller, D. (2009). Children's influences on in-store purchases. *Journal of Retailing and Consumer Services, 16*(2), 145–154.

Egan, J. (2008). *Relationship marketing: Exploring relational strategies in marketing.* Harlow: Pearson Education.

Fan, Y. and Li, Y. (2010). Children's buying behaviour in China: A study of their information sources. *Marketing Intelligence & Planning, 28*(2), 170–187.

Fine, L. (2008). Services marketing. *Business Horizons, 51,* 163–168.

Fisk, R., Brown, S. and Bitner, M. (1993). Tracking the evolution of the services marketing literature. *Journal of Retailing, 69*(1), 61–103.

Fukey, L., Issac, S., Balasubramanian, K. and Jaykumar, V. (2014). Service delivery quality improvement models: A review. *Procedia-Social and Behavioral Sciences, 144,* 343–359.

Garbarino, E. and Johnson, M. S. (1999). The different roles of satisfaction, trust, and commitment in customer relationships. *Journal of Marketing, 63*(2), 70–87.

Geyskens, I., Steenkamp, J. B. E., Scheer, L. K. and Kumar, N. (1996). The effects of trust and interdependence on relationship commitment: A trans-Atlantic study. *International Journal of Research in Marketing, 13*(4), 303–317.

Goksel, A. B., Baytekin, E. P. and Maden, A. G. D. (2013). Kids marketing: An evaluation of Pinar's kids marketing operations. *Gumushane University e-Journal of Faculty of Communication, 2*(2).

Gounaris, S. P. (2005). Trust and commitment influences on customer retention: Insights from business-to-business services. *Journal of Business Research, 58*(2), 126–140.

Grönroos, C. (1984). A service quality model and its marketing implications. *European Journal of Marketing, 18,* 35–40.

Grönroos, C. (1994). From marketing mix to relationship marketing: Towards a paradigm shift in marketing. *Asia-Australia Marketing Journal, 2*(1), 9–29.

Grönroos, C. (2004). The relationship marketing process: Communication, interaction, dialogue value. *Journal of Business and Industrial Marketing, 19*(2), 99–113.

Grönroos, C. (2011). A service perspective on business relationships: The value creation, interaction and marketing interface. *Industrial Marketing Management, 40*(2), 240–247.

Grönroos, C. and Voima, P. (2013). Critical service logic: Making sense of value creation and co-creation. *Journal of the Academy of Marketing Science, 41*(2), 133–150.

Gulla, A. and Purohit, H. (2013). Children's attitude towards television advertisements and influence on the buying behavior of parents. *International Journal of Marketing, Financial Services, 2*(6), 103–117.

Gummesson, E. (1994). Making relationship marketing operational. *International Journal of Service Industry Management, 5*(5), 5–20.

Gummesson, E. (1999). *Total relationship marketing.* Oxford: Butterworth-Heinemann.

Gunter, B. and Furnham, A. (1998). *Children as consumers: A psychological analysis of the young people's market.* London: Psychology Press.

Gwinner, K. P., Gremler, D. D. and Bitner, M. J. (1998). Relational benefits in services industries: The customer's perspective. *Journal of the Academy of Marketing Science*, 26(2), 101–114.

Hanley, S. and Leahy, R. (2009). The effectiveness of relationship marketing strategies in department stores. *International Journal of Business and Management*, 3(10), 133.

Harker, M. J. (1999). Relationship marketing defined? An examination of current relationship marketing definitions. *Marketing Intelligence and Planning*, 17(1), 13–20.

Haryanto, J. O., Moutinho, L. and Coelho, A. (2016). Is brand loyalty really present in the children's market? A comparative study from Indonesia, Portugal, and Brazil. *Journal of Business Research*, 69(10), 4020–4032.

Hawkins, D. I. and Coney, K. A. (1974). Peer group influences on children's product preferences. *Journal of the Academy of Marketing Science*, 2(2), 322–331.

Hennig-Thurau, T. (2000). Relationship quality and customer retention through strategic communication of customer skills. *Journal of Marketing Management*, 16(1–3), 55–79.

Hennig-Thurau, T., Gwinner, K. P. and Gremler, D. D. (2002). Understanding relationship marketing outcomes: An integration of relational benefits and relationship quality. *Journal of Service Research*, 4(3), 230–247.

Holbrook, M. B. and Schindler, R. M. (1991). Echoes of the dear departed past: Some work in progress on nostalgia. *Advances in Consumer Research*, 18, 330–335.

Hougaard, S. and Bjerre, M. (2002). *Strategic relationship marketing*. London: Springer Science & Business Media.

Hur, W. M., Ahn, K. H. and Kim, M. (2011). Building brand loyalty through managing brand community commitment. *Management Decision*, 49(7), 1194–1213.

Ibrahim, E., Joseph, M. and Ibeh, K. (2006). Customers' perception of electronic service delivery in the UK retail banking sector. *International Journal of Bank Marketing*, 24(7), 475–493.

Ji, M. F. and Wood, W. (2007). Purchase and consumption habits: Not necessarily what you intend. *Journal of Consumer Psychology*, 17(4), 261–276.

Johnstone, E. and Dodd, C. A. (2000). Placements as mediators of brand salience within a UK cinema audience. *Journal of Marketing Communications*, 6(3), 141–158.

Judd, V. (1987). Differentiate with the 5th P: People. *Industrial Marketing Management*, 16, 241–247.

Kirkorian, L., Wartella, E. and Anderson, D. (2008). Media and young children's learning. *The Future of Children*, 18(1), 39–61.

Kurniawan, S. and Haryanto, J. O. (2011). Kids as future market: The role of autobiographical memory in building brand loyalty. *Researchers World*, 2(4), 77.

Kushwaha, G. S. and Agrawal, S. (2015). An Indian customer surrounding 7Ps of service marketing. *Journal of Retailing and Consumer Services*, 22, 85–95.

Lemish, D. (2007). *Children and television: A global perspective*. Malden: Blackwell.

Lo, S. C. (2012). A study of relationship marketing on customer satisfaction. *Journal of Social Sciences*, 8(1), 91.

Lovelock, C. and Gummesson, E. (2004). Whither services marketing: In search of a new paradigm and fresh perspectives. *Journal of Service Research*, 7(1), 20–41.

McCarthy, E. (1960). *Basic marketing: A managerial approach*. Homewood, IL: Irwin.

McNeal, J. U (1992). *Kids as customers: A handbook of marketing to children*. New York: Lexington Books.

Miller, S. and Berry, L. (1998). Brand salience versus brand image: Two theories of advertising effectiveness. *Journal of Advertising Research*, 38(5), 77–78.

Mintel. (2015). In-salon hair services. http://academic.mintel.com/display/745817/?highlight (accessed 12 January 2017).

Moore, E. S. and Lutz, R. J. (2000). Children, advertising, and product experiences: A multi-method inquiry. *Journal of Consumer Research*, 27(1), 31–48.

Morales, A. C. (2005). Giving firms an 'E' for effort: Consumer responses to high-effort firms. *Journal of Consumer Research*, 31(4), 806–812.

Morgan, R. M. and Hunt, S. D. (1994). The commitment–trust theory of relationship marketing. *Journal of Marketing*, 58(3), 20–38.

Ndubisi, N. O., Malhotra, N. K. and Wah, C. K. (2008). Relationship marketing, customer satisfaction and loyalty: A theoretical and empirical analysis from an Asian perspective. *Journal of International Consumer Marketing*, 21(1), 5–16.

Neeley, S. and Coffey, T. (2004). Who's your momma? *Young Consumers*, 5(4), 56–61.

Nicholls, A. and Cullen, P. (2004). The child–parent purchase relationship: 'Pester power', human rights and retail ethics. *Journal of Retailing and Consumer Services*, 11(2), 75–86.

O'Dougherty, M., Story, M. and Stang, J. (2006). Observations of parent–child co-shoppers in supermarkets: Children's involvement in food selections, parental yielding, and refusal strategies. *Journal of Nutrition Education and Behavior*, 38(3), 183–188.

Oliver, R. L. (1999). Whence consumer loyalty? *Journal of Marketing*, 63, 33–44.

Palan, K. M. and Wilkes, R. E. (1997). Adolescent–parent interaction in family decision-making. *Journal of Consumer Research*, 24(2), 159–169.

Palmer, A. J. (1996). Relationship marketing: A universal paradigm or management fad? *The Learning Organization*, 3(3), 18–25.

Park, S. Y. and Lee, E. M. (2005). Congruence between brand personality and self-image, and the mediating roles of satisfaction and consumer–brand relationship on brand loyalty. *Asia Pacific Advances in Consumer Research*, 6, 39–45.

Purcarea, V., Gheorghe, I. and Petrescu, C. (2013). The assessment of perceived service quality of public health care services in Romania using the SERVQUAL scale. *Procedia Economics and Finance*, 6, 573–585.

Radley, A. (1996). Relationships in detail: The study of social interaction. In D. Miell and R. Dallos (eds), *Social interaction and personal relationships* (pp. 23–100). London: Sage.

Rafiq, M. and Ahmed, P. (1995). Using the 7Ps as a generic marketing mix: An exploratory survey of UK and European marketing academics. *Marketing Intelligence and Planning*, 13(9), 4–15.

Raggio, R. D. and Leone, R. P. (2007). The theoretical separation of brand equity and brand value: Managerial implications for strategic planning. *Journal of Brand Management*, 14(5), 380–395.

Ramzy, O., Ogden, D. T., Ogden, J. R. and Zakaria, M. Y. (2012). Perceptions of children's influence on purchase decisions empirical investigation for US and Egyptian families. *World Journal of Management*, 4(1), 30–50.

Ross, J. and Harradine, R. (2004). I'm not wearing that! Branding and young children. *Journal of Fashion Marketing and Management: An International Journal*, 8(1), 11–26.

Rubin, D. C. (2006). Autobiographical memory. *Journal of Child and Psychiatry*, 37, 286–329.

Rust, R. T., Zeithaml, V. A. and Lemon, K. N. (2004). Customer-centered brand management. *Harvard Business Review*, 82(9), 110–120.

Saraf, V. (2013). Impact of celebrity endorsement on children through TV advertisements. *International Journal of Marketing & Business Communication*, 2(2), 53.

Shaker, T. I. and Basem, Y. A. (2010). Relationship marketing and organizational performance indicators. *European Journal of Social Sciences*, 12(4), 545–557.

Shamah, R. (2013). A model for applying lean thinking to value creation. *International Journal of Lean Six Sigma*, 4(2), 204–224.

Shanker, R. (2002). *Services marketing: The Indian perspective*. New Delhi: Excel Books.
Shostack, G. (1977). Breaking free from product marketing. *Journal of Marketing*, *41*(2), 73–80.
Skalen, P. (2009). Service marketing and subjectivity: The shaping of customer-oriented employees. *Journal of Marketing Management*, *25*(7–8), 795–809.
Skalen, P. (2011). Service marketing control as practice: A case study. *Qualitative Market Research: An International Journal*, *14*(4), 374–390.
Smit, E., Bronner, F. and Tolboom, M. (2007). Brand relationship quality and its value for personal contact. *Journal of Business Research*, *60*(6), 627–633.
Šramová, B. (2014). Media literacy and marketing consumerism focused on children. *Procedia – Social and Behavioral Sciences*, *141*, 1025–1030.
Šramová, B. (2015). Marketing and media communications targeted to children as consumers. *Procedia – Social and Behavioral Sciences*, *191*, 1522–1527.
Srivastava, R. K., Shervani, T. A. and Fahey, L. (1998). Market-based assets and shareholder value: A framework for analysis. *The Journal of Marketing*, *62*(1), 2–18.
Strizhakova, Y., Coulter, R. A. and Price, L. L. (2011). Branding in a global marketplace: The mediating effects of quality and self-identity brand signals. *International Journal of Research in Marketing*, *28*(4), 342–351.
Szmigin, I. and Bourne, H. (1998). Consumer equity in relationship marketing. *Journal of Consumer Marketing*, *15*(6), 544–557.
Taherdoost, H., Shamsul, S. and Neda, J. (2014). 'Features' evaluation of goods, services and e-services: Electronic service characteristics exploration. *Procedia Technology*, *12*, 204–211.
Tynan, C. (1997). A review of the marriage analogy in relationship marketing. *Journal of Marketing Management*, *13*(7), 695–703.
Udegbe, S. E., Idris, A. A. and Olumoko, T. A. (2010). Relationship marketing and customer loyalty: A customer service approach in Nigerian companies. *Manager Journal: Faculty of Business & Administration, University of Bucharest*, *12*, 167–176.
Valkenburg, P. and Cantor, J. (2001). The development of a child into a consumer. *Journal of Applied Developmental Psychology*, *22*(1), 61–72.
Vyas, V. and Raitani, S. (2015). A study of the impact of relationship marketing on cross-buying. *Journal of Relationship Marketing*, *14*(2), 79–108.
Wood, L. (2000). Brands and brand equity: Definition and management. *Management Decision*, *38*(9), 662–669.
Yi, Y. (1990). A critical review of consumer satisfaction. *Review of Marketing*, *4*(1), 68–123.
Zeithaml, V. A., Berry, L. and Pararsuraman, A. (1990). *Delivering quality service: Balancing customer perceptions and expectations*. New York: The Free Press.
Zeithaml, V. A., Bitner, M. J., Gremler, D. D. and Pandit, A. (2008). *Services marketing: Integrating customer focus across the firm* (4th edn). New Delhi: Tata McGraw-Hill.

13
SEGMENTING THE CHILDREN'S MARKET

Mahama Braimah, Cynthia A. Bulley and Janet A. Anore

Introduction

Marketing finds its essence in being able to provide solutions to customer needs, doing so at a profit and in such a way as not to harm the society and environment at large. What is critically important is that, the solutions that marketers provide, must be based on the needs of consumers, whether children or adults (Kotler and Armstrong, 2010), and this is what makes for great marketing. Great marketers are marketers that produce goods and services based on identified needs of consumers, and getting these consumers to chase after these products, thereby enabling the marketers to build brand communities (Tapp, 2001).

Apple is a good example of a great marketing company. Apple is greatly adept at marketing, evidenced by the creation of many ground-breaking products, which broke the roof as far as sales and profits are concerned (Kane and Sherr, 2011). Such feats can only be achieved by knowing your target market and creating products that sit well with the characteristics of the identified target market. This is where market segmentation becomes crucial to the marketer's task and the success of the firm. Market segmentation enables marketers to identify the differences between consumers and categorise these differences into identifiable groups. Furthermore, market segmentation enables the marketer to clearly identify the similarities between consumers, and based on these commonalities, group them into units that can form the basis for marketing strategy. Segmentation is indeed an important marketing activity that can be the catalyst for marketing success.

Kjeldgaard and Askegaard (2006) note that segmentation is not something that marketers chance upon – markets are not automatically segregated according to the various bases for segmentation. It takes the efforts of marketers to identify the differences and similarities in markets, and to segment them accordingly. Segmentation is critical to marketing strategy. Segmentation enables a marketer to plan and focus his/her efforts on a particular group of consumers with a defined need. Lynn (2011) shares this sentiment and notes that there can be no marketing success if segmentation is flawed. Segmentation acts as a guiding post to ensure that firms do not create goods and services in a vacuum and expect that consumers will buy nonetheless. The huge nature of new product development and the massive budgets that they draw, warrant firms to do due diligence to ensure that there is a market available and ready for the product. This argument calls for the development of effective and viable market segments.

The development of viable market segments is of critical significance to firms, whether the products are targeted at children or adult consumer markets. Children, who constitute a large block of consumers, are unique. For instance, children can influence the purchase decisions of their parents/guardians even in instances where the products to be purchased are for the consumption of others.

The gap in the literature

Scholars have variously studied and written about market segmentation in journals and marketing textbooks all over the world. However, in spite of the plethora of articles and books on the subject, attention has not been fully focused on the children's market. This chapter is therefore an attempt to fill this gap. Children, though relatively constrained by a lack of income, are among the most powerful group of consumers. Interestingly, this is not just because of their volumes of consumption, or the kinds of goods and services they consume, but more especially, because of the influence they wield. Children are highly influential when it comes to the kinds of expenditure their parents (who have earning ability) make. Thus, even though parents are the ones who pay for products and services, children are sometimes the hidden forces that pull the strings and influence the purchase decisions. Children are sometimes able to influence the purchase decisions of their parents or guardians with respect to the goods and services that they (children) consume and even those that are for the consumption of their parents or guardians. This is what makes it imperative to examine the children's market and how it can be segmented. Research interest in the children's market has been on the rise in recent times. There are increasing studies that have been devoted to examining the concept of market segmentation in the light of how it applies to children and teens. Studies by scholars such as Patino et al. (2012), as well as Veloso and Campomar (2012) indicate that researchers are beginning to realise the significance of the children's market to marketing practice as a whole. Brands and firms stand to benefit from more of such research as an understanding of the children's market could be the key to unlocking this huge market.

The rather huge children's market has and is being mined by organisations and entities that have a shrewd marketing eye. Herman (2012) reports that firms like Lego understood the vastness of the children's market right from the outset, and that has led to the creation of a behemoth brand that has transcended generations and still remains relevant. Thomas (2016) also observes that the Disney Empire is rooted on an understanding of what makes children happy, and the epiphany that, in every adult still remains a child, yearning for adventure and for freedom of expression. These two examples of mighty global brands suggest that the children's market is no small market. Firms that are able to understand its dynamics are likely to reap the benefits of a generational cash haul, all other factors held constant. The children's market is as relevant to marketing literature as any other concept, and it is high time further studies are conducted to determine the inner workings of the children's market and other factors that affect child consumption patterns and behaviour.

This chapter is organised into eight sections. The preceding section is the introduction to the chapter and provides an overview of the chapter. This section identifies the gap that exists in the market segmentation literature as far as the children's market is concerned. Subsequent sections examine the concept of market segmentation and the factors that are used in segmenting the market. The children's market is also discussed, noting the uniqueness of the children's market and the characteristics of children. The bases that should underline the segmentation of the children's market are proposed and discussed. The implications of the segmentation of the children's market for marketing activities are also discussed. Finally, the chapter ends with a conclusion, which also makes suggestions for possible future studies.

Market segmentation: a conceptual overview

Having introduced the concept of market segmentation and its relevance in the children's market in the previous section, this section seeks to delve deeper into the concept of market segmentation. According to Kotler and Keller (2012), market segmentation can be described as an attempt at dividing the market into smaller units of buyers with distinct needs, characteristics or behaviours that might require separate marketing strategies or mixes. This description makes it clear that market segmentation enables firms to divide markets into manageable segments of consumers with identical needs. This enables firms to design effective and very specific marketing programmes to cater for the needs of these segments.

Smith (1956) has been credited as the father of the concept of market segmentation. Like him, other scholars have pointed out that segmentation is relevant because markets are not always homogenous, and as such, require separation and targeting by firms (Beane and Ennis, 1987). Marketers have long recognised the variances in markets and have tried to develop different marketing programmes to suit each market, depending on the characteristics of individuals dwelling in those markets. Lambin (2000) believes that segmentation is crucial to firm success as it enables firms to first of all identify which larger market to operate in, and then further divide that larger market into units that can be catered for with respect to the resources of the firm. Segmentation can thus be influenced by the resources a firm has at its disposal. Toor (2014) offers another insightful definition of segmentation.

He describes market segmentation as a marketing strategy to divide broad markets into subsets of consumers with common needs or priorities and strategising to target them. The essence of segmentation is to guide firms in their division of the market. A careful look at Toor's (2014) and Kotler and Keller's (2012) definitions, suggest that firms must be careful to consider the needs and priorities of consumers, and these needs could differ depending on whether the consumers are adults or children. Developing products that are not based on the needs of consumers is likely to lead to a failure in marketing efforts. This is because marketing starts and ends with the consumer (Kotler and Armstrong, 2010).

If firms correctly identify and effectively segment the right market, they can create timeless products that will not only generate huge volumes of sales, but also create timeless brand identities that will transcend generations. Without segmentation, firms will spread their resources thin and would not achieve their targeted results. The curious case of the Kantanka brand of cars, manufactured and marketed in Ghana on the West Coast of Africa comes to mind. The firm launched its vehicles, which were greeted with excitement in the country. Unfortunately, the excitement and publicity that greeted the launch has so far not manifested in sales. What could have gone wrong? Though there could be several reasons for the poor sales performance of the vehicles, a closer observation of the scenario reveals a poor fit between the products and the company's primary market (the Ghana market). For instance, the prices of the vehicles are on the high side, considering that their prices are within the same price-range of more established and prestigious brands. A poor understanding and segmentation of the market might have caused the poor performance of the product. Probably, the company did not ask itself the hard question 'what type of customers will drive my car?' Market segmentation could have helped the automobile manufacturer identify specific segments and target those segments with specific type of vehicles, supported by specific marketing programmes.

Segmentation is not a simple marketing activity. It is a complex process. That is why it is imperative for firms to ensure they get their segmentation spot on to avoid costly mistakes. Toor's (2014) observation on this issue is instructive. He argues that market segmentation is often used to assess the potential market, identify the ideal target market segment and to design the marketing mix to effectively reach the targeted segment. The objective of these activities, Toor (2014) notes, is to maximise returns with optimal use of a company's limited resources. This observation highlights an important consideration for marketers – *limited resources*. Firms cannot afford to produce goods and services that are not tailored to specific needs, because that would result in a waste of resources if the market acceptance is low. There could be low market acceptance for a product if, for instance, that product, which could otherwise have achieved a high market acceptance among children, is supported by a marketing mix programme, which is not tailored to the specific needs of children.

Gilboa and Vilnai-Yavetz (2012) in their study on 'segmenting multicultural mall visitors', noted that segmentation was an important activity that had many consequences for marketers. The authors observed that it was important for firms to profile their target market in order to not just identify, but also understand the type of consumers they were dealing with, and what their (consumers') motivations were. The motivation of young consumers might differ from adult consumers. This, according to them, would help firms identify the triggers of successful behavioural outcomes. Indeed, the study of consumer behaviour is an intricate affair, which is why segmentation holds an important place in the study and practise of marketing. Sherley et al. (2014) believe that it is important to segment so that marketers can know how to shape their corporate communications. The communications strategy targeted at children might not be suitable for mature consumers. The twenty-first century has become very competitive as far as corporate communications and advertising is concerned. This has become especially pronounced due to the advent of social media (Mangold and Faulds, 2009). Firms thus need to segment and profile their customers in order to know which type of communication will best suit their needs.

Targeting and positioning

Scholars have identified a triad of interactions that result in firms getting the best out of their marketing efforts. This triad of concepts, segmentation, targeting and positioning are commonly referred to as the STP model (Kotler and Armstrong, 2010). Lynn (2011) notes that segmentation on its own cannot lead to the effective servicing of the needs of consumers in a given market. He believes that for segmentation to be effective it must be accompanied by effective targeting and astute positioning. Dibb and Simkin (1991) defined targeting as a process that follows after segmentation, where firms target the most attractive segment in a market to focus their marketing offerings and efforts on. Targeting gives meaning to segmentation because, after a firm has identified the various groups of customers in the market, it needs to select the most attractive one to satisfy at a profit. Several factors guide firms in selecting the segments to focus their efforts and attention on. The extent to which the size and characteristics of the market can be measured as well as how accessible the particular market segment is, are factors to consider in targeting market segments. Market segments must be capable of responding differently to different marketing programmes. Each segment must be profitable enough to be served and it should be possible to formulate marketing programmes to attract each market segment (Kotler and Keller, 2012). It is therefore important that in segmentation, the characteristics of the children's market segment be measurable, accessible, profitable and capable of responding differently to different marketing programmes.

Having identified which segment of the market is attractive, marketers must then move to position their goods and service offering. Positioning enables a market segment to recognise the offering of a particular firm. Positioning is about designing a firm's offering and image to occupy a distinctive place in the minds of the target market (Ries and Trout, 2000). The aim is to maximise the potential benefit of the firm as a good brand positioning helps guide marketing strategy and efforts (Kotler and Keller, 2012). Marketers must effectively differentiate their products and services and direct marketing efforts to ensure their offerings achieve a long-lasting and positive perception from the target market; and this is even more important for the children's market as they are expected to have a longer life ahead of them.

This approach suggests that the mass market consists of a number of relatively homogeneous groups, each with distinct needs and desires. The STP activities attempt to identify those market segments, direct marketing activities at the segments that the marketers believe their company can satisfy better than their competitors and position their product offering so as to appeal to the targeted segments.

Conventional bases for segmenting consumer marketing

Marketers may choose to segment a market based on different criteria. These factors help marketers to divide a market into various groups of relatively homogenous consumers who have similar tastes and preferences, and may be treated to a unique marketing approach. Generally, certain factors are noted as bases for segmentation. Factors such as demographic, psychographic, behavioural and geographic segmentation have been recognised as being effective in helping marketers divide markets into smaller units (Kotler, 2002). In this section, four main bases that are used for market segmentation will be discussed, thus: demographic, geographic, psychographic and behavioural factors. Toor (2014) also confirms these as the bases for marketing segmentation, noting that these factors could further be broken into several variables. For instance, geographic factors include such variables as regions, countries, languages, cities, postal codes; demographic factors include items such as age, gender, income, race, marital status; while behavioural variables include knowledge of, attitude towards and usage rate or response to a product. Market segmentation can play an important role in determining customer targets and positioning to achieve growth in an otherwise stagnant market. Each of these segmentation factors are explained below.

Demographic

Consumers may be segmented based on demographic variables like age, gender, religion, income and race, among others. This means that a group of people or customers with similar personal (demographic) characteristics are believed to behave in similar ways and have similar needs and wants, which may be leveraged upon by marketers to satisfy them (customers) together. For example, a product may be made to satisfy the needs of a specific age bracket, which might not necessarily be equally attractive to an older segment.

Geographic

Another method of segmenting consumers is on a geographical basis, where groups of consumers who live in particular locations are grouped together and considered to have similar tastes and preferences. This segmentation may be on the macro level, for example, regions or continents, or as low down as cities, communities or even streets. A good example may be an organisation like Nestle, who has regional offices in different parts of the world, and offers slightly different versions of its products to each region.

Psychographic

A third basis for segmentation is psychographic. In this instance, consumers are divided according to such factors as their lifestyles, activities, values, opinions and attitudes. People have different outlooks on issues and these can be used as a method of differentiating groups of consumers. For example, a company that sells bicycles could consider customers who like riding their bikes as a hobby, versus those who ride their bikes as a mode of transportation, versus those who use bicycles for health reasons.

Behavioural

A fourth basis for market segmentation is the behaviour of consumers towards the offering(s) of a firm. How often consumers use the product, what they use it for, when they use it and why they use it, as well as which specific benefits they are seeking to gain from the usage of the product, are all valuable clues that distinguish groups of consumers from others. Marketers may exploit these in order to know which segments to target their products and services.

The children's market

The children's market is a unique market with unique opportunities for marketers. McNeal (1969) observed that the children's market is composed of children aged 5–13. He also later noted that the children's market could include children aged 4–12 (McNeal, 1992, 1999). Literature suggests that there is a general consensus among a good number of scholars with regards to McNeal's suggestion of the age range that constitutes children (Acuff and Reihner, 1997; Siegel et al., 2001; Lindstrom, 2003; Montigneaux, 2003). Children have for centuries been the target of marketers. Several unique products and services have been developed for them, with the likes of cartoons and animations being the most popular. Toys, decorations, clothes and other products have been developed for children and have seen some individuals become millionaires in the process. This section examines the children's market and discusses the uniqueness of the children's market, characteristics of children and bases for segmenting the children's market.

Uniqueness of the children's market

The children's market finds its uniqueness in the vastness of the population of children. According to reports from the Population Reference Bureau (2014), there are over 143 million births per year. Though some children unfortunately die before their fifth birthday due to various factors including poverty and lack of adequate and quality health care, this number is relatively small. It can therefore be argued that the population of children is a huge market that can be tapped. Reports from the United Nations Population Fund (UNFPA) (2014) indicate that there are more young people today than at any point in the history of mankind. By implication, there are many more children today as well. What this means is that the children's market represents a vast playing field for marketers and their organisations. The presence of these young consumers presents an opportunity for the satisfaction of needs. Whether it is food, clothing, shelter, education, toys and other necessities or even luxuries of life, the children's market is unique in its sheer size and potential.

It is also important to observe that parents are by nature and also by law required to protect their children and care for their needs, and this is one of the things that makes the children's market unique. This consequently makes child expenditure a very important part of the budget of parents. Thus, if firms are able to tap into this market, huge revenue and profits await them. Children are influential when it comes to the spending patterns of their parents, making the parents vulnerable when it comes to purchase decisions. Through crying and wailing for a new toy, for instance, children can get their parents to purchase that toy for them. This influence is what also makes the children's market unique; the emotional ransom that children can hold their parents to, and the guarantee that loving parents will go to any lengths to make their children happy. Montigneaux (2003) shares in this line of argument and opines that children have become a huge consideration when it comes to purchase decisions. Parents may opt to buy or not to buy certain products because of their children. This suggests that children can influence the purchase decisions of their parents even for products and services meant for the consumption of the parents. Thus, children may have an even greater say for products and services meant for their own consumption. Schor (2004) thus sees the children's market as an important market segment that needs to be profiled thoroughly in order to determine how to create and deliver products and services of value to them. It is important to note that while children would be consuming the products/services, parents would be paying for them in most cases. The issue of quality is therefore one major factor that must never be compromised or taken for granted.

The potential for marketers to reap mega rewards from ploughing the fields of the children's market is all too obvious. In 2014, it is reported that revenue obtained from the sale of toys in the United States amounted to $23 billion by the close of the year. It has further been estimated that the toy industry yields an annual turnover of around $80 billion (www.worldatlas.com). This goes to show the revenue firms are likely to make when they focus their marketing efforts on the children's market. The above cited example is only one of several instances where targeting the children's market can lead to massive sales revenue. Toys are not the only products that can be positively impacted by effectively targeting the children's market. There are other product categories where segmenting the children's market can open doors of opportunity for firms. Some of these product categories include such products as clothing, food, jewellery, stationery, religion and many others. Table 13.1 shows a list of firms that have capitalised on the vast opportunities present in the children's market.

Table 13.1 lists firms that have been hugely successful at developing market offerings and operating in the children's market. These firms have built entire business models based on the children's market, and they have reaped massive benefits while doing so. Lego, Cartoon Network, Disney, Warner Brothers and Hasbro are huge global brands with a huge following and a massive plethora of products and sub-brands developed for children.

Scholars believe that the influence of children on household expenditure cannot be missed. The household budget increases more when children come into the picture than when parents are single and living alone (McNeal, 1992; Vecchio, 2002). Bannon (1998) believes that firms have responded to this segment by increasingly developing products targeted at children and their parents. Another unique thing about the children's market is the fact that it comprises essentially of individuals who are at a sensitive stage in their development, both emotionally and physically (Veloso and Campomar, 2012). This realisation means that there are several opportunities for marketers to target the various physical and emotional needs of children in order to meet them. One such example is that of the 2017 movie release of *The Lego Batman Movie*. This swashbuckling animation grossed over US$179 million by the end of February 2017 (www.the-numbers.com). The movie combined two favourite children's products, Lego and Batman, and created a movie that would hold massive appeal not just for children but even for adults who have nostalgic feelings about their childhood experiences with Lego as well as the Batman series. Mendelson (2017) also confirmed the epic success of the Lego Batman movie, reporting that it grossed more than US$55 million on its debut at the box office. Quite clearly, the study of the children's market is important for firms that seek to compete in segments that hold massive growth and market potential.

TABLE 13.1 Companies that have capitalised on the children's market

Brand	Product category
Lego	Toys
Cartoon Network	Animation
Disney	Animation and branded merchandise
Warner Brothers	Animation, movies and branded merchandise
Hasbro	Toys, animation and movies

Characteristics of children

Having examined the uniqueness of the children's market, it is imperative to examine the characteristics of children. Children are often adventurous, naïve, fragile, excitable, eager, physically strong and of bubbly character. Children can also be demanding, excessive, tantrum-throwers and fast learners. These characteristics make children a very interesting segment for marketers. So many needs can be identified at this stage, both physically and emotionally, which can be the bases for product design and development. Children by their very nature require different sort of products and services that vary from what adults would need or prefer. Children, for example, are likely to prefer products with brighter colours of blue, pink and green (Boyatzis and Varghese, 1994; Hemphill, 1996; Burke and Grosvenor, 2015). Adults tend to prefer dull colours, depending on the temperament of the adult. Children's products (non-consumables) also tend to be made out of plastic for protection and safety reasons. Marketers who do not consider the characteristics of children when developing products are likely to encounter hiccups along the way, or fall short of the law.

Children's needs must be the prime consideration in the design of products that target them. Clothing for example, must be designed in a way that does not cause body harm or exacerbate any medical conditions. Appropriate labels must be placed on products meant for children to guide their use and prevent harm. Drugs manufactured for children must be tested and certified thoroughly before being released into the market. Children are emotionally vulnerable and this means that in the development of products such as television shows, cartoons and movies, it is imperative that the right language and mannerism are used in order not to negatively influence the developing child. It has already been established that children are fast learners, and due to that reality, information that is meant to develop children with the right mindset and approach to life is what must be conveyed to them. A famous adage said: 'train up the child the way they must go and when they grow, they will not depart from it'. It is time for marketers to carry this moral responsibility and ensure that all content meant for children is devoid of depressive elements and immoral insinuations that could 'poison' the minds of children. It is argued that some nations suffer from the adverse effects of gun crimes as a result of the type of development children in such nations and communities were exposed to when growing up.

Children have the propensity to be rebellious, and this characteristic must be carefully handled in the development of products and services. This becomes especially important when it comes to the cinematic experience. Movies, cartoons and shows must not portray that it is 'cool' to disrespect parents or be rude to parents. Whatever children pick up early in their lives, they are likely to stick to for the rest of their lives. The characteristics of children make it a matter of moral obligation that marketers put in their best efforts to develop content that will have a positive impact on the children that may be exposed to it. This line of argument also means that when an effective segmentation of the children's market is done, and the needs of children are satisfied, the firm may have a loyal customer for life. Toor (2014) believes that in segmentation, adults should be targeted and treated differently from children. The children's market is a unique market, and firms that operate in that market must be able to recognise the peculiarities of this segment and develop products and services accordingly. The characteristics of children are summed up in Figure 13.1 to afford a better pictorial description.

Segmenting the children's market

Traditionally, the bases for segmenting a market include demographic, geographic, psychographic and behavioural factors (Kotler and Armstrong, 2010). These bases have informed marketing decision-making for decades and have proved useful to firms in their quest to reach out to a particular market and cater for their needs. These four bases for segmenting consumer markets have been discussed earlier in the chapter. However, the key question here is should they be lifted and applied directly to the children's market? If yes, what could the justification be? Alternatively, are there other variables that can be used to segment the children's market? The answers to these questions are not simple or straightforward. The nature and characteristics of children, as well as certain considerations such as the income level of parents, make segmenting the children's market a tricky endeavour. While it is undeniable that the four cornerstone bases for segmentation can be applied to the children's market, there still remains the possibility to further examine other potential bases for segmenting the children's market. Three additional bases for segmenting the children's market are proposed in this chapter: temperament, interests and cultural disposition.

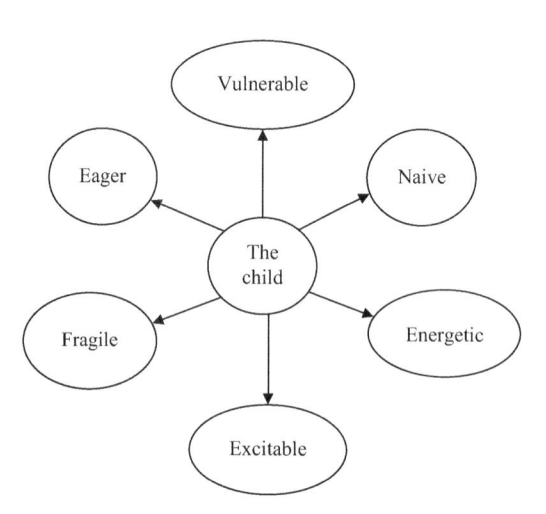

FIGURE 13.1 Characteristics of children

Temperament

According to Shiner and DeYoung (2013), humans display a wide range of individual differences in their typical behaviour, emotions and thoughts. The authors argue that 'beginning in infancy, individuals vary in traits such as energy and activity level, positive emotional engagement with others, feelings of distress and irritability, and persistent attention and interest in absorbing tasks' (Shiner and DeYoung, 2013, p. 113). This suggests that temperaments are important bases for segmenting consumers. When it comes to children, the influence of temperament on choices cannot be discounted or dismissed. Temperaments influence children. Children who are more outgoing, for example, will tend to prefer different types of products or services to children who are introverts. Marketers therefore need to engage in in-depth research to determine how big a role temperament is in children's decision-making. Scholarly work and evidence exists to suggest that temperaments play a big role in children's decisions (Saudino, 2005; Rothbart, 2007; Ganiban *et al.*, 2011). It can also be argued that parents consider the temperaments of their children when buying them gifts. Marketers must therefore be mindful of the different types of temperaments and associated behaviour patterns. McAdams and Pals (2006) have noted that traits show some stability across time and situations. This suggests that if a child belongs to one category of temperament, that temperament is likely to influence their behaviour over a long period of their lives, until some external influence or factors act as a catalyst of change as far as behaviour is concerned.

Interests

Cook (2009) noted that the interests of children can be a good base for segmenting them. Some children are adventurous, while others are timid. Some children are attracted to wildlife, while others are scared to death of animals. Some children like pets, others like toys. The various interests of a child will determine what type of product will satisfy them. Marketers cannot take for granted that all children are the same and have similar interests. Interests vary, and when they are properly identified can serve as a good base for segmenting the children's market.

Cultural disposition

Mattila (1999) strongly believes that the cultural disposition of a person affects their purchase behaviour. This assertion cannot be far from the truth as a North American child who has no experience or knowledge about the rich culture from Ghana may not be interested in donning apparel made of *kente* (a local fabric woven from cotton with intricate patterns). However, this same child may love the gift of a Batman toy figure because he/she is familiar with that. Cultural disposition thus becomes a strong base for segmenting the children's market. Every nation has people with unique cultural backgrounds and this must be taken into consideration when designing products for children. A child from Malaysia will have a different set of tastes from a child who hails from Papua New Guinea. These differences do not suggest inferiority, but rather uniqueness. Marketers would do well to factor this into strategic thinking, product design and market segmentation.

It can be argued from the above discussions that, conceptually, the children's market can be effectively segmented using seven variables. These variables are an integration of the four conventional bases for segmenting the consumer market and three variables proposed in this chapter. Thus, as depicted in Figure 13.2, the following are the relevant factors for segmenting the children's market: demographic, geographic, psychographic, behavioural, temperament, interests and cultural disposition.

Implications for marketers

Marketers have for decades focused their attention on milking the cow, that is, adult consumers. Adequate attention has not been paid to the children's market and how influential and potentially beneficial that market can be. Segmenting the children's market throws up a lot of relevant issues for the marketer. For instance, as observed earlier, effective targeting and positioning is essential if any firm hopes to succeed in the marketplace. The children's market is no different. Marketers must assess whether the market segments they are interested in are accessible, measurable, actionable, sustainable and capable of responding differently to different marketing programmes as suggested by Kotler and Keller (2012). An effective positioning strategy must also be designed, developed and activated. The ability of the marketer to gain a differentiated, positive and sustained perception of his/her products and image are critical for long-term success. These are particularly relevant because of the unique characteristics of children.

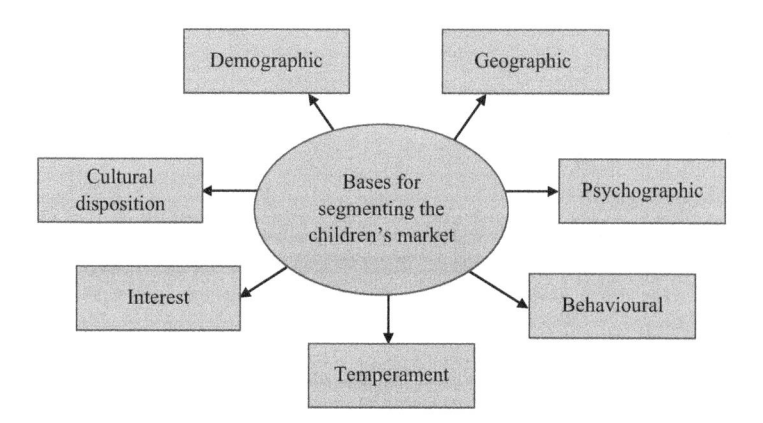

FIGURE 13.2 Segmenting the children's market

The children's market also places an onus on marketers to expand their creative juices to cater for marketing communications campaigns that will appeal to children and have the desired effect in terms of stimulating children to influence their parents to make purchase decisions. A failure to cater for this all-important element of the marketing mix could result in the development of products that would fail to achieve high sale rates because promotional campaigns failed to ignite the interest of children and their relevant audience. For instance, in the use of celebrity endorsement, it is critical that marketers select celebrity endorsers that appeal to children. If celebrity endorsers appeal to parents but not to children, it can create a scenario where parents may be attracted to the product but children may have no interest in it.

Conclusions and directions for future research

Children are unique and represent a massive market for marketers. The differences in attributes with respect to children and adults are vast and illuminating. Children have so many things about them that make them different in terms of needs and wants compared to adults. Even though there is a saying that 'there is a child in every adult', it cannot be said that there is an adult in every child. As a result, it has become imperative for marketing literature to discuss unique approaches to segmenting this all-important market. This chapter has highlighted how the characteristics of children make it important for marketers to consider a different approach to segmenting their markets and noted how the bases for segmenting consumer markets can still be applied to segmenting the children's market. Three new bases for segmenting the children's market have been proposed, namely: temperament, interests and cultural disposition. These three new bases provide marketers with additional concepts that can be effectively employed in the segmentation of the children's market. The study thus concludes on the grounds that the children's market is not only unique but has massive potential, which if firms properly harness and effectively tap into can reap massive profits and build brand empires in the process.

Future researchers can test the new bases for segmenting the children's market proposed in this study. Empirical studies and interviews with firms engaged in the children's market can provide further insight into the validation or disconfirmation of the proposals made here. For instance, future research can consider testing the proposals and evaluating their impact on outcome variables (such as sales performance) to determine the effectiveness of the suggested segmentation variables. It would also be interesting to examine the impact of the characteristics of children on the marketing strategy of firms, with specific reference to branding and promotion.

References

Acuff, D. S. and Reiher, R. H. (1997). *What kids buy and why*. New York: The Free Press.
Bannon, L. (1988). Cresce participação de crianças na economia. *O Estado de S. Paulo*, São Paulo, 19 de outubro.

Beane, T. and Ennis, D. (1987). Market segmentation: A review. *European Journal of Marketing*, 21(5), 20–42.

Boyatzis, C. J. and Varghese, R. (1994). Children's emotional associations with colors. *The Journal of Genetic Psychology*, 155(1), 77–85.

Burke, C. and Grosvenor, I. (2015). *The school I'd like – revisited: Children and young people's reflections on an education for the 21st century*. London and New York: Routledge.

Cook, D. T. (2009). Children as consumers. In J. Qvortrup, W. Corsaro and M. Honig (eds), *The Palgrave handbook of childhood studies* (pp. 332–346). Basingstoke: Palgrave Macmillan.

Dibb, S. and Simkin, L. (1991). Targeting, segments and positioning. *International Journal of Retail and Distribution Management*, 19(3), 4–10.

Ganiban, J. M., Ulbricht, J., Saudino, K. J., Reiss, D. and Neiderhiser, J. M. (2011). Understanding child-based effects on parenting: Temperament as a moderator of genetic and environmental contributions to parenting. *Developmental Psychology*, 47(3), 676–692.

Gilboa, S. and Vilnai-Yavetz, I. (2012). Segmenting multicultural mall visitors: The Israeli case. *Marketing Intelligence & Planning*, 30(6), 608–624.

Hemphill, M. (1996). A note on adults' color–emotion associations. *The Journal of Genetic Psychology*, 157(3), 275–280.

Herman, S. (2012). *A million little bricks: The unofficial illustrated history of the Lego phenomenon*. New York: Skyhorse.

Kane, Y. I. and Sherr, I. (2011). Secrets from Apple's genius bar: Full loyalty, no negativity. *Wall Street Journal*, 15 June.

Kjeldgaard, D. and Askegaard, S. (2006). The globalization of youth culture: The global youth segment as structures of common difference. *Journal of Consumer Research*, 33(2), 231–247.

Kotler, P. (2002). *Marketing places*. New York: Simon & Schuster.

Kotler, P. and Armstrong, G. (2010). *Principles of marketing*. Upper Saddle River, NJ: Prentice Hall.

Kotler, P. and Keller, K. L. (2012). *Marketing management*. Harlow: Pearson Education.

Lambin, J. J. (2000). *Marketing estratégico*. Portugal: McGraw Hill.

Lindstrom, M. (2003). Tweenspeak: The new branding language. *Advertising & Marketing to Children*, 4(3), 35–42.

Lynn, M. (2011). Segmenting and targeting your market: Strategies and limitations. http://scholarship.sha.cornell.edu/articles/243 (accessed 14 February 2017).

McAdams, D. P. and Pals, J. L. (2006). A new Big Five: Fundamental principles for an integrative science of personality. *American Psychologist*, 61, 204–217.

McNeal, J. U. (1969). The child consumer: A new market. *Journal of Retailing*, 45(2), 15–22.

McNeal, J. U. (1992). *Kids as customers*. New York: Lexington Books.

McNeal, J. U. (1999). *The kids market: Myths and realities*. New York: Paramount Books.

Mangold, W. G. and Faulds, D. J. (2009). Social media: The new hybrid element of the promotion mix. *Business Horizons*, 52(4), 357–365.

Mattila, A. S. (1999). The role of culture and purchase motivation in service encounter evaluations. *Journal of Services Marketing*, 13(4/5), 376–389.

Mendelson, S. (2017). Box office: 'LEGO Batman Movie' tops weekend with strong $55.6 million debut. *Forbes*. 12 February. www.forbes.com/sites/scottmendelson/2017/02/12/box-office-lego-batman-movie-tops-weekend-with-strong-55-6m-debut/#279a577a2c77 (accessed 21 February 2017).

Montigneaux, N. (2003). *Público alvo: Crianças*. Sao Paulo: Negócio Editora.

Patino, A., Kaltcheva, V. D., Lingelbach. D. and Pitta, D. A. (2012). Segmenting the toy industry: A study of preteen millennials. *Journal of Consumer Marketing*, 29(2), 156–162.

Population Reference Bureau. (2014). 2014 World population data sheet. www.prb.org (accessed 21 February 2017).

Ries, A. and Trout, J. (2000). *Positioning: The battle for your mind, 20th anniversary edition.* New York: McGraw-Hill.

Rothbart, M. K. (2007). Temperament, development, and personality. *Current Directions in Psychological Science, 16*(4), 207–212.

Saudino, K. J. (2005). Behavioral genetics and child temperament. *Journal of Developmental and Behavioral Pediatrics, 26*(3), 214–223.

Schor, J. B. (2004). *Born to buy.* New York: Scribner.

Sherley, C., Morrison, M., Duncan, R. and Parton, K. (2014). Using segmentation and prototyping in engaging politically salient climate-change household segments. *Journal of Nonprofit & Public Sector Marketing, 26*(3), 258–280.

Shiner, R. L. and DeYoung, C. G. (2013). The structure of temperament and personality traits: A developmental self and other. In P. Zelazo (ed.), *The Oxford handbook of developmental psychology* (pp. 113–141). New York: Oxford University Press.

Siegel, D. L., Coffey, T. J. and Livingston, G. (2001). *The great tween buying machine.* Chicago, IL: Dearborn Trade.

Smith, W. R. (1956). Product differentiation and market segmentation as alternate marketing strategies. *Journal of Marketing, 21*(1), 3–8.

Tapp, A. (2001). The strategic value of direct marketing: What are we good at? Part 1. *Journal of Database Marketing & Customer Strategy Management, 9*(1), 9–15.

The Numbers. (2017). *The Lego Batman Movie.* www.the-numbers.com/movie/Lego-Batman-Movie-The#tab=summary (accessed 21 February 2017).

Thomas, B. (2016). *Magician of the movies: The life of Walt Disney.* New York: Theme Park Press.

Toor, T. (2014). Market segmentation for penetrating deeper into the contact lens market. *Strategic Direction, 30*(5), 34–36.

UNFPA. (2014). *The power of 1.8 billion adolescents, youth and the transformation of the future.* New York: UNFPA.

Vecchio, G. D. (2002). *Creating ever-cool: A guide to a kids heart.* Gretna, LA: Pelican.

Veloso, A. R. and Campomar, M. C. (2012). Segmentation and positioning in the Brazilian kids market: A case study on the bottom of the pyramid. *Revista Administração em Diálogo – RAD, 14*(1), 122–153.

WorldAtlas. (2017). *7 countries that spend most on toys: How much should you spend on your kids?* 9 February. www.worldatlas.com/articles/countries-that-spend-most-on-toys-how-much-should-you-spend-on-your-kids.html (accessed 21 February 2017).

14
AMPLIFYING THE VOICES OF YOUNG CONSUMERS IN FOOD ADVERTISING RESEARCH

Anna Maria Sherrington, Steve Oakes and Philippa Hunter-Jones

Introduction

This chapter examines the ethics and practicalities of conducting research with young consumers in a food advertising context. To do this, the chapter draws upon a longitudinal research study conducted with English and Swedish consumers, who at the beginning were aged 12, at the end aged 14. The orienting frame of reference was that of social marketing, a prime directive of which is *client orientation* – the seeking of a well-grounded understanding of people and their behaviour in order to encourage behavioural change (Hastings and Domegan, 2014). The primary aim of this research study was to ascertain the characteristics of a creative advertising strategy for healthy eating likely to resonate with the age group. This was achieved by conducting research from the perspective of the young consumers themselves.

The chapter will review a number of aspects of relevance. The rationale for the research study will be addressed. This will be followed by a discussion of the role of the young consumers in the research process, after which fundamental aspects associated with ensuring the ethicality of the research are reviewed. The research methodology adopted will then be explained, followed by detailed descriptions of the research methods and data analysis. Here the emphasis will be on demonstrating how the research study was designed in order to give voice to the young consumers. Finally, an evaluation of conducting longitudinal research with a young research population is provided.

The term *young consumers* will be used to denote the research population. Where the discussion refers to aspects of childhood more generally (rather than consumer behaviour specifically), *children* will be used.

Rationale for the research

The *United Nations Convention on the Rights of the Child* (UNICEF, 1989) states that a fundamental right of children is the right to the enjoyment of the highest attainable standard of health. Children are also entitled to high standards of research about their lives, which gives due consideration to their views. Some 25 years after the introduction of the *United Nations Convention on the Rights of the Child*, the *State of the World's Children* report (UNICEF, 2014) calls for innovative approaches for addressing problems affecting children and highlights that the most insightful propositions often emerge from children themselves.

This research study responded to a recommendation for a re-orientation of food advertising research to address how advertising may be used to encourage the adoption of healthier diets (Cairns *et al.*, 2013). The research was prompted by the urgent issue of childhood obesity, described by the World Health Organization (WHO) as having reached 'alarming proportions' in many countries, posing an 'urgent and serious challenge' (World Health Organization, 2016, p. 8). One striking characteristic of the childhood obesity debate is that the voices of the main stakeholder group – children – rarely feature. Hence, this research study sought input from young consumers with the aim of representing their voices through a range of fieldwork activities.

The role and status of the young consumers in the research process

This research study was guided by social constructionism, a research philosophy that holds that our sense of meaning and reality is discursively constructed through language (Hackley, 1998). The consumer remains an autonomous individual, but one whose development of individuality and subjectivity, as well as behaviour, depends upon social interaction. Social constructionism frames research from the perspective of the consumer, rather than the researcher (Hackley, 2001). In the context of childhood obesity this takes on particular prominence, where young consumers' voices need amplifying, with their views of direct relevance to policy makers, food producers and advertisers (Mehtha *et al.*, 2010). Sparrman (2009, p. 299) recognises the contrasting views of children as 'naïve' versus 'competent' research participants (see Figure 14.1).

The perception of children as *innocent/naïve* and in need of protection emanates from developmental psychology and developmental stages. Accordingly, John (1999) proposes that children proceed through three sequential stages associated with their development as consumers and that each stage involves significant cognitive shifts from pre-school to adolescence: the *perceptual stage* (3–7 years), the *analytical stage* (7–11 years) and the *reflective stage* (11–16 years). By early adolescence, their skill set includes reflective thinking. Improved reasoning skills are

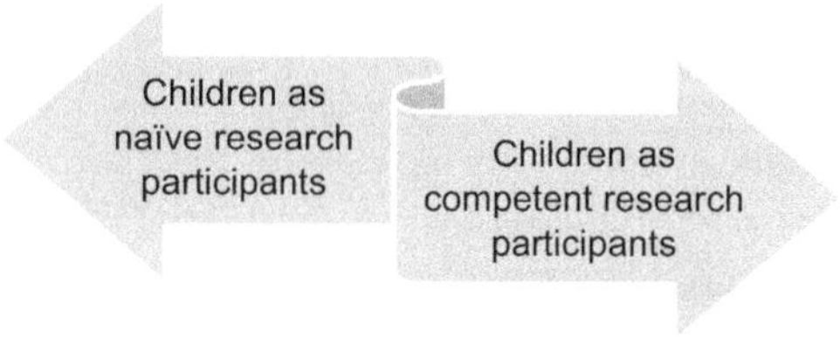

FIGURE 14.1 Contrasting views of children as research participants

Source: Sparrman (2009).

accompanied by more complex marketplace knowledge as well as heightened social awareness, including the ability to recognise the perspectives of others.

The notion of the *competent child* is based upon a socially and culturally constructed child, perceived as an agentive social citizen (Prout and James, 1997; James et al., 1998; Christensen and Prout, 2005). The model of the *social child* (James et al., 1998) sees children as adopting the role of social actors in their own lives, making meaning through interacting with other children and adults alike. This research study positioned the participants as 'social actors within the study context' (Davis, 2010, p. 62). This focus upon children's lived experience has been facilitated by the theoretical move of social constructionism and assisted by the introduction of the *United Nations Convention on the Rights of the Child* (Christensen and Prout, 2005; Kellett, 2010). Accordingly, children are provided with *conceptual autonomy*, regarded as the direct and primary unit of study. Westcott and Littleton (2005) maintain that explicit consideration of the notions of *competence* and *power* is required. James et al. (1998) describe children's competencies as different, not inferior to adults. Kellett (2014) recognises that the *Convention on the Rights of the Child* has resulted in a transfer of power as manifest in research epistemology. It follows that children are gaining the status of 'co-creators of knowledge' (Kellett, 2010, p. 24). Within their own subculture of childhood, children enjoy an insider perspective, investing them with power in their position as *gatekeepers* to the knowledge therein (Kellett, 2010).

The viewpoint of the young consumers as participating research subjects, in combination with this research study's social constructionist epistemological assumptions, meant that the fieldwork was regarded as a series of events in a co-constructive process of meaning-making (Heath et al., 2009; Bucknall, 2014; Fraser et al., 2014). It was thought that *participatory research* (as opposed to data gathering) would assist the process of knowledge production (Kellett, 2010). Figure 14.2 synthesises the discussion in terms of the young consumers' role and status in this research study.

Ensuring the ethicality of the research study

The researcher's duty of care to deliver high-quality research as prescribed by the *United Nations Convention on the Rights of the Child* (UNICEF, 1989), has been

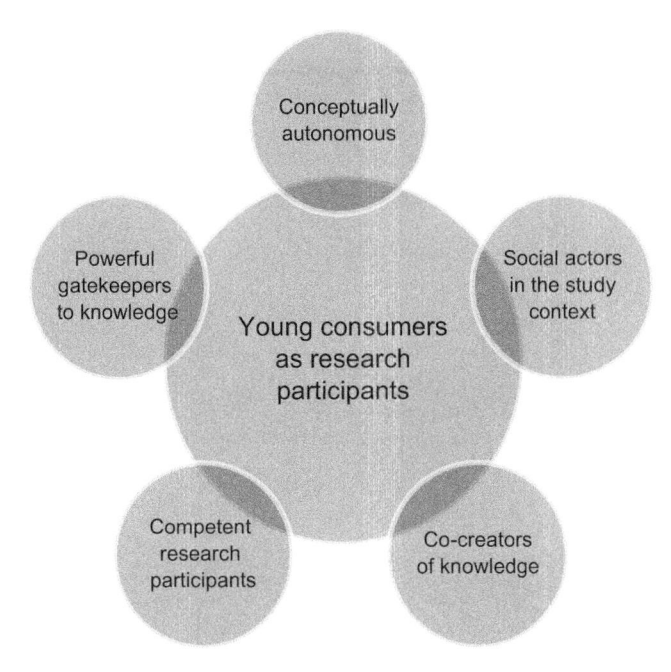

FIGURE 14.2 Young consumers' role and status in the research process

[Diagram shows "Young consumers as research participants" in the center, surrounded by: Conceptually autonomous, Social actors in the study context, Co-creators of knowledge, Competent research participants, Powerful gatekeepers to knowledge]

noted already. Accordingly, this research study adopted the perspective of the young consumers with the aim to amplify their voices. The well-being and safety of the young participants during the research needs to be ensured. Figure 14.3 depicts the various research guidelines of relevance to this and similar research.

ESOMAR (World Association of Opinion and Marketing Research Professionals; formerly, European Society for Opinion and Marketing Research) describes itself as an organisation that aims to encourage, advance and elevate market research worldwide (ESOMAR, 2016). The *ICC/ESOMAR Code on Market and Social Research* was developed jointly with the International Chamber of Commerce (ICC) and contains a guideline (ESOMAR, 1999) on conducting research with children. In addition to outlining more specific detail on special care and precautions during the research process, the guideline recognises children's welfare as the overriding priority. The Market Research Society, the world's largest market research association, supports research for commercial purposes and public policy (Market Research Society, 2016). The *Market Research Society Code of Conduct* (Market Research Society, 2014) requires the permission of a responsible adult for a child to participate in research. Before research affiliated with a university can commence, it needs approval by the ethics committee of that institution. Furthermore, in the UK, researchers require a DBS certificate (Disclosure and Barring Service, n.d.) to conduct research with children.

Obtaining *informed consent* represents a critical stage in the research process and amounts to potential participants being fully briefed via an information sheet about

250 Anna Maria Sherrington *et al.*

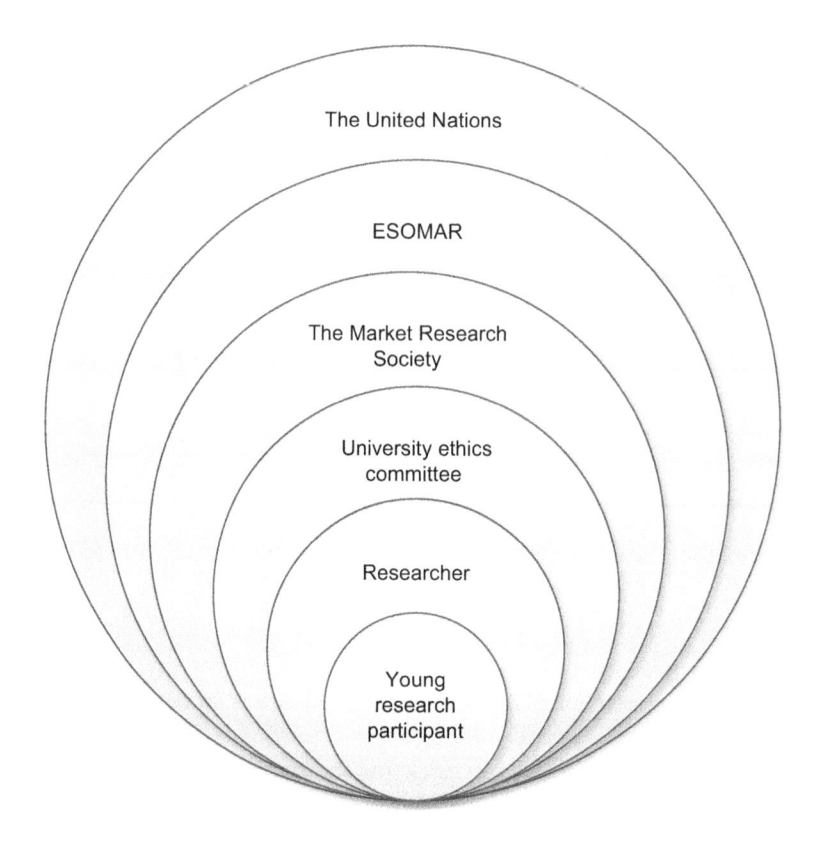

Concentric circles from outermost to innermost:
- The United Nations
- ESOMAR
- The Market Research Society
- University ethics committee
- Researcher
- Young research participant

FIGURE 14.3 Protective layers safeguarding young research participants

the nature of the research and how the findings may be used (Hill, 2005; Heath *et al.*, 2009; Alderson, 2014). This research study used different information sheets for parents and young consumers, the latter of which used simple language to ensure understanding. The notion of gaining informed consent recognises children's agency (c.f. the *competent child* (Prout and James, 1997)), in terms of their competency to engage with research and ability to decide whether to take part (Heath *et al.*, 2009). The *Market Research Society Code of Conduct* (Market Research Society, 2014) stipulates their entitlement to decline, even if a parent has granted permission. Furthermore, the right to withdraw at any stage should be respected. Being longitudinal, this research study re-negotiated consent for each stage, commensurate with the requirement for 'ongoing consent' (Kellett, 2010, p. 25). It recognised the entitlement to *anonymity* – protection of the specific identities of research participants (Heath *et al.*, 2009).

The fieldwork was conducted in a school environment. Schools as research sites may attract criticism based upon potential existence of a power relationship created by teacher–pupil authority. However, many studies involving children tend to recruit through schools, in a bid to satisfy ethics concerns and reflecting ease of access (Banister and Booth, 2005). Importantly, schools enable insight into the participants' behaviour in a social environment (Banister and Booth, 2005), a characteristic commensurate with this research study's social constructionist perspective.

On completion of a study, it is appropriate to share the findings with the participants. Heath *et al.* (2009) maintain a large volume of research with young participants notwithstanding, dissemination targeted specifically at them as a primary audience is uncommon. Recognising the duty of reporting back as part of an ethics contract, this research study shared academic papers written at the completion of a research stage with the participating schools. In terms of dissemination targeted specifically to the participants, a dedicated talk upon completion of all the fieldwork was offered. Figure 14.4 depicts fundamental ethics requirements met at each stage.

Listening to the voices of young consumers

The following sections will account for the research philosophy underpinning this research study, justifying its interpretivist perspective and outlining its social constructionist assumptions.

Adoption of an interpretivist perspective

This research study sought qualitative, in-depth understanding of the young consumer group and their discourses around food advertising. It has been proposed that perceptions of healthy eating are specific to the *context* and the *age group* of the research participants, making an interpretivist approach with a focus upon understanding and interpretation appropriate (Chan *et al.*, 2009). Further support for interpretivism comes from Pettersson and Fjellström (2006), who maintain that the understanding of food in everyday life and the use of food in social interaction represent culturally specific forms of knowledge. Hackley (2001, p. 49) accounts for interpretivist marketing research as placing the emphasis upon 'lived experiences of consumers in engagement with social practices of consumption' and claims that critical, sophisticated and culturally informed scholarship of this nature offers the richest opportunity for social scientific investigation.

Figure 14.5 offers an overview of the approach adopted by this research study. Accordingly, interpretivist research methodology was employed to explore the

FIGURE 14.4 Fundamental ethics considerations for each research study stage

meaning co-created by the young consumers in a range of fieldwork activities, which simulated social environments in order to gain access to their *lived experiences*. This was achieved by conducting all stages of the research using a group context; focus groups for discussions and workshops for the hands-on activities of collage construction and advertisement design. The research was conducted from the perspective of the young consumers, with the spotlight turned upon language. The research design recognised that the participants would benefit from a range of outlets for their opinions and ideas, with the opportunity to express themselves both verbally and visually.

The resulting verbal and visual data were then analysed, providing *understanding and interpretation* in the form of deep participant-centred insight. Essentially, the empirical research involved listening to, interpreting and, eventually, representing the voices of the young consumers. The longitudinal perspective allowed listening to their voices over time and showed how their discourses around food advertising developed and changed in tandem with their acquisition of more sophisticated market persuasion knowledge.

Ontology of social constructionism

Within the overall interpretivist perspective, the research design was influenced by Hackley's (1998, 2001) ideas on social constructionism. Unlike 'mainstream marketing', which tends to promote a scientific research approach concerned with establishing statistical support for empirical truths, social constructionism

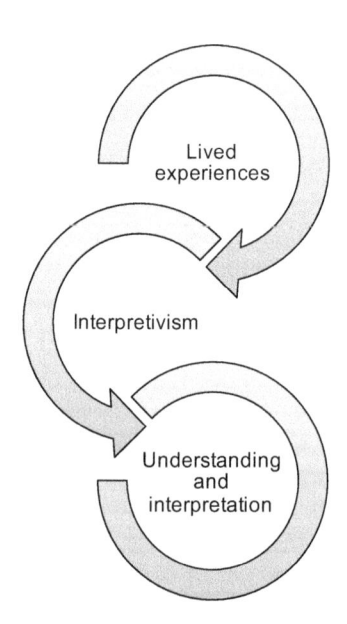

FIGURE 14.5 Interpretivist perspective to the study of young consumers and food advertising

seeks to reveal a realm of marketing practice as a 'complex literary construction', where *language* plays a central role (Hackley, 2001, p. 2). It follows that *meaning* is a social construction and that our sense of meaning and reality is discursively constructed through the 'constitutive language of the everyday' (Hackley, 1998, p. 21). On a similar note, Berger and Luckmann (1967) contend that the most important vehicles of reality maintenance are those of language and conversation. De la Ville and Tartas (2010) claim a more comprehensive understanding of children's consumption activities to follow from a focus upon children's everyday language. Similarly, Moisander and Valtonen (2006) maintain that meaning is constructed discursively in social interaction using text, talk, sounds and images as well as signifying practices.

The social constructionist epistemological model of the consumer sees them as self-directed entities, who actively seek meaning through symbolic engagement with the world (Hackley, 2003). In the realm of food and food consumption, family and friends are the most powerful agents of socialisation, including socialisation for preference and choice of different foods for young consumers (Young, 2003). When it comes to objects of empirical analysis, textual and visual materials provide sites where meanings and forms are accessible to the researcher (Moisander and Valtonen, 2006). Figure 14.6 depicts the main social constructionist assumptions of relevance to this research study.

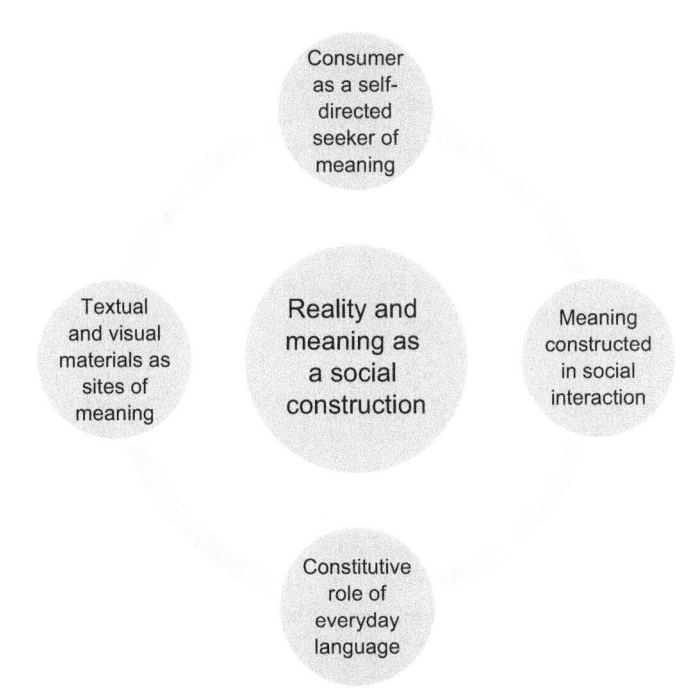

FIGURE 14.6 Social constructionist assumptions of relevance to this research study

Social constructionist perspective on the distributed self

The second stage of the fieldwork concerned research participants' perception of themselves and amounted to their constructing audience profiles of a 'typical 13-year-old consumer'. The design of this stage was influenced by Wetherell and Maybin's (1996) proposition that the *self* is *socially constructed*. This view argues for a merged view of the person and their social context, 'where the boundaries of one cannot be easily separated from the boundaries of the other' (Wetherell and Maybin, 1996, p. 222). It follows that the self is continually shaped and re-shaped through interactions with others within a social world by everyday conversations, current social practices and so on. People move across different sites and so find themselves in different social contexts with different identity possibilities. As a consequence, the self may be described as *distributed*, continually spreading and changing across a relational and social field. It follows that the self is also *contextual* as well as *emergent*, due to its fluid and continuously changing format. Wetherell and Maybin (1996) claim that language, talk and discourse provide important raw materials for the construction of the self and that our identities are, in part, discursive products. In the course of its use, language constructs the world and the self. Meaning is a joint accomplishment and the self a product of collaborative, provisional and contextual negotiation.

Stages in the co-constructive process of meaning-making

Hackley's (2003) ontological assumption that advertising can be seen in a socially constructed light was central to the study, requiring varied and creative research techniques (Hackley, 2001). Seeing young consumers as socially and culturally situated calls for localised, sensitive and flexible research methods (O'Donohoe and Tynan, 1998), which may be achieved by a 'child-centric' approach to research within marketing (Banister and Booth, 2005, p. 157) or what Bartholomew and O'Donohue (2003) refer to as the adoption of a 'child's eye view' (p. 441). Consequently, this research study sought to embrace the participants' active participation in an array of research techniques. The three research stages will now be explored in turn.

Stage 1: exploratory research

Stage 1 of the research study sought to explore the 12-year-old participants' understanding and perceived importance of the concept of healthy eating. Their role as current food customers with their own spending power and their fulfilment of an influence market with impact upon household food purchases (McNeal, 1992) was also of interest, as was their perceived influence of socialisation agents upon their food choice. Further, insight regarding their perception of food advertising in various media was collected. This stage was regarded as *formative*, influencing the direction of the following two research stages.

Given the importance of the social context in the realm of food and food consumption (Young, 2003) and the adoption of a social constructionist ontology, it was established that a group context would be appropriate for all three research stages. Hence, focus groups would be used due to their methodological assumption that social knowledge is produced in interaction with others (Smithson, 2000; Tonkiss, 2004). The focus groups were seen as simulating those routine communicative contexts where meaning is socially constructed through everyday talk (Lunt and Livingstone, 1996), essentially providing a 'collecting tank' for relevant discourses (Puchta and Potter, 2004, p. 126). The suggestion that focus groups may address any power imbalance between the researcher and young participants, as they allow for the group to be collectively powerful, was another imperative for their use (Smithson, 2000; Hennessy and Heary, 2005).

A focus group is 'focused' in that it performs some form of collective activity (Oates, 2000, p. 186). Each focus group addressed a number of tasks, guided by a semi-structured interview guide. The purpose of the session was explained, stressing the absence of correct/incorrect answers. The tasks involved a discussion of print advertisements for healthy/unhealthy food/drinks, followed by an exploration of the meaning of healthy/unhealthy foods. In a card sorting activity, the participants negotiated the order of importance of cards containing images/names of socialisation agents (family, school, peers, shop environment, television advertising, print advertising, the Internet, text messaging) in terms of their influence upon their food choice, followed by a discussion of the nature of such influence. After a discussion of food brands' websites, the participants played an advergame on a branded website hosted by a breakfast cereal brand. This was followed by a discussion of the purpose of advergames. Preceded by a discussion of their use of YouTube, the participants viewed television advertisements for healthy/unhealthy food/drinks, used to anchor a discussion on television advertising. Finally, the participants filled out an anonymous exit questionnaire collecting data on their television viewing behaviour, Internet usage, etc. The groups were audio recorded. Figure 14.7 provides an overview of the research activities used.

Stage 2: collage construction

The following year, when the participants were 13, the research study sought insight into their perception of themselves in terms of their characteristics and what motivates them as consumers. In the spirit of Wetherell and Maybin's (1996) contention that the self is socially constructed, resulting from a collaborative, provisional and contextual negotiation, consumer collages were constructed jointly by groups of participants. The participant-centred approach to visual research (Emmison *et al.*, 2012) described here and for Stage 3, allowed for active involvement of the participants. Importantly, in this style of qualitative research visual materials may be used as a tool to decrease the power differential between the researcher and the young participants (Emmison *et al.*, 2012).

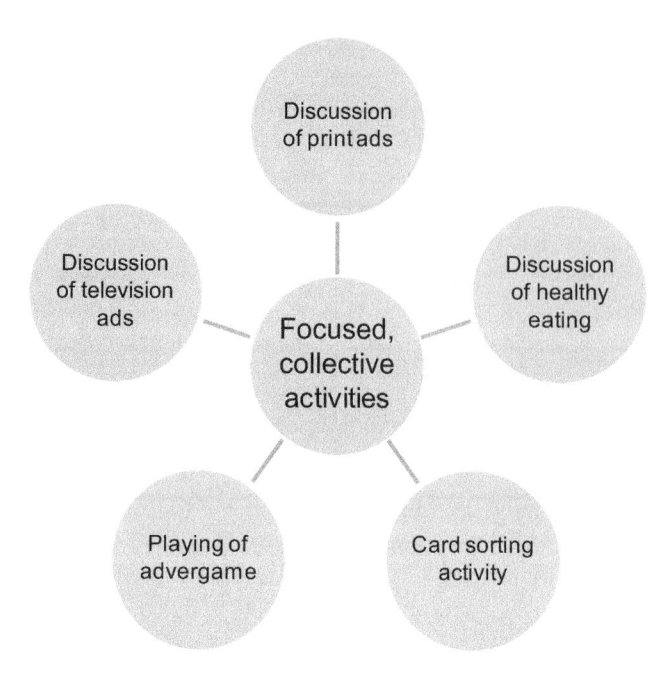

FIGURE 14.7 Research activities used within the Stage 1 focus groups

Moisander and Valtonen (2006) describe collages as a 'product of discursive practice'. As such, collages represent 'visual language' and can be read as 'visual cultural stories' (p. 26). Further, Moisander and Valtonen (2006) claim that 'collaborative and reflexive use of visuals' (p. 96) provides research participants with increased voice in representing study phenomena, which supported the aim to empower the participants and meant that the research was conducted from their perspective. Emmison *et al.* (2012, pp. 20–21) refer to 'participatory visual approaches' as a more 'emancipatory style of qualitative research', where participants take on the role of image-makers and may engage in 'visual storytelling'. For consumer profiling, the technique makes participants' 'inner representations of experiences as ideas, imagery, and consumption practices' accessible (Zaltman and Coulter, 1995; Belk *et al.*, 2003; Cherrier, 2012, p. 93; Siemieniako and Kubacki, 2013) and may enhance their engagement (Havlena and Holak, 1996). Siemieniako and Kubacki (2013) claim collages make the social side of the research issue visible. The motives of this research study were similar to those of Siemieniako and Kubacki (2013), namely, ensuring that communications campaigns reflect the reality of the motivations and perceptions of the particular consumer group to deliver more targeted and effective communications (c.f. Havlena and Holak, 1996; Martin and Peters, 2005). The sum of these qualities were in line with this research study's social constructionist ontology.

Each workshop constructed a collage using images and words in order to describe 'a typical 13-year-old consumer' (boy and girl). The participants were instructed to fill a poster sheet with images and words in response to a set of questions delivered verbally and on a worksheet. For instance, the questions prompted consideration of such aspects as the interests and aspirations of these young consumers, as well as their relationship to food brands and attitudes towards such concepts as organic food and Fairtrade. The absence of right and wrong answers was pointed out. Magazines and other suitable materials were made available, as well as scissors, coloured pens and glue sticks. The materials were selected to ensure availability of a wide variety of images suited to the worksheet questions. The workshops were audio recorded.

Stage 3: advertisement evaluation and design of a healthy eating advertisement

The objective of the final stage was two-fold. It took place a year later and sought the participants' (aged 14) reactions to current television advertisements promoting healthy eating/a healthy lifestyle, in order to identify their dominant discourses in relation to this topic. What is more, the participants devised communication strategies appropriate for advertising healthy eating/foods to their own age group by designing their own advertisements.

For the advertisement evaluation, a similar approach to that used by Chan and Tsang (2011) was employed. Chan and Tsang (2011) measured Hong Kong youths' attitudes to television advertisements promoting green lifestyles. Chan and Tsang's interview questions were adapted for use in this research study. The participants watched two television advertisements. After each one, questions were posed and, equipped with tablets, the participants engaged in a discussion on Padlet (www.padlet.com). Padlet may be described as an online wall, which allows contributors to share their thoughts on what works somewhat like a virtual piece of paper. On advice from the participating schools, Padlet would be acceptable to parents' frequent concern about the Internet and child safety (Newman and Oates, 2014).

Hackley (2003) claims the value of having consumer insights frame and direct creative work to be well established. While this practice is common within the advertising industry, few academic studies report on this aspect. Bartholomew and O'Donohue (2003) describe a research initiative using focus groups, where children provided verbal suggestions for advertising strategies for an imaginary soft drink. In this research study, the participants produced a range of poster- and film-style advertisements. A worksheet was provided to guide the design work. Figure 14.8 provides an overview of the three research stages.

Representing the voices of young consumers

Hackley (2001) argues that *social texts* (for this research study: focus group transcriptions, collages, Padlets and participants' advertisements) are open to differing interpretation and recommends the use of discourse analysis within a social constructionist ontology. Simunaniemi *et al.* (2012) recognise that people gain knowledge

258 Anna Maria Sherrington et al.

- Formative research
- Focus groups
- Meaning-making through focus group interaction
- Output = talk

Stage 1 – exploratory research

Stage 2 – collage construction
- Consumer profiling
- Workshop format
- Collage construction
- Output = collages of images and text

- Advertisement evaluation
- Online discussion board
- Output = text
- Advertisement design
- Design workshops
- Output = images, text, talk, music and moving images

Stage 3 – advertisement evaluation and design

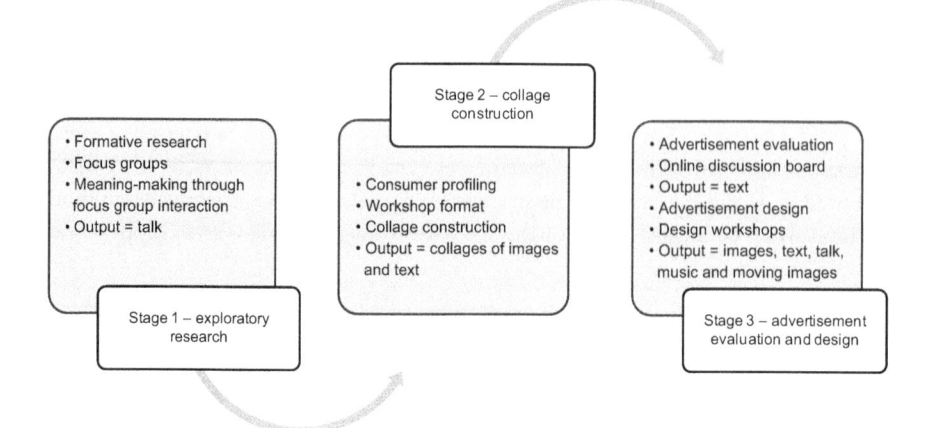

FIGURE 14.8 The three stages of the research study

in social communication and maintain that perceptions of healthy eating represent 'a product of social practices in which language plays a central role' (p. 67). Essentially, in a social constructionist spirit, discourse analysis entails a focus on the use of language in context. Bucknall (2014, p. 72) maintains that 'voice' is not an autonomous but a social production, requiring communication to be recognised as a local, interactional activity. Alldred and Burman's (2005) notion of discourse similarly points to the importance of *context*. Consequently, accounts that young consumers give researchers need contextualising by explicit reference to the social context. Further, context in a physical sense may impact on the researcher–researched relationship. As previously recognised, the predisposition of schools to reinforce adult–child power (Westcott and Littleton, 2005; Kellett, 2010) must be recognised.

A widely used general process of interpretation is that of the *hermeneutic circle*, a concept based on the idea that in order to understand the part (e.g. a detail of discursive practice), the interpreter needs to apprehend the whole (e.g. transcripts of focus group talk, relevant cultural discourses, the discursive context). The process of interpretation proceeds through a series of back and forth, part to whole iterations. The goal of *hermeneutic interpretation* is to produce different interpretations in order to bring about change. The researcher should challenge the obvious and provide new ways of interpreting the world (Moisander and Valtonen, 2006). This process, however, is circular and never ending, as we continuously re-evaluate and revise our understanding of the social world (Clarke, 2006).

The fieldwork produced verbal and visual data. Hearn and Thomson (2014) recognise that images can be counted and categorised, but also seen as discourse and narrative. Scott (1994, p. 264) proposes that advertising images may be understood as a 'discursive form' much like writing and capable of delivering subtle nuances in communications. Moisander and Valtonen (2006) recommend that visual images be analysed as *texts*, based on a particular visual vocabulary and a

The part:
A comment about a food advertisement

The whole:
Transcript of a focus group

Cultural discourses around food

Discursive context in relation to a healthy lifestyle

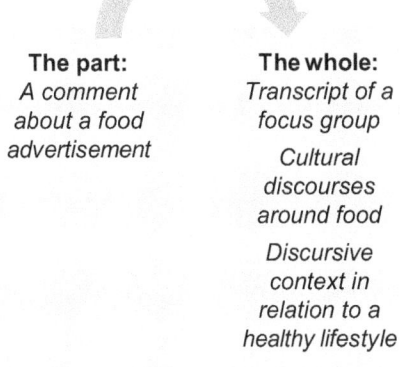

FIGURE 14.9 The adoption of a hermeneutic approach to data analysis

visual grammar. Hence, the analysis proceeded hermeneutically (see Figure 14.9), paying close attention to verbal and visual aspects.

The following sections briefly account for the method of data analysis used in each stage (see Figure 14.10 for an overview).

Analysis of stage 1: the exploratory research

The data collected during this stage was 'talk', which was analysed using discourse analysis (Brown and Yule, 1983; Paltridge, 2012). Hence, the transcribed text was

- Discourse analysis

Stage 1 – exploratory research

Stage 2 – collage construction
- Categorisation of images
- Discourse analysis
- Reading of visual cultural story

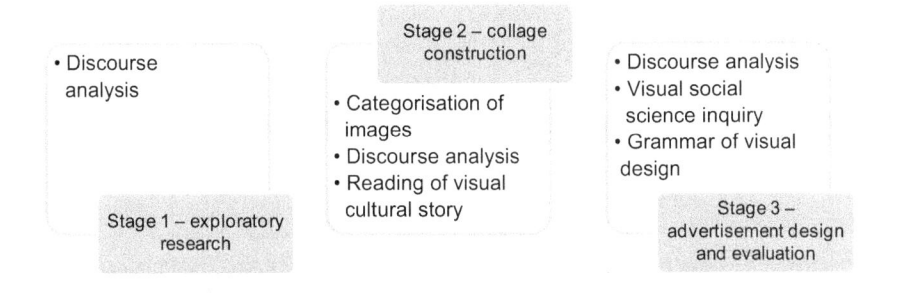

- Discourse analysis
- Visual social science inquiry
- Grammar of visual design

Stage 3 – advertisement design and evaluation

FIGURE 14.10 Approaches to data analysis

read closely in order to identify dominant themes, which in turn were analysed in order to establish *discourses* or particular ways of talking about healthy eating and aspects of food advertising. Fairclough (2003) proposes that a discourse is a particular way of representing some part of the social world, with alternative discourses associated with different groups of people. Establishing discourses central to food and food advertising among young consumers was seen as essential in order to inform the promotion of healthy foods to the age group.

Analysis of stage 2: the consumer collages

The analysis followed the overall guidance of Pachler (2014) of using a hermeneutic interpretation procedure (see Figure 14.9). Accordingly, in the analysis used, 'parts' referred to single elements in the collages (images and words), whereas the 'whole' referred to the collages in their entirety and the context in which they were constructed. The first stage of the analysis used *categorisation*, essentially mapping the 'parts'. Units of data – images and words – were classified as representing a more general category (Spiggle, 1994), each of which received a *label*. The visual images were not analysed in their own right, but allowed a means for the participants to communicate aspects of their lives, experiences and identities (Emmison *et al.*, 2012). As such, the collages were seen to represent *visual language* to be read as a *visual cultural story* (Moisander and Valtonen, 2006). The emerging themes – verbal and visual – were analysed using discourse analysis (Brown and Yule, 1983; Paltridge, 2012). This analysis took place within the socially constructionist perspective of the *distributed self*, important assumptions of which are that the self is continuously shaped and re-shaped through interactions with others and that language, talk and discourse provide raw materials for the construction of the self (Wetherell and Maybin, 1996).

Equipped with the collage labels ('parts') and the audio-recordings of the collage construction workshops, including the participants' verbal summaries of the 'typical consumers' delivered at the end (part of 'the whole'), the researcher wrote 'narrated vignettes' of 12 named (the participants gave each of their consumers a name), 'typical 13-year-old consumers' emerging from the data. This process was informed by insight picked up during the Stage 1 focus groups (another part of 'the whole'). The vignettes, in their position as 'empirically sourced narratives', described *socially constructed consumers* as portrayed in the collages and spoken about by the research participants. The purpose was for the collages and narrated vignettes combined to bring the consumers to life (Quinn and Patterson, 2013, p. 730).

Analysis of Stage 3: the advertisement evaluation and the participant-designed advertisements

The analysis of the Padlets used a format similar to that described by Simunaniemi *et al.* (2012) in their analysis of discourses in a sample of fruit and vegetable-related weblog texts. Accordingly, the analysis began by reading the postings on the discussion wall with an open mind in order to identify recurrent patterns in the data. A number of *preliminary themes* were identified and coded into thematic categories. Following further reading of the postings, in the second phase the preliminary themes were crystallised into *themes*. In the third stage, the themes were categorised into a range of *main discourses*.

The advertisements designed by the research participants varied in their type of presentation from poster advertisements to simple films. Accordingly, the analysis employed discourse analysis (Brown and Yule, 1983; Paltridge, 2012) for the verbal elements. The images contained in the advertisements were thought of as 'like language' and were 'read' in order to interpret their meaning in a similar way to the advertising copy (Hall, 1997, p. 5). In common with Emmison *et al.*'s (2012, p. 113) principles, the analysis looked for 'manifest themes' across images, while simultaneously exploring the social aspects displayed. The analysis then used aspects of Emmison *et al.*'s (2012) approach to *visual social science inquiry*. Accordingly, the visual data were approached 'sociologically' with the aim of investigating how the data may serve as 'sources of concrete visual information about the abstract concepts and processes which are central to organising everyday social life' (Emmison *et al.*, 2012, p. 63).

The analysis also employed Kress and van Leeuwen's (2006) *grammar of visual design*, a particular approach to visual semiotics, where the visual representation is set within the theoretical framework of *social semiotics*. In *social semiotics*, the focus is upon *sign-making* (rather than the use of ready-made signs). Kress and van Leeuwen's *visual grammar* concentrates on the way in which visual elements combine in *visual statements* into *meaningful wholes*, with attention paid to representational, interactive and compositional patterns. The resulting visual structures refer to particular interpretations of experience and forms of social interaction.

The value of longitudinal research

There were particular reasons for this research study's use of a longitudinal perspective. First and foremost, the objectives were ambitious and could not have been fulfilled within one fieldwork session alone. Spacing the research out over a longer time period enabled the adoption of gradually more challenging research techniques. What is more, it allowed appreciation of the participants' development of persuasion knowledge (Wright *et al.*, 2005; Saunders *et al.*, 2016). Importantly, the longer-term perspective meant that the research study could evolve over time, with the possibility of adaptations to changing circumstances.

There are, however, challenges associated with longitudinal research. Accordingly, the recruitment process was more challenging with the field sites having to commit to research taking place over a three-year period. Ongoing relationship maintenance was needed to ensure co-operation of the schools. Parental and participant consent had to be sought for each event. Some attrition followed with a small number of participants deciding not to take part in subsequent stages. Overall, the research study required substantial time and financial investment. The advantages and challenges of a longitudinal approach as perceived from this research study are summarised in Table 14.1.

TABLE 14.1 The advantages and challenges of longitudinal research with young consumers

Suitable for studies with ambitious objectives	Recruitment of research participants more challenging due to longer-term commitment
With children, allows the adoption of gradually more challenging research methods	Parental and participant consent to be re-obtained for each event
Allows the observation of children's development over time	Relationship management required to maintain participation
Makes the research process more flexible, with the possibility to make adaptations	Adaptations may require further applications for ethics consent
Allows the researcher to develop their insight over time, leading to more informed fieldwork	Attrition likely, with strategy of participant replacement needed
	Demands higher investment in terms of time and finance

Conclusion: amplifying the voices of young consumers

This chapter has reported on a research study with young consumers, where the research methodology decisions were driven by the quest to give voice to this consumer group. The adoption of a social constructionist perspective, which sees meaning and reality as discursive constructions in social interaction, turned the focus upon *language* (Hackley, 1998; Moisander and Valtonen, 2006). This final section will highlight the main methodological insights gained during this research study, both in terms of successes and points of learning. Recommendations for future research approaches of a qualitative nature within the domain of food advertising will be provided, aspects of which may be transferred to other areas of relevance to young consumers.

In terms of amplifying the voices of the young consumers, this was achieved by conducting the research from their perspective and through careful consideration of how to facilitate their expression. Altogether, the various stages of the research study – focus group discussions, collage construction, Padlet discussions and advertisement design – allowed the young consumers to express their voice in a variety of languages – verbally, visually and in text – in a manner that allowed factual, emotional and creative expression of their opinions, feelings and ideas. The resulting fieldwork data could then be analysed by means of discourse analysis for talk, text and copy and more specialist methods for visual elements, music and movement.

The exploratory focus groups provided access to a wealth of discourses around healthy eating and food advertising. The 'typical consumers' in the collages provided deep insight of a kind denied to a positivist research orientation. The collages in combination with the narrated vignettes helped to bring the socially constructed consumers alive. By virtue of a longitudinal design, more demanding research activities could be introduced over time. In the final stage of the research study, Padlet provided yet another mouthpiece for the young consumers to express their own voice and so effectively provided access to their discourses around advertisements promoting healthy eating/living. What is more, the young consumers expressed their creative ideas in complete creative concepts that resulted in poster-style and film advertisements.

The research methods literature highlights the risk of a power differential between young participants and a research team. However, this research study saw the young consumers as 'competent research participants' (Sparrman, 2009, p. 299), who in their position as 'co-creators of knowledge' (Kellett, 2014, p. 24) were gatekeepers to valuable information relating to their age group. What is more, use of a group context is likely to have made them collectively powerful (Smithson, 2000). Additionally, the use of visual materials in the collage construction and the advertisement design may have facilitated further reduction of any power differential (Emmison *et al.*, 2012).

The research process resulted in points of learning that provide opportunities for future research. Accordingly, the narrated vignettes were authored by the researcher and so, unlike all the other data, did not represent the first-hand voice of the young consumers. Future studies could task young consumers with writing consumer stories around typical consumers their own age. Further, despite their richness and illuminating variety, the collages still represented mosaics of visual and verbal snippets, a snapshot at a point in time. While still recruiting through school, future research could take the fieldwork away from the school environment and accompany young consumers to various consumption contexts, such as a visit to a fast-food restaurant. This ethnographic approach would allow the researcher to tap into young consumers' discourse around fast food in a social context, enabling exploration of aspects of marketing communication in situ. It would also assist in getting round the precise time allocation frequently allocated to research by schools (e.g. Verhellen *et al.*, 2014), a by-product of their main priority of achieving academic benchmarks.

While the research design described in this chapter did assist in amplifying the voices of the young consumers, there are ways in which research may strengthen the *impact* of their voices. One approach is simply to continue to conduct research *with* young consumers, from their perspective. The academic community is in a powerful position to conduct research with young consumers that is inclusive of the group. Recognising as a responsibility the need to conduct research that is accessible to young consumers, may enable and empower them to contribute towards a critical, society-wide conversation around issues such as childhood obesity and the role of food advertising. Such research would benefit further from a cross-national perspective. Platforms such as Padlet offer safe and inexpensive platforms for conducting such research, with the online environment in a position to amplify their voices and spread the conversation further and wider.

References

Alderson, P. (2014). Ethics. In A. Clark, R. Flewitt, M. Hammersley and M. Robb (eds), *Understanding research with children and young people* (pp. 85–102). London: Sage.

Alldred, P. and Burman, E. (2005). Analysing children's accounts using discourse analysis. In S. Greene and D. Hogan (eds), *Researching children's experience: Approaches and methods*. London: Sage.

Banister, E. N. and Booth, G. J. (2005). Exploring innovative methodologies for child-centric consumer research. *Qualitative Market Research: An International Journal*, 8(2), 157–175.

Bartholomew, A. and O'Donohue, S. (2003). Everything under control: A child's eye view of advertising. *Journal of Marketing Management*, 19(3–4), 433–457.

Belk, R. W., Ger, G. and Askegaard, S. (2003). The fire of desire: A multi-sited inquiry into consumer passion. *Journal of Consumer Research*, 30(3), 326–351.

Berger, P. L. and Luckmann, T. (1967). *The social construction of reality: A treatise in the sociology of knowledge*. Harmondsworth: Penguin.

Brown, G. and Yule, G. (1983). *Discourse analysis*. Cambridge: Cambridge University Press.

Bucknall, S. (2014). Doing qualitative research with children and young people. In A. Clark, R. Flewitt, M. Hammersley and M. Robb (eds), *Understanding research with children and young people* (pp. 69–84). London: Sage.

Cairns, G., Angus, K., Hastings, G. and Caraher, M. (2013). Systematic reviews of the evidence on the nature, extent and effects of food marketing to children: A retrospective summary. *Appetite*, 62(1), 209–215.

Chan, K., Prendergast, G., Grønhøj, A. and Bech-Larsen, T. (2009). Adolescents' perceptions of healthy eating and communication about healthy eating. *Health Education*, 109(6), 474–490.

Chan, K. and Tsang, L. (2011). Promote healthy eating among adolescents: A Hong Kong study. *Journal of Consumer Marketing*, 28(5), 354–362.

Cherrier, H. (2012). Using projective techniques to consider the societal dimension of healthy practices: An exploratory study. *Health Marketing Quarterly*, 29(1), 82–95.

Christensen, P. and Prout, A. (2005). Anthropological and sociological perspectives on the study of children. In S. Greene and D. Hogan (eds), *Researching children's experience: Approaches and methods* (pp. 42–60). London: Sage.

Clarke, S. (2006). *From enlightenment to risk: Social theory and contemporary society*. Basingstoke: Palgrave Macmillan.

Davis, T. (2010). Methodological and design issues in research with children. In D. Marshall (ed.), *Understanding children as consumers* (pp. 61–78). London: Sage.

de la Ville, V.-I. and Tartas, V. (2010). Developing as consumers. In D. Marshall (ed.), *Understanding children as consumers* (pp. 23–40). London: Sage.

Disclosure and Barring Service. (n.d.). Disclosure and barring service: About us. www.gov.uk/government/organisations/disclosure-and-barring-service/about (accessed 23 October 2016).

Emmison, M., Smith, P. and Mayall, M. (2012). *Researching the visual* (2nd edn). London: Sage.

ESOMAR. (1999). ESOMAR World research codes and guidelines: Interviewing children and young people. www.esomar.org/uploads/public/knowledge-and-standards/codes-and-guidelines/ESOMAR_Codes-and-Guidelines_Interviewing-Children-and-Young-People.pdf (accessed 23 October 2016).

ESOMAR. (2016). Homepage: About ESOMAR. www.esomar.org/about-esomar.php (accessed 23 October 2016).

Fairclough, N. (2003). *Analysing discourse: Textual analysis for social research*. London: Routledge.
Fraser, S., Flewitt, R. and Hammersley, M. (2014). What is research with children and young people? In A. Clark, R. Flewitt, M. Hammersley and M. Robb (eds), *Understanding research with children and young people* (pp. 34–50). London: Sage.
Hackley, C. (1998). Social constructionism and research in marketing and advertising. *Qualitative Market Research: An International Journal*, *1*(3), 125–131.
Hackley, C. (2001). *Marketing and social construction: Exploring the rhetorics of managed consumption*. London: Routledge.
Hackley, C. (2003). How divergent beliefs cause account team conflict. *International Journal of Advertising*, *22*(3), 313–331.
Hall, S. (1997). Introduction. In S. Hall (ed.), *Representation: Cultural representations and signifying practices* (pp. 1–11). London: Sage.
Hastings, G. and Domegan, C. (2014). *Social marketing: From tunes to symphonies* (2nd edn). London: Routledge.
Havlena, W. J. and Holak, S. L. (1996). Exploring nostalgia imagery through the use of consumer collages. *Advances in Consumer Research*, *23*(1), 35–42.
Hearn, H. and Thomson, P. (2014). Working with texts, images and artefacts. In A. Clark, R. Flewitt, M. Hammersley and M. Robb (eds), *Understanding research with children and young people* (pp. 154–168). London: Sage.
Heath, S., Brooks, R., Cleaver, E. and Ireland, E. (2009). *Researching young people's lives*. London: Sage.
Hennessy, E. and Heary, C. (2005). Exploring children's views through focus groups. In S. Greene and D. Hogan (eds), *Researching children's experience: Approaches and methods* (pp. 236–252). London: Sage.
Hill, M. (2005). Ethical considerations in researching children's experiences. In S. Greene and D. Hogan (eds), *Researching children's experience: Approaches and methods* (pp. 61–86). London: Sage.
James, A., Jenks, C. and Prout, A. (1998). *Theorizing childhood*. Cambridge: Polity Press.
John, D. R. (1999). Consumer socialization of children: A retrospective look at twenty-five years of research. *Journal of Consumer Research*, *26*(3), 183–213.
Kellett, M. (2010). *Rethinking children and research: Attitudes in contemporary society*. London: Continuum.
Kellett, M. (2014). Images of childhood and their influence on research. In A. Clark, R. Flewitt, M. Hammersley and M. Robb (eds), *Understanding research with children and young people* (pp. 15–33). London: Sage.
Kress, G. R. and van Leeuwen, T. (2006). *Reading images: The grammar of visual design*. London: Routledge.
Lunt, P. and Livingstone, S. (1996). Rethinking the focus group in media and communications research. *Journal of Communication*, *46*(2), 79–98.
McNeal, J. U. (1992). *Kids as customers: A handbook of marketing to children*. New York: Lexington.
Market Research Society. (2014). The market research society code of conduct. 1 September. www.mrs.org.uk/pdf/mrs%20code%20of%20conduct%202014.pdf (accessed 23 October 2016).
Market Research Society. (2016). Homepage: About MRS. www.mrs.org.uk/mrs/about-mrs (accessed 23 October 2016).
Martin, M. C. and Peters, C. O. (2005). Exploring adolescent girls' identification of beauty types through consumer collages. *Journal of Fashion Marketing and Management*, *9*(4), 391–406.

Mehta, K., Coveney, J., Ward, P., Magarey, A., Spurrier, N. and Udell, T. (2010). Australian children's views about food advertising on television. *Appetite*, *55*(1), 49–55.

Moisander, J. and Valtonen, A. (2006). *Qualitative marketing research: A cultural approach*. London: Sage.

Newman, N. and Oates, C. J. (2014). Parental mediation of food marketing communications aimed at children. *International Journal of Advertising*, *33*(3), 579–598.

Oates, C. (2000). The use of focus groups in social science research. In D. Burton (ed.), *Research training for social scientists* (pp. 186–195). London: Sage.

O'Donohoe, S. and Tynan, C. (1998). Beyond sophistication: Dimensions of advertising literacy. *International Journal of Advertising*, *17*(4), 467–482.

Pachler, P. (2014). *How collages reveal your deepest thoughts*. Hamburg: Anchor Academic.

Paltridge, B. (2012). *Discourse analysis*. London: Bloomsbury.

Pettersson, A. and Fjellström, C. (2006). Responsible marketing to children and their families. *Young Consumers*, *7*(4), 13–18.

Prout, A. and James, A. (1997). A new paradigm for the sociology of childhood? Provenance, Promise and Problems. In A. James and A. Prout (eds), *Constructing and reconstructing childhood: Contemporary issues in the sociological study of childhood* (2nd edn, pp. 7–33). London: Routledge.

Puchta, C. and Potter, J. (2004). *Focus group practice*. London: Sage.

Quinn, L. and Patterson, A. (2013). Storying marketing research: The twisted tale of a consumer profiled. *Journal of Marketing Management*, *29*(5–6), 720–733.

Saunders, M., Lewis, P. and Thornhill, A. (2016). *Research methods for business students* (7th edn). Harlow: Pearson Education.

Scott, L. M. (1994). Images in advertising: The need for a theory of visual rhetoric. *Journal of Consumer Research*, *21*(2), 252–273.

Siemieniako, D. and Kubacki, K. (2013). Female students' drinking seen through collages and diaries. *Qualitative Market Research: An International Journal*, *16*(3), 296–314.

Simunaniemi, A.-M., Sandberg, H., Andersson, A. and Nydahl, M. (2012). Normative, authentic, and altruistic fruit and vegetable consumption as weblog discourses. *International Journal of Consumer Studies*, *37*(1), 66–72.

Smithson, J. (2000). Using and analysing focus groups: Limitations and possibilities. *International Journal of Social Research Methodology*, *3*(2), 103–119.

Sparrman, A. (2009). Ambiguities and paradoxes in children's talk about marketing breakfast cereals with toys. *Young Consumers*, *10*(4), 297–313.

Spiggle, S. (1994). Analysis and interpretation of qualitative data in consumer research. *Journal of Consumer Research*, *21*(3), 491–503.

Tonkiss, F. (2004). Using focus groups. In C. Seale. (ed.), *Researching society and culture* (2nd edn, pp. 193–206). London: Sage.

UNICEF. (1989). United Nations convention on the rights of the child. www.ohchr.org/EN/ProfessionalInterest/Pages/CRC.aspx (accessed 17 October 2016).

UNICEF. (2014). The state of the world's children 2015: Executive summary. Reimagine the future. Innovation for every child. www.unicef.org/publications/files/SOWC_2015_Summary_and_Tables.pdf (accessed 17 October 2016).

Verhellen, Y., Oates, C., De Pelsmacker, P. and Dens, N. (2014). Children's responses to traditional versus hybrid advertising formats: The moderating role of persuasion knowledge. *Journal of Consumer Policy*, *37*(2), 235–255.

Westcott, H. L. and Littleton, K. S. (2005). Exploring meaning in interviews with children. In S. Greene and D. Hogan (eds), *Researching children's experience: Approaches and methods* (pp. 141–157). London: Sage.

Wetherell, M. and Maybin, J. (1996). The distributed self: A social constructionist perspective. In R. Stevens (ed.), *Understanding the self* (pp. 219–280). London: Sage.

World Health Organization (WHO). (2016). Report of the Commission on the Ending of Childhood Obesity. http://apps.who.int/iris/bitstream/10665/204176/1/9789241510066_eng.pdf (accessed 17 October 2016).

Wright, P., Friestad, M. and Boush, D. M. (2005). The development of marketplace persuasion knowledge in children, adolescents, and young adults. *Journal of Public Policy & Marketing*, 24(2), 222–233.

Young, B. (2003). Does food advertising make children obese? *Young Consumers*, 4(3), 19–26.

Zaltman, G. and Coulter, R. H. (1995). Seeing the voice of the customer: Metaphor-based advertising research. *Journal of Advertising Research*, 35(4), 35–51.

PART IV
Young consumers in social and cultural contexts

15
REFERENCE GROUPS AND OPINION LEADERSHIP IN CHILDREN'S CONSUMPTION DECISIONS

Ayodele C. Oniku and Achi E. Awele

Introduction

The effect of reference group influence on purchase and consumption decisions, and buying patterns have been a popular study in adults among researchers, thus little contribution has been made to the topical issue regarding children, especially in developing markets (Bearden and Etzel, 1982; Page and Ridgway, 2001; Pechmann and Wang, 2010; Lombe *et al.*, 2011; Mau *et al.*, 2016). Reference groups are fundamental in studying the behavioural aspect of marketing in order to understand how consumers shape their personal buying behaviours based on consumption patterns and behaviours of someone they reverence or avoid. In a way, reference groups are a social phenomenon in that, typically, consumers naturally belong to a particular social group, which knowingly or unknowingly influences demand patterns and consumption decisions in certain areas of living. Thus, it becomes a force that consumers obey; and marketers seek to understand in order to satisfy consumers in market. By and large, consumers' decisions are shaped or influenced by demand and consumption behaviours of others who they are close to or from a distance, or people they see from an aspirational point of view because of their admirable consumption patterns, or otherwise in terms of avoidance or rejection of certain buying or consumption behaviours.

The work of Reza and Valeecha (2013) succinctly captures the operations and concept of reference groups as 'the reference points from where we take cues to configure our values and standards' (p. 197). This definition invariably buttresses the functions and roles of reference grouping as a basis of comparison for a consumer's purchase decision or patterns in order to form effective demand in the marketplace. Also, according to Bearden and Etzel (1982), the earlier work of Hyman (1942) invented the term in a study of social status in the course of understanding and determining what people or group respondents compared themselves with. Thus, the operations of reference groups are applicable and relevant in consumer buying decisions and purchase patterns irrespective of colour, age, sex, nationality, profession, etc. because they solely operate on the pedestal of comparison with groups or individuals.

Types of reference group

The trio of informational, utilitarian and value-expressive influences is very strategic to understanding how reference groups shape the buying decision of consumers and how they help organisations to understand the manners and patterns by which individual consumers express or exhibit reference group influence in market. The informational reference group influence uses information, advice, instruction or counsel to influence the buying decisions of others, thus the roles of experts, celebrity, consultants, etc. to influence consumers' purchase decision with their wealth of knowledge, experiences and consumption levels. In other words, they are seen as competent persons to provide reliable information, advice, guidance or directives that would better their experience and expectation, hence, consumers rely on the group's influence (Reza and Valeecha, 2013). Bearden and Etzel (1982) stress the work of Park and Lessig (1977) that consumers need to make informed decisions so they seek reliable information to avoid uncertainty.

Utilitarian reference groups focus on adherence to or compliance with other people's wishes in order to avoid punishment or receive reward. This is strategic in that where an individual finds out that the product involved is crucial to his/her personality he/she will comply to receive reward or to avoid punishment. According to Kelman (1961) it follows the rule of compliance process (Reza and Valeecha, 2013) because consumers believe that the experience is worthy and so everything must be done to achieve reward or avoid punishment. For instance, many young consumers pay huge membership fees to belong to certain associations like gymnastic or other sports clubs for the benefits to both their health and social well-being, or to a social club like AIESEC, popular among economics and business students in higher institutions, in order to enjoy a particular social status in a society.

Value-expressive influence groups are described by Kelman (1961) as an 'identification process' (Reza and Valeecha, 2013, p. 199). It is a reference group process that stresses 'psychological association with a person or group and is reflected in the acceptance of position expressed by others' (Bearden and Etzel, 1982, p. 184). This is an aspiration pursuit that consumers desire many times in their consumption patterns, e.g. particular attendance of particular educational institutes, club membership, acquisition of certain elitist goods, etc. In all categories of age or demographics there is always a value-expressive reference point that consumers seek (Peter and Olson, 1999; Dibb *et al.*, 2001; Adebowale *et al.*, 2013; Reza and Valeecha, 2013).

Reference groups and buying patterns

The work of Bearden and Etzel (1982) clearly shows the roles and influence of reference groups on products and brand purchase decisions. The study premises its findings on the dimensions of luxury and necessity and private and public goods to understand product and brand buying decisions. Thus, product categorisation into public luxury and public necessity and private luxury and private necessity was determined (Peter and Olson, 1999). Products are fixed into the different dimension to determine the effect of reference groups' influence on consumers' buying patterns and consumption decisions. According to Bearden and Etzel (1982, p. 186),

> a public product is one that other people are aware that you possess and use. If they want to, others can identify the brand of the product with little or no difficulty, a private product is one used at home or in private at the same location. Except for your immediate family, people would be unaware that you own or use the product.

Bearden and Etzel (1982, p. 186) also found that 'luxuries are not needed for ordinary, day-to-day living. Necessities were described as being necessary for ordinary day-to-day living.' The findings of the study show that the degree of conspicuousness is different among the product categories though tests reveal that they are all significant on the three subscales of informational, value expressive and utilitarian. Finally, the study reveals that there is a huge difference in consumer perception of reference group influence on the four product categories. Therefore, the operation of reference groups or the way reference groups influence purchase decisions and consumption patterns is different across the four product categories. Also, it is of note that Veblen's (1899) assertion of conspicuous consumption is ubiquitous in the influence of a reference group in a certain product category (Reza and Valeecha, 2013). For instance, the use of expensive items among youths to command a certain status among colleagues, which is becoming more popular in fashion, jewellery and cars, e.g. wearing designer shoes, clothes and bags, and driving certain brands of cars, e.g. BMW.

According to Bourne (1957),

> Publicly Consumed Luxury (PUL) is a product consumed in public view and not commonly owned or used (e.g. golf club) . . . Privately Consumed luxury (PRL) is a product consumed out of public view and not commonly owned or used (e.g. trash compactor) . . . Publicly Consumed Necessity (PUN) is a product consumed in public view that virtually everyone owns (e.g. wristwatch) . . . Privately Consumed Necessity (PRN) is a product consumed out of public view that virtually everyone owns (e.g. mattresses).
>
> *(Bearden and Etzel, 1982, pp. 184–185)*

It is further shown that publicly consumed luxuries have strong influence on both sides of measurement as a product and a brand; a privately consumed luxury will have strong influence as a product because it is a luxury item, but weak influence as a brand because it is not consumed in public view. Also, a publicly consumed necessity would have influence that is weak as a product but strong as a brand, because it is seen by others; the privately consumed necessity would have influence that is weak as a product because it is a necessity and likewise the influence as a brand will be weak because it is not seen by others (Bearden and Etzel, 1982; Peter and Olson, 1999; Reza and Valeecha, 2013).

The study of Reza and Valeecha (2013) further shows that there are other salient factors that determine influence of reference groups on purchase decisions, for instance, the roles of formal and informal reference groups in purchase decisions (Lombe et al., 2011; Singh, 2015). Thus, the questions of what, who, why and how are imperative in understanding how reference groups can be a potential source to influence consumption decisions and purchase patterns. In other words, every consumer knows what they want and they seek the right person as a reference point to corroborate, inform or give credence to their buying decisions either directly or indirectly. Therefore, the modus operandi of a reference group is not just about product but more importantly, it further provides answers to the issue of who is the right reference point; when it is appropriate to use the product; how best to use the product/brand and the reason why the product/brand is used (Bansal et al., 2005). The finding of Reza and Valeecha (2013) on automobile demand among young executives reveals the presence of both formal and informal influences but formal influence is stronger than informal factors/influences. This is comprehensively analysed as prominence of value expression that leads to conspicuous consumption over other variables like informative function and utilitarian factor.

Likewise, the study of Bansal et al. (2005) shows that the acceptability of cigarettes and creating effective demand for cigarettes has to rely on using reference groups to project aspirational and behavioural factors among consumers. For instance, the study emphasises that the market is segmented along the threshold of upper SES, middle class and lower SES and the theme of advertisements is expressed through aspirational motives like the Western lifestyle, being hardworking, upward mobility and strength among men, and elegance and Western lifestyle among women.

Studies have also shown that the operations of reference groups to determine or influence purchase decisions and consumption patterns is not limited to commercial activities or profit-oriented ventures/businesses. Other areas of relevance and application for reference group strategy are found in medical/health issues, educational placement/pursuit, social behaviour and smoking campaigns, etc. (Bansal et al., 2005; Pechmann and Wang, 2010; Lombe et al., 2011; Adebowale et al., 2013). Studies have shown that reference groups can be potentially instrumental in instilling good character and behaviours among people through peer influence. And wrong peer influence can lead to vices and dangerous lifestyles or cultivating potentially bad habits, such as alcohol abuse among youths, sexual promiscuity and exposure to sexually transmitted diseases, etc. For instance, the study of Adebowale *et al*. (2013) reveals the extent to which peer influence, region of residence, education attainment or level of literacy in communities and wealth-circle identity can influence condom acceptability and usage among male unmarried youths. Equally, the study by Lombe *et al*. (2011) shows that the influence of family background and parent attitude, peer pressure and exposure to delinquency can instigate alcohol consumption among youths. These clearly show that the influence of reference groups is multi-faceted in that it can be used to improve business performance and can equally be used to instill good character or achieve behavioural changes in both social and business settings, and where it is unchecked or negative it may lead to social decadence.

Reference group and marketing strategy

Based on the three types of reference group, marketing organisations leverage on the factors to develop appropriate marketing policies and strategies that are expressed through the marketing mix. In other words, promotional tools are used to express aspirational motives or pursuits that create desire in consumers to seek consumption of a product. Bansal *et al*. (2005) record the strategy used in the cigarette industry in India whereby firms in the industry through print media, bill boards and advertising media create images of success, affluence, Westernisation and rich and Westernised Indians to appeal to different segments of consumers to create effective demand for cigarettes. Besides promotional tools, product decisions are also developed to complement this where a product becomes a reference point through association with promotional appeal. However, it is important to note that reference groups do not influence all products and brand purchase decisions at the same level (Berkman *et al*., 1996; Peter and Olson, 1999; Pechmann and Wang, 2010). To a large extent, effective use of promotional tools to entrench reference points enhances brand purchase intention and ultimately behavioural intention (Peter and Olson, 1999).

Opinion leadership

The work of Rogers (1962) titled *Diffusion of Innovations* gives rise to the popularity of opinion leadership and other adopter categories with the sole aim of understanding how new products and innovations are diffused or adopted by consumers. The adopter categories in the order of operation are: innovators, early adopters, early majority, late majority and laggards. Early majority is alternatively called opinion leadership and the adopter plays the role of adopting new products and innovations to influence other consumers' consumption patterns. According to Dibb *et al*. (2001, p. 462) opinion leadership is described as a process whereby 'early adopters choose new products carefully and are viewed as "the people to check with" by those in the remaining adopter categories'.

The roles of opinion leaders are strategic in businesses especially in developing promotional policies that rely on word of mouth, celebrity endorsement and social network campaigns. Importantly, studies have shown that the roles and strategic functions of opinion leaders are the same irrespective of industry or nation (Hazeldine and Miles, 2010; Sarathy, 2011; Meng and Wei, 2013). Opinion leaders' functions are in the areas of professional knowledge, product involvement and fame (Meng and Wei, 2013). Opinion leadership roles further involve technical competency and polymorphism and monomorphism (Chakravarthy and Prasad, 2011). Also, Hazeldine and Miles (2010) chronicle that opinion leadership is about influence, interpersonal word-of-mouth communication, expertise and innovative behaviour (Myers and Robertson, 1972; Feick and Price, 1987; Flynn, Goldsmith and Eastman, 1996). In the online and virtual communities, Zhang and Dong (2008) and Meng and Wei (2013) submit that opinion leadership roles cover professional knowledge, product involvement, interactivity, visual cues, fame, timeliness, functional value, emotional value and network word-of-mouth communication. The work of Sarathy (2011) shows that the roles of opinion leadership cannot be mingled with non-leader professionals in that the roles of opinion leadership strategically involve media exposure, social involvement, product knowledge, innovativeness and IT-compliant usage in the real estate industry/markets. In recent times, the use of celebrity and world-acknowledged leading sportsmen is becoming more popular in the fashion, automobile and airline industries. For instance advertisements such as David Beckham in Armani men's boxers; Tiger Woods in the Rolex wristwatch commercial; Didier Drogba and Turkish Airlines; President Gorbachev, the last leader of the old USSR with a Louis Vuitton designer bag, which clearly expresses social involvement and style with the aim of influencing the upper-middle class and upper-upper class tastes and buying decisions. All of these emphasise the strategic roles of opinion leadership in influencing consumers' purchase decisions and buying patterns.

Some studies, such as those by Iyengar et al. (2011) and Zhang and Dong (2008) have raised questions regarding the efficacy and effectiveness of opinion leadership in influencing other people's consumption patterns and buying behaviours. For instance, can heavy users be regarded as opinion leaders? Does being an opinion follower necessarily evolve into becoming an effective opinion leader? What is the efficacy level between social network opinion leadership and word-of-mouth opinion leadership? The answers to the above questions are critical in contemporary practice and usage of opinion leadership in many industries and economies or markets. Iyengar et al. (2011) recommend that heavy users in the pharmaceutical industry are good as opinion leaders because they are continuously in use of the product and can make good recommendations that opinion leaders in the industry who are not heavy users of the product involved cannot do. Iyengar et al. (2011) agree that opinion followership is fundamental to becoming effective and efficient opinion leaders because true opinion leaders seek information from everyone relevant irrespective of educational, financial and prestige status. However, other studies are not specific on the issue of opinion leadership but rather affirm that opinion leadership entails professionalism in a specialty and taking part in both formal and informal social activities (Zhang and Dong, 2008; Chakravarthy and Prasad, 2011). The argument on word-of-mouth and social network opinion leadership differs and this may be attributed to the peculiarities of industry. Iyengar *et al.* (2011), Zhang and Dong (2008) and Meng and Wei (2015) directly and indirectly emphasise the importance of social networks or online opinion leadership. Other studies (Armitage, 2005; Fabricius *et al.*, 2007; Chakravathy and Prasad, 2011; Sarathy, 2011) stress the role of word of mouth as effective and strategic in real estate, consumer goods, etc. Currently, former British Prime Minister Tony Blair is being featured by CNN to project and popularise the newly founded World Freedom Day on the Cable news, which is directly focused on children, adolescents and adults. Also, the involvement and roles of Madonna and Bono of U2 in campaigns to support awareness about HIV in order to reduce the spread of the deadly sexual disease and to garner support for victims throughout the world, but especially in Africa, is a pointer to the roles and functions of opinion leaders. In fact it has unprecedentedly reduced the spread of the disease and created more awareness about the need for responsible sexual behaviour among youths.

Hypotheses

Hypotheses were developed based on Park and Lessig (1977) and Flynn *et al.* (1996) as follows:

- H1: Young consumers' preferences and choices are not influenced by close friends in school or church/mosque.
- H2: Sources of information that influence preferences and choices of young consumers are not family members.
- H3: Product influences that entrench inner feelings of being 'cool' when making product choices are not trusted.
- H4: The dominant opinion on preferences and choices is not from friends but that of the individual young consumers.

Methodology

The scale used for the study was adapted from the work of Park and Lessig (1977), the choice is influenced by the previous works that the scale had been used to achieve (Bearden and Etzel, 1982; Reza and Valeecha, 2013). The scale was based on the three phases of reference group influence on purchase decisions – informational, utilitarian and value-expressive influences. Also, the scale was adapted through reconstruction of the original statements to fit into children's level of assimilation and understanding. Flynn *et al.*'s (1996) scale was employed to test opinion leadership; primarily the scale was developed to test the influence of opinion leadership in children's consumption decisions and patterns. A four-point Likert scale was used so as remove the chances of the children taking a 'neutral' stance in their response.

The selection of children for the study was fixed at age ranges of 10–15 years, so they fall into Piaget's concrete operational stage (Rossiter, 1977; Riecken and Samli, 1981; Page and Ridgway, 2001; Mau et al., 2016). Piaget's concrete operational stage recognises the Likert scale but in a simplified way of administration whereby it would be read to the children for them to write their responses through the assistance of the teachers (Riecken and Samli, 1981; Langrial et al., 2014), and in few cases children were allowed to seek the assistance of the parents to complete the questionnaire (Chan and McNeal, 2003). A specific school was selected for the study because of the diversity of the students in the school – the International Secondary School, University of Lagos. The pupils are of different backgrounds – from parents of professors to low-cadre staff in the University and importantly children of non-University staff are also admitted into the school.

Importantly, the products considered for the research work are basically items consumed by pupils for educational purposes, like the choice of brand of backpack, school sandals/shoes, the type of sweets and the choice of school uniforms either local tailor-made or imported ready-made.

Results

Demographic background of participants

TABLE 15.1 Respondents' profile analysis

Variable		Frequency (%)
Gender	Boy	137 (50.2)
	Girl	136 (49.8)
	Total	273 (100)
Age	7–10 years	134 (49.1)
	11–13 years	139 (50.9)
	Total	273 (100)
Status of the parents	Single parent	121 (44.3)
	Married	111 (40.7)
	Divorced	41 (15.0)
	Total	273 (100)
Class in school	JSS 1–3	139 (50.9)
	SSS 1–3	134 (49.1)
	Total	273 (100)

Reliability test

Table 15.2 displays the reliability test output for the scales used in the study after a pilot study with 35 respondents was conducted. The Cronbach's alpha coefficients computed above indicate that the scales are acceptable for the study.

TABLE 15.2 Reliability test

Constructs	Alpha coefficients (α)
Utilitarian influence	.803
Informational influence	.773
Value-expressive influence	.752
Opinion leadership	.801
Children consumption decision	.793

Mean and standard deviation

TABLE 15.3 Standard deviation statistical analysis

Constructs	N	Mean	Standard deviation
Utilitarian influence	273	3.1044	.6535
Information influence	273	3.0491	.5745
Value-expressive influence	273	3.0579	.5791
Children's consumption decision	273	4.0696	.8218
Opinion leadership	273	4.1282	.7474

Hypothesis testing

H1: Young consumers' preferences and choices are not influenced by close friends in school or church/mosque.

TABLE 15.4 Young consumers' preference/choices and influence of close friends

		Children's consumption decision	Close friends (value-expressive influence)
Children's consumption decision	Pearson correlation	1	−.046
	Sig. (2-tailed)		.453
	N	273	273
Close friends (value-expressive influence)	Pearson correlation	−.046	1
	Sig. (2-tailed)	.453	
	N	273	273

** Correlation is significant at the 0.05 level (2-tailed).

Results show that the preferences and choices have a weak negative association (r = −.046) with the influence of their close friends in school and church/mosque while p-value is <0.05. This implies that the more influence close friends try to have on children's purchases, the more likely the children will tend to listen to or heed their advice, though the relationship is not that strong. Hence, the null hypothesis is rejected. The influence of reference groups is positive but not that strong and this may be attributable to the different clusters formed by the students to express reference groups among themselves.

H2: Sources of information that influence preferences and choices of young consumers are not family members.

TABLE 15.5 Information from family members and young consumer choices

		Children's consumption decision	Family members (informational influence)
Children's consumption decision	Pearson correlation	1	.064
	Sig. (2-tailed)		.289
	N	273	273
Family members (informational influence)	Pearson correlation	.064	1
	Sig. (2-tailed)	.289	
	N	273	273

** Correlation is significant at the 0.05 level (2-tailed).

Table 15.5 reveals that a weak positive correlation (r = .064) exists between the preferences and choices of the respondents and family members on what to buy. Moreover, since the p-value is <.000, the hypothesis is significant. Hence, the hypothesis that sources of information that influence preferences and choices are not family members is accepted. This invariably reveals that the youths rely on themselves to form reference groupings with less or no influence of parents on them

H3: Product influences that entrench inner feelings of being 'cool' when making product choices are not trusted.

TABLE 15.6 Feeling of being 'cool' and young consumer choices

		Children's consumption decision	Feeling of 'cool' (utilitarian influence)
Children's consumption decision	Pearson correlation	1	.023
	Sig. (2-tailed)		.703
	N	273	273
Feeling of 'cool' (utilitarian influence)	Pearson correlation	.023	1
	Sig. (2-tailed)	.703	
	N	273	273

** Correlation is significant at the 0.05 level (2-tailed).

Table 15.6 shows a weak positive correlation (r = .023) between influences that entrench inner feelings of being 'cool' and the respondents' preference in buying. Moreover, since the p-value is <.000, the hypothesis is significant. Hence, the hypothesis that respondents do not trust products' influences that entrench inner feelings of being 'cool' when making product choices is supported.

H4: The dominant opinion on preferences and choices is not from friends but that of the individual young consumers.

TABLE 15.7 Friends' opinions and young consumer decisions

		Children's consumption decision	Dominant opinion
Children's consumption decision	Pearson correlation	1	.471**
	Sig. (2-tailed)		.000
	N	273	273
Dominant opinion	Pearson correlation	.471**	1
	Sig. (2-tailed)	.000	
	N	273	273

** Correlation is significant at the 0.05 level (2-tailed).

Table 15.7 shows a positive correlation (r = .471) between the dominant opinion of the children and their ability to influence people around them in terms of their buying preferences and choice. Hence, there is a direct relationship between the dominant opinion of the children and its ability to influence people around them in terms of their buying preferences and choice. Also, since the p-value is <.000, the hypothesis is significant. Hence, the hypothesis that an individual's dominant opinion on their preferences and choices is not from friends but from the individual young consumer is supported.

Summary of correlations and inter-correlations

TABLE 15.8 Summary of correlation results among the constructs

Constructs	1	2	3	4	5
1. Children's consumption decision	1				
2. Feeling cool (utilitarian influence)	.023	1			
3. Family members (informational influence)	.064	−.041**	1		
4. Close friends (value-expressive influence)	−.046	.357**	.094	1	
5. Dominant opinion	.471**	−.011	−.006	−.069	1

Discussion and conclusion

Largely, previous studies have looked into the roles of opinion leadership in buying decisions and consumption patterns of adults across industries and social life but rarely in the buying decisions and consumption patterns or behaviours of young children. This study helps us to understand how young consumers form judgements on opinion leadership and followership and the impacts of reference groups on their buying and consumption behaviours.

First, the study reveals and upholds that the three pedestals of informational, utilitarian and value-expressive reference groups are valid in children's buying decisions and consumption patterns. The analysis shows that informational reference groups among children are not dependent on family members who may include the biological parents, older siblings and grandparents. In other words, informational reference groups are not sourced from parents and other family members of children, and alternatively they found informational reference groups among friends and contemporaries. This is in support of other findings (Lombe et al., 2011; Reza and Valeecha, 2013) that the influence of reference groups is within clusters and not external influence or outside of the clusters. Thus, in spite of factors such as age, level of economic dependency and vulnerability of children, the reference group influence that affects their buying decisions and consumption patterns is generated among contemporaries or within the circle of contemporaries.

The decision on compliance process in children's reference group influence (also known as the utilitarian reference group) from the findings shows a weak positive correlation whereby the decision of children on products that make them feel 'cool' is not based on personal preference or assessment but a function of reference group influence. To a greater extent, the finding reveals that children depend on what is in vogue among their contemporaries to make decisions on product choice and preferences. Our physical observation during questionnaire administration reveal that from backpacks to shoes to sweets during break-time, they all have similar identification, and among the junior class we observed comparison of items among pupils to show to their friends the new things they have just got for the new academic session. The finding supports other studies that were based on adults' purchase decisions and consumption decision influence. For instance the work of Reza and Valeecha (2013) on automobile acquisition and purchase decision among young executives shows that work colleagues have greater influence on the decision than friends or other informal groups. Also, Adebowale et al. (2013) reveal that peer influence is one of the stronger influences on condom acceptability and usage among unmarried male youths. Importantly, the punishment or reward for the compliance factor may be stronger in children because the physical observation during the research activity shows that some pupils are to a level 'ostracised' because they are not compliant with what is in vogue or acceptable to the group. And for the 'ostracised' pupils, they are willing and have desires to be part of the consumption patterns but cannot afford the products due to parents' financial challenge or other social reasons.

The value-expressive reference group, which is also referred to as the identification process, emphasises that people are willing to express themselves in a manner that makes them identified with a desired group or association. Thus, the finding in the study reveals that children are influenced by the purchase decision or consumption patterns of close friends in school or church/mosque. Thus, each child belongs to a specific reference group that influences his/her purchase decision and this may be people they meet in church/mosque or meet occasionally. However, children identify and understand that it is possible for a friend to be wrong in consumption patterns and buying decision when it is out of tune with conformity to their reference group. The importance of reference groups is built on the concept of comparison of one's purchase decision with a group one belongs to or aspires to belong to, thus, a close friend found in a church/mosque may not belong to the same school and if it happens that different consumption patterns or behaviours exist in the respective schools, then reference group influence would be different among friends. Also, from observation it was found that a close friendship at school may be built on academic performance and not on social interest, hence a reference group influence may not bind two close friends together and this would therefore lead to different purchase decisions or consumption patterns or behaviours.

The study further looks into opinion leadership position and influence among children and the findings show that the role of opinion leadership is embraced among children. However, the modus operandi of opinion leadership might be different from the characterisations or functions that lead to determination of opinion leadership in a sector, market or product. The findings show that the average child positions or sees him/herself as an opinion leader in that he/she wants to influence a group with his/her new product to affect the buying decisions and consumption patterns of others. However, the study does not go into finding the factors that determine the characters or features of opinion leadership in children, thus the study would not state the reasons why every child sees him/herself as an opinion leader in a group. Nonetheless, studies have shown that opinion leadership features and characters are largely determined by the following factors: product knowledge, product involvement, interactivity, media exposure, expertise, information sharing, etc. (Zhang and Dong, 2008; Hazeldine and Miles, 2010; Meng and Wei, 2015).

In conclusion, the study has elicited certain facts about the effects and operation of reference groups' influence in the demographic category – children. Importantly, the effects and operations of the three phases or types of reference group are discussed and studied and the results affirm that reference group effect and influence is relevant and strategic in determination and understanding of children's purchase decisions, buying patterns and consumption behaviours. Indeed, the study highlights how business decision makers can apply and strategise with reference group influence in children's products and markets.

The role of opinion leadership is equally found to be imperative in children's buying decisions and buying behaviours, hence organisations and business decision makers should not overlook the relevance to achieve improved performances in the children's product industry, especially where innovations and new products are involved. The study does not cover the area of determination of features and characteristics of opinion leadership in children, however, the strategic importance in new product and innovation diffusion in the market cannot be downplayed. The physical observation during the research study reveals that children are conversant with new products and innovations in their needs and wants, hence opinion leadership is strategic.

The roles of reference group and opinion leadership are strategic in business, and importantly the study's findings have shown that they are not only strategic in the adult market but also relevant and strategic in the children market as well. It is noteworthy that organisations should realise that children have a stronger tendency to form reference groups among regular associations and meeting forums, e.g. school, hence casual associations and meetings or occasional gatherings may not provide a forum to determine children's reference group potential.

Also, opinion leadership among children is not as straightforward and definite as in adults because each child shows a tendency to assume that role among the groups, this therefore calls for a different strategy different from what is possible in the adult market, in order to explore opinion leadership in children's buying behaviours.

References

Adebowale, S. A., Ajiboye, B. V. and Arulogun, O. (2013). Patterns and correlates of condom use among unmarried male youths in Nigeria. *African Journal of Reproductive Health*, *17*(3), 149–159.

Armitage, D. (2005). Adaptive capacity and community-based natural resource management. *Environmental Management*, *35*(6), 703–715.

Bansal, R., John, S. and Ling, P. M. (2005). Cigarette advertising in Mumbai, India: Targeting different socioeconomic groups, women and youths. *Tobacco Control*, *14*, 201–206.

Bearden, W. O. and Etzel, M. J. (1982). Reference group influence on product and brand purchase decisions. *Journal of Consumer Research*, *9*(September), 183–194.

Berkman, H. W., Lindquist, J. D. and Sirgy, M. J. (1996). *Consumer behaviour.* Chicago, IL: NTC.

Bourne, F. S. (1957). Group influence in marketing and public relations. In R. Likert and P. S. Hayes (eds), *Some applications of behavioural research.* Switzerland: UNESCO.

Chakravarthy, S. and Prasad, G. V. B. (2011). The impact of opinion leader on consumer decision-making process. *International Journal of Management and Business Studies*, *1*(3), 61–64.

Chan, K. and McNeal, J. U. (2003). Parent–child communications about consumption and advertising in China. *Journal of Consumer Marketing*, *20*(4), 317–334.

Dibb, S., Simkin, L., Pride, W. M. and Ferrell, O. C. (2001). *Marketing: Concepts and strategies* (4th edn). Boston, MA: Houghton Mifflin.

Fabricius, C., Folke, C., Cundil, G. and Schultz, L. (2007). Powerless spectators, coping actors, and adaptive co-managers: A synthesis of the roles of communities in ecosystem management. *Ecology and Society*, *12*(1), 29.

Feick, L. F. and Price, L. L. (1987). The market maven: A diffuser of marketplace information. *Journal of Marketing*, 51, 83–98.

Flynn, L. R., Goldsmith, R. E. and Eastman, J. K. (1996). Opinion leaders and opinion seekers: Two new measurement scales. *Journal of the Academy of Marketing Science*, 24, 137–147.

Hazeldine, M. F. and Miles, P. M. (2010). An exploratory role analysis of opinion leaders, adopters, and communicative adopters with a dynamically continuous innovation. *Journal of Applied Business Research*, 36(4), 117–130.

Hyman, H. H. (1942). The psychology of status. *Archives of Psychology*, 269, 94–102.

Iyengar, R., Van den Bulte, C., Eichert, J., West, B. and Valente, T. W. (2011). How social networks and opinion leaders affect adoption of new products. *New Theories*, 3(1), 17–25.

Kelman, H. C. (1961). Processes of opinion change. *Public Opinion Quarterly*, 25, 57–78.

Langrial, S., Kashif, M. and Ehsan, U. (2014). Exploring attitudes of Pakistani and Canadian children towards television advertisements: A cross-cultural comparative analysis. *Asia-Pacific Journal of Management Research and Innovation*, 10(3), 191–201.

Lombe, M., Yu, M., Nebbitt, V. and Earl, T. (2011). Understanding alcohol consumption and its correlates among African American youths in public housing. *Social Work Research*, 35(3), 173–182.

Mau, G., Schuhen, M., Steinmann, S. and Schramm-Klein, H. (2016). How children make purchase decisions: Behaviour of the cued processors. *Young Consumers*, 17(2), 111–126.

Meng, F. and Wei, J. (2015). What factors of online opinion leader influence consumer purchase intention? *International Journal of Social Science and Technology*, 16(3), 151–158.

Myers, J. H. and Robertson, T. S. (1972). Dimensions of opinion leadership. *Journal of Marketing Research*, 9, 95–99.

Page, C. and Ridgway, N. (2001). The impact of consumer environments on consumption patterns of children from disparate socioeconomic backgrounds. *Journal of Consumer Marketing*, 18(1), 21–40.

Park, C. W. and Lessig, V. P. (1977). Promotional perspectives of reference group influence: Advertising implications. *Journal of Advertising*, 7(2), 41–47.

Pechmann, C. and Wang, L. (2010). Effects of indirectly and directly competing reference group messages and persuasion knowledge: Implications for education placements. *Journal of Research Marketing*, 47(February), 134–145.

Peter, J. P. and Olson, J. C. (1999). *Consumer behaviour and marketing strategy* (5th edn). New York: Irvin/McGraw Hill.

Reza, S. A. and Valeecha, S. (2013). Influence of social reference groups on automobile buying decisions: Research on young executives. *World Review of Business Research*, 3(4), 197–210.

Riecken, G. and Samli, A. C. (1981). Measuring children's attitudes toward television commercials extension and replication. *Journal of Consumer Research*, 8(1), 57–61.

Rogers, E. M. (1962). *Diffusion of innovation*. New York: Free Press of Glencoe.

Rossiter, J. R. (1977). Reliability of a short test measuring children's attitudes toward TV commercials. *Journal of Consumer Research*, 3(4), 179–184.

Sarathy, P. S. (2011). Opinion leaders in real estate markets. *International Real Estate Reviews*, 14(3), 354–373.

Singh, R. (2015). Ethics in food advertising to children in India: A parental perspective. *Journal of Food Products Marketing*, 21(2), 141–159.

Veblen, T. (1899). *The theory of the leisure class*. New York: Macmillan.

Zhang, X. and Dong, D. (2008). Ways of identifying the opinion leaders in virtual communities. *International Journal of Business and Management*, 3(7), 21–27.

Appendix

Correlations

		Consumer decision	Utilitarian influence	Informational influence	Value-expressive influence	Opinion leadership
Consumer decision	Pearson correlation	1	.023	.064	−.046	.471**
	Sig. (2-tailed)		.703	.289	.453	.000
	N	273	273	273	273	273
Utilitarian influence	Pearson correlation	.023	1	−.041	.357**	−.011
	Sig. (2-tailed)	.703		.499	.000	.854
	N	273	273	273	273	273
Informational influence	Pearson correlation	.064	−.041	1	.094	−.006
	Sig. (2-tailed)	.289	.499		.121	.923
	N	273	273	273	273	273
Value-expressive influence	Pearson correlation	−.046	.357**	.094	1	−.069
	Sig. (2-tailed)	.453	.000	.121		.258
	N	273	273	273	273	273
Opinion leadership	Pearson correlation	.471**	−.011	−.006	−.069	1
	Sig. (2-tailed)	.000	.854	.923	.258	
	N	273	273	273	273	273

** Correlation is significant at the 0.01 level (2-tailed).

Gender

		Frequency	%	Valid %	Cumulative %
Valid	Boy	137	50.2	50.2	50.2
	Girl	136	49.8	49.8	100.0
	Total	273	100.0	100.0	

Age

		Frequency	%	Valid %	Cumulative %
Valid	8–10 years	134	49.1	49.1	49.1
	11–13 years	139	50.9	50.9	100.0
	Total	273	100.0	100.0	

Parental status

		Frequency	%	Valid %	Cumulative %
Valid	Single parent	121	44.3	44.3	44.3
	Married	111	40.7	40.7	85.0
	Divorced	41	15.0	15.0	100.0
	Total	273	100.0	100.0	

Educational status

		Frequency	%	Valid %	Cumulative %
Valid	JSS 1–3	139	50.9	50.9	50.9
	SSS 1–3	134	49.1	49.1	100.0
	Total	273	100.0	100.0	

	N	Mean	Standard deviation
Utilitarian influence	273	3.10440	.653468
Informational influence	273	3.04908	.574528
Value-expressive influence	273	3.05788	.579064
Consumer decision	273	4.0695971	.82175757
Opinion leadership	273	4.12821	.747440
Valid N (list-wise)	273		

16
YOUTH SUBCULTURAL THEORY

Making space for a new perspective

Ofer Dekel, Elizabeth Dempsey and Emily Moorlock

Introduction

Youth subcultures appear in the marketing literature in various ways, including pre-teens (Patino *et al.*, 2011), tweenies (Harris, 2005; Brown *et al.*, 2012), chavs (Mason and Wigley, 2013), rappers, hip hoppers, homies (Arthur, 2009) and surfers (Gupta *et al.*, 2008). This research has predominately focused on the unique identity of subcultures, differences from other groups and members' collective desires and buying power. The extant discussion on subcultures has focused on setting up clear boundaries for the identity of young people, with researchers seeking to identify group members that share a similar identity from those who diverge from the mainstream 'norm'.

Culture and youth consumer behaviour

According to Craig and Douglas (2005, p. 322), 'Culture has a profound influence on all aspects of human behaviour'. This suggests the way that we behave as consumers is grounded in our general approach to life. Culture, for Williams (1958) was a whole way of life, with Chaney (2004) adding that its dynamic helps us understand our experiences, thus it becomes central to exploring consumption. Consumer culture essentially involves developing our understanding and exploration of the role of goods and their significance in our contemporary world (Featherstone, 1987). Thus suggesting that to understand the society within which young people live, deriving the meaning of material items and related consumption activities is integral. Wallendorf and Arnould (1988, p. 535) argue that 'objects serve as the set and props on the theatrical stage of our lives and as markers to remind ourselves of who we are'. This focus on objects and material items is a central theme in consumer culture research, with a mutual dialogue between culture and consumption. Craig and Douglas (2005) support this idea, noting that objects can also be a reflection of culture. Therefore, not only can culture impact on what we consume but what we consume can inherently reflect our culture. Arnould and Thompson (2005, p. 868) recognise this connection as part of the work of consumer culture theory (CCT) where they propose that this work 'refers to a family of perspectives that address the dynamic relationships between consumer actions, the marketplace and cultural meanings'. The style of CCT, despite not being consistent in approach or proposing a meta-narrative, suggests that the relationship between culture and consumption is complex and multi-faceted but more importantly is significant and fundamental in our understanding of consumer behaviour (Arnould and Thompson, 2005).

Humans globally share the need to belong (Gentina *et al.*, 2014) and this is particularly prevalent at the adolescent phase of life (Erikson, 1968), where teenagers are conscious of needing to fit in with their social groups (Isaksen and Roper, 2008). Consumption activities, such as the ownership of brands, often allow young people to successfully achieve social acceptance (Haytko and Baker, 2004; Isaksen and Roper, 2008). Thus the relationship between culture, subculture and teenagers is particularly interesting and significant.

Marketing approaches adolescence as a transitional stage between childhood and adulthood, with this stage being the most important cycle of identity crisis individuals experience over their lifetime (Erikson, 1995; Khallouli and Gharbi, 2013). Marketers have consequently approached young consumers as a subculture with unique needs and desires characteristic of their stage of life. It is therefore imperative to better understand 'youth', and their cultural consumption practices at this significant life stage.

Despite the significant contribution to understanding the workings of youth, identity and conceptualisation of subculture, subcultural theory has been subject to much criticism with subsequent research seeking to find a more appropriate method of defining subculture (Hesmondhalgh, 2005). This chapter explores the development of youth subculture, from traditional subcultural theory to more contemporary approaches to understanding youth, namely post-subcultural theory and post post-subcultural explanations. In that there has been a shift in the attention of marketers from the objectivist accounts of youth as a universal life stage (in line with Erikson's (1995) work), where adolescents are categorised into a homogenous group with inherent features (Kjeldgaard and Askegaard, 2006) to a more social constructionist view that problematises 'youth' as a product of Western humanist psychology (Foucault, 1980).

Understanding youth as a subculture

The explanation of youth as a discreet life stage was originally proposed by Abrams (1959) at a time when young people had more leisure time and propensity to consume. Youthful behaviour and related activities were reserved for holidays, as young people were contributors in the production process (Janssen et al., 1999). This suggests the idea of a 'youth' culture is inextricably connected to notions of consumption, in that with more time on their hands young people seek to entertain themselves.

Rice (1996) postulates that with increasing amounts of time to spare, young people attempt to create their own unique, but collective identity through the consumption of music, clothes and other material objects. The Birmingham Centre for Contemporary Cultural Studies (CCCS) arguably provoked interest in the study of young people with their work in the 1970s around working-class youth (Shildrick and MacDonald, 2006; Martin, 2009). The research of the CCCS focused on the study of popular music and youth which generated the seminal work on subcultural theory (Hesmondhalgh, 2005), termed the 'subcultural approach' (Shildrick and MacDonald, 2006, p. 126).

Early CCCS researchers were engaged with understanding how youth struggle to differentiate themselves both from their parents' working-class culture and the dominant bourgeoisie culture. Subcultures provided agency to overcome the mundanity (Hebdige, 1976) and demise of community (Clarke, 1976) exacerbated by the volatile socio-economic environment. Williams (2007, p. 576) describes, 'subcultural youth formed sites of resistance on the street corners, in the dance halls, on the open road, and in the weekend holiday spots'. Within this struggle, subcultures appropriated and inverted cultural meanings, often through the consumption of clothing, music, and other leisure commodities. Hebdige (1979, p. 103) explains: 'Through rituals of consumption . . . the subculture at once reveals its "secret" identity and communicates its forbidden meanings. It is basically how commodities are used in subculture, which marks the subculture off from more orthodox cultural formations.'

Examples of youth subculture research in marketing

Marketing literature treats youth as a homogenised segment with uniform consumption habits – their clothing styles, music tastes and media habits (Kjeldgaard and Askegaard, 2006, p. 231). One example is the research of Mason and Wigley (2013, p. 173) that demonstrates the existence of the 'chav phenomenon' in youth culture. They describe chavs as a market segment part of the wider teenage consumer group. For example, chavs used the brand Burberry to convey their own identity but also their economic capability (Mason and Wigley, 2013). It is noted when studying this phenomenon that subcultures of consumption are important, highlighting that this youth group named 'chavs' have been clearly identified by the media, if not by marketing academics. In the style of the CCCS, it is claimed that chav subculture members have demographic consistencies in education, employment and criminal behaviour (Mason and Wigley, 2013). The members of the chav subculture are mutually consistent in their backgrounds of family attrition (Mason and Wigley, 2013). This is very much aligned with the subcultural approach where Cohen (1972) argues that young people are joined together by both their social circumstances and collective style.

Equally, Ha and Park (2011) suggest that subculture in Korea allows adolescents self-expression and identity projection. By differentiating themselves from the mainstream culture, youth subcultures have unique clothing styles (Ha and Park, 2011). The same argument, as presented by Mason and Wigley (2013) noted that the choice of brands made by the subculture is a significant facet of their consumption activities and key in their collective identity. Ha and Park (2011) also identify the importance of ethnicity in singling out Korean adolescents as a 'materialistic' generation who hold a strong propensity towards 'groupist' tendencies. In researching pre-teens and teen television audiences, Patino et al. (2011) group together these young people as a market segment that can be effectively targeted by marketers who have insight into their media habits. Essentially treating them as a homogenous group. Their research supports this, with participants holding similar psycho-demographic attributes and the same attitudes towards reality television programmes (Patino et al., 2011). In researching the London Asian music scene, Kim (2016) explores how members of this subculture endure the experience of post-racial Britain. Similarly to Ha and Park (2011), this suggests that ethnicity itself can become a feature of youth groups, but more significantly in the subcultural style, her research demonstrates rejection of the contemporary meta narrative around racism in the UK (Kim, 2016). There is a clear thread of resistance and subversion in Kim's research findings that was also present in the early CCCS subcultural studies.

Recent work on youth subcultures (e.g. Hodkinson, 2004; Goulding and Saren, 2007; Ulusoy and Firat, 2016) has, however, claimed that subcultural 'membership' is increasingly becoming a radical cultural mosaic due to individual agency and negotiation of individual identities. The literature on youth subcultures has also seen the introduction of post-subculturalist theory that seeks an alternate path and alternative consumption explanation to the shared consumption activities described by subcultural theory (e.g. Goulding et al., 2013).

Post-subculturalist criticism of the subcultural approach

Critics of subcultural theory emphasise the complexity and shifting nature of current youth culture. These critics (e.g. Garber and McRobbie, 1975; Ulusoy and Firat, 2016) claim that the structuralist description that views youth subcultures as discrete, identifiable youth social arrangements, needs to be reconsidered. They explain that the sheer diversity of styles, forms and practices found in the living reality of young people today make the existing description of youth subcultures obsolete. In the next part of this chapter we review some of the limitations of subcultural theory, offering a post-subculturalist account of youth culture.

Exclusion of important social categories

The first criticism of subculture theory focuses on the categories of youth excluded from structuralist analysis, rather than those included. Despite the emergence of subcultural theory out of the wider social, political and cultural movements of the 1960s and 1970s, including feminism and anti-racism, women and black youth have received, at best limited attention in early subcultural studies (subcultureslist.com, 2017).

Lack of attention to females

Garber and McRobbie (1975, p. 105) highlight the failure of subculture literature to provide accounts of girls' involvement in subcultures:

> Very little seems to have been written about the role of girls in youth cultural groupings. They are absent from the classic subcultural ethnographic studies, the pop histories, the personal accounts and the journalistic surveys of the field. When they discuss young women it is either in ways which uncritically reinforce the stereotypical image of woman with which we are now so familiar or else they are fleetingly and marginally presented.

McRobbie (1978) claims that we cannot simply assume girls resist dominant cultural norms in a unified way. In her research on female skinheads and punks, McRobbie (1980) demonstrates that these girls might go against the mainstream culture of femininity; however, at the same time, within skinhead subculture, traditional gender divisions are still maintained. Garber and McRobbie's (1975, p. 213) research on 'culture of the bedroom' – which involved young girls experimenting with make-up, listening to music, reading magazines and chatting, it is seen that even when the girls share similar cultural experiences, they do so privately, making individual interpretations. Our claim is that common cultural forms do not necessarily generate common meanings. Instead, we argue that the meaning of a particular cultural experience, for a particular individual, in a particular context is produced through the negotiation between available discourses, rather than determined by a single semiotic system.

Ignoring ethnicity

Many scholars claim that subcultural theory has ineffectually dealt with categories of race and ethnicity (e.g. Carrington and Wilson, 2004; Khalaf and Khalaf, 2009). Research of youth subcultures with ethnic backgrounds, especially among Muslim youth, has not yet reached the same level of research as traditional youth cultures such as mods, punks or ravers (Gazzah, in Khalaf and Khalaf, 2009). Furthermore, not only do ethnic subcultures not receive enough attention, subcultural theory fails to capture the diverse contexts ethnic young people inhabit (cf. Hebdige, 1976). This is inclusive of the increasingly globalised and transactional nature of youth consumption and the pluralising dynamics at play in culturally diverse societies (Nilan and Feixa, 2006). Consequently, when these categories are drawn into subcultural analysis they are often treated as rigid forms of demographic divisions, not dynamic and fluid forms of cultural identity (Wyn and White, 1996; Bennett and Hahn-Harris, 2004).

Examples of the rigid treatment of non-white subcultures in Britain can be seen in the works of Hebdige (1979) and Jones (1988), who looked at Reggae, Rasta and Rudies. These studies present black youth as victims of racism or objectify them as a source of white stylistic appropriation (see Chambers, 1976; Hebdige, 1979; Brake, 1980; Jones, 1988). Clarke (1976, p. 88) claims that British subcultural theory has forced Afro-Caribbean youth to follow a 'coded recording' of race relations where they had to choose either Jamaican culture or British. This demonstrates the inflexibility and rigidity of subcultural theory in the 1970s and 1980s.

One of the main criticisms of subcultural research on Muslim youth subculture comes from Marranci's (2001) research on North African youth culture in France. According to Marranci (2001), Rai music offers young French Muslims the opportunity to differentiate themselves simultaneously from the identities of their parents, other ethnic minority youth subcultures and white popular subcultures. Similarly, De Koning (2008) found that although Islam is an important aspect in the lives of Dutch-Moroccan youth, it is not their only point of reference. Ethnic backgrounds, specific sociocultural imaginary and individual Dutch political affiliations along with Islam affect the nature and content of the Dutch-Moroccan musical choice of young people in the Netherlands.

Omission of 'ordinary' youth

It is often argued that youth culture research places a disproportionate emphasis on the most excluded or most spectacular communities of young people, neglecting the experience of 'ordinary' young people (Laughey, 2006; Roberts, 2011; Woodman, 2013). This significant group of young people has been systematically neglected in empirical youth research, with subcultural research being in danger of producing a distorted and incomplete portrayal of contemporary youth culture (Shildrick and MacDonald, 2006, p. 128).

This criticism of subcultural theory offers a growing body of work, focusing upon ordinary youth. Having been pioneered by McRobbie's (1990) work on ordinary teenage girl cultures, Jenkins' (1983) book *Lads, Citizens and Ordinary Kids*, and Willis et al.'s (1990), examinations of the everyday creativity of 'common culture' are now more prominent in the existent literature. The approach to ordinary youth research is now more widespread, such as Laughey's (2006) UK study of music tastes and identities based on inclusive school-based research, Nayak's (2003) exposition of a range of white working-class cultural identities in North East England, Lincoln's (2012) ongoing work on youth and private space, Cantillon's (2015) research into Australian mainstream clubbing, Pilkington's (e.g. 2002) extensive research on Russian youth cultures, the wide range of work on youth and gender (e.g. Allen and Mendick, 2013; Smith et al., 2014), and youth consumption of social media (Bennett and Robards, 2014). This work insists that 'culture is ordinary, in every society and every mind' (Williams, 1989, p. 3) and we should understand it as a whole way of life. Thus, the challenge for studying culture is to understand that signification process and 'lived culture' coexist in every corner of our lives. It is clearly an oversimplification to reduce the experience of culture to those meanings that are most visible.

Empirical limits of subcultural theory

Subcultural theory sees youth subcultures as structures that are patterned by cultural meanings and practices and that these meanings have significance only with reference to the particular community of intentional agents (Berry *et al.*, 1997, p. 87). The main empirical criticism of subculturalist theory is therefore that it is not the task of subcultural research to make ontological claims about what is the 'real' identity of the members of subcultures. Care needs to be taken when making predictions based on such ontological descriptions of consumers' beliefs or lives. In this chapter we do not dispute the patterns found by the aforementioned researchers. Our claim is that these subcultures might appear homogenic at highly abstracted levels; however, this is actually the living reality if its members are fragmented.

Mungham and Pearson (1976, p. 1) explain that this is partly an epistemological issue, as these categories are produced by reductive research that co-opts participants into specific positions to fashion argument: 'the gap between the sociologists' abstract account of youth culture and the explanations one would be likely to get from the subculture themselves'. Redhead (1990, p. 25) claimed that 'authentic subcultures were produced by subculturalists not the other way round'.

Huq (2006) illustrates this empirical blindness when she discusses Clarke's research (1976, p. 100) on skinheads. In his research, Clarke argues that the violent behaviours of skinheads are derived from the fragmentation of traditional working-class communities as a result of slum housing clearance programmes, industrial decline, dwindling employment opportunities and corrupt central and local government. These processes are given as reasons for skinheads' attacks on 'scapegoated outsiders' (Clarke, 1976, p. 102), i.e. immigrant youth. Huq (2006) points out that Clarke's explanation did not even consider other alternative explanations, such as questioning why skinhead aggression could not be channelled against the authorities responsible for their grievance rather than powerless immigrants.

Post-subculture

This discussion on the limits of subcultural theory brings the 'second wave' (Roberts, 2005) of British youth culture research, which is termed 'post-subcultural studies' (Muggleton and Weinzierl, 2003). This post-subculture idea, initiated by Redhead (1990) and later developed by Muggleton (2000), distances itself from what was deemed a reductionist approach of subcultural theory. The main effort here is to uncover newer concepts and theories with which to explain contemporary youth cultural identities (Redhead, 1993, 1997; Bennett, 2000, 2004; Miles, 2000; Muggleton, 2000, 2005). In contrast to the rigid, economic focused analysis of subcultural theory, post-subcultural work focuses around individual lifestyle and consumption choices. Young people are described as moving swiftly through styles 'like tins of soup on a supermarket shelf' (Polhemus, 1996, p. 143).

While the scholars of this area still take account of the influence of social structures, their main interest is the fragmented and individualised ways in which young people construct their cultural identities. Post-subcultural studies should not be understood as a 'unified body of work' (Muggleton, 2005, p. 214), with a number of key themes being recognised: music subcultures (Bennett, 2000; Stahl, 2003), dance (Malbon, 1999; St John, 2003) and stylistic groups (e.g. Muggleton, 2000). These works use key terms such as: the 'postmodern experience' (Redhead, 1997, p. 95), 'post-modern persona with multiple identifications' (Shields, 1992, p. 16) or the 'heterogeneous and individualistic stylistic identification' (Muggleton, 2000, p. 158).

One of the leading works of this new way of thinking is Bennett's (2000) research on British urban dance music, such as house, hip-hop and bhangra. Bennett explains that Maffesoli's (1995) concept of the 'tribus' (what Bennett named 'neo-tribe') can help us to understand the fluid and multiple individualities and collectivities expressed by stylistic and musical choices found within the clubbing context: 'clubbing appears to be regarded less as a singularly definable activity and more of a series of fragmented, temporal experiences as they move between different dance floors and engage with different crowds' (Bennett, 2000, p. 83).

Back (1996) found similar complex and hybrid forms of cultural identities in research with ethnic youth subcultures, terming these 'new ethnicities'. Back (1996, p. 4) states: 'These new ethnicities not only challenge what it means to be "black" but they also call into question the dominant coding of what it means to be British'. Back's research presents an anti-essentialist notion of the black subject and challenges the structuralist division between urban black and white youth subcultures (Sharma *et al.*, 1996). As Back (1996, p. 217) explains:

> the boundaries between these cultural forms are fast becoming more difficult to identify. They do not exist as mutually exclusive 'subcultures' but rather provide a variety of resources that can be switched into and out of by black young people.

Many scholars in marketing and social sciences (e.g. Kjeldgaard and Askegaard, 2006; Ulusoy and Firat, 2016) increasingly claim subcultural youth theory to be empirically and theoretically insufficient. However, it is important to note that a post-subculturalist explanation should be considered in the context of the wider social-cultural change. British society, along with other parts of the post-industrial world, has undergone a period of extraordinary change. This transformation presents a number of challenges to current subcultural orthodoxy in marketing. The literature on this transformation can be divided into two main themes: individualisation and globalisation.

Individualisation of youth culture

An important concept here is 'risk society', being the manner in which modern society responds to risk. The term is closely associated in particular with Ulrich Beck (1992) and Anthony Giddens (1998), being coined to describe social concerns associated with modernity: 'a society increasingly preoccupied with the future (and also with safety), which generates the notion of risk' (Giddens, 1998, p. 209).

Beck and Beck-Gernsheim (2009) describe contemporary youth as the 'global generations'. He explains that the structural transformation associated with modernity hits younger workers in 'a particularly drastic way' (Beck and Beck-Gernsheim, 2009 quoted in Roberts, 2012, p. 389). This increasing insecurity is experienced by youth globally, transcending borders, with the decline of a united culture.

Beck (2003) highlights individualisation as the main outcome of this crisis, stating that: 'poverty, social peril, structuralized un-employment; divorce and illness are all "individualized away"' (p. 63). In post-industrial society, social problems turned into personal failures, with the individual blamed for the lack of ability to see through and utilise the institutional possibilities available to them (Beck and Beck-Gernsheim, 2002). This can, according to Beck, create a very specific, concrete reaction: 'the social problems turn into immediate psychological dispositions, into personal inadequacy, guilt, anxiety, psychological conflicts and neuroses' (Beck and Beck-Gernsheim, 2009, p. 236). One possible outcome is 'radicalised individualisation' – the idea that individuals have been increasingly disembedded from the different types of collectivities and organisations that had structured social and political life during an earlier period of modernity (Beck, 1997; Castells, 1997, 2000). Beck (2003) claims that this radical individualisation might, at some point, turn into 'full-fledged atomization' (p. 80) of youth subcultures: 'Society can no longer look in the mirror and see social classes'. In that 'the mirror has been smashed and all we have left are the individualized fragments' (Beck and Willms, 2014, p. 107), with subcultures having been replaced by new, individualistic, self-determined sociocultural forms of community. These are youth subcultures based on 'Cosmopolitical individualism' (Beck, 2000, p. 89). Social scientists now need to explore how young people can combine individualisation with other duties and commitments to others (Beck and Beck-Gernsheim, 2002, p. 212).

Globalisation

In the marketing literature, youth has been held up as the prototypical example of a global segment (see Hassan and Katsanis, 1991; Tully, 1994; Geyer et al., 1999). Marketers assume global uniform consumption patterns of young people – their clothing styles, music tastes and media habits (Kjeldgaard and Askegaard, 2006). Kjeldgaard and Askegaard (2006) explain that youth culture is increasingly shaped by global cultural flows, using Appadurai's (1990) landscape metaphor to illustrate these flows: 'ethnoscapes' (the flow of people), 'technoscapes' (the flow of technology), 'finanscapes' (the flow of finance and capital), 'mediascapes' (the flow of mediated images) and 'ideoscapes' (the flow of ideas and ideologies). These flows increase the availability of symbols and meanings in young consumers' everyday lives in such a way that much of what is available in one place is also available in any other place (Waters, 1995). This leads to homogenisation of the world under popular culture or Western consumerism.

In this environment of global flows, young people are encouraged to play with 'sign value' to construct their individual identity (Baudrillard and Poster, 1988) – a process that Featherstone (2007, p. 64) expresses as the 'aesthetication of everyday life', where style and identity are inextricably mixed. Pennycook (2007, pp. 6–8) explains: 'transcultural flows – the ways in which the cultural forms move – change and are reused to fashion new identities'. The economic demographic logic of subcultural marketing has been replaced by categorisation of youth that is related to lifestyle – be it the young cosmetics and beauty market, the youth fashion market, or the latest music fad (Holt, 1997).

In this post-subcultural market, the global youth segment is discursively constructed as sharing a similar, global set of desires. Through the impact of globalising effects of information technology, postmodern marketing, consumerism and mass media, adolescent perceptions, expectations and experiences – many countries are linked, sometimes becoming somewhat homogenised (Giroux, 2005). This construction does not deny that there are differences, but differences are of such a kind that nothing general can be said about them (Kjeldgaard and Askegaard, 2006, p. 231).

Brake (1985) argues that in globalised youth culture the 'authentic' local culture is replaced by 'borrowed' culture. He offers the examples of the borrowing of hip-hop by black Canadian youths from the Afro-American culture, and the borrowing of punk hairstyles from the UK by white youths. These identities are expressed through the use of clothing or the consumption of particular commodities rather than being substantively derived from aboriginal or class-based experiences.

In this new reality marketers will not target 'segments' or 'categories' but instead work with 'neo-tribes' (Bennett, 1999) – a type of relatively loosely defined collective, which individuals can choose to participate in for a period of time. Consequently, marketers should use the concept of tribalism to analyse how young people form temporary alliances and move from group to group, looking for alternative identities through their membership in loose networks or by attending new cultural short-term events and groups.

Post post-subculture

Critics of the post-subcultural approach (e.g. Nwalozie, 2015) claim it has failed in its quest to bring about the improvements to subculture theory in that it has brought about limited advancement from what is already known about subculture, with the focus being on making somewhat trivial semantic changes (e.g. 'neo-tribes'). The ascent to post-subculture was intended to solve the problems created by subculture, as defined earlier in the chapter. However, a clear distinction between subculture and post-subculture remains vague, with it being apparent that studies in the subcultural and post-subcultural domains are on the same continuum (Nwalozie, 2015, p. 11). In turn, the inherent limitations of both subcultural and post-subcultural theories call for a rethink that, among other things, champions the withdrawal from the overemphasis on specific cultural identities, as found in the Anglo-American subcultures. This reconsideration of the subcultural and post-subcultural approaches should take a more holistic and fluid view, recognising subculture to entail elements of individualisation and collectivism.

In this alternative point of view, individualisation need not preclude the existence of collectivist forms of subculture. As Zygmunt Bauman (2001) explains, the 'non-linear' individual has to develop the ability to be part of social networks, to construct alliances and negotiate with others to be able to gain stability in a 'risky' unstable socio-economic reality. In this line of research we can see few examples that emphasise that youth are still looking to be part of networks. A good example is the research of Aaltonen (2013) on young Finns' attempts to take control of their lives beyond the completion of compulsory education, which emphasises the importance of family relationships, peer networks and institutional resources for her participants. A further example is in Evans' (2002) study, where participants believed that personal networking constituted a key part in the creation of one's own success – with participants making their social connections work for them forming a central strand of their individualised approach to their anticipated employment trajectories. The importance of personal networking is also demonstrated in Chua's (2013) study of networked individualism in Singapore, in which he explores the complexity that characterises the contemporary requirement to balance personal autonomy with active networking in order to forge and maintain the 'right' connections.

We take inspiration from the work of Cuzzocrea and Collins (2015) on 'collaborative individuality', which describes young people's attempts to define their identities as simultaneously self-reliant and in need of support and collaboration. This notion of collaborative individuality reflects the diversity of potential future pathways and lifestyles open to young people; recognising, but not demanding, the frequent overlap or intersection of these pathways or lifestyles among those attempting them; and acknowledging the transience of these intersections, which may only last for as long as all parties involved benefit from the alliance. Similarly, current marketing literature on subculture (see Hodkinson, 2016; Ulusoy and Firat, 2016) is progressively attuning to the need to balance both the structuralist and the individualistic perspectives of subculture. This perception is of great significance to marketers, in that young consumers have been found to like being part of collectives, yet they still desire movement between them (Hodkinson, 2016).

A post post-subcultural approach to marketing

In recognising that young people seek to belong to collectives yet desire easy movement between multiple collectives, marketers can facilitate young consumers in this, recognising their evolving, temporal and multiple identities. Brands that evolve with consumers during their adolescent years, growing with them as they mature, have the opportunity to develop strong and enduring relationships with consumers (Moorlock, 2016). We now build on this notion, exploring the implications of post post-subculture theory for marketers.

It is important that marketers circumvent mass cultural stereotyping, and accordingly the categorisation of young consumers into groups based on their predisposed characteristics, such as age, gender, social class and ethnicity. Earlier, we set out that in today's postmodern, globalised era, marketing needs to re-evaluate its approach to youth culture (and subculture) to avoid isolating young consumers. Marketers need to recognise that young consumers are at critical stages in their lives where they are assembling who they are (Erikson, 1995). This is of particular relevance for marketers desiring to build long-term relationships with young consumers in a globalised, unstable and complex consumption society (Baudrillard, 1998).

In taking the ideology presented in this chapter, that the cultural grouping of young people is not fixed, marketers need to consider assemblage and intersectional approaches to better understand and build strong relationships with young consumers. In perceiving the assemblage of youth to be fluid – with these so called 'groupings' having ephemeral and porous boundaries – this is consistent with an anti-essentialist approach to marketing, and the notion that young people no longer align themselves as belonging to one group (Robards and Bennett, 2011).

Accordingly, marketers need to understand that young people belong to multiple groups, from which they selectively interact and draw from (Robards, 2015). It is this notion of young consumers having multiple identities that many marketers have negated to pay due respect to.

Earlier, we highlighted that young people draw their identity and values from a multi-cultural, globalised and somewhat fragmented consumer society. By attuning to the differences in young consumers, marketers can better understand how to target 'ordinary' young consumers, building cumulative knowledge of how individual consumers construct their social reality. Young consumers are not passive recipients of meaning, they are proactive negotiators with inconsistent, somewhat volatile and multiple ways of behaving. Thus, taking a fixed, single and stable approach to establishing and maintaining relationships with young consumers is likely to lead to marketing failure (Firat *et al.*, 1997). This is consistent with the recognition of marketing practitioners and scholars alike, that there has been a paradigmatic shift from mass marketing to that of mass customisation and individualisation methods (see Gilmore and Pine, 2000; Dekel, 2013). Marketers might achieve this through using the principles of co-creation, actively involving young consumers in unique experiences, and thus creating an active dialogue that enables the consumer to co-construct different personalised experience with the brand (Prahalad and Ramaswamy, 2004).

Post post-subcultural branding for youth

The body of research focusing on the relationship between culture and consumption has augmented in the last two decades in correspondence with the widespread acknowledgement that modern culture is exponentially dominated by materialism and the conspicuous consumption of goods and services (Roper and Shah, 2007). Young consumers in particular have been found, globally, to be driven by brand culture, with young consumers being arguably the most brand-conscious and obsessed consumers to date (Lindstrom and Sybould, 2004; Roper and Shah, 2007). Consumers as young as 7 years old use brands to determine their multiple identities in different contexts, such as at home, school and in society, identifying brands that they perceive can verify or enhance their street credibility and provide security (Achenreiner, 1997; Elliott and Wattanasuwan, 1998; Schor, 2004). This demonstrates the importance of marketers recognising that young consumers associate themselves with different brands dependent on how they construct their self-concept in different social and private settings. In that they may wish to associate themselves with a brand in a particular 'setting' and dissociate their self from it in another context, such as with a different group of people. This illustrates the need for marketers to understand that young consumers desire to be part of multiple collectives, with these collectives being somewhat transient. Through developing a brand that allows young consumers the flexibility to attune it to fit their individual identity, which is dependent on a particular 'setting', a brand can look to create stronger relationships with young consumers.

In exploring age subculture in the youth market, scholars have found that as young consumers mature, their association with a brand evolves from functional to symbolic in nature (see Dittmar, 1992; Gentry *et al.*, 1995; Achenreiner and John, 2003). This further demonstrates the temporality and fluid nature of brand culture for young consumers. To account for the complex and multitude of roles that a brand can take in young people's lives, a solution is for a brand to take an approach that is indefinite and provides the consumer with the space and freedom to manoeuvre within the consumer–brand relationship. This approach allows for the fluid and ever-changing nature of the young consumers' identities, and the transference of the brand across cultures and ages. For this approach to be successful the brand needs to ensure that it is not so ambiguous and vague that the brand is ineffectual and incoherent, with young consumers not identifying with the brand.

In an exploration of the social impact of branding on Kenyan and British young consumers, Roper and Shah (2007) found young people in both countries expressed a desire to be 'cool' and 'fashionable' through association with the latest branded goods. They found top brands to be ephemeral in nature, with young consumers feeling under pressure to keep up to date with the latest developments and 'in' brands. This demonstrates the pressure young consumers put themselves under to associate themselves with socially accepted brand names in order to fit in with their peers. A solution here lies in social marketing, wherein marketing is considered a social institution, with marketers having the responsibility to not take advantage of young consumers. In doing so, practitioners need to recognise that 'collectively, firms' branding efforts shape consumer desires and actions', shaping how young people 'think and feel through branded commercial products' (Holt, 2002, p. 71). This is particularly important for marketers to ruminate with young consumers, with marketers needing to recognise that their marketing efforts can have a profound impact on the formation and development of young consumers' identities. Cross-cultural differences must not be ignored, however, can be overcome by marketers allowing young consumers to construct brands and integrate them into their lives, providing them with the power to use the brand in a way that is consistent with their self-concept in certain contexts.

Conclusion

In this chapter we have demonstrated that treating 'youth' as a well-defined, homogeneous group, and treating young people as a fixed 'grouping' based on their predisposed characteristics is an outdated and erroneous ideology. The notion of youth culture as a summation of homogenous norms, values and practices is therefore obsolete in modern society (Rice, 1996). In turn, treating young people as individuals is not the answer, in that young people look to belong to collectives. The solution is that of collaborative individuality, which we consider to be a post post-subcultural approach. This approach recognises that young people negotiate the collectives they want to be part of, having multiple temporal collectives to which they belong or seek to belong.

The implication for marketing practitioners and scholars alike is the need to recognise that consumers have multiple identities and cannot be categorised into a singular fixed group. Young consumers are not passive victims for marketers to take advantage of but are active agents in the construction of meaning (see Elliott, 1997). Young consumers are going through life events where they are continually defining and redefining who they are. The assumption that all young consumers share the same collective worldview and in turn consumer preferences is inappropriate in today's society. A post post-subcultural approach offering an alternative perspective that recognises that young people share some collective consumption activities, which are seen to be transient in nature.

References

Aaltonen, S. (2013). 'Trying to push things through': Forms and bounds of agency in transitions of school-age young people. *Journal of Youth Studies*, *16*(3), 375–390.

Abrams, M. (1959). *The teenage consumer.* London: London Press Exchange.

Achenreiner, G. B. (1997). Materialistic values and susceptibility to influence in children. *Advances in Consumer Research*, *24*, 82–88.

Achenreiner, G. B. and John, D. R. (2003). The meaning of brand names to children: A developmental investigation. *Journal of Consumer Psychology*, *13*(3), 205–219.

Allen, K. and Mendick, H. (2013). Young people's uses of celebrity: Class, gender and 'improper' celebrity. *Discourse: Studies in the Cultural Politics of Education*, *34*(1), 77–93.

Appadurai, A. (1990). Disjuncture and difference in the global cultural economy. *Theory, Culture & Society*, *7*(2), 295–310.

Arnould, E. and Thompson, C. (2005). Consumer culture theory (CCT): Twenty years of research. *Journal of Consumer Research*, *31*(March), 868–882.

Arthur, D. M. (2009). The symbolic consumption of subcultures: An ethnographic study of the Australian hip-hop culture. Doctoral dissertation, University of Adelaide.

Back, L. (1996). *New ethnicities and urban culture: Racisms and multiculture in young lives.* London: UCL Press.

Baudrillard, J. (1998). *The consumer society: Myths and structures* (Vol. 53). London: Sage.

Baudrillard, J. and Poster, M. (1988). *Selected writings.* Edited by M. Poster. Cambridge: Polity Press.

Bauman, Z. (2001). Consuming life. *Journal of Consumer Culture, 1*(1), 9–29.

Beck, U. (1992). From industrial society to the risk society: Questions of survival, social structure and ecological enlightenment. *Theory, Culture & Society, 9*(1), 97–123.

Beck, U. (1997). Democratization of the family. *Childhood, 4*(2), 151–168.

Beck, U. (2000). The cosmopolitan perspective: Sociology of the second age of modernity. *The British Journal of Sociology, 51*(1), 79–105.

Beck, U. (2003). *Globalization: Culture and identity.* Edited by Roland Robertson and Kathleen E. White. New York: Routledge.

Beck, U. and Beck-Gernsheim, E. (2002). *Individualisation.* London: Sage.

Beck, U. and Beck-Gernsheim, E. (2009). Global generations and the trap of methodological nationalism for a cosmopolitan turn in the sociology of youth and generation. *European Sociological Review, 25*(1), 25–36.

Beck, U. and Willms, J. (2014). *Conversations with Ulrich Beck.* London: John Wiley & Sons.

Bennett, A. (1999). Subcultures or neo-tribes? Rethinking the relationship between youth, style and musical taste. *Sociology, 33*(3), 599–617.

Bennett, A. (2000). *Popular music and youth culture: Music, identity and place.* Basingstoke: Macmillan.

Bennett, A. (2004). Virtual subculture? Youth, identity and the internet. In A. B. and K. Kahn-Harris (eds), *After subculture: Critical studies in contemporary youth culture* (pp. 162–172). Basingstoke: Palgrave Macmillan.

Bennett, A. and Kahn-Harris, K. (2004). *After subculture: Critical studies in contemporary youth culture.* Basingstoke: Macmillan.

Bennett, A. and Robards, B. (2014). *Mediated youth culture: The internet, belonging and new cultural configurations.* Basingstoke: Macmillan.

Berry, J. W., Poortinga, Y. H. and Pandey, J. (1997). *Handbook of cross-cultural psychology, Vol. 1: Theory and method.* Boston, MA: Allyn & Bacon.

Brake, M. (1980). *Sociology of youth subcultures: Sex and drugs and rock 'n roll.* Abingdon: Routledge.

Brake, M. (1985). *Comparative youth culture: The sociology of youth cultures and youth subcultures in America, Britain and London.* London: Routledge and Keagan Paul.

Brown, S., McDonagh, P. and Shultz, C. (2012). Dark marketing: Ghost in the machine or skeleton in the cupboard? *European Business Review, 24*(3), 196–215.

Cantillon, Z. (2015). Polyrhythmia, heterogeneity and urban identity: Intersections between 'official' and 'unofficial' narratives in the socio-spatial practices of Australia's Gold Coast. *Journal of Urban Cultural Studies, 2*(3), 253–274.

Carrington, B. and Wilson, B. (2004). Dance nations: Rethinking youth subcultural theory. In A. Bennett and K. Kahn-Harris (eds), *After subculture: Critical studies in contemporary youth culture* (pp. 65–78). Basingstoke: Palgrave.

Castells, M. (1997). *The information age: Economy, society and culture. Vol. 2: The power of identity.* London: Blackwell.

Castells, M. (2000). *The rise of the network society: Economy, society and culture (Vol. 1).* Oxford: Wiley-Blackwell.

Chaney, D. (2004). Fragmented cultures and subcultures. In A. Bennett and K. Kahn-Harris (eds), *After subculture: Critical studies in contemporary youth culture* (pp. 36–48). Basingstoke: Macmillan.

Chua, V. (2013). Contextualizing 'networked individualism': The interplay of social categories, role relationships and tasks. *Current Sociology*, *61*(5–6), 602–625.

Clarke, J. (1976). The skinheads and the magical recovery of community. In S. Hall and T. Jefferson (eds), *Resistance through rituals: Youth subcultures in post-war Britain* (pp. 99–102). London: Hutchinson.

Cohen, B. (1972). Towards understanding our 'youth culture'. *Youth and Society*, *4*(3), 441–458.

Craig, S. C. and Douglas S. P. (2005). Beyond national culture: Implications for cultural dynamics for consumer research. *International Marketing Review*, *23*, 322–342.

Cuzzocrea, V. and Collins, R. (2015). Collaborative individualization? Peer-to-peer action in youth transitions. *Young*, *23*(2), 136–153.

de Koning, M. J. M. (2008). *Zoeken naar een'zuivere'islam: Geloofsbeleving en identiteitsvorming van jonge Marokkaans-Nederlandse moslims*. Amsterdam: Bert Bakker.

Dekel, O. (2013). Anti-essentialist marketing an alternative view of consumers' identity. Doctoral thesis, Manchester University, Manchester.

Dittmar, H. (1992). *The social psychology of material possessions: To have is to be*. New York: St Martins Press.

Elliott, R. (1997). Existential consumption and irrational desire. *European Journal of Marketing*, *31*(3/4), 285–296.

Elliott, R. and Wattanasuwan, K. (1998). Brands as symbolic resources for the construction of identity. *International Journal of Advertising*, *17*(2), 22–27.

Erikson, E. H. (1968). *Identity: Youth and crisis*. New York: W. W. Norton.

Erikson, E. H. (1995). *Childhood and society*. Alma, CO: Vintage.

Evans, K. (2002). Taking control of their lives? Agency in young adult transitions in England and the New Germany. *Journal of Youth Studies*, *5*(3), 245–269.

Featherstone, M. (1987). Lifestyle and consumer culture. *Theory, Culture & Society*, *4*(1), 55–70.

Featherstone, M. (2007). Postmodernism and the aestheticization of everyday life. In *Theory, Culture and Society: Consumer culture and postmodernism* (pp. 64–80). London: Sage.

Firat, A. F., Shultz, I. and Clifford, J. (1997). From segmentation to fragmentation, *European Journal of Marketing*, *31*(3–4), 183–207.

Foucault, M. (1980). *Power/knowledge: Selected interviews*. New York: Pantheon.

Garber, J. and McRobbie, A. (1975). *Girls and subcultures: An exploration*. In S. Hall and T. Jefferson (eds), *Resistance through rituals* (pp. 209–222). London: Hutchinson/Centre for Contemporary Cultural Studies.

Gentina E., Butori, R., Rose, G. and Bakir, A (2014). How national culture impacts teenage shopping behavior: Comparing French and American consumers. *Journal of Business Research*, *67*(April), 464–470.

Gentry, J., Baker, S. M. and Kraft, F. B. (1995). The role of possessions in creating, maintaining and preserving one's identity: Variation over the life course. *Advances in Consumer Research*, *22*, 413–418.

Geyer, R., Ingebritsen, C. and Moses, J. (1999). *Globalization, Europeanization and the end of Scandinavian social democracy?* New York: Springer.

Giddens, A. (1998). Risk society: The context of British politics. In J. Franklin (ed.), *The politics of risk society* (pp. 23–34). Cambridge: Polity Press.

Gilmore, J. H. and Pine, J. (2000). *Markets of one: Creating customer-unique value through mass customization*. Cambridge: Harvard Business Press.

Giroux, H. A. (2005). The terror of neoliberalism: Rethinking the significance of cultural politics. *College Literature*, *32*(1), 1–19.

Goulding, C. and Saren, M. (2007). Gothic entrepreneurs: A study of the subcultural commodification process. In B. Cova, R. V. Kozinets and A. Shankar (eds), *Consumer tribes* (pp. 227–242). Burlington: Butterworth-Heinemann.

Goulding, C., Shankar, A. and Canniford, R. (2013). Learning to be tribal: Facilitating the formation of consumer tribes. *European Journal of Marketing*, *47*(5/6), 813–832.

Gupta, N., Handa, M. and Gupta, B. (2008). Young adults of India: Online surfers or online shoppers. *Journal of Internet Commerce*, *7*(4), 425–444.

Ha, J. S. and Park, J. (2011). Significance of changing Korean youth subculture styles. *Asian Culture and History*, *3*(1), 23–30.

Harris, A. (2005). In a girlie world: Tweenies in Australia. *Counterpoints*, *245*, 209–223.

Hassan, S. S. and Katsanis, L. P. (1991). Identification of global consumer segments: A behavioral framework. *Journal of International Consumer Marketing*, *3*(2), 11–28.

Haytko, D. L. and Baker, J. (2004). It's all at the mall: Exploring adolescent girls' experiences. *Journal of Retailing*, *80*(1), 67–83.

Hebdige, D. (1976). *Reggae, rastas and rudies: Style and the subversion of form.* Birmingham: University of Birmingham, Centre for Contemporary Cultural Studies.

Hebdige, D. (1979). *Subculture: The meaning of style.* London: Methuen.

Hesmondhalgh, D. (2005). Subcultures, scenes or tribes? None of the above. *Journal of Youth Studies*, *8*(1), 21–40.

Hodkinson, P. (2004). Translocal connections in the Goth scene. In A. Bennett and R. A. Peterson (eds), *Music scenes: Local, translocal, and virtual* (pp. 131–148). Nashville: Vanderbilt University Press.

Hodkinson, P. (2016). Youth cultures and the rest of life: Subcultures, post-subcultures and beyond. *Journal of Youth Studies*, *19*(5), 629–645.

Holt, D. B. (1997). Poststructuralist lifestyle analysis: Conceptualizing the social patterning of consumption in postmodernity. *Journal of Consumer Research*, *23*(4), 326–350.

Holt, D. B. (2002). Why do brands cause trouble? A dialectical theory of consumer culture and branding. *Journal of Consumer Research*, *29*(1), 70–90.

Huq, R. (2006). *Beyond subculture: Pop, youth and identity in a postcolonial world.* London: Routledge.

Isaksen K. J. and Roper S. (2008). The impact of branding of low income adolescents: A vicious cycle? *Psychology and Marketing*, *2*(11), 1068–1087.

Janssen, J., Dechesne, M. and Van Knippenberg, A. (1999). The psychological importance of youth culture: A terror management approach. *Youth & Society*, *31*(2), 152–167.

Jenkins, R. (1983). *Lads, citizens, and ordinary kids: Working-class youth life-styles in Belfast.* London: Routledge.

Jones, S. (1988). *Black culture, white youth: The reggae tradition from JA to UK.* London: Palgrave Macmillan.

Khalaf, R. S. and Khalaf, S. (2009). *Arab society and culture: An essential reader.* London: Saqi.

Khallouli, K. J. and Gharbi, A. (2013). Symbolic consumption by teenagers: A discussion through the optics of appearance and identity. *International Journal of Business and Social Science*, *4*(7), 99–105.

Kim, H. (2016). 'We're just like everyone else!' Rethinking the cultural politics of the London Asian urban music scene. *European Journal of Cultural Studies*, *20*(2), 1–16.

Kjeldgaard, D. and Askegaard, S. (2006). The glocalization of youth culture: The global youth segment as structures of common difference. *Journal of Consumer Research*, *33*(2), 231–247.

Laughey, D. (2006). *Music and youth culture.* Edinburgh: Edinburgh University Press.

Lindstrom, M. and Seybould, P. (2004). *BRANDchild: Remarkable insights into the minds of today's global kids and their relationships with brands*. London: Kogan Page.

Lincoln, S. (2012). *Youth culture and private space*. New York: Springer.

McRobbie, A. (1978). *Jackie: An ideology of adolescent femininity*. Birmingham: Centre for Contemporary Cultural Studies.

McRobbie, A. (1980). Settling accounts with subcultures: A feminist critique. In S. Frith and A. Goodwon (eds), *On record: Rock, pop and the written word* (pp. 37–49). London: Routledge.

McRobbie, A. (1990). *Feminism and youth culture from* Jackie *to* Just Seventeen. New York: Routledge.

Maffesoli, M. (1995). *The time of the tribes: The decline of individualism in mass society (Vol. 41)*. London: Sage.

Malborn, B. (1999). *Clubbing: Dance, ecstasy, vitality*. London: Routledge.

Marranci, G. (2001). A complex identity and its musical representation: Beurs and rai music in Paris. www.muspe.unibo.it/period/ma (accessed 28 August 2017).

Martin, G. (2002). Conceptualizing cultural politics in subcultural and social movement studies. *Social Movement Studies*, *1*(1), 73–88.

Martin, G. (2009). Subculture, style, chavs and consumer capitalism: Towards a critical cultural criminology of youth. *Crime, Media, Culture*, *5*(2), 123–145.

Mason, R. B. and Wigley, G. (2013). The 'chav' subculture: Branded clothing as an extension of self. *Journal of Economics and Behavioral Studies*, *5*(3), 173–184.

Miles, S. (2000). *Youth lifestyles in a changing world*. London: McGraw-Hill Education.

Moorlock, E. (2016). Constructing brand relationships: The Generation Y perspective. Doctoral thesis.

Muggleton, D. (2000). *Inside subculture: The postmodern meaning of style*. London: Berg.

Muggleton, D. (2005). From classlessness to club culture: A genealogy of post-war British youth cultural analysis. *Young*, *13*(2), 205–219.

Muggleton, D. and Weinzierl, R. (2003). *The post-subcultures reader*. London: Berg.

Mungham, G. and Pearson, G. (eds) (1976). *Working class youth culture*. London: Routledge.

Nayak, A. (2003). Last of the 'real Geordies'? White masculinities and the subcultural response to deindustrialisation. *Environment and Planning D: Society and Space*, *21*(1), 7–25.

Nilan, P. and Feixa, C. (eds). (2006). *Global youth? Hybrid identities, plural worlds*. London: Routledge.

Nwalozie, C. J. (2015). Rethinking subculture and subcultural theory in the study of youth crime: A theoretical discourse. *Journal of Theoretical and Philosophical Criminology*, *7*(1), 1–16.

Patino A., Kaltcheva, D. V. and Smith M. F. (2011). The appeal of reality television for teen and pre-teen audiences: The powers of connectedness and psycho-demographics. *Journal of Advertising Research*, *51*(1), 288–297.

Pennycook, A. (2007). Language, localization, and the real: Hip-hop and the global spread of authenticity. *Journal of Language, Identity, and Education*, *6*(2), 101–115.

Pilkington, H. (2002). *Looking West? Cultural globalization and Russian youth cultures*. University Park: Penn State Press.

Polhemus, T. (1996). *Style surfing*. London: Thames Hudson.

Prahalad, C. K. and Ramaswamy, V. (2004). Co-creation experiences: The next practice in value creation. *Journal of Interactive Marketing*, *18*(3), 5–14.

Redhead, S. (1990). *The end of the century party: Youth and pop towards 2000*. Manchester: Manchester University Press.

Redhead, S. (1993). *Rave off: Politics and deviance in contemporary youth culture*. Aldershot: Avebury Press.

Redhead, S. (1997). *Subculture to club cultures: An introduction to popular cultural studies*. Oxford: Blackwell.

Rice, F. (1996). *The adolescent: Development, relationships and culture* (7th edn). Boston, MA: Allyn & Bacon.

Robards, B. (2015). Vernacular subculture and multiplicity in everyday experiences of belonging. In S. Baker, B. Robards, B. and R. Buttigieg (eds), *Youth cultures and subcultures: An Australian perspective* (pp. 125–136). London: Routledge.

Robards, B. and Bennett, A. (2011). My tribe: Manifestations of belonging on social network sites. *Sociology*, *45*(2), 303–317.

Roberts, C. (2011). *Ordinary differential equations: Applications, models, and computing*. Boca Raton: CRC Press.

Roberts, K. (2005). What's the point in studying youth cultures? Paper presented to the Annual British Sociological Association Conference University of York, 23 March.

Roberts, S. (2012). One step forward, one step Beck: A contribution to the ongoing conceptual debate in youth studies. *Journal of Youth Studies*, *15*(3), 389–401.

Roper, S. and Shah, M. (2007). Vulnerable consumers: The social impact of branding on children. *Equal Opportunities International*, *26*(7), 712–728.

Schor, J. B. (2004). *Born to buy: The commercialized child and the new consumer culture*. New York: Scribner.

Sharma, S., Hutnyk, J. and Sharma, A. (1996). *Dis-orienting rhythms: The politics of the new Asian dance music*. London: Zed.

Shields, R. (1992). *Lifestyle shopping: The subject of consumption*. Abingdon: Routledge.

Shildrick, T. and MacDonald, R. (2006). In defence of subculture: Young people, leisure and social divisions. *Journal of Youth Studies*, *9*(2), 125–140.

Smith, E., Jones, T., Ward, R., Dixon, J., Mitchell, A. and Hillier, L. (2014). *From blues to rainbows: The mental health and well-being of gender diverse and transgender young people in Australia*. Melbourne: La Trobe University.

St John, G. (2006). Electronic dance music culture and religion: An overview 1. *Culture and Religion*, *7*(1), 1–25.

Stahl, G. (2003). Tastefully renovating subcultural theory: Making space for a new model. In D. Muggleton and R. Weinzerl (eds), *The post-subcultures reader* (pp. 27–40). Oxford: Berg.

Subculture List. (2017, 21 August). Subculture Birmingham. http://subcultureslist.com/subculture-theory/subculture-birmingham/ (accessed 28 August 2017).

Tully, S. (1994). Teens the most global market of all. *Fortune International*, *16*(May), 34–41.

Ulusoy, E. and Firat, A. F. (2016). Toward a theory of subcultural mosaic: Fragmentation into and within subcultures. *Journal of Consumer Culture*, 1–22.

Wallendorf, M. and Arnould E. (1988). 'My favourite things': A cross-cultural inquiry into object attachment, possessiveness, and social linkage. *Journal of Consumer Research*, *14*(March), 531–547.

Waters, M. (1995). *Globalization*. London: Sage.

Williams, J. P. (2007). Youth-subcultural studies: Sociological traditions and core concepts. *Sociology Compass*, *1*(2), 572–593.

Williams, R. (1958). *Culture and society 1780–1950*. London: Chatto & Windus.

Williams, R. (1989). *Resources of hope*. London: Verso.

Willis, P. E., Jones, S., Canaan, J. and Hurd, G. (1990). *Common culture: Symbolic work at play in the everyday cultures of the young*. Milton Keynes: Open University Press.

Wyn, J. and White, R. (1996). *Rethinking youth*. London: Sage.

Woodman, D. (2013). Researching 'ordinary' young people in a changing world: The sociology of generations and the 'missing middle' in youth research. *Sociological Research Online*, *18*(1), 7.

17
YOUNG CONSUMER MISBEHAVIOUR

A perspective from developing countries

Richard Shambare, Nyasha Muswera and Jane Shambare

Introduction

The literature reveals that a wide array of negative consumer behaviours (e.g. copyright infringements, video piracy, substance abuse, shoplifting and fraudulent returns) are prevalent (Tonglet, 2002; Evans *et al.*, 2006; Harris and Dumas, 2009). Most studies that report on these negative consumer acts appear across multiple disciplines, for instance, in social work, criminology and psychology journals; but, less so in marketing literature (Fullerton and Punj, 2004). Despite a wealth of research that recognises the existence of consumer misbehaviour the reporting of such behaviours among young consumers, particularly those in emerging economies, has largely been ignored by marketing researchers (c.f., Tonglet, 2002; Evans *et al.*, 2006; Harris and Dumas, 2009).

This paucity of research almost appears to be a denial, on the part of marketers, that young consumer misbehaviour is a legitimate field of inquiry. Having said that, the last two decades have seen a significant rise in research attention in consumer misbehaviour. There is a steady increase in articles and chapters of consumer misbehaviour and negative consumer behaviour in marketing journals and textbooks. Of note, the *Journal of Global Fashion Marketing (JGFM)* in January 2016 invited papers for a special issue focusing on negative consumer behaviours in the retail fashion industry. Some of the topics of interest included:

- return fraud;
- labour abuses in manufacturing/retailing;
- consumer misbehaviour during massive sales;
- merchandise borrowing;
- production/consumption of fakes;
- overconsumption;

- historical perspectives on consumer misbehaviour;
- cross-cultural differences in the formation of expectations for consumer behaviour in the marketplace;
- vandalism;
- tag-switching;
- compulsive consumption;
- shoplifting;
- consumers' verbal and/or physical abuse toward retail employees or organisational property.

Through the special issue, the *JGFM* (2016, p. 1) concedes that there is '[an enormous] dark side' and misbehaviour in the marketing of fashion. The editors of the journal explain that the special issue seeks to:

> provide opportunities to share research findings, innovative teaching strategies, and concept papers that explore and investigate issues related to the dark side of fashion. As there are many phases to fashion from ideation, design, production, distribution, sale, consumption, and ultimately disposal, there are many instances where misbehavior can occur . . . within the consumption [of clothes and fashion] (e.g. hoarding, merchandise borrowing, stealing, buying items that are never used, retail therapy, return fraud, compulsive shopping).
> (JGGM, *2016, p. 1*)

Overall, calls for increased research in consumer misbehaviour such as that of the *JGFM* example, above, are encouraging. However, research focusing on youths and young consumers, particularly those from developing countries, is still limited. Much of what is known about negative young consumer actions is based on knowledge from other disciplines such as criminology, deviant behaviour (Cromwell and Thurman, 2003) and psychology (Milavec, 2012). The marketing literature, therefore, suffers a huge gap in need of immediate attention (Holbrook and Hirschman, 1982; Fullerton and Punj, 2004; Evans *et al.*, 2006; *JGFM*, 2016, p. 1). The aim of this chapter is, thus, to encourage debate and discourse in young consumer misbehaviour. It is anticipated that this chapter will stimulate research in consumer behaviour in developing countries and, more specifically, young consumer misbehaviour. Collectively, these efforts will contribute towards addressing the gap within the broader consumer behaviour literature.

The purpose of the chapter

The foremost argument of this chapter is that young consumer misbehaviour is an important branch of marketing in general and consumer misbehaviour, specifically. It also goes without saying that mainstream marketing research, until very recently, largely overlooked discussing young consumer behaviour issues from developing countries. As a corollary, the chapter further argues that increased levels of debates and discourse into the young consumer misbehaviour phenomenon are needed and necessary. For this reason, the purpose of this chapter is three-fold. First, the chapter seeks to (re)introduce young consumer misbehaviour as a fruitful research area within the mainstream marketing (and consumer behaviour) research agenda. Second, the chapter promotes the argument that behaviours such as consumer rage, shoplifting, piracy, alcohol and substance abuse and addictive behaviours are rightfully a distinct form of consumer behaviour – consumer misbehaviour; hence, these should be understood as such. In other words, the cause and effects of these actions are of a marketing nature. Third, the chapter seeks to encourage future research deliberation into the consumer misbehaviour phenomenon by proposing avenues for further research.

To achieve these objectives, this chapter is structured into five sections. The next section presents the nature and extent of young consumer misbehaviour in developing countries. Thereafter, the following section attempts to proffer definitions of young consumer misbehaviour. Next, some explanations on why cases of young consumer misbehaviour are increasing are provided. Following that, some marketing implications of young consumer misbehaviour are discussed. Lastly, the chapter concludes by proposing some areas for further research.

Evidence and the extent of young consumer misbehaviour

There once was a time when it was believed that 'the customer was always right'; the Japanese even extended this to a religion and held that 'the customer is a god'. While this might have been true, for some time, new empirical evidence clearly demonstrates that consumers are neither gods nor sweet angels. Customers are not always right (Tran, 2016). The sad reality is that customers are sometimes, dishonest, abusive, vandals and even shoplifters.

It is not uncommon that individuals do not always behave in conduct befitting their role as consumers (Tonglet, 2002; Evans et al., 2006; Harris and Dumas, 2009), they sometimes misbehave. Thus, consumer misbehaviour refers to actions or behaviours that provide excessive rewards to misbehavers and, simultaneously, result in negative effects to other market players such as retailers, producers and other consumers (Evans et al., 2006). The literature documents a wide array of behaviours that can indeed be considered to fall within the ambit of consumer misbehaviour, which occur in various settings and in virtually all industries (Fullerton and Punj, 1998, 2004; Ojikutu et al., 2011; *JGFM*, 2016; Tran, 2016; Wafula, 2016). Although not exhaustive, some examples of consumer misbehaviour include:

- shoplifting;
- queue jumping;
- price-tag switching;
- verbally abusing salespeople;
- fraudulent returns;
- reckless driving, including speeding and road rage;

- vandalism;
- credit card fraud;
- insurance fraud.

Consumer misbehaviour manifests whenever customers act outside acceptable parameters. As such, there are as many variants of consumer misbehaviour as there are products (Fullerton and Punj, 2004; *JGFM*, 2016). Young consumer misbehaviour, on the other hand, refers to negative conduct that is committed by youths and consumers who are approximately 35 years old or younger.

To qualify as legitimate consumer misbehaviour, one basic criterion of the action is that there ought to be an identifiable market actor that suffers material loss or psychological damage. It is against this background that Fullerton and Punj (2004) propose a classification system that identifies five groups of market players (i.e. marketers' employees, marketers' merchandise, marketers' financial assets, and other consumers) through which consumer misbehaviour can be categorised. Consequently, Figure 17.1 demonstrates a typology of five classifications of consumer misbehaviour.

However, given the social nature of consumption, the question of the appropriateness of consumer acts so as to infer misbehaviour is predicated on societal norms. This, in other words, means that what might be accepted as a norm within a particular market might be regarded as misbehaviour in another. Nevertheless, there are some universal expectations through which consumers are expected to

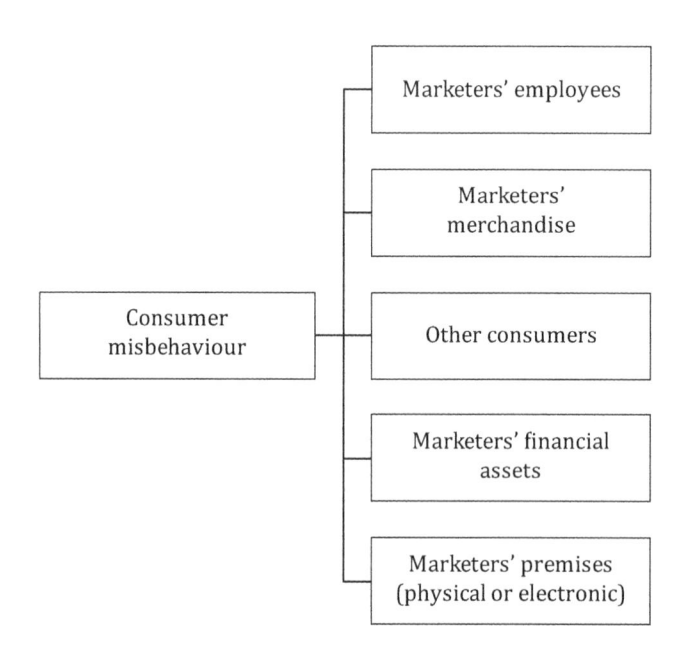

FIGURE 17.1 A typology of consumer misbehaviour

Source: Adapted from Fullerton and Punj (2004).

abide by in consumption situations. Since societal norms ultimately define misbehaviour, the next section provides a more detailed discussion on the issue of norms and consumer expectations before we move on to describing the various typologies of misbehaviour.

Societal norms and consumer misbehaviour

The fact that certain behaviours are labelled as 'misbehaviours' indicates that such actions fall beyond or outside acceptable norms (Fullerton and Punj, 2004). So, when consumers are misbehaving, they would, in fact, be operating outside acceptable parameters, as expected of consumers in the concerned settings. It is critical, however, to concede that there are no specific rules that guide how consumers ought to behave. Instead, this chapter contends that market players including consumers and retailers operate only on informal but widely accepted societal norms. To illustrate, a retailer might offer for sale products at a certain price. Customers will trust that the goods for sale are indeed offered in a good working condition and at fair value. In turn, the retailer would expect that the consumer will pay for the goods. This mutual trust between retailers and consumers is important to ensure trade and exchange.

Sociologists such as Shapiro (1987) argue that economic transactions, such as the one stated in the hypothetical transaction above, are based on a special form of trust known as impersonal trust (Shapiro, 1987, p. 624). Impersonal trust refers to cooperation among people, especially those without close social relations for the purposes of achieving common goals. From the foregoing, this chapter postulates that impersonal trust refers to a social contract among market players that they will interact and transact fairly with each other. This sentiment is echoed by Fullerton and Punj (2004, p. 1241) who explain that the norms in 'consumer conduct in exchange situations are founded upon expectations held by both marketers and consumers. These expectations reflect a trust that each consumer's actions will remain within bounds.'

Following on from this premise, this chapter thus maintains that within the marketing and consumption contexts, impersonal trust governs that:

a) Producers will use ethical manufacturing processes to manufacture products and services.
b) Retailers will sell the best quality products at fair market prices.
c) Consumers will compensate retailers or producers for the acquisition of products and services.
d) All market players (i.e. government, producers, retailers and consumers) will not cause undue harm to the environment in the manufacturing, marketing, and consumption processes.

It is therefore expected that consumers ought to conduct themselves within the dictates of market systems in a manner that promotes fairness – being fair not only to themselves, but to other market actors (e.g. retailers, retailers' employees and the environment). Consequently, in exchange situations, consumers are expected to conduct themselves in a manner that does not cause harm or disadvantage to other market actors (Fullerton and Punj, 1998, 2004; Evans *et al.*, 2006). From this school of thought, it can be concluded that market systems impose four expectations on acceptable consumer behaviour. Table 17.1 summarises the expectations with respect to consumer conduct and behaviour in consumption and exchange situations.

Considering the foregoing discussion, it is concluded that consumer misbehaviour is not only culture specific, but a multi-faceted phenomenon. Consumer misbehaviour refers to externally directed behavioural acts by consumers that violate generally accepted norms and standards of exchange environments. By violating generally accepted norms of exchange, it is meant that such negative behaviour:

a) disrupts impersonal trust and the normal consumption order;
b) negatively affects other market players resulting in either material loss or psychological damage; and
c) allows the misbehaving consumers to draw undue benefits from such exchange incidents.

TABLE 17.1 Expectations of consumers in exchange environments

Consumer expectation	Example	Citation of expectation
Marketers' expectations of consumers	• Consumers will not steal their products • Consumers will not abuse their products or use them for purposes that they were not designed for • Consumers will not unduly influence or spread inaccurate information about the marketer or their products to other consumers	Do not spray people with Doom, Tiger Brands tells prophet of doom (Drum Digital, 2016)
Consumers' expectations of marketers and their employees	• Marketers will sell quality products • Marketers will not test products on animals • Marketers' employees will treat them with respect	Progress toward replacing animals in toxicity testing for cosmetics (Nye, 2006)
Consumers' expectations of other consumers	• When in a queue, other consumers will not abuse them (i.e. stealing from them or verbally abusing them) • When in a queue, other consumers will not jump the queue	Foreigner yells at person cutting in line in three Chinese dialects (Liu, 2016)
The market's expectations of general consumer conduct	• In all exchange situations, consumers will not cause harm to market actors and stakeholders including other consumers, the environment	

Source: Adapted from Fullerton and Punj (2004).

A typology of young consumer misbehaviour in developing countries

Following Fullerton and Punj's (2004) five-variant typology of consumer misbehaviour model, this chapter proposes a typology of eight varieties of young consumer misbehaviour as being consistent with a non-Western and particularly a developing world context. As in Fullerton and Punj (2004), this chapter considers using the market players to which the misbehaviours are directed as means to distinguish one form of negative behaviour from another.

Table 17.2 provides an account of the categories of young consumer misbehaviours as well as some examples. Also, citations of each form of misbehaviour within developing countries are provided in the last column of Table 17.2, which demonstrates the pervasiveness of misbehaviour across various settings in the developing world.

TABLE 17.2 Typologies of young consumer misbehaviour in emerging markets

Misbehaviour categories:		*Citation of misbehaviour*
Acts directed towards . . .	Examples	
Marketers' employees	• Consumer rage • Verbal, emotional and physical abuse against a retailer's or producer's employees	A South African student activist tells a white waitress that he will give her a tip after 'you return the land' (Groundup, 2016)
Marketers' merchandise	• Fraudulent returns • Shoplifting • Price tag switching	Confessions of a returnaholic: the extreme tactics one woman uses to get a refund after wearing her clothes once – no matter how old they are (Mail Online, 2013) University student caught shoplifting (*Zimbabwe News*, 2016)
Marketers' financial assets	• Insurance fraud • Credit card fraud • Defrauding cashiers	Another ATM fraud victim speaks out (De Villiers, 2015) 55% of people in Nigeria view taking too much change from a shop as either acceptable or borderline behaviour (Ojikutu et al., 2011)
Marketers' premises (physical or electronic)	• Vandalism • Hacking • Arson database theft	Worryingly, South African credit card fraud picked up by 23% according to the SABRIC report (Oberholster, 2014) Rate payers in in Kenya vandalise power utility's infrastructure (Wafula, 2016)

(continued)

TABLE 17.2 *(continued)*

Misbehaviour categories:		Citation of misbehaviour
Acts directed towards . . .	Examples	
Other consumers (different age group)	• Intimidation and violence towards other elderly consumers • ATM fraud	Confessions of a bank card scammer, who has been stealing bank cards and pins since his schooling days in 2008 till now (eNCA, 2016) Foreigner yells at person cutting in line in three Chinese dialects (Liu, 2016)
Other young consumers	• Showing-off contests also known as *skothane*	Groups of young, poor, often unemployed black South Africans drape themselves from head to toe in designer brands, which they then destroy after the showing-off contest (Clayton, 2013)
Disregard of societal values	• Stealing money from parents/grandparents or relatives • Refusing to reserve seats for elderly people on a bus or train • Bullying	'These days our children no longer have the fear and respect we had for our parents' (Djanie, 2014)
The environment	• Littering	'Plastics don't litter, people do' (Kieser, 2011)

Source: Adapted from Fullerton and Punj (2004).

As shown in Table 17.2, there is evidence of the existence of eight varieties of young consumer misbehaviour in developing countries. These range from disregard of social values to bullying their peers and even elderly consumers. Given that historically developing nations tend to be less individualistic and communally oriented (Hofstede, 1980, 2011), it was important to separate relations among consumers of the same age (i.e. other young consumers) and elderly consumers (i.e. other consumers – different age) as cultural norms in collectivist societies often impose additional burdens on how the elderly should be treated (Hofstede, 2011). This separation, therefore, is an attempt to indicate the unique aspects of young consumer misbehaviour in developing countries. On that note, the focus of the chapter now turns to providing a more formal definition of young consumer misbehaviour, at least, from a developing country's perspective.

Re-defining young consumer misbehaviour

By now it is clear that consumer misbehaviour is not entirely a new phenomenon. It is just that the marketing literature has until recently not considered the subject matter as a fruitful area for research. As such, there are no definitive conceptual models for defining misbehaviour. Basically, the literature contends that the diverse range of consumer behaviours that disrupt widely accepted functional exchanges of consumption are deemed to be consumer misbehaviour (Tonglet, 2002; Evans *et al.*, 2006; Harris and Dumas, 2009).

It is critical to note that this approach of defining consumer misbehaviour is 'quick, rough and dirty'. Nevertheless, such a simple and basic definition is helpful in highlighting the fundamentals of consumer misbehaviour; its downside, however, is that it tends to be too generic. Since much about consumer behaviour is reported from a Western perspective, the problem of a lack of specific conceptualisation becomes amplified when trying to understand the phenomenon from a non-Western perspective. Given the cultural context of young consumer behaviour, it becomes fruitful to incorporate specific cultural aspects in its definition. Moreover, localised definitions are important to get a full grasp of the phenomenon and also instrumental to theory building research.

Since this chapter concerns itself with young consumers' (mis)behaviour in emerging markets, a localised definition of the phenomenon becomes critical. This is primarily so because a significant proportion of the research on consumer misbehaviour originates from developed countries. Naturally, conceptualisation of consumer misbehaviour contains cultural assumptions of the Western world. For instance, HBD Chick (2013), commenting on the variations of culture across nations seems to indicate that European countries tend to be individualistic. On the other hand, Latin American, Asian and African countries are more collectivist. HBD Chick (2013) specifically mentions that

> all of the Anglo nations are in the top ten wrt to individualism (79+) . . . nearly all the Latin American/Caribbean nations clump towards the bottom, and many of the East/Southeast Asian nations are down there [in the collectivist scale].

Clearly, a developing country-specific definition is befitting.

The narrow definition of young consumer misbehaviour: perspectives from developing countries

Mainstream definitions of young consumer misbehaviour seem to revolve around the notion of disruptive behaviours by consumers. But, what exactly does disruptive behaviour mean? To answer this, one has to consider the socio-cultural environment of the consumer. Since this chapter is concerned with young consumers in the developing and emerging markets, collectivist and communal values should be considered and incorporated in definitions of young consumer misbehaviour. For instance, when defining consumer misbehaviour within an African context, it might be fruitful to consider generally accepted *Ubuntu*[1] African virtues (i.e. humanness, caring, sharing, respect and compassion) in consumption situations.

Using the above-mentioned African Ubuntu example, consumers ought not to draw undue or excessive benefits beyond what they are morally entitled to in their capacity not only as consumers, but also as 'young adults' within society. This, naturally, extends to disadvantaging other market players and vulnerable individuals such as children, the disabled and elderly persons.

In summary, in defining young consumer misbehaviour within the emerging market's context, two additional criteria are included to the traditional definition. These are (1) violation of societal virtues and (2) non-caring behaviour and disrespectful attitudes towards vulnerable population groups. Figure 17.2 teaches that the generic criteria – committing disruptive acts – for consumer misbehaviour apply. However, there are two additional criteria with respect to societal values and vulnerable peoples.

Some explanations to the upsurge of young consumer misbehaviour in developing countries

To understand consumer misbehaviour as well as its motives, it is crucial to understand consumerism. The concept of consumerism has greatly transformed over the years. Purchases are no longer just based on product functionality alone. The appearance, prestige and status associated with products or services are equally important in purchase decisions. Primarily due to television, social media and the Internet, youths in the developing world are increasingly being exposed to the

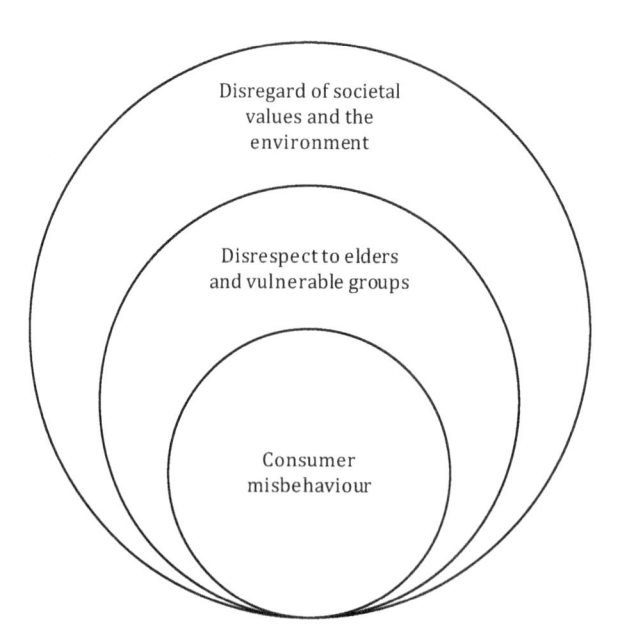

FIGURE 17.2 Young consumer misbehaviour

Source: Author.

so-called glamorous consumer life of the West. Advertisements that were initially intended for, say, the American market, through the power of the Internet, can easily be viewed by youths even those in the rural areas of Chiweshe in Zimbabwe, with the reverse also being true.

Due to technological advancements, youths in developing countries are increasingly embracing the consumerism culture (Clayton, 2013; *Zimbabwe News*, 2016). Youths in developing countries desire to purchase more, spend more and stand out more as people and as consumers (Clayton, 2013). From this, a vicious cycle of consumption emerges, where young consumers continually desire to acquire goods and services in ever-increasing quantities. The desire to accumulate products triggers consumers to increase the number of products they purchase. More purchases lead to greater consumption, which in turn motivates young consumers to desire to earn more. Collectively, as depicted in Figure 17.3, these inter-linking steps are known as the vicious cycle of consumption.

Perspectives of consumerism and consumer misbehaviour in developing countries

The vicious cycle of consumerism clearly demonstrates that the world today is a consumer society. Consumerism is part of our everyday life (Kazi and Indermun, 2014). Consumer spending forms the critical part of the world's economy. Advertising today teaches consumers that the more they spend, the more they live. Television, radio, print media and Internet advertisements bombard consumers and

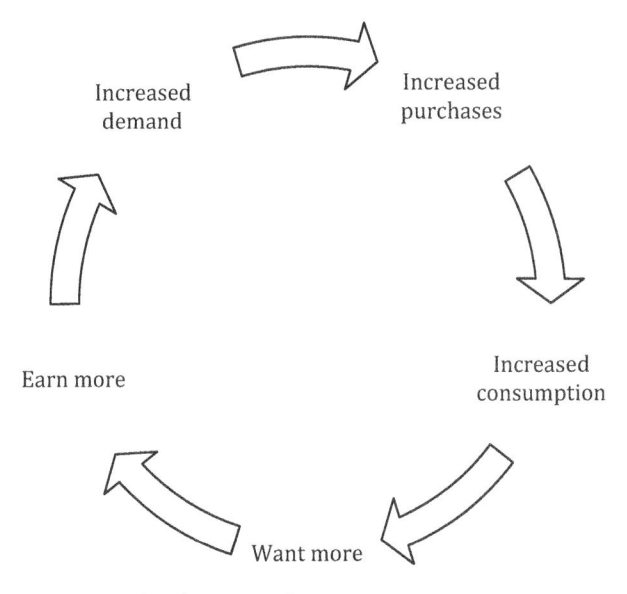

FIGURE 17.3 Vicious circle of consumption

Source: Adapted from Clayton (2013) and Naqad (2013).

encourage spending. This culture of spending is consumerism. From these increased calls for consumerism, consumers sometimes tend to succumb to increased marketing pressure (Fullerton and Punj, 2004).

Consequently, some young consumers tend to over-consume products in such a manner that they become addicted. One such example is that of mobile phone addiction observed by Shambare *et al.* (2012, p. 577). These authors established that 'mobile phone usage', among youths, 'is dependency-forming, habitual and addictive'.

Yet another example of young consumer misbehaviour promoted by increased consumerism is the *skothane* phenomenon in South Africa. The *skothane* movements (or simply *skothane*) are showing-off contests among students and youths. Essentially, these young consumers spend huge sums of money to buy branded clothes to show off their wealth to their peers in choreographed public contests in townships. Clayton (2013) explains that 'often groups of poor often unemployed black South Africans drape themselves head-to-toe in designer brands which they then destroy after the showing-off contest'. More often than not, '*skothaneism*' is usually associated with other acts of consumer misbehaviour such as shoplifting, binge drinking, reckless driving over and above demoralising other consumers.

Clearly, the consumerism ideology is not new. Its roots emerged in the early 1880s in North America when the Western industrial revolution was at its peak, and persisted all the way after World War II. Consumerism, according to Fullerton and Punj (1998), manipulates the masses into the so-called 'democratic consumers'. A democratic consumer society is a collection of individuals with an unusually high appetite for consuming mass produced goods (Fullerton and Punj, 1998). '*Skothaneism*' is one such example of consumers who exhibit a high appetite for consumption.

Advancements in sociology and psychology, in particular, the work by Sigmund Freud, have helped marketers create democratic consumer societies. Of note, Freudian psychoanalytic theories were (and still are) instrumental in manipulating consumers' subliminal perceptions.

Consumers and consumerism revisited

Marketing theory teaches us that consumption is an attempt by people to satisfy the multiple needs and wants encountered in the natural course of life. In today's modern society, this satisfaction process involves acts of purchasing, using and disposing of products and services. A consumer is thus any individual person who seeks to alleviate his or her needs or wants by purchasing goods or services for personal use.

According to Abram Maslow's propositions, people experience five basic needs (i.e. physiological, safety, social, esteem and self-actualisation needs) that they seek to satisfy. Thus, at any given point in time, consumers in one way or another are trying to provide solutions for at least one of these five needs. Some examples of how consumers seek to address these needs are shown in Table 17.3.

TABLE 17.3 Maslow's needs

Maslow's need	Examples of consumer acts to address the need
Physiological	• The acquisition of products whose purpose is to safeguard consumers' physical bodies (e.g. buying food, clothes or building (buying or renting) a house)
Safety	• Purchasing products or services aimed at protecting consumers from physical or emotional harm (e.g. insurance services to ensure that assets are kept safe or if they are lost they can be replaced)
Social	• The need for belonging or being affiliated to a social system or simply to a group of people (e.g. a ring for a partner/spouse, a Harley Davidson motorcycle so as to be admitted into a riding club, to join a Facebook group)
Self-esteem	• Self-esteem is all about affirming one's confidence and ambitions (e.g. wearing and using branded goods. As opposed to just a pair of shoes as in physiological needs, to maintain self-esteem, a consumer might choose to wear designer Louis Vuitton shoes)
Self-actualisation	• Similar to self-esteem. The only difference is that consumers, in this category, continually seek to improve their skills, sense of purpose (e.g. enrolling for a second PhD degree, buying a vintage bottle of wine)

Source: Adapted from Huitt (2007).

Effectively, routine tasks such as buying a pair of jeans or dining at a restaurant are all attempts at satisfying basic human needs. Hence, the desire to satisfy human needs therefore forms the building blocks of human behaviour, which in turn culminates into consumption – the act of purchasing, using and disposing products and services. In other words, consumption and behaviour are closely related.

Freudian psychoanalytic theory and consumerism

Psychoanalytic theories and philosophies have had a major influence on numerous disciplines including psychology, social sciences, medicine and marketing, specifically, consumer behaviour. Of note, Held (2009, p. 32) illustrates that 'Sigmund Freud, the father of psychoanalysis and critic of all things American, was an unwitting contributor to the rise of Western consumer culture'. Fundamentally, the psychoanalytic theories provided marketers with tools that enabled them to understand human behaviour, and by extension, consumer behaviour. For instance, the example from Held (2009) in which American women in 1929 were encouraged to break taboos and begin smoking in public. By manipulating public opinion, indirectly, marketers would be influencing an individual consumer's superego. In other words, this means that consumers can easily change their minds about what is acceptable and what is not acceptable. Extending this to consumption, this might signal which products and how to consume them (Held, 2009).

Freud's psychoanalytic theory postulates that the unconscious nature of personality influences an individual's behaviour. Personality in turn, is a result of the interplay among the three personality forces; namely, id, ego and superego. Figure 17.4 below depicts how these three variables interact to define personality, which in turn influence consumer behaviour or misbehaviour.

Id, as shown in Figure 17.4, is the raw unorganised inborn element of personality. Id is akin to uncontrolled and unregulated animal instinct that guides behaviour towards the primary desire of maximising pleasure and avoiding pain. However, the id unrestrained impulses cannot be expressed without violating societal values (see Figure 17.4).

The superego is the individual's conscience or moral voice. It can be regarded as the internal representative of society that regulates right and wrong behaviour. Lastly, an individual's ego acts as a moderator that finds a way to gratify the id in a way that will be acceptable to society. The manner in which the ego guides the primitive drives of the id and the moralistic demands of the superego accounts for the variety in personalities, interests, motives, attitudes and behaviour patterns of individuals (Kassarjian, 1971). And as shown in previous sections, behaviour leads to consumer patterns. As a corollary, personality or psychoanalysis affects consumerism.

Factors that promote young consumer misbehaviour in developing countries

Largely, consumer behaviour studies are based on cognitive and behavioural theories. The behavioural approach investigates the link between stimulus and response, whereas the cognitive approach focuses on the mental processes of learning such as memory, information processing and thinking. From these two schools

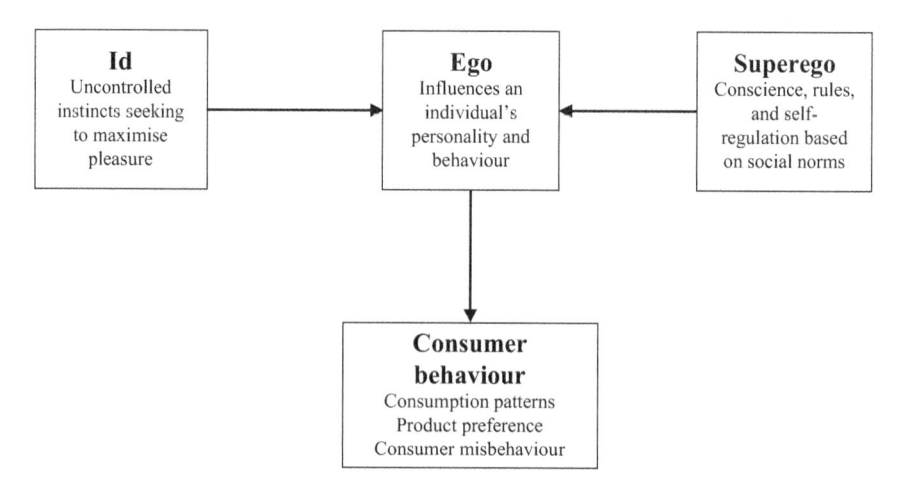

FIGURE 17.4 Id, ego and superego

Source: Author.

of thought, it can be concluded that various forms of consumer behaviour including misbehaviour are results of cause and effect relationships. So, in the context of misbehaviour, there are triggers (stimuli) that result in individuals misbehaving (responses). It, therefore, follows that most misbehaviours are triggered by some stimuli. This can be in the form of an event, action or situation. Although not exhaustive, in this chapter, we identify eight factors that trigger young consumers to misbehave. These are discussed in the following sections.

Poor service

Poor service is among the leading causes of customer dissatisfaction. Incidents of poor service often result when retailers, for one reason or another, fail to live up to consumers' expectations. The literature on customer satisfaction and consumer complaint patterns explains that after experiencing poor service encounters, consumers resort to three forms of responses, namely private actions, third-party and voice responses (Singh, 1998; Lerman, 2006; Shambare et al., 2010). Private actions represent a category of non-confrontational response actions from customers. Shambare et al. (2010) explain these three consumer actions as follows. Private actions usually range from consumers deciding not to take any action to negative campaigns to boycotting the retailer. In third-party responses, consumers engage 'third parties' such as lawyers and consumer groups to engage the retailer. Lastly, voice responses are those incidents when consumers confront the retailer or salesperson to register their complaint or dissatisfaction.

Past research on consumer complaint patterns reveal that young consumers have very high expectations and as such, have an impoverished tolerance for poor service; as such, they are more likely to raise a complaint about the poor service than other consumer groups (Shambare et al., 2010). In addition, the latter study, found that young consumers were more inclined towards confrontational actions – voice responses – in instances of poor service. It is from this confrontation that retailers and their employees become susceptible to abuse, verbally and emotionally. Consequently, poor service can act as a trigger to consumer misbehaviours such as abusing retailers' employees.

The need for revenge against a marketer or its brand

It is not uncommon for young consumers to feel cheated or badly treated by marketers. Feelings of, say being over-charged or being neglected by retailers might trigger a desire on the part of young consumers to 'get even' with marketers. In this context, getting even refers to inflicting harm to marketers' products and brands with a view to causing financial losses. Since the consumers feel that marketers have deprived them of something they want – access to a product they want or simply enjoyment, they, in turn, will also act in reciprocation by denying marketers the one thing that they desire – profits. To inflict harm on marketers or retailers, aggrieved young consumers commit acts that can range from calling for a widespread boycott of a marketer's products to vandalising a marketer's assets to hacking a marketer's website. These acts of revenge vary greatly; regardless of which action is taken by consumers, their commonality is that revenge seeks to destroy marketers' brand image and profitability. The need for revenge can, thus, encourage young consumers to act in a manner that negatively affects other market actors including marketers and their property.

In other extreme cases, geo-political crises among nation states sometimes spill over into the marketing arena. Because of country of origin effects, consumers often extend their frustrations about a country to the brands originating from that country. To illustrate, in 2014, a group of Russian youths took out their frustrations about the US-led sanctions against Russia on American brands such as McDonald's and Coca-Cola (BBC.com, 2014). These youths felt that American establishments were unfairly treating Russia over the Ukraine crisis. In response, the youths resorted to institute their own 'financial sanctions' against the US by publicly campaigning against the consumption of American products.

Thrill-seeking

Young consumers' need for excitement and enjoyment has also been cited as a trigger for several acts of consumer misbehaviour (Evans *et al.*, 2006). Some of the misbehaviours that result from thrill-seeking are reckless driving, vandalism, price-tag switching, fraudulent returns, alcohol and substance abuse. '*Skothaneism*' is yet another example of thrill-seeking behaviour by youths. In most cases, thrill-seeking behaviours are often unplanned and random.

Moreover, thrill-seeking behaviours, other than other types of misbehaviour, tend to be illegal as well as immoral actions. Authors such as Fullerton and Punj (2004, p. 1244) explain that 'for some consumers, misbehaving is an indescribable thrilling experience in which they defy basic legal and moral strictures to lash out at imposing institutions'.

Peer pressure

In the case of young consumer's misbehaviour, peer pressure refers to the collective incitement from other consumers to act. Because young consumers seek to fit in and become part of a larger grouping of individuals, they sometimes resort to activities for the purposes of demonstrating their loyalty. For instance, some fraternities or gangs require new members to undergo rites of passage as part of their initiation ceremonies. These actions such as shoplifting or committing acts of vandalism are designed to prove and enforce loyalty (Evans *et al.*, 2006). In other words, this collective commission of crimes ensures that individual members will not report activities of the group to authorities, since they would also be guilty of the same crime.

In reality though, peer pressure on its own does not trigger misbehaviour. Peer pressure, however, acts as a catalyst that promotes and magnifies acts of misbehaviour.

Consider the Coca-Cola protests discussed earlier in the chapter, it was not necessarily peer pressure that triggered the protests, but peer pressure was, however, a necessary ingredient to facilitate the protests. By this it is meant that one disgruntled Russian youth could have staged the Coca-Cola protest (i.e. consumer revenge), but because the act was executed by a collective – a group of young consumers – the effect of the action was magnified. It is this catalytic effect that makes peer pressure a trigger of consumer misbehaviour.

Absence of moral constraints

The absence of moral constraints, according to Fullerton and Punj (2004, p. 1244), is the 'lack of powerful internal inhibitions against conduct perceived to be wrong'. Because of this, consumers fail to differentiate normal conduct from misbehaviour. Consequently, consumers are unable or fail to see the negative consequences of their actions and go on to act in a manner that is detrimental to other market players. Examples of behaviours committed due to the absence of moral constraints include excessive speeding, vandalism and shoplifting among others. For instance, when motorists drive in excess of the recommended speed limits because they do not realise that excessive speeds are a threat not only to themselves, but also to other motorists and pedestrians. In the case of vandalism, for example, removing signposts, the misbehavers might not fully appreciate that replacing the signposts costs governments and local authorities. Furthermore, it makes navigation challenging for those individuals relying on the information provided by the street signposts.

Calculating opportunism

While the absence of moral constraints might be a result of consumers not being able to differentiate acceptable conduct from unacceptable behaviour, calculating opportunism is essentially the same, the only difference is that consumers willingly and knowingly commit acts of misbehaviour. In the latter, consumers ignore their ethical constraints. Consumers weigh the risks and rewards of misconduct (Fullerton and Punj, 2004, p. 1244); if the rewards outweigh the risks, the consumer continues with the misbehaviour. Alternatively, such behaviours are discouraged when the risks outweigh the benefits. Examples of acts of misbehaviour that result from calculating opportunism are fraudulent returns, credit card fraud, queue jumping and price-tag switching.

Provocative situations

Provocative situations are scenarios that are likely to result in emotional outbursts and irrational behaviour. Examples of provocative situations that would cause consumers to act irrationally are crowded areas such as stadia, amusement parks, airports, bus and train stations. In these situations, consumers' emotions, more often than not, are usually high. So, when they come into contact with other consumers and marketers' employees they have a tendency to engage in unbecoming behaviour, willing or otherwise. For instance, young consumers generally might take the opportunity of the big crowd to show off (i.e. *skothane*). In other cases, consumers might take out their frustration on flight attendants for a delayed flight by verbally abusing them (Fullerton and Punj, 2004, p. 1245). In crowded places, peer pressure can also easily manifest itself and drive a number of acts of misbehaviour.

Marketing forces

In their study, Fullerton and Punj (1998) reveal that modern marketing culture and the resultant consumerism culture are in fact huge driving forces for a variety of consumer misbehaviour. The authors seem to argue that the notion of democratic consumerism, which advocates for increased consumerism rights overemphasises consumers' rights. At the same time, very little, if any, is mentioned of consumer obligations and responsibilities. As such, young consumers tend to over-use or even abuse the age-old mantra that 'the customer is always right'. To this effect, Fullerton and Punj (1998) identified seven core characteristics of the consumption culture accounting for much of the consumer misbehaviour. These are briefly discussed next.

1. *Centrality of consumption:* the consumer's self-image and identity is strongly influenced by the products and services acquired. Hence, consumers continue purchasing more products for approval and recognition from the outside world. Through aggressive advertising and promotion of goods consumers are enticed to purchase even more products to feel better about themselves, resulting in a vicious circle of consumption. As previously discussed, the vicious cycle of consumption often leads to addictive behaviour (Shambare *et al.*, 2012). Other examples of increased consumption pressures are the *skothane* culture of taunting other consumers in the showing-off contests.
2. *Changing moral values:* traits once considered as part of the 'deadly sins' such as envy, pride, greed and lust are now considered legitimate personal aspirations and drives to personal fulfilment. To young consumers, this could easily be construed as opportunities to make as much money as possible, legally or otherwise. Thus, this drives young consumers towards limited moral constraints and calculating opportunism, which in turn trigger consumer misbehaviours such as credit card fraud. All this is done to fuel consumption and greed.
3. *Insatiable desire:* marketers nowadays do not just react to signals by consumers of preferred goods and services but proactively stimulate wants and desires that even the consumers did not know they had. In the previous sections, the issue of how marketers seek to induce demand for products was discussed. This is achieved by manipulating public opinion, which in fact is changing individual

consumers' superego. Consumers are, thus, encouraged to buy more, desire more and consume more. Ultimately, insatiable desire can easily lead to addiction, hoarding and binge shopping (Held, 2009).

4. *Social meaning of goods:* possessions have become an extension of the individual. Consumers' self-image and identity is linked to the products they consume. The products and services that one can purchase have become a means to maintain parity with others. Young consumers in South Africa, for instance, prefer conspicuous consumption and are not afraid to violate other consumers for the sake of demonstrating their 'wealth,' social standing and personality in the community through '*skothaneism*'.

5. *Hedonism:* since the 1920s businesses and marketers have reshaped consumer ethics from a utilitarian outlook into a pleasure-minded ethic (Marchand, 1985). Undoubtedly, hedonism or pleasure-seeking tends to lead consumers to activities such as alcohol and substance abuse among youths.

6. *Impulsive buying:* impulse buying is a widespread consumer behaviour, which was greatly encouraged by marketers over the years through enticing displays, easy access to credit, self-service, 24-hour shopping and online or home shopping networks. These generally emerge as a result of peer pressure and because goods bought through impulse are often thrill-seeking substances such as alcohol, which can then lead to alcohol abuse and in turn result in drink driving and speeding.

7. *Openness of exchange environment*: exchange institutions have become settings for social interaction and expression. Teenagers in particular nowadays spend most of their time in shopping malls, where they can be socialised into the culture of consumption (Fullerton and Punj, 1998). The shopping centres and malls thus represent themselves as provocative situational factors leading to misbehaviour including abuse of marketers' employees, shoplifting and abuse of other consumers.

From the above-mentioned marketing factors, it can be concluded that the deepening consumerism culture is associated with some acts of consumer misbehaviour. Figure 17.5 summarises the link between the culture of consumerism and consumer misbehaviour.

Marketing implications of young consumer misbehaviour

The previous sections of the chapter highlighted several aspects of young consumer misbehaviour and demonstrated that consumer misbehaviour often results in negative effects on various stakeholders in the marketplace. Evidence also indicates that consumer misbehaviour, especially negative consumer acts committed by youths and young people, is on the incline. This is particularly true for developing countries, where the growing number of cases of young consumer misbehaviour present several marketing implications.

```
┌─────────────┐
│  Marketing  │
│  activities │
└─────────────┘
       ⇩
┌─────────────────────────────────────────────────────────────────────────┐
│ Culture of consumption              Motives for consumer misbehaviour   │
│                                                                         │
│ Centrality of consumption    ←——→   Unfulfilled aspirations             │
│                                                                         │
│ Changing moral values        ←——→   Deviant thrill-seeking              │
│                                                                         │
│ Insatiable desire            ←——→   Absence of moral constraints        │
│                                                                         │
│ Social meaning of goods      ←——→   Calculating opportunism             │
│                                                                         │
│ Hedonism                     ←——→   Provocative situational factors     │
│                                                                         │
│ Impulsive buying             ←——→   Differential association            │
│                                                                         │
│ Openness of exchange environment ←——→ Pathological socialisation        │
└─────────────────────────────────────────────────────────────────────────┘
```

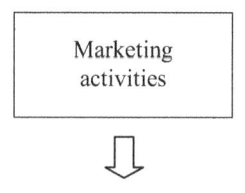

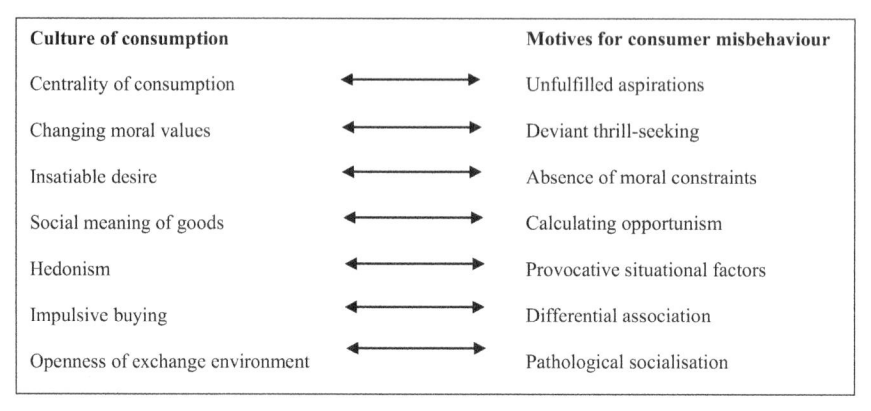

FIGURE 17.5 Motives of young consumer misbehaviour

Source: Adapted from Fullerton and Punj (1998, p. 404).

Attempts to profile the misbehaving young consumer

Profiling and segmenting customers is an important imperative of marketing. Empirical evidence clearly demonstrates that not all consumers are the same. Consumers' tastes are usually distinguishable enough so as to define distinct market segments. It is for this reason that marketers rarely attempt to market their products to all customers; the practice is usually that a marketer establishes a niche and, subsequently, designs its marketing strategy to target that market. Undoubtedly, segmenting is one of the fundamental principles of marketing. But, consumer behaviourists such as Fullerton and Punj (1998, 2004) are of the opinion that consumer misbehaviour violates the 'segmentation principle'. Years of research into consumer misbehaviour has led Fullerton and Punj (2004) to conclude that:

> Misbehaving consumers are as diverse a group as consumers in general. They are in fact representative of consumers overall and not a group apart. It is difficult to distinguish the misbehaviour prone from other consumers on the basis of socioeconomic factors, lifestyle, physical characteristics, or gender.
>
> *(Fullerton and Punj, 2004, p. 1241)*

Furthermore, consumer misbehaviour is not exclusive only to one country or region; it is pervasive across different cultures, religions, and nationalities. More importantly, profiling a typical misbehaving consumer is a difficult exercise (Ojikutu et al., 2011). An exception to this, however, seems to be that of incidents involving calculating opportunism including insurance and credit card fraud. Since these types of fraudulent acts (of misbehaviour) often require certain levels of skill and education, naturally, Fullerton and Punj (2004) and later Ojikutu *et al.* (2011) found evidence suggesting that incidents involving calculating opportunism including insurance and credit card fraud are most likely to be committed by highly educated consumers. In all other incidents of misbehaviour except for calculating opportunism, the profile of a misbehaving consumer is difficult to come by. To that effect, Fullerton and Punj (2004, pp. 1241–1243) concluded that:

1. *Misbehavers cannot be profiled accurately.* The exceptions seem to be in cases of highly planned and sophisticated eventualities such as insurance or credit card fraud and, to a certain extent, hacking and cyber-attacks on marketers' websites.
2. *In most cases, misbehaving is not a continuous behaviour.* It does not necessarily mean that once a misbehaviour, always a misbehaviour. For instance, many adolescents and young adults have shoplifted or vandalised a retailer's premises. Once that misbehaving act has been committed, say, for a gang initiation or simply to pull a prank, it is highly unlikely to be continued.

It might, therefore, be instructive that the inability to profile misbehaving consumers is an indication that all consumers are capable of misbehaving (Fullerton and Punj, 2004, p. 1241). This is not a far-fetched assumption. Consider if you will that a majority of individuals throughout their lifetime, at least on one occasion have either shoplifted, 'taken' linen from a hotel, 'taken' a pen from a bank, verbally (or even physically) abused a retailer's employee, vandalised or abused a marketer's shopping cart. The critical question then becomes: what can marketers do to stop or at least manage young consumer misbehaviour? The next section provides some strategies to manage young consumer misbehaviour.

Managing young consumer misbehaviour

In totality, the foregoing discussions point to the managerial complexities of consumer misbehaviour (Harris and Daunt, 2013). To remain profitable, marketers, on the one hand, should balance consumer needs and expectations with maintaining a good brand image. On the other hand, they also need to accommodate ever-increasing customer needs as well as those of their employees while, at the same time, navigating a highly competitive marketplace.

The negative effects of consumer misbehaviour are undeniable, and several of these have been illustrated in this chapter. Overall, misbehaviour leads to financial loss, depravation, and an uncomfortable consumption experience. Hence, managing or minimising consumer misbehaviour constitutes a matter of paramount importance to marketers (Fullerton and Punj, 2004; Harris and Daunt, 2013). To this effect, three major approaches to managing misbehaviour are proposed, namely increased customer education, deterrence and improved human resources management practices. These strategies are discussed in turn next.

Consumer education as a means to manage negative consumer behaviour

Evidence shows that few consumers dispute the negative effects of consumer misbehaviour. However, two aspects about consumer misbehaviour that might be fully appreciated by a majority of customers, particularly young consumers, are that consumer misbehaviour (1) is not victimless and (2) can result in severe negative consequences not only to marketers, but to other consumers. As such, these consequences need to be communicated to consumers. Communication could be in the form of posters or billboards in shops, malls or even large outdoor billboards. Television and radio campaigns could also be used to spread the call for responsible consumerism.

Deterrence as a control measure to consumer misbehaviour

Studies in criminology and policing demonstrate that deterrent measures such as threats to prosecution, police and security visibility, physical and electronic surveillance systems, among others, have been noted to reduce the prevalence of crime (Grealy *et al.*, 1978; McCaney, 2011). Some of these measures have proved to be quite successful in reducing criminal-related consumer misbehaviours such as shoplifting (Harris and Daunt, 2013). Although these measures are not 100 per cent foolproof, retailers could adopt these strategies to deter opportunist young misbehavers, such as those seeking to pull off initiation pranks. Some deterrent measures that retailers can employ include:

- *CCTV cameras:* installing electronic surveillance cameras in strategic locations both inside and outside of shops will likely show customers that they are being monitored. Such knowledge usually serves to deter unbecoming behaviour.
- *Increased staff on the shop floor:* in addition to electronic technology, physical surveillance has been reported to be quite effective. To make physical surveillance even more effective, Harris and Daunt (2013) found that special uniforms for shop floor employees tends to make them more visible, and as such, much more effective in their role that 'big brother is watching'.
- *Redesigned servicescapes:* changing shops' layout and servicescapes has also been observed to provide positive results in combatting consumer misbehaviour. Examples of these include installing glass barriers or screens to shield clerks working at returns counters from irate customers. Another useful tactic is positioning experienced and elderly employees, especially those that look commanding and authoritative, at stations where volatile encounters with customers are likely to occur (Harris and Daunt, 2013, p. 288). The rationale being that, in general, customers are less likely to abuse service clerks that seem authoritative and commanding.

Empowering customer-contact employees through improved human resources management practices

Given its widespread pervasiveness, it is imperative for marketers not only to realise, but also to accept that consumer misbehaviour is an inextricable part of conducting business in the twenty-first century (Fullerton and Punj, 1998, 2004; Held, 2009; Ojikutu *et al.*, 2011; Harris and Daunt, 2013; *JGFM*, 2016; Tran, 2016; Wafula, 2016). Accordingly, marketers should take proactive measures to counteract negative consumer behaviour. One such approach is to empower its customer-contact staff into dealing with consumer misbehaviour situations effectively (Harris and Daunt, 2013, pp. 287–289). Some of the consumer misbehaviour-centric human resources management practices are:

- *Hiring self-confident employees:* since evidence shows that employees with high levels of public self-confidence are less likely to be affected by abusive customers, it is not a bad strategy to recruit such employees as customer service specialists. Other traits to be considered when hiring customer service personnel include those possessing social and vocal skills. Such employees tend to be able to diffuse tense situations better.
- *Consumer misbehaviour awareness and training:* once appointed, marketers ought to invest in training their employees (existing and new) on consumer misbehaviour. Employees are more likely to be able to deal with negative consumer behaviour if they are empowered to (a) identify it and (b) resolve it.
- *Improved remuneration packages for customer service staff:* considering that customer service personnel perform specialised tasks – dealing with tense and volatile customer service issues – they should be recognised accordingly. These employees, therefore, should be rewarded with appropriate reward packages.

This section identified numerous approaches to manage acts of misbehaviour. It should be noted, however, that each marketer's situation is unique and needs careful analysis of these strategies. Also, no one strategy should be seen as a silver bullet for misbehaviour; a consolidated approach of various strategies is advised.

Unresolved questions: directions for further research

Any research work hardly exhausts all issues of a phenomenon. Likewise, this chapter cannot claim to have addressed all the aspects of young consumer misbehaviour in developing countries. Moreover, from the onset, this chapter sought to stimulate discourse within the area of young consumer misbehaviour. The question of consumer misbehaviour is wide and broad; this chapter attempted to address some of these issues, albeit in a more generic style. More detailed and specific research into young consumer misbehaviour is needed. This chapter, therefore, would be incomplete if it does not set out an agenda for further research.

Accordingly, we propose that future researchers consider the following as possible areas for further inquiry to enrich the discourse of young consumer misbehaviour.

1. Look into possible strategies or approaches to segment misbehaving consumers.
2. Increase in disposable income is often associated with increased levels of consumerism. To that effect, it would be interesting to determine whether misbehaviour and income levels are linked. Also, it would be interesting to determine if the proportion of misbehaviours in a market, economy or country is related to that country's GDP level.
3. The effect of collectivist philosophies, such as the African philosophy of Ubuntu, have been noted to have an influence on consumerism. As such, determining the influence of these non-Western cultural philosophies, as they relate to young consumer behaviour is an interesting field of inquiry. Conducting an empirical study on its effect on consumer behaviour is likely to enrich the literature.
4. Comparison studies on motives for negative young consumer behaviour between youths from developing and developed countries might help in providing new insights into the phenomenon.
5. Essentially, acts of misbehaviour are categorised in terms of the market players they affect. In other words, all misbehaviours directed at the merchandise such as price-tag switching and shoplifting are classified into one variety. Likewise, those targeting marketers' employees are categorised separately. Is this categorisation efficient and applicable for young consumers in developing countries?
6. Investigate whether young consumer misbehaviour can be traced to the differences in cultural orientation. Empirical research into comparisons of, say, migrants from developing countries in Western countries is likely to provide useful insights. For instance, comparing Middle-Eastern and African immigrants into Europe will provide cross-cultural perspectives into the phenomenon.

Concluding remarks

The aim of this chapter was to (re)introduce young consumer misbehaviour in developing countries as a fruitful area for research. As common in consumer behaviour works, the chapter drew insights from the literature across multiple disciplines to conceptualise young consumer misbehaviour. One of the critical aspects highlighted in the chapter was that the social setting in many developing countries is different from that of the West. This distinction was of paramount importance because consumer (mis)behaviour is a socially embedded construct, the different socio-cultural nuances between the West and non-Western world will most likely result in numerous ramifications on how the notion of young consumer misbehaviour is understood. This, in turn, will have serious implications on how the problem is dealt with, both at theoretical and practical levels. Following this line of thought, it was, therefore, necessary for the chapter to propose a definition for young consumer misbehaviour that is befitting of the context of developing countries.

Having said that, it is also important to acknowledge that the term 'developing nations' is generic and does not do justice to the many different nation states and cultural dispositions present in the multiplicity of countries that are labelled as developing countries. Therein, there are African, Asian, Caribbean, Latin American and Middle Eastern countries that all have traces of similarities and differences, both within and among themselves. As such, this fact simply beckons the importance of encouraging research, hence the reason the previous section was dedicated to proposing some areas of future research.

Overall, the implications and significance of this chapter are many. First, it introduced the concept of young consumer misbehaviour as a viable research area in the developing world. Second, the chapter highlighted the strategic importance of young consumer misbehaviour as a critical part of the marketing effort. Third, some managerial complexities surrounding young consumer misbehaviour were discussed. Fourth, strategies on how to deal with these managerial challenges were proposed.

Finally and more importantly, the chapter was able to distinguish that young consumer misbehaviour in developing countries is fundamentally different from that experienced in developed countries. Because consumer behaviourists took these differences for granted, the specific and unique elements of young consumer misbehaviour in non-Western settings has, thus, been largely ignored from mainstream marketing research. As such, the chapter puts forth the argument that now is the time to introduce the debate on young consumer misbehaviour in other non-Western regions, and more particularly, in developing countries.

Note

1 Ubuntu can be loosely translated in English as 'humanness or being human'. In other words, Ubuntu is best described as 'an African philosophy that seeks to promote harmonious relations and interaction among people. This philosophy suggests that a person can only truly and fully exist if he or she co-exists with others in his or her community. In other words, this means that one should always have a strong sense of consideration for others' (Shambare, 2016, p. 217).

References

BBC.com. (2014). Russia: Group calls for Coca-Cola boycott. www.bbc.com/news/blogs-news-from-elsewhere-27680865 (accessed 30 March 2017).

Clayton, J. (2013). Flash mob: South Africa's township youth strut their stuff – in pictures. *Guardian*. www.theguardian.com/world/gallery/2013/may/03/izikhothane-south-africa-pictures-petterson (accessed 27 January 2017).

Cromwell, P. and Thurman, Q. (2003). The devil made me do it: Use of neutralizations by shoplifters. *Deviant Behavior*, *24*, 535–550.

De Villiers, R. (2015). Another ATM fraud victim speaks out. http://randfonteinherald.co.za/189103/another-atm-fraud-victim-speaks-out/ (accessed 27 January 2017).

Djanie, A. (2014). What happened to our youth? http://newafricanmagazine.com/happened-youth/ (accessed 27 January 2017).

Drum Digital. (2016). Do not spray people with Doom, Tiger Brands tells prophet of doom. www.drum.co.za/news/do-not-spray-people-with-doom-tiger-brands-tells-prophet-of-doom/ (accessed 26 January 2017).

eNCA. (2016). Bank card fraud hitting SA consumers. www.enca.com/south-africa/bank-card-fraud-hitting-sa-consumers (accessed 27 January 2017).

Evans, M., Jamal, A. and Foxall, G. (2009). *Consumer behaviour*. West Sussex: John Wiley & Sons.

Fullerton, R. A. and Punj, G. (1998). The unintended consequences of the culture of Consumption: An historical-theoretical analysis of consumer misbehaviour. *Consumption Markets & Culture*, 1(4), 393–423.

Fullerton, R. A. and Punj, G. (2004). Repercussions of promoting an ideology of consumption: Consumer misbehaviour. *Journal of Business Research*, 57, 1239–1249.

Grealy, J. I., Kaplan, H. M. and Hoover, S. S. (1978). Crime prevention through environmental design. *Security World*, 15(9), 60–64.

Groundup. (2016). 'We will give you tip when you return the land', waitress told. Sowetan Live. www.sowetanlive.co.za/news/2016/04/29/we-will-give-tip-when-you-return-the-land-white-waitress-told (accessed 23 January 2017).

Harris, L. C. and Daunt, K. (2013). Managing customer misbehavior: Challenges and strategies. *Journal of Services Marketing*, 27(4), 281–293.

Harris, L. C. and Dumas, A. (2009). Online consumer misbehaviour: An application of neutralization theory. *Marketing Theory*, 9(4), 379–402.

HDB Chick. (2013). National individualism: Collectivism scores. Available at: https://hbdchick.wordpress.com/2013/09/07/national-individualism-collectivism-scores/ (accessed 28 March 2017).

Held, L. (2009). Psychoanalysis shapes consumer culture. *Monitor on Psychology*, 40(11), 32.

Huitt, W. (2007). Maslow's hierarchy of needs. *Educational Psychology Interactive*. Valdosta, GA: Valdosta State University. www.cdpsycintcractivc.org/topics/regsys/maslow.html (accessed 14 December 2016).

Hofstede, G. (1980). *Culture's consequences, international differences in work-related values*. Beverly Hills, CA: Sage.

Hofstede, G. (2011). Dimensionalizing cultures: The Hofstede model in context. *Online Readings in Psychology and Culture*, 2(1), 11.

Holbrook, M. B. and Hirschman, E. C. (1982). The experiential aspects of consumption: Consumer fantasies, feelings, and fun. *Journal of Consumer Research*, 9, 132–140.

Journal of Global Fashion Marketing. (2016). Call for papers: Special issue of *Journal of Global Fashion Marketing* on 'Behind the glamor of fashion'. http://c.ymcdn.com/sites/itaaonline.org/resource/resmgr/Calls_and_Announcments/JGFM_SPECIAL_ISSUE_darkside_.pdf (accessed 24 January 2017).

Kassarjian, H. H. (1971). Personality and consumer behavior: A review. *Journal of Marketing Research*, 8(4), 409.

Kazi, T. B. and Indermun, V. (2014). Consumerism, consumption and consumer education. *International Journal of Innovative Research in Management*, 3(5), 1–16.

Kieser, J. (2011). Plastic litter still soils our beaches. http://thegreentimes.co.za/plastic-litter-still-soils-our-beaches/ (accessed 27 January 2017).

Lerman, D. (2006). Consumer politeness and complaining behaviour. *Journal of Services Marketing*, 20(2), 92–100.

Liu, C. (2016). Foreigner yells at person cutting in line in three Chinese dialects. https://thenanfang.com/expat-puts-queue-cutter-place-perfect-style/ (accessed 23 January 2017).

McCaney, K. (2011). Do surveillance systems reduce crime? GCN Online. https://gcn.com/articles/2011/09/20/surveillance-cameras-effect-on-preventing-crimes.aspx (accessed 1 April 2017).

Mail Online. (2013). Confessions of a returnaholic: The extreme tactics one woman uses to get a refund after wearing her clothes once – no matter how old they are. www.dailymail.co.uk/femail/article-2514675/Confessions-returnaholic-The-extreme-tactics-woman-uses-refund-wearing-clothes-matter-old-are.html#ixzz4WwZse9Wn (accessed on 27 January 2017).

Marchand, R. (1985). *Advertising the American Dream: Making way for modernity, 1920–1940.* Berkeley, CA: University of California Press.

Milavec, B. (2012). An analysis of consumer misbehavior on Black Friday. Bachelor of Science in Psychology Dissertation. University of Delaware.

Naqad. (2013). *Societal evolution: Families and consumerism.* https://naqad.wordpress.com/2013/11/11/societal-evolution-families-and-consumerism (accessed 26 January 2017).

Nye, M. B. (2006). *Progress toward replacing animals in toxicity testing for cosmetics.* https://dash.harvard.edu/bitstream/handle/1/8852184/Nye06.html?sequence=2 (accessed 26 January 2017).

Oberholster, T. (2014). *2014 credit card fraud statistics.* www.banking.org.za/docs/default-source/publication/banker-sa/banker-sa-13.pdf?sfvrsn=10 (accessed 27 January 2017).

Ojikutu, R. K., Yusuf, T. O. and Obadala, M. A. (2011). Attitude and perception about insurance fraud in Lagos State, Nigeria. *European Journal of Scientific Research*, 57(4), 615–625.

Shambare, R. (2016). Consumer adoption of e-government in South Africa: Barriers, solutions, and implications. In A. Gbadamosi (ed.), *Handbook of research on consumerism and buying behavior in developing nations* (pp. 190–217). Hershey, PA: IGI Global.

Shambare, R., Frouws, M. and Naidoo, V. (2010). South African consumers' complaint patterns. *Journal of Business Research*, 4(1/2), 65–71.

Shambare, R., Rugimbana, R. and Zhowa, T. (2012). Are mobile phones the 21st-century addiction? *African Journal of Business Management*, 6(2), 573–577.

Shapiro, S. (1987). The social control of impersonal trust. *Journal of Sociology*, 93(3), 623–658.

Singh, J. (1988). Consumer complaint intentions and behavior: Definitional taxonomical issues. *The Journal of Marketing*, 52(1), 93–107.

Tonglet, M. (2002). Consumer misbehaviour: An exploratory study of shoplifting. *Journal of Consumer Behaviour*, 1(4), 336–354.

Tran, J. M. (2016). When customers behave badly: Psychological antecedents and dynamics of value co-destruction in service experiences. DBA Dissertation. College of Business, Louisiana Tech University.

Wafula, P. (2016). Kenya power arrests 257 for vandalism and theft. *Standard Digital.* www.standardmedia.co.ke/business/article/2000214323/kenya-power-arrests-257-for-vandalism-and-theft (accessed 23 January 2017).

Zimbabwe News. (2016). Midlands State University student caught shoplifting. www.thezimbabwenewslive.com/crime-courts-29980-midlands-state-university-student-caught-shoplifting.html (accessed 23 January 2017).

18
FAITH, RELIGION AND YOUNG CONSUMER BEHAVIOUR

Eddy Kurobuza Tukamushaba and Dan Musinguzi

Introduction

The successful marketing decisions by commercial and non-commercial organisations depend on the knowledge about consumer behaviour. Hawkins and Mothersbaugh (2010) argue that consumer behaviour involves the study of individuals, groups or organisations and the processes used to select, secure, use and dispose of products, services, experiences or ideas to satisfy their needs.

Religion is one factor that influences consumer decision-making behaviour and the way individuals interact with other consumers within society (Delener, 1994). Understanding and anticipating consumer behaviour of various consumer categories helps in developing effective marketing strategies, planning for and managing the ever-changing marketing environment and influencing socially desirable behaviour.

In addition, understanding young consumers' behaviour helps service providers make decisions on what they purchase and where and why they purchase certain products and services and leave out others. Religion influences consumer behaviour across all demographic characteristics. Schwartz and Huismans (1995) argue that based on a Christian theology perspective, religion involves an orientation towards and dependency on God and a transcendence of material concerns and temporary affective desires. It involves respect for God expressed through regular worship and personal control over material and affective desires.

A number of studies have explored the influence of religion/faith and religiosity on consumer behaviour, such as purchasing decisions (Essoo and Dibb, 2004; Choi *et al.*, 2013; Siala, 2013; Mathras *et al.*, 2016), consumption of different products and services (Fontaine *et al.*, 2000; Potluri *et al.*, 2010; Sukhwal and Suman, 2013), but only a few have synthesised the influence of religion on young consumers' behaviour (Eren, 2013; Potluri *et al.*, 2010). This chapter bridges the existing knowledge gap by synthesising the literature to uncover how faith/religion or religiosity impacts on the behaviours of young consumers. The central research question is: to what extent does faith/religion influence young consumers' purchasing decision-making process and consumption of products and services?

In order to answer this question, case studies associated with food, clothing and education are used. Although a number of religions exist such as Christianity, Judaism, Islam, Buddhism, Toaism, Hinduism, only those categorised as being Western religions (Christianity, Judaism, Islam) believe that God created nature and therefore God and humans hold a superior position to nature, making man dominant over it (James, 1902/2004). This study uses the Islamic and Christian perspectives to demonstrate the influence of faith/religion on young consumers' behaviour.

Literature review

Consumer behaviour is hinged on key frameworks consisting of personal, psychological, cultural and social factors that influence consumption of various products and services. A number of factors that influence the consumer behaviour are categorised into external influencers (culture, subculture, demographics, social status, reference groups, family marketing activities and internal influencers (perceptions, learning, memory, personality, emotions and attitudes). These factors influence different aspects of human behaviour such as lifestyle and decision-making.

Religion is part of the external influencers of culture described by Hawkins and Mothersbaugh (2010) as a complex whole at the levels of knowledge, belief, art, law, morals, customs and any other capabilities acquired by humans as members of society. Additionally, religion influences different human behaviour such as high-involvement purchasing behaviour, shopping behaviour and consumer switching behaviour (Essoo and Dibb, 2004; Shah et al., 2011; Choi et al., 2013; Siala, 2013). Evidence from literature suggests that the teachings of most religions directly or indirectly influence the behaviour of the followers. The different religious beliefs and teachings about aspects of life influence personal and social lives and lifestyle. For example, Charseatd (2016) indicates that religious beliefs have a positive influence on the attitude towards prosocial activities, such as blood donation among young people.

Religion is associated with how individuals choose goods and services to consume and information to use when making purchasing decisions (Delener, 1994; Essoo and Dibb, 2004). A number of studies have been conducted on how Islam as a religion has influenced its believers on what to purchase and the attitude towards certain products and services (Potluri et al., 2010; Alam et al., 2011; Bakar et al., 2013; Razzaque and Chaudry, 2013; Sukhwal and Suman, 2013; Khalek, 2014; Charseatd, 2016). Kamil et al. (2012) argue that Islamic faith is anchored on three basic tenets of life such as Shariah (Islamic law and regulation),

Aqidah (basic beliefs) and Akhlak (morals and values). These basic tenets are used to guide individuals' practices or actions within the Islamic faith and are therefore benchmarked in analysing how followers of Islam make decisions associated with food, clothing and education.

Religion and food-buying behaviour

Food is one of the most important basic needs required by humans for survival. It is a great medium of cultural sharing for humanity. Decisions on what food to buy, where to buy and how food is processed are critical to most religions. The following section discusses the Islamic and Christian perspectives on food.

The global Muslim population exceeds 1.6 billion, has been growing at twice the rate of the non-Muslim world and is expected to reach 2.2 billion by 2030 (Pew Research Centre, 2011). This rapid growth has led to the high demand for halal food products and services globally (International Trade Center, 2015). For the purposes of this study, halal refers to food and beverages that are permissible for use and consumption by Muslims. The Islamic faith has rules and guidelines based on the Sharia law that regulates how food should be prepared and handled. For example, Islam rules mandate humane treatment of animals as well as other special preparation. This special attachment to food has resulted in different estimates being made by different organisations. For example, the *Global Islamic Economy Report* (2015/2016) estimated the value of halal food and beverages at US$1,128 billion in 2014, which is a sharp rise from what the Global Halal Food Market (2011) estimated at US$667 million net worth of the halal food industry (Hassan, 2007).

Hamdan *et al.* (2013) explain that halal food does not contain swine or pork (or its by-products), alcohol, blood, certain types of animals and all kinds of meat should be slaughtered following the Islamic procedures. The implication on this aspect is that in societies where Islam is the main faith, young Muslim consumers are highly influenced by the religious teachings on the consumption of certain foods and drinks.

Hamdan *et al.* (2013) found that consumers of all ages in Malaysia made decisions on food purchase based on their familiarity with the process the food goes through, especially for processed food products, and halal label certification is a major consideration for food choice. This shows that religion plays a critical role in influencing Muslims' decisions on purchasing food.

Religiosity within the context of Arabic Islamic collectivist culture has a strong relationship with consumer behaviour, such as boycotting of particular products and services. For example, it is common for some religious organisations to call for the boycott of products and services that are believed to be provided by companies that support subversive activities like waging war and other political considerations (Dekhi *et al.*, 2017). These religious campaigns that call for product and services boycotting also influence young consumers' decisions on what to purchase and consume when it comes to foods produced by blacklisted companies.

Izberk-Bilgin (2012) narrates how some conservative Muslims in Turkey have coined a term 'Infidel brands' to facilitate campaigns to boycott products and services perceived to be produced under unethical dimensions. For instance, various fatwas from popular Islamic scholars direct followers of Islamic faith not to carry out any transaction with a company that uses its profit to help propagate war or advance corruption and immorality (Beekun and Badai, 2005). The consumer decision-making process is influenced by need recognition, search and evaluation of alternatives, purchase decisions and post-purchase evaluation. The need among the followers of the Islamic faith to consume healthy food and halal is linked to religion (Fontaine *et al.*, 2005). The Islamist quest to moralise the market based on Islamic principles is not unlike Christian activism that targets corporations such as Disney and Home Depot for promoting paganism and homosexuality (Izberk-Bilgin, 2012).

The argument that religion has a greater influence on the attitude of followers is further expounded by Khalek (2014). In his study, younger Muslims had positive attitudes towards halal food outlets and the food products with halal certification from Malaysia's Department of Islamic Development. The consumption of halal food is considered important for keeping a religious obligation and setting standards of food offered to consumers, which should be prepared, processed or manufactured in safe and hygienic conditions. These standards ensure safe consumption of food. The teachings about preserving the health of food consumers is vital for the lives of adults and young consumers.

The Christian perspective on food is not as strict as the Islamic requirements. However, different opinions exist on what food a Christian should or should not consume. Some Christians follow the guidelines on what is considered as clean and unclean foods in the Bible, in Leviticus 11: 1–46. Devoted Christians use Leviticus 11 as a yardstick when considering what food to buy. On the other hand, some Christians use Genesis 9: 3 to argue that whatever God created is food, and being strict on food is equated to conservativism. Overall, in the Bible, the books of Leviticus and Deuteronomy have the Jewish law on food (Giorda *et al.*, 2014), that some take into consideration when purchasing and consuming food. Most Christians follow the biblical counsel in 1 Corinthians 10: 31 that, 'So, whether you eat or drink . . . do it all for the glory of God'.

Overall, as with Islamic faith, Christian teachings have both direct and indirect influence on young consumers when making purchasing and consumption decisions. Also, religions that emphasise healthy eating habits such as vegetarian diets are likely to influence their followers in making decisions about the food types to buy. For example, most Seventh-day Adventists emphasise vegetarian diets compared to other Christians (Fontaine *et al.*, 2000; Choi *et al.*, 2013).

Religion and clothes-buying behaviour

Ahmed (1992) asserts that Islam as a religion advocates for modesty in choice of what to wear by its followers across all genders and ages. For instance, a tight dress that shows the contours of the torso violates the Islamic code of dressing (Ahmed, 1992). Arguably, the sitting position for Muslims with legs tucked under the body requires loose garments and would be uncomfortable for worshippers to wear tight jeans. This may explain why tight jeans have failed to get a market within the Muslim countries among the young consumers irrespective of gender because it is considered *haram* (forbidden) (Ahmed, 1992). Ahmed (1992) opines that in a consumer cultural context, the Islamic requirement of wearing loose clothes is a lifestyle that contrasts with the Western consumer culture where skin-tight clothing is the norm.

Ahmed (1992) presents the failure of blue jeans to 'catch on in Muslim countries' as an illustration of the opposition of Islam and consumerism. He further points out that:

> Islam is specific about modesty in men and women. A dress which looks best when 'skin-tight' and is intended to indicate the contours of the torso violates this injunction. Besides, the sitting prayer position, with legs tucked under the body, requires loose garments. Tight jeans would be sheer lumbar agony.
>
> *(Ahmed, 1992, p. 192)*

Islamic clothing is one aspect of modesty that reflects behaviour, manners, speech and appearance in public (Varul, 2008). A dress is considered as an aspect of a total human being that reflects the inner person's heart (Huda, 2016). Islam rules affirm that males and females become responsible and accountable for their behaviours at the age of puberty. For example, females are exclusively required to start wearing Hijab and males to wear clothes that cover between the naval and the knee.

In general, Islamic teaching on modesty is the guiding principle for men and women when choosing what to wear, irrespective of where a Muslim consumer lives, the decision on what to purchase is governed by the level of commitment to Islamic faith (Razzaque and Chaudhry, 2013). 'Wearing loose and long clothes that cover the body provides a reward and forgiveness to those who obey the principles of worshipping through modest clothing' (Quran 33: 35). Any clothing perceived offensive is not limited to Islamic faith, but also other religions prohibit the public display of male and female bodies. Such religious expectations determine the marketing efforts within certain countries when it comes to advertising other products that are considered offensive (Fam *et al.*, 2004; Hamzah *et al.*, 2014). In predominantly Muslim countries, the youth wear clothes that are considered appropriate when going for prayers at all times. Elders are always on the look out to ensure that norms for Islamic dressing are adhered to at all times by all believers. Being modelled at a young age to adhere to Islamic ways of dressing influences young consumers' choice of how they dress later in life.

Clothing/dressing in the Christian denominations is expected to be guided by the principles of simplicity and modesty to reflect the humble character of believers. From the biblical viewpoint, dressing among Christian women is not expected to be very expensive to the point of showing off and causing attention to self in public and places of worship. This expectation is reflected in 2 Timothy 2: 9, which states that women should 'dress modestly, with decency and propriety, adorning themselves, not with elaborate hairstyles or gold or pearls or expensive clothes'. Committed Christian young consumers such as women brought up under strict observance of biblical teachings follow this advice, and this influences their choices for certain products over others. For example, among the Seventh-day Adventists, jewellery and certain hairstyles are not encouraged among women, as such products could breed the vice of showing off (Kapitzke, 1995). However, the locations of believers determine the dressing requirements. For example, believers living in urban areas are believed to be more liberal in matters of dressing than their counterparts. Religious groups in collectivist cultures such as Islam, Judaism and Christianity, usually tend to dictate what is considered acceptable or prohibited behaviour and followers usually respond with strict conformity and obedience to the set rules (Iannaccone, 1995). This has implications for young consumers when making purchasing decisions that comply with the rules defined by their religious doctrines (Schiffman and Kanuk, 2009).

Another example of modesty in dressing in Christianity is found within the Catholic Church, as illustrated by Hart (2015, p. 29):

> Dear Catholic ladies, you must clearly understand that, while not all men are tempted in the same way or to the same extent, in general, bare thighs, midriffs, shoulders, and backs; low cut, sheer or see-through blouses and shirts; and dresses with long slits are all sources of temptation. Therefore, all these must all be absolutely avoided to avoid serious sin.

Such advice has an influence on what clothing devoted/strict young Catholic female consumers choose to buy.

Following fashions in dressing is contentious among young consumers in some Christian denominations. A number of them find no problem in going with the latest fashion trends, but some Christians remain cautious of fashions, as Hart (2015) has advised that those who serve God should not follow fashions.

On the other hand, Deuteronomy 22: 5 prohibits women from dressing in men's clothes and men not to dress in a garment that belongs to a woman. As in Islam, most Christian denominations expect decency and modesty in the dressing of men and women, but this remains a challenge in a number of Christian groups due to the influence on modernity and lack of strict adherence to biblical principles. Overall, globalisation and Westernisation of beliefs and some cultures through increased access to the Internet and social media has encouraged more liberal clothing choices in some hitherto conservative societies of the world.

Young consumer behaviour and education

Parents' choice of schools for their children is largely dependent on the level of religiosity (Cohen-Zada, 2006). He argues that religious parents send their children to a particular religious-based school in order to instill particular values proclaimed by a particular religion (Cohen-Zada, 2006). This observation is common within the private school education system. Cohen-Zada and Sander (2008) conclude that religion and religiosity have a significant effect on the demand for private schools. Parents play a central role in determining which school a child should attend in order to maintain values taught by the religion to which they subscribe (Saroglou et al., 2004). Basically, most young consumers have little control due to no or the limited ability to pay for themselves.

In some other situations, religion alone was not a sufficient factor in influencing the choice of a private school. For example, Cohen-Zada and Sander (2008) found that Catholic religiosity increased the demand for Catholic schools and religion had no effect on the demand of other types of private schools in the US. The same observation seems to apply to other religious denominations around the world. Additionally, households with no religion are more likely to choose non-sectarian private schools for their children.

Denessen et al. (2005) provide some reasons that explain choice of school in Denmark. Notable among them was religion of the parents and school denomination. In Muslim migrant parents, there was a strong preference for an Islamic education for children, suggesting that this posed a risk of self-segregation among the Muslim migrants.

From the Christian perspective, the purpose of education is to equip young learners with the relevant skills to serve God and the human race (Matthew 20: 26–28; Acts 16: 30–34; Acts 2: 45–47). Similarly, proper education does not put wealth creation and material consumerism as the key anchors for human existence. Yuengert (2009) argues that humans sometimes turn wealth into idols to worship instead of worshipping God. Christians are cautioned that 'material goods are "good" but they are not good absolutely; they are good only when they are placed at the service of a person's ultimate ends – life with God and in community' (Yuengert, 2009, p. 34).

It should be noted that one's religious orientation can have an influence on how he/she evaluates the relevance of education institutions. For example, the Seventh-day Adventists emphasise the need for young people to acquire a holistic education. Holistic education enables the learner to acquire skills and knowledge in spiritual, intellectual, physical and social spheres (Arego et al., 2014). The successful implementation of holistic education requires the input of different stakeholders, specifically teachers. White (1995, cited in Arego et al., 2014, pp. 95–96) recommends that 'teachers for Adventist schools should be selected from the very best class. They should be experienced Christians who are balanced in mind, men and women who have learned the lesson of self-control.' This has resulted in Seventh-day Adventists preferring to take their children to church-founded schools or other schools that to some extent embrace the philosophy of the Seventh-day Adventist church. The preference for church-based schools for education of young people is not only limited to Adventists but also other Christian denominations. This demonstrates the influence of religiosity on choices of education institutions that directly affect the young consumers.

The Christian perspectives on education, dressing and food are grounded in 1 Corinthians 10: 31, which states that 'So whether you eat or drink or whatever you do, do it all for the glory of God.' Similarly, Namanya (2015) succinctly states that:

> Christianity is moderation. Moderation in everything: how you live, what you say, what you eat, what you drink, how you dress, what you wear, car you ride, house you live in, what you use and so on. When you are in Christ, you don't show off yourself, because your self is death, you don't show your body, your riches, your pride; you show Christ and Him alone.

Sood and Nasu (1995) argue that the greater consideration of price, willingness to buy foreign brands and being less convinced by advertising messages among protestant consumers is related to the protestant beliefs that promote values such as the need to be excellent, honest and rational while at work.

Discussion

The influence of faith and religion across denominations on consumer behaviour is generally associated with the restriction on consumption of certain foods such as pork (Muslims, Jews and Seventh-day Adventists), beef (Hindus) and alcoholic beverages that are not acceptable to most religions. Varul (2008) argues that Islam markets the health benefits of the tradition of fasting during Ramadan. Islamic literature affirms that Islam as a religion purifies the soul of self-seeking, egotism, tyranny, wantonness and lack of discipline. Buying halal food is considered as obedience to the religious command and a way of expressing a chosen identity of Islamic religion (El-Bassiouny, 2016). This identity is collective and to some extent individual and transcends the immediate existence and location of self in a wider view (Luckmann, 1967). The young consumers cannot therefore act in isolation from what their parents' faith/religion prescribes to as guidelines for healthy living and what is collectively viewed as acceptable within a given community.

The need for a healthy lifestyle that halal food standards require, such as having food prepared in hygienic conditions, triggers the need of young consumers to favour the purchase and consumption of products or services that meet minimum basic standards as per Islamic rules and regulations (Potluri et al., 2010; Khalek, 2014). However, in some other circumstances, young consumers may be influenced by the environment they stay in (Eren, 2013). For example, staying in a country that predominantly follows Islamic faith provides no other alternatives to young consumers compared to those who live in secular countries where there is some level of flexibility (Varul, 2008).

Another factor that augments the influence of religion on young consumers' behaviour is the available alternatives on where to search for information on what to buy. Tauber (1972) argues that consumer behaviour involves activities of shopping, buying and consuming. Shoppers tend to be categorised into: economic, where price is central to decisions to purchase; personalising, where consumers consider shopping as an opportunity to interact with other consumers; and apathetic consumers, who shop only out of necessity. Depending on the type of the consumer, different sources are available such as online shopping sites that provide some level of privacy and can facilitate buying and consumption of goods considered offensive to religion such as alcohol consumption in Islamic countries (Nazlida and Mizerski, 2010; Sukhwal and Suman, 2013).

Another area where religious rules determine what to consume (such as food and wearing of certain clothing) is in businesses licensed to serve or provide services in private. For instance, if a group of young consumers are exploring a destination for holiday, they would choose destinations where rules that restrict their freedom to wear jeans and consumption of certain foods is permissible, and not considered as offensive (Eid and El-Gohary, 2015). In countries where there is no firm control of religious rules, such as in Western countries, individual conscience prevails. In such countries young consumers evaluate the available alternatives and their faith/religion becomes relevant when making the final purchasing decision (Charseatd, 2016; Vai et al., 2016). To some extent the young consumers would be bothered about ethical consumption and remaining faithful to their religion where parents and other fellow believers are not present or not involved in making purchasing decisions (Essoo and Dibb, 2004; Ritchie, 2011; Bakar et al., 2013; Mathras et al., 2016).

Whereas people belonging to the same age group differ in many ways, and tend to share a set of values and common cultural experiences. Religious subcultures have been shown to exert an impact on consumer variables such as personality, attitudes towards sexuality, birth rates and household formation, income and political attitude (Delener, 1990; Solomon et al., 2006). All these aspects of life influence consumer behaviour on what to purchase and consume.

Socialisation occurs largely within the family setting and religion has traditionally guided the norms and values on which attitude and other behaviours are based. In some cases, family and religion are inseparable and exert considerable influence on the members and traditional aspects of behaviour manifestations are dominant during decision-making by any member regardless of gender and age (Pargament and Hahn, 1986).

Conclusion

Although the literature provides evidence of the impact of religion on consumer behaviour in general, little is dedicated to how religion influences young consumers' behaviour. We argue that since children and teenagers grow and are nurtured by adults, who already profess a given religion/faith, the influence by the adults can be immense. The adult influence on young people can have a direct and indirect effect on their purchasing decisions. This influence is especially predominant in decision-making concerning what to eat, wear and from where they choose to go for further studies when they are in a position to make their own independent decisions as adults. Religion therefore has a direct and subconscious influence on young consumers' ability to make various marketing related decisions.

The more religiously involved individuals are, irrespective of religion or faith, the more the predisposition they have to portray behaviours that influence decisions when choosing food, clothing and schooling for their children (Muhamad and Mizerski, 2010). However, it should be noted that tension exits between religion and globalisation. For example, Lehmann (2002) argues that globalisation flattens out cultural differences, erodes local customs and beliefs and spreads a secular, capitalist way of life that is at odds with most religions.

The growth of online marketing where producers of products and services are in direct contact with consumers in private has had tremendous influence on young consumers who are technologically adept. However, religion has to some extent remained a strong force that keeps check on the effects of globalisation on societies throughout the world. It is noteworthy to conclude that the relationship between religion and globalisation is antagonistic and will remain one of struggle and conflict for some time and continue to have formidable influence on marketing efforts. The exposure of children to information from various contexts will continue to have influence on the ability of religion to have a lasting influence on their consumption behaviour, such as food, clothing and education choices.

The discussion points raised in this chapter have both marketing and practical implications. The recognition that religion still has influence on consumer behaviour and individuals at all stages of life cannot be overlooked by both manufacturers and marketing organisations. Policies aimed at regulating consumption of certain products such as food, clothing and education in certain countries should acknowledge that some issues of faith and religion are part and parcel of human life and must be recognised at all times.

References

Ahmed, A. S. (1992). *Postmodernism and Islam: Predicament and promise*. London: Routledge.

Alam, S. S., Mohd, R. and Hisham, B. (2011). Is religiosity an important determinant on Muslim consumer behaviour in Malaysia? *Journal of Islamic Marketing*, 2(1), 83–96.

Arego, S., Role, E. and Makewa, L. N. (2014). Factor influences in the implementation of adventist wholistic education in Mara Conference, Tanzania. *International Journal of Humanities and Social Science*, 4(1), 38–49.

Bakar, A., Lee, R. and Rungie, C. (2013). The effects of religious symbols in product packaging on Muslim consumer responses. *Australasian Marketing Journal*, 21(3), 198–204.

Beekun, R. I. and Badai, J. (2005). Balancing ethical responsibility among multiple organizational stakeholders: The Islamic perspective. *Journal of Business Ethics*, 60, 131–145.

Charseatd, P. (2016). Role of religious beliefs in blood donation behavior among the youngsters in Iran: A theory of planned behavior perspective. *Journal of Islamic Marketing*, 7(3), 250–263.

Choi, Y., Paulraj, A. and Shin, J. (2013). Religion or religiosity: Which is the culprit for consumer switching behavior? *Journal of International Consumer Marketing*, 24(4), 262–280.

Cohen-Zada, D. (2006). Preserving religious identity through education: Economic analysis and evidence from the US. *Journal of Urban Economics* 60, 372–398.

Cohen-Zada, D. and Sander, W. (2008). Religion, religiosity and private school choice: Implications for estimating the effectiveness of private schools. *Journal of Urban Economics*, *64*, 85–100.

Dekhi, F., Boulebech, H. and Bouslama, N. (2017). The effect of religiosity on luxuary consumer behaviour. The case of the Tunisian Muslim. *Journal of Islamic Marketing*, *8*(1), 1–27.

Delener, N. (1990). The effect of religious factors on perceived risk in durable goods purchase decisions. *Journal of Consumer Marketing*, 7(Summer), 27–38.

Delener, N. (1994). Religious contrasts in consumer decision behaviour patterns: Their dimensions and marketing implications. *European Journal of Marketing*, *28*(5), 36–53.

Denessen, E., Driessena, G. and Sleegers, P. (2005). Segregation by choice? A study of group-specific reasons for school choice. *Journal of Education Policy*, *20*(3), 347–368.

Eid, R. and El-Gohary, H. (2015). The role of Islamic religiosity on the relationship between perceived value and tourist satisfaction. *Tourism Management*, *46*, 477–488.

El-Bassiouny, N. (2016). Where is 'Islamic marketing' heading? *Journal of Business Research*, *69*(2), 569–578.

Eren, S. S. (2013). Young consumers' attitudes toward American products. *Procedia – Social and Behavioral Sciences*, *99*, 489–495.

Essoo, N. and Dibb, S. (2004). Religious influences on shopping behavior: An exploratory study. *Journal of Marketing Management*, *20*(7/8), 683–712.

Fam, K. S., Waller, D. S. and Erdogan, B. Z. (2004). The influence of religion on attitudes towards the advertising of controversial products. *European Journal of Marketing*, *38*(5/6), 537–555.

Fontaine, R. J., Duriez, B., Luyten, P., Corveleyn, Z. and Hutsebaut, D. (2005). Consequences of a multidimensional approach to religion for the relationship between religiosity and value priorities. *International Journal for the Psychology of Religion*, *15*(2), 123–143.

Fontaine, R. J., Luyten, P. and Corveleyn, J. (2000). Tell me what you believe and I'll tell you what you want: Empirical evidence for discriminating value patterns of five types of religiosity. *International Journal for the Psychology of Religion*, *10*(2), 65–84.

Giorda, M. C., Bossi, L. and Messina, E. (2014). *Food and religion (in public food service)*. Italy: Consorzio Ristecon.

Global Halal Food Market. (2011). *The global Halal industry: An overview*. http://gifr.net/gifr2013/ch_13.PDF (accessed 21 March 2017).

Global Islamic Economy Report. (2015/2016). *State of the global Islamic economy report 2015/16*. www.iedcdubai.ae/assets/uploads/files/global_islamic_report_1443601512.pdf (accessed 21 March 2017).

Hamdan, H., Issa, Z. M., Abu, N. and Jusoff, K. (2013). Purchasing decisions among Muslim consumers of processed halal food products. *Journal of Food Products Marketing*, *19*(1), 54–61.

Hamzah, S. R., Suandi, T., Hamzah, A. and Tamam, E. (2014). The influence of religiosity, parental and peer attachment on hedonistic behavior among Malaysian youth. *Procedia – Social and Behavioral Sciences*, *122*, 393–397.

Hart, R. T. (2015). Attention Catholics: Helpful reminders for Catholics living in modern confusion. http://sicutincaelo.org/downloads/AC_Read.pdf (accessed 21 March 2017).

Hassan, W. M. (2007). Globalising halal standards: Issues and challenges. *The Halal Journal*, July–August, 38–40.

Hawkins, D. I. and Mothersbaugh, D. L. (2010). *Consumer behavior: Building marketing strategy*. New York: McGraw-Hill/Irwin.

Huda. (2016). *Islamic religious clothing requirements*. http://islam.about.com/od/dress/p/clothing_reqs.htm (accessed 22 January 2017).

Iannaccone, L. R. (1995). Risk, rationality and religious portfolios. *Economic Inquiry*, *33*, 285–295.

The International Trade Centre (ITC). (2015). From niche to mainstream: Halal goes global. www.intracen.org/uploadedFiles/intracenorg/Content/Publications/Halal_Goes_Global-web%281%29.pdf (accessed 21 March 2017).

Izberk-Bilgin, E. (2012). Infidel brands: Unveiling alternative meanings of global brands at the nexus of globalization, consumer culture, and Islamism. *Journal of Consumer Research*, *39*(4), 663–687.

James, W. (1902/2004). *The varieties of religious experience*. New York: Touchstone.

Kamil, I., Zainol, B. and Ram, A. S. (2012). Islamic religiosity measurement and its relationship with business income zakat compliance behavior. *Journal Pengurusan*, *34*, 3–10.

Kapitzke, C. (1995). *Literacy and religion: The textual politics and practices of Seventh-Day Adventism*. Amsterdam/Philadelphia: John Benjamins.

Khalek, A. A. (2014). Young consumers' attitude towards Halal food outlets and JAKIM's Halal certification in Malaysia. *Procedia – Social and Behavioral Sciences*, *121*(September), 26–34.

Lehmann, D. (2002). Religion and globalisation. In L. Woodhead, P. Fletcher, H. Kawanami and D. Smith (eds), *Religions in the modern world: Traditions and transformations* (pp. 348–366). London/New York: Routledge.

Luckmann, T. (1967). *The invisible religion: The problem of religion in modern society*. New York: Macmillan.

Mathras, D., Cohen, A. B., Mandel, N. and Mick, D. G. (2016). The effects of religion on consumer behavior: A conceptual framework and research agenda. *Journal of Consumer Psychology*, *26*(2), 298–311.

Muhamad, N. and Mizerski, D. (2010). The constructs mediating religions' influence on buyers and consumers. *Journal of Islamic Marketing*, *1*(2), 124–135.

Namanya, A. A. (2015). How men and women should dress in Christianity. www.linkedin.com/pulse/how-women-men-should-dress-christianity-asanasio-asher-namanya (accessed 21 March 2017).

Nazlida, M. H. and Mizerski, D. (2010). Exploring Muslim consumers' information sources for fatwa rulings on products and behaviors. *Journal of Islamic Marketing*, *1*(1), 37–50.

Pargament, K. T. and Hahn, J. (1986). God and the just world: Causal and coping attributes in the health situations. *Journal for Scientific Study of Religion*, *25*, 193–207.

Pew Research Center. (2011). *The future of the global muslim population*. www.pewforum.org/2011/01/27/the-future-of-the-global-muslim-population/ (accessed 21 March 2017).

Potluri, R., Pool, G. R. and Tatinbekovna, S. (2010). Young Kazakhstan consumers: Catch them if you can. *Young Consumers*, *11*(1), 47–56.

Razzaque, M. A. and Chaudhry, S. N. (2013). Religiosity and Muslim consumers decision-making process in a non-Muslim society. *Journal of Islamic Marketing*, *4*(2), 198–217.

Ritchie, C. (2011). Young adult interaction with wine in the UK. *International Journal of Contemporary Hospitality Management*, *23*(1), 99–114.

Saroglou, V., Delpierre, V. and Dernelle, R. (2004). Values and religiosity: A meta-analysis of studies using Schwartz's model. *Personality and Individual Differences*, *37*(4), 721–734.

Schiffman, L. G. and Kanuk, L. L. (2009). *Consumer behavior*. Harlow: Pearson Education.

Schwartz, S. H. and Huismans, S. (1995). Value priorities and religiosity in four Western religions. *Social Psychology Quarterly*, *58*, 88–107.

Shah, S., Rohani, A., Hisham, M. B., Alam, S. S., Mohd, R. and Hisham, B. (2011). Is religiosity an important determinant on Muslim consumer behaviour in Malaysia? *Journal of Islamic Marketing*, 2(1), 83–96.

Siala, H. (2013). Religious influences on consumers' high-involvement purchasing decisions. *Journal of Services Marketing*, 27(7), 579–589.

Solomon, M., Bamossy, G., Askegaard, S. and Hogg, M. (2006). *Consumer behaviour: A European perspective* (3rd edn). Upper Saddle River, NJ: Prentice Hall.

Sood, J. and Nasu, Y. (1995). Religiosity and nationality: An exploratory study of their effect on consumer behaviour in Japan and the United States. *Journal of Business Research*, 34(34), 1–9.

Sukhwal, M. and Suman, L. N. (2013). Spirituality, religiosity and alcohol related beliefs among college students. *Asian Journal of Psychiatry*, 6(1), 66–70.

Tauber, E. (1972). Marketing notes and communications: Why do people shop? *Journal of Marketing*, 36, 46–59.

Vai, N. M., Leong, S., Mizerski, D., Muhamad, N. and Leong, V. S. (2016). Consumer knowledge and religious rulings on products: Young Muslim consumer's perspective. *Journal of Islamic Marketing*, 7(1), 74–94.

Varul, M. Z. (2008). After heroism: Religion versus consumerism. Preliminaries for an investigation of Protestantism and Islam under consumer culture. *Islam and Christian Muslim Relations*, 19(2), 237–255.

White, E. G. (1995). *Pastoral ministry*. Silver Spring, MD: The Ministerial Association.

Yuengert, A. M. (2009). Elements of a Christian critique of consumer theory. *Faith and Economics*, 54, 31–56.

19
CHILDREN'S CONSUMER BEHAVIOUR IN DEVELOPING COUNTRIES IN THE TWENTY-FIRST CENTURY

Ndivhuho Tshikovhi and Richard Shambare

Introduction

Consumption is a universal phenomenon; it permeates virtually all aspects of society. Irrespective of our status, age, gender, lifestyle or nationality, we consume one product or another (Gbadamosi, 2016, p. 1). These consumption decisions are linked to the values we derive from being members of the society and environment; these shape our needs and our decisions. Consumer behaviour is a discipline in the social sciences, which deals with why consumers buy, or do not buy, products or services. Solomon *et al.* (2013, p. 15) define consumer behaviour as the study of the processes involved when individuals or groups select, purchase, use or dispose of products, services, ideas or experiences to satisfy needs and desires. Consumers are all different in many ways demographically, emotionally, culturally or in other ways – hence they act differently to the same stimulus (Calvert, 2008; Gbadamosi, 2016). The shift to a modern lifestyle and globalisation in the twenty-first century has made massive contribution to the children's consumer behaviour phenomenon in developing countries. Although the term 'developing countries' has received several backlashes recently, it is still commonly used to define countries with low income per capita of population. Akam and Muller (2013, as cited by Gbadamosi, 2016) similarly define developing countries as nations characterised by a lower stage of development compared to industrialised countries in terms of economy, politics and sociocultural issues (Ogbah, 2011).

Consumer behaviour, despite age, race or gender involves the psychological processes that consumers go through in recognising needs, finding ways to solve these needs, making purchase decisions (e.g. whether to purchase a product or not and, if so, which brand and where), interpret information, make plans and implement these plans (e.g. by engaging in comparison shopping or actually purchasing a product). Several steps take place during consumers' decision-making processes.

The first is *problem recognition*, when you realise that something is not as it should be; perhaps, for example, your car is getting more difficult to start and is not accelerating well. The second step is *information search*, when you ask yourself a question like: what are some alternative ways of solving the problem? In addressing this, you might buy a new car or used car, or take your car in for repair, ride the bus, take a taxi or ride a skateboard to work. The third step involves an *evaluation of alternatives*. A consumer, therefore, after identifying alternatives will not assess them. A skateboard, for example, is inexpensive, but may be ill-suited for long distances and for rainy days. Finally, we have the *purchase* stage and sometimes a *post-purchase* stage (e.g. you return a product to the store because you did not find it satisfactory). In reality, people may go back and forth between the stages. Therefore, a person may resume alternative identification while evaluating already known alternatives.

Consumer behaviours vary greatly from country to country. Even when looking at the most developed countries, children's consumer behaviour, as a phenomenon has not been fully explored, as it is highly individualistic due to any number of reasons, including cultural beliefs, education level and economic situations. Consumer behaviour is largely dependent on cultural factors consisting of mutually shared operating procedures, unstated assumptions, tools, norms, values, standards for perceiving, believing, evaluating and communicating (Marsiglia, 2010). Globalisation has brought the world closer to each other in many ways, however, the behaviour of consumers, particularly children in developing countries is a subject yet to be fully explored in consumer behaviour literature. It is against this background that this chapter explores children's consumer behaviour in developing countries in the twenty-first century.

The purpose of the chapter

In this chapter, it is argued that children's consumer behaviour is an important branch of marketing in general and consumer behaviour specifically. Increased levels of debates and discourse into children's consumer behaviour in developing countries are needed. For this reason, the purpose of this chapter is to discuss children's consumer behaviour in developing countries in mainstream research in the field of consumer behaviour. Second, the chapter promotes the argument that issues such as consumers' age, the Internet, globalisation, culture and parenting styles, result in a distinct form of consumer behaviour in the developed world. In this regard, several effects of these characterisations on consumer actions are presented.

To achieve these objectives, this chapter is structured into four sections. The next section presents the idea of children as consumers from an early age, discusses the theoretical dimensions of children's consumer behaviour and elaborates on the various typologies of consumer behaviour relevant to emerging economies. Lastly, to encourage future deliberations into the phenomenon, some areas for further research on children's consumer behaviour are proposed.

Children as consumers

Parents are responsible for raising their children with a character strong enough to stand up to the complexity of modern life, and for teaching them the behaviour and values required for making economic decisions. The gradually increasing role of children in a consumption economy means that their training to be 'conscious' consumers – developing responsible buying behaviour – should be considered at an early age (Gbadamosi, 2016). Interactions between individuals, especially communication within the family, have an influence on how children learn to be consumers. The family influences the models of behaviour for a child within and outside the family and also influences the consumption behaviour of the children, specifically with respect to products, the decision-making processes and consumers' characteristics. Children in the twenty-first century are fast becoming economically, sociologically and psychologically aware of their needs at an early age as opposed to that of previous years. This fact can be diagrammatically presented as shown in Figure 19.1.

Economically, children have various demands and a certain purchasing power to satisfy such demands. Psychologically, children have needs and they are capable of reflecting such needs in the market. Sociologically, children are consumers who perform a set of collective activities, defined as consumer roles, and they are expected to show a natural development in line with other social characteristics, as they grow older. Commercially, children are consumers who plan purchasing activities, who collect pre-purchase information, who realise the purchase activity, who usually spend their own allowances and who make the after-purchase evaluation. Previous studies such as those by Cristea *et al.* (2014) and Ali *et al.* (2012) have demonstrated that children play an active role in consumption: the children who assume the role of consumer at the age of 4–5 years begin to become conscious consumers at the age of 9–10 years and take their place in society as full consumers at around 12 years of age.

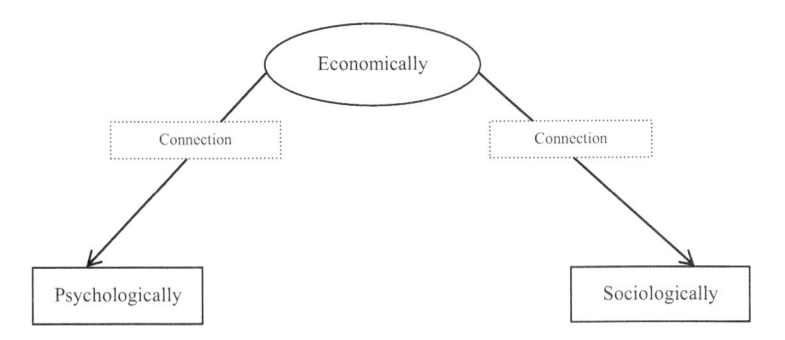

FIGURE 19.1 Economical, psychological and sociological demands

Source: Author.

Gerber and Bothma (2008) argue that in South Africa young consumers spend most of their money on clothes, magazines, CDs and entertainment. Furthermore, the study found that children have a big influence on the products their parents buy, so, for example, parents will buy breakfast food because it has a toy, or sweets in it, or buy magazines with Barbie or Superman on the cover. In developing countries, however, marketers tend to focus on children as consumers as dictated by social or family income differences (Cassim, 2010). For example, in South Africa, stores such as Pep and Shoprite mainly advertise their products with a specific focus on children from lower-income households. According to Gerber and Bothma (2008), in South Africa children as consumers are also affected by their ethnic groups. For example, advertisements targeting black children will be on the television channel South African Broadcasting Corporation (SABC), SABC 1 and SABC 3, whereas on SABC 2 one is likely to find advertisements targeted at white children.

Societal implications of household influences on children

Household influences may have a stabilising effect on children's views of and interaction with society, especially when the parents are either authoritarian, with high control over children; democratic, with balanced control over children; or permissive, with little control over children. These parental types tend to closely influence children's activities and exercise varying degrees of control over their children's purchases and preferred advertising (Assael, 2004). Advertising for children has been a subject of close scrutiny for years due to the possibility of advertisement material that is harmful to the young consumers.

Brucks et al. (1988) suggests that advertising to children involves four major issues:

- Is advertising to children inherently unfair?
- Does advertising to children cause them to make poor consumer choices?
- Is parent–child conflict increased because of advertising to children?
- Does advertising have a negative effect on children's socialisation?

These issues appear to be mitigated when parents help children to understand advertisement's boundaries of reality in addition to teaching children the realities of making sound economic decisions such as considering opportunity costs. Brucks et al.'s (1988), school of thought resonates today, particularly in developing countries.

Realisation of children's consumer behaviour

Early research on children's consumer behaviour has focused on the intellectual and saving-oriented forms of behavioural characteristics of child consumers in order to demonstrate the initial stages of consumer behaviour patterns (McNeal, 1979 as cited by Özgen and Gönen, 1989). Furthermore, these researchers have indicated that the concept of money is formed around the age of 5; while the receipt of a regular allowance and saving began usually at 7 years of age and by the age of 9, the child is a practising consumer. The research also demonstrated that the differences between the sexes of the children, their behaviour, knowledge and activities are related to consumer behaviour. Munn (1958) found that children between the ages of 2 and 8 years were influenced by the commercials on television intended for children their age (for example, cartoons) and these were the most effective means of advertisement. Furthermore, Munn (1958) reports that parents have also admitted that their children do influence their purchases. The research also suggested that for children from middle- and low-income levels, between the ages of 5–8 years, 78 per cent first knew of a toy from seeing it on the television and 22 per cent first knew of a toy from information from friends.

Evidently, television experience in children's formative years was found to be particularly effective in encouraging purchase decisions (Gbadamosi, 2016). This point is in agreement with Cassim (2010) who suggested that in the absence of hard data in South Africa, it is reasonable to assume that children are exposed to the media to a certain extent, but most notably television is still an accessible source of information for most parts of developing countries. African Advertising Research Foundation's (SAARF) 2003 and 2005 statistics, for example, show that among South African children aged 7 to 15, approximately 2.5 hours of television is watched per day. Children watch television well beyond the watershed time of 9 p.m. Using this information, it may be calculated that South African children are exposed to approximately 24 minutes of advertising (or 48 × 30-second commercials) per day in 2003 to 2005 (Cassim, 2010, p. 183). Children from the developing world, therefore, are already informed about what products to buy before they even leave their homes for shopping.

Family influence on children's consumption

Media, family and peers are key agents that build in children the knowledge, skills and attitudes required to function in the marketplace. The process of consumer behavioural traits starts in children while accompanying their parents to stores, shops and malls. In the beginning the children make requests for their own choices in the stores. At the age of 5, most of the children make purchases with the help of their parents, but by the age of 8 they become independent consumers (Ali *et al.*, 2012). Childers and Rao (1992) argue that children receive influence from their families based on products. They also discovered that family influence was less for publicly consumed luxury and necessity products as children learn price sensitivity and brand loyal behaviours from their parents. Family influence on children's consumer behaviour can also be associated with family status, for example, children from well-educated families are likely to perceive intent in advertisements more easily as opposed to those from less-educated families.

A study looking into consumer patterns in India and Mexico found that children from poor homes loved the advertisements but felt uncomfortable knowing that the advertisements' world was an illusion far removed from the harsh realities of their lives (Kaur and Singh, 2006). Children from wealthy homes, on the other hand, disregarded some of the propaganda in the advertisements. Children from the middle class were more deeply influenced than both the poor and rich, by the promises advertisers make (D'Silva et al., 2007). Children from a poor background, therefore, are more likely to believe that purchasing a product that will change their skin complexion within a week as advertised is likely to occur, whereas children from a rich background may question the probability of the changes happening within the prescribed period. The influence, therefore, that family background has on consumer choice and ability to purchase in countries such as South Africa, India and Mexico still plays a major role in children's consumer behaviour.

Transaction knowledge

Advertising plays an early role in the consumer socialisation of children, but so do other consumer experiences such as shopping (John, 1999). For most children, their exposure to the marketplace comes as soon as they can be accommodated as a passenger in a shopping cart at the grocery store. From this vantage point, infants and toddlers are exposed to a variety of stimuli and experiences, including aisles of products, shoppers reading labels and making decisions and the exchange of money and goods at the checkout counter. These experiences, aided by developing cognitive abilities that allow them to interpret and organise their experiences, result in an understanding of marketplace transactions. Children learn about the places where transactions take place (stores), the objects of transactions (products and brands), the procedures for enacting transactions (shopping scripts) and the value obtained in exchanging money for products (shopping skills and pricing). This set of knowledge and skills as discussed by John (1999), which we refer to here as transaction knowledge, are explored in more detail below.

Structural knowledge

Between early and middle childhood, children learn a great deal about the underlying structure of product categories. Although children learn to group or categorise items at a very early age, they shift from highly visible perceptual cues to more important underlying cues as a basis for categorising and judging similarity, or otherwise, among objects, as they grow older.

Symbolic knowledge

Middle to late childhood is also a time of greater understanding of the symbolic meanings and status accorded to certain types of products and brand names. During this time, children develop a preference for particular brands, even when the physical composition of the products is quite similar in nature.

Retail store knowledge

Children are frequent visitors to retail stores at a young age. Convenience stores, discount stores, and supermarkets are the favourites of younger children (5–9 years), while specialty stores, such as toy or sporting goods stores are favourites with older children (10–12 years).

Shopping scripts

Understanding the sequence of events involved in shopping is clearly one of the most important aspects of transaction knowledge. As noted earlier, children acquire a vast amount of experience as an observer or participant in the shopping process at very early ages.

Shopping skills

We use the term 'shopping skills' to refer to a wide array of abilities used for comparing product value prior to purchase.

Pricing knowledge

Despite the fact that children have substantial shopping skills by middle childhood, they pay relatively little attention to prices as an aspect of the marketplace. By the time children are 8 or 9 years old, they know that products have prices, know where to look for price information, and know that there are price variations among products and stores.

These elements of transactional knowledge are fundamental signals of children's exposure to consumer behaviour at an early age, irrespective of their societal status or class. In most developing countries, however, the age at which a child realises his/her transactional knowledge varies according to social background. For instance, Gbadamosi (2016) suggests that children in Asia and Africa are brought up with the understanding that only the elders know what is right for them, as a result the knowledge transfer in this case will always be bias towards what the parents decide, with minimal influence and understanding from the children.

Internet influence on consumer behaviour

Children spend increasing amounts of time online, and television has to a great extent been replaced by the Internet both as an information source and a leisure activity among youngsters. The Internet has also overtaken television as the medium for advertising in most parts of the world, and children are increasingly exposed to online marketing practices. Jourová (2016) conducted a study in an attempt to understand the impact of online marketing on children's consumer behaviour in Europe, and found the following;

Two behavioural experiments with children from 6 to 12 years old found that online marketing practices have significant effects on children's behaviour.

- The first experiment found that embedded advertisements have a subliminal effect on children – they affect children's behaviour without them being aware of it.
- The second experiment found that exposure to prompts to make in-app purchases has a significant impact on children's purchasing behaviour.

For centuries, marketers have used television as a key source for advertisements as it affords access to children at a much earlier age than other sources of advertisements can achieve. This is largely because textual learning development does not happen until many years after children get converted to regular television viewers (Kaur and Singh, 2006).

For example, a study in cross-cultural child consumers in which the researchers compared Japan, the Netherlands, the US and the UK, revealed a positive relationship between children's demands for merchandise advertised on television and the Internet (Davies, 2010). Television has long been the staple advertising media for children and youths. Children view approximately 40,000 advertisements each year (Alvy and Calvert, 2008). The products marketed to children including sugar-coated cereals, fast-food restaurants, sweets and toys have remained relatively constant over time, but marketers are now directing these same kinds of products to children online (Alvy and Calvert, 2008).

Although the kinds of products marketed to children have remained much the same, the buying power of children has increased exponentially over time. Children also shape the buying patterns of their families as argued before; from vacation choices to car purchases to meal selections, they exert tremendous power over the family pocket book (Calvert, 2003). Rapid growth in the number of television stations and online venues has also led advertisers to market directly to children and youths. Because children and youths are heavy media users and early adopters of newer technologies, therefore, media marketing and advertising campaigns using both television and newer media are efficient pathways into children's homes and lives (Roberts et al., 2005).

Although television is still the preferred medium for reaching children and youths, marketers are now also exploring how to reach this age group online using cell phones, iPods, game platforms and other digital devices (Calvert, 2008). In developing countries, however, marketers are still constrained to using hardcopy magazines or news outlets to reach their consumers, because the majority of consumers are not exposed to the newest technological devices. Children are the least expected to access information through online platforms, because, in some developing countries, the Internet is still considered a luxury and mostly unaffordable to poor and ordinary citizens (Bruegge et al., 2011).

In the developed countries, marketers are already exploring a variety of techniques to attract audiences and increase product purchases, online. Traditional marketing techniques in television commercials including repetition, branded characters, catchy and interesting production features and celebrity endorsements are still much used in developing countries (Ogbah, 2011). The theory behind the new technique is that advertising is most effective when consumers do not recognise it as advertising. All these practices are designed to create or enhance branded environments that foster user loyalty (Calvert, 2008). Table 19.1

TABLE 19.1 Television and Internet marketing techniques: definition and use patterns

Marketing technique	Definition	Used on television	Used on Internet
Repetition of the message	Repeating the same commercial message over and over	X	X
Branded characters	Popular animated characters used to sell products ranging from cereal to vacations	X	X
Attention-getting production features	Audio-visual production features such as action, sound effects and music	X	X
Animation	Visually drawn moving images	X	X
Celebrity endorsements	Popular actors, athletes and musicians are either depicted on the product itself or are shown using and approving of the product	X	X
Premiums	Small toys or products that are offered with product purchase; for example, a toy in a Happy Meal or screen savers for filling out an online survey	X	X
Product placement	Placing a product within programme content so it does not seem to be an advertisement; for example, E.T. eating the sweets Reese's Pieces	X	X
Advergames	Online video games with subtle or overt commercial messages		X
Viral marketing	The 'buzz' about a product that is spread by word of mouth		X
Tracking software and spyware	Software that makes it possible to collect data about time spent on a website		X
Online interactive agents	A virtual form of stealth advertising where robots are programmed to converse with visitors to a website to maintain and increase interest in the site and its products		X
Integrated marketing strategies	Marketing products across different media; for example, the toy in a cereal box is also a product placement in a film	X	X
Video news releases	Circulated stories to news media about a product that are broadcast as a news release	X	X

Source: Calvert (2008).

identifies and defines most television and Internet marketing strategies targeted at child consumers globally.

In summary, although television is still the dominant venue for advertising even in developing countries, marketers are exploring new ways to market to children through online media and wireless devices, often using stealth techniques whereby consumers are immersed in branded environments, frequently without knowing that they are being exposed to sophisticated marketing campaigns (Calvert, 2008). Marketers carefully analyse children's interest patterns, focusing on games for teenagers as well as communication software. Tracking these patterns provides extensive information that marketers now analyse in aggregate form, but that can, in the future, be used for one-on-one relational marketing strategies directed at specific individuals (Solomon, 2013). Ultimately, content analyses of online marketing practices reveal similar patterns. One study of children's online advergames found that sugar-coated cereals dominated those sites and that advertisers used animation to provide a perceptually interesting and enjoyable online gaming experience.

Technological advancement has in some cases replaced child-minders in full-time jobs to become observers of children in developing countries, since children have access to the Internet at home and in some cases even at school. For instance, children who do not own a smartphone in Africa can still access advertisements when playing games from their parents' smartphones (Jenyo and Soyoye, 2015). As a result, marketers have access to children through television, Internet and in some instances, even in remote areas of some developing countries such as South Africa, Limpopo Province, through radio advertisements. Limpopo Province is one of the two poorest provinces in South Africa according to Statistics South Africa (2016), and as a result the majority of its population receive information through radio. Children even imitate the voice-overs they hear on the radio advertisements. For example, children know the word 'OMO washing powder' through listening to advertisements on radio. So, although, the Internet and technological advancements have received much attention from marketers, in some parts of developing countries, radio still has a fair share of influence.

Social class in children's consumption

Social groups, although they do not come up in a formal process, are formed by individuals with a similar lifestyle. There are several features of social class. First, the behaviour of members of the social class structure, education levels, attitudes, values and communication styles are similar, and these characteristics are different from other social-class members (Hoyer and MacInnts, 1997). Generally, these groups determine their social norms without clear intent, this is apparent in most developing countries, where a gap between the rich and poor or upper- and lower-class societies prevail. Children are the direct beneficiaries of their class and find themselves being groomed to fit into classism at an early age, eventually shaping their consumer behaviour to subscribe to the social class to which they belong (Durmaz et al., 2011).

Social classes are groups who share similar values, interests and behaviours, which are relatively homogeneous and continuous. Social classes pronounce preferences in clothing, home furnishing, entertainment, gaming activities, automobiles and certain products and brands. Some marketers focus their efforts on only one social class. Social classes are also different in their choice of media. Upper-class consumers prefer books and magazines while sub-class consumers prefer television (Durmaz et al., 2011). With TV programmes, the upper-class consumers prefer news and dramas, but lower-class consumers prefer films and sport programmes. There are also language differences between social classes. Advertisers should be conversant with the language that is spoken in the social class. Therefore, marketers should apply specific communication channels and communication styles by determining the social class (Calvert, 2008).

The gap between the rich and the poor is more apparent in developing countries than developed countries. Classism persists in children in such a way that children from poor family backgrounds have negative experiences of rejected requests for new products as opposed to their counterparts from rich family backgrounds. Children become aware of their social class as early as when they are born, for example, through crying over a product and getting exactly that product, or getting close to that product, to getting no product. The rise of middle-class families in China, India and South Africa has managed to create a new wave of child consumers who are rapidly becoming consumers at an early age (Lareau, 2011).

Does exposure to advertising affect children's behaviour?

Children can also become cynical as they begin to understand the underlying persuasive messages of advertisements (Calvert, 2008). For example, sixth and eighth graders who understand more about commercial practices, such as using celebrity endorsements, are more cynical about the products. Even so, children who are repeatedly exposed to attractive messages about 'fun' products still want them, even if they are aware of advertisers' selling techniques. The implication is that even though children and adults too, for that matter, may know that something is not what it seems, that does not stop them from wanting it. Many advertisements targeted at children are for foods that are high in calories and low in nutritional value, hence concerns have been raised that food advertisements are partly to blame for children being overweight and obese (Institute of Medicine, 2006). Another purported, though rarely studied, outcome of children's commercial exposure is an increased emphasis on materialism among younger children. An American Psychological Association task force has argued that heavy advertising and marketing campaigns are leading to the sexualisation and exploitation of young girls (Durmaz et al., 2011).

A study conducted in South Africa looking into the influence of television programmes on violent behaviour found that television programmes do influence children towards crime and violence (Centerwall, 1992). Although, the programmes are not direct advertisement, the influence that television has on children is related to consumption choice (Assael, 2004; Buijzen, 2009; Bruegge et al., 2011). In developing countries, the level of advertisement effect on children's consumer behaviour depends largely on the products and affordability of the product, and, to some extent, the willingness of the parents to purchase the product. Ultimately the advertisement will grasp the attention needed, the action therefore depends on need and affordability. For example, children who see a new iPad on television or an online advertisement, might ask the parents to purchase the product, however, the parents, depending on the affordability and need, can decide whether or not to purchase the product.

Consumer attitudes

An attitude is a mental position taken towards a topic, a person or an event that influences the holder's feelings, perceptions, learning processes and subsequent behaviour (Fishbein and Ajzen, 1975). Attitudes can drive purchase decisions. A consumer holding a positive attitude towards a brand is more likely to buy it, therefore, someone who enjoys an advertisement, and other elements of marketing communications, will be more likely to purchase a product. The theory of planned behaviour (Ajzen, 1991), however, shows that there is generally a gap between attitudes and behaviour. For instance, research shows that many consumers have positive attitudes towards locally grown organic food. But barriers to purchase exist, such as the premium price, lack of availability, seasonality, lack of variety and the inconvenience associated with buying the food at farmers' markets and organic stores (McCarthy, 2016). In other words, there are high levels of interest in locally grown organic food, and this interest seems to be spreading across groups and countries, but it is a long road between concern and action.

Attitudes consist of three components: (1) affective (feelings); (2) cognitive (beliefs); and (3) behavioural (response tendencies). This model is referred to as the tri-component attitude model (Quester et al., 2014, p. 337). The affective component consists of the feelings or emotions a child has about the object. The cognitive component refers to a child's mental images, understanding and interpretations of the object or issue. The behavioural component contains an individual's intentions, actions or behaviour (see Figure 19.2).

One common sequence of events that takes place in attitude formation is: Cognitive → Affective → Behavioural (Clow and Baack, 2010). Most of the time, a child first develops an understanding of an idea or an object. In the case of marketing, this understanding revolves around the features and benefits of the product or service. These thoughts, understandings or beliefs emerge from exposure to marketing communications or to word-of-mouth advertising, which are arguably largely practised in developing countries. The affective part of the attitude refers to the general feelings or emotions a child attaches to something. Products and services can generate an emotional reaction. Decisions and action tendencies are the behavioural parts of attitudes.

```
Cognitive  →  Affective  →  Behavioural

Affective  →  Behavioural  →  Cognitive

Behavioural  →  Cognitive  →  Affective
```

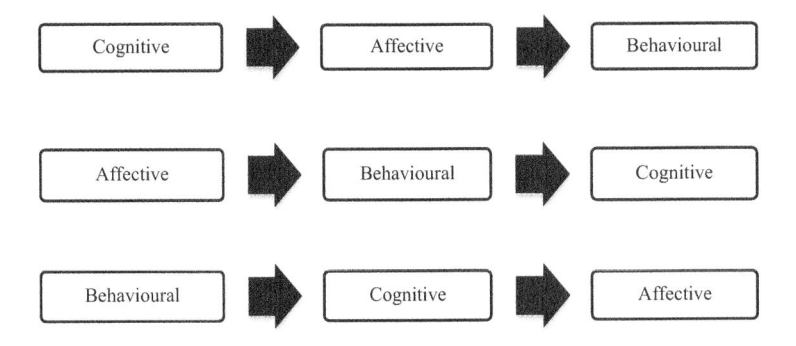

FIGURE 19.2 Development of attitudes: alternative models

Source: McCarthy (2016).

Attitudes, however, develop in other ways. An alternative process is: Affective → Behavioural → Cognitive (McCarthy, 2016). Marketing communications can first appeal to the emotions or feelings held by consumers in order to move them to 'like' a product and purchase it (the behavioural component). Cognitive understanding of the product comes after the purchase. Some attitudes result from a third combination of the components, as follows: Behavioural → Cognitive → Affective (Clow and Baack, 2010). Purchases that require little thought, have a low price, or do not demand any emotional investment might follow this path. Children in the twenty-first century find themselves confronted with this dilemma of developing attitudes towards a product or service based on its marketing exposure.

Consumer attitude in developing countries is still attributed to an individual's level of education, wealth and social class. Children depend on their parents to make sense of the world, therefore, the attitude towards a product or advertisement can be influenced by the learned behaviour of the parents. Gbadamosi (2016) suggests that in developing countries, parenting is still largely traditional, whereby parents tell the children what to do and what to buy, as opposed to in the developed countries. Therefore, children's customer attitude in developing countries will be influenced by the level of parents' willingness to decentralise decision-making on product purchases.

Cognitive development theory

Cognitive development theory has been identified as one of the theories that apply when studying children's behaviour. Piaget's theory of cognitive development provides relevant insights into children's understanding of consumables. Despite technological influence over the years, children still realise the four stages of cognitive development as described by Piaget (1971). Cognitive development theory focuses on child's development in terms of information processing, conceptual resources, perceptual skill, language learning, aspects of brain development and cognitive psychology as compared to an adult's point of view (see Table 19.2). In the developing world, researchers have also relied on this theory to further explore consumer behaviour of children in the twenty-first century (c.f. Kaur and Singh, 2006; D'Silva et al. 2007; Ali et al., 2012).

Alvy and Calvert (2008) argue that children below the age of 8 years old believe that the purpose of commercials is to help them in their purchasing decisions; they are unaware that commercials are designed to persuade them to buy specific products. The shifts that take place in children's understanding of commercial intent are best explained using these theories of cognitive development, as shown above. During the stage of preoperational thought, roughly from age 2–7, young children are perceptually bound and focus on properties such as how a product looks. Young children also use animistic thinking, believing that imaginary events and characters can be real. For instance, during the Christmas season, television is flooded with commercials that foster an interest in the toys that Santa will bring in his sleigh pulled by a flying reindeer. Young children 'buy in' to these fantasies and the consumer culture they represent. Preoperational modes of thought put young children at a distinct disadvantage in understanding commercial intent and, thus, in being able to make informed decisions about requests and purchases of products (Valkenburg and Cantor, 2002).

With the advent of concrete operational thought, between age 7 and 11, children begin to understand their world more realistically. They understand, for example, that perceptual manipulations do not change the underlying properties of objects. More importantly, they begin to go beyond the information given in a commercial and grasp that the intent of advertisers is to sell products. By the stage of formal operational thought, about age 12 and upward, adolescents can

TABLE 19.2 Theory of cognitive development

Stages	Age range	Description
Sensorimotor	Birth–2 years	Identifies object performance, the object still exists when out of sight
		Recognition of ability to control object and acts intentionally
Preoperational	2–7 years	Begins to use language
		Egocentric thinking difficulty seeing things from other viewpoints
		Classified objects by single feature, i.e. colour
Concrete operational	7–11 years	Logical thinking
		Recognises conversation of numbers, mass and weight
		Classifies objects by several features and can place them in order
Formal operational	11 years onward	Logical thinking about abstract propositions
		Concerned with the hypothetical and the future
		Create hypotheses and test

Source: Piaget (1971).

reason abstractly and understand the motives of advertisers even to the point of growing cynical about advertising. Fewer theories address the ways in which commercial messages influence children in interactive media exchanges. Research on how children learn from interactive media builds on developmental theories such as those of Jean Piaget, who argued that knowledge is constructed through interactions between the knower and the known.

Although such interactions do occur as children view television and movies, including advertisements, they are different in the newer interactive technologies, which allow for greater user control and interchanges. Interactive technologies are based on dialogue and turn-taking; a child takes a turn, then a computer responds and takes a turn, then the child takes a turn again. In essence, a conversation is taking place in which each response made by a child leads to potentially different content being shared (Calvert, 2008). Learning takes place through contingent replies, responsiveness to the user, and turn-taking; tools that can enhance learning in any kind of interaction, whether human or simulated with intelligent artificial agents. The nature of the conversation that can take place, however, depends on the child's developmental level. For instance, children under age 8 may well believe that they are really interacting with branded characters while older youth understand the differences between what is real and what is imaginary.

The trend towards increased advertising online makes children more vulnerable to marketing. Once a television viewer watches an advertisement, that viewer must act on the message if a product purchase is to occur. That action can involve multiple steps: requesting the product from a parent, pulling it from a shelf while shopping with a parent and making a purchase. The delay between seeing an advertisement and being in a store where the product can be purchased is also a potential disruption to a purchase. By contrast, newer interactive interfaces involve a user directly in the content; actions can range from clicking on a television icon to transport a child directly to a website where he can purchase the advertised product, to having a mobile phone elicit purchase-oriented behaviours (Alvy and Calvert, 2008). In newer technologies, the distinctions between the commercial and programme content can be blurred in a seamless presentation. The time between being exposed to the product and purchasing it can also be greatly diminished. These changes have major implications for children, who are more vulnerable to commercial messages than adults are, despite these children's social background.

Consumer behaviour education

Since children are the future of a society, due consideration should inevitably be given to the subject of consumption, in the preparation of an education programme intended for their specific needs and interests. Education of schoolchildren should involve accumulation of knowledge related to consumption and information on the responsibilities of consumers, to help them to become responsible adults. Parents can be involved in their children's television viewing in three ways – in co-viewing, parents simply watch programmes with their children without discussing content; in active mediation (also called instructive guidance), parents discuss the programme with their children to help them understand the content or the intent of advertisements; in restrictive mediation, parents control the amount or kind of content that their children view.

The gap between the challenges of the market and the development of consumer literacy in children has increasingly raised questions: Under which circumstances do children need the protection of the law? What can help them acquire the skills to use the market offerings according to their own needs and objectives (Mau *et al.*, 2014). Frequently, policy makers and caregivers refer to a need for an improvement of children's market knowledge as a key to bridging the gap between the challenges of the market and the development of consumer literacy. The assumption behind this proposition is often that children can react as competent consumers if they understand the mechanisms of the market and are aware of persuasive attempts by retailers and manufacturers. Especially with a view to protecting children from undesired effects of advertising, this strategy seems to be prominent while other more restrictive strategies seem to be less suitable for protecting children (Buijzen, 2009).

There is a general sense of lack of customer education among parents in developing countries, which ultimately translates to children not being informed about the risks that come with twenty-first-century consumer behaviour.

The need for further research

A literature analysis on children's consumer behaviour in developing countries remains a quest in the field of consumer behaviour research. Below are proposed areas for future research on this phenomenon.

- Are there any barriers that traditions and modern-day lifestyles have on children's consumer behaviour in developing countries?
- Has the Internet posed security and health threats to children's well-being, as consumers?
- How do TV commercials and in-store experiences influence children's consumer behaviour?
- Do children depend on upon commercial sources rather than interpersonal sources in order to find out about new products?
- In addition to the perceived importance to food purchase of interpersonal influences (i.e. recommendation from parents and peers) what else could be an influence on children?
- Are interpersonal information sources posing higher or lower credibility to commercial sources as the most reliable source of information for children in developing countries?

- Are positive attitudes to and the desire for advertised food products significantly related to the children's level of exposure to the commercial environment, such as hours spent on watching TV and playing games online as well as the amount of attention paid to advertisements?
- Does gender difference have any effect upon children's consumer socialisation?

Conclusion

Marketing to children has become a way of life in the twenty-first century worldwide, which in turn influences children's consumer behaviour from all walks of life. Children from higher- and middle-class families in developing countries have both their own disposable income and influence over what their parents buy, and marketers attempt to determine how that money should be spent. Television now reaps most of the advertising revenue, but the Internet has been providing new ways for marketers to reach children in recent years. Marketing practices such as repetition, branded environments and free prizes are effective in attracting children's attention, making products stay in their memory and influencing their purchasing choices. Immature cognitive development, however, limits the ability of children, younger than 8, to understand the persuasive intent of commercials; thus, public policy regulates how advertisers can interact with children via television. Online environments are now and probably always will be less heavily regulated than more traditional media. Marketing and advertising fuel the large corporate economy and the cost of that economic success requires considerable scrutiny.

In conclusion, this chapter shows that consumer behaviour of children is somewhat spontaneous from numerous elements that form their society, be it parents, classism, exposure and access to the Internet. Children learn how they must behave and what attitude they must adopt in the purchasing activities of their family. Experts think that children and young people are influenced in the decision-making and purchasing processes in which the family members are involved. The influence, however, is not unidirectional from parents to children, but family members influence each other and sometimes take purchasing decisions together. Researchers are encouraged to investigate families' buying style, their preferences and the way in which purchasing takes place in families. Decisions are not taken at random by families: they are mainly determined by the cultural heredity (i.e. values, knowledge, habits and preferences) transmitted in the family from grandparents and parents to children (Cristea *et al.*, 2014). Evidently, consumer behaviour of children is influenced by various factors, namely cultural, economic and social factors. Each society establishes different relationships and hierarchies between its members, and culture plays a crucial part in this process. In the modern and contemporary period, advertising messages have influenced the consumer behaviour of children, as well as their social behaviour. Nowadays children are encouraged to be independent, assertive, dynamic and cool. These messages with which consumers are constantly beset have brought about cultural changes and are regarded as a consumer phenomenon, typical of the Western society. This phenomenon, however, now characterises the developing countries too.

The change in economic conditions is affecting consumers' behaviour and attitudes worldwide, most notably those of children in developing countries. Marketers are forced to come up with strategies based on an understanding of their consumers in the twenty-first century. As discussed earlier in this chapter, child consumers have a variety of characteristics that define their behaviour in several different ways and there are various underlying attitudes and values that govern these changes. It is critical, therefore, for us to re-examine the children's consumer behaviour phenomenon with a particular focus on developing countries, in order to deepen our understanding and fine-tune the marketing strategies for today's children. Also, it is important to note that not all child consumers in the developing countries react to the technological changes in the same way; different child consumers have different reactions to advertisements, product choices, among other understanding.

References

Ajzen, I. (1991). The theory of planned behaviour. *Organizational Behavior and Human Decision Processes*, 50(2), 179–211.

Ali, A. Batra, D. K, Ravizhantan, N., Mustafa, Z. and Rehman, S. U. (2012). Consumer socialization of children: A conceptual framework. *International Journal of Scientific and Research Publications*, 2(1), 1–5.

Alvy, L. and Calvert, S. L. (2008). Food marketing on popular children's websites: A content analysis. *Journal of the American Dietetic Association*, 108(4), 710–713.

Assael, H. (2004). *Consumer behavior: A strategic approach*. Boston, MA: Houghton Mifflin.

Brucks, M., Armstrong, G. M. and Goldberg, M. E. (1988). Children's use of cognitive defences against television advertisement: A cognitive response approach. *Journal of Consumer Research*, 14(4), 471–482.

Bruegge, C., Ido, K., Reynolds, Serra Vallejo, T. C., Stryszowski, P. and Van Der Berg, R. (2011). *The relationship between local content, Internet development and access prices*. OECD. www.unesco.org/new/fileadmin/MULTIMEDIA/HQ/CI/CI/pdf/local_content_study.pdf (accessed 28 August 2017).

Buijzen, M. (2009). The effectiveness of parental communication in modifying the relation between food advertising and children's consumption behaviour. *British Journal of Developmental Psychology*, 27(1), 105–121.

Calvert, S. L. (2003). Future faces of selling to children. In E. L. Palmer and B. M. Young (eds), *The faces of televisual media* (pp. 347–357). London: Routledge.

Calvert, S. L. (2008). Children as consumers: Advertising and marketing. *The Future of Children*, 18(1), 205–234.

Cassim, S. B. (2010). Food and beverage marketing to children in South Africa: Mapping the terrain. *South African Journal of Children Nutrition*, 23(4), 181–185.

Centerwall, B. S. (1992). Television and violence: The scale of the problem and where to go from here. *Journal of the American Medical Association*, 267, 22–25.

Childers, T. L., Rao, A. R. (1992). The influence of familial and peer based reference groups on consumer decisions. *Journal of Consumer Research*, 19, 198–211.

Clow, K. and Baack, D. (2010). *Integrated advertising, promotion, and marketing communications*. Harlow: Pearson Education.

Cristea, A. A., Apostol, M. S. and Dosescu, T. C. (2014). The impact of mass media on consumer behaviour among children and young people. *Knowledge Horizons*, 6(3), 107–110.

Davies, M. M. (2010). *Children, media and culture*. Milton Keynes: Open University Press.

Durmaz, Y., Celik, M. and Oruc, R. (2011). The impact of cultural factors on the consumer buying behaviours examined through an empirical study. *International Journal of Business and Social Science*, 2(5), 109–114.

D'Silva, M. U., Futrell, A. and Reyes, G. V. (2007). Children's consumer behaviour in the age of globalisation: Examples from India and Mexico. *Intercultural Communication Studies*, XVI(2), 253–259.

Fishbein, M. and Ajzen, I. (1975). *Belief, attitude, intention, and behaviour: An introduction to theory and research*. Boston, MA: Addison-Wesley.

Gbadamosi, A. (2016). *Handbook of research on consumerism and buying behavior in developing nations*. Hershey, PA: IGI Global.

Gerber, K. and Bothma, N. (2008). *Consumer behaviour: FET college series level 3*. South Africa. Cape Town: Pearson Education.

Hoyer, W. D. and MacInnts, D. J. (1997). *Consumer behavior*. Boston, MA: Houghton Mifflin.

Institute of Medicine. (2006). *Food marketing to children and youth: Threat or opportunity?* Edited by J. M. McGinnis, J. A. Gootman and V. I. Kraak. Washington DC: National Academies Press.

Jenyo, G. K. and Soyoye, K. M. (2015). Online marketing and consumer purchase behaviour: A study of Nigerian firms. *British Journals of Marketing Studies*, 3(7), 1–14.

John, D. R. (1999). Consumer socialization of children: A retrospective look at twenty-five years of research. *Journal of Consumer Research*, 26, 183–213.

Jourová, V. (2016). *The impact of online marketing on children's behaviour*. European Commission: Directorate-General for Justice and Consumers.

Kaur, P. and Singh, R. (2006). Children in family purchase decision making in India and the West: A review. *Academy of Marketing Science Review*, 8, 1–30.

Lareau, A. (2011). *Unequal childhoods: Class, race and family life*. Berkeley, CA: University of California Press.

McCarthy, B. (2016). *Consumer behaviour and PR* (1st edn). Bookbon.com.

McNeal, J. (1965). *Dimensions of consumer behaviour*. New York: Meredith.

McNeal, J. (1979). Children as consumers. *Journal of the Academy of Marketing Science*, 7, 346–359.

Marsiglia, A. J. (2010). Cultural effects on consumer behaviour. www.lead-inspire.com/Papers-Articles/Leadership-Management/Cultural%20Effects%20on%20Consumer%20Behavior%20Paper%20122610.pdf (accessed 28 August 2017).

Mau, G., Schramm-Klein, H. and Reisch, L. (2014). Consumer socialization, buying decisions, and consumer behaviour in children: Introduction to the special issue. *Journal of Consumer Policy*, 37, 155–160.

Munn, M. (1958). The effect of parental buying habits on children exposed to children's television programs. *Journal of Broadcasting*, 2(2), 253–258.

Ogbah, E. L. (2011). *Handbook of research on information communication technology policy: Trends, issues and advancements*. Nigeria: Delta State University Library.

Özgen, Ö. and Gönen, E. (1989). Consumer behaviour of children in primary school age. *Journal of Consumer Studies and Home Economics*, 13, 175–187.

Piaget, J. (1971). *The theory of stages in cognitive development*. New York: McGraw-Hill.

Quester, P., Pettigrew, S., Kopanidis, F., Rao Hill, S. and Hawkins, D. (2014). *Consumer behaviour: Implications for marketing strategy* (7th edn). North Ryde, New South Wales: McGraw Hill.

Roberts, D., Foehr, U. and Rideout, V. (2005). *Generation M: Media in the lives of 8–18-year-olds*. Menlo Park: Henry J. Kaiser Family Foundation.

SAARF. (2005). Investment and growth in the television sector for the past five years. www.saarf.co.za (accessed 28 August 2017).

Solomon, M. R., Russell-Bennett, R. and Previte, J. (2013). *Consumer behaviour buying, having, being* (3rd edn). Melbourne: Pearson.

Statistics South Africa. (2016). Community survey 2016 in Brief. www.statssa.gov.za/?page_id=1854&PPN=03-01-06&SCH=6809 (accessed 28 August 2017).

Valkenburg, P. and Cantor, J. (2002). The development of a child into a consumer. In L. S. Calvert, A. B. Jordan and R. R. Cocking (eds), *Children in the digital age: Influences of electronic media on development* (pp. 201–214). Westport, CT: Praeger.

PART V
Social marketing and consumerism

Perspectives on young consumers

20
SOCIAL MARKETING AND THE PROTECTION OF THE YOUNG CONSUMER

Chahid Fourali

Introduction

The excesses generated by an irresponsible application of the marketing principles affect all our society. However they can be most pernicious if directed at the young[1] population given that this population may not have developed the critical abilities to withstand the marketing onslaught (Surgeon General, 2012; Hastings and Domegan, 2014). This challenge is compounded by the multiplication of patchy solutions generated by an ever-increasing scientific specialism. So we have various physical, live and social sciences that, in turn, may have many sub-specialisms, and the experts in each may not look at the bigger picture of the broader and long-term effects of each of the specialist areas of studies. This problem has been recognised by many well-established researchers who are only too aware of the limitations of a too restrictive disciplinary focus. Indeed, a recent report by the Academy of Medical Science (2016), confirmed the need to combine advice from other disciplines and especially ones that support preventative measures, to promote healthier societies. The leader of its working group, Professor Anne Johnson (Riddaway, 2017) eloquently put her argument on the importance of protection of children to pre-empt future multiple health conditions (morbidities), as follows:

> We know, from research done by population scientists and epidemiologists that the kids today in our schools who are obese – and a significant fraction of children are leaving school overweight or obese – are already stacking their risks going into the future, in terms of diabetes, heart disease, cancer and so on. Those kids now, they may be 15, 16 but they're going to start getting really sick within 25 years. If you want to think about that long-term trajectory, we have to intervene now.
>
> *(Riddaway, 2017, p. 35)*

As well as highlighting the importance of addressing social problems at a very young age, the report went on to highlight the importance of capitalising on all relevant disciplines, including natural and social sciences, urban planning and the arts. Such an argument is very much the argument of social marketing, which may be termed differently to minimise unwelcome negative associations with 'commercial marketing' and demonstrate the need to capitalise on all supportive disciplines to help address the social problem at hand (Fourali, 2016b). Indeed marketing itself is very much a multi-disciplinary approach. So it is even more urgent for social marketers to highlight the multi-disciplinary nature of their enterprise.

In order to highlight the need for more awareness among professionals about the urgency and legitimacy of social marketing as a worthwhile discipline to pursue, let us first consider the purpose of marketing and contrast it with some of its alleged excesses.

Marketing has always been associated with commercial situations where its purpose, as traditionally put by the now 30-year-old CIM definition, is to 'serve needs profitably'. However, marketing should be seen more as a philosophy of understanding and serving needs irrespective of commercial value. In fact there is an adverse effect of over focusing on commercial benefit as this may align this very effective discipline with socially irresponsible practices. Consider the following question: 'Can marketing be a source of good?' Such a question may attract three types of answers (Fourali, 2016a).

Answer 1: 'Certainly not. Marketing is the cause of many of our problems.' The argument goes on to list the multiple miseries perpetrated against society throughout the world by irresponsible marketers whose primary aim is to increase the profit for their organisations. According to this view the young population is not an 'off limit' target group. Indeed among the resulting adverse impacts on the young population of such irresponsible 'professional' behaviour one may list child obesity, tooth decay, alcoholism, anorexia, smoking, etc. (we will list later some more of such social ills that social marketing managed to address effectively). Moreover, marketing has been accused of promoting a new social concept of success underpinned by greed and valuing people according to their material wealth (Lazonick, 2014). Such condition has been labelled as 'affluenza' (James, 2007).

Answer 2: 'Yes if organisations are responsible companies.' The focus here is on companies that respect what came to be known as the triple bottom line (Elkington, 1998) and how social environmental responsibilities also mean good business (Kotler, 2012; Laloux, 2014).

Answer 3: 'Yes if the powerful techniques of marketing are used for the good of mankind.' Generally speaking, marketing has been primarily associated with the above first and second responses and hardly the third one. The third answer, which reflects what came to be known as the social marketing perspective, is the subject of this chapter. It comes under the broad banner of 'societal marketing' but with the primary focus on social welfare rather than 'profit as well as social responsibility' as these two aims are not always compatible with each other (e.g. consider the tobacco industry). Social marketing is seen as a historical development following from the previous pre-marketing stages (production, product quality, selling and marketing). It is worth noting that such stages of developments have been seen in other disciplines including those advanced by Philosophers, scientists, educators, spiritual teachers and management gurus. For instance very recently Laloux (2014) argued that human organisations are in their fifth stage of development where 'wholeness' and self-management are key representatives of this stage (compared, for example, to previous stages that included management through fear, in Stage 1, or management through empowerment, in Stage 4). Although such broad views tend to suggest that the future is for a more egalitarian, self-managing society, it is worth reminding that this may be an erroneous representation of the trajectory of social organisations. Indeed the fact that Karl Marx argued the case for the Communist stage as the expected future did not make it happen. Conversely, the reality seems to show that 'more humane approaches' may be dropped in favour of more profit-making approaches to management. As theories about the future are just that (theories) it may be useful for our future leaders to look at the broader aims of business and what a happy society looks like, then work together to help fulfil that vision. Once the welfare of humans becomes non-negotiable then the aims of business become clear.

The above three answers may also be inter-dependent. For instance, a lack of social responsibility (the first answer) may lead to environmental degradation, which in turn requires more corporate social responsibility (CSR) (the second answer) and would require more social marketing initiatives. As an illustration we know that air pollution can have multiple effects on babies and children that may last all their life. Among adverse effects are premature births, birth defects, higher probability of early death; brain, respiratory and digestive problems; delayed growth and, even in adulthood, risk of heart disease and diabetes) (Ritz and Wilhelm, 2008). One might assume that public bodies and government departments would prioritise such issues for remedial action. Unfortunately experience shows that this is not always the case as recently demonstrated by ClientEarth NGO through showing that although the UK Government knows that air pollution causes 40,000 of premature deaths (and we are not mentioning the other consequences) it is dragging its feet in enforcing laws that would prevent such deaths (Thornton, 2017).

In the light of such etiological factors, social marketing becomes even more necessary to not only undertake projects to influence authorities to take action but also encourage prevention by working with affected populations.

So what is social marketing and how does it relate to the issue of consumer behaviour of the young population?

In trying to answer this question we will explain the social marketing concept, demonstrate its effectiveness and look at how it is being applied in a children context. However to start off, it may be useful to look at how this concept is both similar and different from the general concept of marketing.

What is social marketing?

As many marketers know, there is a general tendency to mistake marketing for one of its sub-areas. This seems to be another case of the fable of the blind men and the elephant where each blind man mistakes an elephant for the particular part of its anatomy (ear, leg, etc.) that they may be touching. Indeed, how many times have business people mistaken marketing (or social marketing) for 'marketing communication'? In the context of social marketing there is a significant number of academics/researchers who, not unusually, mistake social advertising for social marketing as argued by a number of authors (e.g. McDermott *et al.*, 2005; Hastings and Domegan, 2014; French and Gordon, 2015). Indeed Hastings and Domegan (2014) highlighted another confusion in the form of mistaking social marketing for 'social media marketing'. They remind us that communication (using traditional or new social media) is only a tiny part of a social marketer's effort, if the communication part is needed at all (as this will depend on the type of problem and needs being addressed). To drive their point home, they argue that such an error is the equivalent of saying that Coke domination of the drink industry is exclusively due to advertising campaigns (Hasting and Domegan, 2014) thereby overlooking the multitudes of other aspects of marketing such as marketing research, strategy or the broader dimensions of the marketing mix. Hence despite such errors, which, incidentally, are also well reflected in research engine outcomes if we type the word social marketing, it is important to clearly differentiate marketing first, from commercial marketing and, second, from any part of it. Linked to this issue is obviously the need to consider renaming 'social marketing' to minimise such confusions. A number of social marketers have already suggested alternative names (Kotler, 2013; Fourali, 2016b) and the proverbial jury is still out on this.

Clearly social marketing is a relatively new science that developed, and is still closely linked to, marketing. A number of social marketers trace back the origin of the social marketing concept to a paper by Wiebe (1952) that asked whether it was possible to 'sell brotherhood like soap'. Another key milestone in the development of this discipline was an article by Kotler and Levy (1969) entitled 'Broadening the Concept of Marketing', which announced the advent of social marketing. Since then a lot of work has been carried out to develop the concept further into a separate and mature discipline, as described later.

Social marketing is different from either business-related concepts such as cause-related marketing (corporate funding of a social cause); societal marketing (responsible business practices); and pro-social marketing to promote a social cause (NSMC, 2006). The latter is similar to a promotional campaign for a social cause that is akin to 'social advertising' rather than social marketing. Social marketing is also different from activism, advocacy or lobbying (Kotler, 2013).

In order to understand social marketing it is best to contrast it with 'marketing'. To do so we will consider both a descriptive definition as well as a 'functional definition' (based on the key purpose of the discipline of marketing). Here they are (see Table 20.1):

TABLE 20.1 Comparing marketing to social marketing

	Definition (what is marketing)	Functional definition (key purpose of marketing)
Marketing	Marketing is the management process responsible for identifying, anticipating and satisfying customer requirements profitably (CIM, 2016)	Marketing's key purpose is to advance the aims of organisations (whether private, public or voluntary) by providing direction, gaining commitment and achieving sustainable results and value through identifying, anticipating and satisfying stakeholder requirements (Fourali, 2008)
Social marketing	[Social marketing is] a process that applies marketing principles and techniques to create, communicate, and deliver value in order to influence target audience behaviours that benefit society (public health, safety, the environment and communities) as well as the target audience (Kotler et al., 2006, pers. comm. reported by Smith, 2008)	To apply marketing alongside other concepts and techniques in order to influence individuals, organisations, policy makers, and decision makers to adopt and sustain behaviour that improves people's lives (Fourali, 2008)

There are many marketing definitions. The above selected definition from the Chartered Institute of Marketing, 'Marketing is the management process responsible for identifying, anticipating and satisfying customer requirements profitably' (CIM, 2016), is well established and has survived for 30 years despite some attempts to improve it. Although not perfect, it has the parsimony principle on its side as it is simple and reflects the key focus of marketing: profitable customer satisfaction. The functional definitions have become fashionable among educators as they help identify the key purpose of a discipline that, in turn, provides the main reference for identifying the various functions and sub-functions that make up the various roles of marketing professionals. In the UK such key purposes became the basis for developing the national occupational, or competence, standards that inform the professional qualifications (Fourali, 2016b). If we now consider the social marketing definitions we will note that while the focus of marketing is about achieving value and profitability through serving customer (or more broadly, stakeholders') requirements, social marketing's primary aim is about benefitting society as a whole. The other differentiating factor for social marketing is that it does not have to rely exclusively on applying the marketing principles. Indeed the functional definition establishes this clearly through the words 'apply marketing alongside other concepts and techniques'. This point was also clearly indicated in the work of the National Social Marketing Centre (French and Blair-Stevens, 2005). Social marketing may be seen as the integration of the long-held debate about the arguments between the Sophists and Plato (Perloff, 2017) about the nature, accessibility and purpose of persuasion. The Sophists argued that anybody can learn persuasion (or in our days 'advertising') and set out to make it available to all. While Plato argued that the issues of substance, such as consequence of our actions and true justice, appear to be sacrificed in the process of focusing on how to be persuasive irrespective of whether the end message (or in our marketing speech 'the offer') is a just one. While commercial marketing starts with an identified need or want that primarily serves individual interests and then sets out to persuade its target group that its 'product' is best suited for them, good social marketing starts with what benefits society as a whole and only then sets out to convince people about it.

In the light of this key difference, social marketers argued that a number of key concepts associated with marketing need to be adjusted as shown in the next section.

Consumption versus human welfare: adjusting the conceptual tools

Given that the aim of social marketing is primarily social/human welfare, a number of concepts may need adjusting for this purpose. In particular the following need particular attention (Peattie and Peattie, 2003; French and Gordon, 2015; Fourali, 2016b):

Consumer

Although the word 'consumer' is used routinely in both social marketing and commercial marketing, clearly the meaning in the context of social marketing is different. 'Consumer' is used more in the sense of a 'client' with a vulnerability that may affect either their health (in the broadest sense), the health of those around them or, as in most cases, both. If we are particularly focusing on the younger populations then we need to differentiate between primary and secondary/intermediate targets. For instance if there is a higher level of sexually transmitted diseases (STDs) among the young populations, then a number of influential stakeholders will need targeting as well (e.g. parents, teachers, etc.).

The exchange concept

Rather than talking about customer satisfaction and profit, social marketing perhaps combines individual and social satisfaction. Additionally social marketing makes a clear difference between what the clients wants versus what s/he needs. An obese child may want a big bar of chocolate but what s/he needs is to address the obesity problem.

The concept of competition

In social marketing the competition is not between products, services or company brands. Rather they focus on the battle for attention and winning ideas and lifestyles with a view to induce sustainable attitudinal and behavioural change. Accordingly social marketers are aware that there are many messages that vie for the attention of the young population and they have to be as creative as possible to get the message across and effect a change of behaviour.

Marketing mix versus 'social marketing mix'

There are two broad approaches available to the social marketer. One approach is to adapt the traditional marketing mix to a social marketing context as shown in Table 20.2.

However, a number of social marketers have argued that the traditional marketing mix, even with adaptations, is not satisfactory. It was argued that it comes across as something that is done to the clients rather than derived consultatively to maximise relevance and trust. Consequently they suggested a number of alternatives. Among these are the following:

- 4Cs: Suggested by Lauterborn (1990) including consumer, cost, communication, convenience.
- 7Cs: Suggested by Shizumu (2003) with commodity, cost, communication, channel, corporation, consumer and circumstances.
- COM-SM model (Tapp and Spotswood, 2013): This model argued that motivation, opportunity and capability are key factors to determine the level of success of a social marketing offer.

TABLE 20.2 Marketing versus social marketing mixes

Marketing mix	Social marketing mix
Product	Social and individual value proposition (benefits versus costs) linked to lifestyle/behavioural change (e.g. eat less fatty food)
Price	Cost of involvement (including psychological cost) (for a child a cost of change of behaviour could mean embarrassment in front of peers)
Place	Accessibility of resources for life-style change (e.g. school meals options)
Promotion	Communication value proposition (e.g. for a girl, quitting smoking would lead to an attractive girl without 'ashtray odours')
People	Stakeholders' support; leading by example (e.g. use of school psychologists)
Physical evidence	Can be tangible (e.g. vaccination, nicotine patches, clinics, etc.) or intangible (service, value of idea) to support change
Processes	These should minimise efforts and reflect integrity and responsibility (e.g. recognition of signs and reference to supporting services)

- Types of encouragement (French, 2011): In this model the types of 'encouragements' could be in the form of hugging, smacking, nudging and shoving.
- Five-element model (Gordon, 2012): This model advocated focusing on five decisive dimensions to determine the adequacy of a social marketing programme. These are: (1) circumstances of the situation being faced; (2) the organisational and competition issues (stakeholders and competing challenges); (3) cost of change (or status quo); (4) process issues (programme design and theoretical backup); and (5) channels and strategies of implementation.

The above are only a few examples and as research develops new models will no doubt be offered to help maximise the success of the implementation of a social marketing programme. Further details can be gleaned from Fourali (2016b).

Despite the adjustments made by social marketers to standard marketing approaches the overall social marketing programme for change plan is not too dissimilar to a marketing approach. Perhaps the main reason for this similarity is that, like marketing, social marketing pursues a strategic approach that moves from purpose to means. Having said that, some authors argue that social marketing is more difficult than marketing because of the higher level of complexity of information that social marketers have to deal with (Fourali, 2016b).

Social marketing programme of change

Although there are different approaches in designing and implementing a social marketing programme, Fourali (2016b) argued that overall there are recurrent steps that are expected in most, if not all, social marketing programmes. After reviewing a number of studies, he derived 11 steps that should be present in every social marketing programme. These steps are presented below with a minimal adjustment consisting in positioning Step 6 (objectives) after Step 5 (target group/s). This was

TABLE 20.3 Social marketing planning steps

Social marketing step	Explanation
1. Problem identification	This is a social problem that appears to affect a significant number of people. The problem may be highlighted by government, NGOs or any pressure group that lobbies for action
2. Problem planning	At this explorative stage the social marketer aims to first develop his/her understanding of the complexity of causes of the problem and, second, identify a list of potential stakeholders that may contribute to the problem resolution
3. Develop the project purpose/ mission	At this stage the social marketer clarifies the purpose and scope of the project. This may include raising awareness, change of attitudes or change of behaviours and lifestyles. The size of the target population is also decided at this stage
4. Situation analysis/market research	At this stage an in-depth analysis of the problem at hand is undertaken with a view to understanding causes and opportunities and challenges to change

5.	Target groups	Following the previous analysis it will become clear which groups are most affected by the problem at hand and what obstacles will need addressing. Consequently a decision is taken at this stage as to the target group/s that should mostly benefit from the project
6.	Objectives	At this stage the social marketer defines the SMART objectives that need targeting and how the level of success will be measured (in the case of addressing obesity the objectives may include, e.g. exercise, diet, loss of weight by a certain deadline)
7.	The customer proposition	At this stage the social marketer focuses on designing an attractive offer to the target group/s that would be appealing enough to entice the group to exchange their existing behaviour/lifestyle for the alternative lifestyle (this clarifies the exchange principle in the form of pros and cons of change or no change). It would also be important for the design of the offer to take into account the views of significant stakeholders (including family members)
8.	Selecting a marketing mix	At this stage a marketing mix reflecting the offer is designed either in terms of the traditional marketing mix (4/7Ps) or any of the alternatives suggested by social marketers (e.g. 7Cs or COM-SM model). In this marketing mix all three dimensions of the 'product' (core, actual and augmented) are considered
9.	Implementation of the campaign	At this stage arrangements are made to put into action the marketing mix. This will involve planning the action stages, recruiting contributors, designing and testing posters to raise awareness about the programme and finally launching it at an appropriate event (taking into account resource availability as shown in the next stage)
10.	Resources	This stage is in fact relevant to all stages as the scope and effectiveness of a social marketing project is dependent on the level of support received. However, the resource issue becomes particularly relevant from Stage 9 when all types of support for the programme are needed. Accordingly the programme would welcome any support that helps achieve its aims. This may come from academics, government departments, NGOs, businesses, etc. As suggested in Step 7 above, social marketers may also need to build strong arguments for selling the programme to stakeholders (e.g. schools, employers, significant family members, etc). For instance, one argument could be 'a healthy diet means less sick absences and more energy for better results at school'
11.	Monitoring/ evaluation	This is a recurrent issue among funders of marketing, and in this case social marketing projects. It is important that social marketers demonstrate the tangible and intangible benefits of their programme with clear evidence. This means that social marketers need to establish monitoring arrangements that take into consideration before, during and after the implementation of the programme. Such arrangements are also needed to follow how the programme is doing and make adjustments as and when needed rather than wait until the end of the whole programme

Source: Based on Fourali (2016b).

undertaken as it seems to make more sense to first identify the target group/s and then determine SMART objectives.

Perhaps a simpler way of understanding social marketing is through what may be called the 3-step process (see Figure 20.1).

Figure 20.1 shows that any problem needs defining. Depending on the definition of the problem in terms of a chosen paradigm or discipline of choice (medical, psychological, social, economical, etc.) the causes and solutions would be affected by the answers. The diagram can be illustrated via a downward arrow technique that takes into consideration 'problem drinking among youth' (note the above definition of 'youth' that includes children) and may proceed as follows:

Step 1: What is the problem we are facing?

We may reasonably assume that the problem reflects some unhealthy development affecting, for example, an adolescent, his/her environment or both. In the case of problem drinking it is reasonable to assume that both individual and environmental factors are at the receiving end.

Step 2: What is causing the problem?

Again here the cause/s can be found at individual, environmental levels or both. In the case of problem drinking it is reasonable to assume that both individual and environmental factors are at play.

Step 3: How can we address the problem?

Depending on the previous diagnosis of the problem and associated paradigm, which can take the form of medical, psychological, social, economical, political, etc.

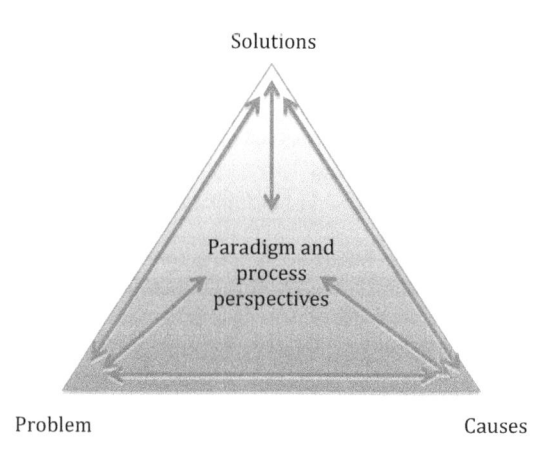

FIGURE 20.1 The 3-step process

terms, the solution will be derived accordingly. This is why we have the 'paradigm and process perspectives' intervening at the centre of the diagram. For instance if we consider a purely medical perspective, a GP addressing the symptoms caused by problem drinking, may suggest that the patient take a number of medicinal drugs to treat the problem or mitigate against the destructive factors of drinking. A GP may also suggest referral to a counsellor in cases of repeated 'relapse' or chronic problems.

A social marketer would advise that if we are to deal with, say, 'youth drug addictions' we will need to take into consideration all dimensions that could directly or indirectly affect the problem. This means that all advice from as many perspectives as possible would be considered with a view to zoom into the key causes of the problem (direct and indirect). The more multi-level/multi-disciplinary and mutually supportive are the actions, the higher the chances of success. The causes and solutions may be tangible (e.g. lack of a job, individual skills or lack of opportunity/investment by the state) or intangible (e.g. lack of information, social and psychological support such as, respectively, friends/family and the individual's values and beliefs about importance for change and ability to sustain discomfort).

Clearly, although the social marketing approach suggests a multi-level, multi-disciplinary approach to defining the problem, identifying the causes and suggesting attractive solutions, this is not always possible (due, for instance, to lack of resources). However, awareness of key influential factors may help 'recruit' decisive stakeholders in addressing the problem in the short and long term. Despite the reality of most human problems being complex, the media generally prefer simple (with one or two factor) answers. This may be partly due to a perceived need for simplifying the message, prioritising the issues at hand or political pressures in the broadest sense. However, these reasons should not divert us from being as accurate as possible as to how to represent the problem and likely solutions.

The above steps are pretty similar to a commercial marketing planning approach. This is no surprise as the effectiveness of the marketing philosophy and techniques has been demonstrated and it is strongly advisable for social marketing to be eclectic in its approach as long as such eclecticism is theoretically enlightened (Fourali, 2016b). The similarities have also been reflected in the criteria that Andreasen (2002) identifies as 'genuine social marketing' initiatives (McDermott *et al.*, 2005; NSMC, 2010). Indeed like most marketing approaches, social marketing is expected to particularly focus on *behavioural change*, supported by *consumer research*, highlighting the *exchange principle* (benefits that motivate the change of behaviour), *segmenting and targeting* specific groups and taking into account the *competition* offered by alternative behaviours. Improvements to these criteria have also been offered such as the ones by NSMC that argued for more systematic use of theoretical frameworks and a variety of methods (NSMC, 2010). The above listed steps integrate such criteria as well.

Some reviewers when they hear of a new discipline may expect a difference of approaches. For instance, after reviewing a new book on social marketing (Egan, 2016), Professor Egan expressed his disappointment that the book makes use of marketing concepts advanced by established authors, such as Kotler. It seems that such expectations assume that a new discipline means starting from a *tabula rasa* and inventing new tools from scratch. In fact this is quite unreasonable since all disciplines tend to emanate from other broader 'disciplines'. Additionally social marketing is a very young 'science' and is yet to cut-off its umbilical cord attached to marketing, if at all. After all, why should there ever be an artificial distancing between these two disciplines if several tested marketing concepts continue to serve the purpose of the social marketing projects? As the saying goes, 'If it ain't broke, don't fix it.' In the case of social marketing, if a concept is relevant and proven effective then why create a new one? Accordingly, the social marketing approach should be eclectic and make use of any conceptual tool that may help it to achieve the purpose of the project at hand. However, the approach should be a theoretically consistent eclecticism. That is an eclecticism that still needs to demonstrate the relevance of any selected tool to the overall thrust of the guiding theoretical framework. This situation is not new as other disciplines routinely make use of the concepts of adjacent disciplines, as demonstrated in the psychotherapy field where cognitive behavioural therapy (CBT) routinely borrows concepts from other counselling orientations (Fourali, 2016b). Additionally it is important to allow a good degree of flexibility to social marketing workers as, while for some workers one model may better serve their purpose, for others the model may be turned down in favour of another. Hence there is an argument for considering various conceptual tools before zooming into one. As shown above, in the section on adjustments of marketing concepts to suit the social marketing purpose, while a social marketing worker may be happy with the traditional marketing mix, another may feel the purpose may be better served by an alternative to such mix (such as 7Cs or COM-SM).

Nevertheless it is worth asking at this junction whether social marketing has fulfilled any promises as advocated by its early proponents such as Wiebe (1952). Indeed one of the mainstays of traditional marketing is its evidence-based success in helping businesses achieve their aims (Pelham, 2000; Jobber and Ellis-Chadwick, 2016). Can this be argued for social marketing? This is the subject of the next section.

Effectiveness of social marketing

Since its early days in the 1960s, social marketing has developed tremendously to become a powerful force for good. Fourali (2009) identified many areas that benefitted from social marketing (see Table 20.4) and further applications are being added.

Most of the issues listed in the table applied to different ages (i.e. including young populations) depending on which age group was considered most affected by a social ill in any particular country or region. For example Duane and Domegan (2014) studied health problems (such as obesity) of the population in Ireland and realised that among the most affected groups were the truckers (long-distance truck drivers). Consequently this group was the primary target group of a social marketing programme.

TABLE 20.4 Issues addressed by social marketing

Blinding trachoma	Physical activity
Community involvement	Racism
Diabetes	Reducing prison numbers
Doping in sport	Safe driving
Energy and water conservation	Smoking cessation (or drug abuse)
Environmental protection	Smoking in pregnancy
Fighting abuse and inequality	Social enterprise
HIV/AIDS prevention	Social exclusion
Injury prevention	Sugar-free medicine
Junk-food advertising	Suicide and domestic violence
Mental health	Transportation
Obesity	Waste prevention and recycling
Oral and bowel cancer prevention	

Source: Courtesy of Fourali (2008).

Many studies demonstrated the effectiveness of social marketing through empirical evidence. These include:

- A systematic analysis of 54 interventions associated with health issues such as smoking, drug avoidance and obesity (Stead *et al.*, 2006).
- A review of 81 case studies and 21 literature studies, which showed that the areas that mostly benefitted from social marketing projects tended to be in public health. They argued that social marketing is an ideal tool for encouraging sustainable behaviour. The study identified individual (psychological), environmental (finding synergies, involvement of leaders and champions, financial incentives, raising awareness and regulation (NESTA, 2008). More recently 22 studies (carried out by the Centre for Disease Control and Prevention) focusing on health-related products (such as child safety seats, nicotine replacement therapy and use of condoms) associated with 25 different groups demonstrated effectiveness of all campaigns in achieving the intended behaviour change (see Robinson *et al.*, 2014; Community Guide, 2015).

Given the complexity of factors associated with a social marketing programme and the challenges presented by counter activities, already in 1981 Bloom and Novelli argued that social marketing faces much bigger challenges than commercial marketers. Given the comparatively scarcer resources available to social marketing it is reasonable that social marketers will need to be more creative to maximise the effect of their programmes.

Fourali (2016b) argued that perhaps some of the key areas that could benefit from social marketing, if supported by many stakeholders, are developing citizenship and the prevention of wars. Regarding the latter, as the potential benefits of targeting such an issue are immense affecting all groups, ages and regions, despite the huge challenges, it makes such a target very promising and worthwhile pursuing. Such an issue is particularly important as the child population is among the most vulnerable to human disasters (e.g. consider the current problem of immigration from war zone areas in the Middle East that is affecting millions of children).

Given the focus of this book on the younger population, the next section will review some studies associated with this target group.

Social marketing initiatives specifically targeting the young population

There is convergence of opinion that children and teens are particularly vulnerable to advertising (Common Sense Media, 2014). Already in 2010, Rideout *et al.* (2010) estimated that children aged 8 years old and above spend about 7 hours being exposed to on-screen media information from computers, video games and handheld devices. Even children as young as 2–8 spend about 2 hours a day with screen media (Common Sense Media, 2014). These same authors note that many campaigns that cross several platforms make it difficult to estimate the degree of children's exposure to advertising. Despite recurrent support for the view that adverts do affect both preferences and consumer choices of children and youth, they recommend that more in-depth studies should be carried out to have a closer understanding of the effect of advertising on such populations. In this section we will present a number of initiatives and evaluations that demonstrate the effect of social marketing in preventing or reducing the impact of a social problem.

Diet and nutrition

It is not surprising to discover that evidence suggests that the marketing communication landscape that primarily aims to make a profit can have some seriously harmful effects on the younger population. Research (Stead *et al.*, 2006) demonstrated that food promotion affects children's food preferences and purchases (and, indirectly, those of parents as well).

This has particularly been demonstrated with the effect on poor diets (Cairns, 2012). The marketing of food products constantly makes use of evocative branded products (as done by Coca Cola and McDonald's) that exploit the younger populations' attraction towards symbolism and link it to the development of their identity through their products (Stead *et al.*, 2011). The effects are particularly significant among low-income teenagers as they tend to be more brand-loyal. Indeed research (Stead *et al.*, 2011) suggests that this group is least likely to have a healthy diet that includes fruit, vegetables or wholegrain bread. Rather they tend to go for foods that are high in sugar, fat and salt.

Substance misuse including smoking and alcohol

Several studies were undertaken highlighting the effect of social marketing on substance misuse. It is important to remember that sometimes what differentiates between the degree of uptake of a substance compared to another may be primarily due to the law of the land as opposed to the degree of harm that the substance may do to the user's body or the environment. Indeed one might argue that there is a disproportionate focus by the media on relatively benign 'events' compared to the seriously harmful effects of smoking on our society. For example, estimates suggest that 5 million people are killed globally *each year* by smoking, which relates to 1 in 10 deaths among adults worldwide (World Health Organization, 2008). Indeed there are those who argue that the issue is about freedom of mature people and so, they continue, it is important to fight against the nanny state that wants to overtake people's lives by discouraging them from smoking. Before addressing such arguments, it is worth noting that in most cases smoking is taken up very early in life. This is confirmed by a US study that suggests that 88 per cent of US smokers take up the habit before the age of 18 (and close to 100 per cent before age 21) (Surgeon General, 2012; Hastings and Domegan, 2014). The study also reveals that three-quarters of all smoking adults regret they have taken up smoking early in life and would prefer to quit but are strongly discouraged by their nicotine addiction. Among these adults, 50 per cent will become one of the 5 million casualties of smoking unless they find a way to break the habit. Once the addiction sets in the law may be quite limited when it comes to protecting its young citizens. For instance, research shows that 75 per cent of tobacconists sell tobacco to young people under the age of 18 (Gallopel-Morvan and Leroux, 2014).

The prevention of smoking

Stead *et al.* (2006) reviewed 21 studies (14 of these were school based, 5 were community based involving several variables and 1 was media based) to determine whether interventions made a difference in terms of prevention of smoking. These studies were evaluated either according to short-term or medium-term effects. Of the 21 studies that evaluated the short-term (up to 1 year) prevention initiative, 13 showed significant effects. Among the studies that evaluated the medium-term effects (over a year and up to 2 years), 7 showed significant positive effects. Hence there is a clear benefit in undertaking preventative initiative.

Alcohol prevention

Some 15 studies on alcohol prevention were reviewed (Stead *et al.*, 2006). Among these 10 were school based, 4 were community based involving several variables and 1 delivered in a family setting. Of these, 8 out of the 15 showed significant short-term, up to 1 year, positive effects. Among the 7 studies evaluated for medium-term, up to 2 years effect, 4 showed significant effects. There is a need for follow-up beyond the 2 years as some studies showed mixed effects with some interventions showing more intensity of impact while there may be some decrease of effect for others.

Illicit drugs

Some 13 studies examined the effect of intervention on illicit drug taking. Of these, 12 (mainly school-based programmes) showed short-term impact and of the 6 that examined the medium-term impact 2 reported significant effects. The studies highlighted challenges in sustaining a long-term impact.

Fighting obesity

A study by Gracia-Marco *et al.* (2011) studied the effectiveness of social marketing obesity prevention programmes targeting children and adolescent populations. They concluded that in the period 1990–2009, 25 of 27 social marketing programmes were effective in inducing behavioural change. They also concluded that the more systematic the application of social marketing benchmark criteria (such as the social marketing planning steps shown above), the more effective it is.

Other social marketing initiatives

There are many more social marketing initiatives undertaken within each country. For example, among key initiatives that took place (or are still in progress) in the UK, one might list the following as promising (SMG, 2016):

- *Mums for health*: This initiative focused on the challenge of encouraging family and children to develop good life skills that value health. This included developing positive behaviours as social norms supported by key family influencers (mums, grandmas, sisters, aunts, etc.). The programme involved community and social media support.
- *Sleep safe*: This initiative focused on researching the problem of unexplained sudden death of infants (SUDIs) and developing strategies, involving key stakeholders, to minimise its occurrence.
- *Children's social work matters*: This initiative focused on supporting the work of children social workers and increasing interest in this career. Among outcomes were the creation of an engaging website, staff-focused portal with webinar and career support facilities.
- *Domestic abuse*: This initiative helped identify the various forms of abuse and supported the targeted community and its various constituents (including teenagers) to stand against it.
- *Free childcare*: This initiative targeted certain parents who met certain criteria to offer them help with the childcare of their 2-year-old children. The aim is to help their children develop healthier lifestyles as well as increase their success chances in life.
- *Knowsley headstart*: This initiative, which is still in development, helps set up a sustainable prevention and early intervention programme for 10–16 year olds to help them cope with life challenges by supporting them emotionally and mentally.

- *Dental health*: This initiative, which is still in development, aims to address the significant problem of tooth decay that was estimated to be the highest cause of children's admissions to hospital in the UK. Currently studies are being carried out to identify the causes of tooth decay and help enlist key stakeholders (especially the parents) in addressing the problem.

In light of the above argument about interference of commercial marketing (competing with social marketing programmes both in terms of individualistic, hedonistic philosophy and incentives offered to young consumers) there is an urgent need for undertaking social marketing programmes at least to counter the effect of destructive advertising. Regarding the impact of social marketing initiatives there appears to be a general trend towards positive effects of the interventions at least in the medium term. Nevertheless there are clear methodological challenges. For instance, it is worth perhaps comparing social marketing initiatives with unilateral initiatives. Indeed, how effective is psychological counselling compared to social marketing that encourages support at multi-level? As they say, the devil is in the detail. There is an argument for weighing up the costs of intervention versus the outcomes both in terms of recovery and long-term economic savings such as through minimising future costly health care interventions. In this respect Fourali (2016b) argued that some of the key advantages of social marketing compared to other alternative problem solutions (such as counselling) is the reach and 'collateral' effect at social and theoretical levels. Indeed the comparisons may be fraught with difficulties in comparing like with like given the complexity of factors involved (e.g. consider the effect of level of motivation, level of environmental support of those recruited for the interventions and their effects at individual and social level in the short, medium and long term). There is also the need to standardise what counts as a comprehensive social marketing intervention. Accordingly, the above highlighted social marketing programme steps provide a good framework for such comparisons. Despite all the above challenges social marketing does offer a much more promising alternative to address social ills.

Criticism of social marketing

Like all disciplines there are several areas of criticisms that have been levelled at social marketing. One criticism involves using deceptive means to induce change. This may be in the form of overlooking significant factors (i.e. being economic with the factors of influence by producing a simplistic view of reality). The extremity of taking such a position would lead to 'blaming the victim', for instance by overlooking some key socio-economic environmental factors that may, at best, discourage individuals to change. Such a position tends to be underpinned by a neoliberal view that people are responsible for and readily able to manage the conditions of key aspects of their lives. Such a view puts the blame squarely on the already suffering individual to heed expert views and voluntarily make significant changes in their lifestyle to turn things around in various aspects of their lives (e.g. health, education, etc.). Perhaps the adage comes to mind here that 'willing' does not necessarily mean 'able' and 'ready'.

Language and associated assumptions linked to social marketing programmes have also been seen as potentially counter-productive (Fourali, 2016b; Lupton, 2014). For instance, some portrayal of certain 'unhealthy conditions' have been perceived as stigmatising as done for example with certain ads where 'fatness is constantly associated with diseases and negative imagery'.

Perhaps a broader criticism levelled against social marketing is whether it should be recognised as a valid academic discipline. All criticisms against social marketing may be seen as normal challenges that are raised against any discipline still in its infancy and should help its development into a mature discipline. Nevertheless, social marketing still seems to be fighting on two fronts to legitimise its existence. On the one hand, we have the orthodox side that likes to see social marketing as just another dimension of marketing (and at worst just a promotional approach) and, on the other, we have the 'promoters of academic discourse' challenge arguing that the discipline lacks reflexivity and critical discourse (Tadajewski and Brownlie, 2008). Regarding the latter, some researchers may consider the marketing concept in general, and social marketing in particular, as primarily anthropocentric in approach (consider the neoliberal view) and only give scant consideration to critical and ecological considerations in their research (Kilbourne *et al.*, 1997; Bourdieu, 1998a, 1998b; Tadajewski, 2016). Although challenges from both fronts have been and are being addressed (Ong and Blair-Stevens, 2009; Gordon, 2011) as the discipline develops and more researchers join its ranks there will naturally be more arguments and supporting theories that will be produced in its defence. In fact the natural focus of social marketing on social health and emancipation should facilitate its weathering of the challenges from the critical studies.

Conclusions and the way ahead

Social marketing is a new, developing discipline that may not be seen as a theory but rather a powerful eclectic methodology that helps us to understand the causes of social ills and design effective actions to counter their destructive effects. Although it has firm roots in marketing, it has 'diversified' its methodology to include all manners of social theories (such as social influence, educational, clinical psychological, management and community intervention theories, among others) that take into consideration micro, meso and macro factors (Fourali, 2016b; Stead *et al.*, 2006). Accordingly, Fourali (2013; also reported by McNiff, 2016) argues that social marketing should clearly adopt an action research perspective as it is a practice-orientated, problem-solving discipline. He suggests that social marketers and action researchers should work more closely together, capitalising on the richness of both approaches to increase the effectiveness of their results. McNiff (a world authority on action research) welcomed Fourali's view by arguing:

> Perhaps we should see the mix of different approaches as this forming of alliances. Perhaps we need to remember that the broad family of action research

is itself part of a broader family that is engaged in a global conversation about how we can find ways to live more peacefully with one another.

(McNiff, 2016, p. 50)

Social marketing has been applied to many social ills with significant positive results. In particular it has helped address several social problems that afflict the younger populations. These include obesity, infant sleep sudden deaths, drug/alcohol addictions and domestic violence. There are many more areas that could benefit from this young field of study.

The social marketing approach has been developed significantly since the early 1970s when the field was in its infancy and there is plenty of room for improvements as the targeted social areas are so diverse. Undertaking a social marketing project has been likened to climbing a Himalayan peak to illustrate the complexity of the SM challenges (Stead *et al.*, 2006). This involves careful planning, making use of the latest available information and tools (maps, navigational aids) to reach clear, achievable objectives while continually monitoring progress and being ready to make adjustments to the routes as necessary. Social marketing goals are broad and relative and require a continuous battle that aims to involve all sectors of society to help improve it.

As highlighted above there are several criticisms levelled against social marketing. However, the principles that underpin its goal of protecting and addressing social problems while aiming to support a happier society, should make it easier for this discipline to take up any challenge of either positioning it as simply within the 'orthodox marketing' or accusing it of lacking the necessary critical discourse to make it a recognisable, mature field of inquiry.

Social marketing is a welcome development that helps address the excesses of unfettered profit-based marketing. Indeed, as demonstrated in this chapter, the younger population has been and will probably be the target of many products that, if not responsibly monitored can lead to destructive results in the very society that marketers broadly set out to serve in the first place. Nevertheless even if marketers creatively try and combine commercial with social benefits (for example consider Amazon's recent ad raising awareness about its brand but also encouraging a more integrated society by showing how representatives of two religions can help each other through using Amazon's products) there will still be the need for social marketing, as ultimately social marketing aims to help create healthier, inclusive and happier societies first and foremost and is therefore free from any potential conflict of interest that involves a covert or overt commercial agenda.

Note

1 Note that youth includes 'child', which according to the UN Convention on the Rights of the Child defines a child as everyone under 18 unless, 'under the law applicable to the child, majority is attained earlier' (Office of the High Commissioner for Human Rights, 1989).

References

Academy of Medical Science. (2016). Improving the health of the public by 2040: Optimising the research environment for a healthier, fairer future. www.acmedsci.ac.uk/policy/policy-projects/health-of-the-public-in-2040 (accessed 21 January 2017).

Andreasen, A. R. (2002). Marketing social marketing in the social change marketplace. *Journal of Public Policy and Marketing*, 21(1), 3–13.

Bloom, P. N. and Novelli, W. D. (1981). Problems and challenges in social marketing. *Journal of Marketing*, 45, 79–88.

Bourdieu, Pierre (1998a). *Cette utopie, en voie de réalisation, d'une exploitation sans limite: L'essence du néolibéralisme.* Le Monde Diplomatique. Mars. www.monde-diplomatique.fr/1998/03/BOURDIEU/3609 (accessed 15 January 2017).

Bourdieu, P. (1998b). *Acts of resistance: Against the tyranny of the market.* Translated by R. Nice. New York: The New Press.

Cairns, G. (2012). Evolutions in food marketing: Quantifying the impact and policy implications. Appetite. http://dx.doi.org/10.1016/j.appet.2012.07.016%20) (accessed 6 January 2017).

CIM. (2016). *What is marketing?* www.cim.co.uk/more/getin2marketing/what-is-marketing (accessed 20 March 2016).

Common Sense Media. (2014). *Advertising to children and teens: Current practices.* www.commonsensemedia.org/research/advertising-to-children-and-teens-current-practices (accessed 24 August 2017).

Community Guide. (2015). *Health communication and social marketing: Health communication campaigns that include mass media and health-related product distribution.* www.thecommunityguide.org/healthcommunication/campaigns.html (accessed 10 July 2015).

Duane, S. and Domegan, C. (2014). Get your life in gear. In G. Hastings and C. Domegan (eds), *Social marketing: From tunes to symphonies.* Abingdon: Butterworth Heinemann/Elsevier.

Egan, John (2016). Book shelf – Professor John Egan on 'The promise of social marketing' by Chahid Fourali. *Marketor: The Livery Company Magazine for Marketing Professionals*, 73(Autumn), 20.

Elkington, J. (1998). *Cannibals with forks: The triple bottom line of 21st century business.* Oxford: Capstone.

Fourali, C. (2008). *World-class national occupational standards in social marketing.* First International Conference on Social Marketing, 29–30 September. Brighton and Hove, UK.

Fourali, C. (2009). Developing world-class social marketing standards: A step in the right direction for a more socially responsible marketing profession. *Social Marketing Quarterly*, 15(2), 14–24.

Fourali, C. (2013). Action research and social marketing: Joining the forces of two powerful potential allies. Third International Conference on 'Value and virtue in practice-based research: Influencing policy through enhancing professionalism'. York: York St John University.

Fourali, C. (2016a). Social marketing: A proven tool for improving the human condition. Conference on 'A company with a soul', 24 October, Warsaw.

Fourali, C. (2016b). *The promise of social marketing: A powerful tool for changing the world for good.* London: Routledge.

French, J. (2011). Why nudging is not enough. *Journal of Social Marketing*, 1(2), 154–162.

French, J. and Blair-Stevens, C. (2005). *Social marketing pocket guide.* London: National Consumer Council.

French, J. and Gordon, R. (2015). *Strategic social marketing.* London: Sage.

Gallopel-Morvan, Karine and Leroux, Christophe (2014). The National League Against Cancer's 'You Kill, You Pay' campaign: How to fight the tobacco industry. In G. Hastings and C. Domegan (eds), *Social marketing: From tunes to symphonies* (pp. 394–401). Abingdon: Butterworth Heinemann/Elsevier.

Gordon, R. (2011). Critical social marketing: Assessing the cumulative impact of alcohol marketing on youth drinking. PhD, University of Stirling.

Gordon, R. (2012). Re-thinking and re-tooling the social marketing mix. *Australasian Marketing Journal*, 20, 122–126.

Gracia-Marco, L., Vicente-Rodriguez, G., Borys, J. M., Le Bodo, Y., Pettigrew, S. and Moreno, L. A. (2011). Contribution of social marketing strategies to community-based obesity prevention programmes in children. *International Journal of Obesity*, 5, 472–479.

Hastings, G. and Domegan, C. (2014). *Social marketing: From tunes to symphonies.* Abingdon: Butterworth Heinemann/Elsevier.

James, O. (2007). *Affluenza: How to be successful and stay sane.* London: Vermilion.

Jobber, D. and Ellis-Chadwick, F. (2016). *Principles and practice of marketing* (8th edn). London: McGraw-Hill.

Kilbourne, W. E., McDonagh, P. and Prothero, A. (1997). Sustainable consumption and the quality of life: A macromarketing challenge to the dominant social paradigm. *Journal of Macromarketing*, 17(Spring), 4–24.

Klein, N. (2000). *No logo*. London: Flamingo.

Kotler, P. (2012). Confessions of a marketer. Presentation at the Chicago Humanities Festival. www.youtube.com/watch?v=sR-qL7QdVZQ (accessed 14 January 2017).

Kotler, P. (2013). World social marketing conference (WSMC). www.youtube.com/watch?v=aLHgyxW1WD8 (accessed 29 November 2014).

Kotler, P. and Levy, S. J. (1969). Broadening the concept of marketing. *Journal of Marketing*, 33(1), 10–15.

Laloux, Frederic (2014). *Reinventing organizations: A guide to creating organizations inspired by the next stage of human consciousness.* Brussels: Nelson-Parker.

Lauterborn, B. (1990). New marketing litany: Four Ps passé: C-words take over. *Advertising Age*, 61(41), 26.

Lazonick, William (2014). Profits without prosperity. *Harvard Business Review*, 92(9), 46–55.

Lupton, Deborah (2014). 'How do you measure up?': Assumptions about 'obesity' and health-related behaviors and beliefs in two Australian 'obesity' prevention campaigns. *Fat Studies: An Interdisciplinary Journal of Body Weight and Society*, 3(1), 32–44.

McDermott, L. M., Stead, M. and Hastings, G. B. (2005). What is and what is not social marketing: The challenge of reviewing the evidence. *Journal of Marketing Management*, 5(6), 545–553.

McNiff, Jean (2016). *You and your action research project* (4th edn). London: Routledge.

NESTA. (2008). *Selling sustainability: Seven lessons from advertising and marketing to sell low-carbon living.* London: NESTA.

NSMC. (2010). NSMC benchmark criteria. www.socialmarketing-toolbox.com/content/nsmc-benchmark-criteria-0 (accessed 30 December 2016).

Office of the High Commissioner for Human Rights. (1989). UN Convention on the Rights of the Child. www.ohchr.org/en/professionalinterest/pages/crc.aspx) United Nations (accessed 23 August 2017).

Ong, D. and Blair-Stevens, C. (2009). The total process planning (TPP) framework. In J. French, C. Blair-Stevens, D. McVey and R. Merritt (eds), *Social marketing and public health: Theory and practice.* Oxford: Oxford University Press.

Peattie, S. and Peattie, K. (2003). Ready to fly solo? Reducing social marketing's dependence on commercial marketing theory. *Marketing Theory*, 3(3), 365–385.

Pelham, A. M. (2000). Market orientation and other potential influences on performance in small- and medium-sized manufacturing firms. *Journal of Small Business Management*, 38(1), 48–67.

Perloff, Richard, M. (2017). *The dynamics of persuasion: Communication and attitudes in the 21st century* (6th edn). London: Routledge.

Riddaway, M. (2017). 2040: A health odyssey. *Prognosis: The Periodical of the Harley Street Medical Area*, 1, 32–38.

Rideout, V. J., Foehr, U. G. and Roberts, D. F. (2010). *Generation m2: Media in the lives of 8- to 18-year-olds*. Menlo Park: Kaiser Family Foundation.

Ritz, Beate and Wilhelm, Michelle (2008). Air pollution impacts on infants and children. UCLA Institute of the Environment and Sustainability. www.environment.ucla.edu/media/files/air-pollution-impacts.pdf (accessed 21 January 2017).

Robinson, M. N., Tansil, K. A., Elder, R. W., Soler, R. E., Labre, M. P., Mercer, S. L., Eroglu, D., Baur, C., Lyon-Daniel, K., Fridinger, F., Sokler, L. A., Green, L. W., Miller, T., Dearing, J. W., Evans, W. D., Snyder, L. B., Viswanath, K. K., Beistle, D. M., Chervin, D. D., Bernhardt, J. M., Rimer B. K. and the Community Preventive Services Task Force. (2014). Mass media health communication campaigns combined with health-related product distribution: A community guide systematic review. *American Journal of Preventive Medicine*, 47(3), 360–371.

Shizumu, K. (2003). *Symbiotic marketing strategy*. Japan: Souseisha Book Company.

SMG. (2016). Case studies. The social marketing gateway – the behaviour change people. www.socialmarketinggateway.co.uk/case-studies/?cs-name=let-me-sleep-safe (accessed 4 January 2017).

Smith, B. (2008). Save the crabs. Then eat 'em. In P. Kotler and N. Lee (eds), *Social marketing: Influencing behaviors for good*. London: Sage.

Surgeon General. (2012). *Preventing tobacco use among youth and young adults: A report of the Surgeon General*. Atlanta: US Department of Health and Human Services, Centers for Disease Control and Prevention, National Center for Chronic Disease Prevention and Health Promotion, Office on Smoking and Health.

Stead, M., McDermott, L., Angus, K. and Hastings, G. (2006). *Marketing review final report*. Prepared for the National Institute for Health and Clinical Excellence (NICE). Institute for Social Marketing. University of Stirling and The Open University. www.nice.org.uk/guidance/ph6/evidence/behaviour-change-review-6-social-marketing-369664530 (accessed 4 December 2017).

Stead, M., McDermott, L., MacKintosh, A. M. and Adamson, A. (2011). Why healthy eating is bad for young people's health: Identity, belonging and food. *Social Science and Medicine*, 72(7), 1131–1139.

Tadajewski, M. (2016). Critical marketing studies and critical marketing education: Key ideas, concepts and materials. *RIMAR – Revista Interdisciplinar de Marketing*, 6(2), 3–24.

Tadajewski, M. and Brownlie, D. (2008). *Critical marketing: Issues in contemporary marketing*. Chichester: Wiley.

Tapp, A. and Spotswood, F. (2013). From the 4Ps to COM-SM: Reconfiguring the social marketing mix. *Journal of Social Marketing*, 3(3), 206–222.

Thornton, J. (2017). Air pollution plan cannot be delayed, high court tells government. *Guardian*. www.theguardian.com/environment/2017/apr/27/air-pollution-plan-election-campaign-bomb-court-government (accessed 24 August 2017).

World Health Organization (WHO). (2008). *Report on the global tobacco epidemic*. www.who.int/tobacco/mpower/mpower_report_tobacco_crisis_2008.pdf. (accessed 6 January 2017).

Wiebe, G. D. (1952). Merchandising commodities and citizenship on television. *Public Opinion Quarterly*, 15, 679–691.

21

CONSUMERISM AND CONSUMER PROTECTION

A focus on young consumers

Ayantunji Gbadamosi, Kathy-Ann Fletcher, Christiana Emmanuel-Stephen and Idowu Comfort Olutola

Introduction

One of the well-established standpoints in the marketing parlance is that marketing is based on the notion of exchange of value between the marketers on the one hand and the customers on the other. So, it is expected that consumers, whether old or young, should derive optimum satisfaction from the market offerings acquired, and have both short-run and long-run benefits from their various transactions. Nonetheless, a plethora of cases in the business world shows that this is not always the case. The horsemeat scandal that rocked many European countries including the UK in 2013 in which horsemeat was sold to unsuspecting customers as processed beef in various food items; the Volkswagen car emission deception in 2015, which according to the BBC (2015) involved about 11 million cars worldwide; and the mis-sold payment protection insurance (PPI) are some of the examples that show that consumers may not be totally at ease in the care of marketers. So, with these and many more, the need to protect the consumer against the excesses of marketers becomes necessary. This is the main crux of consumerism. In his seminal paper in the *Harvard Business Review*, Kotler (1972, p. 49) provides a very useful definition of consumerism as 'a social movement seeking to augment the rights and power of buyers in relation to sellers'. While the examples cited here are relatively new, Bostan *et al.* (2010) note that the notion of consumer protection is not a new phenomenon as it has taken place in one form or another in the past, citing examples in the fifteenth and sixteenth centuries during which some producers were held responsible for their commercial actions. With reference to Feldstein (1988), it is noted that while the producers of goods and services are relatively few and have resources to organise in relation to their interests, this is not the case for the consumers (Rodwin, 1996). Hence, these challenges uncover the need to organise to protect the interest of the consumers. Rodwin (1996) highlights four main reforms proposed by consumer groups in relation to consumer managed care, which are increased information and market options available to consumers; having oversight for management of managed care plans by accrediting organisations, which could be private, state or federal; ensuring standards for the services and marketing of managed care; and ensuring that consumers who are denied services have due process rights to challenge such decisions. So, evidently, the scope of consumerism and consumer protection is understandably wide, covering physical products and service offerings and the associated activities. Meanwhile, specifically in the context of young consumers that constitute the focus of this chapter, many authors show that protecting young consumers' rights is still being circumvented by businesses in some parts of the world ranging from the types of products designed for them to marketing communications activities that accompany some of these offerings targeted at young consumers. For example, there is evidence of drug and alcohol abuse among young consumers and unfortunately in some cases this could be as a direct result of the marketing strategies of these organisations, which are directed at these vulnerable consumers (Cismaru et al., 2008). Cassim (2005) claims that advertisers have more freedom in their advertising to children in South Africa than they do in developed countries. Similar claims are made by Vadehra (2004) concerning India, while Gbadamosi (2010) argues that a lot is still required to be done in Nigeria towards achieving the global standard on advertising to children especially in terms of the implementation of the existing regulations. So, this chapter revisits this enigma from a holistic perspective. Drawing from the extant literature, the chapter reviews the status quo on consumerism and consumer protection in relation to young consumers and suggests some future directions.

Evolution of consumerism and consumer protection

Consumerism, which uses consumption and production as the root of an economically driven society, ensures the protection of consumer rights to fair trade. Consumer protection uses laws and organisations to establish and maintain the rights of consumers and provide an outline for the ethical operations of companies. Consumer protection measures give the consumer an outlet to bring any grievance for the infringing of their rights as set out by the laws of that respective country (Süle, 2012; Alexandru et al., 2014). Additionally, it has been discussed by writers such as Thomas and Wilson (2012) and Zaharia and Zaharia (2015) as a means through which members of a society aspire to and achieve a certain standard of living. In so doing, consumerism develops the economy of the society, country and region by giving consumers access to products and services that are determined by marketers, politicians and the society at large as a way to improve their lives and achieve their ambitions. In carrying such meaning, Miles (1998) argues that consumerism has evolved into a psycho-social consumption experience for shoppers with the promise of personal freedom. Therefore, it is essential to ensure that consumerism continues to protect the rights of consumers, of all ages, to fair trade, because as an ideology it is driving not only the consumption habits of citizens but also informing how children see themselves and their families within their communities and their opportunities for social progress (Zepf, 2010; Cook, 2013). Consequently, the discussion for laws and organisations that maintain these rights remains crucial within a continuously evolving economy and society.

Extant literature shows that the origin of consumerism can be traced to the United States of America in the early twentieth century. Bostan *et al.* (2010) note that consumer protection arose in line with increased consumption, inspired by mass protests to the unsavoury practices of companies in the early 1900s. The US Federal Government then reacted by introducing rules to provide regulation of industry practices. Other countries across the globe have followed the US template of consumerism to develop the economy as well as providing consumer protection according to their own culture and legal framework. For example, the European Union (EU) has region-wide markers of consumer protection, while individual European states like Norway and Sweden have their own rules and regulatory bodies for this purpose and Saudi Arabia has its own consumer protection based on the Quran (Morris and Dababagh, 2004). Since the 1980s, marketers have noted that children are active consumers and therefore their rights need to be protected as well (Bao *et al.*, 2007). In the case of the US, rules and regulations to restrict advertising to children were introduced in the 1970s and similar regulations followed in the EU and worldwide in the 1980s and 1990s (Buijzen and Valkenburg, 2003; Ene, 2012).

The development of consumerism is rooted in American democracy, however, its catalysts vary based on the culture of the country in which it operates. For instance, in the Indian context, consumerism's evolution is due to increasing wages among young people (Thomas and Wilson, 2012) while Valkenburg and Cantor (2001) credit a higher level of education in other cultures. Several factors are responsible for the evolution of consumerism. Industrialisation and patriotism together with marketing's evolution and policy development (to be discussed in more detail later) are among these factors. But consumer protection is a centuries-old act of marketplace preservation with Bostan *et al.* (2010) identifying several steps within Austria and France to protect dairy consumers as early as the fifteenth century. From the twentieth century onward, countries across the globe in Europe, Asia, Africa and Latin America have followed the US in creating their own consumer protection measures, realising that the interest of consumers are best served by protecting their rights and maintaining a balance of power between consumers and businesses (Ha and McGregor, 2013) including those of child consumers. These consumer protection measures have evolved to include online and mobile shopping as Svantesson and Clarke (2010) show that along with traditional concerns of offline consumers, e-consumers have additional trust issues that have to be considered in the creation of consumer protection regulations. Winn (2016) articulate how these concerns are being addressed worldwide by Internet retailer Amazon based on the 2005 AFFECT, which is a set of 12 principles designed to govern the practice of e-commerce. Amazon has taken the role of enforcing global consumer protection within the digital age, ushering possibly a new era where consumer protection principles are universal across the globe.

What drives consumerism and consumer culture?

Beyond the context of consumer vulnerability and the organised protection highlighted earlier, the term consumerism is also commonly used to explain consumption in the sense of consumer culture or materialism. In this sense, it could be stated that several agents within a society can act as drivers of consumerism. First, marketing is credited due to the influence of advertising on consumer behaviour (Johe and Bullar, 2016). This influence extends to children (Montgomery, 2000), with Valkenburg and Cantor (2001) noting that children are exposed to advertising from as young as 2 years old. Second, Cohen (2016) identifies policy as the greatest driver of consumerism as a means of improving the standard of living of the citizens of a country due to tax revenue that funds the infrastructural improvements for the country's citizens. Additionally, personal ambition and socialisation facilitate an increase in consumerism. Thomas and Wilson (2012) identify socialisation as a facet of conspicuous consumption, which focuses on the visual display or use of products in the presence of others and is a major driver of consumerism. In some societies, an ability to maintain a lifestyle similar to one's neighbours is a fundamental personal ambition and driver of consumerism (Zaharia and Zaharia, 2015).

Consumerism, if used in the context of consumption and materialism, is often linked positively to the development of technological and economic innovations as the consumer's vote in the progression of a society. On the other hand, a consumeristic culture is repeatedly portrayed with malign due to perceived negative effects on a country's social fabric. For example, Cohen (2016) speaks to the criticisms of a materialistic culture in light of the impoverishment of the middle and lower classes to the benefit of the upper classes. Consumerism is often blamed for harmful effects on personal well-being such as anxiety, depression and self-esteem issues, especially among children (Cohen, 2016; Sweeting *et al.*, 2012). However, the creation of a trusting marketplace (Ene, 2012) due to consumerism means that customers fully participate in the consumer process because they feel empowered and respected as key players in their society's economic development. For example, in the case of American consumerism, children globally grow to be productive consumers to enact what it means to be American. A further positive argument for consumerism is the economic development and innovations that are credited with the entrepreneurial environment. For example, the US is a breeding ground for technology and other innovative sectors, which can be linked to their long history of consumerism. Another major benefit of consumerism is a high standard of living due to citizens operating at the top of Maslow's hierarchy of needs in terms of satisfying their needs but living for the purpose of self-actualisation and the promise of social mobility. Meanwhile, in the sense of consumer protection, the ultimate benefit of consumerism is the trust of the consumer in a system that protects their rights against vendors that may have predatory business practices (Day and Aaker, 1970; Alexandru *et al.*, 2014). Such confidence and protectionism is believed to be reflected in the swelling of the middle class (Lee *et al.*, 2010). While Todd (2012) argues that consumerism is a restrictive practice due to its false promise of helping consumers achieve their identity and social goals, consumerism and the consumer protection laws' ability to place consumer and vendor on an equitable standing (Kotler, 1972) translates to a society that ensures the vendors themselves have a viable market for their products and services and customers are not unduly taken advantage of whether by deliberate or negligible actions.

How is the child turned into a consumer?

There has been a noticeable increase in pressures associated with consumerism on children. Pichaud (2008) notes that this increase can be measured by the increase in television programming aimed specifically at children. In light of this increase, studies are increasing to determine exactly when the thrust of childhood consumerism can be first noticed and how a child is turned into a consumer. Valkenburg and Cantor (2001) outline a clear pathway as the child ages from 2–12 years old. Essentially, as shown in this study, children's evolution as an active consumer starts from as young as age 2 when they are first exposed to advertising. In their progression, the child starts making connections between advertising and products in store and can recognise the brands by age 5 and is fully versed in the customs of consumerism by the age of 12 (Montgomery, 2000). There are different factors responsible for the development of such a consumer savvy 12-year-old. These include the education system, religion, peer pressure, family life and marketing messages that exist within a consumer culture. Marketers recognise that children are a viable market and have developed strategies to connect with young consumers making brands instrumental in the development of children into consumers (Sweeting et al., 2012). Under 8 years old, marketing communications are influential on children (Valkenburg, 2001), who become more critical of advertising thereafter. The increasing power of the child consumer is evidenced by the popularity of the term 'pester power', whereby children constantly press their parents either at home or in store to purchase desired products. Children are increasingly influential in the consumption choices of their parents (Hsieh et al., 2006) especially for technological products for which they are seen as well informed.

Another factor in the development of the child consumer is their parents' affluence as well as the child's own increase in spending power (Valkenburg and Cantor, 2001; Vandana and Lenka, 2014). Hamilton (2009) says that this increasing spending power is placing more pressure to yield to the temptations of the marketplace while Hsieh et al. (2006) show that parental brand preferences are passed on to their children. Education is a great tool in the creation of the child into a consumer with Süle (2012) arguing that both formal and informal educational processes play a significant role in shaping who a child becomes as a consumer. Therefore, school plus children's relationships with their parents and peers are strong influences in their development as consumers. As they progress, different aspects of their life influence children differently. In their younger ages, advertising has a strong power, whereas when they get older the opinion of their peers has a stronger role in the choices they make as consumers (Valkenburg and Cantor, 2001; D'Alessio *et al.*, 2009; Süle 2012; Thomas and Wilson, 2012). Vandana and Lenka (2014) note that since children are both influencers and purchasers, advertisers are very interested in them as consumers. There is not only the need to maximise on the profitability of childhood consumption but also to protect children's rights against any potential infringement by unethical vendors. Children have rights and freedoms as well and they need to be protected (Pichaud, 2008). Parton (2014) identifies laws such as The Children's Act 1948, The Children Act 1989 and The Children Act (2004) in demonstrating that child protection has a long history in politics across cultures. Child consumer protection was instituted to ensure that children could participate in the consumeristic society with the same confidence as adult consumers but also to protect them as vulnerable and potentially naïve members of the society (Montgomery, 2000; Pichaud, 2008; Parton, 2014). Since children are active and passive consumers (Valkenburg and Cantor, 2001) they deserve the protection and security available to everyone. So, it is not surprising that several papers have been written on the dynamics of advertising to children in several countries. These include advertising to children in Germany (Schotthöfer, 2002), Mexico (Arochi *et al.*, 2005), Spain (Volz *et al.*, 2005), Switzerland (Hofer and Bieri, 2005), Malaysia (Mirandah, 2005), Nigeria (Gbadamosi, 2010), the UK (Dresden and Barnard, 2003), the US (Koester, 2002) and several others. Ultimately, the point of convergence between these publications is ensuring that marketing communications, especially advertising are effectively and fairly managed in relation to children.

Whose role is children's consumer protection?

From a broad perspective, a number of regulatory frameworks and agencies on consumer protection are in place in many countries. While some relate to children, the scope of others are different. Selected examples of these from some countries are shown in Tables 21.1 to 21.5. Children have a legal right according to the United Nations Convention on the Rights of the Child in 1991 (Nicholls and Cullen, 2004) to participate in the decision-making for consumption that affects them. Consumer protection of children is a collaborative activity with a role for parents, education, government, businesses, consumer rights organisations, researchers and religion among other facets of society. This is demonstrated in Figure 21.1, which argues that the roles and the effort involved towards having acceptable advertising including that directed at children is multi-faceted. While firms are expected to play their role at the micro level, the industry is also expected to complement the existing and emerging legal regulatory framework and self-regulatory framework in ensuring acceptable advertising standards at the threshold in which all stakeholders including children will be adequately protected.

Europe's example provides a strong argument for an integrated approach to consumer protection with consumer education at the core. According to Ene (2012), EU member states begin consumer education via the school curricula as well as

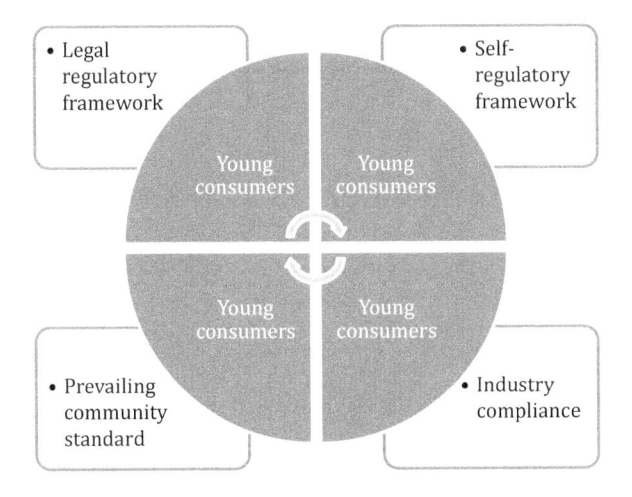

FIGURE 21.1 Acceptable advertising and young consumers

Source: Adapted from Hacker (1998).

online adult education, which allows for the development of wise consumers. Parents' role in consumer protection is very important, as they are often the first intervention in teaching children to be consumers. Parents should include the child in the purchase decisions that affect them (Nicholls and Cullen, 2004) to teach them how to make sound purchase decisions and what their rights are as consumers. Research organisations also have a role to play in laying the foundation for consumer protection measures for children. Montgomery (2000) shows that research can provide the facts needed to inform the development of regulatory framework such as the development of laws like the Children's Online Privacy Protection Act which protects children by revealing the threats of the online world to the rights of vulnerable consumers such as children. This research can also be used by consumer organisations to educate families to speak to their children about the dangers of consumerism especially within today's world of digital media. Digital technologies are equipped with the ability to regulate what is shown to children. These measures are used to protect children from sexual predators and to shield them from excessive advertising. The controls allow parents to monitor their children's access to predatory advertising as a result of activism by consumer organisations and parents that pressurised media companies to include these measures in their technologies such as HDTVs, mobile phones and tablets and the legislation of the Children's Online Privacy Protection Act. A by-product of this technological advancement is social media, which in itself has created a more collaborative method of consumer protection via the use of user-generated reviews on sites like Facebook, YELP and TripAdvisor to educate one another on consumer protection issues and companies that may be infringing upon consumer rights. In this way, consumers show that the wider society has a role to play in protecting one another and children from unscrupulous business practices. Childhood consumer protection is also the role of the companies to ensure that the marketplace they are operating in is sustainable by protecting the rights of consumers they recognise as both influencers and primary consumers. As consumerism is a socialisation process, education plays a sound role in developing the child into an aware consumer. Süle (2012) shows that children who were educated formally in consumer protection were more discerning consumers. These educational activities can be delivered in a variety of methods including regular curricula programming, extra-curricula activities or lifelong learning programmes.

Online child consumer protection includes the right to privacy (Papacharissi and Fernback, 2005) to ensure that private information is not revealed to commercial or other third parties. Papacharissi and Fernback noted as early as 2005 that online data, biometrics and face recognition was a concern with online rights to privacy and behavioural monitoring. In light of those concerns and the desire to protect children especially pre-teens from any predatory behaviour, the Children's Online Privacy Protection Act was implemented and social media sites such as Facebook and Twitter made it a requirement for people to be at least 13 years of age to gain membership of these social networks. This is due to the dangers not only of sexual predators on these sites but also the naïvety of the younger audience to decipher a phishing or other Internet scam that might open the child or the child's parent to high credit card bills or the risk of identity theft (Reid, 2009). For instance, there are cases of children running up high bills on Amazon or eBay on their parents' credit cards because they were not aware of the costs. Online protective acts such as privacy questions and controls allow these children to confidently navigate the online commercial websites without falling into debt for their parents, themselves or the commercial operators. Children are now part of the digital natives, as coined by Prensky (2001), who incorporate digital media into their lives almost seamlessly (Reid, 2009). Therefore, there is a need to protect the children's established right to autonomy as well as guard against their vulnerability (Valkenburg, 2000) as a means of enhancing the safety of children while they are online. Ultimately, the EU has been hailed by Reid (2009) as a leader in the protection of children online from certain inherent dangers of operating within this space, such as harmful content, advertising and increased financial pressures among other concerns, by creating frameworks and conventions at EU-wide and nation-specific jurisdictions to filter and block these kinds of content and to arrange punishments for any reported or discovered infringements. Laws such as the Data Protection Act of 1998 in the UK and the Children's Online Privacy Protection Rule (COPPA) of 1998 in the US, organisations such as the UK's Council for Child Internet Safety (UKCCIS) and educational organisation and website Better Internet for Kids in the EU are essential to evolving the consumer protection measures for children to match the evolving consumerist pressures placed on children by digital media.

TABLE 21.1 US consumer laws

US regulations	Date	Meaning	Source
Federal Trade Commission Act	1914	Outlaws unfair methods of competition and unfair acts or practices that affect commerce. Established the Federal Trade Commission to suggest and enforce trade regulations	www.ftc.gov
(No FEAR Act) Notification and Federal Employee Antidiscrimination and Retaliation Act of 2002	2002	Intended to increase the accountability of federal agencies for acts of discrimination or retaliation against employees, former employees and applicants	www.ftc.gov
Children's Online Privacy Protection Act (COPPA)	1998	Gives parents control over what information websites can collect from their children. Educates businesses and parents about children's consumers rights and company responsibilities	www.ftc.gov
The Equal Credit Opportunity Act	1974	Makes it unlawful to discriminate against any applicant on the basis of race, colour, religion, national origin, sex, marital status or age	www.consumer.ftc.gov

TABLE 21.2 US Protective bodies

US protective bodies	Founded	Purpose	Source
Federal Trade Commission's Bureau of Consumer Protection	1915	A bureau created to stop unfair business practices through complaints, investigations and litigation thus maintaining a fair marketplace and educating consumers and businesses about their rights and responsibilities	www.ftc.gov
Consumer Financial Protection Bureau	2009	A government agency created after the 2008 financial crisis to protect consumers. It aims to empower consumers to make wise financial choices, enforce sanctions against predatory companies and educate consumers from childhood to retirement about healthy financial practices	www.consumerfinance.gov

(continued)

TABLE 21.2 *(continued)*

US protective bodies	Founded	Purpose	Source
US Food and Drug Administration	1906	Protecting, regulating and advancing public health via monitoring of drugs, biological products and medical devices as well as food supply, cosmetics and products that emit radiation. Additionally the FDA regulates the manufacturing and distribution of tobacco products	www.fda.gov
National Consumers League (NCL)	1899	Founded in 1899, NCL is America's pioneer consumer advocacy organisation. It focuses on consumer health and safety protection as well as fairness in the marketplace and workplace	www.nclnet.org

TABLE 21.3 Consumer laws in Europe

Europe regulations	Date	Meaning	Source
Directive on Consumer Rights – European Union	2011	To protect consumers in respect of contracts negotiated away from business premises. To regulate certain aspects of the sale of consumer goods and associated guarantees as well as Directive on unfair terms in consumer contracts remains in force	ec.europa.eu
Charter of Fundamental Rights of the European Union	2010	Provides right to fair treatment. Promises consumers that products must meet acceptable standards. Gives consumers a right of redress if something goes wrong	ec.europa.eu
Consumer Rights Act – UK	2015	Governs what the consumer rights are to redress in terms of faulty goods, digital content, contractual obligations	www.legislation.gov.uk
EU Framework of Laws for Children's Rights	2012	Provides the basis for laws in the EU jurisdiction for the protection of children's rights in a variety of sectors including consumerism	www.europarl.europa.eu

TABLE 21.4 Consumer agencies in Europe

Europe protective bodies	Founded	Purpose	Source
European Consumer Center Network 'ECC-Net'	2005	Aims to provide free of charge help and advice to consumers on their cross-border purchases, whether	ec.europa.eu/consumers/ecc

		online or on the spot within the EU, Norway and Iceland	
BEUC – The European Consumer Organisation	2009	An umbrella organisation that investigates developments that could affect consumers in the financial services, food, digital rights, consumer rights/enforcements and sustainability	www.beuc.eu
Citizens Advice Consumer Helpline – UK	2009	A telephone, email and online service offering information and advice on consumer issues in the UK	www.citizensadvice.org.uk
Better Internet for Kids – European Union	1999	Provides and educational presence online to help children and their caregivers know what their rights are and how to avoid harmful content and scams online	www.betterinternetforkids.eu

TABLE 21.5 Consumer laws across the globe

Global regulations	Date	Meaning	Source
Consumer Protection Act 1992 – Nigeria	1992	Outlines the rights of consumers and the avenues of redress in case of infringement, and establishes the Consumer Protection Council to regulate the process of consumer protection	www.nigeria-law.org
Consumer Protection (Fair Trading) Act – Singapore	2009	Protects consumers against unfair practices and gives consumers additional rights in respect of goods that do not conform to contract, and for matters connected therewith. These include the protection of consumer goods and services for children	statutes.agc.gov.sg/aol
Consumer Defense Code – Brazil	1990	Law governing the rules that protect consumers and determines the responsibilities of providers, establishing penalties for infringement	thebrazilbusiness.com/article/consumer-rights-in-brazil
Consumer protection Act CAP 326D – Barbados	2003	Protects the rights of consumers and prevents harm via unfair trade practices and unfair contract terms as well as misleading advertising while educating and encouraging businesses to comply with the Act	www.commerce.gov.bb

TABLE 21.6 Consumer agencies across the globe

Global protective bodies	Founded	Purpose	Source
Consumer Protection Council – Nigeria	1992	Creates the regulations guiding consumer rights in Nigeria, provides the avenues of redress for wronged consumers. Also educates consumers about their rights and products/services that may be banned in the country. The activities of the council include advocating and providing services especially for the child consumer	cpc.gov.ng
CASE – Consumer Association of Singapore	1971	Tasked with protecting consumer interests using information and education as a means of creating a consumer-friendly marketplace	www.case.org.sg
Conanda (National Council for the Rights of Children and Adolescents) Brazil	2014	Advocacy group for the rights of children and teenagers in Brazil. Credited with leading the advocacy that inspired the law that made advertising to children in Brazil illegal	www.consumersinternational.org
Fair Trade Commission – Barbados	2001	Determines principles, rates and standards of service of regulated service providers, monitors general business conduct, investigating infringements and consumer complaints, enforcing the rights when necessary and educating consumers about their rights	www.ftc.gov.bb

Consumerism and the postmodern consumer

As established earlier in this chapter, it is clear that consumerism compels marketing and businesses in general to engage in activities that will emphasise its significance. As can be inferred from the view of Sheth and Gardner (1982, p. 4), it is geared towards positively adopting better ways of delivering goods and services to consumers, prioritising to manage the friction between producers and consumers and provide an advocacy position in terms of developing and protecting the rights of the consumers. Thus, it is seen as a social movement that seeks to increase the rights and powers of consumers by reinforcing the laws that protect them from producer exploitation. Other activities include regulating activities within the marketplace as well as promoting the customer as the centre of all marketing activities. Meanwhile, from the aforementioned and what we have established earlier in this chapter, it could be logical to argue that here seems to be a link between consumerism and postmodernism. The new intellectual age only means that there is a shift from modernism to postmodernism (Hicks, 2004). Top intellectuals agree that modernism is dead, thus, a revolutionary era is upon us – an era liberated from the oppressive structures of the past, but at the same time disquieted by its expectations of the future (Hicks, 2004; Singh, 2011; Todd, 2012). Similarly, Brann (1992) shows that postmodernism is not a natural, nor a material artefact, it isn't even a theory, that is to say a work of intellectual architecture, freestanding and well founded. Instead it bears the signature of an intellectuals' movement: the 'ism' ending. Advocates of postmodernity figuratively date its birth with the riots in Paris in May 1968, when students with the support of prominent scholars required fundamental changes in a rigid, closed, elitist European university system (Barrett, 1997). Singh (2011) argues that defining postmodernism is difficult because it is a complicated term, or set of ideas, one that has only developed as an area of academic study since the mid-1980s. It is also a concept that appears in a wide variety of disciplines or areas of study, including art, architecture, music, film, literature, sociology, communications, fashion and technology (Singh, 2011, p. 56). It is therefore not surprising that the phenomenon has attracted considerable scholarly attention in the literature (Cova, 1996; Kuntz, 2017) As a phenomenon, it seems to offer some possible choices to linking the global culture of consumption, where commodities and forms of knowledge are offered by forces far beyond any individual's control (Singh, 2011, p. 55). Todd (2012, p. 48) clarifies that we live in the postmodern era and that makes us a postmodern society. Todd's (2012) study reveals that within the postmodern society, few things play significant roles. One of them is consumerism. Considering that the postmodern society consists of various consumers ranging from old to young, it sounds logical to argue that consumerism and the consumer protection right is an appropriate part of societal systems. This is confirmed in the detailed explanation provided by Yannis and Lang (1995), which entails the vital roles of consumerism to the postmodern consumer. According to them, these are delineated into five key meanings that detail its role in postmodernity. These include consumerism as a moral doctrine, a vehicle for economic development, a means for demarcating social status, a public policy and a social movement. All of these meanings are tied to the important role of consumerism to the postmodern consumer. Meanwhile, another useful contribution given by Singh (2011) highlights that the role of consumerism should be linked to the history of how it first began. He adds that in times gone by the principle of *caveat emptor*, which meant buyer beware, governed the relationship between seller and buyer (Singh, 2011, p. 64). This was in the time when buyers and sellers came face to face, sellers displayed their products while buyers had enough time to carefully look at them and then obtained or bought as needed. It was an era where producers were more thorough about what was displayed, they were more careful while engaging in transactions in relation to consumers. The maxim relieved the seller of the obligation to make disclosure about the quality of the product and in addition the relationship between the buyer and the seller was the most important reason for engagement (Singh, 2011, p. 64). This was the case up until the growth of trade and globalisation, which makes it impossible for the buyer to inspect the goods ahead of time and most of the transactions are concluded by correspondence. As a result, the marketplace started experiencing friction while consumers were getting more dissatisfied about what they consumed. Then consumerism was designed to re-emphasise the need to protect consumers. This movement has assumed greater importance and relevance as a universal phenomenon. Its roles are centred on protecting the interests of all consumers including children from all organisations with which there is exchanged relationship. It comprises of all the sets of activities of government, businesses, independent organisations and concerned consumers that are designed to protect the rights of consumers (Venketesh, 1992). As frequently stated, it also consists of the process through which the consumers seek redress, restitution and remedy for their dissatisfaction and frustration with the help of all their organised or unorganised efforts and activities (Featherstone, 1991). Accordingly, consumerism today is an all-pervasive term meaning nothing more than people's search for getting better value for their money, which makes the postmodern young consumer the central point of any business (Sennett, 2006). So, ultimately it is not outlandish to posit that consumerism and postmodernism are becoming increasingly linked in respect of the marketplace roles of children in society and that its place in such a system will continue to be relevant in the foreseeable future.

Consumer protection laws and consumer rights

If considered critically, it could be stated that consumer rights are an essential part of life. Sew (2012, p. 1) calls it 'the consumerist way of life'. He acknowledges that these rights have been used by all consumers at one point or the other whether young or old and suggests that at a time when market resources and influences are growing by the day, young consumers must be aware of their rights (Sew, 2012) – rights that are clearly outlined to protect young consumers from market exploitation. These consumer rights are well defined and within this context we can have agencies like the government, consumer courts and voluntary organisations that work towards safeguarding them (Sew, 2012, p. 1). Kazi and Indermun (2014) note that while consumers are aware of these rights and plan to adopt them, it is significant that the consumer's duty within these rights are not well defined and as such it is difficult to spell out the role of the consumer within this context. Accordingly, Sew (2012, p. 2) defines consumer rights as rights given to the consumer to protect him/her from being cheated by the manufacturer/shopkeeper. Rights listed by Consumer International as the United Nations Guidelines for Consumer Protection (UNGCP) act as an international reference point of the consumer movement (UNGCP, 1985) and are depicted in Figure 21.2 below.

Considering that these rights are well defined to protect the consumer, consumer protection laws, on the other hand, are mapped out to safeguard fair

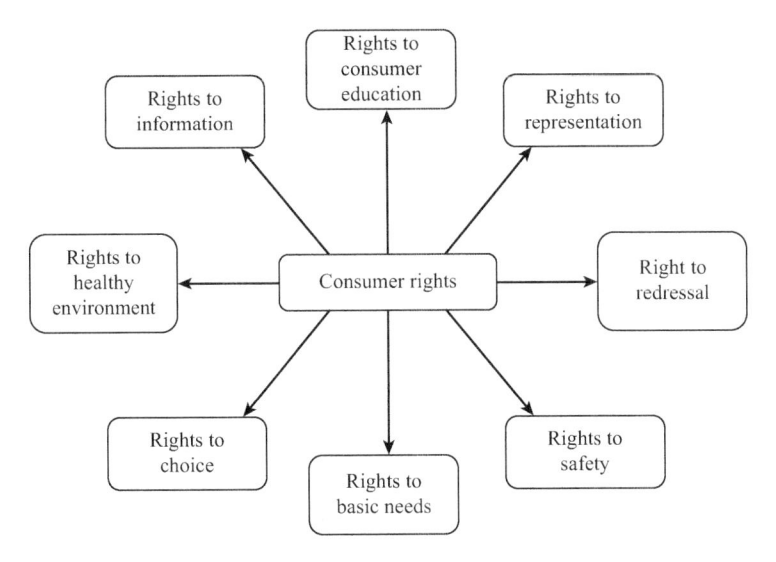

FIGURE 21.2 The UN guidelines for consumer protection

Source: Adapted from Consumer Rights Act (2015).

trade competition and the free flow of truthful information in the marketplace (Sew, 2012, p. 2). McGregor (2005b) adds that these laws are also designed to avert businesses that are involved in fraudulent activities or prejudicial practices from having an edge over competitors as well as offer an added protection for the vulnerable consumers of which children could be listed. In an attempt to enhance the significance of these laws, Sheth and Gardner (1982) explain that consumer protection laws are set up by the government to help protect the rights of all consumers whether weak or not. Extending this viewpoint further, Bello *et al.* (2012) argue that although these laws are set up to protect consumers, they also exist for the purpose of the economy and also to bring the consumer maximum satisfaction as far as possible. Bello *et al.* (2012) emphasise that any goods and/or services manufactured within any country are, in the long run, for the consumer. Hence, the consumer should be protected and also have the right to take decisions about the distribution of resources for their own needs (Sew, 2012). Appreciating this need, the International Organisation of Consumer Unions, now known as Consumers International, took the initiative and under its consistent petitioning, the United Nations adopted a set of Rules for Consumer Protection on 9 April 1985, which were revised in 1999 (Sew, 2012). The Rules address the well-being and requirements of consumers globally and provide a structure for governments, mainly to protect those of developing and newly independent countries to use for elaborating and strengthening consumer protection policies and legislation (Gunter and Furnham, 1998). As such this framework is considered an integrated part of general economic policy decisions (Bostan *et al.*, 2010).

Consumer protection for children: exploring some illustrative examples

The children's market has become more and more important as young people have become more prosperous and have an ever-increasing disposable income (Bostan *et al.*, 2010). A study by Asher (2014) shows that children between 8 and 12 years and adolescents between 13 and 19 years have become a big market because of their wealth and affluence and it is challenging to forecast the likelihood of the children's market. An American survey projects that American children have around $9 billion from their families and directly influence $130 billion of parental purchases (Calvert, 2008). As we experience various developments in the society and the marketplace, these figures will most likely have gone up in recent times. Considering the projections, a lot of laws within the American constitution are aimed at protecting all consumers irrespective of age. In the US, there are a variety of laws at both federal and state levels aimed at regulating consumer affairs. The history of consumer protection in the US is the story of detailed proper legal responses to crises and emergencies that create great public outrage and require a public response. This pattern began against the background of the nineteenth-century common law, which emphasised freedom of contract and *caveat emptor* (let the buyer beware). However, the modern consumer protection movement began in the 1960s with reference to a Consumer Bill of Rights by President Kennedy, the growth of the so-called 'Great Society' programme of the Johnson Administration. This programme highlights the actuality of unsafe products and the significance of having regulations to protect the consumer. The consumer protection law in the US protects the child consumer from unsafe products, fraud, deceptive advertising and unfair business practices through a mixture of national, state and local governmental laws and the existence of many private rights of actions. It also equips them with the knowledge they need to protect themselves (Acosta *et al.*, 2012). In Germany, reports show that at the start of 1990, German children aged 7–15 received 7.5 billion dollars in pocket money and gifts, while the spending power of 12–21 year olds amounted to 33 billion dollars annually (Gladwell, 2000). These are considerable statistics but these figures would still have increased by now. Similarly, this study reveals that in the UK in 1990, it was projected that 14–16 year olds alone had nearly £10 per week in disposable cash. By 1996, the Walls survey showed even 5 year olds had nearly £2.50 per week. The same survey showed that over a quarter save a considerable portion of their money in a variety of places. Even though the kinds of products marketed to children have remained much the same, the buying power of children and adolescents has increased exponentially over time (Calvert, 2008). The affluence of today's children and adolescents has made youth a market eminently worthy of pursuit by businesses (Calvert, 2008, p. 205). Youths now have influence over billions of dollars in spending each year as well as the power to shape the buying patterns of their families (Calvert, 2008, p. 206). From vacation choices to car purchases to meal selections, they exert a tremendous power over the family pocketbook. As a result, to influence the youth could be as good as having access to influencing the entire family's buying decisions. Considering the exposure of children to money, goods and services and the powerful influence on the family's buying pattern, it is right to consider the child as a consumer and make available laws to protect the child consumer (Valkenburg, 2000). While children as consumers should enjoy all consumer rights, there is some argument around what is right for the child and what should be obtainable (Bostan et al., 2010). According to Calvert (2008), government regulations executed by the Federal Communications Commission and the Federal Trade Commission provide some protection for children from advertising and marketing practices. However, children live and grow up in a highly sophisticated marketing environment that influences their preferences and behaviours (Calvert, 2008, p. 207). In Europe, laws are set out to protect the child consumer from a lot of factors, some of which are detailed in Table 21.7, retrieved from evablut.com.

Ethical consumerism and young consumers

Ethical consumerism is the moral ethics and standards by which groups or individuals make decisions on their purchases and how they dispose of goods and services (Muncy and Vitelli, 1992). In a closely related view, it is concerned with

TABLE 21.7 Laws to protect the child consumer in Europe

1	European consumer protection law provides that, under certain circumstances, consumers will have a right of rescission when ordering goods from an entrepreneur via distance selling
2	'Consumer' is defined as any person who is not an 'entrepreneur'. An 'entrepreneur' is any person or entity who operates an enterprise. An enterprise is every organisation of independent commercial activity that is established on a permanent basis, even if not oriented toward making a profit (e.g. this webshop). Legal entities under public administrative law are always deemed 'entrepreneurs' (see Austrian Consumer Protection Act, German acronym: KSchG). Thus, consumers are typically individuals acquiring goods for their personal leisure purposes
3	The Austrian legislature has transposed the requirements under EU law into domestic law primarily through the Distance and Field Sales Act (German acronym: FAGG) and, in respect of legal terminology, has selected the term 'right of rescission'. In other European Union countries, by contrast, the term 'right of cancellation' is more customary
4	Where a consumer is not advised to the contrary during the order process, you, as a customer of our webshop (provided that you are a consumer), have a right of cancellation. That right is described in the text below
5	You have the right to rescind this contract within 14 days' time, without the need to state any grounds of rescission. The rescission period is 14 days from the date on which you or a third party designated by you (who is not the carrier or freight forwarder) took possession of the goods. In order to exercise your right of rescission, you must inform us

Source: Consumer Right Acts (2015).

the actions of consumers when purchasing goods and services; the appropriateness or inappropriateness of decisions made on the purchase. So, it will be interesting and scholarly enriching to explore this within the context of young consumers in this chapter.

It has been previously stated that 1 in every 6 persons worldwide is between the ages of 15 and 19 (Moses, 2000) and there is increased focus on teenage consumers (Rice, 2001). Evidence also shows that this group of consumers tend to spend their money, influence their parents' purchasing decisions and set trends especially in food, fashion and clothing (Martin and Bush, 2000). Therefore, they constitute an attractive market segment for marketers as they double as consumers and influencers of family consumptions (Kim and Lee, 1997). Usually teenagers are able to make their own purchases as they receive allowances from parents and/or jobs. For instance, in a study of teenagers in the USA by Tootelian and Gaedeke (1992), it was revealed that 51.1 per cent of teenagers confirmed they receive some form of allowance. Interestingly, consumers between the ages of 12 and 19 spent an enormous $155 billion in 2001 (National Institute on Media and the Family, 2002), this indicated an increase from seven years earlier with a spend of $63 billion (Zollo, 1995). While this information was obtained some time ago, the trend in recent times suggests that these figures have increased further (Solomon, 2015).

For adolescents, consuming is an integral part of their identity performance in many intersecting ways including their experiences of race, gender and class (Deutsch and Theodorou, 2010). Technology has changed the way they make decisions around purchases. They are very connected and have a lot of access to information and marketers have also changed their strategies in accordance to the behavioural changes in the young consumers. Young consumers are more towards buying online and gather information by using technology. The marketers now focus more on advertising their products on the Internet as it directly targets the young consumers (Carrigan, 2001). They are able to buy more because of the ease of access to products, ready availability and competitiveness of different products available online.

In a study of the consumer attitudes of 15–19 year olds worldwide, Moses (2000) found that teenagers share certain characteristics that she called 'unifiers of global youth culture'. These unifiers are unabated consumerism, passion for technology, unending entertainment, continuous experience and learning, exploration and mobility, sports involvement and observation, respect for global icons, humanism and empathy, hope and trust in the future and self-navigation' (Moses, 2000, p. 37). Young consumers have been known to make decisions on ethical consumption based on three patterns: reserved social conscience, indifference and commitment (Bucic et al., 2012). Usually, ethical consumption is not necessarily a top priority in the decision-making process of what to consume for young people as they are more socially influenced by their peers (Lee, 2008). According to Joergens (2006), ethical issues have low impact on the behaviour of young people especially in fashion and clothing. Young people are growing in a fast-paced, highly networked world characterised by a high number of options and opportunities (Howe and Strauss, 2000). However, this consumer group is not totally averse to ethical consumption as they do have awareness of it. Besides, findings show that they love the hedonic value inherent in ecological products (Gurtner and Soyez, 2016). Their perception of success tends to be expressed through materialism as their purchases tend to be mostly driven by their need for social inclusion and as a status symbol.

Concluding remarks

The notion of consumerism and consumer protection is clearly a popular subject across many societies. And this popularity has remained sustained over the years especially as its main focus is about addressing the excesses of businesses towards ensuring the good well-being of consumers in terms of the protection of their rights. Meanwhile, young consumers also have considerable relevance in marketplace interactions, such as consuming one product or another, participating in the family buying roles, spending money earned from various sources and following the trends in market developments. Hence, they could be susceptible to marketplace turbulence and malpractices. A thorough scan of the marketing environment shows that some businesses engage in unethical business activities. These are in various forms across different elements of the marketing mix. With the prevalence of these notorieties, it makes sense to explore issues around how the rights of young consumers are protected in their various consumption activities. It is noteworthy that a number of regulatory activities, legal frameworks and consumer movements to protect children's rights in relation to consumption are in place but these vary in terms of the scale and effectiveness across different societies. While some are still at the infancy stage, others have made considerable progress towards achieving acceptable levels of young consumer protection. Ultimately, a holistic approach is required for more progress to be achieved on the issue. It is intelligible to argue that all stakeholders involved including parents, governments, business and the industry to which they belong, the society and non-government organisations should be involved in engendering the protection of the rights of young consumers. This will be a robust synergy towards dealing with this conundrum. With such an approach, we can make progress towards the threshold of optimum societal welfare in which consumers of all categories including children have the desired value in their day-to-day marketplace transactions both in the short run and the long run.

References

Acosta, R., Brady, J. and Waller, S. (2012). Consumer protection in the United States: An overview. Working Paper. www.luc.edu/media/lucedu/law/centers/antitrust/pdfs/publications/workingpapers/USConsumerProtectionFormatted.pdf (accessed 28 August 2017).

Alexandru, P. D., Irina, M. and Alice, C. (2014). Consumers' attitude towards consumer protection in the digital single market, as reflected by European barometers. *Amfiteatru Economic*, 16(36), 563.

Arochi, R., Tessmann, K. H. and Galindo, O. (2005). Advertising to children in Mexico. *Young Consumers*, 3, 82–85.

Asher, D. (2014). Child consumer protection: Online child safety case for Kenya. *Briefing Paper*, 1(10), 1–5.

Bao, Y., Fern, E. F. and Sheng, S. (2007). Parental style and adolescent influence in family consumption decisions: An integrative approach. *Journal of Business Research*, 60(7), 672–680.

Barratt, T. (1997). *Modernism and post modernism: An overview with arts examples*. Edited by James Hutchens and Marriane Suggs. Washington DC: NEEA.

BBC. (2015). Volkswagen: The scandal explained. www.bbc.co.uk/news/business-34324772 (accessed 11 May 2017).

Bello, K., Suleiman, J. and Danjuma, I. (2012). Perspectives on consumerism and Consumer Protection Act in Nigeria. *European Journal of Business and Management*, 4(10), 72–78.

Bostan, I., Burciu, A. and Grosu, V. (2010). The consumerism and consumer protection policies in the European community. *Theoretical and Applied Economics*, 17(4), 19–34.

Brann, E. (1992). What is postmodernism? *Harvard Review of Philosophy*, 2(1), 4–8.

Bucic, T., Harris, J. and Arli, D. (2012). Ethical consumers among the Millennials: A cross-national study. *Journal of Business Ethics*, 110(1), 113–131.

Buijzen, M. and Valkenburg, P. M. (2003). The effects of television advertising on materialism, parent–child conflict, and unhappiness: A review of research. *Journal of Applied Developmental Psychology*, 24(4), 437–456.

Calvert, S. (2008). Children as consumers: Advertising and marketing. *The Future of Children*, 18(1), 205–234.

Carrigan, M. (2001). The myth of the ethical consumer – do ethics matter in purchase behaviour? *Journal of Marketing Practice: Applied Marketing Science*, 18(7), 560–578.

Cassim, S. (2005). Advertising to children in South Africa. *Young Consumers*, 2, 51–55.

Cismaru, M., Lavack, A. M. and Markewich, E. (2008). Alcohol consumption among young consumers: A review and recommendations. *Young Consumers*, 9(4), 282–296.

Cohen, J. N. (2016). The myth of America's 'culture of consumerism': Policy may help drive American household's fraying finances. *Journal of Consumer Culture*, 16(2), 531–554.

Consumer Right Act. (2015). www.legislation.gov.uk/ukpga/2015/15/contents (accessed 21 April 2017).

Cook, D. T. (2013). Taking exception with the child consumer. *Childhood*, 20(4), 423–428.

Cova, B. (1996). What postmodern means to marketing managers. *European Management Journal*, 14(5), 494–499.

D'Alessio, M., Laghi, F. and Baiocco, R. (2009). Attitudes toward TV advertising: A measure for children. *Journal of Applied Developmental Psychology*, 30(4), 409–418.

Day, G. S. and Aaker, D. A. (1970). A guide to consumerism. *The Journal of Marketing*, 34(3), 12–19.

Dresden, B. and Barnard, J. (2003). Legal and regulatory controls on advertising and marketing to children in the United Kingdom. *Advertising and Marketing to Children*, October–December, 5(1), 77–83.

Deutsch, L. N. and Theodorou, E. (2010). Aspiring, consuming, becoming: Youth identity in a culture of consumption. *Youth & Society*, 42(2), 229–254.

Ene, C. (2012). Dimensions and perspectives of consumer protection policy in the european union. *The USV Annals of Economics and Public Administration*, 12(1.15), 39–45.

Eze, K., Eluwa N. and Nwobodo, B (2010). The Nigerian consumer @ 50. http://m2weekly.com/cover-cover/the-nigerian-consumer-50 (accessed 13 November 2011).

Featherstone, M. (1991). *Consumer culture and postmodernism*. London and Newbury Park: Sage.

Feldstein, P. J. (1988). *The politics of health legislation: An economic perspective.* Michigan: Health Administration Press.

Gbadamosi, A. (2010). Regulating child-related advertising in Nigeria. *Young Consumers, 11*(3), 204–214.

Gladwell, M. (2000). *The tipping point: How little things can make a big difference.* Abacus: London.

Gunter, B. and Furnham, A. (1998). *Children as consumers: A psychological analysis of the young people's market.* London: Routledge.

Ha, H. and McGregor, S. L. (2013). Role of consumer associations in the governance of e-commerce consumer protection. *Journal of Internet Commerce, 12*(1), 1–25.

Hamilton, K. (2009). Those left behind: Inequality in consumer culture. *Irish Marketing Review, 20*(2), 40.

Hicks, S. (2004). *Explaining postmodernism scepticism and socialism from Rousseau to Foucault* (1st edn). New York: Scholargy.

Hofer, P. and Bieri, J. (2005). Advertising to children in Switzerland. *Young Consumers, 2,* 80–81.

Howe, N. and Strauss, W. (2000). *Millennials rising: The next great generation.* New York: Random House.

Hsieh, Y. C., Chiu, H. C. and Lin, C. C. (2006). Family communication and parental influence on children's brand attitudes. *Journal of Business Research, 59*(10), 1079–1086.

Joergens, C. (2006). Ethical fashion: Myth or future trend? *Journal of Fashion Marketing and Management, 10*(3), 360–371.

Johe, M. H. and Bhullar, N. (2016). To buy or not to buy: The roles of self-identity, attitudes, perceived behavioral control and norms in organic consumerism. *Ecological Economics, 128,* 99–105.

Kazi, T. and Indermun, V. (2014). Consumerism, consumption and consumer education. *International Journal of Innovative Research in Management, 3*(5), 1–16.

Kim, C. and Lee, H. 1997). Development of family triadic measures for children's purchase influence. *Journal of Marketing Research, 34*(August), 307–321.

Koester, J. V. (2002). Legal briefing: Advertising to children in the USA. *Advertising and Marketing to Children, 4*(1), 67–71.

Kotler, P. (1972). What consumerism means for marketers. *Harvard Business Review Issue, 50*(3), 48–57.

Kuntz, M. (2017). Science and postmodernism: From right-thinking to soft-despotism. *Trends in Biotechnology, 35*(4), 283–285.

Lee, K. (2008). Opportunities for green marketing: Young consumers. *Marketing Intelligence & Planning, 26*(6), 573–586.

Lee, M., Pant, A. and Ali, A. (2010). Does the individualist consume more? The interplay of ethics and beliefs that governs consumerism across cultures. *Journal of Business Ethics, 93*(4), 567–581.

McGregor, S. L. T. (2005a). Ideological maps of consumer education. *International Journal of Consumer Studies, 32*(5), 545–552.

McGregor, S. L. T. (2005b). Sustainable consumer empowerment through critical consumer education: A typology of consumer education approaches. *International Journal of Consumer Studies, 29*(5), 437–447.

McGregor, S. L. T. (2005c). Transdisciplinarity and a culture of peace. *Culture of Peace Online Journal, 1*(1), 1–12.

Martin, C. A. and Bush, A. J. (2000). Do role models influence teenagers' purchase intentions and behavior? *The Journal of Consumer Marketing, 17*(5), 441–454.

Miles, S. (1998). *Consumerism as a way of life.* London: Sage.

Mirandah, P. (2005). Advertising to children in Malaysia. *Young Consumers*, 4, 74–76.
Montgomery, K. (2000). Youth and digital media: A policy research agenda. *Journal of Adolescent Health*, 27(2), 61–68.
Morris, D. and Al Dabbagh, M. (2004). The development of consumer protection in Saudi Arabia. *International Journal of Consumer Studies*, 28(1), 2–13.
Moses, E. (2000). *The $100 billion allowance: Accessing the global teen market*. New York: Wiley.
Muncy, J. A. and Vitell, S. J. (1992). Consumer ethics: An investigation of the ethical beliefs of the final consumer. *Journal of Business Research*, 24(June), 297–311.
National Institute on Media and the Family. (2002). Effects of video game playing on children. www.mediafamily.org/facts/facts_effect.shtml (accessed 27 August 2017).
Nicholls, A. J. and Cullen, P. (2004). The child–parent purchase relationship: 'Pester power' – human rights and retail ethics. *Journal of Retailing and Consumer Services*, 11(2), 75–86.
Papacharissi, Z. and Fernback, J. (2005). Online privacy and consumer protection: An analysis of portal privacy statements. *Journal of Broadcasting & Electronic Media*, 49(3), 259–281.
Parton, N. (2014). *The politics of child protection: Contemporary developments and future directions*. London: Palgrave Macmillan.
Pichaud, D. (2008). Freedom to be a child: Commercial pressures on children. *Social Policy and Society*, 7(4), 445–456. doi:10.1017/S1474746408004417.
Prensky, M. (2001). Digital natives, digital immigrants part 1. *On the Horizon*, 9(5), 1–6.
Reid, A. S. (2009). Online protection of the child within Europe. *International Review of Law, Computers & Technology*, 23(3), 217–230.
Rice, F. (2001). Superstars of spending: Marketers clamor for kids. *Advertising Age*, 1, 10.
Rodwin, M. A. (1996). Consumer protection and managed care: The need for organized consumers. *Health Affairs*, 15(3), 110–123.
Schotthöfer, P. (2002). Legal briefing: Advertising to children in Germany. *Advertising and Marketing to Children*, July–September.
Sennett, R. (2006). *The culture of the new capitalism*. New Haven, CT: Yale University Press.
Sew, A. (2012). Consumer protection and consumerism. *International Journal of Transformations in Business Management*, 1(6), 1–5.
Sheth, J. N. and Gardner, D. M. (1982). History of marketing thought: An update. Faculty Working Paper No. 857, College of Commerce and Business Administration, University of Illinois at Urbana Champaign.
Singh, P. (2011). Consumer culture and postmodernism. *Postmodern Openings*, 5(5), 55–58.
Solomon, M. R. (2015). *Consumer behaviour: Buying, having, and being* (11th edn). Upper Saddle River, NJ: Pearson Education.
Soyez, K. and Gurtner, S. (2016). How to catch the Generation Y: Identifying eco-innovators among young customers. In M. Obal, N. Krey and C. Bushardt (eds), *Let's get engaged! Crossing the threshold of marketing's engagement era. Developments in marketing science: Proceedings of the Academy of Marketing Science*. New York: Springer.
Süle, M. (2012). Can conscious consumption be learned? The role of Hungarian consumer protection education in becoming conscious consumers. *International Journal of Consumer Studies*, 36(2), 211–220.
Svantesson, D. and Clarke, R. (2010). A best practice model for e-consumer protection. *Computer Law & Security Review*, 26(1), 31–37.
Sweeting, H., Hunt, K. and Bhaskar, A. (2012). Consumerism and well-being in early adolescence. *Journal of Youth Studies*, 15(6), 802–820.
Thomas, S. E. and Wilson, P. R. (2012). Youth consumerism and consumption of status products: A study on the prevalence of social pressure among students of professional courses. *IUP Journal of Business Strategy*, 9(2), 44.

Todd, D. (2012). You are what you buy: Postmodern consumerism and the construction of self. *University of Hawai'i at Hilo–Hawai'i Community College: HOHONU, 10*, 48–50.

Tootelian, D. H. and Gaedeke, R. M. (1992). The teen market: An exploratory analysis of income, spending, and shopping patterns. *Journal of Consumer Marketing, 9*(4), 35–44.

UNGCP. (1985). Consumer protection. http://unctad.org/en/Pages/DITC/CompetitionLaw/UN-Guidelines-on-Consumer-Protection.aspx (accessed 12 January 2017).

Vadehra, S. (2004). Advertising to children in India. *Young Consumers, 4*, 75–78.

Valkenburg, P. M. (2000). Media and youth consumerism. *Journal of Adolescent Health, 27*(2), 52–56.

Valkenburg, P. M. (2001). Children's preferences for media content. In J. R. Schement (ed.), *Macmillan encyclopedia of communication and information* (pp. 143–147). New York: Macmillan.

Valkenburg, P. M. and Cantor, J. (2001). The development of a child into a consumer. *Journal of Applied Developmental Psychology, 22*(1), 61–72.

Vandana and Lenka, U. (2014). A review on the role of media in increasing materialism among children. *Procedia-Social and Behavioral Sciences, 133*, 456–464.

Venkatesh, A. (1992). Postmodernism, consumer culture and the society of the spectacle. *Advances in Consumer Research, 19*, 199–202.

Volz, G. W., Handschuh, F. B. and Poshtakova, D. (2005). Advertising to children in Spain. *Young Consumers, 1*, 71–76.

Winn, J. K. (2016). The secession of the successful: The rise of Amazon as private global consumer protection regulator. *Arizona Law Review, 58*, i.

Yannis, G. and Lang, T. (1995). *The unmanageable consumer: Contemporary consumption and its fragmentation.* London: Sage.

Zaharia, I. and Zaharia, C. (2015). The growth of environmentally sustainable consumerism. *Economics, Management, and Financial Markets, 2*, 115–120.

Zepf, S. (2010). Consumerism and identity: Some psychoanalytical considerations. *International Forum of Psychoanalysis, 19*(3), 144–154.

Zollo, P. (1995). Talking to teens. *American Demographics, 17*(11), 22–28.

INDEX

Aaker, D. 120, 126, 127, 132, 222
Aaltonen, S. 298
Abercrombie & Fitch 158
Abideen, Z. U. 177–178
Abrams, M. 289
abstract value 59
Academy of Medical Science 369
accommodation 40, 41
accountability 17, 51
Achenreiner, G. B. 144, 148
Acredolo, L. P. 157
action research 386–387
adaptation 40, 41
Adebowale, S. A. 275, 282
Adetunji, Olawale 98–116
adolescents/teenagers 81, 124, 194; attitude formation and persuasion 101, 104–110; Coca-Cola campaign 221; cognitive development 360–361; concept-oriented families 48; consumer misbehaviour 327; consumer socialisation 43, 44; early adulthood 125; emergence of 'teenager' concept 6; ethical consumerism 408; poor diet 382; post post-subcultural approach 298–299; price sensitivity 214; reflective thinking 42, 247; shopping malls 325; smartphones 192; social media 195; subculture 289, 290–291; viral marketing 216
Adugu, Emmanuel 59–78
adulthood, early 125
advergames 50, 355, 356

advertising 25, 32, 33, 170–171; attitude formation 100, 101–104, 110; brand loyalty 216; children's cognitive development 360–361; children's vulnerability to 382; consumer behaviour 350, 363–364; consumer protection 396; consumer socialisation 161; digital marketing 190; as driver of consumerism 394; ethical issues 51, 225; expenditure on 173; family background 351–352; family influence 363; food 218, 246–267; influence on children's behaviour 357–358; Moroccan attitudes to 174, 175–184; multi-tasking 155; Nigeria 98–99; online 44, 353–356, 361, 408; opinion leaders 276; primary markets 209; radio 356; regulation 163, 397, 407; social 372; South Africa 392; targeting of children 172–173; television 46, 101–103, 131, 173, 175–184, 215, 351, 354–356; visual and verbal components 102, 110; words used in 160–161
affordability 140
Africa: brands 134; collectivism 315; consumer protection 393; parental knowledge 353; smartphones 356; Ubuntu 315–316, 330, 331n1
African Americans 6, 176; *see also* black youth
African Youth Charter 66
age: attitudes to advertising 175, 178–179, 181, 182, 351; brand awareness 144; consumer behaviour 348; consumer

culture theory 144–145; consumer socialisation 41–42, 50; evaluation of alternatives 12; influence on family consumption 48, 49; market segmentation 235; marketing by 214; nature of children's purchases 209; reference groups 287; self-congruence 110; *see also* demographics; stages of child development
agency 290, 291
Agrawal, S. 212
Ahmed, A. S. 337–338
Ahmed, P. 211
air pollution 371
Ajzen, I. 99
Akam, M. 347
alcohol 8, 10, 17, 123, 392; consumer misbehaviour 309, 322; Facebook 172; impulse buying 325; peer influence 92, 274–275; religious beliefs 341, 342; social marketing 378–379, 383, 387; teenage rebellion 133
Ali, A. 31, 349
Alldred, P. 258
allowances 408; *see also* pocket money
Allport, G. W. 83, 180
Alvy, L. 360
Amazon 156, 164, 203, 387, 393, 398
American Marketing Association 79
American Psychological Association 357
analytics 189, 190, 196
Anderson, Jennifer 29, 32
Andreasen, A. R. 379
anonymity 250
Anore, Janet A. 230–245
anthropology 5
Appadurai, A. 296
Apple 165, 224, 230
apps 124, 125, 165
AR *see* augmented reality
Aries, Philippe 37
Aristotle 155
Arnould, E. 288, 289
artefacts 87–88
Asher, D. 406
Asia 156, 315, 353, 393
Askegaard, S. 230, 296
aspirational motives 275
assimilation 40, 41
attachment 129, 130
attention, selective 28
attitudes 98, 99–104, 157, 358–359, 408; consumer behaviour 364; Morocco 175–184; relationship marketing 222; study on attitudes and persuasion 104–110
augmented reality (AR) 134
Aurier, P. 149
Austria 393, 407
autonomy 34, 248, 298
Auty, S. 224
Awele, Achi E. 98–116, 271–287
Ayadi, K. 44

babies 123, 157, 163, 173, 209
baby boomers 6
BAC *see* brand adoption curve
Back, L. 295
Backett-Milburn, K. C. 13
Bamber, David 155–169
Bandura, Albert 122
banking services 211, 212–213
Bannon, L. 238
Bansal, R. 274, 275
Barbados 401, 402
Bartholomew, A. 254, 257
Basem, Y. A. 218
Bauman, Zygmunt 298
Baumeister, R. F. 84
Bearden, W. O. 271–272, 273
Beatly, S. E. 104
Beck-Gernsheim, E. 296
Beck, Ulrich 296
Beckham, David 276
behavioural change 379, 384
behavioural segmentation 235, 236, 242
behaviourism 39, 122, 320
Beiersdorf 174
beliefs 86, 87, 99; religious 335; tri-component attitude model 358; Westernisation of 339
Belk, R. W. 85
Bello, K. 405
Bellows, Laura 29, 32
belongingness 10, 60–61, 71–72, 74, 150, 289, 319
Bennett, A. 295
Bennett, P. D. 156
Berger, I. A. 101
Berger, P. L. 253
Berkman, H. W. 102
BERMY *see* brand emotional response model for youth
Berry, L. L. 220
best interest standards 51
Bettman, J. 89
Big Five theory of personality 84
Birmingham Centre for Contemporary Cultural Studies (CCCS) 290, 291

black youth 293, 295; *see also* African Americans
Blair, Tony 277
blogs 14, 166, 195
Bloom, P. N. 381
Blythe, J. 155
Bodenhausen, Galen 27
Boland, W. A. 146
Bono 277
Boots 196
Bosomworth, D. 200
Bostan, I. 391, 393
Bothma, N. 350
Bourne, F. S. 273
Bourne, H. 218
Bowen, M. 140, 147
Bower, T. G. R. 159
boycotts 321–322, 336–337
boys 31–32, 43, 182, 184; *see also* gender
Braimah, Mahama 230–245
Brake, M. 297
brand adoption curve (BAC) 131
brand emotional response model for youth (BERMY) 129–130
brand loyalty 127, 173, 189, 216; consumer style inventory 99; cradle-to-grave 159; digital marketing 206; family influence 351; low-income teenagers 382; loyalty loop 204; personal selling 217; post-purchase evaluation 199; services marketing 214; social media 75
brands/branding 17, 119–137; attitudes towards 101–102, 103, 104–110, 115–116; brand awareness 157–158, 202, 216, 222, 224; brand equity 126, 127, 129, 139; brand image 8, 327; brand names 120, 144, 161; brand symbolism 147, 148–149, 150; characters 128, 157–158, 215, 355; children's role in brand selection 25, 30; communities 128–129; consumer decision purchase loop 199, 202; digital marketing 205–206; evaluation of 99–100; information 104; market segmentation 233; Morocco 174; perceived value 143–145; personification 13; post post-subcultural approach 299–301; price sensitivity 145–146; relationships with 126–127, 129–130, 135, 209–210, 220, 222, 224–225; salience 222; self-identity 89; Snapchat 194; stages of child development 122–125; switching 29; value 126
Brandt, J. 140

Brann, E. 403
Brassington, F. 222
Braun-LaTour, K. A. 133
Brazil 165, 401, 402
Bree, J. 44
Brennan, R. 140
Brenner, J. 5, 15
Bridges, L. J. 180
Brim, Orville G. 40
Bronfenbrenner, Uri 122
Brucks, M. 350
Bucknall, S. 258
Buford, J. A. Jr. 60
Buijzen, M. 144
Bulley, Cynthia A. 230–245
Bullock, L. M. 6
Burger King 223, 224
Burman, E. 258
Burris, V. 141–142
Bush, Alan J. 176
Buskist, W. 159
Butter, E. J. 182

Cadbury's 99, 127
calculating opportunism 323, 324, 326–327
Calvert, S. L.: advertising 183, 184, 215, 216, 360; children's income 176, 208; marketing by age 214; marketing environment 166; regulation 407; stages of child development 42
campaign measurement 190, 196
Campomar, M. C. 231
Canada 9–10, 48–49, 102, 297
cancellation, right of 407
Cantillon, Z. 293
Cantor, J. 122, 131, 176, 208–209, 215, 393–395
capitalism 7
Carlson, L. 44
Carlson, N. R. 159
cartoon characters 29, 128, 173, 223
Cartoon Network 238
Cassim, S. B. 351, 392
Cateora, Phillip R. 6
Cattell, Raymond 83
causality 27–28
caveat emptor 403–404, 406
CCCS *see* Centre for Contemporary Cultural Studies
CCT *see* consumer culture theory
CCTV cameras 328
CDs 16
Cekada, T. L. 6

celebrities 26, 194, 215, 223–224, 243, 276, 355
Centre for Contemporary Cultural Studies (CCCS) 290, 291
Chaffee, S. H. 15, 44
Chaffey, D. 188
Chan, K. 81, 90, 102–103, 257
Chaney, D. 288
Chang, C. 100, 101, 103, 110
change 7
channels 155–169; digital marketing 189, 200; services marketing 212–213, 215
characters 26, 29, 128, 157–158, 173, 215, 223, 355
Charseatd, P. 335
Chartered Institute of Marketing (CIM) 370, 373
'chavs' 290
Childers, T. L. 351
childhood 37, 123–124; definition of a child 38, 387n1; 'valorization of' 25; *see also* stages of child development
Children's Online Privacy Protection Act (COPPA) 166, 397, 398, 399
Childwise 146–147, 158
China: attitudes to advertising 102; brands 134; categorisation of young consumers 81; consumer style inventory 99; middle-class families 357; mobile phones 172; television advertising 46, 215; young consumer market 82
Choi, J. 64
Chomsky, Noam 122
Christianity 334, 335, 337, 338–339, 340–341
Chua, V. 298
Churchill, Gilbert A. Jr. 40
cigarettes 274, 275, 319; *see also* tobacco/smoking
CIM *see* Chartered Institute of Marketing
Clarke, J. 293, 294
Clarke, R. 393
classical conditioning 39, 127
Clayton, J. 318
client orientation 246
clothing 223, 297; religion and clothes-buying behaviour 337–339, 343; subculture 291
clubbing 295
CNN 277
co-creation 14, 17, 132, 299
Coca-Cola 221, 224, 322, 323, 382
codes of ethics 249
Cody, K. 80

cognitive development 122, 159, 217–218, 247, 359–361, 363; consumer knowledge 148; consumer socialisation 31, 41, 145; major theorists 122; perception 28; trust in commercials 182; zone of proximal development 160; *see also* stages of child development
cognitive learning theories 39–40
cognitive processes 320
Cohen, B. 290
Cohen, J. N. 394
Cohen-Zada, D. 339–340
'collaborative individuality' 298, 301
collages 255–257, 258, 259, 260, 262, 263
collective identity 88–90, 92, 93
collectivism 298, 314, 315, 330, 336, 339
Collett, Jessica 26
Collins, R. 298
colour 26, 28–29, 239
commitment 219, 220–221, 222
commodities 59
communication: attitudes to TV ads 102–103; computer-mediated 90; family 15, 43–44, 47–48, 49, 50; market segmentation 234, 243; mothers 45; sign language 157; social class 357; social marketing 372
communities 128–129
competent child concept 248, 250
competition 375, 379
competitive advantage 120, 135, 139
complaints 321
concept-oriented communication 43–44, 45, 47–48, 50, 102, 103
conditioning 39, 88, 127, 155
Coney, K. A. 222
confidentiality 51
consensual families 15, 44, 48, 103
conservative societies 93
conspicuous consumption 273, 274, 299–300, 325, 394
constructivism 40
consumer behaviour 347–366; attitudes 358–359; children as consumers 349–351; cognitive development theory 359–361; definition of 3, 156; education 361–362; family influence 351–353; future research 362–363; Internet influence 353–356; social class 356–357
consumer culture theory (CCT) 144–145, 149, 289
consumer, definition of 81, 374
consumer-driven marketing 205
consumer involvement 61–63, 74–75

consumer life cycle 121
consumer misbehaviour 307–333; examples of 309–310; factors promoting 320–325; future research 329–330; managing 327–329; profiling 326–327; redefining 314–316; societal norms 311–312; typology of 313–314
consumer perception 25–36
consumer protection 391–413
consumer socialisation 6, 40–45, 49–52; attitudes to advertising 175–176; cognitive development 145, 148; definition of 40, 161; materialism 10, 93; media 46; multi-media devices 90; perceived value 143; role of parents 30–31, 34, 44–45; shopping 352; *see also* socialisation
consumer style inventory (CSI) 99
consumerism 29, 139, 163; attitudes to advertising 177; consumer misbehaviour 317–318, 324, 325, 330; consumer protection 391, 392–393, 404, 409; developing countries 316–317; drivers of 394–395; ethical 32, 407–409; postmodernism 403; Western 297
Consumers International 405
consumption 7, 25, 59, 155; centrality of 324, 326; children's influence on parents 237; conspicuous 273, 274, 299–300, 325, 394; consumer misbehaviour 326; culture and 288–289, 290, 299–300; evolutionary 4; family communication 47–48; family influence 15, 351–353; global culture of 403; identity formation 29; perception and 27, 29–30, 33; post-subculture 295; reference groups 277, 279–282, 283; satisfaction of needs 318–319; social context 89; subculture 290; symbolic 148; as universal phenomenon 347; vicious cycle of 317, 324
Converse, P. D. 79
Cook, D. T. 80, 148, 241
'cool' concept 5, 149, 174, 277, 280–281, 282, 300
COPPA *see* Children's Online Privacy Protection Act
corporate social responsibility (CSR) 223, 371
Court, D. 199–200, 202, 203
'cradle-to-grave' marketing 159, 173
Craig, S. C. 288–289
Cram, F. 15–16
credibility 175–176, 180–181
Cristea, A. A. 349

CRM *see* customer relationship management
Cross, G. 5
CSI *see* consumer style inventory
CSR *see* corporate social responsibility
culture 8–9, 98, 288–289; artefacts 87–88; consumer behaviour 348; consumer misbehaviour 315, 330; cross-cultural research 134; evaluation of alternatives 12; globalisation 17; influence of children 48–49; 'ordinary' 293; segmentation by cultural dispositions 241–242; social identity theory 86–87; television advertising 102
customer lifetime value 119, 126, 206
customer proposition 377
customer relationship management (CRM) 189, 191
customer value 142–143
customisation 7, 299
Cuzzocrea, V. 298

Damay, C. 141
Darwin, Charles 5
Daunt, K. 328
Davies, E. 12
Davis, J. 6
Davis, R. 81
Davis, T. 248
De Koning, M. J. M. 293
de la Ville, V.-I. 253
De Pelsmacker, P. 170
decision making 17, 26, 30; BERMY 129; changing dynamics of 52; concept-oriented families 48; consumer decision purchase loop 199–204; consumer socialisation 41–42; digital marketing 196–197, 204–206; family influence 15, 363; mothers' influence 45; price 140–141, 214–215; process of 9–14; purchase funnel 197–199; religion influence 334, 342; stages of 347–348; *see also* purchasing behaviour
Dekel, Ofer 288–306
Delener, N. 180
demographics: attitudes to advertising 105–106, 178; consumer socialisation 43, 49, 50; influence on family consumption 48; market segmentation 235, 242; social media analytics 196; social media and Internet use 66–67
Dempsey, Elizabeth 288–306
Denessen, E. 340
Denmark 340

dental health 385
depression 394
Derbaix, C. 181
desire 130, 131, 324–325, 326
deterrence 328
developing countries 8–9, 59; children's consumer behaviour 347–366; consumer misbehaviour 308, 313–314, 315–318, 320–325, 330–331; definition of 347; price sensitivity 146; social media and Internet use 65–75
developmental psychology 5, 144
DeYoung, C. G. 241
Dibb, S. 234, 275
diet 177–178, 382
diffusion of innovation 275, 284
digital marketing 188–207; decision-making process 196–204; stages of 189–191
digital natives 65, 398
digital technology 7, 165; branding 134; extended self 85; protection of children 397, 398; social identity 86; *see also* mobile technologies; technology
direct marketing 170–171
discourses 259–260, 261, 262
Disney 173, 232, 238, 337
Disneyland 132, 210
display advertising 190
distance selling 407
distributed self 254, 260
Domegan, C. 372, 380
domestic abuse 384, 387
Dong, D. 276–277
Dotson, Michael 30
Douglas, S. P. 288–289
Downes, S. M. 5
Drogba, Didier 276
Droit-Volet, S. 131
drugs 10, 381, 384, 387, 392; *see also* substance abuse
Duane, S. 380
Duff, B. R. L. 155
Dumb Ways to Die 128
DuRant, R. H. 8

e-commerce 51, 165, 393
E-CRM *see* electronic customer relationship management
e-word of mouth (eWOM) 14
early adulthood 125
Easterbrook, M. J. 149
eBay 398
ecological approach 122
ecological products 12, 409

Edell, J. 102
education 159–160; consumer 328, 361–362, 396–398; evolution of consumerism due to 393, 395; impact on consumer attitudes 359; parental 31; reference groups 287; religion influence on 339–341, 343; social media and Internet use 66, 73
Edwards, S. 7
Egan, J. 221
ego 320
Egypt 48
Eighmey, J. 63
Eischen, W. 147
electronic communications 171
electronic customer relationship management (E-CRM) 189, 191
Elliott, R. 147, 149
Ellis-Chadwick, F. 188
Emmanuel-Stephen, Christiania 391–413
Emmison, M. 256, 261
emotions: affective responses 100; branding 127, 129–130; early adulthood 125; provocative situations 323–324; tri-component attitude model 358–359; tweens 124
employees: consumer misbehaviour 308, 310, 313, 321, 329; physical surveillance 328; services marketing 213, 216, 217, 225
employment 13, 45, 66–67, 73
endorsements 26, 124, 215, 223–224, 243, 276, 355
Ene, C. 396–397
engagement 130, 131, 189, 194, 206
enjoyment 127, 129, 130, 131
entertainment 7, 143, 408; attitudes to advertising 175–176, 180–181, 182; China 82; Internet use 63
entrepreneurial marketing 165
environmental misbehaviour 314
Erikson, Erik 122, 159, 289
Escalas, J. E. 89
ESOMAR 249, 250
esteem 10, 60–61, 71–72, 319
ethical consumerism 32, 407–409
ethical issues 50–51; advertising 225; branding 128, 134, 135; manufacturing 311; research 248–251, 262; virtual and augmented reality 134
ethnicity: consumer culture theory 144–145; post-subculture 295; South Africa 350; subculture 291, 292–293; *see also* race

Etzel, M. J. 271–272, 273
European Union (EU) 393, 396–397, 398, 400–401, 407
evaluation: of alternatives 9, 11–13, 208, 348; attitude 99–100; consumer decision purchase loop 199, 203; post-purchase 9, 13–14, 17, 199, 204; social marketing 377
Evans, K. 298
evolutionary perspective 4–5
eWOM *see* e-word of mouth
exchange concept 374
exchange environments 325, 326
exchange principle 379
exhibitions 171
expectations: consumer conduct 310–311, 312; digital marketing 189, 190; 'on-demand' marketing 166; price and quality 140; relationship marketing 219
expenditure by children 16, 124, 157, 172, 208, 408; *see also* purchasing power
experiences 127, 130, 131, 132
expertise 48
exploratory research 254–255, 258, 259–260
extended self 85
Eysenck, Hans 83–84
Eysenck, Sybil 83

Facebook 7, 64, 70, 133, 166, 192; alcohol-related content 172; analytics 196; brand community 128; consumer protection 397, 398; digital marketing 188; FEAT Socks 195; *see also* social media
Fairclough, N. 260
fairness 311–312
faith *see* religion
Fakoussa, Rebecca 155–169
family 12, 14–16; brand behaviour 132–133; changing dynamics of decision-making 52; consumer behaviour 349, 351–353, 363; consumer socialisation 42–45, 51–52; eating behaviour 29; income 150; primary markets 209; religion 342; size of 48, 49, 179, 181, 183–184; *see also* parents
Fan, J. X. 99
Fan, Y. 215
fantasy 143
fashion industry 307–308
Fass, Paula 25
fathers 44, 45
fear 155

FEAT Socks 194–195
Featherstone, M. 297
Feick, L. F. 104
Feldman, H. 157
Feldstein, P. J. 391
Fernback, J. 398
Fill, C. 171
Finland 298
Fishbein, M. 99
Fjellström, C. 251
Flavell, J. H. 159
Fletcher, Kathy-Ann 391–413
Flynn, L. R. 277
FOMO (Fear of Missing Out) 133
food 13, 17, 32; advertising research 246–267; attitudes to advertising 177–178; brand characters 128; influence of role models 29, 32; need recognition 9–10; nutrition education 14; obesity 218, 225, 357, 384; organic 358; pressure on parents 92; regulation 163, 400; relationship marketing 223; religion and food-buying behaviour 336–337, 341, 343; snacks 16; social marketing 382; taxation on 138
football clubs 128
Forrester report (2007) 198
4Ps 211; *see also* 7Ps; marketing mix
Fourali, Chahid 369–390
Fournier, S. 12
Foxman, E. R. 48
France 6, 293, 393
fraud 308, 309, 310, 313, 314, 323, 324, 326–327
French, J. 376
Freud, Sigmund 83, 122, 318, 319–320
Fruchter, B. 109
Fullerton, R. A. 310, 311, 313, 318, 322–325, 326–327
fun 32, 90, 91–92, 131, 143, 192, 194, 357
Furnham, A. 6
future markets 209, 214

Gabel, T. G. 147
Gable, R. A. 6
Gaedeke, R. M. 408
Galvin, K. M. 45
games 4, 192, 356; advertising 173; consumer decision purchase loop 202–203; dangers of 176; loyalty loop 204; Morocco 174–175; online communities 128–129; as promotional tool 223
Gao, T. 172

Garber, J. 292
Gardner, B. B. 79
Gardner, D. M. 402, 405
Gbadamosi, Ayantunji 3–22; consumer protection 391–413; idiosyncratic issues 80; marketing communications 170–187; parents in developing countries 353, 359; pricing 138–154; television advertising 131
gender: adolescents 408; attitudes to advertising 176, 178, 179, 181, 182, 184; consumer culture theory 144–145; consumer socialisation 43, 50; consumption styles 31–32; influence on family consumption 48, 49; Internet use 73; market segmentation 235; reference groups 286; religious beliefs on modesty 338–339
Generation C 65
Generation Y 6
Generation Z 155, 164, 165
geo-location 165
geographic segmentation 235, 236, 242
Gerber, K. 350
Germany 82, 396, 406
Gesell, Arnold 122
Gibb, S. J. 138–139
Giddens, Anthony 296
Gilboa, S. 233–234
girls 31–32, 43, 182, 184, 292; *see also* gender
globalisation 17, 90, 295, 296–297, 339, 347, 404; consumer behaviour 348; post post-subcultural approach 299; religion and 343
Goksel, A. B. 223
Goldin-Meadow, S. 157
Goodwyn, S. W. 157
Google 11, 163, 165, 200, 203
Gorbachev, Mikhail 276
Gordon, R. 376
Gounaris, S. P. 220
Gracia-Marco, L. 384
Granot, E. 149
Grant, I. 172
graphics 26, 28–29
gratifications 63–65, 71–73, 74–75
Gregory, Jane 29
Gresham, L. G. 127
Griskevicius, V. 4
Gronholdt, Lars 30
Grönroos, C. 219
Guest, Lester P. 6
Guildford, J. P. 109

Gulla, A. 182
Gummesson, E. 211, 219
Gunter, B. 6
Gurevitch, M. 64
Gurtner, S. 12
Gwinner, K. P. 220

Ha, J. S. 291
Haas, H. 64
Hackley, C. 251, 252–253, 254, 257
Haynes, J. L. 13
halal food 336, 337, 341
Hamdan, H. 336
Hamelin, Nicolas 170–187
Hamilton, K. 147, 395
Hamley's 164
Hammond, D. 9–10
Hanley, S. 221
happiness 93
harm 51, 311, 312, 321–322
Harradine, R. 149, 222, 223
Harris, J. L. 178, 182
Harris, L. C. 328
Harrison, P. 175, 176
Harry Potter franchise 126
Hart, R. T. 339
Haryanto, J. O. 222–223
Hasbro 238
Hastings, G. 372
Haven, B. 197–199
Hawkes, C. P. 74
Hawkins, D. I. 222, 334, 335
Hazeldine, M. F. 276
HBD Chick 315
health issues 369, 371, 380–381, 382, 384–385; *see also* obesity
Hearn, H. 258
Heath, S. 251
Hebdige, D. 290, 293
hedonic consumption 91
hedonic value 12, 409
hedonism 325, 326
Held, L. 319
Hellman's 196
Helsper, E. 178
Hendon, D. W. 182
Hennig-Thurau, T. 220
Herman, S. 231
hermeneutic circle 258–259
heroes 128, 182, 183
heterogeneity 210, 211
hierarchy of needs 10, 60–61, 71–72, 74, 318–319, 394
Higgins, J. M. 60

Hill, Garett 194
Hill, Jennifer 29, 33
hip-hop music 297
Hofstede, G. 102
Hogg, M. K. 16
Holbrook, M. B. 143, 148, 222
Hollenbeck, C. R. 7
Holt, D. B. 300
Home Depot 337
Honda 158
Honeywell 99
Hong Kong 257
Hong, Yiwen 208–229
Hsieh, Y. C. 395
Hubspot 163
Huegy, H. 79
Hugenberg, Kurt 27
Hughes, Andrew 119–137
Hughes, H. 45
Huismans, S. 334
Huizinga, G. 61
Hultén, B. 163
human resource management 217
humanist psychology 289
Hummerkids.com 158
Hunt, S. D. 218
Hunter-Jones, Philippa 246–267
Huq, R. 294
Hussein, Nashaat H. 25–36
Hyatt, Eva 30
Hyman, H. H. 271–272

ICC *see* International Chamber of Commerce
id 320
ideal self 84–85, 180–181, 183
identity 4, 12, 80, 88–90, 91, 93; adolescents 289, 408; brands 130, 150, 222, 224, 300; centrality of consumption 324; 'chavs' 290; consumption and identity formation 29; cultural artefacts 88; group 82, 88–90, 92; post post-subcultural approach 298–299, 300, 301; sign value 297; social identity theory 86–87, 91, 92; social meaning of goods 325; social media 75; subculture 290, 291, 292; tribalism 297; *see also* self
idiosyncratic issues 80
images 193
IMC *see* integrated marketing communications
immersion 104
impersonal trust 311, 312
impulse buying 325, 326
income 34, 82, 146–147, 208, 406;
attitudes to advertising 183; consumer culture theory 144–145; consumer misbehaviour 330; evaluation of alternatives 12; family 138–139; increase in children's 26, 91; market segmentation 235; perceived value 150; sources of 13; *see also* pocket money
Indermun, V. 404
India: advertising to children 392; brands 134; childhood 37, 38; cigarette industry 275; consumerism 393; influence of family background 351–352; middle-class families 357; mother's role 44–45
individualisation 295, 296, 298, 299
individualism 296, 298, 315
Indomie 99
influence 52, 406–407; brand behaviour 133; children's influence on purchasing behaviour 30, 33–34, 47–49, 147, 149–150, 157, 173, 208, 223, 231, 237, 350; consumer behaviour 349; consumer socialisation 161; opinion leaders 276; peer 91–92; reference groups 271, 272, 279–281; self-categorisation theory 90
information: brand 104, 105, 107–110, 115–116, 131–132; China 82; consumer perception 26; consumer socialisation 31; information search 9, 11, 156, 188, 348; Internet use 63, 67, 68–69, 71, 72
information processing 43, 122, 131–132, 320, 359
informational influence 272, 277, 279–282, 286–287
informativeness 175–176
informed consent 51, 249–250
initial consideration 199, 200–201, 202–203
Inman, J. J. 145
innovation, diffusion of 275, 284
inseparability 210, 212–213
Instagram 64, 128, 166, 188, 195
instant messaging 192, 206
intangibility 210, 213
integrated marketing communications (IMC) 171, 189, 190, 205
interaction 7
interactive agents 355
interest 62, 63; brand adoption curve 131; segmentation by children's interests 241, 242
International Chamber of Commerce (ICC) 249
International Organisation of Consumer Unions 405

Internet 17, 52, 59–60, 89, 158, 159; active-evaluation phase 203; advertising 44, 173, 183, 216, 408; consumer behaviour 348, 353–356, 363; consumer-driven marketing 205; consumer protection 393, 398, 401; customer loyalty 209; developing countries 316–317; digital marketing 188, 191; ethical issues 51; extended self 85; hierarchy of needs 61; online channels 164–165; online communities 128–129, 204, 205, 276; online marketing 32; socialisation 46; use by young consumers 191–192; uses and gratifications perspective 63–65, 67, 68–69, 71–75; Westernisation of beliefs 339; *see also* social media; websites
interpretivism 251–252
Ireland 380
Islam 180, 183, 293, 335–339, 340, 341–342
Israel 38
Italy 126
Iyengar, R. 276–277
Izberk-Bilgin, E. 337

Jadva, V. 43
James, A. 248
Janssen, Sabine 25
Japan 38, 89, 354
Jay, Y. 109
Jenkins, R. 293
JGFM see Journal of Global Fashion Marketing
Ji, Mindy 26, 222
Joergens, C. 408
John, Deborah Roedder 8, 131; brand awareness 144; consumer socialisation 6, 10, 41–42, 143, 145, 148, 161; consumption symbolism 148; stages of child development 122, 247
Johnson & Johnson 174
Johnson, Anne 369
Jones, E. 145
Jones, S. 293
Jorgensen, S. R. 99
Journal of Global Fashion Marketing (JGFM) 307–308
Jourová V. 353
Judaism 335, 339, 341
Judd, V. 213

Kaikati, A. M. 7
Kamil, I. 335
Kantanka 233

Kapferer, J.-N. 62
Kaplan, B. 157
Kashif, M. 102, 109
Katz, E. 64
Kazi, T. 404
KDL *see* kid-dominant logic
Keller, K. L.: brands/branding 120, 126, 127, 129, 130, 143–144; market segmentation 232, 233, 242
Kellett, M. 248, 263
Kellogg's 127, 160–161
Kelman, H. C. 272
Kenrick, D. T. 4
Kenway, J. 159
Kenya 164, 300, 313
Kerrane, B. 16
Khalek, A. A. 337
Khan, T. 138
kid-dominant logic (KDL) 127
Kim, A. J. 7–8
Kim, H. 291
Kisielius, J. 102
Kjeldgaard, D. 230, 296
knowledge: brand 161–162; co-creation of 248, 263; consumer 148; market 362; opinion leadership 283; social construction of 255; stages of child development 42; transaction 352–353; zone of proximal development 160
Ko, E. 7–8
Kopnina, H. 4
Kotex 158
Kotler, P. 232, 233, 242, 372, 379, 391
Kraft 223
Kreitner, R. 60
Kress, G. R. 261
Kubacki, K. 256
Kuhn, M. 147
Kurniawan, S. 222–223
Kushwaha, G. S. 212

laissez-faire families 15, 44, 103
Laloux, Frederic 371
Lambin, J. J. 232
landscape metaphor 296–297
Lang, B. 81
Lang, T. 403
Langrial, S. 102
language 160–161, 253, 258, 262
Larson, R. W. 156
Laslett, B. 5, 15
latency 156
Latin America 315, 393
Laughey, D. 293

Laurent, G. 62
Lauterborn, B. 375
Lea, S. E. 12
Leahy, R. 221
learning 86, 155, 361; behaviourism 39, 122, 320; consumer socialisation 41, 49; theories of 38–40
Lee, E. M. 222
Lee, H. 74
Lee, J. W. 81, 82
legal age of childhood 38
Lego 127, 231–232, 238
The Lego Batman Movie 238
Legoland 132
Lehmann, D. 343
Leigh, J. H. 147
Lenka, U. 396
Leonard, C. 147, 149
Lessig, V. P. 272, 277
Levy, S. J. 372
Lewis, C. 224
Li, Y. 215
life-course model 15
lifestyle: children's perception 29–32; 'collaborative individuality' 298; evaluation of alternatives 12; post-subculture 295, 297; psychographic segmentation 236
likeability 175–176
Lincoln, S. 293
Lindstrom, M. 140–141
littering 314
Littleton, K. S. 248
Livingstone, S. 178
location-based marketing 165, 189
Locke, John 37
logos 144, 157
Lombe, M. 275
longitudinal research 261–262
loop model 199–204
L'Oréal 174
love 10, 60–61, 71–72
Lovelock, C. 211
low-income consumers 145–146, 147, 350, 382
loyalty 209, 224, 355–356; loyalty loop 199, 204; price impact on 212; relationship marketing 219–223; *see also* brand loyalty
Luckmann, T. 253
Lusch, R. F. 127, 132
Lutz, R. J. 103, 110, 222
luxuries 273–274, 351
Lynn, M. 231, 234

m-commerce 165
M-Pesa 164
Madonna 277
Maffesoli, M. 295
Maheshwari, Vish 188–207
Malaysia 336, 337, 396
managed care 391–392
manufacturing 311
Maphar Laboratories 174
market evaluation 189–190
market research 376, 379; *see also* research
Market Research Society 249, 250
market segmentation 3, 230–245; alternative bases for 240–242, 243; characteristics of children 239–240; consumer involvement 62; consumer misbehaviour 326–327; conventional bases for 235–236, 240, 242; definitions of 232–233; digital marketing 190; social marketing 379; targeting and positioning 234–235; uniqueness of the children's market 237–238
marketing: accountability 17; attitudes 99–100, 110; channels 155–169; co-creation of value 14; communications 170–187; consumer behaviour 363; consumer misbehaviour 324–325, 326; consumer perception 26–27; definitions of 370, 373; digital 188–207; as driver of consumerism 394; entrepreneurial 165; ethical issues 50–51; evaluation of alternatives 12; expenditure on 173; increase in marketing to children 25; 'on-demand' 166; online 32; post post-subcultural approach 298–299; primary markets 209; reference groups 275; relationship 121, 218–224; services 211–218; social constructionism 252–253; as source of good 370–371; *see also* advertising; brands/branding
marketing mix 139–140, 147, 149; channels 156; market segmentation 233; services 211–217, 224; social marketing mix 375–376, 377, 380
Marranci, G. 293
Martens, L. 148
Martensen, Anne 30
Marx, Karl 371
Maslow, Abraham 10, 60–61, 71, 74, 318–319, 394
Mason, R. B. 290, 291
mass customisation 299
materialism 10, 93, 299–300, 357; consumerism 394; family communication 44; gender differences 31; Korean

adolescents 291; mothers 45; perceptions of success 409; self-image 81; television advertising 175–176, 177–178
Mattila, A. S. 241
maturation 122
Maybin, J. 254, 255
McAdams, D. P. 241
McCarthy, E. 211
McCarthy, M. 3
McCord, L. 63
McDonald's 215, 220–221, 223, 322, 382
McGinnis, J. M. 102
McGregor, S. L. T. 405
McKinsey 199–200
McLeod, J. M. 13, 15, 44
McNeal, James 16, 26, 30, 82, 102–103, 146, 209, 236
McNiff, Jean 386–387
McQuarrie, E. F. 103–104, 110
McRobbie, A. 292, 293
meaning 4; co-creation of 251–252, 254; cultural 294; social construction of 253, 255, 262; social meaning of goods 325; symbolic 92, 148–149, 150; youth as active agents in the construction of 301
media: attitudes to advertising 175–176, 178, 181; brand characters 223; brand symbolism 149; changing media landscape 7; consumption needs 64; exposure to 82; influence of 32; multi-tasking 163; old 52; social class 357; socialisation 41, 46, 51–52; *see also* social media; television
memory 39, 121, 132, 133; brand names 120; cognitive processes 320; positive brand memories 222–223
Mendelson, S. 238
Meng, F. 276–277
Menzel Baker, S. 148–149
merchandising 126
messages 195–196
Mexico 38, 351–352, 396
Microsoft 128–129
middle class 357, 394
Middleton, S. 147
Miles, P. M. 276
Miles, S. 392
Minaker, L. 9–10
Mingazova, Diliara 138–154
Mininni, Ted 26
misbehaviour 307–333; examples of 309–310; factors promoting 320–325; future research 329–330; managing 327–329; profiling 326–327; redefining 314–316; societal norms 311–312; typology of 313–314
Mitchell, A. A. 101, 102, 110
mobile phones 92, 172, 192, 361; addiction to 318; Coca-Cola campaign 221; consumer protection 397; early adulthood 125; *see also* smartphones
mobile technologies 17, 81, 91, 167; digital marketing 188, 191; Generation Z 164; late childhood 124; location-based marketing 165; multi-tasking 155; word of mouth 14; *see also* digital technology
Moisander, J. 253, 256, 258–259
moments of truth 199, 200–201, 203, 204
money 13, 43, 140–141, 350–351
Montgomery, K. 397
Montigneaux, N. 237
Moore, E. S. 103, 110, 222
Moore, K. A. 180
Moore, R. L. 44, 141
Moorlock, Emily 288–306
moral constraints 323, 326
moral responsibility 239
Morales, A. C. 218–219
Morgan, R. M. 218
Morocco 174–184
Morris, Bethan 188–207
Moschis, G. P. 15, 40, 44, 141
Moses, E. 408
mothers 44–45, 162–163
Mothersbaugh, D. L. 334, 335
motivation 63, 86, 99; consumer misbehaviour 326; definitions of 60; market segmentation 234; research on 79–80; social exchange 90; social media and Internet use 63–64, 71–72; uses and gratifications theory 63
movies 224, 238, 239
Muggleton, D. 294, 295
Muller, C. H. G. 347
multi-channel approach 163, 189
multi-media devices 81, 89, 90, 91–92
multi-tasking 155–156, 163
Mungham, G. 294
Muniz, A. M. 128
Munn, M. 351
music 99, 290, 293, 295, 297
Musinguzi, Dan 334–346
Muslims 180, 183, 292, 293, 336–339, 340, 341–342
Muswera, Nyasha 307–333

Nagarkoti, B. 82
Nairn, A. 143, 144, 149

Namanya, A. A. 341
'narrative transportation' 103–104
Nash, April 183
Nasu, Y. 341
National Social Marketing Centre (NSMC) 373–374, 379
Nayak, A. 293
necessity products 273–274, 351
Neck, H. M. 156
need recognition 17
Needham, A. 14
needs 3, 237, 327; consumer behaviour 347; hierarchy of 10, 60–61, 71–72, 74, 318–319, 394; media consumption 64; need recognition 9–11; satisfaction of 318–319; targeting 238; uses and gratifications theory 63
'neo-tribes' 297
neoliberalism 385
Nestle 99, 127, 236
Netflix 158
Netherlands 293, 354
Neuborne, E. 157
Neulinger, A. 103
new product development 231
New Zealand 126
Newman, J. W. 79
Newman, K. L. 87
news releases 355
Ng, S. H. 15–16
Nickelodeon 159
Nigeria: advertising 98–99, 392; attitude formation and persuasion 104–110; consumer misbehaviour 313; consumer protection 396, 401, 402
Nollen, S. D. 87
noodles 99
norms 87, 89, 301; attitudes to advertising 179, 181; collectivist societies 314; consumer behaviour 348; consumer misbehaviour 310, 311–312; religion 342; social class 356; social exchange 90; social marketing 384
Norway 393
Novelli, W. D. 381
NSMC *see* National Social Marketing Centre
nutrition 177–178, 382

Oakes, Steve 246–267
obesity 32, 247, 357, 369, 374; marketing ethics 225; pricing instruments to counter 138; social marketing 381, 384, 386, 387; television advertising 177–178, 184, 218

objectives 377
objects 288–289
OCEAN 84
Odbert, H. 83
O'Donohoe, S. 172
O'Donohue, S. 254, 257
O'Dougherty, M. 223
O'Guinn, T. C. 128
Ojikutu, R. K. 327
Oliver, R. L. 220
Olson, J. C. 100, 102
Olutola, Idowu Comfort 391–413
omni-channel approach 163–164, 200
Oniku, Ayodele C. 98–116, 271–287
online communities 128–129, 204, 205, 276
online marketing 343
online shopping 342
operant conditioning 39
opinion leadership 275–277, 279, 282, 283–284, 286–287
opportunism 323, 324, 326–327
Opute, Abdullah Promise 79–97
'ordinary' youth 293–294
Otto, A. M. C. 10
Ovaltine 99
own brands 145–146

packaging 26, 28–29
Padlet 257, 260, 263
Pagla, M. 140
Pakistan 102
Pals, J. L. 241
Papacharissi, Z. 63, 398
parents: attitudes to advertising 102–103, 109, 176, 177, 183, 359; brand behaviour 133, 224–225; communication styles 43–44, 47–48, 102–103; consumer socialisation 30–31, 34, 41, 44–45, 50; in developing countries 353, 359; food purchases 92; gatekeeping role 13; growing influence of children on shopping behaviour 30; held to emotional ransom by children 237; involvement in television viewing 361–362; low-income 147; parenting styles 162–163, 348, 350; price sensitivity 146; re-socialisation of 49, 50, 52; reference groups 287; *see also* family
Park, C. W. 272, 277
Park, J. 291
Park, N. 74
Park, S. Y. 222
participatory research 248, 256

Parton, N. 396
past usage 222–223
Patino, A. 231, 291
Pavlov, Ivan 39
payments 165
Pearson, G. 294
Pecheux, C. 181
peer pressure 147, 149, 223, 395; alcohol consumption 275; brands 300; consumer decision purchase loop 202; consumer misbehaviour 322–323, 324; consumer socialisation 30; food preferences 29; impulse buying 325; primary markets 209; viral marketing 216
peers: condom use 282; consumer decision purchase loop 202–203; influence 91–92; peer-to-peer marketing 32; reference groups 274–275; socialisation 41
Pennycook, A. 297
people 211–212, 213, 216, 375; *see also* employees
Pepsi 224
perceived value 141–145, 150
perception 25–36, 86
performance measurement 190
perishability 210, 211
personal care products 16
personal comments 73–74
personal identity 86, 90, 91, 92
personal selling 170–171, 213, 216–217, 224
personalisation 224
personality 29, 82–84, 85–86; brand 120, 132, 222; evaluation of alternatives 12; Freudian theory 320; psychosocial development 122; religious subcultures 342
personification 13
persuasion 98, 100, 103–110, 374
'pester power' 50, 223, 395
Peter, J. P. 100, 102
Peters, Lucas 170–187
Pettersson, A. 251
Pettitt, S. 222
Pew Research Center 65, 66
Phillips, B. J. 103–104, 110
physical evidence 211–212, 213, 217, 225, 375
physiological needs 10, 60–61, 71–72, 74, 319
Piaget, Jean 28, 40, 41, 122, 141, 144–145, 159, 278, 359–361
Pichaud, D. 395
Pilkington, H. 293

Pine, Karen 183
Pinterest 128, 166
piracy 309
Pixar 128
place 163, 211; place branding 132; services marketing 212–213, 215; social marketing mix 375
planned behaviour, theory of 358
Plato 374
PlayStation 128–129
pleasure 62
pluralistic families 15, 44, 48, 103
pocket money 6, 16, 33, 82, 146–147, 208; consumer socialisation 31; Germany 406; late childhood 124; parental motivation 34; price sensitivity 146, 214; *see also* income
point-of-purchase 171
Polhemus, T. 295
pollution 371
poor service 321
popular culture 32, 297
positioning 120, 121, 234–235, 242
Posner, M. I. 131
post post-subculture 297–301
post-purchase evaluation 9, 13–14, 17, 199, 204
post-subculture 291, 294–297
postmodernism 295, 297, 403, 404
preferences 208; preference formation 80–81, 86–88, 91–93; reference groups 277, 279–281
premiums 355
Prendergast, G. 81
price 138–154, 211; brand symbolism 147, 148–149; comparing 26, 30; definition of 140; evaluation of alternatives 11–12; impersonal trust 311; perceived value 141–145; pricing knowledge 353; sensitivity 145–146, 224, 351; services marketing 212, 214–215; social marketing mix 375; strategies 141–142
Price, L. L. 104
price-tag switching 308, 309, 313, 322, 323
pricing *see* price
primary markets 209
print media 189
privacy 51, 64, 195, 342, 398
private products 273–274
problem identification 376
problem planning 376
problem recognition 348
processes 211–212, 213–214, 217, 375
product placement 216, 223, 224, 355

product trial 103
products 211; attitudes to 358–359; brand symbolism 150; consumer involvement 61–63; market segmentation 231, 233, 236, 238; opinion leadership 283–284; perceived value 141–145; price sensitivity 145–146; reference groups 273–274; routine and special 139; services marketing 212, 214; social marketing mix 375; transaction knowledge 352–353
profitability 220, 221
promotion 195, 211, 223; aspirational motives 275; services marketing 213, 215; social marketing mix 375
Pronto 99
protection of children 362, 369, 396–398, 409; *see also* consumer protection
protective families 15, 44
provocative situations 323–324, 326
psychoanalytic theory 318, 319–320
psychodynamic approach 122
psychographic segmentation 236, 242
psychology 5, 87, 91, 144, 289, 318
psychosocial development 122, 159
public products 273–274
public relations (PR) 170, 213
publicity 170
punishment 272, 282
Punj, G. 310, 311, 313, 318, 322–325, 326–327
purchase funnel 197–199
purchasing behaviour 9, 13, 26, 348, 363; attitude formation and persuasion 101, 104–110, 115–116; children's influence on 30, 33–34, 47–49, 147, 149–150, 157, 172–173, 208, 223, 231, 237, 350; consumer style inventory 99; impulse buying 325; reference groups 271, 272, 273–275, 283; religion influence on 334, 342; social media 75
purchasing power 90, 91, 157, 349; digital marketing 206; increase in children's 33, 92, 406; *see also* expenditure by children
Purohit, H. 182

quality: impersonal trust 311; price relationship 140; service 217
queueing 312, 323

race: adolescents 408; attitudes to advertising 175–176; market segmentation 235; *see also* ethnicity
racism 178, 291, 293
radio advertising 356
Rafiq, M. 211

rage 309, 313
Rai music 293
Raitani, S. 219
Ramzy, Omar 25
Rao, A. R. 351
Redhead, S. 294, 295
Reed II, A. 90
reference groups 86, 271–287; buying patterns 273–275; definition of 271; evaluation of alternatives 12; types of 272
regulation 163, 363; children's rights 396; consumer protection 393, 396–397, 398, 399–402, 404–405, 406–407, 409; digital marketing 205; food advertising 218
Reid, A. S. 398
Reisman, D. 6
relationship marketing (RM) 121, 218–224, 356
religion 88, 93, 334–346; attitudes to advertising 180, 181, 183, 184; evolution of the child consumer 395; market segmentation 235
remuneration 329
rescission, right of 407
research: food advertising 246–267; social marketing 386–387
resistance 290, 291
resources 377
retail store knowledge 353
returns, fraudulent 307, 308, 309, 313, 322, 323
revenge 321–322
revenue 237–238
reverse socialisation 47, 49–50, 52
rewards 272, 282, 323
Reza, S. A. 271, 274, 282
Rice, F. 290
Richard, Cliff 155
Rideout, V. J. 382
ridicule 10
rights 392–394, 396, 398, 400, 404–405, 407, 409
risk 62, 63, 124, 143, 145
'risk society' 296
RM *see* relationship marketing
Robertson, T. S. 131
Rodhain, A. 149
Rodwin, M. A. 391–392
Rogers, C. R. 84–85
Rogers, E. M. 275
role models 29, 32, 177
roles of young consumers 16, 17, 33, 49–50, 132–133, 139
Roper, S. 300
Rose, G. M. 143

Roseborough, H. 6
Ross, J. 149, 222, 223
Ross, J. M. 180
Rossiter, J. R. 101, 131, 181
routine products 139
Roy, S. 64
Rubin, M. A. 63
Russia 322, 323
Rust, R. T. 220

S-CRM *see* social customer relationship management
Saad, G. 4
safety needs 10, 60–61, 71–72, 74, 319
Salaria, R. M. 177–178
sales promotions 146, 170–171, 213; *see also* promotion
Sander, W. 340
Saraf, V. 224
Sarathy, P. S. 276
Sasser, W. E. 126
satisfaction: customer loyalty 223; definition of marketing 373; poor service 321; post-purchase evaluation 14; price impact on 212; relationship marketing 221
Saudi Arabia 393
scandals 391
Schiffman, L. G. 3
Schindler, R. M. 222
Schmitt, B. H. 132
schools: brand promotion in 223; research in 250–251, 263; school uniforms 11
Schor, J. B. 237
Schunk, D. H. 39
Schwartz, S. H. 334
Scott, L. M. 258
screen time 382
SDL *see* service-dominant logic
search engine optimisation 190
secondary markets 209
segmentation 3, 230–245; alternative bases for 240–242, 243; characteristics of children 239–240; consumer involvement 62; consumer misbehaviour 326–327; conventional bases for 235–236, 240, 242; definitions of 232–233; digital marketing 190; social marketing 379; targeting and positioning 234–235; uniqueness of the children's market 237–238
selective attention 28
self 80, 81; actual and ideal 84–85, 180–181, 183; attitude formation 100–101; distributed 254, 260; *see also* identity

self-actualisation 10, 60–61, 71–72, 74, 84–85, 319, 394
self-categorisation 86, 89–90, 100–101, 103
self-concept 82, 84–85, 88–89, 91, 300; attitudes 100, 103–104, 108–109, 110, 180–181; branding 301; evaluation of alternatives 12
self-congruence 84–85, 100–101, 103–104, 108–109, 110, 222
self-esteem 4, 61, 84, 89, 150, 319, 394; *see also* esteem
self-image 81–82, 84–85, 100–101, 222, 324, 325
self-referencing 101, 110
selfies 193
senses 33, 163
service-dominant logic (SDL) 127, 132
service quality 217, 321
services, definition of 210–211
services marketing 211–218, 224, 225
servicescapes 328
Sethna, Zubin 155–169
7Ps 211–217, 224, 375; *see also* marketing mix
Seventh-day Adventists 337, 339, 340, 341
Sew, A. 404
sexual behaviour 274–275, 277, 282
Seybold, P. B. 140–141
Shah, M. 300
Shaker, T. I. 218
Shambare, Jane 307–333
Shambare, Richard 307–333, 347–366
Shapiro, S. 311
sharing views 67–71, 72
Sharma, Adya 37–58
Sherley, C. 234
Sherrington, Anna Maria 246–267
Sheth, J. N. 132, 402, 405
Shields, R. 295
Shimp, T. A. 127
Shiner, R. L. 241
Shizumu, K. 375
shoplifting 308, 309, 313, 318, 322–323, 325, 327
shopping: compulsive 92; consumer socialisation 352; mothers 45; scripts 353; supermarkets 161; types of consumer 341–342; *see also* purchasing behaviour
shopping malls 325
showing-off contests (*skothane*) 314, 318, 322, 324, 325
Sidin, S. M. 15
Siemieniako, D. 256

sign language 157
sign value 62, 297
signs 261
Simkin, L. 234
Simunaniemi, A.-M. 257–258, 260
Singapore 298, 401, 402
Singh, P. 403
single-parent families 8, 45
Sinnott, Karl 188–207
situation analysis 376
size of family 48, 49, 179, 181, 183–184
skills: consumer socialisation 31, 41, 43, 49–50; preparation for adulthood 34; reverse socialisation 47; shopping 353; zone of proximal development 162
skinheads 294
Skinner, B. F. 39, 122
skothane (showing-off contests) 314, 318, 322, 324, 325
smartphones 82, 85, 133, 192, 356; *see also* mobile phones
Smit, E. 222
Smith, G. H. 80
Smith, W. R. 232
SMM *see* social media marketing
Smock, A. D. 61
smoking *see* tobacco/smoking
snacks 16
Snapchat 166, 188, 192–195, 196
social acceptance 289
social advertising 372
Social Child model 248
social class 12, 144–145, 356–357, 359, 408; *see also* socio-economic status
social constructionism 247–248, 251–256, 258, 260, 262, 289
social context 89, 255, 258, 263
social customer relationship management (S-CRM) 189, 191
social identity theory 86–87, 91, 92
social marketing 300, 369–390; competition 375; concept of 372–374; consumers 374; criticism of 385–386; effectiveness of 380–382; exchange concept 374; programme of change 376–380; social marketing mix 375–376, 377, 380
social meaning 209, 325, 326
social media 7–8, 17, 59–60, 158, 166–167, 293; Coca-Cola campaign 221; consumer decision purchase loop 202, 203; consumer-driven marketing 205; consumer protection 397; developing countries 316–317; digital marketing 188, 190–191, 195–196,

206; early adulthood 125; extended self 85; hierarchy of needs 61; market segmentation 234; online communities 128–129; purchase funnel 198; research 134; tweens 124, 130, 192; uses and gratifications perspective 64–65, 67–75; Westernisation of beliefs 339; *see also* Facebook; social networking sites; Twitter
social media marketing (SMM) 8
social networking sites (SNSs) 59–60, 82, 166, 192; consumer misbehaviour 312; dangers of 176; hierarchy of needs 61; uses and gratifications perspective 64–65, 67–75; *see also* Facebook; social media; Twitter
social networks 88, 298; opinion leaders 276, 277; stages of child development 124
social norms *see* norms
social responsibility 17, 370, 371
social semiotics 261
social texts 257
socialisation 6, 8, 40–45, 49–52, 208, 217–218; attitudes to advertising 176; conspicuous consumption 394; definition of 40, 161; economic 147; family 15; family ecology 12; food consumption 253, 255; gender differences in consumption styles 31–32; materialism 10, 93; media 46; multi-media devices 90; pathological 326; perceived value 143; price sensitivity 146; religion 342; reverse 47, 49–50, 52; role of parents 30–31, 34, 44–45; shopping 352
socio-economic status 31, 147, 179, 274, 351–352; *see also* social class
socio-oriented communication 43–44, 45, 47–48, 50, 102
sociology 5, 8, 318
software 355
Solomon, M. R. 3, 16, 347
Song, I. 63
Sonstegard, J. S. 99
Sony 128–129
Sood, J. 341
Sophists 374
Soutar, G. N. 143
South Africa: advertising to children 392; children as consumers 350; consumer behaviour 352; consumer misbehaviour 313, 314, 318, 325; middle-class families 357; radio advertising 356; television advertising 351; violence on television 357

South Korea 99, 291
Southall, C. 45
Soyez, K. 12
Spain 396
Sparrman, A. 247, 263
special products 139
sponsorship 32, 171, 223
Spotswood, F. 375
spyware 355
Srivastava, R. K. 220
Staelin, R. 102
Stafford, T. F. 63
stages of child development 159, 209, 247, 360–361, 395; attitudes to advertising 216; brand behaviour 121, 122–125; consumer socialisation 41–42, 148; perceived value 141–142; *see also* cognitive development
Stead, M. 383
'stealth marketing' 216, 356
stereotypes 178
Sternthal, B. 102
stimuli 27–28, 33, 163, 320–321
Stokes, D. 156
store knowledge 353
store layouts 328
store preferences 88
STP model 234, 235
structural knowledge 352
subculture 288–306; criticism of 291–294; evaluation of alternatives 12; post post-subculture 297–301; post-subculture 291, 294–297; religious 342
substance abuse 309, 322, 382–384, 392; *see also* alcohol; drugs; tobacco/smoking
sugar 17
Süle, M. 395, 398
superego 320, 324–325
supermarkets 161, 223, 353
Surf 224
surveillance 328
Svantesson, D. 393
Swanson, D. L. 63
Sweden 393
Sweeney, J. C. 143
Switzerland 396
symbolic interactionism 80
symbolic knowledge 352
symbolic value 92, 147, 148–149
Syrjälä, H. 89
Szmigin, I. 218

tablets 191, 192
Talpade, S. 104
Tapp, A. 375

targeting: digital marketing 189, 190; market segmentation 234; social marketing 377, 379
Tartas, V. 253
Tauber, E. 341
technology 17, 82, 408; consumer involvement 61–62, 63; consumer protection 397; digital play 7; extended self 85; gender differences in consumption styles 31–32; globalisation 90, 297; information search 11; interactive 361; multi-media devices 89, 90, 91–92; services 211; social identity 86; *see also* digital marketing; digital technology; Internet; mobile technologies
Teen Vogue 194
teenagers/adolescents 81, 124, 194; attitude formation and persuasion 101, 104–110; Coca-Cola campaign 221; cognitive development 360–361; concept-oriented families 48; consumer misbehaviour 327; consumer socialisation 43, 44; early adulthood 125; emergence of 'teenager' concept 6; ethical consumerism 408; poor diet 382; post post-subcultural approach 298–299; price sensitivity 214; reflective thinking 42, 247; shopping malls 325; smartphones 192; social media 195; subculture 289, 290–291; viral marketing 216
television: advertising 46, 101–103, 131, 173, 174–184, 215, 351, 354–356; brand characters 157–158; changing habits 158–159; developing countries 316–317; digital marketing 189; exposure to 4, 82; food advertising research 255; increase in children's 395; influence on children's behaviour 357–358; information processing 131–132; multi-tasking 155; need recognition 10; as old media 52; parental involvement in viewing 361–362; as promotional tool 223; services marketing 215; smart TVs 191; social class 357; South Africa 350; toddlers 123; violence on 8, 176–177, 357
Tellis, G. J. 145
temperament 241, 242
temptation 10
theme parks 132
Thomas, B. 232
Thomas, S. E. 392, 394
Thompson, C. 289
Thomson, P. 258
3Es 127
thrill-seeking 194, 322, 325, 326

Ting-Toomey, S. 88
tobacco/smoking 10, 17, 92; reference groups 274, 275; regulation 400; smoking 381, 382–383; women 319
Todd, D. 394–395, 403
toddlers 123, 209, 352
Toor, T. 232–233, 235, 240
Tootelian, D. H. 408
toys 119, 121, 123, 125, 126, 129–130, 237, 351
tracking software 355
trade fairs 171
training: consumer misbehaviour awareness 329; services marketing 213, 216, 217, 225
Tran, Anh N. H. 208–229
transaction knowledge 352–353
transparency 51
trendiness 7
Trentmann, F. 4, 7
Treviño, R. P. 14
tri-component attitude model 358–359
tribalism 297
triggers 199, 200–201, 202
TripAdvisor 397
triple bottom line 370
trust: attitudes to advertising 182, 183–184; brand relationships 222; consumer protection 394; digital marketing 188; e-commerce 393; impersonal 311, 312; relationship marketing 220–221
Tsang, L. 257
Tshikovhi, Ndivhuho 347–366
Tukamushaba, Eddy K. 334–346
Turkey 337
Turnbull, S. 171–172
Turner, J. 140
tweens 124, 130, 133, 157, 158, 192
Twining & Company Ltd. 99
Twitter 64, 70, 166; analytics 196; consumer protection 398; digital marketing 188; FEAT Socks 195; *see also* social media
Tynan, C. 218

Ubuntu 315–316, 330, 331n1
Udegbe, S. E. 219
UI *see* user interface
UNGCP *see* United Nations Guidelines for Consumer Protection
UNFPA *see* United Nations Population Fund
United Kingdom (UK): attitudes to advertising 178; branding 300; children's disposable income 406; consumer protection 396, 401; cultural borrowing 297; digital technology 191; ethnic subcultures 293; horsemeat scandal 391;
London Asian music scene 291; national occupational standards 373; number of children in the 157; post-subculture 295; scholarship 6; Snapchat 192; social marketing 384–385; socio-economic divisions 147; television advertising 354; value of children's market 146
United Nations 250
United Nations Convention on the Rights of the Child 38, 247, 248, 387n1, 396
United Nations Guidelines for Consumer Protection (UNGCP) 404–405
United Nations Population Fund 237
United States (US): advertising regulation 218; allowances 408; children's expenditure 157; Children's Online Privacy Protection Act 166, 397, 398, 399; consumer protection 393, 396, 399–400, 406; consumer style inventory 99; consumerism 393, 394; influence of children 48; obesity 138; online purchases 165; religion 180; scholarship 6; smoking 383; Snapchat 192; television advertising 354
use value 59
user experience (UX) 164
user interface (UI) 164
uses and gratifications 59, 63–65, 67–75
utilitarian influence 272, 277, 279–282, 286–287
UX *see* user experience

Vadehra, S. 392
Valeecha, S. 271, 274, 282
Valkenburg, Patti 25, 122, 131, 144, 208–209, 215, 393–395
Valtonen, A. 253, 256, 258–259
value 89, 149–150; adding 214; brand 126; co-creation of 14, 17, 132; mobile technologies 92; perceived 141–145, 150
value-expressive influence 272, 277, 279–283, 286–287
value for money 143, 404
values: attitudes to advertising 181; brand 120; Christian 341; consumer behaviour 348, 364; consumer misbehaviour 314, 315, 316; consumption linked to 347; culture 87; materialistic 44; moral 324, 326; post-purchase evaluation 14; religious 342; social exchange 90; youth culture 301
Van de Sompel, Dieneke 33
van Leeuwen, T. 261
vandalism 308, 310, 313, 322, 323

Vandana 396
Vargo, S. L. 127, 132
Varul, M. Z. 341
Veblen, T. 273
Veloso, A. R. 231
verbal abuse 308, 309, 313, 321, 324
Verma, S. 156
Vermeir, Iris 33
vicious cycle of consumption 317, 324
video games *see* games
Vilnai-Yavetz, I. 233–234
violence 8, 176–177, 184, 357; attitudes to advertising 178; consumer misbehaviour 314; domestic abuse 384, 387; gun crimes 239
viral marketing 216, 355
virtual reality (VR) 134
visual grammar 258–259, 261
visual language 260
visual social science inquiry 261
Vodafone 164
Volkswagen 391
VR *see* virtual reality
Vyas, V. 219
Vygotsky, Lev 7, 40, 41, 160

Wakefield, K. L. 145
Wallendorf, M. 288
wants 208
war prevention 381–382
Ward, Scott 6, 31, 40, 42–43, 161
Warner Brothers 238
Watson, John 122
Web 2.0 191
'web generation' 155
Webley, P. 10, 141–142
websites 158, 164; active-evaluation phase 203; dangers of 176; food advertising research 255; product placement 224; as promotional tool 223; *see also* Internet; social media
Wei, J. 276–277
Weiten, W. 159
well-being 93, 394
Werner, H. 157
Westcott, H. L. 248
Western culture 8–9, 315
Wetherell, M. 254, 255
WhatsApp 192, 195–196
White, E. G. 340
WHO *see* World Health Organization
Wiebe, G. D. 372, 380
Wigley, G. 290, 291
Williams, J. 140, 143
Williams, J. P. 290

Williams, R. 288, 293
Willis, P. E. 293
Willms, J. 296
Wilson, N. 156
Wilson, P. R. 392, 394
Winn, J. K. 393
Wisenblit, J. Z. 162
WOM *see* word of mouth
women 32, 292, 319, 338–339; *see also* gender
Wood, J. T. 182
Wood, W. 222
Woodruff, R. B. 142–143
Woods, Tiger 276
Woodward, J. L. 79
Woolley, J. D. 143
Wooten, D. B. 10–11
word of mouth (WOM) 7, 14, 202; active-evaluation phase 203; opinion leaders 276, 277; relationship marketing 222; store preferences 88
working-class culture 290, 293, 294
World Health Organization (WHO) 247

X-Men Apocalypse 193
XBox 128–129
Xiao, J. J. 99

Yahoo 11
Yang, Hsiao-Pei 208–229
Yannis, G. 403
YELP 397
YOLO (You Only Live Once) 133
Yoo, B. 139
Young, Bernard 27
youth: concept of 289–290; definition of 65–66
youth subculture 288–306; criticism of 291–294; post post-subculture 297–301; post-subculture 291, 294–297
YouTube 158, 188, 192, 202, 255
Yuengert, A. M. 340

Zaharia, C. 392
Zaharia, I. 392
Zaichkowsky, J. L. 62, 74
Zeithaml, V. A. 140, 143
Zero Moment of Truth (ZMOT) 200, 201, 203
Zhang, C. 81
Zhang, X. 276–277
ZMOT *see* Zero Moment of Truth
zone of proximal development (ZPD) 40, 160–161, 162
Zsoter, B. 103

Taylor & Francis eBooks

Helping you to choose the right eBooks for your Library

Add Routledge titles to your library's digital collection today. Taylor and Francis ebooks contains over 50,000 titles in the Humanities, Social Sciences, Behavioural Sciences, Built Environment and Law.

Choose from a range of subject packages or create your own!

Benefits for you
- Free MARC records
- COUNTER-compliant usage statistics
- Flexible purchase and pricing options
- All titles DRM-free.

Benefits for your user
- Off-site, anytime access via Athens or referring URL
- Print or copy pages or chapters
- Full content search
- Bookmark, highlight and annotate text
- Access to thousands of pages of quality research at the click of a button.

REQUEST YOUR FREE INSTITUTIONAL TRIAL TODAY

Free Trials Available
We offer free trials to qualifying academic, corporate and government customers.

eCollections – Choose from over 30 subject eCollections, including:

Archaeology	Language Learning
Architecture	Law
Asian Studies	Literature
Business & Management	Media & Communication
Classical Studies	Middle East Studies
Construction	Music
Creative & Media Arts	Philosophy
Criminology & Criminal Justice	Planning
Economics	Politics
Education	Psychology & Mental Health
Energy	Religion
Engineering	Security
English Language & Linguistics	Social Work
Environment & Sustainability	Sociology
Geography	Sport
Health Studies	Theatre & Performance
History	Tourism, Hospitality & Events

For more information, pricing enquiries or to order a free trial, please contact your local sales team:
www.tandfebooks.com/page/sales

Routledge Taylor & Francis Group | The home of Routledge books | **www.tandfebooks.com**